THE MECKLENBURG SIGNERS
AND THEIR NEIGHBORS

(ILLUSTRATED)

By
WORTH S. RAY

CLEARFIELD

Reprinted for
Clearfield Company, Inc. by
Genealogical Publishing Co., Inc.
Baltimore, Maryland
1993, 1995, 1997, 2000

Originally published as
The Lost Tribes of North Carolina, Part III
Austin, Texas, 1946
Reprinted: Genealogical Publishing Co., Inc.
Baltimore, 1962, 1966, 1975, 1982
Library of Congress Catalogue Card Number 63-524
International Standard Book Number 0-8063-0268-0
Made in the United States of America

Notice

This work has been reproduced in facsimile from the original publication of 1945. In spite of the uneven type image of the original edition, our printer has made every effort to produce as sharp a reprint as possible.

Publisher's Preface

This is probably the finest genealogical record that could be gathered of the people of Mecklenburg County. The first half of the book consists of various records, while the second part is devoted to family histories much too numerous to mention.

Several maps are included herein, including one locating the homes of the Mecklenburg Signers and their neighbors.

We regret the poor quality of the text, but as this is an exact facsimile reprint of the original edition as published in 1946 by the author, it is the very best we could produce.

GENEALOGICAL PUBLISHING COMPANY

Baltimore, Maryland
1966

PREFACE

This attempt on the part of the writer to study the MECKLENBURG SIGNERS AND THEIR NEIGHBORS is more remarkable for what has been left out than for what it contains.

Collectively, what is here presented is not genealogy, so much as the history of a people — a TRIBE of people — that came to the valley between the Yadkin and Catawba rivers more than two hundred years ago. In these notes the compiler has tried to show, in conformity with the general theme he has had in mind, where these people originated, and finally what became of them and their descendants. In the jealous conservation of space it has been necessary to omit the text of many valuable documents and data which had been collected in the course of years, which would have been appreciated by students; to leave out many convincing citations and authorities and innumerable lengthy charts and lists of grandchildren and great-grandchildren, discarding them as so much surplus weight, in trying to give a brief, though otherwise adequate and understandable account of those families mentioned.

The type is small, PURPOSELY SO, to avoid the manufacture of an unwieldy volume, which the writer abhors; but at that, it can be read much more easily than many of the musty records the author has pored over for years in hot vaults and dusty, neglected archives, seeking the elusive information thus published for the first time. Real research workers who have experienced these inconveniencies will be able to appreciate the point.

The approximately 250 pages (313 to 558) will eventually appear in a larger volume — but not too large — entitled "THE LOST TRIBES OF NORTH CAROLINA," which should be off the press within the year. This separate binding is issued to enable them to be so acquired by persons particularly interested in the Mecklenburg tribes.

WORTH S. RAY

Austin, Texas, June, 1946.

BEGINNING OF A BACKWOODS SETTLEMENT THAT DEFIED THE BRITISH EMPIRE.

More than two hundred years ago a travel-worn frontiersman and his wife and little family drove across the swirling waters of the YADKIN RIVER in the first "wheeled vehicle" ever to have been seen in that part of the country, in search of a new home and a little less government. The crude wagon was of archaic design and the slow moving animals he guided to the South bank of the stream were known as "oxens". When Thomas Spratt reached dry land again, the history of MECKLENBURG COUNTY, NORTH CAROLINA began to take form. This was in 1740 or earlier. He had traveled a "fur piece" considering the transportation facilities of that day and time, leaving behind him the memories of the "Eastern Shore" of MARYLAND and VIRGINIA, and the islands and "poquosons" of SOMERSET. Tired and weary with the long journey he and his family were ready to rest for awhile when they reached the waters of "ROCKY RIVER" in what is now CABARRUS COUNTY, according to tradition, but afterwards "pulled up stakes" and took up lands, it is said, in the neighborhood of the present PINEVILLE, some miles South of the later CHARLOTTE, and almost within hearing distance of the roar of the CATAWBA as it flowed southward to the sea.

A long time afterwards the first court ever held in MECKLENBURG COUNTY was at his home.

Thomas Spratt is buried near the corner of East Fifth and Caswell Road about two miles from the business center of the present City of Charlotte near the Mercy Hospital.

One fine day, near the setting of the sun, a lone foot traveler arrived at the humble cabin of Thomas Spratt with a knapsack on his back. When Spratt met him at the door he recognized the oldest son of a SOMERSET (Maryland) neighbor, one THOMAS POLK. Polk received a warm welcome, settled down in the same general neighborhood and was followed later by several brothers and sisters. Not long afterwards THOMAS POLK married SUSAN SPRATT, a daughter of Thomas Spratt, and WILLIAM POLK, his brother, married her sister. ANN SPRATT married JOHN BARNETT. EZEKIEL POLK the youngest brother of THOMAS POLK married MARY WILSON and he and his wife were the grandparents of JAMES KNOX POLK, President of the UNITED STATES.

JOHN BARNETT and ANN SPRATT were the parents of SUSAN BARNETT, who married GEORGE W. SMART, a contemporary in age with ANDREW JACKSON, REV. FRANCIS CUMMINS and CAPT. JAMES JACK, who carried the MECKLENBURG DECLARATION to the Convention in session in 1775 at PHILADELPHIA, thus being an instrument in the hands of Providence in touching off the sparks that caused the explosion heard round the World and furnished the cue that made the delegates there assembled resolved to "hang together" at the risk of "hanging separately".

Thus the history of a nation had its beginning, which is thus traced to the door of THOMAS SPRATT. Prominent among those whose signatures were attached to the MECKLENBURG DECLARATION OF INDEPENDENCE, which James Jack carried to Philadelphia, was this same THOMAS POLK, the knap-sack traveler, now grown wealthy and influential in this new country, who more than a quarter of a century before had followed the wheel tracks of his old SOMERSET, MARYLAND, neighbor across the YADKIN.

Of these interesting characters SUSAN (BARNETT) SMART outlived them all. When she passed away about 1850 she left an interesting will on record in MECKLENBURG COUNTY. It was dated on June 11, 1850. The following is an abstract (not a complete copy) of the instrument:

1st. To Margaret A. Elliott, daughter of S.N. Elliott.
2nd. To Mary Ann Smith, daughter of Stephen and Martha Smith.
3rd. To Stephen Smith, son of Stephen and Martha Smith.
4th. To Susan Spratt, daughter of Robert Spratt.
5th. To Albert Smith, son of Stephen Smith.
6th. To S. N. Elliott, my book case and library.
7th. To David Cowan, a bed.
8th. To Thomas B. Cowan, son of David Cowan.
9th. To my nephew Samuel N. Elliott.
10th. To Mary Elliott.
11th. To Benjamin Elliott.
12th. To Thomas B. Cowan and John Cowan, sons of David Cowan.
13th. To my friend Samuel Williamson $50.00.
14th. To Ellen, Cynthia and Rebecca Smart, children of Littleberry Smart.
15th. To the children of Samuel Barnett, son of my brother William W. Barnett.
16th. To my niece Ann Jack, wife of James Jack.
17th. To my niece Susan Bowie, wife of Alexander Bowie.
18th. To my niece Jane Jack $200.00.
My friend and relative Samuel N. Elliott, Executor.
Witnessed and proved by B. C. Carson and A. Graham.

The "friend Samuel Williamson" to whom Mrs. Smart left a legacy of $50.00 in the above will was the President of Davidson College and brother of Rev. John Williamson, one time pastor of Hopewell Presbyterian Church.

Andrew Jackson, afterwards President of the United States, and Samuel Polk, father of James Knox Polk, also President, were among Susan Smart's boy friends, and it is stated on good authority that when Susan Smart visited the mother of James K. Polk, shortly after his birth, she predicted that the child, who had an enormous head for one so young, would one day become President of the UNITED STATES.

HOW OLIVER CROMWELL MAY HAVE INFLUENCED THE MECKLENBURG DECLARATION - HIS KIN.

There were many prominent families living in MECKLENBURG COUNTY, NORTH CAROLINA, prior to the signing of the famous DECLARATION, who claimed they were blood kinsmen of the great ENGLISH throne-buster, OLIVER CROMWELL, and if this is true, CROMWELL, who had died more than a century before, may nevertheless have wielded an influence in shaping this great document of human emancipation. This may sound incredible, until one examines the history of the people of MECKLENBURG and their origin.

It has been repeatedly asserted, and by many writers, that the Scotch-Irish were the founders of MECKLENBURG COUNTY, North Carolina, and that this particular race of people were the instigators behind the adoption of the Declaration. Further, that most, if not ALL of the signers of that document were from PENNSYLVANIA.

The compiler does not agree with either statement. Few, IF ANY, of the signers came from the colony of William Penn. As we understand it, the term "Scotch-Irish" applies to SCOTCHMEN, who took refuge in the North of Ireland, where they remained for a time, and later found their way to the AMERICAN COLONIES. The signers were not generally of this type. Some were perhaps from SCOTLAND and some were IRISH, but a study of their origin from the records seems to disclose that the families to which they belong were in the early American colonies BEFORE the so-called "Scotch-Irish" began to arrive in this country. In the days of CROMWELL'S ascendency and the reign of BERKELEY, the ROYAL Governor of the Virginia colony, they are found on the records of Virginia SOUTH OF THE JAMES RIVER, and across the Chesapeake Bay in ACCOMAC and NORTHAMPTON Counties, where they were living to, as much as possible, escape the wrath of BERKELEY and his persecutions.

WILLIAM DURANT, a friend of WILLIAM CLAYBORNE and a member of the Vestry of LYNHAVEN PARISH in Lower Norfolk County, led some hundreds of them out of Norfolk and Nansemond to the KENT ISLAND section of the Eastern Shore of Maryland about the time of the restoration, when BERKELEY became unduly arrogant and bold. GEORGE DURANT, a son of WILLIAM, led another set of them to the vicinity of "DURANT'S NECK" on Albemarle Sound.

In Northampton and Accomac Counties on the Eastern Shore of Virginia, a few puritans and non-conformists followed the Ex-Sheriff, WILLIAM STONE, across the line into MARYLAND, and one STEPHEN HORSEY led another contingent to a haven of refuge, just over the line into what is now SOMERSET COUNTY, Maryland, between the ANNEMESSEX and POCOMOKE rivers. Here, these non-conformists, many of whom were pure IRISH, lived, died and had their being for several decades until they were found and preached to after 1680 by REV. FRANCIS MAKEMIE about whom we will have more to say hereafter in these notes, and those who came after him.

Among these were a number of families of the same name as those whose descendants claim they were blood relatives of OLIVER CROMWELL, and through all those long years, they and their children nursed their grievances without an outlet or an outpouring of their political ills, until finally, still seeking for homes where they could speak their minds and their feelings, their descendants joined a general movement to North Carolina, where lands were cheap, fertile and productive, & where those who had ministered unto them in MARYLAND followed, set up schools, churches, colleges and civic institutions and taught their children the doctrines of free speech, religious tolerance and political science.

Then and there was born the idea that a public officer was a public servant, and that the people themselves and not Kings and Potentates had an inalienable right to rule the World. Thomson and Craighead had sewn the seeds of the Mecklenburg Declaration and it had taken firm root in the minds of the people, but back in their family traditions and history still lingered faint and sometimes livid pictures of the persecutions heaped upon their forefathers in the generations that lay behind. And among them were some of the blood kin of the CROMWELL FAMILY.

WHO WERE THESE KINSMEN OF OLIVER CROMWELL?

The CALDWELLS
The WHITES
The LAWSONS
The McCONNELLS
The BARRYS
The STUARTS

AND their connections, which took in a great many other families in early day MECKLENBURG. In the files of the compiler of these notes there is an old letter, more than a hundred years old in which a kinsman of the WHITE FAMILY makes the claim. In a very informative account of the LAWSONS, CALDWELLS, McCONNELLS, McKISSICKS and HENDERSONS, written by CAROLINE BEALL PRICE many years ago appears authenticated data showing the relationship of these families to the OLIVER CROMWELL strain and discussing the English background of some of these people.

Yes, it is possible. Although at the time the Declaration was written, OLIVER CROMWELL had been dead for a whole century, his influence still lived and wielded an influence.

WHO REALLY DID SIGN THE MECKLENBURG DECLARATION OF INDEPENDENCE?

There is no shadow of doubt but what on May 20, 1775, at a spot approximately where the present day Trade Street crosses Tryon, in the modern City of Charlotte, N. C., at a time when every citizen of Mecklenburg County was supposed to be a "subject" of the King of England and of the mighty empire of Great Britain, a concorse of duly elected delegates from the surrounding country, being fully satisfied that they were carrying out the will of their neighbors and truly voicing the prevailing sentiment of an awakening public in the midst of which they lived, drew up and adopted a ringing set of resolutions couched in plain and unmistakable language repudiating the English Crown and the theory that rulers were the "bosses" of the people, and expressing the opinion, on the contrary, that the people should be the "bosses" of the rulers, and would be from that time on so far as those represented at the convention was concerned.

This was the most startling reversal of governmental policy that had ever been announced since the beginning of time! It was the final thunderclap that shook the thrones of all Europe, as a raging storm shakes the frail vessels at sea. The prior rumblings in the conventions of Virginia and other American colonies had been mere meetings of protest. This was no protest. They were not asking for anything. They were TELLING THE WORLD. Patrick Henry's fervor ran towards a war, as one colony seeking to end a dispute with another, or compromise it. There was no dispute in the Mecklenburg Declaration. It was a statement of facts, springing from breasts and hearts whose minds were foreclosed and settled and called for a complete shifting of the Sovereign powers of the State; a total repudiation of the soverign (?) rights of Kings, making "servants" of so-called rulers and transplanting all powers to the citizen. The fiction of a "Titled Aristocracy", so far as American life was concerned, received its death blow at the corners of Tryon and Trade Streets in Charlotte, N. C. on May 20, 1775, and the brave men who affixed their signatures to the document changed the whole course of human experience. Who were they?

It is indeed strange that there should be any doubt about it, and a sad commentary on the efficiency of historians. Fifty years after this momentous action took place there were those who had the affrontery to assert that the whole incident was a myth, and interested descendants of the courageous signers had to call upon the few scattered, but still living eye witnesses to re-establish the authenticity of the occurrence. Even Legislative research was invoked to "authenticate" the list of signers, some of whom, to this good day are referred to as "reputed" signers.

The writer has personally copied the names of these "signers" from the monument erected in commemoration of the event, which stands in the Mecklenburg Courthouse yard. It is given below. Also set out below is the list published on page 129 of Ramsey's Annals of Tennessee, by Dr. J. G. M. Ramsey in 1853, a grandson of the Secretary of the Convention, Hon. John McKnitt Alexander. Also the list from Francis X. Martin's History of North Carolina. The three lists all appear below:

THE LIST ON THE MONUMENT:	THE J. G. M. RAMSEY LIST:	THE LIST IN MARTIN'S HISTORY:
1. EPHRAIM BREVARD	1. HEZEKIAH ALEXANDER	1. ABRAHAM ALEXANDER
2. HEZEKIAH BALCH	2. ADAM ALEXANDER	2. JOHN McKNITT ALEXANDER
3. JOHN PHIFER	3. CHARLES ALEXANDER	3. EPHRAIM BREVARD
4. JAMES HARRIS	4. EZRA ALEXANDER	4. REV. HEZEKIAH BALCH
5. WILLIAM KENNON	5. WEIGHTSTILL AVERY	5. JOHN PHIFER
6. JOHN FORD	6. EPHRAIM BREVARD	6. JAMES HARRIS
7. RICHARD BARRY	7. HEZEKIAH JAMES BALCH	7. WILLIAM KENNON
8. HENRY DOWNS	8. RICHARD BARRY	8. JOHN FORD
9. EZRA ALEXANDER	9. HENRY DOWNS	9. RICHARD BARRY
10. WILLIAM GRAHAM	10. JOHN DAVIDSON	10. HENRY DOWNS
11. JOHN QUEARY	11. WILLIAM DAVIDSON	11. EZRA ALEXANDER
12. HEZEKIAH ALEXANDER	12. JOHN FLENNIKEN	12. WILLIAM GRAHAM
13. ADAM ALEXANDER	13. JOHN FORD	13. JOHN QUEARY
14. CHARLES ALEXANDER	14. WILLIAM GRAHAM	14. HEZEKIAH ALEXANDER
15. ZACCHEUS WILSON	15. JAMES HARRIS	15. ADAM ALEXANDER
16. WEIGHTSTILL AVERY	16. RICHARD HARRIS SR.	16. CHARLES ALEXANDER
17. BENJAMIN PATTON	17. ROBERT IRWIN	17. ZACCHEUS WILSON JR.
18. MATTHEW McCLURE	18. WILLIAM KENNON	18. WEIGHTSTILL AVERY
19. NEIL MORRISON	19. NEILL MORRISON	19. BENJAMIN PATTON
20. ROBERT IRWIN	20. MATTHEW McCLURE	20. MATTHEW McCLURE
21. JOHN FLENNIGIN	21. SAMUEL MARTIN	21. NEILL MORRISON
22. DAVID REESE	22. THOMAS POLK	22. ROBERT IRWIN
23. JOHN DAVIDSON	23. JOHN PHIFER	23. JOHN FLENNIKEN
24. RICHARD HARRIS	24. EZEKIEL POLK	24. DAVID REESE
25. THOMAS POLK	25. BENJAMIN PATTON	25. JOHN DAVIDSON
26. ABRAHAM ALEXANDER	26. DUNCAN OCHILTREE	26. RICHARD HARRIS
27. JOHN McKNITT ALEXANDER	27. JOHN QUEARY	27. THOMAS POLK
	28. DAVID REESE	
	29. WILLIAM WILSON	
	30. ZACHEUS WILSON	

DISCUSSION OF SOME OF THE DISCREPANCIES
ON THE RAMSEY LIST

The name of RICHARD HARRIS appears as a signer of the MECKLENBURG DECLARATION on all of the three lists shwon on the preceding page, but this compiler, following DR. J. B. ALEXANDER in his HISTORY OF MECKLENBURG COUNTY, has substituted in his stead the name of ROBERT HARRIS, JR. On page 422 of ALEXANDER'S HISTORY appears this statement in this connection:

LOSSING in his "FIELD NOTES OF THE REVOLUTION", corrects the apparent error of RICHARD HARRIS and substitutes the name of ROBERT HARRIS. "It is surprising" writes W. S. HARRIS, who lived all his life in that region, and one of the best chroniclers in that section of the country, "that such an error should have been committed, and the name given as RICHARD; I know that the name should have been ROBERT HARRIS."

WILLIAM DAVIDSON, who is signer No. 11, on the RAMSEY list, does not appear on either of the other lists as a signer. It is surprising that this man was NOT a signer, with all of his prominence and wealth, as well as his numerous connections, but the same might be said about a numer of other persons contemporaneous with him. Not every man who was qualified was selected as a delegate to the convention, and therefore their names do not appear signed to the Declaration. Ramsey, who if not a native of the county, yet was closely connected with its best families, and familiar with the standing of its citizens, may have naturally conceived the idea that WILLIAM DAVIDSON was one of the signers as a matter of course. The person intended was GEN. WILLIAM LEE DAVIDSON, who a few years later was killed in the battle of COWAN'S FORD on the Catawba in the revolution. On his tombstone at Hopewell Church, the name is spelled out in full, WILLIAM LEE DAVIDSON, but, Hunter, I believe, says that the middle name was generally left out in his signing. In the will of GEORGE DAVIDSON, his father, he is called just plain, WILLIAM DAVIDSON, though it is well established that his middle name was LEE.

WILLIAM WILSON, according to the RAMSEY list, signed the DECLARATION. The fact, however, that his name does not appear on either of the other lists and is mentioned by no other historian execpt RAMSEY would indicate that the TENNESSEE HISTORIAN was in error in this case as well as in several other instances.

SAMUEL MARTIN, according to the RAMSEY LIST was also a signer. His name does not appear on the monument, nor does it appear on the list in FRANCIS XAVIER MARTIN'S HISTORY of North Carolina. As a matter of fact, SAMUEL MARTIN was a brother of ALEXANDER MARTIN, one time Governor of North Carolina, and did not live in MECKLENBURG COUNTY in 1775, but was a resident of first, TRYON, and afterwards LINCOLN COUNTY. His home was in the lower part of what is now GASTON COUNTY, perhaps on ALLISON or CROWDER'S CREEK. According to a chart furnished the compiler some years ago, he and his brothers had a sister JANE MARTIN, who married THOMAS HENDERSON, revolutionary soldier of GRANVILLE COUNTY, North Carolina, brother of the famous JUDGE RICHARD HENDERSON. CAPTAIN SAMUEL MARTIN was in command of a LINCOLN COUNTY COMPANY during the revolution. But he was not a signer of the MECKLENBURG DECLARATION OF INDEPENDENCE.

EZEKIEL POLK, the grandfather of President JAMES KNOX POLK appears on the RAMSEY list as a signer of the DECLARATION, but his name does not appear on either of the other lists. ALEXANDER and others say that EZEKIEL POLK was one of the "prime movers" and advocates of the Declaration but not a signer. He was a brother of THOMAS POLK, who was a signer, one being the oldest and the other the youngest of the POLK BROTHERS, who will be discussed later in these notes. EZEKIEL POLK, it is claimed by ALEXANDER, became an INFIDEL before he left North Carolina and moved to the vicinity of BOLIVER, TENNESSEE. The writer is inclined to doubt the statement, which if true, probably represented a m ital state, which righted itself, after he reached the new land of "promise" away out beyond DUCK RIVER, where his brother THOMAS POLK and his sons took up lands, and from where his grandson JAMES KNOX POLK started a political career that led finally to the WHITE HOUSE.

DUNCAN OCHILTREE appears to have been a signer, according to RAMSEY'S ANNALS, and after reading what DR. ALEXANDER'S HISTORY has to say about this man, one is inclined to believe that he may have been a signer, though his name is omitted from all other lists that have been published. It appears that when GEN. CORNWALLIS' army invaded Mecklenburg, DUNCAN OCHILTREE, joined his forces and was commissioned a British Officer, and thus "double-Crossed" his patriotic neighbors. He afterwards sought protection personally from JOHN McKNITT ALEXANDER, who turned him down and denounced him as a traitor to his country. Nobody seems to know just what became of him. (See p. 355).

REV. HEZEKIAH BALCH. This man was a signer, beyond any question. But there were TWO PERSONS by that name in MECKLENBURG COUNTY. Which one was the signer? The writer does not believe that anyone knows. Both were born in HARFORD COUNTY, MARYLAND, on the West side of the SUSQUEHANNAH RIVER, while CECIL COUNTY (where so many other signers came from) was just across on the East side of the same river. One graduated from PRINCETON in 1766, and the other in 1762, according to the accounts that have been written. Both came to MECKLENBURG COUNTY with their parents when they were very young. One married a MISS SCONNEL (?) and settled West of CONCORD on the Beattie's Ford Road & the other married HANNAH LEWIS and was minister of BETHEL CHURCH, just below STEELE CREEK in York COUNTY, S. C. The latter removed to TENNESSEE, and became a contemporary of REV. SAMUEL DOAK.

ABSTRACTS OF SOME ANCIENT ITEMS FROM
THE MECKLENBURG COUNTY RECORDS

JOHN MOORE. Nuncupative will of John Moore, deceased, who was killed at the Eakown in the Middle Settlements of the Cherokee Nation of Indians, recorded in Anson County, North Carolina. Will Book 1 p. 7.

Taken by me, PETER KUYKENDALL, a little time before the said John Moore dyed. He sent for me and told me that he wanted to let me know how he wanted his estate disposed of, and which John Moore then said it was his will and desire that his brother MOSES MOORE and son John should have the place which he bought of JEREMIAH POTTS; and the remainder of his estate of all kinds whatever he left to his own wife Mary. In witness whereof said PETER KUYKENDALL set his hand and seal, August 6, 1760.

DEED BY MARY MOORE, Anson County, North Carolina, February 22, 1762. MARY MOORE, the widow of JOHN MOORE, deceased, to MOSES MOORE, 130 acres, part of a certain tract granted EVAN LEWIS by patent April 10, 1750, containing 600 acres, conveyed by said EVAN LEWIS and MARY his wife to JOHN MOORE, October 25, 1755, then on the 15th day of May, 1758, said JOHN MOORE did reconvey unto JEREMIAH POTTS 170 acres, and unto JOSEPH CLOUD 300 acres, the remaining part being 130 acres. Signed by MARY MOORE. Witnessed by ABRAHAM SCOTT, RICHARD BARRY and JOHN THOMAS. Book 6, page 412.

DEED BY WILLIAM MOORE, Anson County, N. C., dated April 21, 1756. WILLIAM MOORE and MARGARET his wife sell to JOHN HARVEY, consideration 40 pounds, 280 acres on the CATAWBA RIVER, on the South side of CANE CREEK. Signed by William Moore and Margaret Moore. Witnessed by ROBERT McCLENACHAN and ARCH BURWICK. Book 1, page 205-207.

JOHN MOORE DEED. Anson County, North Carolina May 15, 1758. (Deed referred to above). JOHN MOORE, Planter, to JEREMIAH POTTS, 170 acres on INDIAN CREEK. Signed JOHN MOORE. (Indian Creek was in the present LINCOLN COUNTY). Witnessed by SAMUEL BEASON, JOSEPH CLOUD and by FRANCIS BEATY. Book 5 pp. 113-114.

SAMUEL MOORE DEED. Anson County, North Carolina October 19, 1753. Samuel Moore and Sarah his wife to PETER CLUB, for thirty pounds 250 acres on the South side of the CATAWBA RIVER and on both sides of KILLIAN'S CREEK and the line of ROBERT LEEPER. Deed Book 1, p. 370.

HUGH BARRY DEED, Mecklenburg County, N.C. in 1771. HUGH BARRY and MARGARET his wife, to RICHARD BARRY, 420 acres on the North side of the CATAWBA RIVER, on the South side of McDOWELL'S CREEK, where HUGH BARRY now dwells, part of a tract of 540 acres, formerly granted to ANDREW BARRY, Esq., deceased, on February 23rd 1754, sold by the said ANDREW BARRY to the said HUGH BARRY, September 16, 1768. Signed by HUGH BARRY and MARGARET BARRY, and witnessed by GEO. ELLIOTT, VIOLET WILSON and JANNET ELLIOTT.

> The foregoing deed establishes beyond doubt the location of the home of HUGH BARRY; it also shows that one ANDREW BARRY was deceased in 1771, but had been living in September, 1768, and furnishes an approximate date for the following item found on the records of ANSON COUNTY:

ANDREW BARRY. Inventory of his goods, chattels, rights and credits by RICHARD BARRY, administrator. No date given. (This ANDREW BARRY may have been the FATHER of both RICHARD and HUGH BARRY, as it is known that their father was named ANDREW BARRY.)

ROBERT McKINDLEY. Deed in Mecklenburg County, North Carolina, by ROBERT McKINDLEY, Cooper, to WILLIAM McKINDLEY, dated January 17, 1775, to a tract of land on both sides of PAW CREEK, a sub-division from a tract of 600 acres patented to JOHN DAVIS, April 10, 1761, and conveyed to MATTHEW PATTON, July 29, 1763, and conveyed by said PATTON to ROBERT McKINDLEY, on April 18, 1764, containing 200 acres. Signed by ROBERT McKINDLEY and witnessed by DANIEL DACRES and JUSTIS BUCK.

> I dislike to startle the readers and especially the genealogists with the statement that the "McKINDLEYS" of the above deed were the ancestors of a certain WILLIAM McKINLEY, President of the United States, but they were. The William "McKindley" of this deed is buried at STEELE CREEK, and the name on the stone is spelled McKINLEY. See later.

GEORGE CALHOUN, DEED. Mecklenburg County, North Carolina, January 12, 1775. GEORGE CALHOUN and ELIZABETH, his wife, to their son SAMUEL CALHOUN, for a consideration of 100 lbs; a tract of land on the EAST side of CATAWBA RIVER, joining SAMUEL KNOX and JOHN HENDRY'S land, beginning at JOHN BIGGER'S line, thence to CHARLES CALHOUN'S Corner, which was patented by SAMUEL KNOX, and containing 180 acres. Signed by GEORGE CALHOUN and ELIZABETH CALHOUN and witnessed by ANN BROWN and WILLIAM KERR.

> The above land was on the NORTH side of the CATAWBA, but was on the "bend" near CARR'S (Kerr's) creek and in this instance was called "EAST" as it actually WAS East at that particular point. This GEORGE CALHOUN was from Prince Edward County, Virginia & so was JOHN BIGGERS, a descendant of ADAM CALHOUN, relative of the ARMSTRONGS who lived on the other side of the CATAWBA from this land.

JAMES TATE DEED. Mecklenburg County, N. C., April 22, 1772. James Tate and Ann, his wife, executes deed to JAMES SIMPSON, of ROWAN COUNTY, N. C., consideration ninety pounds, to 220 acres on the South side of Four Mile Creek, between JAMES JOHNSTON and HENRY DOWNS, and JOHN RAMSEY. Signed by JAMES TATE and ANN TATE and witnessed by WILLIAM SIMS, JOHN RAMSEY and GEORGE ROSS.

> This deed shows that HENRY DOWNS the "signer" lived in the general vicinity of Four Mile Creek. JOHN RAMSEY belonged at PROVIDENCE and his wife was the mother of ARCHIBALD CROCKETT. See later.

JOHN SHIELDS DEED. Mecklenburg County, North Carolina, October 10, 1771. JOHN SHIELDS and MARGARET his wife, Planter, to DAVID BRADFORD, consideration 52 pounds, a tract of 205 acres, part of an original grant to AMBROSE HARDING, on McGUISTAN'S line to ROBERT MOFFITT, & thence by MOSES ANDREW'S line to JOHN FINLEY'S. Signed by JOHN SHIELDS and MARGARET SHIELDS, & witnessed by JAMES SHIELDS and AGNES SHIELDS.

Both JOHN SHIELDS and JOHN FINLEY mentioned in the above deed married daughters of REV. JOHN THOMSON, who is buried at BAKER'S GRAVEYARD. John Shields married MARGARET THOMSON and the given name of the daughter who married JOHN FINLEY is unknown.

DAVID MOORE DEED. Mecklenburg County, N. Carolina January 21, 1773. DAVID MOORE and ANNA his wife to JONATHAN BUCKALOO, 114 acres on the waters of McALPIN'S CREEK, consideration 38 pounds. Signed by DAVID MOORE and ANNA MOORE. Witnesses were JOHN FORD and a WILLIAM HAMMOND.

The above DAVID MOORE died in 1793.

SELWYN DEED. Mecklenburg County, North Carolina, August 24, 1770. JOHN AUGUSTINE SELWYN, of Mahon in the County of Gloster, in the Kingdom of Great Britain, son and heir of JOHN SELWYN deceased, deeds to ROBERT ROBINSON, of the County of Mecklenburg and the Province of North Carolina, for a consideration of five pounds, fifty acres of land which was granted to JOHN SELWYN, on HENDY CREEK in 1769. Signed by JOHN FROHACK, agent for JOHN SELWYN.

ANDREW DOWNS DEED. Mecklenburg County, N. C., April 25, 1775. ANDREW DOWNS and ANN, his wife, to BENJAMIN MAXWELL, 150 acres of land, part of an original grant to said DOWNS patented December 22, 1768, on the East side of the CATAWBA RIVER, joining lands of JAMES MAXWELL, thence North to WALTER CARSON'S line, thence to BENJAMIN COCKERAN'S corner, consideration fifty pounds. Signed by ANDREW DOWNS and ANN DOWNS, the witnesses being JOHN MAXWELL, THOMAS MARTIN and RICHARD MORROW.

The above ANDREW DOWNS may have been either a son or brother of HENRY DOWNS, one of the "Signers" of the Mecklenburg Declaration, who is said by Dr. J. B. Alexander, to have been born in 1728.

PATRICK JACK DEED. Mecklenburg County, N. C. October 24, 1773. PATRICK JACK, party of the first part, to ROBERT McGOUGH, consideration 60 pounds, sells 150 acres on both sides of McALPIN CREEK, joining ROBERT ELLIOTT and SAMUEL JACK'S land, to where said PATRICK JACK now dwells. It is signed PATRICK JACK and witnessed by JAMES TATE, SAMUEL JACK and EDWARD SHARP.

This PATRICK JACK was the ancestor of all the JACK tribe, including CAPT. JAMES JACK, who carried the "DECLARATION" of the Mecklenburg Patriots to the Continental Congress at Philadelphia. See later.

JOSEPH McKINDLEY DEED. Mecklenburg County, North Carolina, October 26, 1776. In the first year of our being free and independent from the Crown, 1776. JOSEPH McKINDLEY, Planter sells to JAMES BROWN, tanner, consideration 110 pounds, 466 acres joining BIGGERS, opposite the mouth of CROWDER'S CREEK, part of the lands of Biggers granted to him in 1765. Signed by JOSEPH McKINDLEY and MARGARET McKINDLEY, his wife. Witnessed by SAMUEL CHAMBERS and FRANCIS JOHNSTON.

This deed was to lands near the ferry of JOHN BIGGERS established across the CATAWBA RIVER below and West of STEELE CREEK Church, at the junction of CROWDER'S CREEK which empties into the Catawba at that point, flowing Westward and across the line into the present GASTON COUNTY.

SAMUEL JACK DEED. On September 17, 1773 SAMUEL JACK and his wife FRANCIS sold lands in Mecklenburg County by deed to WILLIAM SMITH on the waters of McALPIN'S CREEK.

DAVID HAY DEED. October 9, 1774, in Mecklenburg County, N. C. DAVID HAY and his wife JENN, for a consideration of 200 pounds sold 300 acres of land on the North side of the CATAWBA RIVER to HUGH REID. The land was on SUGAW or SUGAR CREEK, about one mile from the path to JOHN POLL, formerly the Widow MECHUM, to the Catawba; lands formerly patented to HUGH MORROW, May 17, 1754, and conveyed by said HUGH MORROW to SAMUEL YOUNG. Signed by DAVID HAY and JENN HAY, and witnessed by THOMAS POLK and JAMES NEAL.

ISAAC KILLOUGH DEED. In Mecklenburg County, N. C. on April 8, 1764, ISAAC KILLOUGH and his wife MARY deeded lands to JOHN ARMSTRONG, farmer, consisting of 140 acres on the South side of the CATAWBA RIVER, for a consideration of 80 pounds. Signed by ISAAC KILLOUGH and MARY KILLOUGH, and witnessed by ADAM ALEXANDER and JOHN McKNITT ALEXANDER.

I think the notation after the David Stanley deed was intended for this one, since it is certain this land WAS ON that side now GASTON COUNTY. Killough & wife, however, must have lived on the North side and in what is now Mecklenburg. So far as known JOHN ARMSTRONG always lived in LINCOLN or TRYON, the part now GASTON, near the ARMSTRONG FORD. Nearly a hundred years later an ISAAC KILLOUGH died in Texas.

JOSEPH MOORE DEED. August 27, 1795, in Mecklenburg County ADLAI OSBORNE of Iredell Co. attorney for the Trustees of the University of North Carolina deed 190 acres of land to JOSEPH MOORE, of Mecklenburg County.

HUGH NEELY, DEED. In Mecklenburg County, N. C. July 17, 1778, HUGH NEELY, Weaver, and ANDREW ROBINSON and his wife MARGARET executed a deed to lands.

The ROBINSON family to which ANDREW ROBINSON belonged are mostly buried in the original Sugar Creek Churchyard, which see.

CHARLES MOORE from ROGER LAWSON. Indenture dated December 23, 1762 and placed on record in Mecklenburg County in Book 5, page 156 of the Harris Records. ROGER LAWSON, of Halifax District in the Province of Georgia, of the one part and CHARLES MOORE, of ANSON COUNTY, in the Province of NORTH CAROLINA, Schoolmaster, of the other part, a tract of land in ANSON COUNTY, N. C., on the South side of BROAD RIVER and the South side of PACOLET, on a large creek called LAWSON'S CREEK, estimated to be 500 acres, granted to said ROGER LAWSON by a patent dated FEBRUARY 23, 1754. Signed ROGER LAWSON. Witnessed by WILLIAM MESLAND, ROBERT LAWSON or LAW-RENCE and RICHARD BARRY.

> ROGER LAWSON one of the parties to the above deed was the son in law of REV. JOHN THOMSON, and the son of HUGH LAWSON; CHARLES MOORE was the cousin of MRS. MARY GRAHAM, mother of GEN. JOSEPH GRAHAM and his brothers and sisters. Also CHARLES MOORE was a cousin of the ROGER LAWSON (or his uncle) as HUGH LAWSON'S wife was MARY MOORE, the daughter of a CHARLES MOORE & MARGARET BARRY.

GEORGE DAVIDSON DEED. Mecklenburg Co. North Carolina, July 14, 1764. GEORGE DAVIDSON and KATHERINE DAVIDSON, his wife, deed to SAMUEL DAVIDSON, of ROWAN COUNTY, to a tract of 540 acres in the County of Mecklenburg, on MOSES DICKEY'S CREEK, on the South side of the CATAWBA RIVER. Signed by GEORGE DAVIDSON and CATHERINE DAVIDSON, and witnessed by JOHN BYRUM. Recorded in Book 5, page 135 Harris Records.

> GEORGE DAVIDSON, of the above deed, was the brother of GEN. WILLIAM LEE DAVIDSON, and the deed was to another brother SAMUEL DAVIDSON. They were sons of GEORGE DAVIDSON and his wife MARGARET.

MOSES MOORE DEED. This deed dated on April 23, 1765 and recorded in Mecklenburg County. MOSES MOORE, planter, to THOMAS ROBINSON, a tract of land on the South Side of INDIAN CREEK, beginning at JOHN MOORE'S old corner; granted to said MOSES MOORE in 1763. Signed by MOSES MOORE.

MATTHEW McCORKLE DEED. Mecklenburg County North Carolina, May 30, 1772. Matthew McCORKLE and JEAN, his wife, out of their natural love & affection for their son, THOMAS McCORKLE, convey to him 400 acres on the North side of the CATAWBA RIVER, part of a tract of land originally granted to EDWARD GIVENS by His Majesty's patent in 1752, as shown by the records of ANSON COUNTY, commonly known as the McCorkle Plantation, on both sides of BEAVER DAM CREEK. Signed by MATTHEW McCORKLE and JEAN McCORKLE and witnessed by EDWARD GIVENS, ROBERT GRIDDLE and HENRY HENLEY.

JAMES BELL DEED. In 1774 JAMES BELL, of CHARLOTTE TOWN executed a deed to one JAMES ROYALL, of Mecklenburg County. Description of the land sold not copied.

JOHN SELLERS DEED. 1764 in Mecklenburg County, North Carolina. JOHN SELLERS and ELIZABETH his wife in the year 1764, deeded to CHARLES ANDERSON SCOTT, from VIRGINIA, 100 acres of land on the West side of the CATAWBA RIVER. Book 5, Harris.

ANDREW ERA DEED. In 1764 ANDREW ERA of Mecklenburg County deeded lands to HENRY E. McCULLOCH.

JAMES MOORE DEED. In 1764 JAMES MOORE of Mecklenburg County North Carolina, deeded lands to HENRY E. McCULLOGH.

MOSES SCOTT DEED. In the year 1764 in Mecklenburg County, North Carolina, JOHN MOORE and his wife ANNE MOORE, of TRYON CO. deeded lands to MOSES SCOTT of MECKLENBURG COUNTY, 196 acres lying in Mecklenburg County, on the East side of the CATAWBA RIVER. This deed executed in NOVEMBER of 1764. It is signed by JOHN MOORE and ANNE MOORE, and witnessed by JAMES SCOTT, and ROBERT HARRIS, JR., Clerk of the Court.

WILLIAM BRIGHAM DEED. This deed recorded in Mecklenburg but names the parties as of "ANSON COUNTY" (Mecklenburg was established on paper only that year). WILLIAM BRIGHAM, of the County of ANSON, and Province of N. C., of the one part, and JOSEPH MOORE of the County and Province aforesaid, of the other, one tract of land on the head of the North Fork of PAW CREEK on the East side of the Catawba River, being the land granted to the said WILLIAM BRIGHAM, April 10, 1761. Signed by WILLIAM BRIGHAM and the witnesses were MOSES FERGUSON, SAMUEL BRIGHAM and SAMUEL BERRYHILL.

WILLIAM BRIGHAM. A second deed from WILLIAM BRIGHAM to JOSEPH MOORE, of ROWAN COUNTY, dated November 17, 1762, to a tract of 195 acres described as being in "ANSON" County, but the same location as the tract deeded in APRIL above.

MARTIN ARMSTRONG DEED. Executed August 9, 1762, in what was then called ANSON COUNTY, but a little later Mecklenburg County. Martin Armstrong deed to DANIEL McGARTY, of ROWAN COUNTY, tract of 130 acres in ANSON County "opposite to John Armstrong's land". Signed MARTIN ARMSTRONG and witnessed by ADAM BUTNER and WILLIAM ARMSTRONG.

JOHN McDOWELL DEED. Not dated but recorded at about the same time and in the same book No. 5, Harris. Mecklenburg County, North Carolina. JOHN McDOWELL and ANN his wife, to JAMES MOORE of LUNENBURG (or Stevensburg) in VIRGINIA (Colony of), a tract of 204 acres on the waters of CATAWBA RIVER and a branch of McDOWELL'S CREEK, beginning at JOSEPH MOORE'S corner. Signed by JOHN McDOWELL and ANN McDOWELL, and witnessed by RICHARD BARRY, CHARLES MOORE and WILLIAM BARRY. (About 1765).

> For the relationship of the BARRY and MOORE family see hereafter. The Charles Moore, of the subscribing witnesses was the "cousin" of MRS. MARY GRAHAM, mother of Gen. Joseph and the others. The JOHN McDOWELL grantor may have been the ancestor of that family for whom McDOWELL'S CREEK was named.

JOHN McDOWELL DEED. Mecklenburg County, North Carolina, June 8, 1765. Indenture between JOHN McDOWELL and ANN, his wife, of Mecklenburg County, Province of North Carolina of ye one part, and JOSEPH MOORE, late from PENNSYLVANIA. a tract of land estimated to be 190 acres, being part of a tract of 775 acres conveyed from HENRY JUSTICE McCULLOUGH to the said JOHN McDOWELL, on a branch of McDOWELL'S CREEK, on the waters of the CATAWBA RIVER. Signed by JOHN McDOWELL and ANN McDOWELL and witnessed by RICHARD BARRY, CHARLES MOORE and WILLIAM BARRY.

HUGH MOORE DEED. Mecklenburg County, N. C. August 25, 1793. HUGH MOORE and WILLIAM MOORE, at a Sheriff's Sale of land (for taxes) bought from ANDREW ALEXANDER, late Sheriff of Mecklenburg County, two certain tracts of land, containing 150 acres lying on both sides of the old plantation of HUGH MOORE, SR. deceased, and on both sides of GOOSE CREEK. Signed by ANDREW ALEXANDER, Sheriff, and ISAAC ALEXANDER, C. C.

DAVID MOORE DEED. Mecklenburg County N. C. 1767.(Jan. 17). DAVID MOORE, in the 7th year of the reign of KING GEORGE III (1767) deeded to HENRY N. McCULLOUGH, a certain tract of land in Mecklenburg County, beginning at a small post oak in Governor Dobb's boundary line, containing 117 acres. Signed by DAVID MOORE and witnessed by JOHN FROHACK and THOMAS POLK.

JOHN MOORE DEED. Anson County, North Carolina, May 15, 1758. JOHN MOORE to JOSEPH CLOUD, for three shillings Sterling, 300 acres on the North Side of Indian Creek, being a South Branch of the South Fork of the CATAWBA RIVER. Signed JOHN MOORE, Witnessed by SAMUEL BEASON and JEREMIAH POTTS.

DAVID STANLEY - DEED. In Mecklenburg County, N. C. on August 3, 1764, DAVID STANLEY and his wife HANNAH STANLEY executed a deed to JOHN MOORE, consideration 61 pounds of proclamation money, to 200 acres of land on the North side the CATAWBA RIVER, part of the WILLIAM WATSON grant, patented February 28, 1754, which WILLIAM WATSON had conveyed to BENJAMIN HARDIN, who in turn sold the same by deed to DAVID STANLEY. Deed signed by DAVID STANLEY and HANNAH STANLEY and witnessed by JACOB MONEY, FENDERICK MONEY & JOHN LOW. Book 7, p. 20 Harris Records. Notation says "this land now in Gaston County".

STEPHEN WHITE DEED. Executed in Mecklenburg County, North Carolina 1765. STEPHEN WHITE and his wife AGNES WHITE, of Mecklenburg County, to ISAAC McCULLOUGH of said County, 200 acres on the line of _____ Pickens. Signed by STEPHEN WHITE and AGNES WHITE, and witnessed by ROBERT McCLANACHAN, JOHN BIGS and HENRY HOFFER (?).

THOMAS MOORE DEED. Dated January 30, 1765. THOMAS MOORE and ELIZABETH, his wife, of the WAXHAWS in Mecklenburg County, in North Carolina, to THOMAS AMBROSE of said County, 57 acres on the N. side of CATAWBA RIVER, on both sides of a branch of KAIN CREEK. Signed by THOMAS MOORE and ELIZABETH MOORE, and witnessed by ALEXANDER BARNETT, ROGER SMITH and SAMUEL THOMPSON.

The above tract of land now lies in LANCASTER COUNTY. S. C.

WILLIAM MOORE DEED. Mecklenburg County, North Carolina, October 19, 1760. WILLIAM MOORE and MARY MOORE his wife deed land to EPHRAIM MCLEAR(?) Signed by WILLIAM MOORE and MARY MOORE and witnessed by WILLIAM DUNLAP and JOHN WILSON.

This compiler can't help the conviction that the name "Mclear" as it appears in the above deed, is intended for EPHRAIM McLEAN. It is established by family tradition that EPHRAIM McLEAN was a grandson of an EPHRAIM MOORE and a MISS McLEAN.

MAJ. JOHN DAVIDSON DEED. Mecklenburg County, North Carolina. JOHN DAVIDSON and VIOLET his wife,tof Mecklenburg County, North Carolina deeds certain lands to JAMES KEW and JOHN MURPHY, the line of said land beginning at THOMAS McQUOWN'S, and west of HENRY HENDRY'S lands, and containing 228 acres, patented to said HENDRY in 1751. Deed signed by JOHN DAVIDSON and VIOLET DAVIDSON, and witnessed by THOMAS McQUOWN and HENRY HENDRY.

This deed was by Maj. John Davidson, whose wife Violet, was VIOLET WILSON, the daughter of SAMUEL WILSON. The HENRY HENDRY, of this deed was Pfof. HENRY HENDRY, who married ISABELLA DAVIDSON, the mother of Maj. John Davidson, after the death of his father ROBERT DAVIDSON. On the U. S. Census Records this name is spelled HENRY, while in this deed it is spelled HENDRY. The name, however, was perhaps HENRY. HENRY HENDRY or HENRY had four children by his first marriage, but perhaps none by his second.

ANDREW WALKER DEED. This instrument is recorded in Mecklenburg County, dated December 27, 1779. Deed from NATHANIEL WALKER and his wife ELCE WALKER, of the State of South Carolina and County of COLLETON, to ANDREW WALKER of the State of North Carolina and County of Mecklenburg, to certain lands granted in 1760 to NATHANIEL WALKER on a branch of CANE CREEK in the WAXHAW SETTLEMENT, in the County of Mecklenburg, bounded by lands belonging to HUGH McCONNELL. This deed is signed by NATHANIEL WALKER and ELSE WALKER, and witnessed by PHILLIP WALKER and ELIZABETH WALKER.

WILLIAM HENDERSON'S EXECUTORS. Mecklenburg County, N. C. July 4, 1779. Deed between FRANCES JOHNSON and AGNES HENDERSON, the executors of WILLIAM HENDERSON, deceased, and PRUDENCE HAYS, Administratrix and wife of WILLIAM HAYS of the same place, to 32 acres of land on McALPIN'S CREEK. Witnesses were JAMES HAYS, JOHN HARRIS and WILLIAM KERR.

WILLIAM ELLIOTT DEED. Mecklenburg County, North Carolina, March 16, 1780. Deed to lands between WILLIAM ELLIOTT and JOSEPH NICHOLSON, of Mecklenburg County, to lands described by a reference to ROBERT ELLIOTT'S line. This deed was witnessed by JAMES JACK and SAMUEL ELLIOTT.

This was CAPT. JAMES JACK who carried the "Declaration" to Philadelphia after it was adopted May 20, 1775. JOSEPH NICHOLSON married a sister of Capt. James Jack and the daughter of PATRICK JACK, and ROBERT ELLIOTT married MARGARET, the daughter of DAVID MOORE.

JOSEPH WALLACE ESTATE. JAMES BARR and MARGARET WALLACE were the executors of the estate of JOSEPH WALLACE in 1781, and for 850 pounds sold certain lands of the estate to JOHN DAVIDSON, on the 5th day of August 1768 (?). Attested by JAMES WILEY Sheriff of Mecklenburg County.

ARCHIBALD RAMSEY and his wife JEAN RAMSEY executed a deed to certain lands in 1780, which was witnessed by WILLIAM RAMSEY and ISABELLA ROBERTSON.

DAVID CROCKETT DEED. Mecklenburg County, North Carolina, February 19, 1782. Deed by DAVID CROCKETT and ELIZABETH CROCKETT, his wife, to JOSEPH GALBRAITH (all at that time of Mecklenburg County) for a consideration of 100 pounds proclamation money, to 50 acres on the branch of SUGAR CREEK, joing the lands of JAMES REED, being part of a tract of land ALEX MITCHELL now lives on, surveyed September 11, 1777. Signed by DAVID CROCKETT and ELIZABETH CROCKETT and witnessed by MOSES ROBERSON and EDWARD MALERY. Vol 1-2 Alexander p. 91.

JOHN CROCKETT, DEED. Mecklenburg County, N. C. January 6, 1770. Deed by JOHN CROCKETT and his wife MARGARET, to WILLIAM MOORE (all of Mecklenburg County) for a consideration of 20 pounds paid by said WILLIAM MOORE, a certain tract of 162 acres of land on the South side of Waxhaw Creek, joining the lands of WILLIAM NUTT. Signed by JOHN CROCKETT and MARGARET CROCKETT, and witnessed by WILLIAM, JOHN and KATHERINE NUTT. Vol 14 p. 89.

WILLIAM McCORKLE DEED. Mecklenburg County, North Carolina, June 4, 1771. Deed by WILLIAM McCORKLE and his wife ESTHER to THOMAS PUSLEY, to a tract of 200 acres of land on the North Fork of the Waxhaw Creek, including HUMPHREY YARBOROUGH'S improvements, to the corner of the land of JOHN DAVIS. Signed by WILLIAM McCORKLE and ESTHER McCORKLE, in the presence of JOHN DAVIS, HENRY YARBOROUGH and JOHN CROCKETT.

ANDREW CROCKETT, DEED. Mecklenburg County, N. C. November 2, 1772. ANDREW CROCKETT, planter, and his wife MARY CROCKETT, and ARCHIBALD CROCKETT, for a consideration of 100 pounds paid by ARCHIBALD CROCKETT, deed to him a tract of land on the waters of that five mile creek (called SIX MILE -WSR) in NEW PROVIDENCE joining and between JAMES POTTS, WILLIAM DONALDSON, JAMES TATE and BRICE MILLER'S line, containing 140 acres, granted to said ANDREW CROCKETT by patent dated APRIL 25, 1767. The words "given and granted" used in the conveyance. Signed by ANDREW CROCKETT and MARY CROCKETT; also by ARCHIBALD CROCKETT, the grantee. Witnessed by FRANCIS BARNETT, JOHN WILSON and WILLIAM McCULLOUGH.

ANDREW CROCKETT, DEED. June 12, 1772, in Mecklenburg County, North Carolina. ANDREW CROCKETT and wife MARY to HUGH BARNETT, a certain tract of land therein described. Signed by ANDREW CROCKETT and MARY CROCKETT and witnessed by ANDREW NEEL and JOHN MOORE. Recorded at the April term, 1774.

ANDREW CROCKETT, DEED. Mecklenburg County, N. C. December 21, 1773. ANDREW CROCKETT and wife MARY in a deed sell to JOHN STURGEON, a tract of land, beginning at the corner of the land of HUGH BARNETT on the North Side of the West Fork of Twelve - Mile Creek in Mecklenburg County, containing 225 acres. This deed was signed by ANDREW CROCKETT and MARY CROCKETT and witnessed by ARCHIBALD CROCKETT, JOHN WILSON and WILLIAM MILLER.

JOHN PRICE, DEED. A deed by JOHN PRICE and wife MARY for 200 acres of land, dated July 20th, 1774, and by them acknowledged in Court.

AARON MOORE, will. AARON MOORE and wife RACHEL, of Mecklenburg County, North Carolina, convey to PETER CARPENTER, of the same place- 200 acres of land in Mecklenburg County, on both sides of the South Fork of the CATAWBA RIVER, which was granted to AARON MOORE October 3, 1758. Vol 10 p. 271. (See his will later).

ADAM MOORE had a grant of land consisting of 250 acres of land on both sides of a branch of CATAWBA RIVER in Anson County, North Carolina, on November 26, 1757. (This may or may NOT have been in the limits of the present Mecklenburg County.)

CHARLES MOORE, DEED. Charles Moore of TRYON COUNTY, deed to his son in law ANDREW BARRY, a blacksmith, to land on both sides of TYGER RIVER, on Lawson's Creek, bounded by the lands of HUGH LAWSON. (This land was below the line of the present North Carolina, in South Carolina, but at that time was considered a part of TRYON COUNTY). The deed was executed between 1762 and 1779, which was the life-time of TRYON COUNTY. It shows that HUGH LAWSON owned lands in upper South Carilina at the time of his death, which adjoined lands belonging to CHARLES MOORE, Lawson's wife having been MARY MOORE, a sister of CHARLES MOORE, and the daughter of a CHARLES MOORE and his wife MARGARET BARRY, the parents of PROF. CHARLES MOORE.

CHARLES MOORE, according to the Court Minutes of TRYON COUNTY for January 5, 1769, was witness to a deed from JAMES MILLER to WILLIAM SHARP.

DAVID MOORE GRANTS. The records disclose that DAVID MOORE (whose will is to be given in these notes later) owned a tract of land on Four Mile Creek (see Map) in Mecklenburg County in 1779. A later DAVID, his nephew or son, owned lands in 1800 on Twelve-Mile Creek, and in 1822 on GOOSE CREEK.

JAMES MOORE. One JAMES MOORE owned lands consisting of several different tracts in LINCOLN COUNTY, N. C. about 1800, on what was called "Little Catawba River". (This has reference to the South Fork of the Catawba.).

JAMES MOORE, Deed. Dated December 30, 1766. JAMES MOORE and his wife RACHEL (who releases her dower) deeded lands to JOHN MOORE (Both of Mecklenburg County), in consideration of 20 pounds, 137 acres of land on the South side of the CATAWBA RIVER on the waters of the South Fork of FISHING CREEK; bounded by the lands of JOHN MOORE. Deed was witnessed by THOMAS RAINEY, SAMUEL RAINEY, BENJAMIN RAINEY and RALPH BAKER. Book 10 pp. 386-7 Mecklenburg County. (These lands were in what is now South Carolina, in the present YORK COUNTY).

JOHN MOORE. There is a record which says that JOHN MOORE had grants to lands "in Mecklenburg County" located on the South Fork of FISHING CREEK, GUM LOG and the EAST SIDE of the CATAWBA RIVER.

These lands were in what is now SOUTH CAROLINA, although at that time they were believed to have been a part of Mecklenburg County, in NORTH CAROLINA.

Later notes herein will deal with these MOORES and CROCKETTS and their family connections.

DAVID MOORE - HIS WILL. DAVID MOORE, SR. and ANNA, his wife. Will probated in Mecklenburg County, North Carolina, August 4, 1793. In it he mentions "my three youngest children" and six other children, indicating two sets and that he had been twice married.

The "three youngest children" were sons JOSEPH and JACOB and a daughter AGNES. Also he names WILLIAM BROWN and DANIEL BROWN, "sons of my daughter MARGARET MOORE BROWN. He then mentions in addition, the following children:

    ANDREW MOORE
    DAVID MOORE
    JAMES MOORE
    HANNAH MOORE
    ELIZABETH MOORE (the wife of SOLOMON STANFIELD.

His wife AGNES and son JOSEPH MOORE were named as his executors. The witnesses to the will were GEORGE ORR, JOHN McCORKLE and JOHN CRESWELL.

But in connection with the above will the records of Mecklenburg County disclose that DAVID MOORE SR. and his wife ANNA on January 21, 1773, had made a deed to JONATHAN BUCKALOO to 114 acres down on McAlpin's Creek. Apparently this was the same DAVID MOORE who sold lands to Henry E. McCullough and who left the above will in 1793, whose wife was called AGNES at that time.

But here is the will of another, an earlier and a different DAVID MOORE:

DAVID MOORE - HIS WILL. Mecklenburg County, North Carolina, dated February 5, 1778.
He leaves his house and furniture to his wife, MARGARET MOORE.
I appoint my son JOSEPH MOORE and HUGH MOORE to have my land equally divided betwixt them.
My wife MARGARET MOORE.
That JOSEPH MOORE should have the place on which he lives in part of said division.
I will that my son WILLIAM MOORE shall have six pounds currency.
I will that my son DAVID MOORE should have ten pounds currency.
My daughter MARY McRORY shall have choice of three mares on the plantation.
My daughter MARGARET ELLIOTT.
I appoint JOHN HARRIS and JOHN BARNETT as my executors.
Will is signed by DAVID MOORE and MARGARET MOORE, the witnesses being ARCHIBALD CAMPBELL and JAMES MOORE. (W. B. "B" p. 60).

RICHARD SPRINGS - HIS WILL. Mecklenburg Co. North Carolina (Book G p. 158) dated October 25, 1833. Names the following children:
    RICHARD SPRINGS (youngest son)
    JOHN SPRINGS
    ANDREW SPRINGS
    SOPHIA MOORE
    MARGARET SPRINGS
Children of my son ELI SPRINGS, and children of my daughter CYNTHIA DUNKINS and HARRIET MOORE.
JOHN SPRINGS and ANDREW SPRINGS executors.
Witnesses to the will were JOSEPH H. WILSON and WILLIAM CARRILAN (Carrigan?).

All the SPRINGS of Mecklenburg County are descendants of COL. ADAM ALEXANDER "the signer" whose daughter married JOHN SPRINGS, according to DR. J. B. ALEXANDER'S History.

JOSEPH MOORE - HIS WILL. Mecklenburg County, North Carolina (Will Book "B" p. 79) Dated November 3, 1797. Mentions:
My dearly beloved wife MARY MOORE.
Home, farming tools, etc. (one 7th part of the lands) to be divided equally among our six children:
    MINTY MOORE
    JOSEPH MOORE
    JAMES MOORE
    LUCINDA MOORE
    NARCISSA MOORE
    EPHRAIM MOORE
I will and bequeath unto my seven married children:
    JOHN MOORE
    MARY TENNER
    MARGARET L. STONE
    GEORGE MOORE
    JANE HILL
    SARAH DICKSON
My trusty and well beloved friends and neighbors HUGH TENNER, WILLIAM BEANE ALEXANDER and JOHN SHARPE, Executors.

MARTHA MORROW - HER WILL. (Book G p 109) MARTHA MORROW, of the State of S. C. and District of LIMESTONE. Dated September 1, 1830. (It is not plain whether this is the date of the will, or the date of probate). Mentions:
Son, DAVID MORROW.
Grandsons: JOHN W. MORROW
    ELI MORROW
    DAVID MORROW
Grand-daus: JANE MORROW
    MARTHA MORROW
These are mentioned as the children of DAVID MORROW.
My grandson WILLIAM MORROW, the son of JAMES MORROW.
Daughters:
    ANN McCULLOGH
    ELIZABETH PRIDE
    MARGERY HEGANS
    JANE BROWN
And the children of MARGARET WALKUP.
My worthy friends JAMES GORDON and AARON HOUSTON, Executors.
Will was witnessed by ISAAC BAKER, WILLIAM LAWSON and WILSON ALLEN.

ELIZABETH MORROW - HER WILL. Mecklenburg County, North Carolina, June 6, 1832 (Will Book "G" p. 110). ELIZABETH MORROW, of Mecklenburg County. Mentions:
My beloved son McKNIGHT (George) 100 acres of land.
My beloved son JOHN MORROW.
Lands to be sold and delivered among the rest of my children.
I ordain my worthy friend JOHN W. MORROW Executor of this my will.
Signed ELIZABETH MORROW.
In the presence of WILLIAM HILL.

HUGH CARRIGAN - HIS WILL. HUGH CARRIGAN, of Mecklenburg County. Dated June 2, 1795. Mentions:
My beloved girl ELIZABETH CARRIGAN.
My sons:
    WILLIAM CARRIGAN
    HENRY CARRIGAN
This will was witnessed by JOHN HOOD, MOSES WALKER and ANDREW HARMON.

The CARRIGAN FAMILY lived in what is now CABARRUS COUNTY although this will was probated in Mecklenburg County, apparently after Cabarrus County was formed.

ABRAHAM ALEXANDER - HIS WILL. Proved in Mecklenburg County, North Carolina - as I copied it - in 1800. In the will he names his wife DORCAS ALEXANDER, his sons ABRAHAM ALEXANDER, NATHANIEL ALEXANDER, JACOB ALEXANDER and two granddaughters DORCAS ALEXANDER and AMELIA ALEXANDER.

The children named in this will do not agree with those named on page 398 of the History of Mecklenburg County, N. C. by Dr. J. B. Alexander, who says that ABRAHAM ALEXANDER died April 28, 1778, in the 69th year of his age, that his wife was DORCAS and that they had five sons and a daughter:

    Abraham Alexander
    Isaac Alexander
    Nathaniel Alexander
    Elias Alexander
    Joab Alexander, and
    Elizabeth Alexander;

and that the daughter ELIZABETH married WILLIAM ALEXANDER, a son of Hezekiah Alexander.

The date given for ABRAHAM ALEXANDER on his tombstone in the second oldest Sugar Creek Church cemetery is that he died April 28, 1786, aged 68 years. He was the presiding chairman of the Mecklenburg Convention on May 20, 1775.

Here are some other dates from the tombstones relating to Abraham's family:

DORCAS ALEXANDER (the widow) died May 20, 1800, exactly 25 years after the signing of the Mecklenburg Declaration, aged 66 years.
JOAB ALEXANDER died in 1828 aged 58 years.
ELIAS ALEXANDER died September 21, 1812, aged 53 years.

ZEBULON ALEXANDER - HIS WILL. It was probated in Mecklenburg County, March 3, 1784. In it mention is made of his daughter RUTH McREE. No Other person is mentioned.

WILLIAM ALEXANDER - HIS WILL. Proved in Mecklenburg County, North Carolina in the year 1772, witnessed by JOSEPH KENNEDY and ELIAS ALEXANDER.

JAMES ALEXANDER - HIS WILL. Proved in the County of Mecklenburg in the year 1779, and witnessed by BENJAMIN ALEXANDER and ANDREW ALEXANDER. Nothing further.

ARTHUR ALEXANDER - HIS WILL. He is described as "of ANSON COUNTY", the date being December 16, 1763, the year after Mecklenburg County was cut off of ANSON. The witnesses to his will were JAMES ALEXANDER, ABRAHAM ALEXANDER (whom he calls a brother); EZEKIEL ALEXANDER; also brother EZRA ALEXANDER and the testator's son ELIAS ALEXANDER.

EZRA ALEXANDER - HIS WILL. Proved in Mecklenburg County, North Carolina in the year 1798. The will is witnessed by SAMUEL POLK and by WILLIAM POLK.

Now just who can identify and straighten out these ALEXANDERS?

JOHN McKNITT ALEXANDER - HIS LAST WILL & TESTAMENT. Main will was executed July 2nd, 1807; codicil dated Nov. 3rd, 1812; a second codicil dated April 30, 1813. The testator mentions his five children, as follows:

    WILLIAM BANE ALEXANDER
    JOSEPH McKNITT ALEXANDER
    MARGARET McKNITT ALEXANDER
    JANE BANE ALEXANDER
    ABIGAIL BANE ALEXANDER.

In the main will in 1807 he appoints as his whole and sole executors his two sons WILLIAM BANE ALEXANDER and JOSEPH McKNITT ALEXANDER and RICHARD BARRY, ESQUIRE. Among other relatives mentioned in the will are the nine grand-children, children of his son WILLIAM BANE ALEXANDER; his four grand-children, the children of FRANCIS A. RAMSEY, and the six grand-children, children of REV. JAMES WALLIS and his wife POLLY; and the two children of his daughter ABIGAIL and her husband SAMUEL C. Caldwell - JANE BANE CALDWELL and DAVID THOMAS Caldwell; also mentions AMOS ALEXANDER, the son of HEZEKIAH ALEXANDER (said to have been his brother); also MOSES WINSLOW ALEXANDER, the grandson of the testator and son of JOSEPH McKNITT ALEXANDER, who married DOVIE WINSLOW, a daughter of MOSES WINSLOW and his wife JEAN OSBORNE.

WILLIAM BANE ALEXANDER, the son of JOHN McKNITT ALEXANDER, who married VIOLET DAVIDSON in 1791 had a family of fourteen children, seven boys and seven girls. It might be well to set out the names of these children at this point for reference. They were:

JOSEPH McKNITT ALEXANDER (b. 1793).
JANE BANE ALEXANDER (b. 1794)
ROBERT DAVIDSON ALEXANDER (b. 1796).
MARGARET DAVIDSON ALEXANDER (b. 1797).
WILLIAM BANE ALEXANDER (b. 1799).
JOHN RAMSEY ALEXANDER (b. 1801).
REBECCA ELOISE ALEXANDER (b. 1803).
BENJAMIN WILSON ALEXANDER (b. 1805).
SARAH DAVIDSON ALEXANDER (b. 1807).
JAMES McKNITT ALEXANDER (b. 1808).
GEORGE WASHINGTON ALEXANDER (b. 1810).
VIOLET ELIZABETH ALEXANDER (b. 1812).
MARY ABIGAIL ALEXANDER (b. 1813)
ISABELLA SOPHIA ALEXANDER (b. 1816).

JOSEPH McKNITT ALEXANDER, beloved physician and son of JOHN McKNITT ALEXANDER had only one son, MOSES WINSLOW ALEXANDER, who was mentioned in his grandfather's will. He married VIOLET WILSON WINSLOW GRAHAM, a daughter of GENERAL JOSEPH GRAHAM, and he and his wife had twelve children, as follows:

DOVIE WINSLOW ALEXANDER
JAMES GRAHAM ALEXANDER
JUNIUS MONTROSE ALEXANDER
ISABELLA LOUISA ALEXANDER
HAMILTON LAFAYETTE ALEXANDER
MARY SOPHIA ALEXANDER
JULIA SUSAN ALEXANDER
EMILY EUGENIA ALEXANDER
ROCINDA ALEXANDER
WISTAR WINSLOW ALEXANDER
SYDENHAM BENONI ALEXANDER
ALICE LENORA ALEXANDER

MOSES WINSLOW ALEXANDER died in 1845.

ROGER CUNNINGHAM - HIS WILL. Probated and of record in MECKLENBURG COUNTY, North Carolina, January 2, 1806. In it he mentions:
To my wife the house I live in.
To my daughter MARY CUNNINGHAM $100.00.
To my sons WILLIAM CUNNINGHAM and JAMES CUNNINGHAM.
To my daughters MARGARET CUNNINGHAM and ELEANOR CUNNINGHAM.
To my sons in law JOHN SHARP and JAMES SHARP.
To my son ROBERT CUNNINGHAM
Son ROBERT CUNNINGHAM and JOSIAH HARRISON to be executors of my estate.
Signed ROGER CUNNINGHAM.
Witnesses were JOHN SALE and JOSIAH HARRISON.

ROBERT CUNNINGHAM, the son of the above testator and the executor of the will with Josiah Harrison, was the REV. ROBERT MOORE CUNNINGHAM, afterwards a famous Presbyterian Minister, whose first wife was ELIZABETH MOORE, a daughter of CHARLES MOORE, the cousin of MRS. MARY GRAHAM, mother of GEN. JOSEPH GRAHAM and his brothers and sisters. Rev. Robert Moore Cunningham married three times, but had no children by this first marriage. He lived in GEORGIA, ALABAMA and KENTUCKY and left several children by his subsequent marriages.

ROBERT McKNIGHT - HIS WILL. Proved in Mecklenburg County, North Carolina, July 7, 1832 (See W. B. "G" p. 116). Names his wife as MARGARET, and sons JAMES McKNIGHT, ROBERT H. McKNIGHT and JOHN A. McKNIGHT, and his two sisters JANE McKNIGHT and SUSANNAH McKNIGHT. Also the testator names the following daughters:
Catherine C. McKnight
Margaret B. McKnight
Jane P. McKnight
Henry L. McKnight
Mary Anne McKnight
Susan A. McKnight.
The executors of this will, named therein were WILLIAM H. PARKS and son JAMES M. McKNIGHT. Witnesses were J. W. Heron and Robert M. Reams.

These McKnights were either the direct descendants or relatives of REV. JAMES McKNIGHT one of the first ministers of the old GILLIEAD CHURCH in the Beattie's Ford Section of Mecklenburg County.

JAMES CUNNINGHAM - HIS WILL. Probated in Mecklenburg County, North Carolina, on June 28th, 1833. The testator names his wife LETITIA and the following children:

ANDREW CUNNINGHAM
WILLIAM CUNNINGHAM
ROBERT CUNNINGHAM
JAMES CUNNINGHAM
MARY CUNNINGHAM
ELIZABETH CUNNINGHAM.

The witnesses and others mentioned were JAMES G. PORTER, JAMES CUNNINGHAM and one W. A. ARDERY.

This family of Cunninghams lived in the PROVIDENCE SECTION.

JAMES WALKUP - HIS WILL. This will was probated in Mecklenburg County, but the date it was proven is not shown on the abstract the writer took from the records. The date of the will was September 25, 1795, but, I think it was from the tombstone records I learned the date of his death, which was in 1798. He is buried in the old Waxhaw Graveyard, now in South Carolina. The will states that he was "of the Waxhaw settlement in Mecklenburg Co., N. C." He does not name his wife, but from the gravestone we know her name was MARGARET. From other sources that she was MARGARET PICKENS, daughter of ISRAEL PICKENS, who came from Virginia. The following are the names of the legatees under the will:

ISRAEL WALKUP
WILLIAM WALKUP
JOSEPH WALKUP
ROBERT WALKUP
MARGARET WALKUP
SAMUEL WALKUP
JOHN WALKUP
MARTHA WALKUP wife of JOHN FINLEY.
AGNES WALKUP wife of WILLIAM CROCKETT.

"And lastly," says the testator, "I do hereby nominate and appoint my son SAMUEL WALKUP & my brother in law JAMES DAVIS to be the executors of my last will and testament, this the 25th day of September, 1795."
Signed   JAMES WAUGHOP (Seal).
In the presence of JOHN ROGERS, BARBARA ROGERS and JOHN McCORKLE.

JAMES DAVIS - HIS WILL. Probated in Mecklenburg County, N. C., April 18, 1837. (Will Book "E" p. 177). Mentions:

MARIAH HILL, wife of REV. JACOB HILL.
Daughter ESTHER CROCKETT.
Grandson JAMES DAVIS CROCKETT.
Son JOHN NEWTON DAVIS, lands in the fork of McCAPIN and MICKEL CREEK, together with two sections of land lying and being in ERWIN County, GEORGIA, each containing 492 acres.
Son SAMUEL DAVIS, land purchased by me of G. STURGEON.
Grandson JAMES DAVIS, son of SAMUEL DAVIS.
Grandson WILLIAM WEBB, son of JANE WEBB.
Daughter MARY DAVIS, my plantation in YORK DISTRICT, S. C.
Daughter ANGELINE ALEXANDER.
Son JAMES DAVIS, plantation whereon I now live, with mill, etc. on the South side of McCAIPIN'S CREEK, my library, books, etc.
Names JAMES H. DAVIS and JOHN H. DAVIS executors of the will.
Witnesses, JAMES WILLIAMSON and JAMES A. WALKUP.
Codicil witnessed by D. R. DUNLAP.

EDWARD LINTON - HIS WILL. Probated in Mecklenburg County in 1776. (Will Book "D" p. 151). Testator mentions his "dearly beloved wife REBECCA, and makes his son SAMUEL LINTON his sole executor.
Revoking all other wills.
Signed   EDWARD LINTON (Seal).
The witnesses to the will were:
SAMUEL BARNETT
JOHN BARNETT
and
ALEX. BARNETT.

JAMES MARTIN - HIS WILL. Proved in Mecklenburg County, North Carolina, March 22, 1810. (Will Book "B" p. 88).
Names his wife MARGARET and children:
1. HANNAH MARTIN
2. LEMMY (or SAMMY) MARTIN
3. PEGGY L. MARTIN
4. JAMES D. MARTIN
5. ROBERT N. MARTIN
6. BILLY MARTIN
7. THOMAS MARTIN
EXECUTORS: Alexander Stinson, Thomas McGain, John Kerr and wife MARGARET MARTIN.
WITNESSES: HANNAH MARTIN, ESTHER McCLURE and ANDREW MOORE.

ROBERT MORTON - HIS WILL. Probated in Mecklenburg County, North Carolina, July 30, 1779 (Will Book "B" p. 58).
Names his wife SUSANNAH MORTON and Oldest son SAMUEL MORTON.
Third son JACOB MORTON.
Oldest daughter MARGARET MORTON who married a McKINLEY.
Second daughter SUSANNAH MORTON, the wife of a McCALL.
Daughter AGNES MORTON married a HOUSTON.
Witnesses: DAVID WILSON, JOHN BRANHAM and HEZEKIAH ALEXANDER.
Executors: HEZEKIAH ALEXANDER and JAMES BRADSHAW.

ARCHIBALD CROCKETT - HIS WILL. Proved in Mecklenburg County, North Carolina, January 3rd, 1804. (His wife was a KING). Mentions:
1. Son ELIAS CROCKETT. (Land where I live).
2. Daughter: ANN CROCKETT, wife of a MR. TAYLOR. Tract of land where FREDERICK TAYLOR lives. (Evidently ANN married FREDERICK TAYLOR).
3. Son: JOHN CROCKETT. To him I will and bequeath a tract and parcel of land now lying in the hands of COL. THOMAS KING, now living in the State of TENNESSEE in HAWKINS COUNTY, and all the rest of my property except one woman's saddle to be taken out for my daughter MARY ANN.
Executors: Son JOHN CROCKETT and SAMUEL DOWNS.
In presence of ELI CROCKETT and ELIAS CROCKETT.

Above is the will of the grandfather of the celebrated and famous DAVID CROCKETT, his father being the son JOHN CROCKETT mentioned in the will. This will refutes the idea that the father of DAVID CROCKETT was a penniless backwoodsman in Tennessee, and shows that he was a close kinsman of Hon. Thomas King, an uncle, who lived in and helped to organize HAWKINS COUNTY, TENNESSEE, and who served from that district in the Legislature of North Carolina.

ANDREW McKEE - HIS WILL. Probated in Mecklenburg County, North Carolina, January 7th, 1801. In the will he mentions his wife MARTHA and three sons:
1. WILLIAM McKEE
2. RICHARD McKEE
3. JAMES McKEE
and refers to "other children" without naming them. Executors: JAMES McKEE, DR. NATHANIEL ALEXANDER, THOMAS ALEXANDER and SAMUEL BOWMAN.
Witnessed by THOMAS HENDERSON and JAMES McKEE.

ROBERT DAVIS - HIS WILL. Probated in Mecklenburg County, North Carolina, October 7, 1836. (This ROBERT DAVIS was deceased at the time of his father's will (JAMES DAVIS) in 1737, and is not mentioned therein for that reason). He mentions in the will the name of his wife MARGARET DAVIS, and his children:
1. Eldest son ALEXANDER G. DAVIS.
2. Second son: ISRAEL P. DAVIS, to whom he leaves what he calls the "McCrory plantation".
3. Youngest son: John N. DAVIS.
4. Daughter MARGARET DAVIS
5. Daughter AGNES DAVIS.
Executors: Wife MARGARET and son JOHN DAVIS.
Witnesses: ROBERT G. DAVIS, ISRAEL DAVIS and NATHAN COOK.
(Compare this will with that of JAMES DAVIS heretofore shown.)

Another son of JAMES DAVIS and a brother of ROBERT DAVIS shown above was ISRAEL PICKENS DAVIS, who had been dead for some TEN years at the time his brother ROBERT DAVIS died, as is shown by the following tombstone record from page 261 of ACKLEN'S Tennessee Records:

"Sacred to the memory of ISRAEL P. DAVIS, of WAXHAW, Mecklenburg County, N. C., who on returning home from visiting the Western District of Tennessee, departed this life November 5, 1826; aged 45 years."
His remains were interred in what is known as the JOHN MATTHEWS CEMETERY, six miles South of COLUMBIA, TENNESSEE. The following very interesting records in regard to ISRAEL PICKENS DAVIS appears in ACKLEN'S RECORDS:

"The above is a copy of the inscription on one of the early tombs of the MATTHEWS CEMETERY located near the present residence of T. H. NEELY. This was the home of ESQ. JOHN MATTHEWS, who gave the cemetery grounds and whose descendants have composed some of the best citizenship of MAURY COUNTY, TENNESSEE.

"The traveling companion of MR. DAVIS was my father, RICHARD PEEPLES, of MECKLENBURG COUNTY, North Carolina. The two friends had traveled through the mountains of Western N. C., and West Tennessee as far as the CHICKASAW BLUFFS, the site of the present City of MEMPHIS. On their return home they stopped on a Saturday night at the home of their mutual friend and former neighbor, JOHN MATTHEWS, to rest and to resume their journey on Monday morning. But here, far from his home and family, (he was married and had a family at the time), Mr. Davis was taken seriously ill, & after some days, in spite of the tender care of friends true and tried, he died, and his remains were laid to rest in the cemetery near by, there to rest until the resurection. My father resumed the journey homeward alone, taking with him the horse and saddle and other valuables of his deceased friend.

"Some years afterwards the wife and family removed to MAURY COUNTY, TENNESSEE and settled near BIGBYVILLE and became associated with the A. R. Presbyterian Church. JAMES DAVIS, his son, was a ruling elder in HOPEWELL CHURCH at this place and was buried near his father some 83 years ago. (This was written in November, 1909.)

JOHN WYLIE - HIS WILL. Proved in Mecklenburg County, North Carolina, December 27th, 1806. (Will Book "G" page 53).
He mentions his wife ELIZABETH.
Son in law SAMUEL PARKS.
Son JOSEPH V. WYLIE.
Son in law ROBERT WYLIE
Son in law ALEX McKIBBEN.
Son ROBERT WYLIE
Son JOHN GIBSON WYLIE
Son WILLIAM WYLIE
Executors: Wife ELIZABETH and sons ROBERT WYLIE and WILLIAM WYLIE.
Witnesses: SAMUEL BLACK, JANE BLACK and HAMILTON BLACK.

JOHN McCULLOGH - WILL. Proven in Mecklenburg County, North Carolina, May 6, 1848. (Will Book J. page 144).
Mentions his wife DOSY M. McCULLOUGH, to whom he leaves (among other bequests) lands purchased from A. F. WYLIE, known as the "Potts place".
Daughter: KATHERINE ROSINDA McCULLOUGH.
Daughter: SARAH JANE McCULLOUGH
Daughter: NANCY ROSALIE McCULLOUGH
Son: AMOS McCULLOGH.
"Other children provided for".
Mentions "lands from my father" without naming him. Signed
JOHN McCULLOCH (Seal).
Administrator: JAMES B. ROBINSON.
Witnesses: SAM A. DAVIS and WILLIAM ROSS.

JOHN LOVE - HIS WILL. Proved in Mecklenburg County July 23, 1791. Mentions his beloved wife SARAH LOVE, and the following children:
1. JANE REEMY
2. WILLIAM LOVE
3. JOHN LOVE
4. MARY ADAMSON
5. THOMAS LOVE
6. SAMUEL LOVE
7. JOSEPH LOVE
8. CHRISTOPHER LOVE
9. SARAH LOVE
10. ELIZABETH LOVE BANKS.
11. DAVID LOVE, he and CHRISTOPHER are left the planation.
Executors: JOSEPH TODD and JAMES NEEL.
Signed: JOHN LOVE (Seal).
Witnesses: MICHAEL STINSON and JOHN CANNON.

The records indicate that the LOVE FAMILY, of this will, was of a different set than that of the EPHRAIM LOVE branch in Rutherford, Buncomb and Western North Carolina, which was represented by COL. ROBERT LOVE and THOMAS LOVE, of that section. These LOVES were from Virginia to North Carolina, but settled in that part of ANSON which for a time was considered in Mecklenburg County, but later became UNION COUNTY.
The son 11 DAVID LOVE married the winsome lass JEAN BLEWETT, who used to ferry him across the PEE DEE RIVER, when he was an INDIAN TRADER, she being a daughter of CAPT. WILLIAM BLEWETT and his wife SARAH GARTEN. David Love was Captain of a Company in the revolution, and was married to JEAN BLEWETT, it is said in 1772, probably in ANSON COUNTY.
CAPT. DAVID LOVE was a rather eccentric character and sold out his interest in the plantation left him and his brother CHRISTOPHER and moved to GREENE COUNTY, Georgia, near the present historic town of GREENSBORO, where he lived and died. The place he owned there in his lifetime was known as "LOVE SPRINGS", and Dr. T. B. Rice, the historian, has written a very interesting story about that spring and the old revolutionary soldier. Some insight into DAVID'S character may be gleaned from the unusual names he bestowed upon his children, as shown by his will, dated November 29, 1798, proved in Greene County, Georgia. In this will he mentions his wife JANE LOVE and the following children:
1. ROBERTUS LOVE
2. JOSEPHUS LOVE
3. ACHSAN LOVE
4. VIRTUOUS LOVE
5. BELOVED LOVE (Son)
6. CHASTE EASTER LOVE
7. ALLELUJAH LOVE
To these last two daughters he leaves "a tract of land conveyed to me by WILLIAM DANIEL and WILLIAM HOUGHTON in the Appalachie Forks".
8. FRIEND ORTED LOVE
9. My cousin DAVID LOVE who now lives with me, 100 acres in this county surveyed by GEORGE PHILLIPS and joining WILLIAM PHILLIPS of Virginia.
Directs that his son should go to the State of VIRGINIA and get his audited claim or certificate which shall be divided among his children. Such claims are in the hands of JOHN B. SCOTT.
Signed: DAVID LOVE.
Executors: Wife JANE and sons ROBERTUS LOVE and JOSEPHUS LOVE.
Witnesses: WILLIAM PHILLIPS, DAVID PATILLO and CURTIS KING.

WILLIAM WALLACE - HIS WILL. Probated in Mecklenburg County, North Carolina, October 26, 1824. (Will Book "G" page 58). Mentions:
Daughters:
ELIZABETH WALLACE
MARGARET WALLACE
MATILDA WALLACE
MALINDA WALLACE
My beloved son MATTHEW BROWN WALLACE.
My brother MATTHEW WALLACE.
Witnesses: MR. ERWIN and JAMES W. ALEXANDER.

JOHN BARNETT - HIS WILL. Proved in Mecklenburg County, North Carolina in the year 1804. Mentions:
Daughter MARY JACK, wife of JOHN JACK.
Daughter ANN ELLIOTT.
Son: JOHN BARNETT
Daughter: SUSANNAH SMART.
Grandson: JOHN ELLIOTT.
Witnessed by JOSEPH C. McBEE.

(The SUSANNAH SMART, a daughter, was the famous SUSAN, friend of ANDREW JACKSON, who witnessed the signing of the Mecklenburg Declaration in 1775, as testified to by her in later years, and whose will will be found in the pages of these notes.)

WILLIAM BLACK - HIS WILL, dated November 1, 1775. Mentions his daughter FRANCES BLACK and his brother JOHN BLACK.
Witnesses were: WILLIAM PICKENS, WILLIAM HENDERSON and MARTHA BLACK.
Martha may have been his wife.

SAMUEL BROWN - HIS WILL. Probated in Mecklenburg County, North Carolina, April 17, 1772. The testator names his son and daughter:
BENJAMIN BROWN
SOPHIA BROWN
"and the rest of my children" without naming them.
Witnesses: DAVID ALEXANDER, JOHN ALEXANDER and ZACHEUS WILSON.

Three years later the witness ZACHEUS WILSON signed the Mecklenburg Declaration.

RICHARD DANIEL - HIS WILL. Probated in Mecklenburg County, North Carolina October 15th 1823. (Will Book "C"). Does not mention a wife.
Brother: WASHINGTON DANIEL
Sister: MARY DANIEL
Brother: WILLIAM DANIEL
Appoints WILLIAM DANIEL, his brother, administrator of the will. Legacy left also to EPHRAIM KENDRICK. No relation given.
Witnesses: STEPHEN FOX, EPHRAIM KENDRICK and FREDERICK DUNKINS.

WILLIAM DARNALL - HIS WILL. Probated in Mecklenburg County, North Carolina February 13th, 1799. (Will Book "C" page 17).
Mentions his wife PHILLIS DARNALL.
Children: JAMES DARNALL
JOHN DARNALL
POLLY ALEXANDER
Executors: Wife PHILLIS and son JAMES DARNALL. Signed: WILLIAM DARNALL.
Witnesses: FRANCIS SMART and JOSEPH DARNALL.

EDWARD LINTON - HIS WILL. Probated in Mecklenburg County, North Carolina in 1776. (Will Book "D" page 151.
Mentions his "dearly beloved wife" REBECCA to whom he gives a fifth part of his estate. (Indicating that there were four children).
Son SAMUEL LINTON.
Sole Executor, son SAMUEL LINTON.
Revokes all other wills.
Signed: EDWARD LINTON.
Witnesses to the will were ALEX. BARNETT, JOHN BARNETT and SAMUEL BARNETT.

The son SAMUEL LINTON of the above will was a revolutionary soldier, said to have served in South Carolina. He was the father of SAMUEL BROWN LINTON, of GREENE COUNTY, Georgia, who was the ancestor of all of the Georgia Lintons.

JOHN LUSK - HIS WILL. Proved in Mecklenburg County, North Carolina, September 20th, 1777. (Will Book "D" page 152).
Mentions his wife ELIZABETH LUSK.
Will states that he had three sons, but only names one of them, SAMUEL LUSK.
Signed: JOHN LUSK.
Witnesses were ROGER CUNNINGHAM, JOHN BAXTER and GEORGE HOPKINS.

It is believed that the sons of JOHN LUSK moved West to BUNCOMBE County and settled for a time.

WILLIAM KING - HIS WILL. Probated in Mecklenburg County, North Carolina, and dated November 1, 1788. (Will Book "D" page 158).
Mentions "my dear wife MARY ANN KING".
My four children:
1. ARCHIBALD CROCKETT
2. JOHN KING
3. ELIZABETH McCORKLE
4. WILLIAM McCULLOCH.
Executors named are ARCHIBALD CROCKETT and JOHN KING.
Witnesses were ELI CROCKETT, JOHN ELLIOTT and HENRY DOWNS.

This WILLIAM KING lived somewhere East of PROVIDENCE CHURCH of which ARCHIBALD CROCKETT was one of the first elders. He was the Great Grandfather of the famous DAVID CROCKETT of Tennessee and Texas, his daughter having married ARCHIBALD CROCKETT, the grandfather of DAVID CROCKETT. HENRY DOWNS who signed this will as one of the witnesses was a signer of the Mecklenburg Declaration on May 20, 1775.

SAMUEL KNOX - HIS WILL. Probated in Mecklenburg County, North Carolina and dated May 5, 1794.
Mentions first, his "well beloved wife MARY".
Daughter JANE KNOX.
Daughter SARAH KNOX.
Daughter MARY KNOX.
Grandsons: JOHN PETTUS and STEPHEN PETTUS.
Grand-daughter: AGNES PETTUS.
Grand-daughter: MARY PETTUS, daughter of GEORGE PETTUS.
Grand-daughter: MARY CANDISH, daughter of ALEXANDER CANDISH to whom he gives certain lands in S. C. joining GEORGE PETTUS, WILLIAM PETTUS, JOSEPH JACKSON and JESSE KENDON, also a plantation in Mecklenburg County, North Carolina joining DAVID McMEANS, SAMUEL NEELY and MARTIN WEST.
Witnesses: JAMES F. GORDON, JOSEPH KNOX, and GEORGE PETTUS.

At this point, at least, I shall not attempt to un-puzzle the significance of this will in which the PETTUS FAMILY of Eastern Virginia, are apparently badly mixed with the KNOX FAMILY, but let the reader work it out. And at the same time consider the one immediately following:

VIOLET PETTUS - HER WILL. Probated in Mecklenburg County, N. C. dated January 26th, 1828. (Will Book "D" pp. 364). Provides: All my negro property to be hired out until my son STEPHEN PETTUS becomes of age.
HANNAH M. A. PETTUS
JOHN PETTUS.
Signed: VIOLET PETTUS (SEAL).
Witnessed by ROBERT WILSON and SAMUEL WILSON.

JOSEPH BARNARD - HIS WILL. Probated in Mecklenburg County, N. C. dated March 10, 1808.
Witnesses: JOHN MORRIS and DANIEL DENTON.

PATRICK JACK - HIS WILL. Proven in Mecklenburg County, North Carolina, and dated May 19, 1780. (Will Book "D" page 93). Mentions his "well beloved wife" and his FIVE daughters:
1. MARY ALEXANDER
2. MARGARET WILSON
3. CHARITY DYSART
4. JANE BARNETT
5. LYLLY NICHOLSON

Also my grandson PATRICK JACK.
Executors: JAMES JACK and JOSEPH NICHOLSON.
Signed: PATRICK JACK.(Seal)
Witnesses: JOHN NEWTON, DANIEL McDUGALD and JOSEPH WISHARD.

JOHN THOMPSON - HIS WILL. Probated Mecklenburg County, North Carolina, and dated May 25th 1814. Names his wife NANCY and children:
1. LUCY HUTSON
2. MOLLY HUTSON
3. WILLIAM THOMPSON
4. NATHAN THOMPSON

Executors: WILLIAM McKEE and THOMAS MORRIS.
Witnesses: SILAS M. BROWN, BENJAMIN FINCHER and MARY WILSON.

JOHN HANNA - HIS WILL. Probated in Mecklenburg County, North Carolina, September 6, 1765. (Will Book "D" p. 39).
To his wife SUSAN HANNA one-third part.
Son: ANDREW HANNA one-third part.
Son: JOHN HANNA one-third part.
To my daughter-in-law ANN McCRACKEN.
Executors: COL. NATHANIEL ALEXANDER, THOMAS POLK, ESQ. and SARAH HANNA.
Witnesses: J. McKNITT ALEXANDER and ALEX. McCOSTEN.

ANDREW BAXTER - HIS WILL. Probated in Mecklenburg County, North Carolina, and dated on November 23, 1775.
Gives to his "beloved wife" FRANCES BAXTER, the home and plantation whereon she now lives during life.
Names children:
1. ANDREW BAXTER
2. JAMES BAXTER
3. JANE BAXTER
4. ELIZABETH BAXTER
5. JOHN BAXTER
Signed: ANDREW BAXTER (Seal).
Executors: EZRA ALEXANDER and HENRY DOWNS.
Witnesses: JAMES SHANKS and ROBERT McGAUGH.

Both of the named executors to the above will, on May 20 immediately preceding the date of the will had been present and signed the famous Mecklenburg Declaration.

ESTHER WALKER - HER WILL. Mecklenburg Co. North Carolina, May 1, 1843. The testator names the following children: (W. B. "J" p. 168).
1. MARY WALKER
2. JEMIMAH WALKER
3. JOHN WALKER (and daughter ELIZA).
4. ADELINE WALKER.
Executor: Son JOHN WALKER.

GEORGE BAKER - HIS WILL. Probated in Mecklenburg County, North Carolina, and dated in 1814.
Names his wife RACHEL and leaves to her the "plantation where I live".
Names his children:
1. REBECCA MITCHELL, wife of JOHN.
2. ABEL BAKER.
3. JACOB BAKER
4. ISAAC BAKER
5. RACHEL BAKER
6. HANNAH BAKER
7. ELIZABETH BAKER
Executrix, wife RACHEL BAKER.
Signed: GEORGE BAKER.
Witnesses: J. HEGANS and JOHN BYROM.

The above GEORGE BAKER may have been a grandson of SAMUEL BAKER, the son in law of REV. JOHN THOMSON, who married the daughter ELIZABETH THOMSON, who afterwards became the wife of CHARLES HARRIS, but this fact has not been established at this writing.

SAMUEL WILSON, SR. - HIS WILL. Probated in Mecklenburg County, North Carolina, and dated March 9, 1778. His wife at the time of his death, the exact date of which has not been found, was MARGARET. She was one of the FIVE daughters mentioned in the will of PATRICK JACK an abstract of whose will is on this page.

Samuel Wilson was married three times & the names of his wives in the order of marriage were: MARY WINSLOW, the WIDOW HOWARD and MARGARET JACK.
Children by first marriage were:
1. DAVID WILSON
2. BENJAMIN WILSON
3. SAMUEL WILSON
4. SALLY WILSON
5. VIOLET WILSON
6. MARY WILSON
Children by second marriage:
7. MARGARET WILSON.
Children by third marriage:
8. ROBERT WILSON
9. WILLIAM WILSON
10. LILLIE WILSON
11. SARAH WILSON
12. CHARITY WILSON.

The above children are all mentioned in the will of SAMUEL WILSON SR., except those who may have died young and before the will was written. The testator was the father in law of EZEKIEL POLK, who married MARY, daughter by the first marriage; and he was also the father in law of MAJ. JOHN DAVIDSON, the revolutionary patriot, who married the daughter VIOLET.

The executors named in the will were his son in law MAJ. JOHN DAVIDSON, and his sons BENJAMIN and SAMUEL WILSON.
The will was signed:
SAMUEL WILSON.
Witnesses to the will were:
JOHN HENDERSON
SAMUEL BLYTHE
JOHN McKNITT ALEXANDER.

Authority: History of Hopewell Presbyterian Church by C. W. SOMMERVILLE Ph. D.

DAVID WILSON - HIS WILL. Proved Mecklenburg County, North Carolina, dated in September, 1830 (Book "G").
Name of his wife not mentioned in the will.
Children:
1. SAMUEL WILSON
2. MOSES WINSTON WILSON
3. POLLY WILSON married a Mr. WAUGH.
4. BENJAMIN WILSON'S two children, not mentioned by name.
Executors, friends: DANIEL McKNITT and MOSES W. WILSON.

This DAVID WILSON was apparently the oldest son of SAMUEL WILSON, SR. and the brother-in-law of EZEKIEL POLK grandfather of President JAMES KNOX POLK. In the sketch of SAMUEL WILSON SR. in SOMERVILLE'S "Hopewell Church" it is stated that DAVID WILSON had two sons LAWSON WILSON and WINSLOW WILSON. The latter is mentioned in his will but the former is NOT. This account is taken from the records.

ROBERT WILSON - HIS WILL. Probated in Mecklenburg County, North Carolina, and dated on December 14, 1793.
Mentions his wife ELEANOR.
Children:
1. AARON WILSON
2. ZACHEUS WILSON
3. MOSES WILSON
4. THOMAS WILSON
5. JOHN WILSON
6. JAMES WILSON
7. ROBERT WILSON
8. JOSIAH WILSON
Executors: JOHN McDOWELL, DAVID VANN and AARON WILSON, JOHN TAYLOR and WILLIAM IKES.
Witnesses (friends): COL. ROBERT ERWIN, ZACCHEUS WILSON, JAMES SPRATT, SR., JOSEPH SWANN and JOHN McDOWELL.

The above ROBERT WILSON was one of the three brothers of ZACCHEUS WILSON, a "signer" of the MECKLENBURG DECLARATION. His brothers ZACCHEUS and DAVID WILSON in 1796 removed to near the town of GALLATIN, in SUMNER COUNTY, Tennessee. ZACCHEUS WILSON, the witness above, was a "cousin" of the testator, & this fact establishes that the father of the signer ZACCHEUS must have had a brother who came to MECKLENBURG COUNTY (about 1735 or 1740). This family of WILSONS lived in what is now CABARRUS COUNTY, then a part of MECKLENBURG.

AUGUSTINE REED - HIS WILL. Mecklenburg County N. C. dated May 30, 1781. (Will Book "F" page 117.) Names his wife ELIZABETH. Farther provides:
"My children are all and every one of them to be taught and educated in the principles of the Christian religion".
Executors: MARK HOUSE and DANIEL JARRETT.

JOHN MORROW - HIS WILL. Probated in Mecklenburg County, North Carolina, and dated February 16, 1796. (Will Book "B" p. 134).
Wife is mentioned but no name given.
Children named:
1. GEORGE MORROW
2. ROBERT MORROW
3. JOHN MORROW
4. RICHARD MORROW five shillings.
5. JAMES MORROW and his son JOHN.
Executors: WILLIAM HILL and a certain JAMES CURRY.
Witnesses: JAMES CURRY, GEORGE DUCKWORTH and WILLIAM HILL.

In the will of ELIZABETH MORROW (Dated June 6, 1832, and abstracted herein) WILLIAM HILL was one of the witnesses and GEORGE MORROW is referred to therein as GEORGE McKNIGHT or McKNIGHT MORROW.

In the will of ROBERT MORROW March 25, 1800 (Will Book "B" page 145 Mecklenburg County) he names appraisers JAMES MEEK, LEWIS PATTON and JAMES CURRY, and his wife MARTHA "shall have the raising of all the children" without naming them.

MRS. JIMMIE LEE HARRIS, of Mooresville, N. C., is a daughter of a GEORGE McKNIGHT MORROW, JR., who was the son of GEORGE McKNIGHT MORROW SR. & the last was perhaps also a son of a GEORGE McKNIGHT MORROW.

JAMES MORROW, buried in the old Six-Mile Church below PINEVILLE who married SUSANNA WATSON, the daughter of DRURY WATSON, from Virginia, named one of his sons JAMES McKNIGHT MORROW. See later.

DAVID MORROW - HIS WILL. Probated in Mecklenburg County, North Carolina, and dated February 25, 1810. (Will Book "E" page 15).
Does not name his wife.
Children mentioned:
1. JAMES MORROW.
2. DAVID MORROW on Sugar Creek.
3. MARGERY MORROW married HIGGINS or HEGANS.
4. ANN MORROW married a CROCKETT.
5. MARGARET MORROW married a WALKUP.
6. ELIZABETH MORROW married a PRIDE.
7. MARTHA MORROW married a CROCKETT.
8. JANE MORROW married a BROWN.
Grand-daughter MARY K. MORROW.
Executors: Friends BENJAMIN WEATHERS and LEMUEL BIGHAM.
Witnesses: ABNER ALEXANDER and PARIS ALEXANDER.

An abstract of the will of MARTHA MORROW, obviously the widow of DAVID MORROW above will be found a few pages back in this record. It is dated September 1, 1830, but the date of probate is not shown.

WILLIAM McKEE - HIS WILL. Probated in Mecklenburg County, North Carolina, and dated on September 22, 1832. (Will Book "G" p. 111).

Testator fails to name his wife, so it is presumed that he was a widower at the time he executed the will. He mentions:

Grandson WILLIAM, son of JOHN McKEE.
Grand-daughter NANCY, daughter of JOHN McKEE.
Grand-daughter MARGARET C. McKEE, daughter of JOHN McKEE.
Grand-daughter MARGARET, daughter of JAMES McKEE.
Grand-son WILLIAM, son of JAMES McKEE.
Grand-daughter MARGARET, daughter of MORRISON McKEE.
Grand-son WILLIAM, son of MORRISON McKEE.
Grand-son ELLIS, son of MORRISON McKEE.
Grand-daughter RUTH, daughter of MORRISON McKEE.
Grand-daughter POLLY, daughter of MORRISON McKEE.

My daughters:
RUTH McKEE
POLLY McKEE
AMELIA McKEE
ELIZA McKEE
FREDERICK McKEE.

Books to JOHN, JAMES and MORRISON McKEE.
Grandson WILLIAM McKEE and his brother FRANKLIN McKEE.
Grand-daughter ISABELLA, daughter of JOHN McKEE.

Executors: JAMES McKEE, DR. DAVID R. DUNLAP and JAMES N. MORRISON.
Witnesses: WILLIAM REA and JAMES REA.

These McKEES all lived in the PROVIDENCE section of MECKLENBURG COUNTY.

BENJAMIN MORROW - HIS WILL. Probated in Mecklenburg County, North Carolina, and dated on August 5, 1767. (Will Book "X" p. 195). The will was probated many years later in 1875.

Does not mention his wife.
Children:
1. JOHN W. MORROW appointed guardian for my son.
2. HENRY C. MORROW, a bequest to be held in trust until he is 25 years old.
3. BENJ. F. MORROW appointed guardian of my daughter.
4. MATILDA N. MORROW.

Witnesses to the main will, JOHN WALKER & JOHN WOLFE.

Codicil, filed later, provides:
Stock in the South Carolina Railroad Co., to be divided equally between my three sons:
JOHN W. MORROW
BENJAMIN F. MORROW
WASHINGTON MORROW.
And my three grand-children:
MARTHA THOMAS
MARY THOMAS
WILLIAM B. THOMAS
to have (their mother's) a child's portion of my estate.

My friend JOHN E. BROWN made co-executor.
Witnesses: J. N. MORROW and JAMES W. OSBORN.

The above BENJAMIN MORROW was MAJ. BENJ. MORROW of the war of 1812, and the son of JAMES McKNIGHT MORROW of Six-Mile CHURCH below PINEVILLE.

ANDREW REA - HIS WILL. Probated in Mecklenburg County, North Carolina, and dated on May 18, 1801. (Will Book "T" page 60).

Mentions his wife JANE.
Children:
1. JOHN REA and his son ANDREW, a minor.
2. ANN REA married McCLUGHEN.
3. ANTHONY REA.
4. JANE REA.
5. NED REA.
6. THOMAS REA - plantation where I now live.
7. ELIZABETH REA.

Grand-daughter JANE McCLUGHEN.
Executors: My son JOHN REA, JAMES McCLUGHEN and WILLIAM McKEE.
Witnesses: JAMES WALLIS and FRANCES HOUSE.

The witness was the REV. JAMES WALLIS, son in law of JOHN McK. ALEXANDER and the minister of PROVIDENCE CHURCH.

DAVID REA - HIS WILL. Probated in MECKLENBURG COUNTY, N. C. and dated July 13, 1839. (Will Book "T" page 238).

(This testator was a revolutionary soldier and is buried at PROVIDENCE CHURCH, which see).

He names the following legatees:
1. JOHN REA, deceased.
2. JAMES REA.
3. WILLIAM REA.
4. JOSEPH REA.
5. SILAS REA.
6. GEORGE REA.
7. MARTHA REA.
8. MARY REA.
9. HANNAH REA.
10. DAVID REA.
11. JONATHAN REA.
12. ELIZABETH REA.

Daughter in law MARY REA and her daughter MARGARET REA.

Witnesses: *ROBERT PEOPLES and JAMES BLACK.

*See abstract of the will of ROBERT DAVIS and the notes thereunder for the name PEOPLES or PEEPLES, of Mecklenburg County.

ALLEN REED - HIS WILL. Probated in MECKLENBURG COUNTY, North Carolina, and dated June 11, 1814. (Will Book "T" page 75).

Names his wife FANNY.
Children:
1. WILLIAM REED, plantation in LINCOLN COUNTY.
2. JONAS REED, plantation where I live.
3. ALLEN REED, plantation in LINCOLN COUNTY.
4. POLLY C. REED
5. JAMES D. REED.
6. ELIZABETH REED married a DOBBINS.
7. JONATHAN REED.

My sister in law JANE MOORE.*
Executors: Brother JOSEPH REED and ROBERT SLOAN.
Witnesses: JOHN HARRISON and JOSEPH L. CUTHBERT.

*FANNY, the wife of the above testator, ALLEN REED, was FRANCES MOORE, daughter of HUGH. They were married Nov. 2, 1797. JOHN FITTON, Sec.

MOSES SHELBY - HIS WILL. Probated in Mecklenburg County, North Carolina, dated in 1778. (At that time Mecklenburg, but in the part afterwards changed to CABARRUS COUNTY.)
Does not mention name of his wife.
Children:
1. WILLIAM SHELBY
2. JOHN SHELBY
3. EVAN SHELBY
4. THOMAS SHELBY
5. MOSES SHELBY
6. CATHERINE SHELBY
7. MARGARET SHELBY
8. RACHEL SHELBY
9. ISABELLA SHELBY
10. ELEANOR SHELBY married a CARUTHERS.
11. MARY SHELBY wife of OLIVER WYLIE.
Signed: MOSES SHELBY.
Executors: His wife, OLIVER WYLIE and sons EVAN and THOMAS SHELBY.

ROBERT WALKER - HIS WILL. Probated in Mecklenburg County, North Carolina, November 1, 1824. (Will Book "B" page 12).
Does not mention his wife's name.
Children:
1. ANNIE WALKER married a REED.
2. WILLIAM WALKER
3. MARY WALKER married a ERA.
4. JANE WALKER married a REED.
5. JAMES WALKER.
6. ROBERT WALKER.
Executors: WILLIAM WALKER and ROBERT WALKER, his sons.
Signed: ROBERT WALKER.
Witnesses: WILLIAM WALKER and JOHN WALKER.

HUGH REED - HIS WILL. Probated in Mecklenburg County, North Carolina, August 25, 1778. (Will Book "T" page 116.)
Mentions his wife AGNES NEEL and her son WILLIAM. Other legatees named are:
1. JAMES REED
2. JOHN REED
3. THOMAS REED
4. MARY REED married a NEEL.
5. HANNAH REED married a McDONALD.
6. WILLIAM REED, all my lands, etc.
Executors: WILLIAM REED and DAVID REED on SUGAR CREEK, and JOHN REED.
Signed: HUGH REED.
Witnesses: THOMAS ALLISON, SIMON VANN POTTS and DAVID FREEMAN.

HUGH MOORE - HIS FAMILY. HUGH MOORE (Son of DAVID MOORE who left will in Mecklenburg County, North Carolina, dated Feb. 5, 1778, shown in these notes) failed to leave a will but the following DEED gives the names of his five sons:
DEED executed NOV. 3, 1807, by and between DAVID MOORE, of the County of Mecklenburg and the State of North Carolina, of the one part, and a son and heir to HUGH MOORE, deceased, and JOHN MOORE, HUGH MOORE, WILLIAM MOORE and JOSEPH MOORE of the same, and heirs of the said HUGH MOORE, deceased, of the other part, WITNESSETH:
In consideration of the sum of $324.00, in hand paid by the said DAVID MOORE, unto the said JOHN, HUGH, WILLIAM and JOSEPH MOORE, they bargain, sell and convey to said DAVID MOORE, all that certain tract of land lying on BOTH SIDES OF GOOSE CREEK, including the deceased's old improvements (which are carefully described by meets and bounds) containing 324 acres of land, more or less.
Warranted and signed by
JOHN MOORE
HUGH MOORE
WILLIAM MOORE
JOSEPH MOORE
Witnessed by DANIEL L. HALL and by CHARLES T. ALEXANDER.

HUGH MOORE, the father of the five brothers mentioned in the foregoing deed, is on the 1790 Census of Mecklenburg County, N. C., as the head of a family of nine, two males over 16 years old (which included himself) four males under 16 and four females.
HUGH MOORE died intestate between 1790 and 1793, the latter being the date of the deed of August 25, 1793, shown in these notes, when the sons HUGH and WILLIAM purchased a part of the lands described in the above deed from ANDREW ALEXANDER at a sale by the Sheriff - ISAAC ALEXANDER being the Clerk of the Court at that time.
For some reason the estate of HUGH MOORE was not finally settled until 1807, when the above deed was executed, the son DAVID MOORE buying the interest of his four brothers in the land on "both sides of Goose Creek", as shown in the deed.
In the census (of 1790) HUGH MOORE, it will be noted, was on record as having FOUR females in his family. These would have been his wife and THREE daughters, the identity of whom is given below:
PATSY MOORE (probably christened Martha) who is said to have married an IRISHMAN, COL. SMITH, an officer of the revolution. They moved to Greene County, Georgia, where their daughter JANE SMITH married in 1822, ROBERT ERA, a schoolmaster, who afterwards represented that county 19 terms in the General Assembly of Georgia.
MARGARET MOORE, who married ROBERT McKNIGHT, in 1803, is also believed to have been another one of the daughters and a sister of the five MOORE BROTHERS mentioned in the above deed.
FRANCES MOORE, who married ALLEN REED on November 2, 1797, with JOHN FITTON as security, was the other. (The will of ALLEN REED with wife "FANNY" is abstracted elsewhere in the preceding notes).
HUGH MOORE, according to the family tradition, married a MISS FITZGERALD. It is known that he went to GEORGIA and settled & later to Chambers County, Alabama, where he died, and his estate was settled.
WILLIAM MOORE married POLLY FITTON, in Mecklenburg County, North Carolina, on February 19, 1805, with JAMES REED as his security.
JOHN MOORE was the oldest son of HUGH MOORE, the father of all these children. His wife was OLIVIA. He and his wife and their children remained in Mecklenburg County, but they are buried in the old second SIX MILE PRESBYTERIAN CHURCH, which is now just across the State line in South Carolina. This JOHN MOORE died September 2, 1833 and his wife OLIVIA died in 1857 aged 84 years, 9 months and 25 days. JOHN P. MOORE, OLIVIA MILLER and HUGH MOORE, their children are also buried in the same plot. It is believed the Moores and Alexanders were related.

JAMES MOORE - HIS WILL (Son of DAVID MOORE, SR., son of first DAVID) Probated Mecklenburg County, North Carolina and dated July 12 1832. Names his wife CYNTHIA MOORE and the following children:
Daughters:
1. ABELISSIA MOORE
2. MARGARET MOORE
3. JEAN MOORE m. AMZI HOUSTON.
4. MARY MOORE m. LUCKY.
Sons:
5. JOHN MOORE
6. SAMUEL MOORE m. EVALINE CATHERINE WALLACE.
7. ELAM MOORE m. ELFRIEZA CAMPBELL
8. JAMES HALL MOORE.
Executors: Son ELAM MOORE and son in law AMZI HOUSTON.
Witnesses: MATTHEW WALLACE and ROBERT W. PARKS. (W. Book "G" p. 172).

The name of the first wife of JAMES MOORE is not known. He married second CYNTHIA JOHNSON, FEB. 13, 1827, with DAVID PARKS as Security.

ELAM MOORE - HIS WILL. Son of the above JAMES MOORE. Will executed in Mecklenburg County Jan. 29, 1840, the day before his death, in which he named the following legatees:
Sister: MARGARET MOORE
Bros: JOHN MOORE and SAMUEL MOORE.
Children:
JAMES CAMPBELL MOORE
MARGARET CATHERINE MOORE
CHARLES ROBINSON MOORE.
Executors: Brother in law WILLIAM LUCKY, the husband of MARY MOORE.
Witnesses: WILLIAM C. MOORE and JOHN PARKS.

JAMES CAMPBELL MOORE married MARY J. McCORKLE May 1, 1855
JAMES HALL MOORE married KESIAH PARKS, April 6, 1825, with LEVI PARKS, Security.
MARGARET CATHERINE MOORE married JAMES M. CALDWELL Jan. 15, 1851.

ANDREW MOORE - HIS WILL (Son of JAMES MOORE and his wife MARGARET McADEN). Probated Mecklenburg County, North Carolina and dated November 25, 1843. Mentions the following legatees:

His wife JANE(BAIN)MOORE.
Daughters:
1. JENNIE E. MOORE
2. MARGARET R. MOORE
3. MELISSA M. MOORE m. CLARKE
4. HANNAH EMILINE MOORE m. JOHN HARVEY MONTGOMERY.
Sons: 5. ANDREW FLETCHER MOORE
6. AMZI ALEXANDER MOORE
7. JAMES SAMPLE MOORE
Witnesses: WILLIAM F. CHRISTENBURG & JAMES SHIELDS.

The above ANDREW MOORE was the father of the BETHESDA METHODIST CHURCH, the first, it is said, of that denomination between the YADKIN and CATAWBA RIVERS in Mecklenburg County.

JOSEPH MOORE - HIS WILL. Probated Mecklenburg County, N. C. and dated May 13, 1769. The following legatees are mentioned:
Wife : MARY MOORE
Dau: ANNE LEMON.
Son: JOSEPH MOORE.
The son JOSEPH was directed to take care of his mother while she lived and was made executor. Witnesses: JOHN SCOTT, JOHN TODD and WILLIAM McKINLEY.

JOSEPH MOORE - HIS WILL. Probated Mecklenburg County, N. C. November 3, 1797. (This is thought to have been the JOSEPH, son of the JOSEPH above who left will in 1769, but he may have been the son of the first DAVID MOORE and brother of HUGH SR.) Names wife MARY and two sets of children, showing he had evidently been twice married. He mentions
"My seven elder children, already settled off, viz:"
1. JOHN MOORE
2. MARY TANNER
3. MARGARET NELSON
4. GEORGE MOORE
5. JANE HILL
6. SARAH DICKSON
7. ESTHER DICKSON,
to each of whom he leaves the sum of one dollar each.
My neighbors, HUGH TORRENCE, WILLIAM BEAN ALEXANDER and JOHN SHARPE to sell the home place (400 acres), for my widow when she requests it, she to have one-sixth part of the sale price.
Sons JOSEPH, JAMES and EPHRAIM to have 40 pounds each, son GEORGE 20 pounds and remainder to be equally divided to my six youngest children.
Executors, friends: HUGH TORRENCE, WILLIAM BEAN ALEXANDER and JOHN SHARP.
Witnesses: WILLIAM LEECH, JAMES PEEL, SR. and J. W. ALEXANDER.
Signed: JOSEPH MOORE.

CATHERINE ALEXANDER (Widow) - HER FAMILY. She was the widow of THEOPHILUS ALEXANDER, a brother of JOHN McKNITT ALEXANDER and his sister JEMIMAH SHARPE. Catherine died in 1775 in MECKLENBURG and left will. Her children were:
1. REV. JOSEPH ALEXANDER
2. GEORGE ALEXANDER
4. SOPHIA ALEXANDER m. SHARP.
5. MARGARET ALEXANDER m. JOHN CANNON.
6. ANN ALEXANDER m. a CANNON.
7. CATHERINE ALEXANDER m. EZEKIEL SHARP
The father of these children, THEOPHILUS ALEXANDER, is said to have died in CECIL COUNTY, MARYLAND in 1768, before his wife and family and sister and several brothers came to Mecklenburg County.

The above information, furnished by a reliable source, clears up the identity of REV. JOSEPH ALEXANDER, who was known to be a nephew of JOHN McKNITT ALEXANDER and the others. It was this JOSEPH ALEXANDER, one time Minister and classical school teacher in MECKLENBURG COUNTY who established a school on BULLOCK'S CREEK in South Carolina, which place was one of refuge during the American revolution.

JOSEPH DARNELL - HIS WILL. Probated in MECKLENBURG COUNTY, N. C. and dated August 12th, 1812. Names the following legatees:
Sons:
1. JOSHUA DARNELL
2. JOSEPH R. DARNELL
3. JOHN DARNELL
4. WILLIAM DARNELL
Daughters:
5. JENNIE CUNNINGHAM
6. ELIZABETH SMITH
7. SUKEY BOYD
8. POLLY COTHORN
9. PATSY DARNELL
10. WINIFRED SMITH
Wife: WINIFRED DARNELL.
Executors: BENJAMIN PERSONS of YORK, S. C. and the testator's wife WINIFRED.

NATHANIEL CUNNINGHAM - HIS WILL (This is a corrected abstract in lieu of one on another page) Will dated October 26, 1830. Legatees named were:
Daughters:
1. WINIFRED DARNELL
2. ELIZABETH ROBINSON
3. JANE H. RIVES
Son:
4. ELIJAH CUNNINGHAM
GRAND-daughter: ELIZABETH A. M. CUNNINGHAM in a deed of gift with ELIJAH CUNNINGHAM as agent for his children.
Executors: BENJAMIN PERSONS, of YORK, S.C. and his son ELIJAH CUNNINGHAM.

MOSES PARKS - HIS WILL. Probated in Mecklenburg County, North Carolina and dated July 15, 1822. Names the following:
Wife: MARY PARKS.
Children:
1. GEORGE PARKS
2. THOMAS PARKS
3. JOHN PARKS
4. OTTERY PARKS
5. MOSES PARKS
6. JAMES PARKS
7. POLLY PARKS.
Witnesses: MILAS JAY ROBINSON, and ANDREW ERA.
NOTE: JAMES SHARP of GREENE COUNTY, GA. sold lands to GEORGE PARKS, of MECKLENBURG County, N. C. in 1815.

WINIFRED DARNELL - HER WILL. Probated in Mecklenburg County, N. C. and dated in 1829.
Names:
ELIJAH CUNNINGHAM, grandson.
Children of JANE CUNNINGHAM, deceased, including ELIAS and others, the same as in the will of JOSEPH DARNELL, whose widow she was.

JAMES CUNNINGHAM - HIS WILL. Probated in Mecklenburg County, N. C. in 1833. Names the following legatees:
Wife: LETITIA CUNNINGHAM
Sons: ANDREW, WILLIAM, ROBERT and JAMES CUNNINGHAM.
Daughter: ELIZABETH CUNNINGHAM.
Gr. Daughter: MARY LOWRY CUNNINGHAM (Or LOUISE), daughter of son WILLIAM CUNNINGHAM.

WILLIAM CUNNINGHAM - HIS WILL. Probated in MECKLENBURG COUNTY, N. C., and dated June 21, 1842. Names legatees:
Daughters:
1. NANCY D. CUNNINGHAM
2. MARY CUNNINGHAM, to whom he leaves one-third of his McALPIN CREEK plantation.
3. ELIZABETH HAWFIELD
Wife: JANE CUNNINGHAM.
Sons:
4. ROBERT CUNNINGHAM
5. WILLIAM S. CUNNINGHAM
6. JAMES CUNNINGHAM, to whom he leaves the ARNOLD PLANTATION, reserving about fifteen acres woodland on LETITIA CUNNINGHAM'S line.
Grandson: JAMES W. HAWFIELDS.
Executor: Son ROBERT CUNNINGHAM.

THOMAS DOWNS - HIS WILL. Probated MECKLENBURG COUNTY, North Carolina and dated in 1839. Legatees mentions:
Children:
1. MARGARET WYLIE
2. FRANCES GRIFFITH
3. CAROLINE CUNNINGHAM
4. LARKIN DOWNS
5. JONATHAN DOWNS
Grandson: GRIFFITH.
Executor: JONATHAN DOWNS.
Witnesses: JOHN SHARP and AUZIEL SHARP.

NOTE: JOHN SHARP sold lands to SAMUEL DOWNS in 1813, and THOMAS DOWNS witnessed deeds of JOHN, THOMAS and CUNNINGHAM SHARP in 1814.

ISAIAH CUNNINGHAM FITTEN - HIS WILL. This will was proven in GREENE COUNTY, GEORGIA, July 21, 1814. (Deceased from MECKLENBURG CO. N.C.)
Mentions:
1. ISAIAH A. FITTEN, of Greene Co.(self).
Items:
1. My mother, MARGARET SHARP.
2. POLLY CUNNINGHAM
3. ELLEN KERR. Money to be paid to WILLIAM MOORE for the purpose of schooling the children of my sister POLLY MOORE, and $50.00 to SAMUEL KERR for the purpose of schooling the children of my sister, ELLEN KERR.
4. POLLY MOORE $25.00
5. To my beloved friend ROBERT MOORE CUNNINGHAM $75.00 for buying a suit of clothes.
6. My brother JOHN FITTEN, all my clothes
7. After all just debts are paid I allow ISAIAH C. FITTEN, one-half, JAMES FITTEN one-fourth, and ELIZA A. FITTEN, the balance.
8. Part of my negroes (naming them) to work for my mother, and after her death they are to serve JOHN FITTEN.
9. Slave Peter is to serve ISAIAH C. FITTEN, son of JOHN FITTEN.
Executors: JOHN FITTEN and JAMES NESBIT.
Witnesses: JOHN SIMONTON, THOMAS TAYLOR and DANIEL FLYTHEATH.

ISAIAH FITTEN - HIS ESTATE. Account of sale of his estate in Mecklenburg County, N. C.
"ISAIAH FITTEN, late of this County, deceased, March 13, 1783." Endorsed on the back: "Inventory of JOSIAH FITTEN. Purchasers were: EDWARD SHARP, SR. and ROGER CUNNINGHAM.
Certified: Dec. 29, 1783.

MARGARET BARR - HER WILL. Mecklenburg Co. North Carolina. About 1780. Mentions a step-daughter NANCY BARR, daughter MARY GILLESPY (?) and her son JAMES BARR. Executors were JOHN C. BARNETT and JOHN WILSON (Probably John McKamie Wilson's father). Witnesses were ISAAC ORR and JOHN WILSON.

CHARLES CUMMINS - HIS WILL. Mecklenburg County, North Carolina September 13, 1777 (Book A p. 182). Names his wife REBECCA, his sons JOHN and FRANCIS and his daughters ELIZABETH, REBECCA and JEAN CUMMINS. Legacies also (apparently) to EPHRAIM BREVARD, ISAAC ALEXANDER, WILLIAM ALEXANDER (son of HEZEKIAH) and to my son FRANCIS CUMMINS the plantation on which I dwell, after the death of my wife. Executors were my son FRANCIS CUMMINS. Witnesses were DAVID HAY, JOHN HUTCHINS and JOSEPH GRAHAM.

NOTE: Francis Cummins, the son and executor of the above testator, was the Rev. Francis Cummins, famous teacher and preacher, of whom more will be said later in these notes.

NATHANIEL CUNNINGHAM - HIS WILL. Mecklenburg County, North Carolina, dated October 26th, 1830. Mentions his daughter WINNIFRED DARCHOL (?) ELIZABETH ROBINSON and JAMES H. RIVES or RIVERS, son ELIJAH CUNNINGHAM and grand-daughter ELIZABETH M. A. CUNNINGHAM. Witnesses were JOHN NIMS, JAMES NIMS and JAMES BOOTEN.

JOHN DAVIDSON - HIS WILL. Mecklenburg County, North Carolina, January 24, 1778 (Book C p. 14) mentions sons JAMES, JOHN, SAMUEL and THOMAS DAVIDSON; son in law HUGH BRYSON. Executors are JAMES and JOHN DAVIDSON, and witnesses JAMES NASH and ANDREW MORRISON. He married MARY MORRISON.

> JOHN DAVIDSON who made the above will was a son of JOHN DAVIDSON and his wife a MRS. MORRISON, the parents also of MAJ. WILLIAM DAVIDSON, of SWANANOA. The testator's wife was NANCY BREVARD, and he was killed by the Indians according to one account. His sister ELIZABETH was the wife of EPHRAIM McLEAN.

THOMAS DAVIDSON - HIS WILL. Mecklenburg Co. N. C. June 8, 1800. Mentions his wife SARAH and a daughter MARY LONG DAVIDSON, and brothers JAMES, JOHN and SAMUEL DAVIDSON; also his brother in law HUGH BRYSON. The Executors of this will were DR. JOSEPH ALEXANDER, ROBERT DAVIDSON and ROBERT BRYSON, "my nephew". The witnesses were WILLIAM McLEAN, Ephraim B. Davidson and ARCHIBALD FURR.

> This THOMAS DAVIDSON was the son of JOHN DAVIDSON, who made the will just above in 1778.

WILLIAM DAVIDSON - HIS WILL. Mecklenburg County, N. C. OCT. 15, 1780. Mentions his wife as MARY and their children, but only names one son ISAAC DAVIDSON. Mentions his brother GEORGE DAVIDSON. Wife and his brother in law JOHN McCULLOUGH named Executors. Witnesses were JOHN THOMPSON, HUGH DAVIDSON and ISAAC McCULLOGH.

Who was this WILLIAM DAVIDSON?

JAMES ELLIOTT - HIS WILL. Mecklenburg Co. N. C., March 13, 1778. Names his wife MARY & son ROBERT ELLIOTT; also daughters MARTHA and ISABELLA ELLIOTT. Mentions his father ROBERT ELLIOTT and his wife MARY to be his Executors. The witnesses were ANDREW McNEAL and WALTER DAVIS.

SOLOMON ELLIOTT - HIS WILL. Recorded in Mecklenburg County, N. C. in Book G., but the testator was "Of the Province of Pennsylvania and County of Chester. He leaves the sum of THIRTY POUNDS to his father ANDREW ELLIOTT & TWENTY POUNDS money to each of the following named legatees (whose place of residence is not given, but presumably some of them must have been living in MECKLENBURG COUNTY, North Carolina:

My eldest brother JOHN ELLIOTT
My brother ROBERT ELLIOTT
My brother JOSEPH ELLIOTT
My brother ANDREW ELLIOTT
My eldest sister MARGARET ELLIS
My sister MARTHA BOGGS
My sister ALICE ELLIOTT
My sister SARAH McLELLAN
My sister RACHEL ELLIOTT

The balance of my estate to be divided between my brothers ANDREW and JAMES ELLIOTT, and my sisters MARGARET and RACHEL ELLIOTT. Executors brothers JOSEPH and ANDREW ELLIOTT. Witnesses HEZEKIAH JAMES BALCH, LEMUEL PATTON and WILLIAM McWHIRTER.

MOSES MOORE - HIS WILL. Mecklenburg County, North Carolina, OCT. 5, 1785. (Will Book B, page 66). To my wife ANNE MOORE, in lieu of her dowry, 1 feather bed and furniture; one big black mare, four cows, all the sheep and the privilege of living and enjoying the profits of the plantation during her widowhood, and support our THREE CHILDREN, clothe and school them.

Daughter (?) Abigail Robinson, one case of drawers and five shillings.
Son JAMES MOORE
Son WILLIAM MOORE
Dau MARY SCOTT MOORE

All of my estate except my negroes to be sold and divided between MY THREE CHILDREN, JAMES, WILLIAM and MARY SCOTT MOORE, when the sons become of age. My neighbors JAMES HENRY, HEZEKIEL ALEXANDER and JOHN McKNITT ALEXANDER to be my executors.

MY SISTER ABIGAIL ROBINSON.
Witnesses JAMES SHARPE, JEMIMAH SHARPE and J. McKNITT ALEXANDER.

> NOTE: The Clerk in copying evidently made an error, as " My Three Children" are mentioned twice in this will, and ABIGAIL ROBINSON is mentioned a second time as "my sister". Evidently Abigail was his sister.

MOSES and ANNE MOORE are buried at HOPEWELL CHURCH. He died in 1785 at the age of 81 and Ann lived until 1802 and died at the age of 65. The charge has been made in error that this MOSES MOORE was a Tory during the revolution, which charge is refuted by the names of the well known patriots who were named as his NEIGHBORS and EXECUTORS of his will.

MARRIAGE RECORDS AND RELATIONSHIPS
OF MECKLENBURG PEOPLE

ABERNATHY, ELIZABETH m. Jan. 2, 1798 to WILLIAM HENDERSON.

ABERNATHY, DR. JAMES SAMUEL m. (1) LENORA POTTS & (2) HATTIE DAVIDSON (Dau. of JOHN SPRINGS DAVIDSON). No date.

ABERNATHY, JOHN CONNELLY (b. 1820) m. NANCY JOHNSON BLYTHE (Dau. of SAMUEL BLYTHE and ISABELL NANCE).

ABERNATHY, LOCKY T. m. JOSUA T. MOORE, Jan. 6, 1830. ABNER SHARPE, Sec.

ABERNATHY, RICHARD BLYTHE m. ELLA HARRY. No date. He the son of JOHN CONNELLY ABERNATHY.

ABERNATHY, SINA PHARR (b. 1811) m. JAMES ABERNATHY HENDERSON (No date).

ABERNATHY, SYDNEY TURNER m. ELIZABETH CAROLINE DAVENPORT (b. in 1803). No other date.

ABERNATHY, SUSAN ISABELLA m. W. S. McCORD of PAW CREEK. She died in 1914. No other date.

ALEXANDER, ABIGAIL B. m. SAMUEL C. CALDWELL, May 8, 1793.

ALEXANDER, ABRAHAM (one of the signers) married DORCAS (from will). No date.

ALEXANDER, ADAM (one of the signers) m. MARY SHELBY, in Maryland. No date given.

ALEXANDER, AMOS m. MARY SHARP, of MARYLAND, and came to MECKLENBURG COUNTY. He was brother of JOHN McKNITT ALEXANDER, the signer.

ALEXANDER, BENJAMIN WILSON (b. 1805) m. ELVIRA DAVIS McCOY, March 6, 1828.

ALEXANDER, CATHEINE m. EZEKIEL SHARP (son of JERIMAH ALEXANDER SHARP. No date given.

ALEXANDER, DOVIE m. REV. HUGH B. CUNINGHAM. No date. Dau. of MOSES WINSLOW ALEXANDER.

ALEXANDER, ELIZA m. SAMUEL BLAIR Nov. 26, 1823.

ALEXANDER, COL. GEORGE m. MARGARET HARRIS, dau. of CHARLES HARRIS. No date.

ALEXANDER, GEORGE WASHINGTON (son of WILLIAM B. ALEXANDER) m. three times: (1) SARAH PHARR HARRIS Jan. 6, 1842; (2) MINERVA LATITIA GILLESPIE, Aug. 10, 1847; (3) SALLY SHARPE JETTON, Feb. 28, 1855.

ALEXANDER, HELENA m. HUGH MOORE March 19, 1824. ELEAZER ALEXANDER, Sec.

ALEXANDER, JAMES m. HANNAH CLARK, Oct. 16,1798.

ALEXANDER, JAMES McKNITT (son of WILLIAM BAIN ALEXANDER m. MARY LOUISA WILSON, July 16, 1844. His widow m. DIXON KERNS of IREDELL.

ALEXANDER, JERIMAH married THOMAS SHARPE in Maryland "about 1762".

ALEXANDER, JOHN BREVARD m. ANNIE LOWRIE, daughter of SAMUEL LOWRIE in 1858.

ALEXANDER, JOHN McKNITT (one of the signers) m. JANE or JEAN BAKS in MARYLAND "about 1762".

ALEXANDER, JOHN McKNITT (son of JAMES ALEXANDER and wife MARY LOUISA WILSON) married MARY ELIZABETH HENDERSON, June 4, 1872. She a sister of Dr. Harvey C. Henderson.

ALEXANDER, JOHN RAMSEY m. VIOLET JANE DAVIDSON, daughter of MAJ. JOHN DAVIDSON. The date of marriage not found.

ALEXANDER, JOHN R. married HARRIETT HENDERSON, Dec. 14, 1723. Another account says Dec. 19, 1723. He the son of WILLIAM B. ALEXANDER.

ALEXANDER, DR. JOSEPH McKNITT (1774 -1841) son of JOHN McKNITT ALEXANDER, the signer, m. DOVIE WILSON WINSLOW, daughter of Col. Moses Winslow, August 3, 1797.

ALEXANDER, MARGARET McKNITT m. FRANCIS ALEXANDER RAMSEY (father of the Tennessee Historian) April 7, 1789.

ALEXANDER, MOSES WINSLOW m. VIOLET WILSON WINSLOW GRAHAM, daughter of GEN. JOSEPH GRAHAM, Dec. 27, 1821.

ALEXANDER, NATHANIEL (Governor) m. MARGARET BREVARD, daughter of EPHRAIM BREVARD and his wife MARGARET POLK. No Date found.

ALEXANDER, SARAH, daughter of ADAM ALEXANDER (the signer) m. CAPT. JOHN SPRING. No date of the marriage found.

ALEXANDER, SOPHIA, daughter of JOHN RAMSEY ALEXANDER, married JOHN SAMPLE. No date found.

ALEXANDER, MAJ. THOMAS married a MISS MORRISON, sister of NEIL MORRISON (the signer). No date found.

ALEXANDER, ROBERT DAVIDSON m. ABIGAIL BAIN CALDWELL (dau. of Rev. S. C. Caldwell) in 1829. Parents of the HISTORIAN ALEXANDER.

ALEXANDER, WILLIAM BAIN m. VIOLET DAVIDSON, daughter of MAJ. JOHN DAVIDSON, August 25, 1791.

ALEXANDER, WILLIAM BAIN, JR. m. THERESA ALEXANDER, March 10, 1825.

ALLISON, ELLA m. GEORGE HENRY STEPHENS, Dec. 24, 1902.

ALLISON, JOHN m. ELLENER BUCHANAN in July, 1799.

ALLISON, MARGARET m. JAMES TORRENCE, son of JAMES TORRENCE and his wife NANCY DAVIDSON No date found.

ANDREWS, WILLIAM, married BARBARA CALDWELL April 16, 1792.

BAKER, ELIZABETH THOMSON (widow of SAMUEL BAKER) m. CHARLES HARRIS about 1780.

BALCH, ANN (daughter of HEZEKIAH JAMES BALCH the signer) m. SAMUEL CALDWELL, son of ROBERT of Charlotte County, Va., March 6, 1794.

BALCH, HEZEKIAH JAMES m. a MISS CONNELL about 1767. He was one of the signers and his widow married a MCWHORTER and moved to TENNESSEE

BALDRIDGE, ELIZABETH m. WILLIAM STEELE HENDERSON Sept. 18, 1804.

BALDWIN, ALLEN m. ELIZABETH HENDERSON on June 3rd 1818.

BARNES, ELIZABETH m. WILLIAM RICE, July 14, 1803. WILLIAM BURTON, Sec.

BARNETT, ANNE m. JAMES JACK, JR. (b. 1775) but no date given.

BARNETT, ESTHER, married SAMUEL CALDWELL March 11 1818.

BARNETT, JOHN married ANN SPRATT (estimated about 1752-3. Their daughter SUSAN born 1761.

BARNETT, LEVICY C. m. JOHN M. CROCKETT, Sept. 29, 1828. JOHN J. DUNLAP and SAMUEL THOMPSON, Sec

BARNETT, MARY m. CAPT. THOMAS JACK. She born before 1760. No date of marriage.

BARNETT, SUSAN m. GEORGE W. SMART in 1775.

BARR, JOHN m. SARAH HOWELL December 1, 1865.

BARRY, VIOLET m. WILLIAM MONTEITH, Sept. 4, 1807. HUGH BARRY, Sec.

BEATTY, MILLY m. JOHN RODDEN (named spelled ROWDEN on signature) March 1, 1842.

BEATTY, WILLIAM, married CAROLINE REA, Apr. 1, 1841.

BERRYHILL, HANNAH m. WILLIAM REA March 23, 1814.

BIRD, LUCY married JAMES CLARK, Sept. 18, 1805.

BLACK, JOSEPH m. MARTHA MORROW, Aug. 17, 1837.

BLAIR, JOHN m. ELIZABETH SHELL, March 26, 1800.

BLAIR, LAIRD m. MARGARET C. ORR, July 24, 1833.

BLAIR, SAMUEL m. ELIZA ALEXANDER Nov. 26, 1823.

BLAKELY, THOMAS H. m. MARGARET H. MORROW, Sept. 20, 1836.

BLYTHE, ANN m. THOMAS MARTIN, October 17, 1786.

BLYTHE, NANCY JOHNSON m. JOHN C. ABERNATHY. He was born 1820. No date given of marriage.

BLYTHE, SAMUEL m. PATSY BOND, May 9, 1803.

BLYTHE, SAMUEL (1790-1866) m. ISABELLA NANCE and were parents of NANCY JOHNSON BLYTHE. They were married Jan. 8, 1822.

BOATWRIGHT, SAMUEL m. NANCY WEATHERS on August 1, 1792.

BOGGS, ASAHEL (ARCHIBALD?) m. ESTHER McCOY Jan. 25, 1792.

BOND, JAMES m. PEGGY MORROW (or McCULLOUGH) April 27, 1802. Another entry reads Nov. 25, 1802.

BOND, PATSY m. SAMUEL BLYTHE, May 9, 1803.

BOND, POLLY m. ALLEN MOORE Oct. 20, 180__

BOND, THOMAS m. RHODA BOND, Dec. 30, 1790.

BOWERS, ELIZABETH m. GEORGE MORROW, September 23, 1819. WILLIAM BUSBY, Sec.

BOZZELL, POLLY m. JAMES REA in 1809. Exact date omitted.

BRADSHAW, LOUISA m. ROBERT B. MORROW, March 11, 1852.

BREVARD, CAPT. ALEXANDER m. REBECCA DAVIDSON, a daughter of MAJ. JOHN DAVIDSON.

BREVARD, EPHRAIM m. MARGARET POLK, daughter of THOMAS POLK. No date secured.

BREVARD, JOHN (the N. C. ancestor) m. JANE McWHORTER, sister of REV. McWHORTER, the early minister from MARYLAND. Date unavailable.

BREVARD, MARGARET, daughter of EPHRAIM & wife MARGARET POLK, m. NATHANIEL ALEXANDER, the GOVERNOR. Date not found.

BROWN, ADAMS m. JENNIE MORROW, April 28, 1801. (Daughter of DAVID MORROW - See will of 1810)

BROWN, BENJAMIN m. EMMILY McCARTY Jan. 7,1896

BROWN, JOHN m. BETSY SHARP Feb. 22, 1802. WILLIAM WALKER, Sec.

CAIN, ELISHA m. CATHERINE LEWIS Feb. 6, 1805 FRANCIS LEWIS, Sec.

CALDWELL, ALEXANDER (son of DR. DAVID CALDWELL of GUILFORD) m. SARAH DAVIDSON, a daughter of MAJ. JOHN DAVIDSON, signer, OCT. 9, 17_4. ISAAC ALEXANDER and JOHN McKNITT ALEXANDER, Sec.

CALDWELL, ANDREW H. m. SARAH A. WILLIAMS on March 26, 1844 JOHN M. CALDWELL Sec.

CALDWELL, ANDREW m. MARGARET M. QUEARY Feb. 12, 1853. JEREMIAH HOWIE, Sec.

CALDWELL, BARBARA m. WILLIAM ANDREWS, April 16, 1792.

CALDWELL, DANIEL m. ISABELLA SHIELDS Jan. 18, 1826.

CALDWELL, REV. DAVID (Of Guilford) married RACHEL CRAIGHEAD, daughter of REV. ALEXANDER CRAIGHEAD, in 1760. (He was son of an ANDREW CALDWELL and his wife MARTHA, says ALEXANDER).

CALDWELL, DAVID m. MARY SMITH, June 29, 1791. STEPHEN ALEXANDER and JOHN ALLISON Sec.

CALDWELL, DAVID F. m. HARRIETT E. DAVIDSON March 30, 1826. JOSHUA D. BOYD, Sec.

CALDWELL, DAVID A. m. MRS. MARTHA CALDWELL, Dec. 12, 1836. WILLIAM B. ALEXANDER, Sec.

CALDWELL, EDWARD m. ANN E. TORRENCE, August 11, 1828. ANDREW CALDWELL, Sec.

CALDWELL, HUGH M. m. MARTHA A. KERR in 1857.

CALDWELL, JAMES m. MARY DIXON, Feb. 23, 1831. JOHN M. McLEAN, Sec.

CALDWELL, JAMES m. MINTY PARKS, August 12, 1816. ROBERT CALDWELL, Sec.

CALDWELL, JAMES m. MARGARET MOORE, the daughter of ELAM MOORE, Jan. 15, 1851.

> His full name was JAMES M. MOORE & her full name MARGARET C. MOORE.

CALDWELL, JANE, daughter of REV. SAMUEL C. CALDWELL m. REV. W. S. PHARR.

> This is a matter of family history, but we do not find the exact date. They were the parents of REV. SAMUEL C. PHARR.

CALDWELL, J. C. m. LILLA A. HENDERSON, July 1, 1856.

CALDWELL, JEFF m. AMANDA HUNTER Jan. 11, 1866.

CALDWELL, JOHN m. MARGARET HOWIE, Feb. 26, 1823. JEREMIAH HOWIE, Sec.

> The name HOWIE in this family was spelled HUEY on the older gravestones, as we were informed by members of the family and as the gravestones reveal.

CALDWELL, DR. PINCKNEY C. m. SARAH R. WILSON, Dec. 12, 1831.

CALDWELL, ROBERT m. LAVINIAH HOUSTON Dec. 27,1819

CALDWELL, ROBERT m. MARY SHIELDS March 20, 1839 & ISAAC ALEXANDER and WILLIAM ANDREWS were Sec.

CALDWELL, SAMUEL m. ANN BALCH, March 6, 1794.

> He is said to have been the son of ROBERT CALDWELL (son of the original JOHN CALDWELL) of CHARLOTTE COUNTY, Virginia, CALDWELL SETTLEMENT, and she the daughter of HEZEKIAH JAMES BALCH, one of the "signers".

CALDWELL, REV. SAMUEL C. m. ABIGAIL BAIN ALEXANDER in 1792.

> He married as his second wife ELIZABETH LINDSAY, of GREENSBORO, N. C. Another account says he married 1st on May 8, 1793.

CALDWELL, SAMUEL m. ESTHER BARNETT March 11, 1818. AMOS BARNETT, Sec.

CALDWELL, DR. D. THOMAS m. HARRIETT DAVIDSON, a daughter of HON. WILLIAM DAVIDSON. No date found. They had eight children.

CALHOUN, HANNAH m. HUGH ROWAN, May 26, 1792, and THOMAS NEELY was Sec.

CAMPBELL, ELFRIEZA m. ELAM MOORE Jan. 18, in 1826. IRA PARKS, Sec.

CARLOCK, THOMAS m. HANNAH STEVENS, April 26, 1831.

CARRUTH, NANCY m. THOMAS HARRIS (Taken from family History. Date omitted.)

CARRUTHERS, MARY m. ELI CHAPPELL Jan. 7, 1866.

CASHON, HANNAH m. BRITTON RAY, Oct. 4, 1802.

CATHEY, FANNY m. WILLIAM CLARK, July 23, 1818.

CHAPPELL, ELI m. MARY CARRUTHERS, Jan. 7, 1866.

CHEEK, REBECCA A. m. HENRY WASHINGTON MARKS July 24, 1823. WILLIAM A. SMITH, Sec.

CHRISTENBURY, ARMINTA F. m. ANDREW F. MOORE in 1846.

CLARK, HANNAH m. JAMES ALEXANDER, Oct. 16,1798.

CLARK, HELEN M. m. DAVID H. REA in 1848.

CLARK, JAMES m. SARAH M. McCORKLE Nov. 15,1831 Le REA and B. GATES, Sec.

CLARK, JAMES m. LUCY BIRD Sept. 18, 1805.

CLARKE, JAMES m. MELISSA MOORE Nov. 24, 1829. A. A. MOORE, Sec.

CLARK, JESSE m. JANE P. McGIBONY, April 14, 1825.

CLARK, MARY m. WILLIAM COWAN Oct. 14, 1816.

CLARK, WILLIAM m. FANNY CATHEY July 23, 1818.

CLARK, WILLIAM m. LUCINDA MONTGOMERY Jan. 27, 1800.

COCHRAN, JOHN m. MARTHA REA June 16, 1816. JOHN REED and ANDREW REA, Sec.

COFFEY, DAVID S. m. JANE E. KERR July 24,1843.

COFFEY, JOHN M. m. JANE KERR Jan. 7, 1839. DAVID MORROW, Sec.

COLBERT, ROBERT L. m. MARY JANE MASSEY May 20, 1839. J. R. C. MASSEY, Sec.

COLLINGS, MISS SOPHIA m. JOSEPH W. ROSS Feb. 19, 1822. ROBERT H. MORRISON.

COOK, MARY m. ELI MORROW Dec. 19, 1838. A. A. COFFEY, Sec.

COOK, W. S. m. LENORA A. REED Sept. 5, 1848. W. S. DANIEL, Sec.

COOPER, ALEXANDER m. ELIZABETH STINSON March 4, 1824.

COOPER, JOSEPH m. MARY LIVINGSTON March 30, 1791.

COWAN, DAVID m. FRANCES WADDELL May 20, 1835.

COWAN, POLLY m. JACKSON RODEN, Feb. 17, 1810. BENJAMIN RODEN, Sec.

COWAN, WILLIAM m. MARY CLARK, Oct. 14, 1816.

CRAIG, ALEXANDER m. AGNES HUEY March 9, 1804.

CRAIG, MARGARET m. JOHN HUEY March 9th, 1804. (Evidently brothers and sisters had a) (double wedding)

CRAIGHEAD, ALEXANDER, REV. We have been unable to learn the name of his wife, whom he probably married in VIRGINIA on the "Calf Pasture", nor the date of his marriage. He was married before 1780, because his son REV. THOMAS B. CRAIGHEAD was born that year, according to the tombstone records. The son died at NASHVILLE, TENNESSEE, in 1825, having married ELIZABETH B.

> Rev. ALEXANDER CRAIGHEAD was the father in law of REV. DAVID CALDWELL D. D. of Guilford County; another daughter married a DUNLAP, and still another daughter became the wife of a MR. CRAWFORD, of South Carolina.

CRAWFORD, THOMAS m. MARY DAVIDSON, April 27, 1816. SAM W. DAVIDSON and JOHN M. ALEXANDER, Sec.

CROCKETT, ARCHIBALD m. DEBORAH WILSON, Jan. 12, in 1792. WILLIAM POTTS and JAMES DOUGLASS, Sec.

CROCKETT, ARCHIBALD m. ESTHER DAVIS, April 3, 1820 JOHN M. QUEARY and ISAAC ALEXANDER, Sec.

> From the will of JAMES DAVIS, an abstract of which is shown herein, we learn that ARCHIBALD CROCKETT married his daughter ESTHER. This will was probated in Mecklenburg County, April 18, 1837.

CROCKETT, ELIJAH m. MARY DAVIE, presumably in Mecklenburg County. No date.

> MARY DAVIE, who married ELIJAH CROCKETT was a sister of WILLIAM RICHARDSON DAVIE, the famous N. Carolina Statesman and Jurist. This couple left a long line of descendants.

CROCKETT, ELIZABETH m. JOSEPH WALLIS April 10, 1823

> ELIZABETH CROCKETT was the daughter of ELIJAH CROCKETT and MARY DAVIE, and JOSEPH WALLIS was the son of REV. JAMES WALLIS, the son in law of JOHN McKNITT ALEXANDER.

CROCKETT, JOHN M. m. LEVICY C. BARNETT Sept. 29th 1828. JOHN J. DUNLAP and SAMUEL THOMPSON Sec.

CROCKETT, MARGARET m. WILLIAM MORROW March 7, in 1794. ELI CROCKETT, Sec.

CROCKETT, MARGARET m. JOHN McKNITT WALLIS, the son of REV. JAMES WALLIS, in 1813.

CUNNINGHAM, FRANCES m. ROBERT HARRIS (JR.) son of a ROBERT HARRIS on ROCKY RIVER in CABARRUS, or what was afterwards CABARRUS - then Mecklenburg - before 1791. Date not given. ROBERT HARRIS, JR. of this record was a brother of a CHARLES HARRIS who married (2nd) ELIZABETH THOMSON BAKER, daughter of REV. JOHN THOMSON.

CUNNINGHAM, REV. HUGH B. m. DOVIE ALEXANDER, the daughter of DR. MOSES WINSLOW ALEXANDER. The exact date not given.

CUNNINGHAM, JAMES m. MARY JANE REA Dec. 21, 1847. JOHN W. BLAIR, Sec.

CUNNINGHAM, MARGARET, daughter of ROGER CUNNINGHAM m. JAMES SHARP.

> The bride was a sister of REV. ROBERT MOORE CUNNINGHAM. vide

CUNNINGHAM, REBECCA m. JOHN BAIRD. No date of the marriage.

> REBECCA and her husband moved to S. C. and later proceedings show that she was a sister of KEZIAH, JACOB, GEORGE and JOHN CUNNINGHAM.

CUNNINGHAM, WILLIAM K. m. REBECCA C. SWANN on Feb. 10, 1847. JAMES GLOVER, Sec.

CUNNINGHAM, WILLIAM R. m. CAROLINE DOWNS on July 16, 1830. JAMES PARKS, Sec.

CUNNINGHAM, WILLIAM married JANE SMITH Oct. 13, 1808. RICHARD SHARP, Sec.

CURETON, JOHN m. LYDIA E. POTTS, Feb. 29, 1825 JEREMIAH CURETON, Sec.

CUNNINGHAM, ELEANOR daughter of ROGER CUNNINGHAM m. JOHN SHARP. No date.

DAVENPORT, ELIZABETH CAROLINE (b. 1823) married SYDNEY TURNER ABERNATHY. No date.

DAVIDSON, ADAM BREVARD m. MISS SPRING, daughter of JOHN SPRING and his wife SARAH ALEXANDER. No date.

DAVIDSON, HARRIETT E. m. DAVID F. CALDWELL March 30, 1826, JOSHUA D. BOYD, Sec.

DAVIDSON, ISABELLA RAMSEY, widow of ROBERT DAVIDSON (father of MAJ. JOHN DAVIDSON) m. HENRY HENRY, a teacher. No date.

DAVIDSON, ISABELLA S. G. m. JAMES W. MOORE Jan. 19, 1835. A. R. IRWIN, Sec.

DAVIDSON, MARY BREVARD m. ROBERT HARRIS as his second wife. No date.

> This ROBERT HARRIS was the son by his first marriage of CHARLES HARRIS, who married second, ELIZABETH THOMSON BAKER, daughter of the pioneer minister REV. JOHN THOMSON.

DAVIDSON, MARY m. THOMAS CRAWFORD Apr 27, 1816 SAM W. DAVIDSON and JOHN M. ALEXANDER Sec

DAVIDSON, MARY, sister of MAJ. JOHN DAVIDSON m. JAMES PRICE - another account states that his name was JOHN PRICE. Date of this marriage not found.

DAVIDSON, SARAH m. ALEXANDER CALDWELL Oct 9, 17_4. ISAAC ALEXANDER and JOHN McKNITT ALEXANDER Sec.

DAVIDSON, VIOLET m. WILLIAM BAIN ALEXANDER August 25, 1791.

DAVIDSON, MAJ. JOHN m. VIOLET WILSON, June 2 1761. She the daughter of SAMUEL WILSON.

DAVIDSON, WILLIAM LEE (son of GEN. WILLIAM LEE DAVIDSON) m. ELIZABETH DAVIDSON the youngest daughter of MAJ. JOHN DAVIDSON.

> She was called Aunt Betsy Lee DAVIDSON. They moved to ALABAMA, where her husband died in 1863. She is buried at Hopewell. They left no children.

DAVIS, ESTHER m. ARCHIBALD CROCKETT, April 3, 1820. JOHN M. QUEARY & ISAAC ALEXANDER, Sec.

DAVIS, JANE m. DAVID MOORE in CABARRUS COUNTY, Dec. 1, 1834. JAMES H. McCALL, Sec.

DIXON, MARY m. JAMES CALDWELL Feb. 23, 1831. JOHN M. McLEAN, Sec.

DOHERTY, MARY m. SAMUEL RANKIN Nov. 16, 1791. RICHARD RANKIN, Sec.

DOWNS, CAROLINE m. WILLIAM R. CUNNINGHAM, July 16 1830. JAMES PARKS, Sec.

DUNN, ISABELLA m. THOMAS MOORE, Feb. 12, 1793. JOHN TODD, Sec.

DYSART, DR. CORNELIUS m. CHARITY JACK (Daughter of PATRICK JACK) no date. He died in 1800 in GEORGIA. His wife was a sister of JAMES JACK.

EMBERSON, SARAH m. JOSEPH S. MOORE Dec. 20, 1836 STEPHEN EMBERSON, Sec.

FALLS, ISABELLA (widow of COL. FALLS of the Revolution) m. HUGH TORRENCE. (No date found).

FALLS, PEGGY (Dau. of Col. Falls) m. THOMAS McKNIGHT. (No date).

FITTEN, ELLEN m. SAMUEL KERR (Son of SAMUEL KERR SR.) No date found.

FITTEN, JOHN m. POLLY FRANKLIN Feb. 27, 1798.

FITTEN, POLLY m. WILLIAM MOORE, Feb. 19, 1805. JAMES REED, Sec.

FITZGERALD, MILES m. ELIZA PROCTOR, April 11 1836 THOMAS PROCTOR, Sec. (This in LINCOLN CC.)

FLENIKEN, MARY A. m. R. W. REED Nov. 22, 1844. JAMES C. HEA, Sec.

FORD, NANCY m. ISAAC MOORE Nov. 5, 1800. JOHN JOHNSTON, Sec.

FRANKLIN, POLLY m. JOHN FITTEN Feb. 27, 1798.

The FITTEN FAMILY of the above records, moved to GEORGIA, and POLLY FITTEN and WILLIAM MOORE as well as JOHN FITTEN finally found their way to CHAMBERS CO ALABAMA.

GRAHAM, ANN m. THOMAS BARNETT, a revolutionary soldier' She a sister of GEN. JOS. GRAHAM. She died in Jackson, Tenn. in 1841.

GRAHAM, GEN. GEORGE (d. 1826) m. (1) FANNY CATHEY daughter of GEORGE CATHEY; m. (2) MRS. LYDIA POTTS, widow of WILLIAM POTTS.

GRAHAM, ELIZABETH (Dau. of GEORGE) m. WILLIAM M. BOSTWICK. No date.

GRAHAM, JANE m. WILLIAM R. McKEE. She the daughter of GEN. GEORGE GRAHAM. No date found.

GRAHAM, POLLY (Dau. of GEN. GEORGE GRAHAM) married GEORGE CARRUTH. No date found.

GRAHAM, GEN. JOSEPH m. ISABELLA DAVIDSON -1787.

GRAHAM, SARAH (a sister of GEN. JOSEPH GRAHAM) m. ROBERT ALLISON (d. 1904). She died in 1825. No date of marriage found.

GRAHAM, VIOLET WILSON WINSLOW m. MOSES WINSLOW ALEXANDER, Dec. 27, 1821.

The bride was the daughter of GEN. JOSEPH GRAHAM.

GRIER, REV. ISAAC m. ISABELLA HARRIS (b. 1783) No date of marriage found. Family record.

GRIFFIN, JANE m. JACOB RIDDEN, Jan. 25, 1795. UPTON BYRUM, Sec.

HALL, ISABELLA m. JAMES RAMSEY, Feb. 3, 1792.

HAMPTON, GEORGE m. CORNELIA HENDERSON, Feb. 29 1804.

HARPER, MARGARET m. ROBERT HARRIS (b. 1731) a son of JAMES HARRIS and MARY McILHENNY. From family record. Date omitted.

HARGROVE, AGNES m. WILLIAM ROBINSON Oct. 9th 1804. WALTER CARRUTH Sec.

HARGROVE, ANN m. RICHARD RANKIN May 18, 1825. ROBERT WILSON, Sec.

HARRIS, CHARLES m. (1) JANE McILHENNY and (2) ELIZABETH THOMSON BAKER.

The last marriage was about 1760. Elizabeth Thomson Baker was the widow of SAMUEL BAKER, and daughter of the pioneer Presbyterian minister, Rev. JOHN THOMSON, who is buried at BAKER'S GRAVEYARD in upper Mecklenburg County. CHARLES HARRIS lived on ROCKY RIVER in the present CABARRUS COUNTY.

HARRIS, DAVID W. (Son of JOSIAH HARRIS) married ANN E. BUCKNER in 1865, and they moved to DILLEY, TEXAS, below and West of SAN ANTONIC.

HARRIS, HUGH m. MARTHA ROBINSON Jan. 11, 1788

HARRIS, ISAAC ROSS (1813-1887) married EMILY E. HORN. No date furnished.

HARRIS, ISABELL m. REV. ISAAC GRIER. She was born in 1783. No date of marriage found.

HARRIS, JAMES m. MARGARET DAVIDSON, daughter of MAJ. JOHN DAVIDSON. No date furnished. They moved to ALABAMA.

HARRIS, JAMES m. GRACE LEGGITT. He born 1739. m. in CABARRUS territory. NO DATE.

HARRIS, JAMES m. JANE SLOAN HUNTER in 1813. Probably in CABARRUS COUNTY.

HARRIS, JAMES MOORE (1785-1844) m. MARGARET MARY MILLER March 31, 1812.

HARRIS, JAMES m. NANCY HUNTER in 1782, in what is now CABARRUS COUNTY.

HARRIS, JOHN m. MARTHA HUNTER March 31, 1790.

HARRIS, JOHN (b. 1761) m. NANCY MATTHEWS and they moved to TENNESSEE. From family records, and no date of marriage furnished.

HARRIS, JOHN m. JANE MOORE, April 7, 1777. This marriage in what is now CABARRUS COUNTY. No date furnished by the family record.

HARRIS, JOSIAH m. MARGARET M. PURVIANCE, Dec. 25, 1830. They moved to TENNESSEE.

HARRIS, MARGARET m. MATTHEW HENDERSON Mar 6, 1798.

HARRIS, MATTHEW m. HANNAH ROSS in 1784. He was b. in 1754.

HARRIS, ROBERT m. HANNAH BEA in 1811.

HARRIS, ROBERT m. JANE McCAULN in 1779.

HARRIS, ROBERT m. MARY BREVARD DAVIDSON (No DATE)

    This ROBERT HARRIS was the son of CHARLES HARRIS, who married second, ELIZABETH THOMSON BAKER, daughter of REV. JOHN THOMSON. CHARLES was the ancestor of WILLIAM SHAKESPEARE HARRIS.

HARRIS, ROBERT (Son of JAMES HARRIS) m. MARGARET HARPER about 1750. They lived on ROCKY RIVER in what is now CABARRUS COUNTY. He was born in 1731.

HARRIS, ROBERT JR. (Son of ROBERT HARRIS) married FRANCES CUNNINGHAM (Date not furnished.) They lived in what is now CABARRUS COUNTY.

HARRIS, SAMUEL m. JENNETT HOUSTON, Oct. 10, 1782.

    This SAMUEL HARRIS, reported as being of the second generation of the HARRIS FAMILY of ROCKY RIVER, is supposed to have been a son of a SAMUEL HARRIS and his wife DOROTHY WYLIE.

HARRIS, SAMUEL m. MARTHA LAIRD, in what is now a part of CABARRUS COUNTY. No date given.

HARRIS, SARAH ELIZABETH m. HECTOR McNEIL in 1832.

HARRIS, THOMAS m. MARY PATTERSON. He was born in 1740 and died in 1791, and he and his wife MARY moved to GREENE COUNTY, GEORGIA.

HARRIS, THOMAS m. (as his first wife) MARGARET McKINNEY. No date furnished. He was brother of ROBERT HARRIS JR.

HAWKINS, JEMIMAH m. JOSEPH BEA July 15, in 1809. JAMES C. DAVIS, Sec.

HAWKINS, MARY JANE m. BENJAMIN MORROW, April 20, 1847. S. N. ALEXANDER, SECURITY.

    MARY JANE HAWKINS of the above record, was a daughter of HON. WILLIAM HAWKINS, Governor of North Carolina, from 1812 to 1814, who lived in WARREN CO., a son of PHILEMON HAWKINS, JR. The groom was MAJ. BENJAMIN MORROW, of the war of 1812, and a prominent resident of MECKLENBURG, whose father was JAMES McKNIGHT MORROW.

HEIMS, AGNES m. DAVID MOORE, May 9, 1816. MARTIN McWHORTER, Sec.

    The name McWHORTER is spelled McWHIRTER, but we think "o" is right.

HENDERSON, ADALINE (b. 1808) m. ROBERT MILAS SAMPLE. No date found.

HENDERSON, ALEXANDER WOOD m. NANCY. Her last name unknown. He died 1790, and she 1793 Date of marriage not found.

HENDERSON, ANDREW ROBINSON m. RACHEL ROXANA RUTLEDGE, May 26, 1850. He lived in the River Bend in what is now GASTON COUNTY.

HENDERSON, CAIRNES (d. 1793) married ELIZABETH (last name unknown) who died 1806, at the age of 77 years. Date of marriage not found.

HENDERSON, CAIRNES m. LILLY PARKS Jan. 24, 1792

HENDERSON, CORNELIA m. GEORGE HAMPTON Feb. 29 1804.

HENDERSON, DAVID ROBINSON (Of SUGAR CREEK) m. MARGARET DAVIDSON ALEXANDER May 4, 1836.

HENDERSON, ELIZABETH m. ALLEN BALDWIN, June 3, 1818.

HENDERSON, HARRIETT m. JOHN R. HENDERSON Dec. 14, 1823.

HENDERSON, ISAAC m. MARTHA JANE LOUISE HENDERSON, March 8, 1892.

HENDERSON, JAMES ABERNATHY m. SINA FRAZER ABERNATHY. She was born 1811. No date found.

HENDERSON, JANE m. ADAM MILLER april 13, 1804.

HENDERSON, JAMES SAMPLE m. MARGARET HARRY, and they had son HUGH CUNNINGHAM HENDERSON. No date of this marriage furnished.

HENDERSON, JOHN m. REBECCA HENDERSON Jan 38, 1798.

HENDERSON, LILLA A. m. J. C. CALDWELL July 1, 1856.

HENDERSON, MARGARET m. ROBERT ROBINSON Mar. 30 1790. JOHN ROBINSON, SEC.

HENDERSON, MARTHA H. m. E. L. BURNEY, Oct 1, 1851.

HENDERSON, MARY ELIZABETH m. JOHN McKNITT ALEXANDER, June 4, 1872. They were married by REV. S. C. PHARR.

HENDERSON, MATTHEW m. MARGARET HARRIS March 6, 1798.

HENDERSON, RICHARD m. ISABEL JAMISON Feb. 8th, 1798.

HENDERSON, ROBERT B. m. MARTHA CAROLINE SAMPLE Dec. 15, 1832.

HENDERSON, SUSANNAH m. THOMAS RAMSEY Oct 4, 1804.

HENDERSON, WILLIAM m. ELIZABETH ABERNATHY, Jan. 2, 1798.

HENDERSON, WILLIAM m. NANCY (Last name unknown) (died and buried at GILEAD CHURCH in 1813.)

HENDERSON, WILLIAM STEELE m. ELIZABETH BAIRD - RIDGE, Sept. 8, 1804.

HENRY, ROBERT - FIRST PASTOR AT STEELE CREEK.

HILL, WHITMEIL m. MARY SHARP, March 21, 1814; JOHN L. DANIEL, Sec.

HILL, WILLIAM m. HANNAH SHARP, July 24, 1821, with WHITMELL HILL, Sec.

HOUSTON, ELIZABETH m. JAMES KERR, about 1820; the daughter of SAMUEL KERR and MARY SPRATT.

HOUSTON, LORENA m. ROBERT CALDWELL Dec. 27, 1819.

HOUSTON, MARGARET m. CAPT. JAMES JACK, bearer of the MECKLENBURG DECLATION. Date not found.

HOUSTON, MATTHEW M. m. EUNICE McCOY, oldest daughter of JOHN McCOY. Sons in C. S. A.

HOWARD, NANCY m. JOHN M. ORMOND Dec. 22, 1740 (?) (probably 1840.)

HOWIE (HUEY), MARGARET m. JOHN CALDWELL Feb. 25th 1823. JEREMIAH HOWIE, Sec.

HUEY, ELIZABETH m. HECTOR McCOHRON July 26, 1791.

HUEY, JOHN m. MARGARET CRAIG March 9, 1804.

HUNTER, MARTHA m. JOHN HARRIS, March 31, 1790.

HUNTER, NANCY m. JAMES HARRIS in 1782, on ROCKY RIVER in what became CABARRUS COUNTY.

REV. HUMPHREY HUNTER was Minister of STEELE CREEK CHURCH, from 1804 to 1807. See later about the Church, etc.

IRWIN, MARY ANN m. THOMAS MOORE Sept. 20, 1838. JOHN F. IRWIN and A. B. MOORE, Sec.

IRWIN, ROBERT m. ELIZABETH ERA in 1817.

IRWIN, GEN. ROBERT (b. Aug. 26, 1740) m. a daughter of ZEBULON ALEXANDER, at an unknown date and lived in the STEELE CREEK SETTLEMENT.

JACK, CHARITY m. DR. CORNELIUS DYSART (Date not found) and they moved to GEORGIA where he died in 1800.

JACK, CYNTHIA m. A. S. COSBY. She was a daughter of CAPT. JAMES JACK. Date not found.

JACK, JAMES m. MARGARET HOUSTON. Date of marriage not found.

JACK, JAMES HOUSTON JR. m. ANNIE BARNETT. He was born in 1775. Date of marriage not secured.

JACK, JANE m. WILLIAM BARNETT. Date not found.

JACK, PATRICK, SR. m. LILLIUS McADOO, according to family tradition in PENNSYLVANIA. They were the ancestors of all the MECKLENBURG COUNTY JACK FAMILY.

JACK, WILLIAM HOUSTON m. FRANCES CUMMINS, daughter of REV. FRANCIS CUMMINS. Family records fail to give the date.

JACK, PATRICK, JR. m. HARRIETT SPENCER, (no date). He was the son of CAPT. JAMES JACK and grandson of PATRICK JACK. These JACKS moved to GEORGIA, ALABAMA and some to TEXAS.

JAMISON, ISRAEL m. RICHARD HENDERSON Feb. 8, 1798.

JOHN, ABEL m. ISABELLA REED. He was killed in 1825 and widow and family moved to SELMA, ALABAMA.

JOHN, DANIEL m. ELIZABETH McCLENDON. No Date. He the son of DAVID and MARY MOORE JOHN.

JOHN, DAVID m. MARY MOORE. She was daughter of ANDREW MOORE, of BETHESDA. No date.

JOHN, ZEPHANIAH m. MARGARET SHARP Dec. 22nd, 1824. JAMES SHARP, SEC.

JOHNSTON, CYNTHIA m. JAMES MOORE Feb. 13, 1827. IRA PARKS, Sec.

JOHNSTON, MARY (Dau. of PATRICK JOHNSTON) m. SAMUEL LOWRIE, JR. He died 1846 in Mo.

JOHNSTON, PATRICK (Said to have been from IRELAND) m. MISS ANNIE WALL. No date.

JONES, ELIZABETH m. HEZEKIAH MORROW Jan. 5th 1815.

KENNEDY, MARTHA ANN m. SAMUEL A. MOORE, April 16, 1851.

KERNS, JAMES HARPER m. CLARISSA ALEXANDER Aug. 23, 1825.

KERNS, THOMAS McCLURE (1799-1868), son of WILLIAM KERNS and JANE McCLURE, m. JANE McKNIGHT. Date not furnished.

KERR, AARON (Son of SAMUEL and MARY SPRATT) m. MARY SHARP, daughter of JOHN SHARP and ELLEN CUNNINGHAM, Feb. 17, 1823. JAMES SHARP, Sec.

KERR, JAMES (b. 1720) m. SUSANNAH STEPHENSON. No date given.

KERR, JAMES m. ELIZABETH HOUSTON about 1820.

KERR, JANE m. JOHN M. COFFEY Jan. 7, 1839, & DAVID MORROW was Sec.

KERR, JANE E. m. DAVID S. COFFEY July 24th, 1843.

KERR, MARGARET married a man named McMILLAN. Date not stated.

KERR, MARTHA A. m. HUGH M. CALDWELL in 1857.

KERR, SAMUEL m. MARY SPRATT (About 1800). or 1795.

KERR, SAMUEL m. ELLEN FITTEN. No Date found.

KERR, SARAH m. ANDREW L. ROGERS Feb. 9,1835. JOHN MILLER, Sec.

KERR, WILLIAM (Son of SAMUEL KERR and MARY SPRATT) m. JANE SHARP. No Date found.

KIRK, AGNES m. HARRIS ROBINSON May 11, 1795 JAMES HENDERSON, Sec.

KIRKPATRICK, JANE m. SAMUEL V. ROGERS, Feb. 25, 1823.

KNOX, GRACE ELIZABETH m. G. V. ROBINSON. No date of marriage located.

KERR, RACHEL m. JOHN McCAULEY Sept. 12, 1795.

KING, DOLLY m. JAMES REED April 13, 1802. JOSEPH REED, Sec.

KING, POLLY m. JAMES REED, JR. April 13, 1802.

KNOX, JOANNA m. JOHN POLK (No date found) and they were the grandparents of THOMAS POLK, EZEKIEL POLK and others, and ancestors of PRESIDENT JAMES KNOX POLK.

KNOX, JANE m. SAMUEL POLK, before 1795 in MECKLENBURG COUNTY. They were the grandparents of JAMES KNOX POLK who was born Nov. 2, 1795.

KNOX, SAMUEL m. MARY (Last name unknown) He died leaving will May 5, 1794, in Mecklenburg County; which see herein.

KNOX, AGNES (Son of SAMUEL KNOX and wife MARY) m. WILLIAM PETTUS (From Will - no date).

> The wife of JAMES KNOX POLK was SARAH CHILDRESS, daughter of CAPT. JOEL CHILDRESS of Rutherford County, TENNESSEE.
>
> SAMUEL KNOX lived near where the present town of CORNELIUS is located, about two or three miles South of DAVIDSON COLLEGE in MECKLENBURG COUNTY. The claim is made that his grandson JAMES K. POLK was born at that place, tho his parents' home was down around PINEVILLE, below CHARLOTTE, where the POLK FAMILY had originally settled.

LAIRD, MARTHA m. SAMUEL HARRIS (Brother of ROBERT HARRIS, JR.) No Date found.

LANNING, BIDDY m. WILLIAM MOORE in August, 1833.

LEGGITT, GRACE m. JAMES HARRIS (1739-1797) in then MECKLENBURG, now CABARRUS COUNTY. No Date.

LEWIS, CATHERINE m. ELISHA CAIN, Feb. 6, 1805, & FRANCIS LEWIS was Sec.

LIPE, AGNES JANE m. McKAMIE RUDOLPHUS PUCKETT in 1787.

LOWRIE, ANNIE m. JOHN BREVARD ALEXANDER (The Historian) in 1858.

LOWRIE, LILY m. BRAWLEY OATES and lived in CHARLOTTE (No date found).

LOWRIE, POLLY m. DR. DAVID R. DUNLAP, and also resided in CHARLOTTE. No date found.

LOWRIE, SAMUEL JR. m. MARY JOHNSTON (Daughter of PATRICK JOHNSTON. No Date.

LOWRIE, SAMUEL SR. m. MARGARET ALEXANDER, daughter of ROBERT ALEXANDER in 1788; secondly he married MARY NORFLEET in 1811, daughter of MARMADUKE NORFLEET of BERTIE COUNTY.

> Dr. J. B. ALEXANDER says that Miss Lilly LOWRIE who became the wife of BRAWLEY OATES was the prettiest woman in all of MECKLENBURG. Brawley Oates for many years was connected with the office of the County Court Clerk.

MARKS, HENRY WASHINGTON m. REBECCA A. CREEK July 24, 1823. WILLIAM A. SMITH, Sec.

MARKS, THOMAS m. MARGARET E. BUTTON April 21, 1832.

MARSHALL, JOHN m. ANN KINMAN May 21, 1818.

MARTIN, JAMES W. m. HARRIETT D. HEA in 1837?

MARTIN, JOSIAH m. MARY McCLARY (Daughter of ROBERT McCLARY) May 28, 1783.

MARTIN, JAMES m. MARGARET (Mentioned in his will in 1810, with children) NO DATE.

MARTIN, THOMAS m. ANN BLYTHE Oct. 17, 1786.

MASSEY, MARY JANE m. ROBERT L. COLBERT May 20, 1839. J. R. C. MASSEY, Sec.

MASSEY, THOMAS P. m. ELIZABETH WORSHAM Oct. 24, 1823.

MAXWELL, ELLEN m. JOHN ROGERS Feb. 2, 180__. (Exact year illegible).

McADEN, MARGARET m. JAMES MOORE. No date.

> They were the parents of the ANDREW MOORE who established the first METHODIST CHURCH in MECKLENBURG COUNTY and who died in 1843.

McAULEY, ELI HUGH (1851-1934) m. MARY LAURA McCOY Nov. 16, 1876.

McCALL, ELIZA m. JAMES MASSEY Nov. 25, 1837.

McCALL, SARAH JANE m. E. P. ROGERS Sept. 25, 1865.

McCAULE, JANE (McCALL?) m. ROBERT HARRIS in 1779.

McCAULEY, JOHN (McAULEY) JOHN m. RACHEL KERR Sept. 12, 1795.

McCARTY, EMMILY m. BENJAMIN BROWN Jan. 7,1828.

McCLARY, MARY m. JOSIAH MARTIN May 28, 1783

McCLENDON, ELIZABETH m. DANIEL JOHN (A son of DAVID JOHN and his wife MARY MOORE) Date not furnished.

McCLURE, JAMES m. MARY SHARP, April 4, 1803. ANDREW OLIPHANT, Sec.

McCOMBON, HECTOR m. ELIZABETH HUEY July 26, 1791.

McCORKLE, HANNAH m. LEROY HEA, Jan. 8, 1839. ELIAS HANKEY, Sec.

McCORKLE, MARY J. m. JAMES C. MOORE May 1st, 1855.

McCORKLE SARAH M. m. JAMES CLARK Nov. 15th, 1831. LE (LEROY) HEA and BRAWLEY OATES Sec.

McCORKLE, THOMAS J. m. MARY ANN PUCKETT who was born 1825. No date of Marriage.

McCOY, ELVIRA DAVIS m. BENJAMIN WILSON ALEXANDER - March 6, 1828.

McCOY, ESTHER m. ASHAHEL (ARCHIBALD) BOGGS, Jan. 25, 1792.

McCOY, JOHN m. ESTHER FRAZIER in 1798.

McCOY, MARSHALL RUDOLPHUS m. REBECCA ELOISA ALEXANDER May 6, 1827.

    They lived a mile East of HOPEWELL CHURCH.

McCULLOUGH, ESTHER m. HENRY MORROW, Jan. 17, 1830. AMOS McCULLOUGH, Sec.

McCULLOUGH, JENNIE m. DAVID MORROW, Nov. 25th, 1802. ANDREW LOFTIN, Sec.

McDANIELS, JANE P. m. JONATHAN REED in 1822, with ROBERT LINDSAY, Sec.

McEWEN, ELLEN m. JAMES MOORE on June 12, 1795. SAMUEL McEWEN, Sec.

McEWEN, MARGARET m. JOSEPH ROGERS, August 9, 1822. ROBERT McEWEN, Sec.

McEWEN, SARAH J. m. JAMES IRA on July 28, 1837.

McGIBONY, JANE m. JESSE M. CLARK, APRIL 14, 1825.

McILHENNY, JANE m. (as first wife) CHARLES HARRIS No date. Probably by or before 1750.

    The second wife of CHARLES HARRIS was MRS. SAMUEL BAKER, who was the daughter of REV. JOHN THOMSON, the early Minister.

McILHENNY, MARY m. JAMES HARRIS, brother of the preceding CHARLES HARRIS. No Date found.

McKINNEY, MARGARET m. THOMAS HARRIS, another brother of CHARLES and JAMES HARRIS. Family record fails to give dates.

McKNIGHT, HUGH m. PATSY WILSON, daughter of SAMUEL WILSON, JR. He was son of THOMAS McKNIGHT & his wife PEGGY FALLS.

McKNIGHT, THOMAS m. PEGGY FALLS the daughter of a COLONEL FALLS who was killed at RAMSEUR'S MILL in the revolution. No Date found.

McLEAN, REBECCA, daughter of DR. WILLIAM McLEAN of the revolution m. (2) DR. ISAAC WILSON. No date found.

McLEAN, DR. WILLIAM m. MARY DAVIDSON, daughter of MAJ. JOHN DAVIDSON, on June 19, 1792.

McNEIL, HECTOR m. SARAH ELIZABETH HARRIS, sister of ISAAC ROSS HARRIS, in 1832.

McREE, WILLIAM E. m. JANE GRAHAM (No date furnished of this marriage.)

McSPANN, MARGARET m. HARRY S. IRA, March 5th, 1823. ROBERT J. MORRIS, Sec.

MONTEITH, WILLIAM m. VIOLET BARRY Sept. 6, 1807. HUGH BARRY, Sec.

MONTGOMERY, JAMES m. REBECCA CLARK Jan. 8th, 1808.

MONTGOMERY, JOHN HARVEY m. HANNAH EMILINE MOORE. (Dau. of ANDREW MOORE, of BETHESDA)

MONTGOMERY, LAWRENCE HARVEY (Son of above) married ANNIE GORDON JOHN. No date. (Ala.)

MONTGOMERY, LUCINDA m. WILLIAM CLARK Jan. 27, 1800.

MORRISON, REBECCA m. SAMUEL HARRIS. No date. He was born in 1733. Family record.

———

MOORE, ALLEN m. POLLY BOND, October 20, 18__ D. S. MORRIS, Sec.

MOORE, ANDREW m. ARMINTA F. CHRISTENBURG 1845 (sometimes CHRISTENBURY).

MOORE, ANDREW m. JEAN BAIN SAMPLE (Chair-maker) No date. He established the first METHODIST CHURCH in Mecklenburg County.

MOORE, ARMINTA m. JOHN MOORE, Oct. 22, 1800. ROBERT IRWIN, Sec.

MOORE, CATHERINE m. WILLIAM MOORE, Feb. 15th, 1802. ISAAC MOORE and ISAAC ALEXANDER the Secs.

MOORE, CHARLES B. m. CATHERINE RODDEN, June 19, 1807. JACOB RODEN, Sec.

MOORE, DAVID m. AGNES KRIMS, May 9th, 1815. MARTIN McWHORTER, Sec.

MOORE, DAVID G. m. NANCY L. WILSON October 8, 1845. H. I. STEWART, Sec.

MOORE, DAVID m. JANE DAVIS, Dec. 1, 1824 in CABARRUS COUNTY. JAMES H. McCALL, Sec.

MOORE, FRANCES m. ALLEN IRA in 1797.

MOORE, FRANCES m. ALLEN REED Nov. 2, 1797. JOHN FITTON, Sec.

MOORE, ELAM m. ELFRINA CAMPBELL Jan. 12, 1826 IRA PARKS, Sec.

MOORE, GEORGE B. m. CHRISTIAN B. TODD, Jan. 3, 1849. FRANKLIN RILEY, Sec.

MOORE, HANNAH EMILINE m. JOHN HARVEY MONTGOMERY. (No date).

MOORE, HUGH m. HELENA ALEXANDER Mar 19, 1824 EBEASER ALEXANDER, Sec.

MOORE, ISAAC m. NANCY FORD (Spelled FOARD on the record) Nov. 5, 1800. JOHN JOHNSTON Sec.

MOORE, JAMES m. CYNTHIA JOHNSTON Feb. 13, in 1827. IRA PARKS, Sec.

MOORE, JAMES m. ELLEN McEWEN June 12, 1795. SAMUEL McEWEN, Sec.

MOORE, JAMES m. MARGARET McAIDEN (No Date) It is thought they were the parents of the ANDREW MOORE, chair-maker, of BETHESDA Methodist Church.

MOORE, JAMES C. m. MARY J. McCORKLE May 1st, 1855.

MOORE, JAMES W. m. ISABELLA S. G. DAVIDSON Jan. 19, 1835. A. R. IRWIN, Sec.

MOORE, JANE m. JOHN HARRIS, April 7, 1777. He was the son of SAMUEL HARRIS and DOROTHY WYLEY, according to the family records of the HARRIS FAMILY, from which this is taken. CABARRUS HARRIS FAMILY.

MOORE, JOHN m. ARMINTA MOORE, October 22, in 1800. ROBERT IRVIN, Sec.

MOORE, JOHN m. MARY WILLIAMSON (no date) daughter of S. L. and M. P. WILLIAMSON.

MOORE, JOHN V. m. MAGGIE GIBBONS in 1865.

MOORE, JOSEPH (Of CABARRUS COUNTY) m. MARY PARK, Oct. 9, 1795. JOHN PARK, Sec. (PHARR?)

MOORE, JOSEPH S. m. SARAH EMMERSON Dec. 20, 1825. STEPHEN EMMERSON, Sec.

MOORE, JOSHUA S. m. LOCKY D. ABERNATHY in 1830, on JANUARY 6. ABNER SHARP, Sec.

MOORE, MARGARET C. m. JAMES M. CALDWELL, Jan. 15, 1851. Daughter of ELAM MOORE.

MOORE, MARY m. DAVID JOHN (Son of GRIFFITH JOHN, of WELCH NECK). No date given.

MOORE, MELISSA m. JAMES CLARK, Nov. 24, 1839, with A. A. (ANDREW) MOORE, Sec.

MOORE, SAMUEL m. EVELINE C. WALLACE in the year of 1831. JOSEPH Y. WALLACE, Sec.

MOORE, SAMUEL A. m. MARTHA ANN KENNEDY, April 18th 1851.

MOORE, SAMUEL K. m. RACHEL OVERCASH, Jan. 26, 1825. JOHN R. DIXON, Sec.

MOORE, THOMAS m. ISABELLA DUNN Feb. 12, 1793. JOHN TODD, Sec.

MOORE, THOMAS m. MARY ANN IRWIN Sept. 20, 1838 and JOHN F. IRWIN and A. B. MOORE, JR. were Sec.

MOORE, THOMAS m. SARAH STARNES June 24, 1820 (In CABARRUS COUNTY) DAVID ROST, Sec.

MOORE, WILLIAM m. MRS. ANN TODD, April 7, 1821, & ROBERT WILSON was Sec.

MOORE, WILLIAM m. BIDDY LAWING, in August 1833.

MOORE, WILLIAM m. CATHERINE MOORE, Feb. 16, 1802. ISAAC MOORE and ISAAC ALEXANDER, Sec.

MOORE, WILLIAM, m. HANNAH STANFIELD, Nov. 11, 1800 ROBERT STANFIELD, Sec.

MOORE, WILLIAM m. POLLY FITTEN, Feb. 19, 1805 and JAMES REED was Sec.

MILES, ARCHIBALD m. PATSY WASHAM, June 25, 1804. BURREL CASHON, Sec.

MILLER, ADAM m. JANE HENDERSON, April 13, 1804.

MILLER, JANE m. ANDREW ROGERS, Sept. 21, 1801, & ABRAHAM MILLER was Sec.

MILLER, MARGARET MARY m. JAMES MOORE HARRIS, Mar. 31, 1812.

MORROW, ALLEN m. CLARISSA SPEARS, Dec. 3, 1837 & ROBERT POTTS was Sec.

CLARISSA SPEARS was the second wife of ALLEN MORROW, his first wife being a SPEARS. These MORROWS are all buried at SIX MILE CHURCH below PINEVILLE. See later.

MORROW, BENJAMIN m. MARY JANE HAWKINS, April 20, 1847. G. W. ALEXANDER, Sec.

This was MAJ. BENJAMIN MORROW (War of 1812) who is buried in the Presbyterian Church-yard in CHARLOTTE, N. C. MARY JANE HAWKINS was the daughter of GOV. WILLIAM HAWKINS, of WARREN COUNTY and a granddaughter of PHILEMON HAWKINS. BENJAMIN MORROW was a son of JAMES McKNIGHT MORROW and his wife SUSANNAH WATSON, daughter of DRURY WATSON, revolutionary soldier of PRINCE EDWARD COUNTY, Virginia.

MORROW, DAVID m. JENNIE McCULLOUGH, Nov. 25, 1802. ANDREW LOFTON, Sec.

MORROW, DAVID m. MARGARET PARKS, August 20, 1839. JAMES K. DAVIS, Sec.

DAVID MORROW was born in N. C. in 1813. They moved to MISSISSIPPI, where he died in 1881 at the age of 68 years. He served in the C. S. A. They had eight children, including RUFUS MORROW who married JENNIE PHARR in Mississippi and moved to TEXAS in 1884.

MORROW, DRURY m. ESTHER McCULLOUGH Jan. 17, 1820. AMOS McCULLOUGH, Sec.

DRURY MORROW was a brother of MAJ. BENJAMIN MORROW and a son of JAMES McKNIGHT MORROW, mentioned above. The family says he moved to TENNESSEE.

ELI MORROW m. MARY COOK, Dec. 9, 1838, and A. A. COFFEY was Sec.

The members of the COFFEY family are buried with the MORROWS in the old SIX-MILE PRESBYTERIAN CHURCH, built by ALLEN MORROW, a few miles below PINEVILLE. Just how they were related has not been definitely established.

MORROW, ELIZABETH m. ISAAC MORROW Nov. 14th 1820. WILLIAM BUSBY, Sec.

MORROW, GEORGE m. ELIZABETH BOWERS (Or POWERS) Sept. 23, 1819. WILLIAM BUSBY, Sec.

MORROW, HEZEKIAH m. ELIZABETH JONES Jan. 5th 1818. WILLIAM BUSBY, Sec.

MORROW, HEZEKIAH m. ELIZABETH RAY, April 25, 1807. W. T. DAVIDSON & WILLIAM BUSBY as Sec.

MORROW, ISAAC m. ELIZABETH MORROW Nov. 14, 1820. WILLIAM BUSBY, Sec.

MORROW, ISAAC m. SALLIE POWERS July 18,1811. GEORGE MORROW and WILLIAM STEWART, Sec.

MORROW, JAMES m. MARY LEMONS (Or TIMONS) on Feb. 23, 1819. LAIRD H. HARRIS, Sec.

MORROW, JENNIE m. ADAMS BROWN, April 28, 1801.

She was a daughter of DAVID MORROW who left will in 1810.

MORROW, JOHN WHITE m. PATSY WORLEY, Dec. 10, 1807 GEORGE MORROW and ALLEN STEELE, Sec.

MORROW, JOHN W. m. M. A. NUTTALL (Of GRANVILLE COUNTY, N. C.) March 30, 1848.

MORROW, JOHN W. m. JERUSHA ANN ELLIOTT (His second marriage) Nov. 7, 1854.

MORROW, MARGARET H. m. THOMAS H. BLAKELY, Sept. 20, 1836.

MORROW, MARTHA L. m. JOSEPH BLACK, August 17, 1837

MORROW, MARTHA M. m. LEWIS H. RUSSELL Dec. 23, 1847.

MORROW, MARTHA m. STEPHEN W. MORROW Sept. 27, 1841

MORROW, MARY m. WILLIAM BUSBY, March 5, 1812.

MORROW, PEGGY m. JAMES BOND, Nov. 25, 1802.

MORROW, ROBERT m. MARTHA MORROW March 5, 1812. WILLIAM BUSBY, Sec.

MORROW, ROBERT W. m. SARAH WILLIAMS Feb. 4, 1840 JOHN BRINKLEY, Sec.

MORROW, ROBERT B. m. LOUISA BRADSHAW Mar. 11, 1852.

MORROW, STEPHEN W. m. MISS MARTHA MORROW, Sept. 27, 1841. DANIEL BRINKLEY Sec.

MORROW, WILLIAM m. MARGARET CROCKETT March 7, 1794 ELI CROCKETT, Sec.

MASSEY, JAMES m. ELIZA McCALL November 25th, 1837.

MULWEE, MARY m. WILLIAM SHARP, May 2, 1818, with WHITMELL HILL, Sec.

NANCE, ISABELLA m. SAMUEL BLYTHE, Jan. 8th, 1822.

NEELY, JENNIE m. JOHN ROGERS, April 27, 1809

NEELY, MARGARET m. MATTHEW RAMSEY, Jan 29th, 1795 ANDREW WALKER, Sec.

NEWMAN, ANN m. JOHN MARSHALL, May 21, 1818.

NORLEY, PATSY m. JOHN WHITE MORROW, Dec. 10, 1807. (She was PATSY WORLEY, as shown above.)

NUTTALL, MISS M. A. (Of GRANVILLE COUNTY, N. CAROLINA) m. JOHN W. MORROW, March 30, 1848.

> This JOHN WHITE MORROW was the son of MAJ. BENJAMIN MORROW, a son of JAMES McKNIGHT MORROW; and BENJAMIN MORROW also married a GRANVILLE COUNTY girl, MARY JANE HAWKINS, daughter of GOV. WILLIAM HAWKINS.

———

ORMOND, JOHN M. m. NANCY HOWARD Dec. 29th, 1740

ORR, MARGARET C. m. LAIRD BLAIR, July 24, 1833.

ORR, NANCY m. WILLIAM A. REA in 1854. Exact date not located.

OSBORN, JONATHAN m. SARAH M. SHARP Sept. 15, 1848 JOHN T. MULKEE, Sec.

OVERBY, OWEN m. JANE SHARP Nov. 11, 1822. JOHN McQUAY, Sec.

OVERCASH, RACHEL m. SAMUEL K. MOORE Jan. 26, 1825.

PARKS, ANDREW m. ISABELLA WILSON (Dau. ISAAC WILSON) No date furnished.

PARKS, JANE m. HUGH W. ROGERS May 1, 1824. SAMUEL W. McCARTY, Sec.

PARKS, JOHN LINDSAY m. MARGARET McDOWELL McELRATH Sept. 26, 1848.

> In 1859, after her death, he married MRS. SARAH KIBLER BUTLER.

PARKS, LILLY m. CAIRNES HENDERSON Jan. 24, 1792

PARKS, MARGARET m. DAVID MORROW, August 20, 1839 JAMES H. DAVIS, Sec.

PARKS, MARY m. JAMES M. REA, April 21, 1842 HUGH A. MATTHEWS, Sec.

PARKS, MINTA m. JAMES CALDWELL, Aug. 12, 1816 ROBERT CALDWELL, Sec.

PARKS, MRS. A. M. m. SILAS REA, SR. Feb. 28th, 1856. SILAS H. REA, Sec.

PARKS, THOMAS MOORE m. SARAH ALEXANDER (Daughter of JAMES McKNITT ALEXANDER) and settled in MONROE, N. C. No date given.

PARKS, WILLIAM BEATTY m. NANCY ALICE GLUYAS Oct. 9, 1873.

———

PATTERSON, EMILY m. THOMAS ALLEN SHARP, Nov. 13, 1849. MARK ALEXANDER, Sec.

PATTERSON, JOHN m. MARGARET HOUSTON, Feb. 13 1794.

> They lived in the PROVIDENCE CHURCH settlement and both are buried in the churchyard there.

PATTERSON, JOHN NEWELL WILLIAMSON m. MARGARET LENORA SLOAN in 1861.

> He was a Confederate soldier and a son of JOHN PATTERSON and MARGARET HOUSTON.

PATTERSON, MARY m. THOMAS HARRIS. He was born in 1754, and he and his wife went to GREENE COUNTY, GEORGIA.

PATTERSON, ONA ELIZABETH JOSEPHINE m. REV. C. K. CUMMING, D. D. in 1894.

> They were both missionaries and members of HOPEWELL PRESBYTERIAN CHURCH.

PEOPLES, RICHARD (b. 1790) m. JANE HARRIS (b. in 1798) Date of their marriage not obtained.

> Some Tennessee descendants of this family spelled the name PEEPLES.

PETTUS, NANCY m. IRVIN ABERNATHY (Date marriage not found).

PETTUS, WILLIAM m. VIOLET KNOX. (She left a will in 1828, and appears to have been a daughter of SAMUEL KNOX and an aunt of Pres. JAMES KNOX POLK.

POLK, CHARLES m. Daughter of HEZEKIAH ALEXANDER (No date given).

POLK, EZEKIEL m. MARY WILSON, daughter of SAMUEL WILSON and his first wife MARY WINSLOW, the daughter of MOSES WINSLOW. No date given.

POLK, MARGARET m. EPHRAIM BREVARD. She was daughter of GEN. THOMAS POLK. (No date).

POLK, GEN. THOMAS m. SUSANNA SPRATT. She was the daughter of THOMAS SPRATT. (No date).

POTTER, MARY m. JAMES BUCHANAN Dec. 27, 1794.

POTTS, JAMES m. MARGARET McKEE, (No date). He was son of JOHN POTTS, of CODDLE CREEK, who bought land in MECKLENBURG in 1763.

POTTS, LENORA m. DR. JAMES SAMUEL ABERNATHY. (No date furnished.)

POTTS, LYDIA E. m. JOHN CURETON, Feb. 29, 1825 and JEREMIAH CURETON was Sec.

POTTS, MARY m. JAMES POTTS (No date given).

POTTS, WILLIAM GRAHAM m. REBECCA TORRENCE. He was the son of JAMES and MARY POTTS. No date.

POTTS, LYDIA (McKARAHAN) m. (second) GENERAL GEO. GRAHAM. (no date).

POTTS, WILLIAM m. LYDIA McKARAHAN, who after his death married GEN. GEORGE GRAHAM. No date. This WILLIAM POTTS was the son of the second JOHN POTTS.

POTTS, WILLIAM HENRY m. ANNIE CALDWELL. He was a son of WILLIAM GRAHAM POTTS and his wife REBECCA TORRENCE. (No date again).

POTTS, VAN BUREN m. HAZELINE PATTERSON in 1906. He was the son of WILLIAM HENRY POTTS and his wife ANNIE CALDWELL.

> The record of these marriages come from family records and other reliable sources, and although the dates are often not available, they can be estimated, and this lack of data does not destroy their importance as links in the chain of the family history. For that reason they are included in this important record.

POTTS, AGNES m. ALLEN MORROW (As his first wife) Date not obtainable.

PRICE, JAMES m. MARY DAVIDSON She was the sister of MAJ. JOHN DAVIDSON, and is buried at the old BAKER GRAVEYARD not far from BEATTY'S FORD on the CATAWBA river. No date.

PRICE, JOHN DAVIDSON m. JANE BEATTY. He was the son of JAMES PRICE and MARY DAVIDSON. No date found.

PRICE, MARGARET m. EPHRAIM ALEXANDER. No date is given.

PRICE, PATSY m. GEN. THOMAS MOORE of S. CAROLINA son of CHARLES MOORE. No Date.

PRICE, RACHEL m. JOHN HILL, a Blacksmith. NO DATE.

PRICE, THOMAS m. MARY DUCKWORTH. NO DATE.

PRICE, RACHEL m. EZEKIEL ALEXANDER. She was a daughter of JOHN DAVIDSON PRICE. No date.

PRICE, WILLIAM, son of JAMES and MARY DAVIDSON PRICE m. _____. To TENNESSEE.

QUEARY, MARGARET m. ANDREW CALDWELL Feb. 12th 1853. JEREMIAH HOWIE, Sec.

RAMSEY, FRANCIS ALEXANDER m. MARGARET McKNITT ALEXANDER April 7, 1789.

RAMSEY, JAMES m. ISABELLA HALL Feb. 8, 1792.

RAMSEY, MATTHEW m. MARGARET NEELY Jan. 29th, 1795. ANDREW WALKER, Sec.

RAMSEY, THOMAS m. SUSANNAH HENDERSON Oct. 4, 1804.

RANKIN, RICHARD m. ANN HARGROVES May 18, 1825 ROBERT WILSON, Sec.

RANKIN, SAMUEL m. MARY DOHERTY Nov. 16, 1791. RICHARD RANKIN, Sec.

RANKIN, DR. WATSON W. m. SARAH ELIZABETH ALEXANDER, May 25, 1847.

RAY, BRITTON m. HANNAH CASHON, Oct. 4th, 1802.

RAY, ELIZABETH m. HEZEKIAH MORROW, April 25th 1807. W. T. DAVIDSON and WILLIAM BUSBY Security.

REA, ALLEN m. FRANCES MOORE in 1797.

REA, ANDREW m. ELEANOR HENNEGAN in 1797.

REA, AVERY S. m. MARGARET McSPARREN in 1823.

REA, CAROLINE m. WILLIAM BEATTY Apr. 1, 1841.

REA, DAVID H. m. CHARLOTTE SHEPARD in 1836

REA, DAVID H. m. HELEN M. CLARK in 1848.

REA, DAVID N. m. ELIZABETH SPEARS Nov. 29th, 1802.

REA, ELIZABETH m. ROBERT IRWIN in 1817.

REA, EMERY S. m. MARGARET McSPANN March 5th 1823. ROBERT J. MORRIS, Sec.

REA, HARRIETT D m. JAMES W. MARTIN in 1837.

REA, JAMES m. POLLY WALKER March 10, 1814.

REA, JAMES, m. POLLY BOZZELL in 1809.

REA, JAMES M. m. MARY PARKS April 21, 1842 HUGH A. MATTHEWS, Sec.

REA, JAMES m. SARAH J. McEWEN July 28, 1857

REA, JOSEPH m. JEMIMAH HAWKINS July 15, 1809

REA, LEROY m. HANNAH McCORKLE Jan. 8, 1839. ELIAS HANKEY, Sec.

REA, MARTHA m. SAMUEL REA April 5, 1797.

REA, MARTHA m. JOHN COCHRAN Jan. 16th 1815; JOHN REED and ANDREW REA, Sec.

REA, MARY JANE m. JAMES CUNNINGHAM, Dec. 21, 1847 JOHN W. BLAIR, Sec.

REA, SAMUEL m. MARTHA REA, April 5, 1798.

REA, SILAS SR. m. MRS. A. M. PARKS, Feb. 28, 1856 SILAS H. REA, Sec.

REA, WILLIAM W. m. ELIZABETH SHARP, August 28th, 1854. ROBERT H. MAXWELL, Sec.

REA, WILLIAM m. HANNAH BERRYHILL, March 23, 1814.

Rea, WILLIAM A. m. NANCY ORR in 1854.

REED, ALLEN m. FRANCES MOORE, Nov. 2, 1797. JOHN FITTEN, Sec.

REED, CAROLINE m. JOHN M. SHARP, January 22, 1840 JOHN REED, Sec.

REED, HUGH m. ANN WALKER in March 1809. WILLIAM WALKER, Sec.

REED, ISABELL m. ABEL JOHN (No date) He was killed in 1825. His family left and settled in DALLAS COUNTY, ALABAMA.

REED, JAMES m. DOLLY KING April 13, 1802. JOSEPH REED Sec.

REED, JAMES JR. m. POLLY KING April 13, 1802. Both records appear, though there may be some mistake here.

REED, JONATHAN m. JANE P. McDANIELS in 1822. ROBT. LINDSAY, Sec.

REED, LENORA A. m. W. A. COOK, September 5th, 1848 W. S. DANIEL, Sec.

REED, R. W. m. MARY FLENNIKEN, Nov. 27, 1844. JAS. C. REA, Sec.

REED, SILAS m. NANCY MILLER, February 16, 1842. JOHN W. WOODWARD, Sec.

REESE, REV. THOMAS m. JANE HARRIS. She was daughter of CHARLES HARRIS who married ELIZABETH THOMSON BAKER, and a niece of ROBERT HARRIS JR. No date given in the family record.

RHEA, HANNAH m. ROBERT HARRIS in 1811. No other date furnished.

RHODES, MARY m. WILLIAM ROGERS, December 15, 1806.

RICE, WILLIAM m. ELIZABETH BARNES July 14th, 1803 WILLIAM BURTON (Or BARTON) Sec.

ROBINSON, EZEKIEL (b. 1786) m. ELEANOR ROBINSON. No date given.

ROBINSON, HARRIS m. AGNES KIRK, on May 11, 1795 JAMES HENDERSON, Sec.

ROBINSON, CAIRNES HENDERSON m. MARY ABIGAIL ALEXANDER, March 12, 1844.

ROBINSON, MARGARET JANE m. WILLIAM HEZEKIAH VANCE No date of marriage given.

ROBINSON, MARTHA m. HUGH HARRIS, January 11, 1788

ROBINSON, MARY m. BATTE ERVIN. She was daughter of REV. JOHN ROBINSON. No date given.

ROBINSON, ROBERT m. MARGARET HENDERSON March 30, 1790. JOHN ROBINSON, Sec.

ROBINSON, WILLIAM m. AGNES HARGROVE, Oct. 9th, 1804. WALTER CARRUTH, Sec.

RODDEN, ANDREW m. HARRIETT JUDETH ROWDEN Jan. 26, 1835.

In most instances where this name RODEN or RODDEN appears on the Mecklenburg records it is so spelled, but in at least one instance, the signature of the record is written by the applicant himself as ROWDEN, which this writer thinks is the correct spelling. It appears to have been a corruption of the name WROTEN, which was either adopted or restored to use by the family after its migration to Orangeburg and Barnwell Districts in South Carolina. It will be noticed that the bride's name in the above record is spelled ROWDEN.

RODDEN, BENJAMIN m. BETSY WILLIAMS, Dec. 30, 1807. WILLIAM RODDEN, Sec.

RODDEN, CATHERINE m. CHARLES B. MOORE, June 19, 1807. JACOB RODDEN, Sec.

RODEN, JACKSON m. POLLY COWAN, Feb. 17, 1810 BENJAMIN RODDEN, Sec.

RODDEN, JACOB m. JANE GRIFFIN, Jan. 25th in 1795. UPTON BYRUM, Sec.

RODDEN, JOHN m. MILLY BEATTY March 1, 1842. Here JOHN signed his name ROWDEN.

RODDEN, UPTON m. RACHEL PITTMAN May 16th in 1806. JONATHAN BAKER, Sec. (There was some relationship between UPTON BYRUM and UPTON RODDEN, but what?)

RODDEN, WILLIAM m. HANNAH R. ROWDEN, March 18, 1847.

ROGERS, ANDREW m. JANE MILLER, Sept. 21, 1811. ABRAHAM MILLER, Sec.

ROGERS, ANDREW L. m. SARAH KERR, Feb. 9, 1835 JOHN MILLER, Sec.

ROGERS, HUGH W. m. JANE PARKS May 1, 1824. SAMUEL W. McCARTY, Sec.

ROGERS, JOHN m. ELLEN MAXWELL Feb. 2, 18___

ROGERS, JOHN m. JENNIE NEELY, Apr. 27, 1809.

ROGERS, JOHN m. MARGARET RUSSELL, May 12, 1789 DAVID RUSSELL, Sec.

ROGERS, JOSEPH m. JANE LEDLES, April 6, 1825 JOHN L. HAYES, Sec.

ROGERS, JOSEPH m. MARGARET McEWEN, August 9th 1822. ROBERT McEWEN, Sec.

ROGERS, SAMUEL W. m. JANE KIRKPATRICK Feb. 25 1823.

ROGERS, THOMAS m. TABITHA M. SECREST, January 31, 1804. STEPHEN ROGERS, Sec.

ROGERS, WILLIAM m. MARY RHODES on the 15th of December in 1806.

POWERS, SALLY m. ISAAC MORROW July 18th, 1811.

PUCKETT, JAMES m. VIOLET DAVIDSON ALEXANDER, July 14, 1847. He was the son of JOHN PUCKETT of SALEM, VIRGINIA, and she the daughter of WILLIAM BAIN ALEXANDER JR.

PUCKETT, McKAMIE RUDOLPHUS m. AGNES JANE LIPE on February 24, 1887.

PUCKETT, WILLIAM HARRISON m. LOUISE DOWNS about 1870. Exact date not given.

PURVIANCE, MARGARET M. m. JOSIAH HARRIS, December 25, 1830.

ROSS, HANNAH m. MATTHEW HARRIS in 1784. Exact date not found.

ROSS, JOSEPH V. m. MISS SOPHIA COLLINGS, Feb. 19, 1822. By ROBERT H. MORRISON.

ROWAN, HUGH m. HANNAH CALHOUN May 26, 1792, with THOMAS NEELY Sec.

RUMPLE, JOSEPH m. BARBARA LAWRENCE (who was born in 1807). From tombstone. Date missing.

RUSSELL, LEWIS H. m. MARTHA M. MORROW Dec. 23,1847

RUSSELL, MARGARET m. JOHN ROGERS May 12, 1789, & DAVID RUSSELL was Sec.

SAMPLE, MARTHA C. m. ROBERT B. HENDERSON in 1832

SAMPLE, ROBERT MILAS m. ADALINE HENDERSON (who was born in 1808) Date not given.

SAMPLE, WILLIAM m. ELIZABETH ALEXANDER, a half sister of JOHN McKNITT ALEXANDER. No date.

SAMPLE, WILLIAM AZMON (born in 1803) married JANE LOUISA BERRY, Dec. 24, 1829.

SCOTT, JAMES M. m. ELLEN SHARP April 4, 1848, and WILLIAM W. QUINN was Sec.

SCOTT, JANE m. JOHN SHARP, February 20, 1837, and AZARIAH SHARP was Sec.

SECHEST, TABITHA M. m. THOMAS ROGERS January 31, 1804; STEPHEN ROGERS, Sec.

SHARP, BETSY m. JOHN BROWN, Feb. 22, 1802. WILLIAM WALKER, Sec.

SHARP, CAROLINE m. ROBERT J. BYRAM, Sept 3, 1829. GODFREY WILLIAMSON, Sec.

SHARP, ELIZABETH P. m. WILLIAM W. REA, August 28, 1854; ROBERT H. MAXWELL, Sec.

SHARP, ELLEN m. JAMES M. SCOTT, April 4, 1848, & WILLIAM W. QUINN was Sec.

SHARP, EZEKIEL m. CATHERINE ALEXANDER. (No date) She was a sister of REV. JOSEPH ALEXANDER & daughter of THEOPHILUS ALEXANDER, older brother of JEMIMAH and JOHN McKNITT ALEXANDER.

SHARP, HANNAH m. WILLIAM HILL July 24, in 1821; WHITMELL HILL, Sec.

SHARP, JAMES m. MARGARET CUNNINGHAM (No date) She was a daughter of ROGER CUNNINGHAM and sister of REV. ROBERT MOORE CUNNINGHAM.

SHARP, JANE m. OWEN OVERBY November 11, 1822 and JOHN McQUAY was Sec.

SHARP, JEAN m. WILLIAM WALKER, June 1, 1801; JOHN BROWN, Sec.

SHARP, JOHN M. m. CAROLINE REED, Jan. 22, 1840. JOHN REED Sec.

SHARP, JOHN m. JANE SCOTT Feb. 20, 1837, with AZARIAH SHARP Sec.

SHARP, JOHN m. SARAH JANE TAYLOR Sept. 18, 1854 R. J. REED, Sec.

SHARP, JOHN (Son of EDWARD SHARP) m. ELEANOR CUNNINGHAM. No date. He died in 1819 in PROVIDENCE CHURCH community, in Mecklenburg County.

SHARP, MARGARET m. ZEPHANIAH JOHN Dec. 22,1824 JAMES SHARP, Sec.

SHARP, MARY m. AARON (Or ADAM) KERR, Feb. 17, 1823

SHARP, MARY m. JAMES McCLURE, April 4th, 1803; ANDREW OLIPHANT Sec.

SHARP, MARY m. WHITMELL HILL, March 21, 1814. JOHN L. DANIEL Sec.

SHARP, RICHARD SR. m. ANN VAN PELT Nov. 18th, 1807. SAMUEL FLENNIKEN, Sec.

SHARP, SARAH M. m. JONATHAN OSBORN Sept. 15, 1848. JOHN T. MULNEE Sec.

SHARPE, THOMAS m. JEMIMAH ALEXANDER about 1762 Possibly in MARYLAND.

SHARP, THOMAS ALLEN m. EMILY PATTERSON Nov. 13 1849. MARK ALEXANDER Sec.

SHARP, WILLIAM m. MARY MULVEE, May 2, 1818; WHITMELL HILL, Sec.

SHEPARD, CHARLOTTE m. DAVID H. REA in 1836.

SHIELDS, ALEXANDER COWAN (born in 1826) married JANE HENDERSON about 1854.

SHIELDS, COWAN LEMLEY m. JULIA NANCY ALEXANDER Nov. 7th, 1889.

SHIELDS, DAVID HENDERSON (born in 1856) married (1) ANNIE SITTON and (2) LILLIAN KERNER. No dates furnished.

SHIELDS, ISABELLA m. DANIEL CALDWELL January 18, 1826.

SHIELDS, MARY m. ROBERT CALDWELL March 20,1819.

SHIELDS, MARY m. ROBERT ALEXANDER March 20th, 1839; ISAAC ALEXANDER and WILLIAM ANDREWS Sec.

SMART, GEORGE W. m. SUSAN BARNETT in 1775. Exact date not found.

SMITH, JANE m. WILLIAM CUNNINGHAM, October 15 1805. RICHARD SHARPE and JAMES WALLIS as Sec.

SMITH, MARY m. DAVID CALDWELL June 29, in 1791 STEPHEN ALEXANDER and JOHN ALLISON, Sec.

SNELL, ELIZABETH m. JOHN BLAIR March 26th 1800

SPEARS, CLARISSA m. ALLEN MORROW Dec. 3, 1845 ROBERT POTTS, Sec.

SPEARS, ELIZABETH m. DAVID N. REA Nov. 29th 1802

SPENCER, HARRIETT m. PATRICK JACK (Son of CAPTAIN JAMES JACK) No date found.

SPRATT, SUSANNAH m. THOMAS POLK. She the daughter of THOMAS SPRATT. (No date).

STANFIELD, HANNAH m. WILLIAM MOORE Nov. 11th 1800 ROBERT STANFIELD, Sec.

STARNES, SARAH m. THOMAS MOORE June 24, 1820. DAVID BOST, Sec.

STEELE, GRIZZEL m. JOHN HARRIS. (No date found).

STEVENS, HANNAH m. THOMAS CARLOCK April 26, 1831.

STINSON, ELIZABETH m. ALEXANDER COOPER Mar 4, 1834

STRONG, DR. JOHN MASON m. RACHEL ELEANOR HARRIS April 7, 1851. (He married second NANCY GRIER of STEELE CREEK).

SWANN, REBECCA C. m. WILLIAM K. CUNNINGHAM, February 10, 1847. JAMES GLOVER, Sec.

TAYLOR, SARAH JANE m. JOHN SHARP Sept. 18, 1854. R. J. REED, Sec.

THOMPSON, ANN m. WILLIAM CLARK November 2, 1796.

TIMONS (LEMONS) MARY m. JAMES MORROW, February 23, 1819. LAIRD H. HARRIS, Sec.

TODD, CHRISTIAN E. m. GEORGE R. MOORE, January 3, 1849. FRANKLIN RILEY, Sec.

TODD, MRS. ANN m. WILLIAM MOORE April 7, 1821; ROBERT WILSON, Sec.

TORRENCE ANN E. m. EDWARD CALDWELL August 11, 1828 ANDREW CALDWELL, Sec.

TORRENCE, HUGH m. ISABELLA FALLS, the widow of COL FALLS who was killed at RAMSEUR'S MILL. Both HUGH and ISABELLA died in 1816 and are buried at HOPEWELL CHURCH. No date of marriage found.

TORRENCE, JAMES (Son of HUGH) m. NANCY DAVIDSON of IREDELL COUNTY. She died and he married second MARY LATTA (who was born in 1790), and after Mary's death he married third MARGARET ALLISON. (No dates found). His full name was JAMES GALBRAITH TORRENCE.

VAN PELT, ANN m. RICHARD SHARP SR. November 8th, 1807. SAMUEL FLENNIKEN Sec.

VANCE, JOHN DAVID m. BARBARA ANN KILLIAN in May, 1874; he married (2) MARY McAULEY (No date).

VANCE, JOHN FRANKLIN m. HATTIE ELIZABETH PUCKETT (Daughter of WILLIAM HARRISON PUCKETT) Dec. 12, 1893.

VANCE, WILLIAM (BILLY) m. JULIA ANN FULLWOOD July 10, 1879 Of GILLEAD CHURCH.

VANCE, WILLIAM HEZEKIAH m. MARGARET JANE ROBINSON (b. 1820). He died in C. S. A.

VANCE, WILLIAM McILWAIN m. MINNIE VIOLA ALEXANDER August 16, 1905.

WADDELL, FRANCES m. DAVID COWAN, May 20th, 1835.

WALKER, ANN m. HUGH REED in March 1809. WILLIAM WALKER, Sec.

WALKER, MARY m. JAMES REA March 10, 1814.

WALKER, WILLIAM m. JEAN SHARP, June 1, 1801 JOHN BROWN, Sec.

WALLACE, ALBERT to CAROLINE REED, Dec. 1st, 1845. JAMES C. FLOW witness.

WALLACE, ALBERT to CORNELIA L. CROSS, January 21, 1861. SAMUEL P. CALDWELL.

WALLACE, ALEXANDER to PRUDENCE SMITH, July 12, 1817. TELEMACUS ALEXANDER and ISAAC ALEXANDER, Security and witnesses.

WALLACE, ALLEN V. m. ROCINDA G. CHRISTENBURY August 28, 1851, by E. D. ALEXANDER, J. P. SAMUEL N. CHRISTENBURY and JAMES PARKS as Sec.

WALLACE, ANDREW to SARAH ALEXANDER, January 14 1801. WILLIAM ALEXANDER, Sec.

WALLACE, EVELINE C. m. SAMUEL MOORE in 1831. JOSEPH Y. WALLACE, Sec.

WALLACE, EZEKIEL to LYDIA KNOX, April 19, 1797 RUTHY ALEXANDER, Sec. or witness.

WALLACE, EZEKIEL m. ELIZABETH ROBINSON, December 23, 1806. JOHN PARK, JR. and ISAAC ALEXANDER, witnesses.

WALLACE, GEORGE m. SARAH ROGERS, August 28, 1792 SAMUEL WALLACE and ISAAC ALEXANDER witnesses

WALLACE, JAMES to EDNITHA HUNTER, Feb. 1, 1842 WILLIAM B. SLOAN and C. T. ALEXANDER, wits.

WALLACE, JAMES to SARAH E. D. MONTGOMERY, Sept. 30, 1845. WILLIAM G. GARRISON and C. T. ALEXANDER, witnesses.

WALLACE, JOHN m. ELIZABETH WALLACE, April 2nd, 1831. MATHEW WALLACE and WILLIAM BROWN as security.

WALLACE, JOHN m. SARAH JOHNSON Feb. 13, 1833 WILLIAMSON WALLACE, Sec.

WALLACE, JOHN W. to S. E. WALLACE November 10 1859. They were married by A. RANSOM. The witnesses were ROBERT LUCKY and W. K. REED.

WALLACE, JOSEPH m. MARGARET HOUSTON Jan. 7th, 1823. THOMAS G. BARNETT and ISAAC S. ALEXANDER, witnesses and Security.

WALLACE, JOSEPH R. m. ALICE J. MORRIS, October 9, 1865. Married by JOHN F. BUTT. A. N. JOHNSTON and WILLIAM MAXWELL C. C. C.

WALLACE, LAWRENCE M. m. NANCY S. SMITH, Jan. 1 1861, by LORENZO HUNTER, J. P. ALLISON N. BIGGER and W. K. REED C. C. C.

WALLACE, MARQUIS L. m. ELIZABETH M. WILLIAMSON Oct. 31, 1848. NATHAN ORR and SAMUEL A. DAVIS, J. P.

WALLACE, MATTHEW m. PEGGY BARNHILL Oct. 5th, 1811. JOHN Z. BARNHILL and ISAAC S. ALEXANDER, witnesses and security.

WALLACE, MATTHEW B. m. MARY CAROLINE BLACK, Feb 15, 1822. ALEXANDER McLARTY and ISAAC ALEXANDER witnesses and security.

WALLACE, ROBERT B. m. JANE ANN MORRISON, Oct. 16 1865. Married by Wm. McDONALD. P. M. WHITE and WILLIAM MAXWELL, Sec.

WALLACE, ROBERT B. m. MARY ANN BIGHAMS, Jan. 11th 1843. JOHN W. WILSON, Sec.

WALLACE, ROBERT L. m. MARGARET M. JOHNSTON July 21, 1851. Married by JOHN WALKER, J. P. With R. M. NORMANT and BRAWLEY OATES, C. C. C.

WALLACE, WILLIAM m. JEAN MOFFETT, December 1, 1792 SAMUEL MEEK and JOHN ALLISON, Sec.

WALLACE, WILLIAM m. CATHERINE McLARTY Jan. 14th 1800. ROBERT WALLACE and ISAAC ALEXANDER, as Security.

WALLACE, WILLIAM m. SARAH GILLILAND, December 2nd 1806. JOHN GILLILAND and ISAAC ALEXANDER as witnesses.

WALLACE, WILLIAM m. JANE A. KERNS, February 23rd 1810. R. V. KERNS and JAMES PARKS Sec.

WALLACE, WILLIAM M. m. LUCY B. JOHNSTON, January 22, 1846. JOHN PHELAN and BRAWLEY OATES the witnesses, etc.

WALLACE, WILLIAMSON m. MARY MORRIS, August 21st, 1848. JOHN T. REED and SAMUEL J. LOWRIE as witnesses, etc. REED spelled REID.

WALLACE, EZEKIEL C. m. MARY PARKS, December 17, 1839. CYRUS L. ALEXANDER and BRAWLEY OATES as witnesses.

The above EZEKIEL spelled his name WALLIS, as did the WILLIAM WALLIS in the two items that follow, which was the spelling adopted by REV. JAMES WALLACE, who had it changed to WALLIS.

WALLIS, WILLIAM to REBECCA ALEXANDER, February 29 1804. WILLIE M. BEATTY, Security.

WALLIS, WILLIAM m. HANNAH JULIAN March 14, 1809. NATHAN ORR, Security.

WALLIS, REV. JAMES m. JEAN BAIN ALEXANDER, before August 4, 1793 when a child was born.

WALLIS, JOSEPH (b. 1801) m. ELIZABETH CROCKETT April 10, 1823. (Dau. of ELIJAH CROCKETT)

WALLIS, JAMES (Son of REV. JAMES WALLIS) married ANN CROCKETT (Date not found.)

WALLIS, JOHN McKNITT (Son of Rev. James) married MARGARET CROCKETT in 1813.

WASHAM, PATSY m. ARCHIBALD MILES June 25, 1804. BURRELL CASHON, Sec.

WEATHERS, NANCY m. SAMUEL BOATWRIGHT, Aug. 1, 1792

WEIR, DR. CALVIN STUART m. ISABELLA SOPHIA ALEXANDER March 31, 1839.

WHITNEY, ROBERT DAVIDSON m. first, SARAH ESTHER McCOY, and second (Sept. 8, 1868) MARTHA ELIZABETH McCOY.

WILLIAMS, BETSY m. BENJAMIN RODDEN, Dec. 30, 1807 WILLIAM RODDEN, Sec.

WILLIAMS, HANNAH m. LEWIS RODDEN, Sept. 7th 1802. WILLIAM RODDEN, Sec.

WILLIAMS, REV. JOHN CUNNINGHAM (From LAURENS COUNTY, S. C.) m. MISS ELIZABETH A. R. CHILES, July 2, 1844.

WILLIAMS, SARAH m. ROBERT W. MORROW, February 4, 1840. JOHN BRINKLEY, Sec.

WILLIAMS, SARAH A. m. ANDREW N. CALDWELL Mar. 26, 1844. JOHN M. CALDWELL, Sec.

WILSON, CYNTHIA m. JOSEPH WADE HAMPTON, July 2, 1844.

CYNTHIA WILSON was the daughter of ROBERT WILSON, the son of SAMUEL WILSON. She was the niece of MRS. EZEKIEL POLK and of MRS. MAJ. JOHN DAVIDSON. Her husband, JOSEPH WADE HAMPTON went to Texas, where he died in the City of Austin, and after his death CYNTHIA and her children returned to MECKLENBURG COUNTY, where she died and is buried at Hopewell Church.

WILSON, DEBORAH m. ARCHIBALD CROCKETT, Jan. 12 1792. WILLIAM POTTS and JAMES DOUGLASS Sec.

WILSON, DOVIE, daughter of WILLIAM WILSON and grand-daughter of SAMUEL WILSON married DR. HAMILTON DOUGHERTY (No Date found).

WILSON, DR. ISAAC m. VIOLE_ ELIZABETH ALEXANDER, Dec. 27, 1831. After her death DR. WILSON m. REBECCA McLEAN.

VIOLET ELIZABETH ALEXANDER was a daughter of WILLIAM BAIN ALEXANDER and grand-daughter of JOHN McKNITT ALEXANDER. REBECCA McLEAN was daughter of DR. McLEAN revolutionary soldier and surgeon.

WILSON, LILLIE m. JAMES CONNOR. She was the daughter of SAMUEL WILSON and MARGARET JACK, the third wife of SAMUEL WILSON & the daughter of PATRICK JACK.

WILSON, MARY m. EZEKIEL POLK the grandfather of President JAMES KNOX POLK. She was a daughter of SAMUEL WILSON and his first wife MARY WINSLOW.

WILSON, MARY m. ROBERT HARRIS (No date found). He was the son of CHARLES HARRIS who married second, ELIZABETH THOMSON BAKER.

WILSON, NANCY m. DAVID G. MOORE Oct. 8, 1845. N. E. STEWART, Sec.

WILSON, ROBERT (Son of SAMUEL WILSON and his third wife MARGARET JACK) married MARGARET ALEXANDER, the daughter of THOMAS ALEXANDER "of Sugar Creek". No date found.

WILSON, SALLIE, daughter of SAMUEL WILSON and MARY WINSLOW m. BENJAMIN McCONNELL. No date found.

WILSON, SARAH m. LATTA McCONNELL (No date) After their marriage they moved to Tennessee. She was a daughter of SAMUEL WILSON and MARGARET JACK.

WILSON, SARAH R. m. DR. PINCKNEY C. CALDWELL Dec. 12, 1831.

WILSON, SAMUEL m. (1) MARY WINSLOW, daughter of MOSES WINSLOW and his wife JEAN OSBORN, by whom he had six children; m. (2) the widow HOWARD, by whom he had one daughter MARGARET HOWARD, who married JOHN DAVIDSON, of S. C.; (3) MARGARET JACK, daughter of PATRICK JACK and sister of CAPT. JAMES JACK, by whom he had five children.

> The above statement in regard to the several marriages of SAMUEL WILSON is obtained from several sources, but particularly from page 196 of the History of HOPEWELL CHURCH by CHARLES WILLIAM SOMMERVILLE, Ph. D. 1939. If these statements are correct then SAMUEL WILSON had two daughters, VIOLET, who married MAJOR JOHN DAVIDSON, and MARGARET (by his second marriage) who became the wife of another JOHN DAVIDSON "Of South Carolina". That is, he was the father in law of two different JOHN DAVIDSONS.

WILSON, SAMUEL, JR. m. HANNAH KNOX. (No date has been found). He was a son of SAMUEL DAVIDSON and his wife MARY WINSLOW.

WILSON, VIOLET (Also a daughter of SAMUEL WILSON and MARY WINSLOW) m. MAJ. JOHN DAVIDSON.

WILSON, ZACCHEUS is said to have married LIZZIE CONGER, who was the widow of NICHOLAS ROSS. Nicholas Ross and ZACCHEUS WILSON lived in the STEELE CREEK SETTLEMENT. The latter was one of the "signers" of the Mecklenburg Declaration. See later.

WORLEY, JOSHUA m. a MISS CALDWELL. According to a statement on page 141 of Vol. 1, Habersham Chapter D. A. R. Historical Collections, she was the daughter of JOHN CALDWELL, of CHARLOTTE COUNTY, Virginia.

WORLEY, PATSY m. JOHN WHITE MORROW, December 10, 1807. GEORGE MORROW and ALLEN STEELE Sec.

HARRISON FAMILY MARRIAGES IN MECKLENBURG COUNTY, NORTH CAROLINA

HARRISON, DANIEL m. ESTHER HUTCHINSON, November 20, 1820. WILLIAM ALEXANDER and ISAAC ALEXANDER, witnesses and security.

HARRISON, HIAM m. ELLEN C. FLOW, on August 26 1847. THOMAS N. ALEXANDER, Sec.

HARRISON, GRIFFIN m. SUSAN HARRISON July 24th 1820. THOMAS HARRISON and ISAAC ALEXANDER, witnesses and sureties.

HARRISON, JOSEPH m. SARAH E. HILL, March 28th 1833. ALEXANDER DOBBIN, Sec.

HARRISON, JOSEPH m. FANNIE D. CHRISTENBURY on June 21, 1854. Married by R. D. ALEXANDER, with SAMUEL GARRISON and W. K. REED, witnesses and sureties.

HARRISON, ROBERT m. CATHERINE WILSON March 16 1841. JACKSON WALLACE & BRAWLEY OATES Sec.

HARRISON, WILLIAM m. MARY BURNETT, May 31, in 1831. JOSHUA SIKES and WILLIAM H. SIMPSON, witnesses and sureties.

HARRISON, EDMUND (Spelled HARR (I) SS, and may have been HARRISON) m. PATSY SMARTT December 17, 1800. ROBERT SAVILLE Sec.

HARRISON, NEHEMIAH m. POLLY WILSON July 5th 1815. SAMUEL WILSON and ISAAC ALEXANDER witnesses and sureties.

> The identity of this family of HARRISONS down in Mecklenburg County has not been determined as this is written, but the ancestor may have been one JOSIAH HARRISON who came there early.

SOME DEEDS TO LANDS IN MECKLENBURG COUNTY BETWEEN MEMBERS OF THE WALLACE FAMILY

JAMES AND JEAN WALLACE. (Deed Book 7, page 508) JAMES and JEAN WALLACE deed 28 acres in Mecklenburg County to ZACCHEUS WILSON, August 27, 1774. The witnesses to this deed were THOMAS HARRIS and DAVID WILSON.

THOMAS WALLACE - HIS DEED. (Deed Book 15 page 243) THOMAS WALLACE, of CHESTER COUNTY, SOUTH CAROLINA executes a deed to certain lands for the sum of one hundred pounds to ANDREW OLIVER, of MECKLENBURG COUNTY, North Carolina, dated December 6, 1796. Signed THOMAS WALLACE.

THOMAS WALLACE - HIS DEED. On December 23, 1796, the above THOMAS WALLACE of Chester County, S.C. executed another deed to WILL GRAY of Mecklenburg County, North Carolina, in which he conveys to said Gray 159 acres of land. This deed also signed THOMAS WALLACE.

EZEKIEL WALLACE - HIS DEED. (Deed Book 18, page 286) EZEKIEL WALLACE, of MECKLENBURG COUNTY, North Carolina, gave certain lands to his "beloved son James"; also gave his said son a negro boy named Stephen aged 9 years, and another negro boy named Joe aged 4 years. This instrument is witnessed by ISAAC ALEXANDER, Clerk, Nathaniel Alexander and JAMES WILLIFORD. September 10, 17_3. (Evidently about 1793).

MATTHEW WALLACE - HIS DEED. (Deed Book 18, page 330) MATTHEW WALLACE and JACOB ALEXANDER of Mecklenburg County, North Carolina, and STEPHEN FOX are parties to an indenture, which is of record in the book and page above cited. The signature is thus: _____ WALLIS.

LIST OF PUBLIC OFFICIALS OF MECKLENBURG COUNTY (N.C.) FROM THE YEAR 1775 TO 1785.

The following list contains the names of those persons who resided in Mecklenburg County, North Carolina, as militia officers, tax assessors, tax collectors, justices of the peace, road overseers, jurors and other public officers appointed for the different CAPTAINS' COMPANIES, after an order of the Court of said County held in July, 1777, as well as a partial list of the militiamen of the County from 1775 to 1785, as shown by the County Records:

AKER, ADAM.
ALEXANDER, AARON, Constable.
ALEXANDER, ABRAHAM, justice, chairman of the County Court, ranger (1778) and Captain in 1779.
ALEXANDER, ADAM, J. P., lieutenant colonel and tax collector.
ALEXANDER, ANDREW, SR.
ALEXANDER, ANDREW, JR.
ALEXANDER, BENJAMIN, tax assessor in 1778.
ALEXANDER, CHARLES, SR.
ALEXANDER, CHARLES, JR. tax assessor in 1782.
ALEXANDER, DAVID, road overseer 1779.
ALEXANDER, ELIJAH, tax assessor in 1778 and tax collector in 1781.
ALEXANDER, EZEKIEL tax assessor from 1777 to 1781 and tax collector in 1781.
ALEXANDER, EZRA, road overseer in 1778.
ALEXANDER, GEORGE, Captain and Major 1776, and Captain 1782; tax collector in 1783.
ALEXANDER, HEZEKIAH, J. P.
ALEXANDER, ISAAC, entry taker.
ALEXANDER, JAMES, Captain in 1777, and tax collector in 1778 and 1779.
ALEXANDER, JOHN JR. road overseer 1778.
ALEXANDER, JOHN SR.
ALEXANDER, JOHN McKNITT, Captain in 1777; J. P.; tavern keeper and tax collector 1781; Clerk of the Court, 1781; road overseer in 1778; tax collector 1781; county trustee in 1781; Commissioner of confiscated estates in 1781.
ALEXANDER, MATTHEW.
ALEXANDER, MOSES, road overseer in 1781.
ALEXANDER PHINEAS.
ALEXANDER, STEPHEN, constable and tax assessor in 1781.
ALEXANDER, THOMAS, Captain 1781 to 1785.
ALEXANDER, WILLIAM, Captain 1778 to 1785.
ALEXANDER, ZEBULON.
ALLEN, JOHN, tax assessor in 1777.
ALLISON, JOHN, tax collector in 1783.
ARMSTRONG, JOHN.
ARMSTRONG, MATHIAS, constable in 1779 and 1780.
ARTERS, ROBERT.

BAKER, JOHN.
BALY (BAILEY) JOHN.
BARBARA, CHRISTOPHER.
BARBARA, JOHN.
BARNES, PETER, tax collector in 1783.
BARNETT, ABRAHAM, J. P. and tavern keeper.
BARNETT, HUGH assessor in 1777.
BARNETT, JOHN, tax collector in 1783.
BARNETT, ROBERT, constable.
BARNETT, SAMUEL.
BARNETT, WILLIAM, road overseer and Captain in 1778 and 1779.
BARNHILL, WILLIAM, assessor 1778.
BARNHILL, CHARLES
BARR, JAMES, road overseer in 1778 and Captain in 1777 to 1779.
BARRINGER, GEORGE tax assessor in 1778.
BARRINGER, JOHN road overseer in 1778 and tax collector in 1783.
BARRINGER, PAUL, overseer of the poor in 1779; tax assessor in 1779, road overseer in 1778 and a constable in 1785.

BAXTER, ANDREW tax assessor and constable in 1780.
BAXTER, JOHN.
BEATTY, JOHN.
BEATTY, WALLACE.
BEATTY, WALTER.
BEAVER, MATTHEW, Captain in 1779.
BELL, JAMES, constable.
BELK, JAMES, Captain 1782 to 1784.
BELK, JOHN, JR. tax assessor in 1781 and tax collector in 1783.
BENNELLEW, JONATHAN, constable 1775.
BERRY, RICHARD (BARRY?) J. P.
BERRYHILL, WILLIAM.
BIGGERS, JOHN, constable in 1785.
BIGHAM, JOHN.
BLACK, JOHN, constable in 1778.
BLACK, WILLIAM, constable 1779 and 1780.
BLACKWELDER, ISAAC.
BLAIR, WILLIAM, assessor in 1777, constable in 1778, 1779 and 1780.
BLYTHE, SAMUEL tax assessor 1779 to 1781, tax collector 1781 and road overseer in 1778.
BONDS, SAMUEL.
BOST, GEORGE.
BOST, JACOB.
BRADLEY, FRANCIS, collector in 1777, and road overseer 1778.
BRADSHAW, JAMES, assessor in 1778 and tax collector in 1778.
BRATTON, JAMES.
BREDON, ISAAC.
BREDON, JOHN, tavern keeper and road overseer in 1778.
BREVARD, EPHRAIM, J. P.
BREVARD, ZEBULON.
BROUSTER (BREWSTER) JOHN.
BROWN, JAMES, constable 1777 and 1778.
BROWN, SAMUEL.
BROWNFIELD, JOHN, Captain 1781 to 1785.
BROWNFIELD, ROBERT.
BUCHANAN, JOHN, constable 1777 to 1778.

CAIRNS, ALEXANDER.
CALDWELL, CHARLES, constable.
CALDWELL, JOHN.
CALDWELL, SAMUEL.
CALDWELL, WILLIAM.
CAMPBELL, ROBERT, assessor in 1777, and constable and road overseer in 1779.
CAMPBELL, ANDREW.
CANNON, CHARLES, constable 1779 and 1780.
CANNON, JOHN.
CARRIGAN, JAMES, assessor in 1777.
CARSON, JOHN, constable.
CARRUTH, JAMES, assessor 1779 and 1781 and tax collector in 1781.
CARUTHERS, ANDREW.
CATHY, JOHN, assessor in 1777 and road overseer in 1781.
CATHY, GEORGE, JR.
CATHY, GEORGE, SR., collector in 1777, and constable in 1774 to 1778.
CLARK, JAMES, road overseer in 1781.
COCHRANE, ROBERT.

352

COOK, ABRAHAM.
COOK, ISAAC, Captain in 1779.
CRAIGHEAD, ROBERT, constable
CHESMAN, MITCHELL, Assessor, 1777.
CROCKETT, ARCHIBALD.
CROZIER, LEVI.
CRUZINE, GEORGE.
CRUZINE, LEVI.
CUNNINGHAM, ROGER, constable.

DAVIDSON, JOHN, second major in 1775 and 1776, major in 1776, and tax assessor in 1778.
DAVIS, JOHN, road overseer in 1781.
DAVIS, ROBERT, tax assessor in 1778.
DAVIS, DeARMOND.
DAVIS, JOHN, tax collector.
DOWNS, HENRY, tax assessor in 1777 and 1778, and overseer of the poor in 1779.
DOUGLAS, JOSEPH, assessor in 1777 and tax collector in 1778.
DRAFFIN, JAMES, road overseer in 1778.
DRESHILL, JOHN.
DRESSER, JAMES.
DRY, GEORGE.
DUCKWORTH, JOHN, constable 1777 to 1778.
DUNLAP, GILBERT, tavern keeper.
DUNN, ANDREW.
DYSART, JOHN, road overseer in 1778.

EDWARDS, JOSEPH.
EDDENTON, NATHANIEL, constable in 1778.
ELLIOTT, GEORGE, tax collector in 1783, and road overseer in 1778.
ELLIOTT, THOMAS.
ELLIOTT, WILLIAM, tax assessor in 1778.
ERWIN, NATHANIEL.
EVENSHINE, REYNOLDS.

FAGGATT, JACOB, road overseer in 1784.
FAGGATT, HENRY.
FANNER, JAMES.
FARRER, JOHN.
FERGUSON, THOMAS, road overseer in 1778.
FERGUSON, ALEXANDER.
FINDLEY, GEORGE, constable in 1777.
FINDLEY, THOMAS.
FINNEY, ALEXANDER.
FISHER, CHARLES, road overseer in 1778.
FLENNIKEN, DAVID.
FLENNIKEN, JOHN, J. P. and road overseer in 1778.
FLENNIKEN, SAMUEL, Captain in 1777 to 1785.
FORD, JOHN, J. P.
FORD, JOSEPH.
FOSTER, JOHN, Captain in 1779 to 1781, and Commissioner to lay off roads in 1779.
FOSTER, ROBERT.
FRAZIER, WILLIAM, constable in 1778.
FREEMAN, ALLEN.
FURR, JOHN, assessor in 1778.

GALBRAITH, WILLIAM.
GARDNER, _ Captain 1781 to 1785.
GARDNER, WILLIAM, tax collector in 1778.
GARDNER, MITCHELL.
GARMON, GEORGE.
GARNATT, DANIEL tax collector in 1783.
GARDNER, LEONARD, tax collector in 1783.
GARRISON, ARTHUR, tax Assessor in 1777.
GARRISON, JOHN, tax assessor 1778 and also tax collector in 1778.
GIFFORD, JAMES, assessor in 1778.
GILES, EDWARD, J. P.

GILMORE, JAMES, constable in 1779.
GILMORE, MITCHELL.
GILMORE, NATHANIEL.
GINGLES, SAMUEL, constable in 1774.
GIVENS, EDWARD.
GIVENS, SAMUEL, tax assessor in 1778, Captain in 1779 to 1781 and Major in 1783.
GIVENS, WILLIAM, tax assessor in 1778.
GOODMAN, CHARLES.
GOODMAN, JOSEPH.
GOODNIGHT, GEORGE, tax assessor in 1778.
GOODNIGHT, MICHAEL, constable in 1775.
GORDON, JOHN, constable in 1775.
GRAHAM, JOHN.
GRAHAM, JOSEPH, Sheriff in 1784.
GRAHAM, ROBERT.
GRAHAM, WILLIAM, assessor 1777 to 1778, tax collector in 1783, and constable in 1785.
GRAY, JACOB, constable 1777 to 1779.
GREEN, JOHN.
GRIER, ANDREW, tavern keeper.
GREER, THOMAS tax collector in 1783.
GREER, JOHN, tax collector in 1783.
GRIBBLE, THOMAS.

HAMBLETON, JAMES.
HAMBLETON, JOHN, tax assessor in 1778, and tavern keeper.
HAMBLETON, PATRICK.
HAGLER, JOHN.
HALL, THOMAS.
HARGETT, HENRY, road overseer in 1778.
HARKEY, MARTIN.
HARRIS, GEORGE.
HARRIS, JAMES (Of Rocky River) Captain in 1777, to 1782, and major in 1783.
HARRIS, JAMES (Of Clear Creek) Captain 1777 to 1779, and tax collector in 1778.
HARRIS, JOHN.
HARRIS, ROBERT, JR., J. P. 1778.
HARRIS, ROBERT, SR., J. P. and Colonel in 1774 also register.
HARRIS, SAMUEL, constable in 1785, tax assessor in 1777, and overseer of the poor in 1779.
HARRIS, THOMAS (Of Rocky River) Sheriff in 1782.
HARRIS, THOMAS (Of Providence) Sheriff in 1774.
HARRIS, WILLIAM.
HART, DAVID.
HAYES, CONRAD.
HAYES, DAVID, SR.
HAYES, DAVID, JR., constable in 1775.
HAYES, ROBERT.
HAYES, WILLIAM, constable 1777 to 1778, Captain 1782 to 1785.
HAYNES, DAVID.
HENRY, _ , Captain 1782 to 1785.
HENRY, JAMES, constable.
HENRY, JOHN.
HENRY, WILLIAM, assessor 1777 to 1779.
HENDERSON, JOHN.
HENDERSON, KERNS, road overseer in 1782.
HENDERSON, WILLIAM, road overseer from 1778 to 1784.
HENDERSON, WILLIAM, JR.
HERRON, FRANCIS.
HILL, JOHN.
HILL, WILLIAM, road overseer in 1777.
HISS, CONRAD, road overseer in 1778.
HOEY, JOHN, constable in 1775, and tax assessor in 1779.
HOGANS, JOHN, constable in 1778.
HOGANS, WILLIAM, Captain 1777 and 1778.
HOLBROOK, CALEB.
HOLBROOKS, JOHN, road overseer in 1778.
HOLLAND, WILLIAM.
HOOD, TUNIS, SR.
HOOD, TUNIS, JR.

HOOVER, WILLIAM, tax assessor in 1777.
HOPE, ROBERT.
HORLASHER, CHRISTOPHER, constable.
HOUSE, ELISHA.
HOUSE, MARK, tax collector in 1778.
HOUSE, WILLIAM.
HOUSTON, ARCHIBALD, Captain 1778, tax assessor in 1780 and 1781, and tax collector in 1783.
HOUSTON, HUGH.
HOUSTON, JAMES, road overseer in 1779.
HOUSTON, JOHN, road overseer 1778 to 1784.
HOUSTON, WILLIAM.
HUGHIE, JOHN.
HUNTER, HENRY.
HUNTER, JOHN, road overseer 1778 to 1784.
HUNTER, ROBERT, tax collector.
HUTCHINSON, WILLIAM, tavern keeper, jailer 1777, and road overseer in 1782.

IRVIN, CHRISTOPHER.
IRVIN, NATHANIEL.
IRVIN, ROBERT, J. P. and Captain 1777, and tax collector in 1783.
IRVIN, WILLIAM, tax assessor in 1779.
(This name appears as ERWIN and IRWIN at different places on the records.)

JACK, JAMES, tavern keeper 1774 to 1782, Captain 1777 to 1782; tax collector 1781.
JACK, JOHN, tax assessor in 1777.
JARRETT, DANIEL, tax collector in 1781.
JETTON, LEWIS.
JOHNSTON, JAMES.
JOHNSTON, PETER.
JOHNSTON, WILLIAM.

KAIRNS, ALEXANDER, tax collector in 1783.
KAIRNS, DANIEL.
KELIAH, JOHN, tavern keeper and constable.
KELIAH, SAMUEL.
KENNEDY, DAVID.
KENNEDY, JAMES, constable in 1780.
KENNEDY, JOSEPH, physician and tavern keeper.
KERR, JAMES.
KERR, JOHN.
KERR, JOSEPH.
KERR, ROBERT, tax assessor and constable 1778.
KILPATRICK, JOHN.
KING, JOHN.
KENNON, JAMES.
KNOX, JAMES.
KNOX, MATTHEW, constable 1777 and 1778.
KNOX, SAMUEL tax assessor in 1778, and Captain in 1781 to 1785.
KYSER, GEORGE.

LASHLEY, SAMUEL, constable in 1774 and 1775.
LAWING, JOHN.
LEGGATT, JACKSON.
LEGGATT, MICHAEL, tax assessor in 1777, and commission to lay off road in 1779.
LEMOND, WILLIAM, constable in 1775.
LENOIR, ROBERT, road overseer in 1778.
LEOPARD, JOHN, Captain in 1775 and 1778; tax collector in 1778, and tax assessor in 1780 and 1781.
LEWIS, ALEXANDER.
LEWIS, ROBERT, tavern keeper and Captain 1781.
LITAKER, PHILLIP.
LOCK, FRANCIS, constable in 1778, and road overseer in 1781.
LONG, JOHN.
LONG, DAVID.
LONG, HENRY.

LOWERY, BENJAMIN.
LUCAS, HUGH.
LYTLE, WILLIAM, tavern keeper.

MACK, JAMES, road overseer 1781.
MAYLER, JOSEPH.
MARTINDALE, THOMAS, road overseer in 1778.
MARTIN, ALEXANDER, lawyer.
MARTIN, JAMES.
MARTIN, RICHARD.
MARTIN, SAMUEL, Clerk of the Court.
MASON, CHARLES.
MASON, RICHARD, tavern keeper and road overseer in 1782.
MATTHEWS, WILLIAM, tax collector in 1783.
MAXWELL, JAMES.
MAXWELL, JOSEPH.
MEANS, JOHN.
MEANS, WILLIAM.
MEEK, ADAM, tax collector.
MEEK, MOSES.
MEISENHEIMER, JOHN.
MILLIER, ABRAHAM, road overseer 1778.
MITCHELL, THOMAS.
MITCHELL, GEORGE, tax collector in 1777.
MITCHELL, HENRY, constable 1779 and 1780, and tax collector in 1778.
MITCHELL, ROBERT, tax assessor in 1777.
MOFFATT, ROBERT, constable in 1775.
MONTGOMERY, JOHN, constable in 1777 and 1779, and road overseer in 1781.
MOORE, DAVID.
MOORE, FRANCIS, tax assessor in 1777, Captain and overseer of the poor in 1779.
MOORE, JAMES.
MOORE, JOSEPH.
MOORE, MOSES, tax assessor in 1780 and 1781.
MORRIS, WILLIAM, tax assessor in 1778.
MORRIS, JAMES, constable in 1775.
MORRISON, JOHN, constable in 1785.
MOYER, ADAM.
MUIRKE, JOHN.
MURPHY, JOHN, constable in 1775.
MYERS, JACOB, Captain in 1778 and tax assessor in 1778.
MYERS, ADAM, constable.

McANNULTY, _____, Captain in 1781 to 1785.
McCAFERTY, JAMES.
McCAFERTY, JEREMIAH, tax assessor in 1777.
McCAIN, HUGH, constable in 1778 and 1779, and commissioner to lay off roads 1779.
McCALL, FRANCIS, JR., tax assessor in 1778.
McCALL, FRANCIS, SR., constable in 1779.
McCALL, JAMES.
McCALL, WILLIAM.
McCALL, HUGH.
McCARDESS, JOHN.
McCLERRY, ROBERT, tax assessor in 1777.
McCLURE, MATTHEW, road overseer in 1778 and tax assessor in 1777.
McCLURE, ROBERT, constable.
McCLURE, THOMAS.
McCLURE, WILLIAM, tax collector in 1783.
McCOMBS, SAMUEL, tavern keeper and constable in 1777.
McCOMBS, JAMES.
McCORD, DAVID, road overseer in 1778.
McCORD, JAMES, road overseer in 1781.
McCORD, ROBERT, road overseer in 1778.
McCONKIE, JOHN, tax assessor in 1777 and tax collector in 1781.
McCONKIE, THOMAS, road overseer in 1778.
McCOY, BEATTY, road overseer in 1784.
McCOY, JOHN, tavern keeper.
McCOY, SPRUCE (McKAY? or McCAY?) lawyer in 1778.

McCREE, DAVID, road overseer in 1778.
McCREE, ROBERT, tax assessor and constable 1778.
McCREE, JOHN, Captain in 1777.
McCREE, WILLIAM, road overseer in 1778.
McCULLOCH, JOHN, constable in 1774, tax assessor in 1778 and tax collector 1783.
McCULLOCH, WILLIAM, constable and road overseer in 1778 and constable in 1780.
McCURDY, ALEXANDER, Captain in 1782 to 1785.
McDOWELL, PATRICK.
McELROY, JOHN, tax assessor in 1778.
McELROY, ROBERT, road overseer in 1781.
McELROY, WILLIAM tax assessor in 1778.
McFADDEN, THOMAS.
McKEE, ALEXANDER.
McKEE, WILLIAM.
McKNIGHT, ROBERT, Captain 1779 to 1781.
McNEELY, JOHN.
McREA, JOHN, Captain 1778.
McREA, ROBERT, tax assessor 1778.
McWHORTER, AARON, constable.
McWHORTER, HENRY.

NAILOR, JOHN.
NEAL, JAMES.
NEAL, HENRY, road overseer in 1784.
NEAL, ANDREW, constable in 1779.
NEELY, JOHN.
NEELY, THOMAS.
NEWELL, FRANCIS, tax assessor 1777.
NEWELL, WILLIAM.
NEWMAN, JOHN.
NICELER, JOHN.
NICHOLSON, GEORGE.
NICHOLSON, JOSEPH, tavern keeper.
NICHOLSON, JOHN, road overseer in 1781.
NUTT, JOHN, Captain in 1778, and tax assessor in 1780 and 1781.

OCHILTREE, DUNCAN, appointed to take care of the courthouse in 1780.
ORR, JAMES, JR.
ORR, JAMES, SR., tavern keeper.
ORR, JOHN.
ORR, NATHAN, tax assessor 1777.
ORR, WILLIAM.
OSBORN, __, Captain, 1779 to 1785.
OSBORN ADLAI, lawyer.
OSBORN, JAMES, tax assessor in 1778.
OSBORN, JOHN.
OSBORN, NOBLE, constable.

PARKS, JOHN, SR.
PARKS, JOHN, JR.
PARKS, DAVID, constable.
PARKS, DAVID, Captain 1782 to 1785.
PATTERSON, JOHN, tax assessor in 1778.
PATTERSON, WILLIAM, tax assessor and tax collector, and tavern keeper 1777 and 1783.
PATTON, BENJAMIN tax assessor 1780 and 1781, tax collector 1781, and overseer of the poor in 1779.
PATTON, MATTHEW.
PATTON, ROBERT.
PATTON, SAMUEL, assessor in 1778.
PEEL, JAMES tax assessor in 1777.
PENNY, WILLIAM, constable in 1779 to 1780.
PERKINS, SAMUEL.
PERKINS, WILLIAM tax collector 1777 to 1780.
PHIFER, JOHN, Major in 1775 and 1776; colonel in 1776; tavern keeper and colonel in 1778.
PHIFER, MARTIN, J. P. and Constable.
PHIFER, ROBERT, constable in 1778 and 1780.

PHIFER, WALLACE, constable in 1779.
PHILLIPS, ROBERT, constable 1778 and 1779, & road overseer in 1781.
PHILLIPS, WILLIAM.
PICKENS, __, Captain 1781 to 1785.
PICKENS, SAMUEL, constable in 1778.
PLYLER, JEREMIAH, constable in 1778, and Captain in 1782 to 1785.
POLK, EZEKIEL, tax assessor in 1778, J. P., tavern keeper and Sheriff in 1782.
POLK, THOMAS, Colonel 1775 and 1776, commissioner of Confiscated estates in 1781; General in 1782.
POLK, JOHN, road overseer in 1778.
PORTER, ____, (Of Catawba River) Captain 1782 to 1785.
PORTER, ROBERT, Captain from 1782 to 1784.
POTTS, JOHN.
POTTS, WILLIAM, Captain 1781 to 1785; tax collector in 1783.
PRICE, ISAAC.
PRICE, JOHN, tax assessor in 1778.
PRICE, REESE.

QUERY, JOHN, constable 1779 to 1785; tax assessor 1777 to 1782; tax collector 1783.
QUERY, WILLIAM, road overseer 1778.
QUITMAN, PETER.

RABB, JOSEPH, constable.
RABB, WILLIAM, road overseer in 1778.
RAMSEY, WILLIAM.
REA, ANDREW, Captain 1782 to 1785; tax assessor 1777 and 1778, and road overseer in 1781.
REA, DAVID, tax assessor in 1782.
REA, WILLIAM, road overseer in 1779.
REED, DAVID, road overseer 1778, Captain 1779 to 1781.
REED, GEORGE.
REED, JAMES, JR., road overseer 1781.
REED, JAMES, constable 1778.
REESE, DAVID, tax assessor 1777 to 1779; Justice and commissioner 1782.
REESE, JAMES, Captain 1782 to 1785, and tax collector in 1778.
REESE, GEORGE.
RICHEY, JACOB.
RITCHISON, JAMES.
ROBINSON, ANDREW.
ROBINSON, DAVID, road overseer 1781.
ROBINSON, JOHN.
ROBINSON, WILLIAM, road overseer in 1781.
ROBINSON, JAMES.
ROBINSON, ROBERT, road overseer in 1778.
ROGERS, JAMES, Captain 1782 to 1785.
ROGERS, JOHN, tax collector in 1783.
ROGERS, JOSEPH, constable.
ROGERS, ROBERT, tax collector 1778.
ROSS, GEORGE.
ROSS, JOSEPH.
ROSS, JAMES.
ROSS, WILLIAM.
RUSSELL, DAVID.
RUSSELL, ROBERT.
RUSSELL, JAMES, road overseer in 1778.

SADLER, JOHN.
SAMPLE, JOHN.
SAMPLE, WILLIAM, constable.
SCOTT, JAMES, tax assessor in 1777, road overseer in 1778 and Captain 1779.
SCOTT, WILLIAM, J. P.
SCOTT, JOSEPH, constable.
SECREST, JACOB.
SHANKS, JAMES.
SHARP, JAMES.

SHELBY, EVAN.
SHELBY, EZRON.
SHIELDS, WILLIAM.
SHINN, JOSEPH, Captain 1783 to 1784.
SHORT, PETER.
SIMPSON, JAMES.
SIKES, CHRISTOPHER, constable 1775, and road overseer in 1778.
SLOAN, JAMES.
SLOAN, ROBERT.
SLOAN, DAVID.
SMALL, ROBERT.
SMITH, ROBERT, constable and tavern keeper.
SMITH, SAMUEL, road overseer and constable 1778.
SPEERS, WILLIAM, tax collector 1783; constable & road overseer in 1778.
SPRATT, ANDREW, constable.
SPRATT, JAMES, constable.
SPRIGGS, JOHN, Captain 1781; road overseer 1782.
SPRIGGS, RICHARD.
STAFFORD, JAMES, constable.
STARR, ARTHUR.
STEEN, __ , Captain 1779.
STEVENSON, JOHN.
STEVENSON, RICHARD, road overseer in 1781.
STARRETT, WILLIAM, tax assessor in 1777.
STARRETT, ALEXANDER.
STINSON, RICHARD.
STEWART, ALBERT.
STEWART, MATTHEW, tax collector in 1783.
STEWART, JOHN, tavern keeper.
SWANN, JOHN, constable 1777; tax collector in 1778.
SWANN, MOSES tax assessor in 1780 and 1781.
SWANN, ROBERT, tavern keeper.

TANNER, JOHN.
TAYLOR, JOHN, road overseer 1781.
TAYLOR, WILLIAM, road overseer in 1782.
TEMPLE, MAJOR.
TEMPLETON, JAMES.
TEMPLETON, SAMUEL, tax assessor in 1777.
THOMAS, DRURY.
TODD, JOSEPH.
TODD, WILLIAM.
TYGERT, JAMES, Captain 1782 to 1785, and constable, also, in 1785.

VOGLE, THOMAS.

WADDLE, WILLIAM.
WALLACE, ALEXANDER.
WALLACE, EZEKIEL, tax assessor.
WALLACE LODOWICK.
WALLACE, JAMES, tax assessor in 1780, tax collector in 1781 and constable in 1779.
WALLACE, THOMAS, tax collector in 1777, and a road overseer in 1778.
WALKER, ANDREW, Captain 1782 to 1785.
WALKER, JOHN.
WALKER, PHILLIP, constable 1778.
WALKUP, JAMES (Waughup) tax assessor in 1778 and Captain in 1779.
WEEKS, PHILLIP.
WHITE, JAMES, constable 1774, tax collector in 1777, Captain in 1779 and Sheriff in 1779 and 1780.
WHITE, JOHN.
WHITE, ARCHIBALD.
WHITE, SAMUEL.
VIER, JOHN.
WILLIAMS, ISAAC tax assessor in 1780 and 1781; tax collector 1781.
WILSON, BENJAMIN.
WILSON, DAVID, Captain 1777.
WILSON, JAMES.
WILSON, JOSEPH.
WILSON, WILLIAM, Captain 1777 to 1778; J. P. and coroner in 1778.
WILSON, JOHN, tax collector 1783.
WILSON, SAMUEL.
WILSON, ROBERT.
WILSON, ZACCHEUS, Captain 1778, and surveyor.
WINNCOFF, JOHN MICHAEL, constable 1777 to 1778.
WINSLOW, MOSES.
WISENER, MICHAEL, constable.
WITHERSPOON, JAMES, constable 1780; tax collector 1783.
WOLFE, PHILLIP.
WOODS, JOHN.
WYLIE, JOHN, constable 1778 to 1781.
WYLIE, OLIVER, tax assessor 1777.
WYLIE, WILLIAM, road overseer 1778; collector 1783.
YANDELL, WILLIAM.
YOUNG, WILLIAM
YOUNG, JOSEPH, road overseer 1781.

MECKLENBURG COUNTY, N. C. - FIRST U. S. CENSUS, IN 1790
By DISTRICTS. Followed by MAP and GENEALOGICAL NOTES

Column 1, males over 16; Column 2, males under 16; Column 3, females; Column 4, other free persons; Column 5, Slaves

DISTRICT NO. 1

Name	1	2	3	4	5	Name	1	2	3	4	5
Allison, Robert	1	3	4		3	Hanks, Thomas	1	1	1		
Allison, Archabald	3	1	3			Isler, Nicholas	2		2		
Allison, David	1					Jackson, Shadrick	2	7	1		
Alexander, Wᵐ, Jr	2	1	3			Kirkes, Thomas	1	2	1		
Alexander, Ezra, Senʳ	3	1	3			Kerr (Widow)		1	3		1
Elga, Francis	1	2	1			Kithcart, John	1	2	1		
Allison, Joseph	1		3			Love, John	2		2		
Allen, John	3	3	4			Love, Samuel	1		1		
Alexander, Able	2	2	2			McCord, John	4	1	4		1
Alexander, Phenias	1	3	4			McCord, Robert	2	1	4		
Berryhill, Wᵐ	1		4		1	McClarey, Wᵐ	2				
Barnet, Robert, Juʳ	1	1	1		2	McDowell, John	1	3	4		5
Bryan, Mathew	2	5	4			McClarey, Michael	2	2	1		3
Brown, Patrick	4		2			McDowell, Esther	1		3		
Beaty, John, Juʳ	1	2	4		9	McKinley, William	1	4	7		
Beaty, John, Senʳ	2	3	5			McKnight, Robert	2	1	8		
Baker, George	1	4	3			McKnight, James	1	8	1		
Buan, James	1	3	2			McNeely, James	1	4	3		
Brown, David	3	1	3			Moore, Joseph, Seʳ	3	1	5		
Berryhill, John	3	3	3			Montgomery, James	1	4	3		
Clark, Jessey	2	3	2		2	McNeely, Andʷ	1		2		
Davis, George	1	2	2			McClure, John, Juʳ	4	1	2		
Cooper, Doctor	1	1	2			McClure (Wid̄)	1	1	2		
Clarke, Robert R	1	3	3			Clelland (Widow)			4		
Clarke, William	3		3		3	McKee, Andʷ	1		3		6
Campbell, Robert	1	1	6			McKee, John	1	2	5		
Cathey, George, Senʳ	3	1	3		5	McGee (Widow)	3	1	3		
Cathey, Esther	2	3	5			McCormack, William	1	1	1		
Cathey, Alexander	2	1	3			Mariner, John	1				
Cummins, John	1		2			McClure, Moses, Juʳ			1	1	
Cooper, John	2		2			McClure, Thomas, Juʳ	1		1	1	
Carson, John	1					McDonald, David				1	
Castillo, Miles	1	2	4			Nation, Thomas	1	3	4		
Carroll, Joseph	3	2	2		3	Null, James, Seʳ	1	2	6		
Cathren, Robert	1	4	5			Nicholson, John, Senʳ	2	1	5		2
Coreham, William	1	3	3			Nicholson, George	1				
Clayton, James				1		Owens, James	1	4	5		
Carroll, James	1		2			Van Pelt, Simon	2	5	4		
Cattor, George	1		1			Pierson, Henry	3		4		
Currethers, Edmond	1	1	1			Parks, Hugh	1	2	4		2
Coreham, Robert	2	1	3			Porter, John	1	3	4		
Freemon, Michael	1		4		1	Plummer, Zepheniah	1		4		
Freemon, David	3	2	5			Plummer, Thomas				1	
Freemon, Reuben	2		1			Reed, James, Senʳ	3	2	2		
Griffey, Aron	1		3			Reed, James	1	1	2		1
Gibbeney, Nicholas	1	2	4		6	Reed, James (midde)	1	4	4		1
Greene, John	2	2	4		2	Reed, Robert	2	1	2		1
Graham, Maj Joseph	1	1	2		8	Reed, Thomas	1		2		1
Graham, George	1	2	2		4	Reed, John	1	4	4		
Graham, James				1		Sloan, John	1	1	3		
Hucheson, John	1		1			Sloan, James	1	2	3		1
Hern, Jesse	1	3	4			Sumter, John	2	1	1		5
Hucheson, George	2	1	1		1	Spratt, James	2	1	4		
Hargrove, Thompson	1	2	5			Stinson, John	1		3		2
Hargrove, John	2	1	3			Stinson, Michael					
Hunter, John, Seʳ	2	1	2		6	Shields, David				1	
Hunter, Robert	1	3	2		3	Tagert, James	2		2		
Hogden Nehemiah	1		2			Wilson, John	3	2	2		5
Haynes, David	3	2	3		2	Walker, John	2	3	4		
Hepworth, John	1		5			Walker, William	1	2	4		
Hann, Margret & Son				2		Wilkeson, George	1		2		
McFalls, John				1		Verner, John	1			5	

DISTRICT NO. 2

Name	1	2	3	4	5	Name	1	2	3	4	5
Alexander, Judith	1	1	1			Barnet, Robert, Senʳ	1	3	4		
Alexander, James	1		3			Barnet, John, Seʳ	1		3		1
Bigham, John	2	3	3		4	Barnet, John, Juʳ	1		3		
Bigham, James, Sʳ	1		3			Blackwood, James	2	2	4		1
Bigham, Robert	1	1	2			Brownfield, Robert	1		1		
Bigham, Samuel, Sʳ	2		1			Brownfield, William	1	3	3		
Bigham, Samuel, Jʳ	1	4	4			Brown, Richard					1
Bigham, William, Juʳ	2	1	4			Cathey, Andʷ	1		1		
Bigham, James, Juʳ	2	2	1			Cathey, George	2	1	3		5
Bigham, Hugh	1		1			Carruthers, James	2	3	2		2

Carruthers, Robert	1	2	5		1	Neely, John	2	3	7		6
Carruthers, John	1	3	2			Neely, Thomas, Ju^r	1	4	2		2
Calhoone, Charles	1	1	5		3	Null, James, Ju^r	1		2		2
Calhoon, Samuel	1	3	5		9	Neely, Samuel	2		2		2
Cheek, Silas	1				9	Neely, Moses		1	4		3
Calhoon, George	1		1			Nicholson, John, Ju^r				1	
Davis, Walter	3	4	5		8	Porter, William	1	4	5		4
Davis, John L	3	1	2			Porter, Alexander	1	1	7		
Dunn, William	1	2	4			Porter, Joseph	1	1	4		
Darnell, William	1	5	4			Porter, Hugh	1	1	1		
Darnell, Joseph	1	3	5		6	Porter, James	1	2	4		4
Dinkins, John	2	3	3		12	Patterson, William	2	2	2		
Ferguson, Thomas	1		1		1	Price, Isaac	4	4	3		7
Ferguson, William	1					Howe, Joseph				1	
Gilmore, William	1		3			Price, John	2	1	3		13
Gilmore, Margret	1	2	3			Reed, Joseph	1		2		
Gillan, John	1		3			Ramey, Thomas	1		4		
Greer, Thomas	1	2	3		5	Robison, Richard	1		2		1
Greer, James	2		2		2	Robison, David	1	2	5		
Herron, And^w	2		2			Robison, Mathew		4	5		
Hart, James	1					Ramey, William	1		2		
Hart, Joseph	1	1	1			Ramey, William, Senr	2	1	1		
Hart, David	1					Smart, George	2		1		4
Harris, Hugh	1	2	3			Smart, Littleberry	2				2
Herron, Hugh	1	2	4		5	Smart, Elijah	2	1	2		9
Herren, Allen	1	2	3			Smart, Francis	2		2		9
Herron, Samuel				1	3	Swann, Joseph	1	4	3		
Erwin, Robert	2	2	6			Speers, James	1	3	6		
Knox, James	2		1		2	Scott, James	1		4		
Knox, Samuel, Ju^r	1		1			Shepperd, William				1	
Knox, Mathew	2		2		5	Thomas, Benj^a	2	4	2		9
Knox, Samuel, Senr	3		3		9	Taylor, John	3	3	3		4
Knox, John	1		2			Vance, David	2	4	3		2
Kindrick, John	1	3	1		2	Whitsitt, John	1	5	2		
Kindrick, William	1		2		2	West, Martin	1	2	4		
McClarey, Robert	2	2	5			Walker, John	6		2		
McCormick, Robert	2		4			Wilson, Robert			4		
McCrum, Rachel		2	3		6	Wilson, Zachias	1	1	1		2
McKee, Robert	3	3	6		1	Wilson, Isaac	1		3		
McKee, James	1	3	2		8	Wilson, William	1	3	3		
McGill, Thomas				1		Wilson, Joseph	1				
McKee (Widow)	1	4	7			Wilson, James	1				
Maxwell (Widow)	2	4	4		1	Withers, Reuben	2	1	5		4
Null (Widow)	1	1	4		3	Yurce, Francis	1	3	2		

DISTRICT NO. 3

Alexander, Isaac, Esqr	1				1	McCulloch, William	2		2		1
Bigham, John	1	5	2			McClary (Widow)		1	1		
Barnhart, Henry	1	2	3			Martin, Thomas	1	2	1		
Cook, Isaac	2	2	3		8	McNabb, Duncan	1	1	3		
Cooper, Joseph				1		McKee, David	2	5	3		3
Emerson, Henry	1	1	1			Martin, Ephraim	1	1	2		
Elliott, Samuel	2	3	4		4	Cliver, George	1	2	3		
Elliott. Thomas	3		2		2	Polk, William	1		1		21
Henderson, D^o Thomas	1	1	6		2	Polk, Thomas	5		4		47
Hutcheson, William	2	4	2		3	Polk, Charles	2	2	1		9
Isham, John	1		3			Pattison, William	2	1	3		5
Holt, William			1			Riley, John	1	3	4		
Kennaday, James	2	1	4			Rice, George	1	1	6		
Kennaday, Esther	3		1		1	Robison, James	1	1	1		
Kennaday, Samuel				1		Stuart (Widow)			2		
Lefeever, Joseph	2		2			Springs, John	3	3	2	5	50
Luckey, William	1	3	3		1	Wisehart, Joseph	1		2		1
Mason, Richard	2	4	2		5	Wright, William				1	
McCombs. Samuel	1	1			3						

DISTRICT NO. 4

Alexander, Darkus	2	1	2		8	Allen, Agnes		1	2		6
Alexander, W^m, Se^r	3				11	Allen, George, Senr	1				1
Alexander, Ezekiel, Senr	2	2	6			Alexander, Ezekieh, Esqr	4	2	3		13
Alexander, David	1		1			Alexander, Capt Andrew	2				9
Alexander, Ezekel, Ju^r		2	2			Bailey, Richard	1	3	3		4
Alexander, Daniel	1	2	3			Batey, Samuel	1	2	4		
Alexander, Elijah	1	1	2			Barlow, Amrose				1	
Alexander, Elias, Ju^r	1	3	3		6	Braley, Thos C	1		1		
Alexander, Capt Thomas	1					Batey, William	1	3	1		
Alexander, D^o James	1					Balch, Thomas	1	1	2		2
Alexander, John						Campbell, Alexander				1	
Alexander, Capt (B) William	2	4	2		9	Carney, Patrick					
Alexander, Charles	1	4	3			Davis, Samuel	1		1	7	4
Alexander, Benjamin	2		1			Fipps (Widow)			7		
Alexander, George, Ju^r	1	1	1			Daker, Christopher	3	2	4		

Goforth, William	2	2	6		Parks, David	4	2	3	4
Graham, Samuel	1			1	Parks, John, Junr	1		2	3
Gipson (Widow)	2	2	4		Parks, Samuel	1	1	2	
Houston, Henry	1		2	1	Reed, George	1	4	2	
Henderson, Cairns	3		1	1	Richey, David	2	1	5	
Houston, William	2	2	2		Richey, John	1		3	
Henderson, Andrew	1	1	3		Ross, George	2		3	
Johnston, William	3	3	5	2	Robison, John	1	1	2	1
Johnston, David	1	1	3		Robison, Robert, Senr	1			
Kennaday, David	2	2	2		Robison, Robert, Jur	1	2	7	
Kewer, Henry	1	2	2		Robison, Moses	1		1	
Lemons, Robert	1	3	2		Robison, David	3	1	1	
Luckey, Robert	1	3	3		Robison, James, Senr	1		1	2
Mitchell, John	1		1		Robison, Wm & Richard	2		3	
McGee, John	2	2	1		Rogers, David	1		2	
Mitchell, Robert	3		3	2	Shields, William	1		3	
McCulloch (Widow)		1	2		Stuart, David	1	3	4	
McGintey, Alexander	1		1	2	Strachback, Daniel	1		1	
Montgomery, John	1		1		Sample, Samuel	2	1	3	
Montgomery, Robert	1	3	5		Starling, James				1
McClure, Thos Senr	2	1	1		Tasey, Alexander	1	1	2	
Mekee, Wm, Junr	1		1	1	Wise, Thomas	2	2	5	
McDowell, Archabeld			1		Wallace, Ezekel	2		3	4
Miller, Samuel			1		Wallace, Mathew	1	1	3	1
Neely, Hugh	2	3	3		Wallace, William	1	1	1	
Neely, Thomas			4	1	Wallace, George	1	1	3	
McCall, James	2	2	4		Wallace, Alexander	3		1	
Orr, Nathan, Senr	3	1	6		Wiley, William	3		3	2
Orr, Wm	1	1	7	9	Wiley, John	1	4	3	
Orr, James (Jockey)	1	4	3	6	Williamson, Benjamin	1	1	3	
Orr, Nathan, Jur	1	3	1	1	Watson, William	1	1	4	
Orr, James (white)	1	2	2		Wiley, Joseph	1		1	
Parks, John, Senr	3	3	4	3					

DISTRICT NO. 5

Alexander, Col George	3	1	5	11	Irwin, Robert	1	2	2	1
Archabeld, Rev. Robert	1	1	3	4	Kelugh, Samuel	2	3	4	3
Alexander, Abraham	1	1	2		Meek, Adam	2		2	3
Alexander, William	2	3	5	1	Meek, Moses	1	2	5	
Alexander, Moses	3	7	2	1	McClain, Joseph	2		2	
Alexander, Benjamin, Jur	2	2	5		McCandeless, John	1	1	2	3
Alexander, Moses, Jur	1				McCay, Michael	1		3	
Alexander, Andw	1	3		6	McCallister, John	1	2	4	
Alexander, Hezekiah	1		2	1	Meek, Robert	1	1	1	
Alexander, Abijah	2	1	5		Newman, John	1	3	3	
Bouchfriend, George	1		2		Query, Alexander	3	2	4	
Brown, James	1	2	3	7	Reed, John	1	3	4	
Black, William	2	1	3		Robison, Alexander	2		2	
Buckhanon, Robert	3	2	4		Russell, James	1	1	3	
Cowden (Widow)	1		2		Pickens, William	1		1	2
Caldwell, Charles	1		1	2	Smith, Col Robert	1	1	3	15
Caldwell, Capt David	1				Sharpe, Ezekel	2		7	3
Craighead, Robert	2	4	3	4	Smith, James	1		2	
Clark, Eliner	1		1		Sloan, John	1	1	3	
Doherty, James	2	3	1	1	Sloan, James, Senr	1	1	2	
Edmiston, John	1	2	4		Sloan, James, Jur	1	2	2	
Giles, Edward, Esqr	4	1	6	2	Sloan, Thomas	1	2	4	
Gardner, James	1	1	4		Simmons, William	1	1	6	4
Gilmore (Widow)	1	3	3		Shelby, Evan	1			
Gilmore, Nathaniel	2	1	5		Strain, Dor Wm	1			
Gardner, William	2	2	4		Simmons, Thomas	1	3	5	
Gardner, John	1	1	2		Wallace, James	2		3	6
Galliway, Thomas	1	5	2		Wilson, Zachias, Senr	1	1	1	
Garrison, David		3	5		Wallace, John	1	2	1	1
Giles, Nathaniel	1	1	3		Woods, John	1		2	
Hunter, Henry	2	7	3	2	Young, Joseph	2		7	5
Hunter, John	1		3	1	Young, William		3	8	2
Hope, Robert	3	5	4	6	Montgomery, David	1	3	3	
					Winings, Peteter	1	1	2	1

DISTRICT NO. 6

Alexander, John Mns, Esqr	3		1	16	Beach, Justice	2	3	4	
Alexander, William, Senr	3	1	3		Blackwood, William	1	2	5	2
Atkins, Samuel	1	2	5		Bradley (Widow)	1	1	4	
Alexander, Ezekel	1	3	4	2	Blackwood, Thomas		3	3	1
Abernathey, Miles	1	2	4		Cannon, John	3	1	1	
Aldridg, Isham	1		2		Clark, James	1			
Aldridg, William		3	2		Cannon, Margret	1	1	2	2
Bradshaw, Josiah	2	1	5	1	Cannon, Joseph	1	1	5	
					Cannon, James, Senr	1	1	1	

359

Crocket, Robert	1	1	7			McCoy, Beaty	4	5	3		5
Dunn, Andrew, Senr	2		2		2	Moore, Joseph	2	3	5		2
Dunn, Robert	1	1	2			McClure, John, Junr	1	2	4		
Dunn, James	1					McCracken, James	2	2	7		
Dunn, John	1		1			Maxwell, Ann	1		4		
Doherty (Widow)			4		2	Montieth, Jane	3		4		2
Davidson, John (Mercht)		1	4			Montieth, Nathaniel	1				
Ewart, Joseph	2	3	4		9	Moore, James	1	3	6		
Elliot, George	1		3			McClure, William	3	2			
Elliot, William	3	3		1	3	Moore (Widow)	2		3		3
Frazer, Joseph	1	4	3			Mullen, Harris	1	1			
Frazer, Samuel	1		2			McGinn (Widow)	3		3		
Frazer, James	1					McClure, Moses (Thoson)	1	2	3		
Ferrill, John	1	2	1			Moffitt, William	1		1		
Ferrill, Gabriel	1	1	2			Nation John	2	2	6		
Flenniker, Charles	1		2			Nighten, John	1	1	3		
Gailbraith, Martha	1	3	2		1	Patten, Charles	2		1		1
Garrison, John	1	1	2			Parker, Isaiah		4	6		
Gibson, John	1	3	2		2	Peoples, John	1	2	1		
Henderson (Widow)		2	4			Robison, Mathew	1	2	2		
Henry, James	1	4	3			Robison, George	1	1	2		
Hudson, Richard	1	2	5			Robison, Alexander	1	2	6		3
Hammond, Mathias	1	1	4			Russell, David	1	2	6		3
Hipp, Stephen	2	1	3			Ramsey, William	2	3	4		
Hipp, Valentine	1	2	1			Raphil, John	1	1	2		
Jimeson, Robert	1		2			Stephenson, Richard	3		1		
Johnston, Nathaniel	1	3	5			Sharpe, James	1	1	2		3
Jemison, Arthur	1	4	4			Sharpe, John	5	3	2		1
Jemison, Thomas	1		2			Steele, Peter	1	1	1		
Erwin, Edward	1		5			Sample (Widow)	1	1	6		
Johnston, Isaac	1	4	4		1	Sullivan, Patrick	1	1	3		1
Johnston, John	1	2	4		1	Sullivan, Jeremiah	1		1		
Kerr, Joseph	1	2	6			Thompson, John	1	1	6		
Knox, Capt James	2	1	3		15	Thompson, Gideon	2		2		2
Kerr, Robert	1	3	4			Thompson (Widow)	4	1	3		
Kerr (Widw)	1	2	5		3	Todd, William	3		4		
Lewing, William	3		5			Todd, Adam		2			
Lewing, Andrew	1		4			Todd, Joseph	2		2		1
Lather, Robert				1		Todd, John		1	2		
Long, Capt John	3	2	3		1	Williams, Billy	1	1	2		
McClennahan, Reuben	1	2	2			Woods, Robert	1	2	3		
McClure, Capt Mathew	3		2		6	Woods, Mathew	2	1	2		
McIntire, James	1		2		1	Watkins, James	1	2	2		

DISTRICT NO. 7

Alexander, Amos	1	4	3		6	Givvins, John, Junr	1	2	2		
Alexander, Moses	2		1			Givvins, Edward	2		2		11
Alexander, Aron	2	3	4		2	Givvins, Jno Ruther	1	4	3		
Alexander, David	5		4			Garrison, Samuel	1	1	2		4
Alexander, Daniel	1	1	2			Graham, William	3	7	3		3
Alexander, Joel	1		1			Harper, William	1	2	3		3
Alexander, Isaac				1		Henderson, John	1	1	1		3
Bryson, Hugh	2	4	4			Henderson, John, Jur	1	1	6		
Bell, John	1					Henderson, William, Senr					
Black, Thomas	1		5			Henderson, William, Jur	2	2	2		3
Berry, Capt Richard	4		6			Hill, William	2	4	4		6
Bailey, Francis	1	1	5		2	Hansill, John	1	3	2		
Blythe, Samuel		2		1	1	Hampton, Patrick	3	1	4		9
Blythe, Richard	1		2			Henry, Capt Henry	2	4	5		
Bell, Walter	1					Harris, May Thos	3		5		7
Brodinax, John	1	3	3		16	Hunt, Turner	1	1	6		15
Currey, James	1	3	4			Hunnsycut, Howell	1		1		
Caldwell, William	1	4	2		4	Hamilton, William				1	
Cathey, Capt Archabeld	1	1	3		11	Jetton (Widow)			1		1
Cochran, Benjamin	1		1			Jetton, Lewis	4	4	5		3
Conner, James	3		4			Johnston, John	3	4	1		
Cooke, James	2	5	4		6	Irwin, Samuel	1		1		1
Carson, Jane			2			Kelly, Thomas				1	
Conner, William	1	2	2			Knox, Allison	2		6		
Doherty, David	1	1	5			Latta, Joseph		1	5		
Davidson, Thomas	1		2			Lucas, Hugh	1	3	1		
Davidson, Samuel	1	2	6			Lowrance, Michael	1	1	2		
Davidson, May John	2	2	6		26	Jetton, Abraham	1	1	2		2
Duck, John	1	1	3			Morrow, John	2		2		
Duck, Simon	1	2	3			Morrow, Robert	2	2	3		
Duck, George	1	4	2			Morrow, John, Jur	1	1	2		
Duck, Abel	1	2	4			Maxwell, James	2	4	2		
Duck, Absalom	1	3	1			Maxwell, Benjamin	2	4	3		
Duck, George, Jur				1		McDugal, Thomas	1				
Davis, David	1	1	5			McCorkle, Thomas	2		3		6
Davis, Daniel				1		Meek, James, Esqr	1		3		
Evitts, William	2	1	3			Meek, James, Jur	1	1	2		
Forsyth, Robert	3	3	4			Montieth, Henry			2		
Gillaspie, Joseph			2		1	Montieth, Samuel	1	2	4		
Gillaspie, James		2	2		2	Martin, Thomas	1	1	2		
Gilmore, Patrick	1	7	1			McNair, James	1		2		
Givvins, John, Senr	2					Osborn, John			4		

peele, James, Ser	2	1	1	5	Taylor, Elijah	1	3	3	
peele, James, Jur	1	1	2		Wilson, David	1	4	2	1
Potts, Robert	1	5	3	10	Wilson, Benjn	1	1	2	9
Potts, Jonathan	2	1	7	1	Wilson, Samuel, Jur	1		2	1
price, James	1	3	5		Wilson, John	1			
price, John	1		4		Wilson, Joseph	1			
price, Robert	1		1		Wise, John	2	4	4	
Sloan, David	1	4	2		Wise, William	1		1	
Sloan, John	1		3		Walls, Abin				1
Clark, Benjamin	1		4		McCong, Thomas				1
Hutchison, David	1		1		Willie, John	1		4	
Shelds, Robert	1		1		Willie, William	1	2	3	
Clark, Joseph	1		2		Wilson, William			1	1
Wilson, Samuel, Senr	1	1	3		Waddle, William	1	3	4	1
Sloan, Robert	2		2		Wilson (Widow)	1	1	2	
Stanford, Samuel	2	1	4		Williams, Jas L.			1	4
Stanford, Isaac	1				Emmerson, James	1	1	4	
Smith, David	1		1	5	Christenberry, Nicholas	2		3	
Smith, James			1		Christenberry, Moses	1		1	
Torrence, Hugh	1	1	5	12	Wilson, John, Junr	1		1	
Tucker, William	2	1	1						

DISTRICT NO. 8

Andrews, Robert	2	2	7		Hamilton, Hugh	1	1	2	
Anderson, Robert	2		5		Harris, Robert, Esqr	2	1	4	11
Alexander, Capt Stephen	2	1	7	2	Henderson, John	2		2	
Alexander, Josiah	1	3	2	2	Harris, Oliver	1		2	1
Brown, Benjn	2	2	2		Harris, Robert	1		6	1
Brown, Samuel	2		2		Harris, James	2	1	2	
Bradford, Mary	2	1	3		Irwin, Thomas	1	2	4	
Benson, Thomas	1	2	2		Lewis, Benjamin		2	1	4
Benson, Robert	2	2	2		Moffit, Martha	3		3	2
Bell, James				1	McCulloch, John	1	2	6	
Bradford, James					Morton, Samuel	4		1	
Bowman, Samuel	1	1	5	3	Martin, Robert	2	1	3	
Bartley, Daniel	1	1	6		McOwn, Margt		1	3	1
Carrigan, James	2		2	2	McCabb, James	1	3	2	
Cooper, John	1	2	2		Null, John	1		6	
Copeland, Dennis	1		3		Null, James	2	4	6	13
Casey, Mary	1		1		Prule, Reese	1		2	
Carruthers, John	3	3	3		Penney, John		1	2	
Davis, Isaac	1		2		Penney, William	1		2	
Davis, John, Senr	2		2		Pickens, Capt Samuel	1	3	4	5
Davis, David	1		2		Ross, William	1	4	3	
Flemming, Mitchell	1	2	2		Ross, Joseph	1	2	5	
Farr, Margt	2		2	6	Ross, George	1	2	2	
Gilliland, John	2		2		Stevenson, Jas			5	
Gilmore, Archabeld	1		1		Steele, John	1		2	2
Gillaspie, James	1	1			Templeton, David	1	4	3	2
Houstin, John	1	3	4	1	Tanner, James	1	4	3	
Houstin, Capt Archabeld	2		1	3	Wells, William	1	2	1	
Houstin, David	1		2	2	Wilson, John	1		5	
					Andrews, Moses	1	1	2	

DISTRICT NO. 9

Allison, John, Esqr	3	1	3	5	Houston, David		1	2	
Armstrong, John	1		1		Hall, Morgan	1	1	3	
Armstrong, John, Jur				1	Hosey, Jonathan	1		2	
Alexander, Francis	1	1	2		Holbrook, Valtch	1	2	3	
Baker, John	1	5	4	3	Kyles, James	1		4	5
Berry, George	1		2		Lock, Francis	1	2	2	
Baker, Christopher	2	3	3		Lingo, Daniel	1		4	
Baker, Joshua	1	1	3		McClartey, Archabeld	1		4	
Biggers, Robert	1		2		McClartey, Alexander	2	1	4	
Barns, William	1	5	4		Means, John	3	2	4	4
Booker, Joseph	1	2	5		Martin, Robert	2	3	2	
Campbell, Thomas	1				Martin (Widow)			2	
Carruthers, Andw	3	1	8	1	Morrison, William		1		1
Creaton, James	1		1		McCray, William	1	2	5	1
Cannon, James	1		1	3	Martin, Richard	1	4	5	
Doherty, James			1		McKinley, David	1	2	3	
Frazer, William	1	3	6		McKinley, John	2	1	2	
Glover, Ezekel	1		2		Murphey, John			5	
Glover, John				1	McRea, Arthur			3	
Glover, William	1		1		Martin, William	1	2	2	
Gaseway, John	1	4	2		Phifer, Col Caleb	1		6	19
Houston, Capt William	2	2	3	4	Phifer, Capt Martin	1	2	4	16
Holbrook, John	2		2		Patton, Benjamin	2		2	
Holbrooks, Caleb	1	2	2		Patton, Samuel			3	
Holbrooks, William	1	3	1		Patton, Joseph	1	3	1	

Patterson, Samuel	5	2	3		Russell, David	1	2	1	
Patterson, Alexander	2		4	3	Rogers, John	1	1	1	1
Patterson, Robert	1		1		Scannell, John	1		1	
Phifer, Henry	1		2		Scales, John				
Pasinger, Thomas	1	2	2	1	Skitleton (Widow)				1
Reese, Solomon	1		4		Taylor, John	1	2	4	
Rogers, Joseph	1	3	4	3	Wallace, Ludwick	1	3	2	
Rogers, Moses	1	1	3		Wallace, Jediah	1		9	
Rogers, Thomas	1	2	1		Wallace, John	1	1	1	
Rogers, James, Junr	1		2		Wodington, John	1		1	
Rogers, Seth	1	3	1		Goodman, Jacob	1	1	2	
Ross, Francis	2	5	2			1	2	4	

DISTRICT NO. 10

Blackwelder, Charles	1	2	3		Lewis (Widow)	1	1	6	
Blackwelder, John	1	1	6		Mitchell, Mathias, Senr	2	2	2	
Black, Thomas	1	2	2		Miller, William	2	1	4	
Bawyers, Adam	2		3		Minster, Frederick	2	2	3	
Bryance, Henry, Senr	1				Misenhimer, Jacob	1	3	4	
Bryance, Henry, Junr	1	2	3		Mock, Thomas	2	2	3	
Bryance, William	1	2	2		Masters, George	2	3		1
Barnhart, Mathias	1	2	1		Morgadine, John	1	1	1	
Barnhart, George	1		2		Mitchell, Jacob	1		1	
Barbrick, Leonard	1	1	5		Mitchell, Mathias, Junr	1	1	2	
Barnhart, Christian	1		1		Moyer, Elias	1	2	4	
Barnhart, Christian, Junr	1	1	3		Murph, Jacob	1	2	3	
Blackwelder, Jno Adam	1		1		Nichler, John	3	4	4	
Coleman, Mark	1	6	5		Phifer, Martin, Senr	2		1	14
Cerlaugh, George	1	1	4		Phifer, Jacob	2	1	2	
Campbell, James	1	1	5		Plott, George	3	3	3	
Cook, Nicholas	3		2		Phifer, George	1	1	2	
Chamberlain, John	1	1	7		Rogers, George	2	1	6	
Clerice, George	1	2	2		Russell, James	2		5	7
Corzine, George, Senr	3	1	5		Russell, Robert	1	3	3	7
Corzine, Levil	1	3	4		Russell, John	1	3	5	
Corzine, Nicholas	1	1	4		Rogers, Nat	1		3	
Corzine, George, Junr	1	2	4		Shinn, Capt Joseph	3	3	5	6
Corzine, Samuel	1	1	3		Shinn, Benjamin	1	5	5	1
Caster, John	1		2		Shive, Phillip	1	2	3	
Kerlock, Fredrick	1		1		Smith, John	1	2	1	1
Cook, Nicholas, Junr	1	1	1		Shaver, John	2	6	4	
Deaton, Mathew	1		2		Scott, James	1	5	4	
Eagley, Phillip	1	2	3		Siminer, John	1		1	6
Farr, Walter	2	5	4	1	Shelhoas, John	1		2	
Farr, John	1	5	6		Shank, Manas				
Ferguson (Widow)			2	5	Tedford, James	1	4	1	
Furr, Henry	1	1	3		Slowgh, Martin		3		1
Faggenwinter, Christian	1		1		Voyls, William	2	5	2	
Goodnight, Christian	1	4	6		Voyls, James	1	3	2	
Groner, Jacob	3	1	2		Walter, Paul	1	2	3	
Gonder, George	2	4	4		Walter, Nicholas	1		3	
Haddock, James	1	1	2		Winesaugh, Michael	1		1	3
Hadley, Joshua	3	1	4		Winesaugh, Michael, Junr	1	4	3	
Hartman, George	1	1	6		Wiley, John	2	1	1	
Hobley, John	1	3	2		White, William	1	2	3	1
Townsand, Dudley	1	2	2		Young, John	1		3	
Townsand, George	1	4	3		Young, Martin	1	1	3	
Long, John	1	1	5		Yewman, John			2	
Lewis, Jacob	1	2	5		Townsand, Henry	1	2	1	
Lewis, Christor	2		1		Townsand, William	1	1	4	
					McGraw, William	1	1	1	

DISTRICT NO. 11

Bless (Widow)	2	2	3		Cox, Moses	1		2	
Boger, Daniel	1	2	3		Cox, John	1		3	
Boger, Peter	1	2	5		Cox, William	1		1	
Best, John	1	1	2		Coble, Peter	1		4	
Bussard, John	2		3	1	Dolin, Henry	1	2	3	
Berger, John	1	3	3		Dry, Martin	2	2	2	
Beck, Fredrick		3	8		Evalt, Michael	1	4	2	
Baringer, Mathias	3	3	6	2	Adelman, George	1		1	
Cottiser, Henry			1		Evalt, Jacob	2	2	2	
Cruse, Andrew	1	1	1		Esenhart, George	1	1	3	
Cruse, Adam	1	1	2		Fesperman, Fredrick	1		4	
Clonts, Jeremiah	1	3	2		Fesperman, Michael	1	4	5	
Clonts, George	1	1	3		Fosterman, Henry	1		1	
Closian, Jacob	2		3		Ferterman, John	1	1	2	
Christman, George	1	1	1		Goodman, George	1		2	
Caple, Peter	2	1	2		Goodman, Michael	1		1	
Culp, John	2	2	4		Goodman, Elizabeth	2		2	

Gregory, Christian	1	3	3	
Goodman, Christopher	2	2	2	
Goodman, Michael, Jur	1	2	4	
Goodman, Christopher, Jur	1	2	4	
Heso, Conrad	1	3	5	
Herron, Elijah	2	3	3	1
Herron, Jesse	1	3	6	3
Harris, Ephraim D	2	1	6	
Juke, John	1	3	5	
Creps, Tobias	1		3	
Creps, Phillip	1	2	4	1
Lippard, John	3	4	5	5
Lippard, William	1	2	2	
Long, Henry	3	2	4	
Lingle, Jacob	1		4	
Lingle, Conrad	1		4	
Lingle, Casper	1	2	3	
Misenhimer, John	1	1	5	
Moyer, Adam	2		1	
Misenhimer, Abraham	2	1	5	
McMahan, James	1	3	4	
Minsinger, William	1	1	3	
Netterhever, Paul				1
Ovenshine, Rinholt	1	1	2	
Ovenshine, Christian	1		1	
Aurey, Martin	1	2	3	
Pence, Jacob	1	2	6	
Props, Henry	1	3	1	1
Perry, Jacob	3		1	
Brineger, Erasmus	2	1	1	
Slaugh, Jacob	1	2	4	
Seferit, Barnhart	1	1		
Seferit, Charles	2		4	
Semions, John	1	1	6	
Stierwalt, Adam	1	1	1	
Speck (Widow)	3		3	
Sides, Michael	1	4	5	
Isenhaker, Nicholas				1
Rigey, George	2		2	
Richey, Jacob	1		3	
Richey, Henry	1	5	2	
Rogers, Benjamin	1	3	4	
Wolf, Phillip	3	5	3	
Wisel, Michael	2	1	3	
Walker, Fredrick	1	1	2	
Foil, George	3	2	1	
Goodman, Jacob	1	2	4	
Rosberry, Benjamin	1	3	2	
Clemments, Samuel				1
Allen, Thomas	2	1	2	
Christman, George	1	1	1	
Hartis, John	2	2	4	
Ashley, John	1	2	4	
Brown, William	1	3	3	
Cresco, William	1	3	3	

DISTRICT NO. 12

Barringer, Paul	1	4	4	13
Barenhart, Charles	3	5	4	
Bost, George	2	3	1	
Bost, Jacob	1	1	5	
Blackwelder, Caleb	1	1	4	
Blackwelder, Isaac	1	4	2	
Bost, Elias	1	3	3	
Bostion, Jonas	1		5	
Blaster, Abraham	2		1	
Barringer, John	1	5	4	2
Blackwelder, Martin	1	1	1	
Blackwelder, Jacob	1	2	1	
Bever, Daniel	1	2	1	
Caigle, Charles	2	3	5	
Casey, Jacob	1	1	5	
Carriger, George	1	3	4	
Carriger, Andrew	1	3	3	
Carriger, Phillip, Senr	1	2	1	
Carriger, Phillip, Junr	2		1	
Coile, John	1	2	3	
Clots, Tobias	1		2	
Croul, Peter	2		2	
Cline, Michael	1		5	
Coan, Lewis	1		3	
Caigle, Charles, Junr	1		1	
Dry, Charles	1	2	3	
Dry, Owen	1	3		
Dry, Phillip	1		1	
Dove, Caleb	1	1		
Gruff, William	1		2	
Eafrit, Jacob	1	1	2	
Clain, George	1	2	2	
Furr, John	2	6	2	3
Furr, Paul	1	3	4	1
Fogleman, Melcher	3	2	3	
Fisher, Lewis	1		4	
Fink, David	1	2	2	
Faggett, Jacob	2	2	3	
Foil, John	1		4	
Folk, William	1		1	
Fink, George	1		1	
Fruseland, George	1	1	3	
Faggott, Valentine	1		2	
Briges, James	4	1	4	
Hagler, John	2	3	6	
Hartwick, Conrad	1	3	2	
Hardman, George	1		2	
House, John	2	2	2	
House, Elias	1		2	
Hagler, Jacob	1	4	4	
Huber, Jacob	1	3	4	
Hardwick, George	1		3	
Hennager, Michael	1	3	3	
Hise, George	1	2	5	
Hurlaugher, Christor	3		3	
Hargey, Martin	1	3	3	
Hoan, Henry	1		5	
Hineman, William	1	1	5	
House (Widow)			6	
Hartsel, John	2	2	4	
Jarret, Daniel	3	2	5	
Little, James	1	1	1	
Honeycut, Thomas	2		2	
Kerlock, Fredrick	2		2	
Kerlock, George	1	1	4	
Krepps, John	1	3	2	
Little, Daniel	1	2	4	
Kneese, Bolser	2		2	
Lidaker, Conrad	1		2	
Linker, Henry	1	2	2	
Loften, Isaac	1	3	2	
Lidaker, Phillip	2	2	5	1
Lierly, Christopher	1	2	3	
Lype, Jonas	1		5	
Lype, Godfryt, Senr				1
Lype, Godfryt, Junr	1	1	1	
Lierly, Zamah	1	3	1	
Mathews, Andrew	1	4	3	
McGraw, James	3	4	1	
Moyer, Mathias	1		2	
Melcher, John	3	1	6	
Misenhimer, George	1	2	3	
Misenhimer, Peter	1	2	3	
Miller, Jacob	1	3	3	
Neusman, Revd Mr	1	2	4	
Oudy, Conrad	1	4	3	
Ourey, George	1	3	3	
Ourey, Godfryt	1		1	
Ourey, Barenhard	1	1	3	
Price, Henry	1		4	
Piller, Fredrick	1	2	2	
Piller, Henry	1		5	
Starns (Widow)		2	3	
Quilman, Peter	1	2	2	
Rape, Agustian	1		2	
Reed, John	1	3	3	
Ridenaur, Nicholas	1	3	7	
Redland, Geo M	2		8	
Rinhart (Widow)		2	2	
Rigsbey, Thomas	1	3	2	
Sell, Phillip	2	1	2	
Smith, George	1		3	
Smith, Henry	2	2	3	
Stough, Andw	1	1	3	1
Sides, Andw	4			
Sides, Henry	1	1	1	
Smith, Henry	2	2	3	
Starns, Conrad	1	3	5	
Stucker, Daniel	1	1	2	

Sides, Christian	2		1		Weaver, Jacob	1	1	1	
Bell, Peter	1		3		Weaver, Henry	1	3	4	
Starns, Charles	1	1	1		Weaver, Peter	1		2	
Tucker, George, Sr	3	3	5		Walker, Michael	1		10	
Tucker, George, Jur	1	1	3		Walker, Adam	2	1	2	
Teem, Jacob	2		1		Cook, Jacob	1	3	3	
Teem, Adam	1	4	2		Suther, David			2	
Voyls, Thomas	2	2	5		Suther, John	1	3	2	
Wilhelm, George	1	4	6		Miller, George	2	2	2	
Witenhouse, Martin				1	Winchester, William	2	2	4	
Wiser, Phillip, Jur			2		Caigle, John	2	3	6	
Wiser, Phillip, Senr	3		1		Winchester, Dugles	2	3	3	
Wagginor, William	1	5	2						

DISTRICT NO. 13

Andrews, William	1		2		Morgan, Enoch	1	2	1	
Armstrong (Widow)		1	4		McCammon, Charles	2		2	
Alexander, William S	1	3	2	4	Morrison, Robert	4	1	5	
Allen, Alexander, Jur	1	4	2		Morrison, William	2	1	3	1
Allen, Alexr, Senr	1	3	2		Morris, Griffin	1	4	5	
Burns, James	2	1	6		McClelland, John	1	3	3	
Bradshaw, James	2	4	6		Mash, Ebenezer	2		2	
Biggers, Joseph	3	1	5		McGinnis, Charles	3		3	
Bean, Robert	3	4	5		McCurdey, Capt Archabeld	1	4	5	6
Black, James	2		2		Maxwell, James	2	4	1	
Black, Wm	1	3	2		Newill, Francis	1	1	4	
Black, John	1		3		Newill, William	3		3	
McClain, Allen	2	2	4		Newill, David	1		1	
Carruthers, Hugh	1	3	2		Plunket, James, Senr	1		1	6
Carruthers, James	1	1	4		Plunket, James, Junr	1	4	1	
Colland, William	3		1	2	Purviance, John	3	1	2	1
Crumel, James	1	1	2		Purviance, Joseph	1	1	2	
Crumel, John	1	2	5		Purviance, James	1	4	1	1
Coldwell, Daniel	1	4	1		Purviance, John	1	1	3	
Coldwell, Robt	1		2		Russell, James	1		1	3
Cochran, Benja	1	4	2		Ross, William	2	2	5	3
Cochran, Robert	1	2	6		Ross, James	1			1
Campbell, Andw	1	2	2		Scott, James	2		2	
Cochran, Wm	2		1		Scott, Alexander	1	2	4	
Cochran, Paul		4	2		Simons, John	1	5	2	
Cochran, John	1	2	1	1	Stuart, Samuel	1	3	5	
Corruthers, Robert	3	3	6		Spears, William	4	2	4	
Davis, Robt	1	6	5		Stafford, James, Senr	2			1
Dunn, Simon				1	Stafford, James, Junr	1	4	3	1
Davis, Thomas	2	4	4		Scott, William, Esqr	3		2	
Davis, Andrew	3		6		Stuart, William	1	2	4	
Davis, William				1	Stuart (Widow)	1		4	
Ferguson, Alexander	1	4	2	3	Taylor, William	1	2	3	
Harris, William, Jur	1	4	5		Taylor, David	1		3	
Hays, Patrick	1	2	2	1	Wite, John	2	4	3	2
Harris, John	6		4	6	White, Thomas	1	3	2	1
Harris, Capt James	1	2	1		White, William	1	3	5	
Harris, Robert, Junr	1	2	1	11	Wiley, Oliver	1	4	6	4
Harris, Samuel	2	1	6	2	Widington, Samuel	1	1		
Harris, William, Senr	1	3	5		Wallace, Aron	1		2	8
Gingles, John	1		1		White, Archabeld	3	1	2	
Harris, Capt Robert	1		1	3	White, David	1	2	3	4
Howell, Joseph	3	3	2		White, James	2		1	
Howell, John	1		3		Watson, Thomas	4	2	3	
Kirkpatrick, Valentine	1	3	2		White, Joseph	1		3	
Kimmins, Hugh		2	5		Wallace, Moses	1		3	
Kimmins, Alexander				1	Dorton, Charles	1	6	2	
McClelland, Rebeca	1	1	3		Davis, George	1	6	4	1
McCinley, David	1		7		Morgan, Robert	1		3	
McCinley, Charles	1	3	2		Stuart, John	1		3	
McKentire, Capt William	2	4	3		Harris, Samuel, Junr	1		4	1
McMurray, Francis	1		2	3	Welch, Joseph	1	1	2	
McMurray, Robert	1		1		Eager, Adam	2	1	3	3
McCahern (Widow)	1		6		Eager, Hugh	1	2	4	
McFadian, Thomas	1	1	1						
Morrison, James	3	2	2	2					

DISTRICT NO. 14

Alexander, Col Adam	3	1	3	5	Bailey, Joseph	1	1	2	
Alexander, Evan	1		4		Brandon, John	1	3	2	
Bean, William	3	1	4		Brown, James	1		1	
Bugg, William	1	2	3		Bryan, Kiah	1	3	1	
Bean, Daniel	1		2		Cuthbertson, John		1	3	
Barnhill, Robert	1	1	2		Crowle, Samuel	2	2	3	

Cuthbertson, David	1	1	2		Pickens, William	1	2	3	
Crowle, Samuel, Junr	1	1	2		Pyron, William	2	2	5	
Carruthers, John	1		2	7	Powell, David	1	2	2	
Clay, Isham	1		3		Pyron, John	1	2	2	
College, Henry	1		4		Powell, John			2	
Freemon (Widow)		3	2		Polk, William, Jur	3	4	2	
Dickson, James	1	1			Polk, William, Senr	1		1	2
Davis, James	1	2	2		Polk, Capt Charles	2	3	3	4
Freemon, Allen, Junr	1		2		Powell, Abel	1		2	
Freemon, Allen, Senr	1	3	3	12	Purser, John	2	2	5	
Freemon, Gidion	1	1	4	1	Polk, John, Junr	1	1	2	
Flaugh, David	2	3	5		Polk, Thomas, Junr	1	1	3	
Ford (Widow)	1	1	4		Rabb, Capt William	2	4	3	3
Freemon, William	1	1	4		Rogers, James	1		3	5
Freemon, Elyburn	1		2		Rogers, Hugh	1	1	3	2
Garmon, Michael	1	1	7	9	Ramsay, William	1	3	6	
Garmon (Widow)	1	1	8		Rodgers, Joseph	1	1	7	
Guiliams, Travis	1		2		Simpson, William	1	3	2	
Harkey (Widow)	1		3		Snell, Francis	1		4	1
Hall, James	1	2	3		Smith, Thomas	1		4	
Harbison, William	1	1	4		Smith, William	1		3	6
Hall, Thomas	1	3	4		Shelley, Capt Thomas	1	1	3	
Harris, Majr James	4	1	3	13	Stansill, John	1	2	2	
Hall, John	2	3	2		Smith, Samuel, Senr	2	1	2	4
Johnston, William	2	2	2		Self, Jacob	1	3	1	
Johnston (Widow)	1	1	3		Smith, Samuel, Junr				
Kiser, Fredrick	1	3	3		Smith, Saml (son of Saml)				
Kiser, George	1	4	3		Talley, Priar	1		1	
Kyger, George A	1	2	2		Townsand, William	1	1	3	
Long, James	1		2		Warden, Samuel	1	2	2	
Mulls, John	1	1	2		Witherford, Wilks	3	3	2	
McMurray, James	1	4	5	1	Witherford, William	1	1	3	
Miney, Martin	1	3	2		Wise, Benjamin				1
McCracken, John	3	3	2		Watts, Andrew	2		2	
McClartey, Alexr					Reed, John		3	2	
Murphey, John	2	1	5		Totter, George	2	3	2	
McCoy, John	1	1	5	2	Crawford, John	1		6	
Miller, Phillip	2		2		Miller (Widow)	1		6	
Mitchell, William	1		5		Miller, Mathew		2	3	
McGuist, John	2	4	3		Miller (Widow) Senr	1		1	1
Masser, George	1		2		Clay, James	1	1	1	
McGehey, Amos	1		2		Caegie, Henry	1	4	1	
Nelson, John	1	1	2						
McCummons, John	2	3	4	1					

DISTRICT NO. 15

Blair, William	3	3	5		Morris, William	3	3	3	1
Buckhannon, Samuel	3	2	2		Montgomery, John	1	3	3	
Black, John	2	1	6	2	McCall, William	3		3	
Black, Ezekel	1	1	6	2	Moore, Hugh	2	4	4	
Black, Samuel	1		2		McCombs, James	2		5	5
Black, William, Sr	2		2	1	Miller, Abraham	3	1	5	
Carragan, Thomas	1	1	1		McCollum, Malcom	1	3	2	
Charles, Henry	1	1	3		McCraven, John, Jur	1		3	
Crum, Conrad	1		3		McGintey, James	1	2	4	
Contz, Lewis	1	2	4		Moore, Andw	1	2	3	
Donaldson, John	1	2	5		Moore, David, Jur	1	1	4	
Ford, Zeblin	1	5	1		Nail, John	1	4	4	
Fisher, George		2	2	7	Orr, James (whistling)	2	5	3	
Ford, John, Esqr	2	1	2		Orr, James	1	3	3	1
Glass, Robert	1		2		Phillips, Adam	1	1	1	
Glass, Francis	2	4	1		Query, William, Senr	3		1	
Grubble, Thomas	1	2	5		Quary, John	3		1	
Gooder, Lewis	2			7	Quary, William, Jur			4	
Hood, Tunis, Senr	1				Ray, Isaac	1	2	5	
Hood, Capt Tunis	1	4	4	4	Routh, Edward	1		1	
Hood, Reuben	1	2	5	2	Stansill, Jesse	1		4	
Harrison, Nebemiah	1	3	2		Stansill, John	1		2	
Hartwick, Conrad	2		2		Shaver, Fredrick	2	5	4	1
Harkey, John, Senr	1	1	2		Stuart, Mathew	2	1	4	
Hartis, Lewis	3		3		Stevens, Emmanuel	1	4	3	
Irwin, William, Senr	1		2		Stains, James				1
Irwin, Thomas	1	3	2		Stilwell, Jesse			3	
Kenneday, William	1	3	5		Walker, William	2		2	
Kidwell, William	1	1	2		Wilson, James	3	4	4	
Leagh, Henry			6		Wilson, Thomas		4	3	
Lippe, Leonard		1	2		Walker, Capt Archabeld	2	1	2	
Laigh, Jacob	1	3	2		Walker, Mathew, Senr			6	
Lemmonds, John	2	3	3		Vance, Andw	1		1	
Mcjersion, John				1	Irwin, William, Jur	1	1	2	
McIntire, William	1		4		Ormond, James	1			1
McGinnis, Peter	3	1	3		Carrigan, William			1	
					Walker, Moses	1		1	

Wilson, Thomas, Senr	1		1		Duglass, James, Esqr	1	3	3	1
Coul, James				1	Dunbarr, Nathaniel			1	
Vance, Valentine	1				Craig, John			2	
Culbertson, William	2	3	5		Elkins, Shadrick	1	1	3	
Darbey, Charles	1		1		Eakins, John			4	
Dunn, James	2	1	2		Bradshaw, Samuel			2	
Dunn, Andrew	1	2	6		Bradshaw (Widow)		2	1	2
Demsey, John	1	1	6		Crye, William	1	3	2	

DISTRICT NO. 16

Appleton, William	2	2	2		Lawson, Moses	1		1	
Adams, Charles	3	2	5		Leggit, Esther	2	3	4	2
Blythe, James	1	6	3		Lawson, Thomas	2		2	
Basdill, Reuben	1	3	3	3	Leggit, William	2	2	2	1
Barnet, Robert	1	3	3		Linn (Widow)	2	1	3	
Bonds, George	2	3	2		McNeely, John	2			1
Bickett (Widow)	3		3		McCall, Francis	1		3	
Crye, John	3	1	2		McCorkle, John	1	1	3	
Craige, Moses	2	2	4		McCallum, John	1		2	
Cochran, Thomas, Senr	2	2	1	1	McCablum, Thomas	1	1	2	
Cochran, Thomas, Junr	1	5	7		McCabben, Mighty	1	1	5	
Crye, James	3		2		McCain, Hance	1		2	
Courtney, William	2		1		McWhorter, Aron	2	1	4	
Cochran, John	1	1	3		McCauslin, James	1		4	
Chainey, William	1	4	2		Mcquistion, Joseph	1		4	
Fincher, James	1	4	2		Morrison, Dr William	1		1	2
Fincher, Richard	1	2	4		McCrorey, Hugh	1	1	2	
Finley, James			2		McCain, John				1
Fincher, Jonathan	2	3	6		Newton, Robert	1	2	5	
Fowler, John	2	1	2		Orr, George	1	1	5	1
Forsythe, Hugh	1	2	3		Osborn, William	3	1	7	
Finley, William				1	Ormond, James	1	2	2	
Finley, Charles				1	Orr, David	2	4	4	
Forbers, Hugh	1		3		Osborn (Widow)	2	1	4	
Givvins, William	1	1	4		Ormond, Jacob	1	2	4	1
Gibbens, John	1	4	2		Porter, William	1		1	
Givvins, Samuel	1	2	1		Paxton, Moses	1	2	2	
Gray, Jacob	3	1	1		Potts, John	1	1	5	3
Gray, Sherrod	1	2	2	2	Potts, William	1	1	3	14
Gordin, John	3		3		Porter, Capt Robert	2	3	5	
Gillaspie, Jacob		1			Richardson, Edward	3	2	3	
Hargitt, James		1	1		Rape, Peter	1		4	
Hellums, George	1	3	3		Ramsay, Robert	1	3	3	
Hellums, John	1	2	4		Rich, James	1	2	2	
Hellums, George, Senr				1	Rape, Henry	1	2	2	
Houston, Hugh	3		1	4	Rederick, Shadrick	1	2	3	
Hargitt, Henry		1	2		Redford, John	4	2	4	
Helms, Jacob		1	4		Rogers, John, Senr	1		2	
Houston, William, Senr	1		3	1	Ramsay, Alexander	1	1	1	
Houston, William, Junr	1		3	1	Rich, John, Junr	1		2	
Howey, George		2	2		Shepperd, John	1	1	3	
Howard, William	1	1	3		Shepperd, James	1		1	
Helms, Tilmon	1	2	2		Shepperd, Edward	1	2	1	
Hargitt, Henry, Junr		6	2		Secrist, Michael	1		3	2
Hise, Leonard	1	3	3		Secrist, John	1		3	
Howey, William	2	1	1	1	Rich, James, Senr	2	3	5	
Henninger, Dennis	2	3	6		Stuart, Joseph	1	1	2	
Howey, John	1		3	5	Storey, James	1		3	1
Houston, James	3	1	2	5	Secrist, Jacob	2	4	4	
Heggins (Widow)	2	1	2	4	Stevenson, James	1		4	
Harris, John	1		5		Thompson, Elijah	3	1	4	
Hellums, Isaac	1		2		Tanner, Thomas	1	2	4	
Izel, Fredrick	2	1	3		Thompson, John	1	2	5	
Queban, John	1		2		Spratt, Andw	1	5	5	
King, Robert	1	3	2		Williamson, James	1	5	2	
Lawson, John	1		2		White, Thomas	1	2	1	
Lewis, William		2	4		West, Benjamin	1	2	3	
Lewis, Martha	1	1	1		Yarbrough, Joshua	3	3	5	1
Lewis, James	1	5	3		Uans, Robert	1		1	

DISTRICT NO. 17

Avent, James	1	1	6	5	Cairns, Alexander	1	4	5	4
Abbott (Widow)			4		Coak, Robert	1		2	3
Allen, Andw	1	3	2		Coak, Charles	1		6	3
Allen, Thomas				1	Cairns, Daniel	2	1	4	
Blue, Stephen	1	2	3		Davis, James	2		6	1
Broom, John	3		2		Dosher, James	2	1	5	
Belk, John, Esqr			1	8	Davis, Capt Robert	2	3	6	4
Belk, Darling	1	3	2		Findly, John	1		2	
					Forster, Capt Joseph	1			4

Fisher, Paul	1		1		Haggins, John	1	1	1	
Fisher, William	1	1	2		Gillaspie, John	1	4	4	
Fisher, John	1	2	2		Kendrick, Philad	1		3	
Fisher, Charles	1		1		Hughey, John	1		6	
Fisher, Fredrick	1	2	2		Lathlin, Samuel	1		2	
Gantt, William	1		4		Lathlin, John	1		3	
Gillaspie, Andʷ	1		1		Lasley, James	1	2	3	1
Gantt, Thomas	1		5		Lackey, Robert	1		2	
McCain, William	1	1	4		Lackey, Thomas	1	3	3	1
Yerbey, Avent	1	3	2		Lesley (Widow)	2	1	1	
McCammon, John	3	3	5		Lanley, George	1	2	4	1
McCorkle, Archabeld	1		1		McWhorter, John	1		1	
McWhorter, James	1	1	2		Myars, Hermon	1	1	1	
Odum, May	1		2		McElroy, John	4	2	2	
Orr (Widow)		3	7		McElroy, James	1	3	3	1
Potts, Joshua	1	1	1		McWhorter, Moses	1	2	5	
Rogers, Hugh	1	5	3		McCorkle, James	1	4	2	
Rogers, Mathew	1	3	4		McWhorter, George	3		2	
Ramsay, John	1	3	2		McCorkle, Owen	1		2	
Rogers, John	1	3	2		McCain, Andʷ	1	1	1	
Rowan, Henry	1		2		Meller, Bule	1	3	4	
Faggett, Moses	1	2	4	1	McCain, John	1	1	4	
Rogers, William	2	4	3		McCain, Hugh	3	1		3
Starns, Fredrick	1		3		McCain, Thomas, Junr	1	3	1	
Starns, David	1	3	1		Vinen, Drury	1	5	3	4
Stevenson, John	1	4	3	1	Washam, Jeremiah	2	1	3	
Sibley, John	1	2	3		Walker, Capᵗ Andʷ	1	1	6	3
Shannon, James	1	1	1		Williams, John	1	2	1	
Titus, Dennis	1	1	7		Wahaub, James	3	2	3	9
Thompson, Alexander	1		5		Williams, Ishmael	1	2	2	
Thompson, Obediah	1	1	3		Walker, John	3		1	
Vinan, Thomas	1	5	3		Walker, Thomas	1	1	1	
Vinan, William	1		3		Griffin, Richard	1	3	1	
Gillaspie, Charles	1	1	1		Redick, Barnabas	1	4	1	
					Oats, Michel	1	1	3	

DISTRICT NO. 18

Bruster, James	2	2	3	5	Null, Jesse	1	1	1	1
Barnet, Hugh	3	1	5		Null, Andʷ	1		2	
Black, James	2	3	5		Osborn, Robert	1	2	2	
Black, William, Junr	1		3		Osborn, Alexander	1	1	3	
Batey, Walter	2	1	5	2	Ormond, Adam	1		1	1
Chambers, James	1	1	1		Osborn Able	1		1	
Crocket, Archabeld	4	1	5	2	Parks, Moses	3	3	3	
Coningham, Roger	2	1	2		Patson, Simon	2		3	
Currey, James	1	4	3		Potter, Gordon	3	3	4	
Dawns, Henry	2			3	Patterson, John				1
Dawns, Samuel	1		2	1	Ray, Andrew, Senr	2	2	4	
Dawns, Thomas	1	1	1	1	Reed, James	1	2	4	
Donaldson, Robert	1	2	1		Ray, John	1	1	1	
Greer, John	1		1		Reed, Joseph	2	3	2	2
Guire, John	1	1	3		Robison, John	1	5	3	2
Hoge, Francis	2		4		Ray, David	1	3	4	
Harkness, George	1	3	6		Robison, Thomas	1	2	5	
Hadden, George	1	2	1		Stuart, William	2		2	
Hodge, John	1	1	2		Slitt, William	2	5	2	
Housten, David	1		1	1	Simeson, Capᵗ John	1	1	1	
Harrison, Isaiah	1	3	3	2	Shanks, James	1	1	6	4
John, Daniel	1	1	3	1	Sharpe, John	1	2	2	
McSparren, James	1		4		Stevenson, John				1
Means, William	1	3	5	1	Stuart, John	2	3	4	
McKee, William	1	3	2	6	Springs, John, Senr	1		2	2
Miller, John	1	2	2		Stevenson, David				1
McCauley, Daniel	1		3		Tawns, Elijha	2		2	
McKee, Alexander	1	3	4		Wyatt, Sylvester	1	2	2	
Moore, Phillip	2	1	4		Wylle, James	1		2	1
Montgomery, George	1	4	1		Valch, William	1	4	3	
Moore, David, Senr	4	4	6	1	McBoyd, Patrick	1	2	3	
Miller, George	1		2		Smith, John	1	2	2	1
McGoughen, James				1	Gailbraith, Robert	2		5	
Morrison, Alexander	2		2	1	Hendricks, William	1		1	1
Mathews, William, Esqr	1	3	1	1	Cleymon, Simon	1	1	4	
					Cleymon, Richard	1	1	6	

DISTRICT NO. 19

Alexander, Capᵗ Charles	3	1	4	6	Alexander, Levine	3		2	
Alexander, Abner	1	1	3		Alexander, Samuel	2		2	
Alexander, George	1	1	2		Bigham (Widow)	3		2	

Bays, James	3	2	3		Sturgeon, John	2	2	2	
Bonham, Daniel	1	3	4	1	Smith, John	1	1	3	
Brown, James	2	1	1		King, John	2	3	4	
Brown, William	1	2	6		Sharpe, Edward, Senr	1		2	
Barnett, John	1	1	3		Swann, John	4		2	1
Baxter, James	1		4	1	Sharpe, James	2	2	5	
Cuningham, William	1	2	3		Sharpe, Edward, Junr	1		2	
Cuningham, Nathaniel	1	1	2	1	Walker, Robert	1	1	2	
Cook, Joseph	1		5	2	Weeks, Phillip	2		3	
Dermond, James	1	2	3		Wilson, William, Esqr	2	2	3	1
Esselman, James	1	2	2		Wilson, Robert	1	2	2	
Flemmekan, David	1	8	3		Wilson, John	1	2	2	
Graham, William	1		2		Washingtown, John				1
Gaston, Thomas	1	2			Wotherspoon, William	1	1	1	
Hays, Robert	2	1	4		Walker, John	1	1	1	
Kirkpatrick, John	3		3	3	Yandell, James	1	3	4	
Knox, David				1	Yandel, William	4	4	7	
Erwin, Christor	1		6		Yandel, Andrew	1	4	3	
McCulloch, John	5	2	4	3	Jinkins, John	3	2	3	
Menson, William	1		3		Smith, James	1	3	3	
Mulwee, John	2	2	6		Robison (Widow)		3	4	
Merchant, William	1	2	7		Lindsey, Walter	1		3	
Osborn, Capt James	1	4	6		Wilson (Widow)	1		2	4
Osborn, John	2	2	2	3	Alexander, Eli	1	2	3	1
Phillips, Robert	1	1	2		Wallace, George	1		3	
Page, Nicholas			2	1	Wallace, Mathew	1	2	3	
Rogers, John	1	3	2		Wallace, William	1	2	3	
Reed (Widow)	2	2	5		Miller (Widow)	1		1	

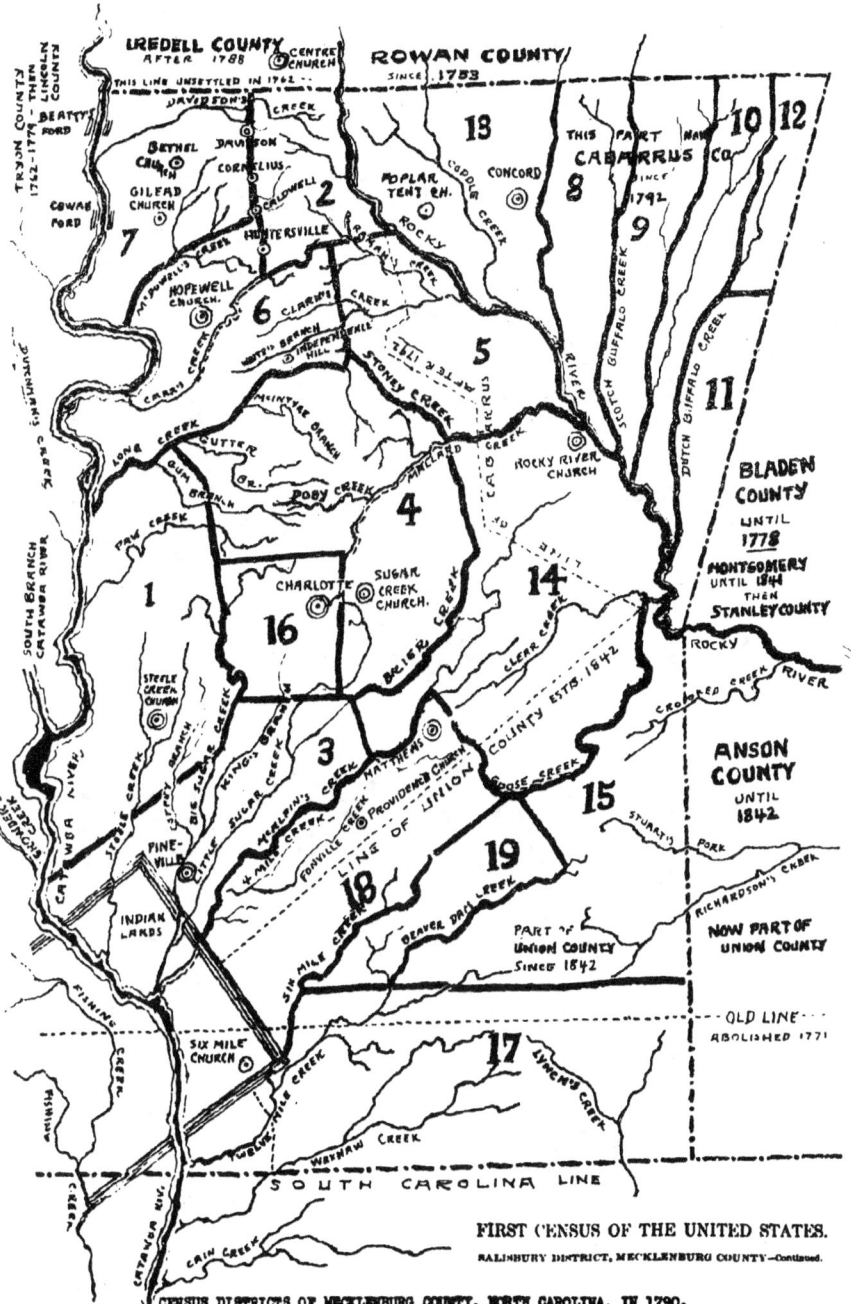

FIRST CENSUS OF THE UNITED STATES.
SALISBURY DISTRICT, MECKLENBURG COUNTY—Continued.

CENSUS DISTRICTS OF MECKLENBURG COUNTY, NORTH CAROLINA, IN 1790.

The boundaries of the above Districts are not of record so far as this compiler knows, but are delineated from information obtained from deeds, wills, court records, church records and tombstone inscriptions indicating the place of residence of those whose names appear on the census at approximately the time it was taken. No pretence is indulged that it is other than a substantial guide. See the notes which follow.

GENEALOGICAL NOTES PERTAINING TO CENSUS RECORDS OF MECKLENBURG COUNTY

DISTRICT NO. 1

The Census Districts shown on the accompanying map have been segregated from the original list as published, using the alphabetical grouping that was followed as the main key, although the published list was all jammed and jumbled together when finally made up for publication by the United States Census Bureau; other keys used was knowledge obtained from contemporaneous records of various kinds found by the compiler in doing his research on the lives and families of the older Mecklenburg families. The job now undertaken by the writer is to take this long, tedious list of names apart to "see what makes it tick" and reassemble it in some semblance that would conform somewhat to the known facts otherwise revealed.

District No. 1 may be properly called the "Steele Creek District", since both the creek of that name and the famous "Steele Creek Church" intersect and is located within the area, the Southwest corner of which started at the JOHN BIGGERS FERRY on the Catawba River, opposite the mouth of what is known as CROWDER'S CREEK. This District, in 1790, was the home of at least one of the "Signers" of the Mecklenburg Declaration - EZRA ALEXANDER. The grave of this signer has never been located, and Dr. J. B. Alexander in his "History" declares (p. 78) that he may have gone with EZEKIEL POLK to Tennessee, where possibly he found his last resting place. If so, he perhaps settled in Sumner County in that State with Zaccheus Wilson, another of the "signers" who is known to have died there.

The writer, in trying to analyze the lives of some of these families has discovered that the members were sometimes scattered over the Mecklenburg area, some owning lands in one part of the county and others of the same name and family being located in another part. So it is we find that GEORGE CATHEY, SR. and his wife ESTHER, and ALEXANDER CATHEY lived in this Steele Creek District, while some of the other Catheys were listed in other Districts, further up the CATAWBA and elsewhere. "Cathey's Meeting House", if the Historian FOOTE can be relied upon, was located somewhere in what has been designated on our map as District No. 7. The graves of some of the Catheys will be found at Steele Creek, including a younger JOHN BEATTY who was born in 1790, the year the Census was taken. Also many of the members of the COFFEY FAMILY are interred at the old Steele Creek burial ground, the family for which COFFEY BRANCH - an arm of Big Sugar Creek was named. NICHOLAS GIBBONY, entered on the list is also buried there, as are CAPT. HUGH PARKS and JOHN and ESTHER McDOWELL. On this list will also be found the names of the three celebrated and distinguished brothers, GEORGE, JAMES and MAJ. JOSEPH GRAHAM. Neither of these men are buried at Steele Creek Church, but at least one of them is known to have had his home on PAW CREEK, West of Charlotte, perhaps in 1790 within the bounds we have laid off for the Steele Creek District. Moore will be said about all of these families later on in this work. ROBERT IRWIN was "signer" from this District.

DISTRICT NO. 2

This District apparently embraced that territory lying East of a line passing through Huntersville, Cornelius and Davidson as presently located and extending to Rocky River on the East and a point South of the present Huntersville. A certain ZACCHEUS WILSON is listed on this roll, but as there were several Wilsons of that name we cannot be sure that this Zaccheus was the "signer". The home of EPHRAIM BREVARD, Secretary of the Convention, is known to have been in this area, somewhat South and East of the present town of DAVIDSON, where the College is located, but since he died at the home of his friend JOHN McKNITT ALEXANDER, when trying to reach his home after a long illness in prison during the revolution, he was not alive at the time the census was taken. Dr. Brevard married in Mecklenburg, though the Brevards lived somewhat North of the unsettled line between it and Iredell. District No. 2 is therefore credited with being the home of the celebrated EPHRAIM BREVARD, the "Signer" and Secretary of the Mecklenburg Convention of May 20, 1775.

This District was also the home of the KNOX FAMILY, and of JAMES KNOX, the grandfather of President JAMES KNOX POLK. The names of JAMES, SAMUEL KNOX SR., SAMUEL JR., MATTHEW and JOHN KNOX will be noticed on this list. The claim is made that President Polk was born near the town of Huntersville at the home of his grandfather, JAMES KNOX, while others claim he was born at the old POLK HOMESTEAD East of PINEVILLE in District No. 3. It is at the latter place the marker designating his birthplace has been located.

Another family of considerable importance whose members are listed as residing in this District was that of the SMARTS. This family was related to the BARNETTS and SPRATTS, who were among the first families. Several members of the SMART family moved West and settled in Tennessee. GEORGE SMART married SUSAN BARNETT, and LITTLEBURY SMART appears to have been one of his sons, who was unmarried at the time the census was taken.

DISTRICT NO. 3

This was the PINEVILLE DISTRICT. It was somewhere within the bounds of this territory, according to tradition, that the pioneer THOMAS SPRATT finally settled prior to 1750. There was no Pineville there in those days, nor until long afterwards. It was a cross-roads known as the "Morrow Turn-Off" located near the lands of the Indian reservation and what is now the line of South Carolina. Prominent names to be found on this list are those of WILLIAM, THOMAS and CHARLES POLK, representatives in 1790 of that family which produced JAMES KNOX POLK, a President of the United States. A short distance East of this little "cross-roads" town stands the marker designating the birthplace of the President. About five or six miles almost due South of this point lived the parents of another distinguished President of the United States - ANDREW JACKSON, between two branches of what is known as Twelve-Mile Creek. Members of the old MORROW FAMILY still reside at PINEVILLE.

DISTRICT NO. 4

This is the SUGAR CREEK CHURCH DISTRICT, and was the home of the Chairman of the Mecklenburg Convention which adopted the famous "resolves", although at the time the census was taken in 1790, he was deceased, and only the name of his wife, DORCAS ALEXANDER, appears on the list, who had at that time four sons and two daughters in her household; according to Dr. Alexander's History of Mecklenburg County he died April 28, 1778, though his tombstone says 1786. The latter is perhaps correct. Dorcas Alexander, his widow, died May 20, 1800. The grave of both HEZEKIAH and ABRAHAM ALEXANDER may be found in what is known as the second oldest Sugar Creek burying ground, just across the road from the present churchyard. (There are three Sugar Creek burying grounds). The reader will note that there were no less than fifteen heads of families listed in this District No. 4, bearing the name of ALEXANDER. The name of HEZEKIAH ALEXANDER does not appear on this list, although he was obviously alive at the time the census was taken, he having lived until July 16, 1801. (Tombstone). There does appear on the list however an "EZEKIAH ALEXANDER, ESQ.", with five sons & two daughters and with thirteen slaves, all of which indicates that this entry was intended for Col. HEZEKIAH ALEXANDER, the signer of the Mecklenburg Declaration. This shows that the Sugar Creek District (No. 4) was the home of at least two of the signers. The relationship between these several Alexanders of Sugar Creek Church and who were living in different parts of Mecklenburg County about the time the U. S. Census was taken, has never been accounted for by any student or writer, so far as this compiler knows. This problem will be discussed in these notes later.

On this list appear the names of an old family of ROBISONS, including ROBERT, SR. and JR., JOHN, MOSES, DAVID, JAMES SR. and WILLIAM and RICHARD ROBISON. The graves of these ROBISONS are, some of them, in the oldest Sugar Creek Churchyard, including DAVID ROBISON who died in 1808 at the age of 82 years, which would throw his birth back in 1726. The ROBISONS married muchly into the HENDERSON FAMILY, of which CAIRNS HENDERSON (also listed) appears to have been the ancestor, so far as the Sugar Creek Church Hendersons were concerned. JOHN McGEE, whose name is shown on the list of heads of families in this District was a son of ROBERT McGEE, who is buried in the original Sugar Creek Churchyard, and who died October 9, 1775 ate the age of 75 years, being born therefore in the year 1700. So far as noticed this appears to be the oldest person in point of date of birth, whose grave is to be found therein. Other important families represented by two or more "heads" on the list, were the PARKS, ORRS, MONTGOMERYS, RICKEYS, SAMPLES and WALLACES. Chief among the latter was EZEKIEL WALLACE, father of REV. JAMES WALLIS, of PROVIDENCE CHURCH, who married one of the daughters of the patriot JOHN McKNITT ALEXANDER.

DISTRICT NO. 5

District No. 5 lay South of the BREVARD-KNOX District and between Stony Creek and ROCKY RIVER. The list is headed, in this instance also, by a number of ALEXANDERS, chief among them being MOSES ALEXANDER, who was the father of NATHANIEL ALEXANDER, who was elected and served as Governor of North Carolina, beginning in 1805. (Alexander's History p. 98). Nathaniel Alexander married a daughter of COL. THOMAS POLK, but the same authority says: "He left no children -neither son or daughter - to inherit his name or keep his name fresh as it passes down the stream of time." We found his grave - well marked - in the Old Presbyterian Churchyard, in the very heart of the City of Charlotte, one of the oldest burial places in the bounds of the City.

The list of "heads of families" in this District are not so very numerous, but they are of exceeding interest to the student of genealogy. By the way, among them is a HEZEKIAH ALEXANDER — the only one we have found on the list - but he appears to have been a very young man, having a wife and one child, a daughter, and the owner of one slave. Since it is stated on good authority by several sources that Hezekiah "the signer" was a brother of JOHN McKNITT ALEXANDER, the writer is constrained to believe that this particular Hezekiah was a nephew, or the son of the "signer", and not the one who attached his name to the Mecklenburg Declaration. Another person of interest whose name is written here is ROBERT CRAIGHEAD, doubtless a son of the patriarchial ALEXANDER CRAIGHEAD who it is claimed, more than anyone else sent forth the seed of political and religious freedom from which sprang the almost spontaneous "resolves" of 1775, that sent Capt. James Jack speeding on that momentous mission to Philadelphia. If Robert Craighead was his son, then he was a brother in law of the famous DR. DAVID CALDWELL, who had married his sister, and a brother of REV. THOMAS CRAIGHEAD, the famous minister of Nashville, Tennessee.

The name of ALEXANDER QUERY appears on this list, blessed with a family of four sons and three daughters, evidently a relative in some degree of JOHN QUEARY, another one of the famous "signers" of the Declaration. Another name is that of WILLIAM PICKENS, evidently ayoung man, married, but without children, who may have been a son of CAPT. SAMUEL PICKENS who lived in an adjoining district on the other side of ROCKY RIVER, of whom see later.

The name of EZEKIEL SHARPE appears on this list, obviously a nephew of JOHN McKNITT ALEXANDER and one of the sons of JEMIMAH SHARPE, a sister of John McKnitt Alexander, who was named for his distinguished uncle.

The names of JOHN, JAMES, Sr., JAMES Jr., and THOMAS SLOAN, appearing on this list among the others brings forth a long list of connections in many of the Western and Southern States, who claim, and have established, connection with the Sloan family of North Carolina, between the YADKIN and the CATAWBA.

DISTRICT NO. 6

This District was the home of the Secretary of the Mecklenburg Convention of May 19th and 20th 1775 - HON. JOHN McKNITT ALEXANDER. His home was near WHITE'S BRANCH and the waters of CLARK'S CREEK, some nine or ten miles North of "Charlotte Town" and the District embraced all of the territory between his home, which he called "INDEPENDENCE HILL", and the Catawba River, including the land lying in the bounds of HOPEWELL PRESBYTERIAN CHURCH, in which he was a life long member. The width of the District was evidently measured by the meanderings of LONG CREEK on the South and McDOWELL'S — sometimes called BARRY'S - CREEK, on the North. The names on this list are interesting because of the fact that within its bounds resided the patriots who made Mecklenburg County, what General Tarlton declared it to be, a "regular hornet's nest" for the British Army, during the revolution. Not all of the membership of the Hopewell Presbyterian Church, however, resided in the bound. of this District, because some lived farther away and the membership of that famous place of religious worship lapped over into District No. 5, No. 7 and others adjoining. It was at Hopewell Churchyard that General William Lee Davidson was buried at the dead hours of midnight by his faithful friends, after he was shot from his horse at Cowan's Ford on the Catawba in District No. 7, as shown on the map. Matthew, George and Alexander Robison, kinsmen of the Sugar Creek Robisons, resided in this District, as did the Elliotts, another prominent family, the Galbraiths, some of the Crocketts, Mathias Hammond, the McClures, David Russell, John Peoples and John and James Sharpe, nephews of the old Secretary of the Convention. It is probable that Mrs. Jemimah Sharpe, their mother, resided close to Huntersville, and near her brother John McKnitt Alexander, but whether in District 6, 5 or 4, is problematical. At any rate she was not far away from "Independence Hill", the home of the old Secretary. A much better idea of just who lived and died in the bounds of the District may be gleaned from the Cemetery Records of Hopewell Presbyterian Church, which will be found later herein, with dates, etc.

DISTRICT NO. 7

To the writer District No. 7, as portrayed on the accompanying map, is one of the most interesting of all the several areas in Mecklenburg County. Thousands of people all over the Southern States can trace their ancestry to the "heads of families" that appear on this list, and it is a heritage of which they may well be proud. To delve into the background and history of these men has been an absorbing past-time for this compiler, though many long years, and it will be a difficult task to set down these facts without a certain display of partiality in favor of the subjects. At least two "signers" of the Mecklenburg Declaration lived (for the greater part of their lives) and died in the bounds of this strip of territory. They were RICHARD BARRY and MAJOR JOHN DAVIDSON. Many of the members of numerous patriotic Societies, including the Daughters of the American Revolution proudly ride into membership on the coat tails of these two outstanding patriots of the American Revolution. Richard Barry was one of the faithful followers of General William Lee Davidson, who under cover of darkness and at the risk of their lives and liberty, helped to deposit his remains in the old churchyard at Hopewell Presbyterian Church where they rest today, properly marked, after many years of neglect. The story of the BARRY and DAVIDSON families will be inadequately told in the remaining pages of this volume, somewhere, if the writer lives to set it down in his crude and awkward way.

Here lived at least seven of the members of the famous Alexander family, who were then heads of families, namely! AMOS, MOSES, ARON, DAVID, DANIEL, JOEL and ISAAC. Here lived the BLYTHE family, with SAMUEL and RICHARD heading the two families of the name; Hugh Bryson, a relative of the Davidsons by marriage; John and Walter Bell, JAMES CURRY and WILLIAM NILL, a bunch of patriots named DUCK, David and Daniel DAVIS, Joseph and James Gillespie; the Gilmores and GIVENS families, and WILLIAM GRAHAM, another one of the famous "Signers" - making three who lived in this district in 1790. (This shows that these temporary census districts did not co-incide with the Districts from which men were elected as delegates to the convention in 1775, from which only two members were elected by the residents).

This District (No. 7) was also the home of the POTTS FAMILY, the PEELES, who came from Northeastern N. C., JAMES, JOHN and ROBERT PRICE, one of whom married MARY DAVIDSON, sister of MAJ. JOHN DAVIDSON; also living in this section in 1790 were DAVID and JOHN SLOAN, DAVID HUTCHINSON, BENJAMIN and JOSEPH CLARK, the distinguished SAMUEL WILSON, father in law of MAJ. JOHN DAVIDSON, and Great Grandfather of JAMES KNOX POLK, who was the grandson of his daughter MRS. EZEKIEL POLK. Other WILSONS on the list include JOHN, JOSEPH, DAVID and BENJAMIN. These relationships may be discussed later on. This was also the home of JOHN and WILLIAM WYLIE, though the name is spelled "WILLIE" or "WILIE" on the U. S. records.

Between Cowan's Ford and Beattie's Ford, on the Catawba, and a short distance from the old river itself, as attempted to be portrayed on the map, is the burial place of that early religious patriot and missionary REV. JOHN THOMSON, known as Baker's Graveyard. In this place also sleep the last remains of MARY PRICE, sister of Maj. John Davidson; HUGH LAWSON, father in law of HUGH BARRY and SAMUEL BAKER. Up to some fifty years ago there were crude head and foot stones, on one of which was carved the initials "H-L" marking the grave of HUGH LAWSON. Now the spot is a shambles, yielding at last to the ravages of centuries, its enclosing stone fence torn down to build a highway for the modern, speeding generations. The stately oaks, under which Rev. John Thomson delivered his stirring pioneer sermons between 1751 and 1753, no longer spread their sacred foliage to the Catawba breezes, but there are still signs of unmistakable import that they once marked the hallowed spot, now passing into the oblivion of forgotten history.

DISTRICT NO. 8

These numbered Districts (arbitrarily numbered by the compiler, in the order in which the several distinguishable groups of names are officially published by the Government) now shift to the Northern side of ROCKY RIVER, in which all of the territory covered is now in CABARRUS COUNTY, which was erected out of Mecklenburg the next year (1791) after the Census was taken. If there was a "signer" of the Declaration who resided in this District (No. 8) it was ROBERT HARRIS, ESQ., who is accredited with a wife and family consisting of two sons and two daughters, and whose standing was marked in the community by being the owner of eleven slaves. The ROBERT HARRIS, whom JOHN BREVARD ALEXANDER, in his History, declares was properly listed as a signer (instead of RICHARD HARRIS, whose name is on the monument in the courthouse yard) was a brother of JAMES HARRIS, whom we identify as probably CAPT. JAMES HARRIS, of District No. 13, although there is another James Harris who lived in THIS DISTRICT. The family Historian, MISS CLARA HARRIS, of Concord, N. C., in a letter to the compiler, admits that the real identity of neither JAMES HARRIS or RICHARD or ROBER! HARRIS

372

has never been positively determined, since there were so many persons of the same name living contemporaneously in the same section, the task has been well nigh an impossible one.

This District, like many of the others, has representatives of the numerous Alexander family listed on the 1790 census, two heads of families being CAPTAIN STEPHEN and JOSIAH ALEXANDER. In this District lived two BROWNS, Benjamin and Samuel, two of the BENSONS, Thomas and Robert, James Bell and James Bradford and JAMES CARRIGAN, DENNIS COPELAND, and ISAAC, JOHN and DAVID DAVIS; John and ARCHIBALD GILMORE, JAMES GILLESPIE and three members of the HOUSTON family in the persons of JOHN and DAVID and CAPT. ARCHIBALD HOUSTON. DAVID TEMPLETON is also on this list, which indicates that some of these families lived in the upper section of the District, near ROWAN COUNTY, which was the home of many of the name HOUSTON. MOSES and ROBERT ANDREWS are also on the list.

Another interesting name on this list is that of CAPT. SAMUEL PICKENS, who in 1790 had three sons under 16 years of age and three daughters. One of these sons (b. in 1780) became Governor of the State of Alabama in 1821, the celebrated ISRAEL PICKENS – his brother EZEKIEL also went to Alabama and became a member of the highest court in the State. The latter died an old bachelor, but after a useful and distinguished career as a Judge on the bench of his adopted State. Captain Samuel Pickens was a brother in law of COL. JAMES WALKUP, who lived in District 17, an abstract of whose last will and testament will be found among the will records published in this volume. Colonel Walkup married MARGARET PICKENS, a sister of Captain Samuel.

DISTRICT NO. 9

This District, on the North side of ROCKY RIVER and extending to the line of ROWAN COUNTY, was the home of JOHN PHIFER, whose name does not appear on the 1790 list, but who was a son of MARTIN PHIFER, who had three sons, JOHN (the signer), MARTIN and GEORGE. Martin Phifer, the father, was a student of Hampden-Sydney College in Virginia. In this District also appears the name of a DAVID HOUSTON and that of CAPTAIN WILLIAM HOUSTON; the name of JOHN ALLISON and of JOHN ARMSTRONG SR. and his son JOHN JR., also JOHN, CHRISTOPHER and JOSHUA BAKER, and ROBERT BIGGER; three GLOVERS, three persons named HOLBROOK and ROBERT and RICHARD MARTIN. Samuel, Alexander and ROBERT PATTERSON lived in this District also, with five heads of families named ROGERS, including JOSEPH, MOSES, THOMAS, JAMES and SETH ROGERS; also a JOHN ROGERS. Another interesting set of persons were BENJAMIN, SAMUEL and JOSEPH PATTON, whose sons, some of them, migrated Westward and had much to do with the laying off and building of ASHVILLE, in Buncombe County, the site of which was owned by the firm of PATTON & ERWIN. This District was also the home of LUDOWICK, JEDIAH and JOHN WALLACE.

DISTRICT NO. 10.

MARTIN PHIFER, perhaps the father of CALEB, MARTIN and JOHN PHIFER (the signer) lived in this District. He is listed as "SR", indicating that he had a son MARTIN. He perhaps lived on the East side of "Scotch Buffalo" Creek, while his sons lived on the West side, with just the Creek between them. The name of NAT and GEORGE ROGERS appear also on this list, doubtless of the same breed as those in the Ninth District – just across the creek. We note that there were no less than four "heads of families" by the name of TOWNSEND living in this District – HENRY, WILLIAM, DUDLEY and GEORGE TOWNSEND. There were three persons named LEWIS – JACOB, CHRISTOPHER and the widow LEWIS. I wonder where they fit in the Lewis family History? There were no less than five "heads" by the name of CORZINE, and the only place I have run across that name was among some of the pioneers of early Texas history.

On this list I find the name of CHRISTIAN GOODNIGHT, which suggests the bare possibility that in this Mecklenburg research I may have run across the ancestor of the famous Texas cattle baron, the late CHARLES GOODNIGHT, who died a few years ago full of wealth, years and all the glamorous experiences of the Great plains country. He it was who preserved the almost extinct BUFFALO and kept it from dying out altogether. That his ancestors lived on "DUTCH BUFFALO CREEK" in Mecklenburg County (now CABARRUS), North Carolina, would be quite a coincidence. The entry shows that Christian Goodnight, in 1790, then had FOUR SONS all under 16 years of age. As Captain CHARLES GOODNIGHT lived to near the ripe age of 100 years it would be possible for him to have been a grandson of this entry.

DISTRICT NO. 11

The names on this list are of apparent Dutch origin, and it must have been the character of these settlers which gave the name "DUTCH BUFFALO" to the stream along which they settled. We find the names of ANDREW and ADAM CRUSE, doubtless ancestors of families of the name we have found in various parts of the West. The name BARRINGER appears; several persons named GOODMAN (a very common name throughout the country now); one CHRISTIAN GREGORY, one ALLEN and at least one person by the name of BROWN; otherwise there are few names in this section that one finds mentioned in the numerous "family histories" that have been committed to print. Any of the Anglo names found there may have been simply slightly altered to give them a convenient American sound. LONG, for instance, does not sound "Dutch", but research discloses that there was a family of "Dutchmen" living there at this period bearing the name LONG. HENRY LONG'S name is on this list. JACOB LONG, of the "Dutch family" of the name is found buried in an old cemetery in the Northern part of Union County — one a part of Mecklenburg - near Goose Creek, called "Bethlehem". There were no "signers" living in District No. 11 in 1790, so far as this record discloses.

DISTRICT NO. 12

This list is headed by the name of PAUL BARRINGER, with JOHN BARRINGER listed a few names lower down. Many of the family names on this list are the same as those in District 11, as this part of the District was the home of the same class of settlers as the one below it. It is obvious that the settlement, extending from ROCKY RIVER to the line of ROWAN COUNTY was a long one, and it was found convenient to divide it in taking the census.

DISTRICT NO. 13

This was the CONCORD DISTRICT and the POPLAR TENT CHURCH settlement, now a part of CABARRUS COUNTY, which was cut off from Mecklenburg in 1791, the year after the census was taken. Strange to relate only one ALEXANDER'S name appears on this list, that of WILLIAM S. ALEXANDER. To the writer his identity is uncertain, but he may have been the WILLIAM ALEXANDER who later settled in TENNESSEE. This was the home of the HARRIS FAMILY, including the CAPTAIN JAMES HARRIS, who must have been one of the "Signers" of the Declaration of May 20, 1775. Likewise there was a ROBERT HARRIS, JR. on this list, who could have been the "signer" whom Dr. Alexander in his History declares signed instead of RICHARD HARRIS, whose name was placed on the monument. Another outstanding and numerous family of this settlement was that of the MORRISONS, but these were not the immediate "kinnery" of the signer NIELL MORRISON, who lived in another district. See later.

Still another family, the name of which is mentioned in the revolutionary history of Mecklenburg County, was that of the WHITES. On the list is entered the names of JOHN, THOMAS, WILLIAM, ARCHIBALD, DAVID and JAMES WHITE. These boys furnished a part of the crew who concocted what is called the "gun powder plot" in the days of the "regulator" troubles, joined in the enterprise by "Black Billy" Alexander, who could possibly have been the WILLIAM S. ALEXANDER who almost heads this list, or his son. Space here will not permit a repetition of the thrilling story, which has been related in some detail by other writers.

On this list appears the names of ROBERT and DANIEL COLDWELL. While there appears to be a family bearing the name as thus spelled, on the map drawn by Major Joseph Graham the family of this name in the Cabarrus territory, is spelled CALDWELL, so that may have been the correct way to spell it. Undoubtedly, some of these names are erroneously spelled on the lists, but in a case of this kind one cannot always be sure. The names of STUART, CAMPBELL, COCHRAN, PURVIANCE, RUSSELL, ROSS, SCOTT and WALLACE are familiar ones, found in District No. 13.

Of particular interest, and bearing a decided MARYLAND flavor are the last two names on the list, those of ADAM and HUGH EAGER.

The POPLAR TENT CHURCH, which was located in this District, on the upper reaches of ROCKY RIVER and CODDLE CREEK, is a famous land-mark in Mecklenburg History, better told in the wonderful narratives of the Historian William Henry Foote, on which we shall draw for a more extended notice in the proper place.

Owing to the uncertainty as to the identity of the two "Signers" who bore the name of HARRIS we are unable to say with confidence whether this list contains the names of only one or of two of that distinguished group. As for RICHARD HARRIS, JR., whose name appears on the monument, by the insistance, it is said of the Rev. Humphrey Hunter, if his name appears on the census of Mecklenburg County for 1790, we have overlooked it. He could have resided - especially in 1790 - outside the bounds of the county, or he may have died before the census was taken.

DISTRICT NO. 14

The name of COL. ADAM ALEXANDER, one of the immortal "Signers" of the Mecklenburg Declaration heads this list. The year following the enumeration of the inhabitants in this, the first United States census, CABARRUS COUNTY was established and the territory taken from MECKLENBURG. The line between the two counties is indicated on the map by the dotted boundary, and shows that a large part of District No. 14 was left in CABARRUS COUNTY.

COL. ADAM ALEXANDER is the ancestor of a large number of descendants scattered all over the United States - particularly the South. He was residing on ROCKY RIVER as far back as 1756, when the Rev. HUGH McADEN made his celebrated tour through the Carolinas and on his trip through this section was the guest of Col. Alexander, of whom he speaks most glowingly in his famous diary.

Dr. Caldwell refers to COL. ALEXANDER, when President Washington made his Southern tour in 1792, as "far advanced in life". He died in 1798 at the age of 70 years, and the accounts say that he was buried at ROCK SPRINGS. More space will be devoted to Col. Alexander further along in this work.

On this list appears the name of a SAMUEL CROWIN SR. and JR. The writer is quite sure that the spelling in this instance is erroneous, because on the tombstone records in old cemeteries in the area embraced in this District the name is chiselled CROWELL. Of course the later members of this family may have changed the spelling, but it is more than likely that the census taker was in error at the time he made the enumeration.

The name of DAVID and JOHN CUTHBURTSON, JOHN CARUTHERS, the FIRONS, POLKS and ROGERS appear on this list. As for the POLKS, it will be noticed that the bounds of this District, on the West join District No. 3, where the POLKS are known to have lived, and as there were numerous persons of the name by 1790, it is likely that some of them lived over the line in COL. ADAM ALEXANDER'S DISTRICT. In fact, THOMAS POLK, the "signer" may have been elected to serve in the convention from what was at the time a part of the territory of this District No. 14, as was Col. Adam Alexander.

It is certain that the District had one, and possibly two signers, in the persons of COL. ADAM ALEXANDER and possibly THOMAS POLK. The reader, by consulting the map will see that all that territory in this District immediately North or West of GOOSE CREEK, at the time the census was taken and when the convention was held (1775) was in what is now UNION COUNTY, N. C., which was cut off from Mecklenburg in 1842.

DISTRICT NO. 15

This District was the home of the "signer" JOHN QUEARY - spelled on the census list QUARY. It evidently, also, was the home of still another signer, JOHN FORD, who is listed as JOHN FORD, ESQ. The Historian, JOHN BREVARD ALEXANDER, declares that both QUEARY and FORD, resided in that part of MECKLENBURG COUNTY "which now forms Union County", or, as he intended to say, "now a part of Union County", as shown on the map accompanying these notes.

The writer, of course, is personally interested in the fact that his own family name and kinsman appears on this list, immediately following the names of the QUEARY family, viz, ISAAC

RAY, who appears to have had only one son and about four daughters, while the family of the compiler's wife is also well represented by the HUGH, ANDREW and DAVID MOORE, JR., whose names appear just a few notches above on the same list and residing in the same neighborhood. Other collateral kin of our family were the WALKERS - MATTHEW, WILLIAM, MOSES and CAPT. ARCHIBALD WALKER. JOHN BLACK, near the top of the list, followed by EZEKIEL, SAMUEL and WILLIAM SR., accompanied the writer's RAY ancestry over into Tennessee, early in the nineteenth century, with a lot of others, and settled on adjoining lands and along the same romantic streams that trickle through the Tennessee valleys where, with the kin of SAM HOUSTON, we fished and hunted when a barefoot boy. The reader will, of course, excuse this impulsive reference to personal relationships, set down in a paragraph where it does not properly belong, but District No. 15, for the reasons stated, appeals to the sentiment and romance of a childhood, long since fading into the distance of the years that are now tumbling over each other, as we approach the jumping off place.

DISTRICT NO. 16

This was the District in which the town of CHARLOTTE was erected, and wherein the famous Mecklenburg Convention was held in 1775. A careful study of this list will show that the families represented on it apparently came from various parts of the county. Some are on this list who bear the same surnames as are to be found on the tombstones at Providence Church - in fact, many of them. Some are on the list who perhaps lived at one time in the present CABARRUS COUNTY and along the reaches of ROCKY RIVER. There are also some on the list who undoubtedly had kinnery living down in that part of Mecklenburg which is now UNION COUNTY, and the POTTS names on the list are drawn from as far North as IREDELL COUNTY and on down into the WAXHAW and HELL AIRE section of South Carolina. ANDREW SPRATT probably came to the Charlotte section from down around Pineville in District No. 3, while THOMAS WHITE was perhaps one of the Whites who lived over on Rocky River, and - who knows -may have been one of the confederates who helped "Black Billy" Alexander destroy the ammunition that was being brought in to quell the "regulators" - doubtless being a regulator sympathiser himself. ALEXANDER RAMSEY, we almost know, was of a Providence family, and the FINLEYS lived along the CATAWBA, perhaps somewhere above PAW CREEK and LONG CREEK, or even further up stream.

DISTRICT NO. 17

This is the "WAXHAW SECTION" of Mecklenburg County. So far as we have been able to ascertain neither this of District 16, furnished a "signer" to the Declaration, but both sections furnished a lot of fighters to help make it hot for Cornwallis when he invaded North Carolina. It was from this section that Captain WILLIAM RICHARDSON DAVIE collected many of his brave men who went to the rescue of COL. JAMES WALKUP and his home down on LYNCH'S CREEK, when the British arrived in that section. COL. JAMES WALKUP lived in this section, himself; he and all his family. See his will in previous pages of this work.

COL. JOHN BELK, whose name appears near the head of this list, lived near COL. WALKUP in this District, his home being on the upper branches of Lynch's Creek. He was a man of substance and importance, being the owner of broad acres and many slaves. The BELK name still lives in the Charlotte section and the lower part of Mecklenburg County, there being many descendants, who have played important roles in the subsequent history of the county.

The Old Waxhaw Church, a landmark of three centuries, is over the line in South Carolina only a short distance. This was the home of Captain DAVIE and his ancestors, and here he is buried. The story of the part he played in the history of the Mecklenburg Declaration, particularly its preservation, and his political career in the State of North Carolina, is epochal. After a brilliant career in the Old North State, he returned to the Waxhaw settlement to spend his last years and there died and is buried in the old cemetery at the church, where likewise rest the remains of the father of ANDREW JACKSON, a President of the United States.

DISTRICT NO. 18.

This is the PROVIDENCE CHURCH DISTRICT. The name of one of the immortal "signers" is shown on the list - HENRY DOWNS - with his name spelled wrong - the enumerator having written it as DAWNS, but the fame and glory of his deeds cannot be hidden from the view of the encroaching centuries by a mere error of spelling. That this was intended for the signer there can be no doubt. Dr. J. B. Alexander (p. 420) says that he died October 8, 1798, at the age of 70 years and was buried in PROVIDENCE BURIAL GROUND, twelve miles South of Charlotte.

Besides this signer there are many old revolutionary patriots and soldiers who spent the best years of their lives in this District and are buried in the same place where rest the ashes of HENRY DOWNS. Among these was the old patriarch DAVID RAY. His name is spelled REA and the family have used that spelling for several generations, so far as this particular branch is concerned. Other RAYS of the 1790 period listed in this District were JOHN and ANDREW.

On this list also will be found the name of ROGER CUNNINGHAM, ARCHIBALD CROCKETT, ALEXANDER MORRISON, ROBERT and ALEXANDER OSBORN, the SHARPES, PATTERSONS, GALBRAITHS and others, not to omit the BENDS, each of which names brings to mind long vistas of genealogical interest to one who has made a study of these old families and tried to ascertain where they came from and what became of their descendants. See later notes.

DISTRICT NO. 19

This is just an overflow District adjoining the PROVIDENCE CHURCH DISTRICT, and many members of the same families show up on this list. There were many SHARPES in this Section, and also a set of CUNNINGHAMS. It was in this section where the parents of President ANDREW JACKSON resided and where his mother lived at the time of his birth. The Jackson home was on the waters of BEAVER DAM CREEK, a branch of TWELVE-MILE between the little fork just below the figure "18" on the map.

375

However the famous President was not born in this home. At the time of his birth his father had been deceased for some weeks, and his mother went to visit her sisters in the Waxhaws just a mile or so inside of South Carolina, and it was there his birth occurred. Some rather lurid controversies have been based upon the issue thus raised, as to whether "Old Hickory" was a native of North Carolina or South Carolina, both States claiming the honor.

To the writer, whether this President was born in Mecklenburg County, or across the line in South Carolina, is of less interest than the fact that some five or six miles North of the home of the parents of this President, another President, James K. Polk, was born. Even this remarkable fact has its disputants, who declare Polk was born at the home of his grandparents up around Huntersville. But at any rate none have ever questioned Polk's nativity as being elsewhere than in Mecklenburg County.

MATTHEW, GEORGE and WILLIAM WALLACE were residents of District No. 19, and two other notable names the reader will find thereon are CHRISTOPHER IRWIN and JOHN WASHINGTON, which ought to whet the appetite of the student of genealogy for more information on the members of this remarkable group of people.

SIGNERS OF THE "DECLARATION" AND THE CENSUS DISTRICTS IN WHICH THEY LIVED

ABRAHAM ALEXANDER lived in District No. 4
JOHN McKNITT ALEXANDER, Secretary, lived in District No. 6
EPHRAIM BREVARD, Secretary, lived in District No. 2.

REV. HEZEKIAH JAMES BALCH lived in District No. 13.
JOHN PHIFER lived in District No. 9.
CAPT. JAMES HARRIS lived in District No. 13.
JOHN FORD lived in District No. 15.
RICHARD BARRY lived in District No. 7.
HENRY DOWNS lived in District No. 18.
EZRA ALEXANDER lived in District No. 1.
WILLIAM GRAHAM lived in District No. 7.
JOHN QUERY lived in District No. 15.
HEZEKIAH ALEXANDER lived in District No. 4.
ADAM ALEXANDER lived in District No. 14.
CHARLES ALEXANDER lived in District No. 4.
ZACCHEUS WILSON lived in District No. 2.
WAIGHTSTILL AVERY lived in District No. 16.
BENJAMIN PATTON lived in District No. 9.
MATTHEW McCLURE lived in District No. 6.
NEILL MORRISON lived in District No. 3.
ROBERT IRWIN lived in District No. 1.
JOHN FLENNIKEN lived in District No. 19.
DAVID REESE lived in District No. 9.
JOHN DAVIDSON lived in District No. 7.
ROBERT HARRIS lived in District No. 8.
THOMAS POLK lived in District No. 3.
WILLIAM KENNON lived in Rowan County.

RUMPLE, in his History of ROWAN COUNTY says that the appearance of the name of WILLIAM KENNON on the Mecklenburg Declaration "can be accounted for only on the theory that the Mecklenburg patriots had no rigorous committee on credentials on that occasion."

This compiler's theory about COL. WILLIAM KENNON is that, while he practiced law at Salisbury and was Chairman of the Committee of Safety in that County in 1774, he may have resided in the lower edge of ROWAN in the neck contiguous to CENTRE CHURCH, which afterwards became a part of IREDELL COUNTY (the boundary line at which point remained unsettled for many years after 1762, according to Alexander) and that his home was counted as being in MECKLENBURG, and that he may have actually been a resident of Mecklenburg County and of either District 1 or 2 as laid off for the enumeration as shown on the Census map.

WAIGHTSTILL AVERY'S law office was in District No. 16 in the town of CHARLOTTE, but Dr. Alexander says that he made his home with HEZEKIAH ALEXANDER'S family in District No. 4, in the Sugar Creek settlement, after he located in Charlotte and about the time the Mecklenburg Convention was held. What particular group had elected him to the convention is unknown, because the Districts were not bounded as were those shown on the map, which were mere temporary areas fixed for the enumeration of the census only.

THE LEADING MEN OF WEALTH AND INFLUENCE IN MECKLENBURG COUNTY IN THE YEAR 1790

The First United States Census as shown herein on pages 357 to 369 inclusive contains a lot more information than the mere list of names would indicate. These pages and those preceding it, back to 357, are intended as a study of that enumeration, with the idea in mind to draw from the monotonous columns of names all of the data possible of a historic interest or nature.

By segregating the enumeration into sections, comparing those listed with other and contemporaneous records, we have partially, at least, succeeded in ferreting out where these people lived with respect to the geography of the county, as at that period constituted. This is no small accomplishment. By this means, also, we are able to point out with some certainty, the different communities who sent representatives to the Mecklenburg Convention, and who they elected as delegates to that body. Another service of great value.

We know a lot about some of these great men, because enterprising historians of the past have delved into the subject and given us the benefit of the knowledge they thus acquired. But none of them have attempted specifically to point out to us the more wealthy and influential men of that period when public sentiment against a foreign government was gradually taking form in the mind of these people. Again we turn to the "monotony of names" on the 1790 census to see if they throw any light on this point. We find that it does, because, the number of slaves owned by each resident or head of a family is given. That furnishes the "key" that unlocks the "rating" of the men of that day and time. The number of slaves a man owned in 1790 was as expressive of his wealth and standing financially as the number of dollars in his balance in the banks at the present day. The difference is that nowadays a man can hide his bank balance behind the cloak of banking confidence, but in those days the owner of every slave was known. Taking this as a safe criterion, we are able to turn back to the census list of 1790 and point out the wealthy and influential men in Mecklenburg County in the year 1790, because we can judge their worldly wealth; and then as now, wealth meant influence.

In the year 1790 the two wealthiest and most influential men in Mecklenburg County, according to the records were COL. THOMAS POLK and JOHN SPRINGS, who lived in the general vicinity of PINEVILLE, District No. 3, of the census map. JOHN SPRINGS, a son in law of ADAM ALEXANDER, was the owner of 50 slaves, while COLONEL THOMAS POLK had 47. No other planter in the bounds of MECKLENBURG COUNTY had half as many, save one - MAJOR JOHN DAVIDSON with his 26 to WILLIAM POLK'S 21. COL. THOMAS POLK served in the Convention, but JOHN SPRING did not. Of course, each of these men had large bodies of land, on which to use this slave labor, and accordingly automatically were considered the leading planters in their respective communities.

From here on we will take each census district as shown on the map:

DISTRICT NO. 1.- JOHN BEATY, JR. 9 (slaves); NICHOLAS GIBBONY 9; MAJ. JOSEPH GRAHAM 8; JOHN HUNTER, SR. 6; ANDREW McKEE 6; GEORGE CATHEY, JOHN McDOWELL, JOHN SUMPTER and JOHN WILSON 5 each; GEORGE GRAHAM 4; JOSEPH CARROLL, ROBERT ALLISON, ROBERT HUNTER, MICHAEL McCLARY and JAMES SPRATT each with 3 slaves. A few others scattered with a less number.

DISTRICT NO. 2. - JOHN PRICE (brother in law of MAJ. JOHN DAVIDSON) had 13 slaves & JOHN DINKINS 12; ELIJAH SMART, FRANCIS SMART, BENJAMIN THOMAS, SILAS CREEK had nine slaves each; WALTER DAVIS and JOHN McKEE each had 8; JOHN NEELY, JOSEPH DARNELL and RACHEL McCRUM each had six; SAMUEL KNOX SR. (Father of the wife SAMUEL POLK) had 7; JOHN BIGHAM 4; WILLIAM and JAMES PORTER had 4 each; JOHN BIGHAM, GEORGE CATHEY, THOMAS GREER, HUGH HERRON and MATTHEW KNOX each had 5 slaves; rest scattered 1, 2 and 3 each.

DISTRICT NO. 3. (PINEVILLE) - ISAAC COOK 8; Richard MASON 5; WILLIAM PATTERSON 5; CHARLES POLK 9; WILLIAM POLK 21 and JOHN SPRINGS 50; THOMAS POLK 47. The rest negligible.

DISTRICT NO. 4.- (SUGAR CREEK CHURCH DISTRICT) - EZEKIEL ALEXANDER 13; WILLIAM ALEXANDER 11; CAPT. ANDREW ALEXANDER, CAPT. WILLIAM ALEXANDER and WILLIAM ORR had 9 each; DORCAS ALEXANDER (widow of ABRAHAM) had 8; CAPT. THOMAS ALEXANDER, AGNES ALLEN and JAMES ORR each had 6; SAMUEL BATEY (BEATTY), SAMUEL DAVIS, DAVID PARKS and EZEKIEL WALLACE each had 4, and WILLIAM WYLIE had two. A few scattered.

DISTRICT NO. 5. - COL. ROBERT SMITH had 15 slaves; COL. GEORGE ALEXANDER 11; WILLIAM BLACK 7; ANDREW ALEXANDER and JAMES WALLACE each had 6; JOSEPH YOUNG 5, and REV. ROBERT ARCHIBALD (the preacher owned slaves in those days), ROBERT CRAIGHEAD (son of a preacher), and EVAN SHELBY each had 4.

DISTRICT NO. 6. - JOHN McKNITT ALEXANDER and CAPT. JAMES KNOX owned most of them, the first having 16 and the second 15; JOHN DAVIDSON (merchant John) had 9; MATTHEW McCLURE (the signer) had 6 and BEATY McCOY 5. The rest were 3, 2 and 1 slave owners. Most of them had none.

DISTRICT No. 7. - MAJ. JOHN DAVIDSON had 26 slaves; JOHN BROADWAY had 16 and TURNER HUNT had 15; CAPT. ARCHIBALD CATHEY and EDWARD GIVVENS had 11 each; HUGH TORRENCE was the owner of 12, and ROBERT POTTS owned 10 slaves. PATRICK HAMPTON and SAMUEL WILSON JR. each had 9; JAMES COOK, AMOS ALEXANDER, WILLIAM HENDERSON, JR. each had 6 slaves; JAMES PEELE, SR. had 5; JAMES CONNOR, JAMES EMERSON, SAMUEL GARRISON and WILLIAM GRAHAM (a signer) had 4 each; THOMAS McCORKLE had six; DAVID SMITH had 5. The rest scattering 2s and 1nbs.

DISTRICT NO. 8, across ROCKY RIVER in CABARRUS COUNTY. - Sam BOWMAN 3; REESE PRUIE 13; MARGARET FARR 6; BENJAMIN LEWIS 4, CAPT. SAMUEL PICKENS 5, and ROBERT HARRIS, ESQ. 11. Balance owned one, two or three slaves - just a few more.

DISTRICT No. 9. - COL. CALEB PHIFER owned 19 and CAPT. MARTIN PHIFER 16 (The latter's son JOHN PHIFER was a "signer"); JOHN ARMSTRONG and FRANCIS LOCK owned 5 each; CAPT. WILLIAM HOUSTON and JOHN MEANS owned 4 each, and ALEXANDER PATTERSON and JOSEPH ROGERS each owned 3 slaves.

DISTRICT NO. 10. - MARTIN PHIFER SR., like his relatives across the line in District No. 9, was a considerable slave owner (as well, no doubt, as a land owner), and was the owner of 14 slaves. JAMES and ROBERT RUSSELL owned seven slaves each; Captain JOSEPH SHINN and a JOHN SIMINER each had six slaves, the widow FERGUSON had five and WALTER FARR and WILLIAM WHITE each had one. Not many slaves in this District.

DISTRICT NO. 11. - Only fourteen slaves were owned in this entire District. Apparently the Dutch emigrants who settled East of DUTCH BUFFALO and along the line of MONTGOMERY COUNTY did not believe much in slavery. JOHN LIPPARD had 5, JESSE HERRON 3, MATHIAS BARRINGER 2 and JOHN BUSSARD, ELIJAH HERRON, PHILLIP CREPS and HENRY PROPS each had one slave. That was all.

DISTRICT NO. 12. - There were a total of 20 slaves in this entire District which ran South to ROCKY RIVER, but of these COL. PAUL BARRINGER owned 13, his brother JOHN BARRINGER 2, JOHN FUHR 3 and PAUL FUHR and PHILLIP LIDAKER 1 each.

DISTRICT NO. 13. - This was the POPLAR TENT and CONCORD DISTRICT and the settlers owned lands and slaves somewhat in proportion to the other settlements South of Rocky River. SAMUEL HARRIS was the largest slave owner, with a total of 11, and CAPT. ROBERT HARRIS came next with eight of them, while CAPT. JAMES HARRIS owned six. This places the HARRIS FAMILY of this District at the top of the list of families who were prosperous in those old days, a place that perhaps was consistently maintained throughout the years before and immediately following the revolution. Next to them there was a certain CAPT. ARCHABALD McCURDY who had six slaves, also a JAMES PLUNKETT, SR. with a like number. WILLIAM S. ALEXANDER, OLIVER WYLIE and DAVID WHITE each owned four, while those who had 3 each were ALEXANDER FERGUSON, JOSEPH HOWELL, ROBERT McMURRAY, JAMES RUSSELL, WILLIAM ROSS and ADAM EAGER. JAMES MORRISON and JOHN WHITE had 2 each.

DISTRICT NO. 14. - This was the home of COL. ADAM ALEXANDER, but apparently in 1790 he did not own as many slaves as some of his neighbors. Possibly at that time he had distributed much of his property among his children, since his son in law, COL. JOHN SPRINGS, of the PINEVILLE DISTRICT (No. 3) was the largest slave holder in the entire county, with a total of 50. This may account for the fact that in 1790 COL. ADAM ALEXANDER only had five slaves to his credit. MAJ. JAMES HARRIS with 13 slaves topped the list in DISTRICT 14, and ALLEN FREEMAN SR. came next with a dozen. MICHAEL GARMAN and the "WIDOW GARMAN" each had 9 and 8 respectively, and JOHN CARROTHERS owned 7, CAPT. THOMAS SHELLY owned five slaves and JAMES ROGERS had 5. CAPT. CHARLES POLK and SAMUEL SMITH, SR. had 4 each, CAPT. WILLIAM BAIN owned three and JOHN McCOY and HUGH ROGERS had 2 each.

DISTRICT NO. 15. - This entire District owned only 35 slaves, apportioned as follows: JOHN FORD, ESQ. "the signer" had 7, and TUNIS HOOD, SR. had 7; JAMES McCOMBS had 5, and CAPT. TUNIS HOOD 4. JOHN and EZEKIEL BLACK, and NEHEMIAH HARRISON had 2 each each, and WILLIAM BLACK, SR., WILLIAM MORRIS, FREDERICK SHAVER, JAMES COUL and JAMES DOUGLAS, ESQ. each had 1.

DISTRICT NO. 16. - By far the largest slave owner and the richest man in this District, which comprised the territory in which the present town of Charlotte is located, was CAPT. WILLIAM POTTS, who was the owner of fourteen slaves; his son JOHN POTTS having 3. JOHN HOWIE and JAMES HOUSTON had 5 each, HUGH HOUSTON and the Widow HAGENS had 4 each, REUBEN BASDELL had 3, and SHERROD GRAY and MICHAEL SECREST had 2 each. Those having only one each were THOMAS COCHRAN SR., WILLIAM HOUSTON SR. and JR., MARTHA LEWIS and JAMES STOREY. A few others scattered.

DISTRICT NO. 17. - COL. JAMES WALKUP and JOHN BELK ESQ., were the largest slave owners in the "Waxhaw Section" of Mecklenburg. Walkup had 9 slaves and Belk had 8. JAMES AVENT and DRURY VINCENT had 4 each, as did CAPT. ROBERT DAVIS and CAPT. JOSEPH FORRESTER. ALEXANDER CAIRNS, CHARLES COOK, CAPT. ANDREW WALKER and HUGH McCAIN each had 3 slaves, while MOSES FAGGETT, JOHN STEVENSON, JAMES LASHLEY, THOMAS LACKEY and JOHN McELROY each had one slave.

DISTRICT NO. 18. - WILLIAM McKEE owned six, JAMES BREWSTER 5 and JAMES SHANKS 4 slaves in 1790. HENRY DOWNS "Signer" of the Declaration had 3 slaves only. WALTER BEATY, ARCHIBALD CROCKETT, ISAIAH HARRISON, JOSEPH REED, JOHN ROBINSON and JOHN SPRINGS, SR. each had 2 slaves. There were an even dozen other planters with only one slave each.

DISTRICT NO. 19. - Between Beaver Dam Creek and Six Mile Creek, where ANDREW JACKSON SR. resided, had a total of 11 slave owners in 1790, the largest of which was CAPT. CHARLES ALEXANDER who owned six slaves. The "Widow" WILSON owned 4 slaves, and JOHN KIRKPATRICK, JOHN McCULLOCH and ROBERT PHILLIPS each had three slaves. DANIEL BEHAM, JAMES BAXTER, NATHANIEL CUNNINGHAM, JOHN SWANN, WILLIAM WILSON, ESQ. and ELI ALEXANDER each owned one slave.

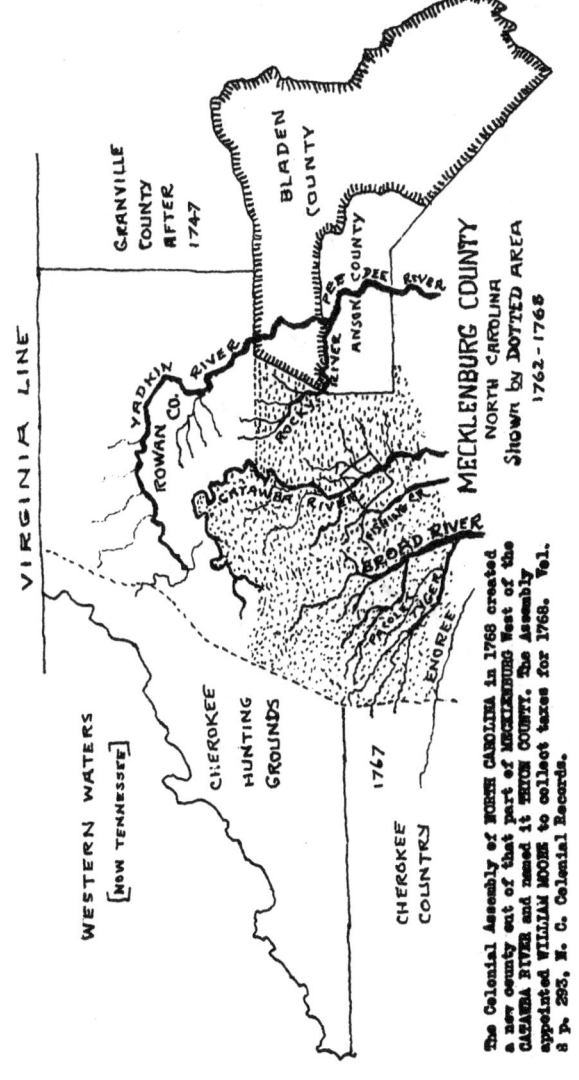

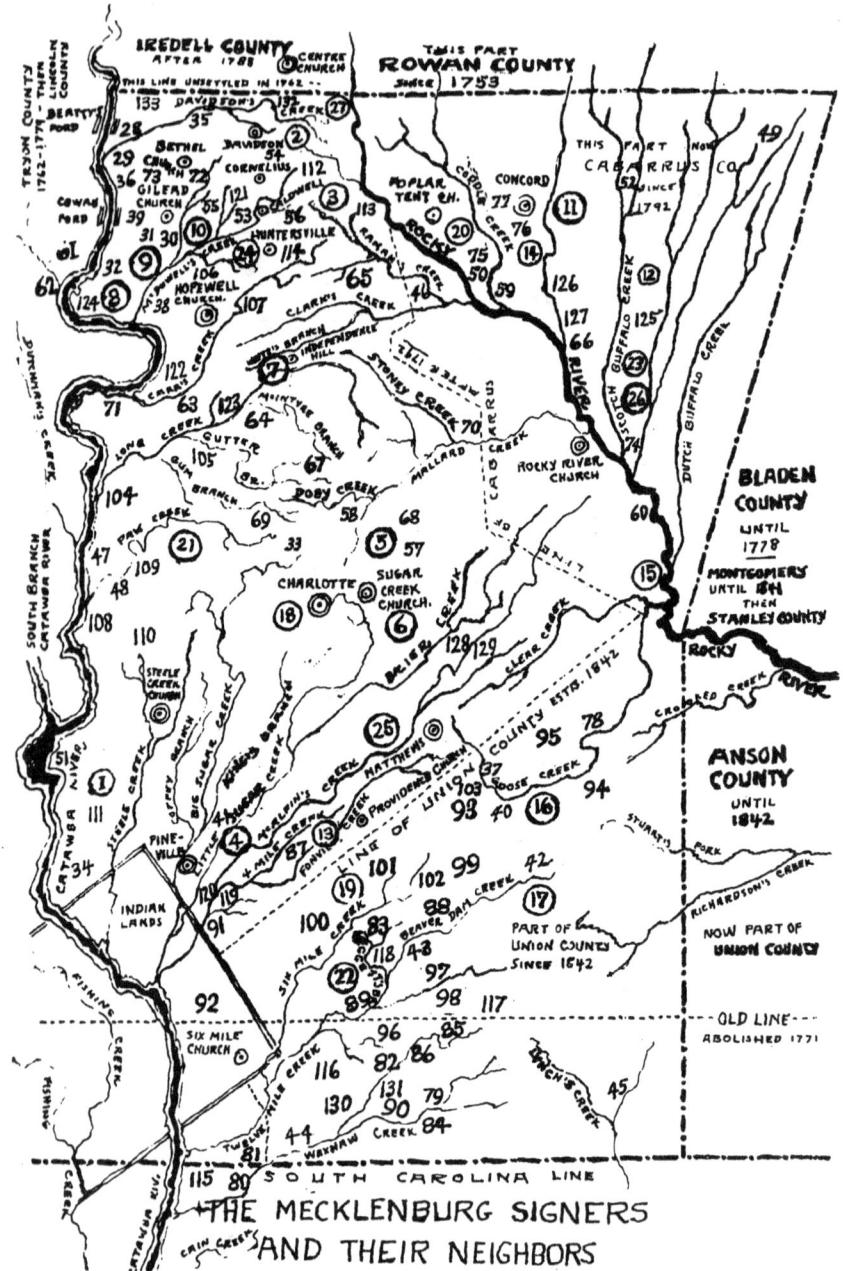

THE MECKLENBURG SIGNERS AND THEIR NEIGHBORS

MAP OF MECKLENBURG COUNTY showing where they lived. The numbers designating the location of the homes of the SIGNERS are RINGED. The "key" to this map will be found on the opposite page. Over 100 families besides the signers are shown. The data for this compilation is based on records of deeds, places of burial, old historical references, and the MAP DRAWN IN JANUARY, 1789 BY MAJOR JOSEPH GRAHAM. Studies of most of these families have been prepared to follow the numbers laid down on MAP.

"KEY" TO THE MAP ON THE OPPOSITE PAGE, SHOWING THE MECKLENBURG SIGNERS AND THEIR NEIGHBORS

THE SIGNERS
(Ringed)

(1) ROBERT IRWIN
(2) EPHRAIM BREVARD
(3) ZACCHEUS WILSON
(4) THOMAS POLK
(5) ABRAHAM ALEXANDER
(6) HEZEKIAH ALEXANDER
(7) JOHN McKNITT ALEXANDER
(8) MAJ. JOHN DAVIDSON
(9) RICHARD BARRY
(10) WILLIAM GRAHAM

CHURCHES

CENTRE CHURCH
HOPEWELL CHURCH
SUGAR CREEK CHURCH
POPLAR TENT CHURCH
ROCKY RIVER CHURCH
STEELE CREEK CHURCH
PROVIDENCE CHURCH
GILLEAD CHURCH

(11) ROBERT HARRIS, JR.
(12) JOHN PHIFER
(13) NEILL MORRISON
(14) COLT. JAMES HARRIS
(15) COL. ADAM ALEXANDER
(16) JOHN FORD

(17) JOHN QUEARY
(18) WAIGHTSTILL AVERY
(19) HENRY DOWNS
(20) HEZEKIAH JAMES BALCH
(21) EZRA ALEXANDER
(22) CHARLES ALEXANDER
(23) BENJAMIN PATTON
(24) MATTHEW McCLURE
(25) JOHN FLENNIKEN
(26) DAVID REESE
(27) WILLIAM KENNON

THEIR NEIGHBORS:

28. SAMUEL BAKER
29. BAKER'S GRAVEYARD
30. HUGH BARRY
31. ANDREW BARRY
32. SAMUEL WILSON
33. MRS. MARY GRAHAM
34. JOHN BIGGERS
35. HUGH LAWSON
36. JOHN MORROW, SR.
37. DAVID MOORE
38. CHARLES MOORE
39. JAMES McKNIGHT
40. ROBERT McKNIGHT
41. EZEKIEL POLK
42. MATTHEW McCORKLE
43. JAMES HARRISON
44. COL. JAMES WALKUP
45. COL. JOHN BELK
46. WILLIAM PICKENS
47. COL. JOSEPH GRAHAM
48. GEORGE CATHEY
49. MATTHEW BARRINGER
50. COL. THOMAS HARRIS
51. JOHN PRICE
52. CAPT. CALEB PHIFER
53. WILLIAM MAXWELL
54. ANDREW CATHEY
55. JOSEPH MOORE, SR.
56. JAMES KNOX
57. ELIJAH ALEXANDER
58. DAVID PARKS
59. COL. ADAM PHIFER
60. ROSS' MILL
61. JACOB FORNEY
62. MILES ABERNATHY

63. JAMES McINTYRE
64. ARCHIBALD McDOWELL
65. JEMIMAH SHARPE
66. CAPT. SAMUEL PICKENS
67. CAIRNS HENDERSON
68. JOHN McGEE
69. ROBERT MONTGOMERY
70. CAPT. DAVID CALDWELL
71. WILLIAM HENDERSON, SR.
72. CAPT. ARCHIBALD CATHEY
73. WILLIAM POTTS
74. ALEXANDER PATTERSON
75. SAMUEL HARRIS
76. ARCHIBALD WHITE
77. ROBERT MORRISON
78. WILLIAM HOUSTON, SR.
79. JOHN FINDLEY
80. MAJ. ROBERT CRAWFORD
81. JAMES CRAWFORD
82. GEORGE McKEMIE
83. ANDREW JACKSON, SR.
84. WILLIAM MOORE
85. JOHN CROCKETT
86. JOHN DAVIS
87. ANDREW CROCKETT
88. JOHN STURGEON
89. HUGH BARNETT
90. JAMES WILLIAMSON
91. JAMES DAVIS
92. JAMES McKNIGHT MORROW
93. ROGER CUNNINGHAM
94. NEHEMIAH HARRISON
95. ARCHIBALD CAMPBELL
96. HUGH McCAIN
97. MOSES McWHORTER
98. JAMES McCORKLE

99. EDWARD SHARPE, SR.
100. DAVID RAY
101. ARCHIBALD CROCKETT
102. DAVID HOUSTON
103. DAVID MOORE, SR.
104. ROBERT ALLISON
105. JOHN CUMMINS
106. ROBERT CROCKETT
107. ANDREW DUNN
108. JOHN BERRYHILL
109. DAVID BROWN
110. JOSEPH CARROLL
111. JOHN LOVE
112. ROBERT BARNETT
113. JAMES SPRATT
114. WILLIAM DUNN
115. OLD WAXHAW CHURCH
116. WIDOW IESLEY
117. JOHN McELROY
118. THOMAS EWING
119. ROBERT GALBRAITH
120. DAVID CROCKETT
121. PATRICK HAMPTON
122. JOHN CANNON
123. JOHN DAVIDSON
124. WILLIAM CALDWELL
125. CHRISTOPHER BAKER
126. SAMUEL BROWN
127. JAMES CARRIGAN
128. JOHN McKEMIE WILSON
129. EZEKIEL WALLACE
130. NATHANIEL CUNNINGHAM
131. WILLIAM CUNNINGHAM
132. MOSES WHITE
133. WILLIAM CONNOR

NOTE: A few names of persons and places are on the list and noted by numbers on the map that were not strictly within the County, such, for instance, as CENTER and OLD WAXHAW CHURCH and Col. Jacob Forney. But they were all "neighbors" in a real sense.

CENTRE CHURCH

Dr. J. B. Alexander, in his fine History of Mecklenburg County, published in 1902, makes the following observation with respect to the boundary line of MECKLENBURG COUNTY, to be considered in connection with the location of CENTRE CHURCH:

> "The boundary of MECKLENBURG was marked off in 1762 - that is, the eastern, southern and western borders; the northern or NORTHWESTERN was not marked off, but was left open to see where it would be settled up, so as to DRAW THE BOUNDARY LINE."

Considering the facts as thus stated, it is easy to see just why many of the early settlers of the upper NORTHWESTERN part of MECKLENBURG COUNTY, in the general neighborhood of the present location of DAVIDSON COLLEGE, were in doubt, perhaps for many years, as to whether they were residents of ROWAN or MECKLENBURG. In Dr. Foote's account of what he calls "Centre Congregation", and in Rev. Hugh McAden's famous diary and account of his visit through Mecklenburg (p. 168 Foote's Sketches), it is plain that the location of the meeting house of CENTRE, was moved about several times from one place to another, and it appears more than probable that for a time, at least it was located on the MECKLENBURG side of the line. Eventually, however, it appears to have been finally located in what is now IREDELL COUNTY, some distance North of the town of DAVIDSON, where the College of that name is situated. McADEN made his trip through the country in 1755, two years after the death of REV. JOHN THOMSON, admitted pioneer minister of Mecklenburg County, whose place of burial has been questioned, a matter that will be discussed under the notes pertaining to BAKER'S GRAVEYARD.

Dr. WILLIAM HENRY FOOTE on page 433 says:

> "The boundaries of CENTRE CONGREGATION were originally large, and with the limits of THIATIRA, filled a broad space from the CATAWBA to the YADKIN; they began at JOHN CATHEY'S, south of BEATTIE'S FORD, on the Catawba; from thence to MATTHEW McCORKLE'S and THOMAS HARRIS'S; from thence to DAVID KERR'S, on the old SALISBURY ROAD; from thence to GALBRAITH NAILS' northeast corner; from thence down the river to the first named place".

It is plain from this that CENTRE CHURCH had its Southwestern boundary at the home of JOHN CATHEY, well down in MECKLENBURG on the CATAWBA RIVER towards the home of RICHARD BARRY and MAJOR JOHN DAVIDSON'S place; that a line (the Southern one) extended East from that point clear to the ROCKY RIVER about where CODDLE CREEK joins that stream from the East, and where THOMAS HARRIS had his mill. From there the Eastern line extended North to the Salisbury road and turned back West towards the Catawba, crossing the territory now in IREDELL COUNTY, then back down the river into Mecklenburg. Thus, it is probable that all of the Northern part of Mecklenburg County, beginning a little above or about where HOPEWELL CHURCH is now located, was in the territory occupied by the membership of CENTRE, and that the area included many miles of what is now IREDELL COUNTY, where the BREVARDS, OSBORNS, WINSLOWS, McCONNELLS and some of the TORRENCES lived. The CARRUTHS also lived in this territory, as we learn from the McADEN JOURNAL.

These early families, occupying the territory immediately above DAVIDSON'S CREEK, and the present DAVIDSON COLLEGE site, were perhaps kept in doubt for some years after 1762, when Mecklenburg County was established, as to just which county they lived in. In fact the records at CHARLOTTE and also at SALISBURY indicate that members of the jury were sometimes drawn from this settlement to serve in both counties; also that wills of persons deceased, who perhaps died in Mecklenburg, were placed on record in ROWAN, and after 1788 in IREDELL COUNTY.

One of the most important historical links in this geographical puzzle is the map made by GEN. JOSEPH GRAHAM, and dated January 16, 1789, after the close of the American Revolution. This map does not specifically draw the line between Mecklenburg and Rowan Counties or IREDELL County, but does depict what is called "Lord Granville's Line", evidently intended to be and treated as the line between these counties at that time (1789). It is from this map that the writer, with the aid of other written accounts, has been able to determine the approximate places of residence of many of the early pioneers of Mecklenburg County, including the home of COL. JOSEPH GRAHAM himself, West of Charlotte and on the banks of the CATAWBA. From the paragraph quoted by the writer from Dr. Foote, above, the home of JOHN CATHEY is located, though later his sons GEORGE and ANDREW relocated themselves on other lands, lower down.

DR. FOOTE further says (p. 433): The first Presbytery that met between the two rivers held its sessions in CENTRE; the first meeting of the Concord Presbytery was in CENTRE, and there too, the "SYNOD OF THE CAROLINAS" was organized. The tradition is, that the first white child born between the two rivers (Yadkin and Catawba) was in CENTRE, in a tent pitched upon a broad, flat rock; the name of the child is not certain, supposed however to be MARY BARNETT, grand-daughter of THOMAS SPRATT, that settled finally near CHARLOTTE, and held the first court of MECKLENBURG COUNTY at his house.

The location of CENTRE meeting house, says Foote also, was a matter of compromise in 1765. By the persuasions of the delegates sent by the Synod of Philadelphia, the various preaching places were given up, and a center spot chosen for the permanent worship of the large congregation, which lies partly in each of two counties, IREDELL and MECKLENBURG.

HOPEWELL PRESBYTERIAN CHURCH

"The History of Hopewell Presbyterian Church", by CHARLES WILLIAM SOMMERVILLE, Ph. D., D. D., published in 1939 by Hopewell Presbyterian Church, says:

"The particular beginning of HOPEWELL was the preaching of the REV. JOHN THOMSON. So far as tradition and incidental evidence go, the organization of the hearers of his preaching into a Church was due to Rev. Alexander Craighead, at RICHARD BARRY'S, not later than 1762, perhaps much earlier."

A note adds that this is the date most popularly accepted and is on the bronze marker erected by Col. E. L. Baxter Davidson on the highway.

The Church was organized several years before any building was erected. Since the earliest organization was probably made at the home of RICHARD BARRY, his house must have been the first shelter until 1765. An old letter states that the East end of Mr. Barry's house was the place of organization; the site usually spoken of being a wide spreading poplar or oak at the West end of the House.

Says DR. ALEXANDER, in his History on page 10:

"In 1752, REV. JOHN THOMSON, a preacher of the Presbyterian faith, held service under a wide spreading oak, near the House of RICHARD BARRY, fourteen miles Northwest of where CHARLOTTE was ten years later laid off, and established as the county seat of Mecklenburg. This was on the Beattie's ford road in the direction of the mountains."

Later notes in this volume will deal more specifically with the life and activities of the Rev. John Thomson above mentioned.

The present HOPEWELL CHURCH is about ten miles North of the City of Charlotte on the Beattie's Ford road and about two miles from the Catawba River. The history of the patriots and citizens of this community cannot be better written than by a list of the inscriptions on the tombstones of those who found their last resting place in the old church yard, which this writer and his wife have visited more than once and personally copied from the old headstones. Another and similar list of these inscriptions were collected for Dr. Sommerville's History, above mentioned, and arranged in alphabetical order for publication in that excellent volume under the supervision of Jane D. Carson, M. A., and Betty Guy Sommerville A. B., and in the following we have followed the published notes, as being more convenient, at the same time checking them with the original notes that we had made:

HOPEWELL TOMBSTONE INSCRIPTIONS

JOHN C. ABERNATHY, born Sept. 15, 1821; departed this life May 13, 1911.

NANCY J. BLYTHE ABERNATHY, wife of JOHN C. ABERNATHAY, born Dec. 2, 1825; departed this life April 5, 1877.

ROSA J. ABERNATHY, wife of W. M. ABERNATHY; b. Sept. 8, 1875; died April 25, 1916.

ELLA A. ABERNATHY, wife of A. L. ABERNATHY; b. July 6, 1864; died Feb. 22, 1901.

A. L. ABERNATHY born Jan. 18, 1860; died Oct. 3, 1889.

E. C. ABERNATHY, his wife (wife of S. T.); Feb. 11, 1828, Sept. 27, 1886.

FRANCIS MONROE ABERNATHY, June 7, 1882, Sept. 23, 1884.

INFANT DAUGHTER of DR. J. S. and HATTIE D. ABERNATHY; Sept. 13, 1911.

JOHN GRAHAM ABERNATHY; May 12, 1880; Sept. 12, 1905.

MARY BELL ABERNATHY; May 20, 1888; Feb. 28th, 1914.

MARGARET CALDWELL ABERNATHY, daughter of DR. J. S. and HATTIE D. ABERNATHY; Oct. 16, 1907; Feb. 1, 1919.

LENORA POTTS ABERNATHY, wife of J. S. ABERNATHY M. D.; Feb. 1, 1856; April 15, 1898.

INFANT DAUGHTER of DR. J. S. and HATTIE D. ABERNATHY; November 27, 1905.

J. S. ABERNATHY, M. D.; Born June 1, 1852; d. June 11, 1925.

HATTIE B. DAVIDSON ABERNATHY, second wife of DR. J. S. ABERNATHY; b. 1871; d. 1933.

RICHARD B. ABERNATHY; born March 7, 1858; died July 14, 1921; his wife SUSAN E. ABERNATHY, born July 13, 1861; died April 5, 1920.

RICHARD B. ABERNATHY; April 16, 1890; died December 9, 1918.

EMERY E. ABERNATHY; born Sept. 4, 1855, d. November 9, 1923.

JANE L. TODD ABERNATHY, wife of E. F. ABERNATHY; born August 15, 1853; died Jan. 30, 1929.

OLA BEATY ABERNATHY, wife of WALTER I. ABERNATHY; born April 5, 1897; died January 14, 1919. Also an infant daughter.

MARY WINSLOW ABERNATHY; born November 3rd, 1897; died Nov. 15, 1897.

CARRIE LEONIA ABERNATHY; born Feb. 29, 1864; died May 2, 1935.

A. C. ALEXANDER, son of JOSEPH McK. and NANCY C. ALEXANDER; born December 25, 1818; died June 15, 1820.

MARY A. ALEXANDER, daughter of JOSEPH McK. & NANCY C. ALEXANDER; born April 3, 1821; died Feb. 25, 1827.

SARAH P. ALEXANDER; born Dec. 20, 1816; died August 6, 1845.

LOUIS McKNITT ALEXANDER, son of G. W. and SARAH ALEXANDER, born March 14, 1856 and died July 1, 1857.

B. J. ALEXANDER, born September 8th, 1860; died Feb. 26, 1934.

WISTER W. ALEXANDER; born 1838; died Feb. 1859.

SARAH S. ALEXANDER, widow of the late G. W. ALEXANDER; born Sept. 21, 1831; died February 7, 1897.

GEORGE W. ALEXANDER; born May 18, 1810; died Nov. 22, 1866.

MINERVA L. ALEXANDER, wife of GEORGE W. ALEXANDER born Dec. 3, 1818; died August 28, 1852.

JUNIUS M. ALEXANDER; born April 18, 1826; died on July 14, 1855.

JAMES GRAHAM ALEXANDER, son of DR. M. W. and V. W. ALEXANDER; born Nov. 5, 1824; died October 8 1840.

DR. M. W. ALEXANDER, son of JOHN McKNITT ALEXANDER, born May 3, 1798; died Feb. 27, 1845.

VIOLET W. GRAHAM, daughter of GEN. JOSEPH GRAHAM, and wife of DR. M. W. ALEXANDER; born Aug. 31, 1799; died March 23, 1868.

JOSEPH McKNITT ALEXANDER, M. D.; born 1771; died Oct. 17, 1841.

LOTTIE A. ALEXANDER, daughter of R. D. and A. B. ALEXANDER, born Jan. 30, 1856; died October 26, 1877.

ABIGAIL B. ALEXANDER, wife of ROBERT D. ALEXANDER born May 10, 1808; died April 29, 1889.

WILLIAM LEE ALEXANDER, son of COL. B. W. and VIRA D. ALEXANDER; born Nov. 5, 1833; died April 20, 1845.

ROBERT DAVIDSON ALEXANDER, born in MECKLENBURG COUNTY, married ABIGAIL BAIN CALDWELL (who died in 1889) as shown above, and they were the parents of DR. J. B. ALEXANDER, the Mecklenburg Historian; another son, WILLIAM D. ALEXANDER, married one of the daughters of DR. J. G. M. RAMSEY, the TENNESSEE HISTORIAN.

JOHN McCOY ALEXANDER, son of COL. B. W. and VIRA D. ALEXANDER; died Sept. 9, 1846 in his 18th year.

B. W. ALEXANDER, died Oct. 17, 1865 in his 61st year.

JOHN McKNITT ALEXANDER, died July 10th, A. D. 1817, aged 84 years.

DOVIE WINSLOW ALEXANDER, died September 6, 1801, aged 25 years.

M. E. R. ALEXANDER, died Feb. 3, 1845, aged 13.

CAPT. FRANCIS R. ALEXANDER, born March 28, 1841, died June 19, 1864, from wounds received in the war. In C. S. A.

MAGGIE A. ALEXANDER, wife of A. H. ALEXANDER; b. July 2, 1840; died December 14, 1861.

MARY A. ROBISON, daughter of WILLIAM BAIN ALEXANDER, born 1813; died April 9, 1845.

VIOLET ELIZABETH ALEXANDER, daughter of J. McK. & MARY L. ALEXANDER; born July 30, 1845; died January 3, 1850.

JAMES ALEXANDER; born December 1, 1808 & died September 29, 1856.

SARAH J. ALEXANDER, daughter of ROBERT DAVIDSON and ABIGAIL B. ALEXANDER; born July 31,1844 and died January 16, 1848.

ROBERT H. ALEXANDER, son of ROBERT DAVIDSON and ABIGAIL B. ALEXANDER; born July 22, 1839; d. December 1, 1839.

ROBERT D. ALEXANDER; born August 26, 1796; died May 8, 1868.

He was the son of WILLIAM BAIN ALEXANDER, and the grandson of JOHN McKITT ALEXANDER; also the father of DR. J. BREVARD ALEXANDER, the Mecklenburg Historian.

MARTHA J. ALEXANDER, daughter of R. D. ALEXANDER and his wife ABIGAIL BAIN CALDWELL; born July 27, 1836; died July 7, 1838.

WILLIAM BAIN ALEXANDER; b. April 1764; d. 1844.

EMILY EUGENIA ALEXANDER, daughter of M. W. ALEXANDER and V. W. ALEXANDER; born October 18, 1832; died May 24, 1844.

WILLIAM DAVIDSON ALEXANDER; born Nov. 26,1840; died April 7, 1927.

SUE RAMSEY ALEXANDER, wife of WILLIAM DAVIDSON ALEXANDER; born April 23, 1843; died April 13, 1890.

She was the daughter of DR. J. G. M. RAMSEY, the TENNESSEE HISTORIAN.

SUE CROZIER ALEXANDER; born June 17, 1877; d. November 11, 1877.

BERTIE ALEXANDER; born Dec. 11, 1868; died Oct. 28, 1878.

EVA TRESCOT ALEXANDER; born Feb. 11, 1872; died January 18, 1873.

ELIZA ROCINDA ALEXANDER; born Sept. 2nd, 1834; died July 4, 1855.

VIOLET D. ALEXANDER; born August 28, 1771; died October 26, 1821.

SARAH D. ALEXANDER; born Feb. 18, 1807; died December 24, 1864.

WILLIAM B. ALEXANDER departed this life January 28, 1846 in his 48th year.

W. A. ALEXANDER died October 14, 1852 aged 14.

BREVARD JETTON ALEXANDER; born Sept. 8th, 1860; died Feb. 26, 1934.

ISABELLA SOPHIA WEIR, youngest child of WILLIAM B. and VIOLET D. ALEXANDER; born Feb. 25, 1816; died May 8, 1845.

JOHN McKNITT ALEXANDER, born June 15, 1850; d. July 24, 1895.

This JOHN McKNITT ALEXANDER was son of JAMES McKNITT ALEXANDER, who was the son of WILLIAM BAIN ALEXANDER - oldest son of the patriot JOHN McK. ALEXANDER. His wife was MARY ELIZABETH HENDERSON, a daughter of ANDREW ROBISON HENDERSON.

HARRIETTE V. ALEXANDER, wife of J. R. ALEXANDER; born Sept. 13, 1804; died Sept. 10, 1882.

J. R. ALEXANDER; born May 24, 1801; died Oct. 13 1873.

A. A. ALEXANDER, died May 30, 1877 aged 64 years.

JANE SOPHINA ALEXANDER, wife of A. A. ALEXANDER (She was a MONTEITH) died in January, 1895 aged 86 years.

GRACE HALYBURTON ALEXANDER, child of W. A. & M. E. ALEXANDER, died 1875, an infant.

VIOLET JANE ALEXANDER; born March 14, 1843; died April 4, 1874.

MISS SALLIE J. ALEXANDER, died August 8,1924, aged 71 years.

THOMAS M. ALEXANDER ("Lame Tom") died in C. S. Army during the Civil War.

MRS. WOODSIDE ALEXANDER, died Nov. 24, 1927, aged 51 years.

MARGARET EMMA ALEXANDER, died August 11, 1845 aged 1 year.

JEAN ALEXANDER, died March 16, 1789, aged 50 years.

W. ABNER ALEXANDER; born Feb. 22, 1847; died April 5, 1913.

LEIGH ALEXANDER; born July 20, 1879; died May 13, 1897.

HARRIET EMMA ALEXANDER, daughter of JOHN R. & HARRIET V. ALEXANDER, died April 4, 1815, aged 1 year.

DAVID ALLEN; born March 13, 1800; died Nov. 30, 1869.

W. H. ALLEN; born June 19, 1835; died Feb. 23, 1887.

R. M. ALLISON, C. S. A. b. 1847, died 1915.

JOHANNA E. BAKER; born Dec. 5, 1852; died Sept. 9, 1928.
GRANDERSON A. BAKER; born Sept. 20, 1857; died on March 8, 1927.
LILLES ALLEN BAKER; born Dec. 16, 1886; died Dec. 18, 1886.
INFANT SON of JOHANNA and GRANDERSON BAKER. Date?
JANE L. BAKER; born June 9, 1859; died December 21, 1918.
MARGARET L. BAKER; born Sept. 19, 1906; d. 1912.
MINNIE HAGER BARKLEY, wife of C. W. BARKLEY; born Nov. 5, 1878; died August 12, 1912.
MOTHER, MARTHA V. BARKLEY, wife of HENRY S. BAKLEY Born Sept. 17, 1880; died July 26, 1910.
GRAHAM N. BARKLEY; born Nov. 18, 1909; died Nov. 20, 1923.
S. P. BARKLEY; died Nov. 29, 1899, aged 23 years.
S. V. BARKLEY; died Nov. 22, 1899; aged 22 years.
MISS MARY ETTA BARKLEY; died Dec. 30, 1933 at the age of 79 years.
HARRY F. BARNETT; born March 17, 1871; died Oct. 25, 1923.
BROWNIE GATHINGS BARNETT, wife of HARRY F. BARNETT born July 4, 1881; died Feb. 10, 1931.
ROBERT SIDNEY BARNETT; born May 1, 1832; died Aug. 1, 1906.
ELLEN HARRY BARNETT, born July 1842; died May 22, 1897.
JOSEPH BARRON, died January 29, 1810, aged 60.
JEMIMAN BARRY died February 21, 1799, aged 27 yrs.
MARGARET McDOWELL BARRY; born April 16, 1782; died June 7, 1816.
MARY M. BARRY; born August 18, 1806; died April 9, 1833.
RICHARD BARRY, died March 22, 1815, in the 50th year of his age.
ANNE BARRY, died February 27, 1842, in the 66th year of her age.
WILLIAM BARRY, died Nov. 8, 1786, in the twenty-fourth year of his age.
ANNE PRICE BARRY, wife of RICHARD BARRY, died August 13th, 1827, in the 92nd year of her age.
RICHARD BARRY died August 21, 1801, in the 75th year of his life.

 RICHARD BARRY was one of the Signers of the Mecklenburg Declaration of Independence on May 20, 1775, & his wife was ANNE PRICE, of Maryland.

JEAN ALEXANDER (Alias BEAN or BAIN) wife of JOHN McKNITT ALEXANDER, died March 16, 1789, at the age of 50 years.

 Her husband, JOHN McKNITT ALEXANDER was also one of the Signers of the Declaration of May 20, 1775.

HUGH BARRY died May 19, 1837, at the age of sixty-six years.
JOSEPH BARTON, died January 22, 1816. His age is not given.
JOSEPH BARRON, died January 29, 1810, aged 60 yrs.
JAMES BEATY died May 13, 1816, aged 56 years.
JOHN BEATY, died Jan. 25, 1804, in the 83rd year of his age.
ARVEN BEATY died Feb. 25, 1797, in the 74th year of his age.
MARTHA E. BLACK, wife of SAMUEL BLACK, died March 31, 1862 aged 75 years and 20 days.
SAMUEL BLACK; born 1799 and died Jan. 17, 1875 at the age of 76.
ELIZABETH BLACK, daughter of SAMUEL and MARTHA E. BLACK; born August 15, 1807; died Oct. 25, 1825.
SOPHIA BLACKWOOD (alias GARNER) died April 23rd, 1893, aged 53 years.
THOMAS BLACKWOOD died April 16, 1793 aged 30 yrs.

CLEMENT N. BLYTHE born 1828; died 1896. C.S.A.
INFANT SON of JOHN E. and MATTIE BLYTHE died Feb. 26, 1923.
R. F. BLYTHE; born March 22, 1824; died Oct. 5, 1885.
MARSHALL McCOY BLYTHE, born July 20, 1855 & died April 8, 1932.
MARY BLYTHE, born Jan. 22, 1868, died Dec. 31, 1928.
VIOLET JANE BLYTHE, wife of R. F. BLYTHE, b. Feb. 28, 1829; died April 18, 1899.
MARY A. SAMPLE BLYTHE, wife of C. N. BLYTHE, born Jan. 31, 1846; died Feb. 10, 1930.
JOHN NIMROD BLYTHE, born Nov. 5, 1861; died March 31, 1864.
DAVID WINSTON BLYTHE, born June 3, 1839; died November 24, 1890.
JAMES COLUMBUS BLYTHE, born in November, 1875; died Feb. 29, 1920.
JOHN NANCE BLYTHE, born Nov. 20, 1830; died September 30, 1896
MARSHALL ALEXANDER BLYTHE; born Jan 5, 1878; died April 15, 1879.
SAMUEL McCOY BLYTHE, born Oct. 6, 1866; died Dec. 8, 1920.
LEROY M. BROWN, born Feb. 17, 1878; died June 22, 1879.
B. F. BROWN; died March 8, 1889; aged 46 years
FRANCIS BRADLEY; died Nov. 14, 1780, aged 37 years.
ABIGAIL BRADLEY, died Sept. 23, 1817, at the age of 69 years.
ELIZABETH BRADLEY, died August 19, 1817; aged 41 years.
ANNA F. BROWN, wife of B. F. BROWN; born Aug. 28, 1841; died March 24, 1896.
T. S. BUTLER; born May 21, 1847; died September 12, 1875.
MATTIE PARKS BUTLER, died May 23, 1903, aged 75 years.
JOHN R. BELL, son of J. and R. BELL, died June 25, 1837, aged 30 years.
ABIGAIL RANE CALDWELL, died May 14, 1802 in her 32nd year.
MARY N. (M?) CALDWELL, wife of JOHN H. CAID-WELL, and oldest daughter of ANDREW SPRINGS Dec. 30, 1833, aged 34 years.
JAMES CANNON died September 8, 1784, aged 53 years.
MARGARET ALEXANDER CANNON, wife of JAMES CANNON, died in 1802.
EDWARD J. CANNON, born Feb. 15. 1810; died Dec. 5, 1844.
JANE E. CANNON, wife of EDWARD J. CANNON, born SEPT. 7, 1812; died Dec. 11, 1843.
MARTHA A. CANNON; died October 8, 1798; aged 64 years.
JOHN CANNON died Jan. 19, 1794 aged 64 years.
SAMUEL D. CANNON died May 27, 1834 aged 27 yrs.
PEGGY THERRESSA CANNON, died Feb. 13, 1805, at the age of 4 years.
JOSEPH CANNON, died April 4, 1803, at the age of 34 years.

 The name CANNON on these tombstones is spelled CANON, with one "N", but other cannon records of the County show the correct spelling to be CANNON as has been used above.

NANCY CAPPS, wife of JOHN CAPPS, died Oct. 7, 1830 in her 55th year.
WILLIAM CAPPS, son of JOHN and NANCY CAPPS, d. January 2, 1833 aged 21 years.
MARY CAPPS, daughter of JOHN and NANCY CAPPS, died Aug. 21, 1837 aged 6 years.
SARAH CARSON died October 4, 1830 aged 53 yrs.
JOHN CARSON died October 18th, 1812 at the age of 50 years.

ANN CARSON died Nov. 13, 1799, aged 30 years.
BARBARA CARR died July 10, 1858 aged 67 years.
ROBERT CARR; born Dec. 17, 1750; died May 10th, 1843.
BARBARA CARR died March 22, 1833, in the 82nd year of her age.
RACHEL CARR, died July 4, 1858, at the age of 64 years and 7 months.
JANE CARR; born Jan. 17, 1789, and died August 14, 1854.
WILLIAM CARR died June 16, 1830, in the 52nd year of his age.
ROBERT WILLIAM CARR, son of J. H. CARR; born Feb. 18, 1852; died March 8, 1855
MARY CARR was born Sept. 7, 1783 and died Jan. 29, 1839, aged 55 years.
JOHN A. CARR, died October 26, 1833 in the 15th year of his life.
MARY M. HENDERSON COLLINS, wife of JAS. S. COLLINS born April 24, 1848; died Feb. 24, 1924.
DR. WALTER P. CRAVEN; born Dec. 29, 1845; died on December 5, 1929.
MARTHA A. VILUYAS CRAVEN, wife of DR. CRAVEN; born August 22, 1859; died January 5, 1903.
REV. CALVIN KNOX CUMMING, D. D., born in Scotland July 1, 1854; died at Davidson, N. C. March 25, 1935; son of SAMUEL and MARGARET CUMMING, who were also born in SCOTLAND. DR. CUMMING was a Missionary to JAPAN.
MARTHA E. CAMPBELL, wife of C. F. CAMPBELL; born April 8, 1828; died Feb. 26, 1901.
C. F. CAMPBELL; died April 1, 1887, aged 65 years.
D. W. CAMPBELL; born June 5, 1859; died July 27th 1896.

Sacred to the Memory of
GENERAL WILLIAM LEE DAVIDSON, OF MECKLENBURG COUNTY, N. C.
Born 1746, youngest son of GEORGE DAVIDSON, of LANCASTER COUNTY, PA. Who moved to Mecklenburg County, N. C. in 1750.
MAJOR
Of the 4th Regiment of North Carolina Troops; promoted to
LIEUTENANT COLONEL;
Severely wounded at COLSON'S MILL. Promoted for bravery to the rank of
BRIGADIER GENERAL.
With 300 men opposing CORNWALLIS and his troops he was killed Feb. 1, 1782.
Erected by Mecklenburg Declaration of Independence Chapter, D. A. R. in 1920.

JANE ELIZABETH DAVIDSON, wife of DR. W. S. M. DAVIDSON; died Dec. 3, 1844, aged 21 years.
JAMES T. DAVIDSON; born Oct. 21, 1843; died March 4, 1874.
W. S. M. DAVIDSON; born Nov. 2, 1817; died Dec. 15, 1873.
ELIZABETH LEE DAVIDSON, died April 27, 1845, aged 62 years and 7 months.
BENJAMIN WILSON DAVIDSON; born May 20, 1787; died September 25, 1829.
LIZZIE DAVIDSON, infant daughter of J. R. and E. O. DAVIDSON. No date.
JOHN W. DAVIDSON, died April 7, 1823, aged 5 mos.
JAMES DAVIDSON, died Sept. 10, 1788, aged 9 mos.
JOHN DOHORTY, died Feb. 26, A. D., 1790 at the age of 46 years.
JANE DOHORTY died Feb. 20, 1824 aged 46 years.
IDA M. KERNS DOUGLASS, wife of J. L. DOUGLASS; b. April 20, 1870; died Oct. 24, 1911.
C. E. DOUGLASS; born Feb. 3, 1832; died March 1, 1919; aged 87 years 1 month.
SAMUEL A. DOUGLASS; born April 17, 1826; and died November 18, 1905.

JOSEPH DOUGLAS, ESQ., died September 4,1805; aged 55 years.
ANDREW DUNN, born October 31, 1791, aged 71.
JAMES DUNN, died August 29, 1813; aged 49 years.
ANDREW ELLIOTT, SR., born March 29, 1765; died March 12, 1855.
WILLIAM ELLIOTT; born Jan. 20, 1816; died July 3, 1856.
MARGARET E. ELLIOTT; born Jan. 15, 1798; died died June 10, 1831.
ANNIE L. ELLIOTT, born Dec. 7, 1809; died on June 16, 1873, aged 63 years.
MARY ELLIOTT born Feb. 10, 1802; died July 1, 1879, aged 77 years.
MISS E. L. ELLIOTT, born August 1813 d. 1891.
ANDREW ELLIOTT JR.; born April 9, 1804; died Jan. 11, 1855.
CATHERINE ELLIOTT; born March 20, 1769; died Sept. 27, 1825.
CATHERINE L. ELLIOTT, born Jan. 18, 1800; d. April 5, 1861.
GEORGE ELLIOTT; born May 17, 1794; died June 21, 1873.
NANCY EMERSON, died Sept. 9, 1816; age 76 years.
MARTHA A. FULHAM; born July 12, 1831; died o April 7, 1905.
ABIGAIL GARRISON, died September 3, 1892 at the age of 73 years.
MARGARET GRAHAM, relict of WILLIAM GRAHAM, d. May 12, A. D. 1821, aged 71 years.
WILLIAM GRAHAM, died July 17, A. D. 1818, at the age of 78 years.

WILLIAM GRAHAM above was one of the signers of the MECKLENBURG DECLARATION of INDEPENDENCE on May 20, 1775.

JANE McCULLOUGH, wife of HUGH A. GREY, died April 5, 1883, aged 49 years.
LAURA J. HANNON, born March 30, 1855; died on September 2, 1870.
FREDDIE McMURRAY GREY; born July 9, 1885; d. Feb. 1, 1887.
JOHN F. HARRY, born August 29, 1829; died Aug. 7, 1871. Ruling elder.
ANN L. HARRY, born Sept. 29, 1839; died Oct. 9, 1843.
CYNTHIA WILSON HAMPTON, born Feb. 23, 1824; d. May 31, 1896.
CHARLES FISHER HAMPTON, born May 4, 1852; d. October 22, 1896.
ROBERT THOMAS HAMPTON, born May 10, 1854; died April 18, 1921.

The last three inscriptions above represents the family of JOSEPH WADE HAMPTON who married CYNTHIA WILSON, whose grandmother was MARGARET JACK, who married SAMUEL WILSON. The two children were born in AUSTIN, TEXAS, where their father died, after which the widow returned to Mecklenburg County with her children. The two sons never married.

SARAH LAWING HARRY, wife of W. B. HARRY; born Dec. 8, 1838; died July 29, 1875.
WILLIAM BATTE HARRY; born Feb. 26, 1834; died June 17, 1889.
HARRY HARRY, infant son of W. B. and SARAH A. HARRY (no date).
DAVID HARRY, born Sept. 30, 1798; died April 24, 1849.
SARAH E. HENDERSON, daughter of A. R. and R. R. HENDERSON; born January 11, 1868; d. September 4, 1878.

HOPEWELL CHURCH AND IT'S ANCIENT TOMBS

Mrs. Worth S. Ray copies inscription on monument of GEN. WILLIAM LEE DAVIDSON - Hopewell Churchyard

Tombstones at Grave of WILLIAM GRAHAM, "Signer" and his wife MARGARET at old Hopewell Churchyard

JOHN HENDERSON; departed this life May 23, 1842 at the age of 62 years and 10 months.
ANN HENDERSON, consort of JOHN HENDERSON, died May 29, 1830, aged 56 years.
WILLIE P. HENDERSON, son of J. S. and M. E. HENDERSON; born July 7, 1863; died Jan. 23rd, 1865.
MARCUS S. HENDERSON, infant son of J. B. and M. E. HENDERSON; born March 3, 1868; d. 1868.
TENNIE HENDERSON, infant daughter of above, born and died in 1862.
NANCY HENDERSON, died June 30, 1793 age 17 mos.
WOODS HENDERSON, died aged 17 months.
ALEXANDER HENDERSON died Aug. 15, 1895, no date.
MARTHA JANE HENDERSON; born Dec. 8, 1887; died June 19, 1911.
MARGARET HENDERSON, died Sept. 13, 1809, age 28.
BETSY HENDERSON died March 14, 1821, age 35 yrs.
SARAH HENDERSON, died Feb. 8, 1808, in the 55th year of her age.
JOHN MILTON HENDERSON, son of R. and M. C. HENDERSON; born July 9, 1855, died Feb. 8th, 1866.
ALICE VIRA HENDERSON, daughter of R. and M. C. HENDERSON; born in 1852; died 1863.
LAWSON P. HENDERSON, C. S. A.; born August 18th, 1839; died August 17, 1861; killed at YORKTOWN, VIRGINIA.
WILLIAM A. HENDERSON, C. S. A.; born August 16th 1844; died May 19, 1863, at RICHMOND, VA. He and LAWSON P. HENDERSON were brothers & sons of R. and M. C. HENDERSON.
CHARISSA P. HENDERSON; died Sept. 11, 1808, in the 19th year of her age.
JOHN HENDERSON; died Sept. 7th, 1809 in the 62nd year of his age (b. 1747).
JAMES SAMPLE HENDERSON; born March 4, 1836; died Nov. 10, 1912.
MARGARET E. HARRY HENDERSON, wife of JAMES S. HENDERSON; born Oct. 1, 1836; died April 7, 1895.
DAVID ROBINSON HENDERSON; born Oct. 26th, 1854; died Feb. 10, 1931.
INFANT SON of D. R. and C. R. HENDERSON; born & died in June 1897.
THERESA CARRIE ROBINSON HENDERSON, wife of D. R. HENDERSON; b. Dec. 14, 1869; died June 18, 1897.
ROBERT HENDERSON, JR.; born March 21, 1804; died Feb. 26, 1863, age 58 years.
MARTHA CAROLINE HENDERSON, wife of ROBERT HENDERSON, JR.; born April 1, 1814; died March 26, 1891; aged 76 years.
DOVIE WINSLOW HENDERSON; born 1850; died in 1851.
ANN HENDERSON and MYRA HENDERSON infant daughters of ROBERT and M. C. HENDERSON born 1841-2.
JOHN HENDERSON; died NOV. 14, 1794, aged 70 years (b. 1724).
ANDREW R. HENDERSON; died Dec. 28, 1901; aged 75 years and six months.
MARY HENDERSON, died Sept. 25, 1825 aged 42 years
MARGARET R. HENDERSON, daughter of A. R. and P. R. HENDERSON; born 1874; died in 1875.
INFANT SON of A. M. and P. R. HENDERSON; born and died in 1905.

The JOHN HENDERSON, 5th above, who died in 1794, appears to be the oldest HENDERSON on this list, since he was born in 1724. In the study of the HENDERSON FAMILY of Mecklenburg County, his identification is of importance. He was evidently the ancestor of many of them.

JOHN MARSHALL HOUSTON; born July 13, 1827; died June 16, 1925.
JANE ELIZABETH SAMPLE HOUSTON, his wife; b. Apr. 10, 1835; died June 14, 1914.

EUNICE McCOY HOUSTON; born 1801; married MATTHEW HOUSTON in 1825; died in the Spring of 1863.
ROBERT S. HOUSTON, young son of J. M. and J. E. HOUSTON; born 1857; died 1861.
IDA B. HOUSTON, daughter of J. M. and J. E. HOUSTON; born in 1866; died 1870.
RACHEL ROXANNA RUTLEDGE, wife of A. R. HENDERSON; born June 19, 1832; died June 18th 1908.
W. M. HOUSTON; born in 1800; died April 1879.
ELIZABETH V. HUNTER; born Dec. 5, 1851; died Dec. 22, 1896.
ESTHER F. HOUSTON; died August 14, 1908; age 75 years.
SARAH E. HUNTER; died Feb. 10, 1838, age 24.
THOMAS N. HUNTER; born April 29, 1854; died on April 24, 1888.
ROBERT IRVIN; died August 11, 1803, aged 17 years.
MARGERY IRVIN; died Oct. 29, 1788; aged 48 yrs
EDWARD IRVIN; died Oct. 10, 1790, aged 54 years
ROBERT JAMISON; born June 30, 1774; died Sept. 13, 1832.
JONAS JAMISON; died June 28, 1867; aged 37 yrs
THOMAS JAMISON, died Dec. 16, 1808.
ANDREW JAMISON; died July 8, 1810, age 32.
SADIE REBECCA JAMISON, daughter of W. A. and A. L. JAMISON; born Nov. 14, 1885; died August 28, 1893.
ELIZABETH JAMISON, died May 31, 1800. Her age in doubt.
ISABELLA JAMISON, died Jan. 30, 1816, in the 41st year of her life.
ANDREW C. JOHNSON; died Nov. 13, 1820 age 7 months.
LOUISA JOHNSON; died Oct. 22, 1841, aged about 50 years.
NANCY A. KENNERLY, wife of E. W. KENNERLY, d. Jan. 20, 1856; aged 21 years.
INFANT DAUGHTER of E. W. KENNERLY, died Nov. 13, 1855 aged 2 months.
J. ABNER KERNS; born June 6, 1858; died July 27, 1932.
FRANCES CHRISTENBURY KERNS, wife of J. ABNER KERNS, died Jan. ____?
JAMES L. KERNS, son of S. A. and F. C. KERNS; born 1890; died 1892.
FANNIE R. KERNS, daughter of J. F. and N. T. KERNS; died Sept 18, 1878, aged 3 years.
MARY KATE McAULEY, wife of R. W. KERNS; born Oct. 23, 1885; died Jan. 14, 1915.
MINNIE I. BARKLEY, wife of N. M. KERNS; born JUNE 2, 1867; died May 19, 1896.
BRICE McK. KERNS, son of N. M. and MINNIE KERNS; born 1896; died 1897.
MRS. W. M. KERNS, died Nov. 24, 1932; aged 65 years.
MARGARET J. KERNS, daughter of T. S. and L. C. KERNS, no date.
J. P. KERNS, died May 9, 1896, aged 3 years.
R. V. KERNS; born July 1, 1826; died September 5, 1901.
J. F. KERNS died May 7, 1896, aged 45 years.
LURA T. KERNS, daughter of J. F. and N. T. KERNS died 1878, age 1 year.
MAC KERNS died May 5, 1887, age 2 months.
P. B. KERNS, died 1896 age 6 months.
M. REBECCA KERNS; born August 30, 1827; died July 15, 1906.
SARAH (J. R.) KERNS, daughter of W. C. and N. V. KERNS; born 1856; died 1858.
MARY A. HUNTER, wife of JOHN W. KERNS; born Feb. 27, 1884; died Jan 14, 1928.
INFANT SON of J. W. and MARY A. KERNS d. 1828.
JAMES D. KERNS; born 1864; died 1868.
JAMES H. KERR; died Dec. 28, 1853, aged 36 yrs
JOSEPH KERR died Dec. 28, 1821 in his 81st yr.
MARGARET KINCAID died October 1, 1788.
ELIZABETH C. HUTCHINSON KING d 1846 aged 18 yrs.

CAPT. JAMES KNOX, died October 10, 1794, aged 42 years.

His daughter married SAMUEL POLK and they were the parents of Hon. JAMES K. POLK, who became President of the United States.

JANE K. LATTA, wife of JAMES LATTA; died July 1, 1864 in the 89th year of her age.
EZEKIEL LATTA; born January 16, 1810; died Nov. 21, 1820.
JAMES LATTA; died October 30, 1837, at the age of 82 years.
ANDREW LAWING; died June 5, 1825; aged 64 years.
ELIZABETH LAWING, died October 8, 1825, aged 26 years.
SAMUEL C. LITTLE, infant son of JOHN F. and JANE LITTLE; died Aug. 10, 1853, aged 3 years.
JANIE McKENZIE LITTLE, infant daughter of J. M. & M. E. LITTLE; died 1879 aged 9 months.
MARY, daughter of J. M. and M. E. LITTLE died in 1888, aged 2 months.
JOHN C. LITTLE, son of J. M. and M. E. LITTLE, d. 1891, aged 3 years.
MINNIE ESTHER McCOY LITTLE, wife of J. M. LITTLE, born Jan. 14, 1866; died August 13, 1895.
PEGGY LONG, died July 19, 1799 aged 30 years.
CAPT. JOHN LONG, died July 4, 1799, aged 55 years.

LONG'S CREEK received its name from CAPT. JOHN LONG.

JOHN WILLIAM LOVE; born June 24, 1855; died May 4, 1894.
ROBERT LUCKEY; born August 29, 1826; died Nov. 26 1900.
MARY A. ABERNATHY LUCKEY, wife of ROBERT LUCKEY; born Jan. 18, 1846; died Jan. 1, 1916.
HANNAH KERR MARTIN, wife of ROBERT MARTIN; born May 10, 1776; died July 12, 1832.
MARGARET N. MARTIN; born Nov. 20, 1807; died Sept 10, 1841.
ROBERT MARTIN, died April 1, 1812, aged 33 years.
JOHN E. McAULEY; born May 21, 1861; died Nov. 27, 1929.
E. H. McAULEY; born Jan. 11, 1851; died Jan. 18th 1934.
MARY L. McCOY McAULEY, born Oct. 2, 1858; d.____
THOMAS J. McCORKLE; born Nov. 12, 1824; died June 5, 1862. Two children:
ROBERT C. McCORKLE 1847-1852.
MARY JANE McCORKLE 1849-1852.
J. M. McCORKLE; born Feb. 9, 1851; died August 25 1915.
MARY ANNA HAMBRIGHT McCORKLE, wife of J. M. McCORKLE; born July 27, 1856; died Sept. 15, 1919
NANNIE McCORKLE, daughter of J. M. and M. A. McCORKLE; born 1884; died 1886.
FRANK H. McCORKLE, son of J. M. and M. A. McCORKLE, died 1873 at age of 10 months.
MAGGIE McCORKLE (child of above) 1895-1897.
FRANKLIN ALEX. McCORKLE; born Sept. 23, 1858; d. Sept. 5, 1935.
MARY ANN PUCKETT McCORKLE; born Dec. 21, 1825; d. July 4, 1862.
M. J. ALEXANDER McCOY, wife of W. L. McCOY; born August 12, 1864; died Dec. 29, 1895.
WILLIAM L. McCOY; born MARCH 7, 1862; died April 26, 1917.
JOHN F. McCOY, son of M. R. and R. McCOY; born Sept. 5, 1830; died in C. S. A. 1863.
M. R. McCOY; born March 10, 1807; died May 12, in 1854.
PEGGY ALEXANDER McCOY, infant; born 1792, d.1793.
JOHN McCLURE; died April 11, 1817, aged 78 years and 10 months.
  Some markers spell it McCLURE and others have it McCLURE.

JANE A. McCLURE, wife of J. A. McCLURE; born June 4, 1856; died April 18, 1991.
ANN McCLURE; died July 12, 1828, aged 75 years
ARTHUR McCLURE; died March 18, 1817, aged 68 years.
JOHN M. McCLURE, died April 11, 1817, aged 78 years.
HUGH McCLURE, died Nov. 10, 1840 in the 59th year of his age.
JEAN McCREAKEN, died August 13, 1786 at the age of 33 years.
JAMES McCRAKEN, died Jan. 18, 1802, aged 52 years.
SAMUEL McELROY; born in March 1803; died Dec. 30, 1874.
WILLIAM EDWARD McELROY; born Dec. 2, 1866; d. March 14, 1925.
IOLA LEE McELROY, son of S. J. and M. J. McELROY; born 1871; died in 1873.
SAMUEL J. McELROY; born Oct. 30, 1840; died Nov. 5, 1927.
MARGARET SAMPLE McELROY, wife of SAMUEL J. McELROY; born August 19, 1846; died Dec. 28, 1928.
JOHN McENTIRE, died Jan. 26, 1824; at the age of 67 years.
HENRY McENTIRE, died Oct. 28, 1827, at the age of 40 years.
ISAAC McENTIRE, died Jan. 22, 1820; aged 46 years.
ANN McGIN, died Nov. 22, 1797 in the 27th year of her age.
MARTHA McKNIGHT, wife of H. F. McKNIGHT, born March 24, 1796; died Aug. 24, 1852.
SAMUEL McNEELY, son of T. N. and I. A. McNEELY (no date)
THEODORE NEWTON McNEELY; born April 30, 1830; died June 12, 1915.
ISABELLA A. HENDERSON McNEELY, wife of T. N. McNEELY; born May 6, 1834; died October 27, 1908.
MRS. ANNIE McNEELY; born 1876; died 1935.
ELIZABETH H. MINCY, wife of WILEY MINCY; born Feb. 24 1844, died Jan. 7, 1921.
WILLIAM MONTEITH; died August 8, 1824 aged 72 years.
FRANKLIN LEE MONTEITH; born Sept. 15, 1815; d. Feb. 21, 1855.
VIOLET P. MONTEITH; died Oct. 17, 1855, at the age of 79 years.
ALEXANDER MONTEITH, died Nov. 15, 1775, aged 45 years.
JANE MONTEITH, died Feb. 27, 1812, age 85 yrs.
HANNAH MONTEITH, died Nov. 22, 1844 at the age of 78 years.
MARY E. MONTEITH; born Dec. 3, 1810; died July 26, 1851.
HUGH ESREN MONTEITH; born Jan. 5, 1818; & died Nov. 26, 1820.
JANE SOPHINA MONTEITH, died in January, 1895 at the age of 86 years.
REV. LYNFORD LARDNER MOORE, born April 22nd, 1869; died August 11, 1929.
SAMUEL MOORE (infant) died Sept. 26, 1933.
MOSES MOORE, died Oct. 30, 1782 at the age of 51 years.
ANN MOORE, wife of MOSES MOORE, died March 3, 1802, aged 65 years.
ELLIE REID MOORE, wife of REV. JOHN W. MOORE, born Oct. 13, 1863; died Nov. 18, 1893.
JOHN W. MOORE; born January 2, 1843; died on Dec. 31, 1923.
MARGARET GIBBON MOORE, wife of JOHN W. MOORE; born August 4, 1840; died Feb. 25, 1896.
MARGARET JEANE MOORE, infant daughter of REV. JOHN W. MOORE b. 1892, died 1893.
MASON EDWARDS MOORE, son of J. W. and K. B. MOORE; born March 26, 1908; died December 21, 1928
FLORENCE NANCE, died Nov. 27, 1895 age 14 yrs.

389

JAMES TAYLOR NANCE; born 1848; died 1925.
M. E. PARKS, daughter of A. D. and I. E. PARKS, died Nov. 14, 1881, aged 18 years.
A. D. PARKS; born July 16, 1835; died January 15 1911, aged 75 years.
ISABELLA S. PARKS, wife of A. D. PARKS; born Apr 3, 1836; died Oct. 4, 1894.
LUELLA TEMPLE PARKS, wife of J. L. PARKS; born July 11, 1882; died Sept. 19, 1913.
ELIZABETH A. PARKS; born Feb. 18, 1827; died July 12, 1904.
SARAH M. PARKS; born April 26, 1822; died Nov. 4, 1876.
DR. THOMAS M. PARKS; born Jan. 18, 1841; died May 30, 1877.
INFANT PARKS, child of DR. T. M. and S. A. PARKS, born and died July 13, 1869.
ERNEST PARKS, same as above, born and died 1874.
THOMAS A. PARKS, same as above, born 1875, and d. Feb. 27, 1877.
MARY ANN PARKS, born Sept. 15, 1811; died March 2, 1883.
ESTHER J. PARKS; died Nov. 29, 1895, aged 72 yrs.
MARTHA N. PARKS, died May 2, 1874, aged 55 years.
WILLIAM BEATY PARKS; born May 13, 1851; died Sep. 17, 1929.
NANCY ALICE GLUYAS PARKS, wife of WILLIAM BEATY PARKS; born May 7, 1853; d. Feb. 12, 1925.
JOHN L. PARKS; born June 25, 1822; died March 8, 1906.
JOHN N. PATTERSON; born Dec. 5, 1835; died Oct. 7, 1912. Confederate Soldier.
LENORA SLOAN PATTERSON, wife of JOHN N. PATTERSON born Oct. 4, 1845; died Oct. 27, 1904.
JAMES N. PATTERSON, died Oct. 6, 1877, aged 2 yr.
GEORGE G. PATTERSON, died July 13, 1878, aged 2 years. Children of J. N. and M. L. PATTERSON.
THOMAS PEEL; died Dec. 8, 1795, aged 19 years.
JOHN PEOPLES, died March 14, 1829, age 65 years.
HANNAH PEOPLES; born Nov. 16, 1823; died June 11 1891.
JOHN PEOPLES; died Oct. 10, 1827, aged 34 years.
JEMIMAH PEOPLES STONE, daughter of JOHN and S.S. PEOPLES; born Sept. 16, 1821; died Nov. 2, 1884.
SARAH E. D. PEOPLES; died March 18, 1848; aged 20 years.
SAMUEL W. PETTUS, son of JOHN and VIOLET PETTUS, died Jan. 14, 1810, aged 9 months and 14 ds
JANE B. PHARR, born Nov. 29, 1796; died August 29, 1839, in her 44th year.
AMANDA TALIULA PHARR; died August 31, 1861, aged 22 years.
MARY ANN PUCKETT; born Dec. 21, 1825; died July 24, 1861.
ROBERT E. PUCKETT; born June 1, 1831; died Feb. 8, 1901.
JAMES PUCKETT, born March 17, 1824; died Oct 31, 1901.
VIOLET D. PUCKETT, born May 7, 1829; died Nov. 13, 1901.
MULVINA D. PUCKETT, born March 19, 1852; died Oct. 29, 1905.
M. R. PUCKETT, born Jan 11, 1862; died August 18 1920.
MARTHA PUCKETT; born August 5, 1851; died April 9, 1887.
MARY ELLA PUCKETT, little daughter of J. P. and M. L. PUCKETT, died 1884 aged 4 months.
JORDAN PRIM PUCKETT; born Dec. 15, 1858; died on March 18, 1894.
MAGGIE LENORA HUNTER PUCKETT, wife of J. P. PUCKETT; born June 7, 1860; died Aug. 24, 1905.
WILLIAM FRANKLIN PUCKETT; born Jan. 9, 1854; d. Nov. 28, 1928.
JANE ELIZABETH PUCKETT, wife of W. F. PUCKETT; born Sept. 17, 1859; died May 12, 1922.
ROSA R. PUCKETT, wife of R. E. PUCKETT; born on July 27, 1836; died Sept. 10, 1875.

W. HAYES PUCKETT; born Dec. 17, 1868; died on Sept. 26, 1893.
JOHN A. PUCKETT, born Jan. 21, 1871; died Oct. 6, 1899, aged 28 years.
KENNETH D. PUCKETT; died April 15, 1934, aged only 11 months.
POLLY RANKIN, with her infant, died January 30 1803, in her 33rd year. She left a husband and five children.
RICHARD RANKIN, died March 23, 1804, at the age of 35 years.
MRS. NANCY L. REID, wife of RUFUS REID; born Feb. 15, 1801; died Nov. 6, 1833.
ELIZABETH L. REID, second wife of RUFUS REID, born Feb. 9, 1797; died May 4, 1838.
MARY A. ROBINSON; born Nov. 9, 1813; died Apr. 9, 1845. Daughter of WILLIAM BAIN ALEXANDER.
ARCHIBALD ROBINSON, died in 1879.
ABIGAIL BARNETT ROBINSON, died May 28, 1888 at the age of 98 years.
JOHN W. RODGERS, son of A. W. and S. J. RODGERS born April 28, 1888; died Feb. 12, 1890.
POLLY TILLY ROSS, daughter of JAMES and CATEY ROSS, died Jan. 31, 1809, aged 2 years.
REUBEN E. ROSS, died Sept. 5, 1824, aged 23.
JAMES ROSS, died April 6, 1809, age 39 years.
DAVID RUSSELL, died March 28, 1802, aged 69 years.
RICHARD SIDNEY SAMPLE, son of WILLIAM A. and J. L. SAMPLE; born Dec. 3, 1830; died Nov. 20, 1831.
M. IDA WILLIAMS SAMPLE, wife of JOHN W. SAMPLE, born July 5, 1851; died Aug. 11, 1889.
JENNIE PEARL SAMPLE; born March 25, 1893; died Oct. 13, 1895.
PAULINE SAMPLE; born Nov. 4, 1894; died Oct. 4 1895.
E. EUGENIA HARRIS SAMPLE, wife of J. McCAMIE SAMPLE; born Aug. 7, 1842; died January 28, 1893.
JAMES McCAMIE SAMPLE; born Jan. 19, 1835; died April 16, 1927, aged 92 years.
JANE L. BARRY SAMPLE, wife of WILLIAM A. SAMPLE born March 29, 1811, died May 11, 1876.
JAMES SAMPLE, born Feb. 14, 1770; died January 7, 1853.

This JAMES SAMPLE, born in 1770, must have been the ancestor of many of the SAMPLES on these records.

WILLIAM SAMPLE, died in September A. D. 1791, aged 55 years.

Probably the father of JAMES SAMPLE, since he was born in 1736.

ELIZABETH ALEXANDER SAMPLE, died August 1, 1822 aged 75 years. (B. 1747).

Probably the wife of WILLIAM SAMPLE just above. She was ELIZABETH ALEXANDER. They were married in the 1760s.

ARAMINTA C. SAMPLE; died July 11, 1794, aged only 5 years.
DAVID IRWIN SAMPLE; born August 5, 1837, and died Jan. 11, 1913, aged 75 years.
MARTHA SAMPLE, wife of JAMES SAMPLE; born Sept. 22, 1777; died Dec. 31, 1861, age 84 yrs.
ROBERT MIDAS SAMPLE, son of JOHN W. and IDA W. SAMPLE; born 1889; died 1890.
WILLIAM A. SAMPLE; born April 15, 1803; died June 29 1877. He was a ruling Elder of Hopewell Church at one time.
LEE HOUSTON SAMPLE, child of D. I. and R. E. SAMPLE, died at the age of 2 years.

REBECCA ELLIE McCOY SAMPLE, wife of D. I. SAM-
PLE; born March 22, 1842; died Feb. 17,1963.
MARTHA E. SAMPLE, daughter of WILLIAM A. and I.
L. SAMPLE; born Sept. 8, 1832; died Sept. 20
1857.
A. C. SHIELDS, born Dec. 27, 1826; died Sept. 9,
1899.
COWAN LEMIY SHIELDS; born July 10, 1863; died
March 21, 1928.
JULIA ALEXANDER SHIELDS, born Sept. 29, 1866; the
wife of COWAN LEMIY SHIELDS.
ALICE ONA SHIELDS, daughter of C. L. and J. N.
SHIELDS; born June 10, 1908; died April 21st
1910.
BANNER JANE SHIELDS, same as above; born Sept.
13, 1895; died March 9, 1915.
JANE A. HENDERSON SHIELDS, wife of A. C. SHIELDS;
born Oct. 24, 1824; died April 22, 1898.
W. R. SHIELDS; born April 16, 1856; died Sept. 20
1893.
KATE NELSON, first born of DR. THOMAS L. GREGORY
and CATHERINE NELSON; born July 11, 1851 at
PIPING TREE, VIRGINIA; married June 20, 1878
REV. JOHN WATKINS DABNEY, of BRAZIL, by whom
she had five children; August 4, 1892 she
married CHAS. WILLIAM SOMMERVILLE, of HAMPDEN-
SYDNEY, VIRGINIA, who became Pastor of HOPE-
WELL CHURCH; she died Jan. 16, 1936.
SALLIE IOEL STEPHENS; born June 3, 1845; died Mar
19, 1908.
ASE E. STEPHENS; born Nov. 4, 1847; died June 19,
1927.
J. L. STEPHENS; born Sept. 18, 1870; died Aug. 18
1901.
ALLEN PRESTON STEPHENS, died March 29, 1930.
SARAH BELL STEPHENS, daughter of ALLEN PRESTON
STEPHENS; born Nov. 20, 1885; died June 17th
1913.
CYNTHIA A. (ALLEN) STEPHENS; born Feb. 28, 1856;
died April 20, 1936.
LAURA S. STEPHENS, daughter of S. J. and M. C.
STEPHENS; born Oct. 4, 1872; died June 29th,
1879.
MOLLIE R. STEPHENS, daughter of S. J. and M. C.
STEPHENS; born Sept. 24, 1871; died Feb. 25,
1879.
SARAH ANN SPENCER; died August 29, 1806, at the
aged of 18 years.
SUSAN C. STEWART; born May 12, 1824; died June
25, 1879.
MARY CLEMENTINE STEWART, wife of S. J. STEWART;
born Sept. 12, 1853; died May 28, 1911.
S. J. STEWART; born Feb. 18, 1840; died May 26th
1921.
MICHAEL W. STINSON, died Jan. 9, 1908, aged 5
years.
H. A. STOWE; died March 21, 1878, aged 7 years.
ISABELLA F. STUART; born Oct. 28, 1826; died Dec.
28, 1896.
THOMAS A. STUART; born Oct. 28, 1826; died Oct.
25, 1895.
NANCY ALEXANDER STUART; born Nov. 2nd, 1835; died
June 24, 1906.
MOLLIE REBECCA STUART; born Sept. 24, 1879; died
Feb. 25, 1880; daughter of S. J. and M. C.
STUART.
LAURA SUSAN STUART, same as above, born 1873; and
died 1879.
SARAH THOMPSON; died Feb. 16, 1828, at the age
of 74 years (b. 1256).
THOMAS THOMPSON; died March 2, 1781, at the age
of 58 years (b. 1726).
JANNETT THOMPSON; died Feb. 2, 1796, at the age
of 69 years. (b. 1727).
CAPT. JAMES THOMPSON, died Jan. 28, 1781, at the
age of 30 years (b. 1751).
JOHN THOMSON (so spelled) died March 13, 1775;
aged 21 years. (b. 1754).

GIDEON THOMPSON, died in October 1796, at the
age of 71 years. (b. 1725).
WILLIAM TODD, died Jan. 8, 1829 at the age of
99 years. (He was born in 1730).
CHRISTIAN TODD, died Feb. 22, 1801, at the age
of 60 years. (b. 1831?).
JOSEPH TODD, died Nov. 7, 1825, at the age of
76 years.
GEORGE W. TODD, a son of JAMES and NANCY TODD
died Aug. 20, 1812, aged 2 years.
WILLIAM NEEL TODD, died April 19, 1819, aged
25 years.
JOHN TODD, died Feb. 23, 1873, in the 75th
year of his age.
HUGH TORRENCE died Feb. 14, 1816, aged 73 yrs.
(He was born about 1743).
RICHARD ALLISON TORRENCE; born Dec. 7, 1833;
died May 22, 1927.
ELIZA GASTON TORRENCE, wife of RICHARD ALLISON
TORRENCE; born Jan. 20, 1843; died June
10, 1916.
JANE ADELINE TORRENCE; born 1811; died in Mar.
1820.
NANCY A. TORRENCE, died Nov. 11, 1818, at the
age of 26 years.
JAMES GALBRAITH TORRENCE; Born Nov. 19, 1874;
died Dec. 12, 1847.
MARGARET ALLISON TORRENCE; born Jan. 6, 1798;
died Jan. 19, 1820.
WILLIAM L. TORRENCE; born Jan. 20, 1822; d.
May 26, 1852.
ISABELLA TORRENCE; died Feb. 1, 1816; aged
76 years. (She born in 1740).

ISABELLA TORRENCE was the wife
of HUGH TORRENCE (see above)
and had been the widow of COL.
FALLS who fell in action at the
engagement at Ramsaur's Mill in
what is now LINCOLN COUNTY, during the revolution.

MARY L. TORRENCE; born Dec. 19, 1799; died Nov
26, 1821.
JOHN ANDREW TORRENCE, born Jan. 28, 1839; d.
Dec. 21, 1904.
JOHN M. UNDERWOOD; born Dec. 9, 1836; died on
May 30, 1929.
CARRIE J. McELROY UNDERWOOD, wife of JOHN M.,
born Sept. 1, 1875; died June 20, 1928.
JNO. D. UNDERWOOD; born Dec. 9, 1836; died
March 1, 1901.
NANCY J. UNDERWOOD, wife of J. D. UNDERWOOD;
born Dec. 9, 1841; died Feb. 22, 1922.
JOHN D. VANCE; born Nov. 28, 1853; died Mar.
1, 1917.
JANE M. VANCE; born Sept. 21, 1820; died on
April 13, 1901.
DAVID VANCE; died Feb. 13, 1827; at the age of
50 years. (He was born 1777).
KATE ESTELLE VANCE; born 1885; died 1887.
KATHERINE VANCE; died Sept. 7, 1826, at the
age of 43 years.
WILLIAM VANCE, died Dec. 10, 1821 at age of 19
years.
MARCUS WILLIAM VANCE; born Oct. 14, 1849; died
July 10, 1928.
ELIZABETH C. VANCE; born Dec. 8, 1851; died
Dec. 22, 1896.
JULIA A. FULLWOOD, wife of M. W. VANCE; born
July 23, 1851; died March 23, 1898.
CORA WARREN, wife of C. E. WARREN; born April
13, 1880; died Sept. 7, 1909.
SIDNEY JOHNSTON WARREN; born June 25, 1902; d.
April 5, 1904.
SARAH C. B. WALLIS; died Dec. 16, 1843 at the
age of 29 years.
ELIZABETH JANE WHARTON, wife of SAMUEL D. WHAR-
TON; died Aug. 4, 1855 aged 27 years.

THOS. A. WHITE; born May 17, 1853; died June 14, 1909.
DAVID H. WHITE. Co. H. N. C. Inf., C. S. A.
MATTIE L. WHITE, wife of THOMAS A. WHITE; born May 28, 1859; died Dec. 4, 1901.
WADE HAMPTON WHITE; died Dec. 8, 1934.
EDNA MAY PARKS WHITE, wife of ARTHUR P. WHITE; b. May 27, 1882; died Nov. 21, 1924.
NEIL M. WHITLEY; died Jan. 30, 1866, age 4 years.
BRAXTON WHITLEY, infant, died Oct. 1866 age 11 months.
ESTHER SALLIE McCOY WHITLEY, wife of R. D. WHITLEY; died July 29, 1867, aged 35 years.
ELLA J. WHITLEY, died Jan. 26, 1866, aged 7 yrs.
JANE B. WHITLEY died Jan. 22, 1865, aged 69 yrs.
J. H. WILLIAMS; born Jan. 17, 1830; d. May 17, 1910.
NANCY STEPHENS WILLIAMS, wife of G. F. WILLIAMS; born Sept. 14, 1880; died July 14, 1917.
ELIZABETH ANN CHILES WILLIAMS, wife of REV. JOHN C. WILLIAMS; born Feb. 18, 1827; died on July 12, 1904.
REBECCA WILLIAMS, daughter of REV. J. C. and RE. A. WILLIAMS; born 1862; died 1872.
REV. JAMES L. WILLIAMS; borr Oct. 16, 1854; d. March 5, 1885; son of Rev. JOHN C. WILLIAMS and ELIZABETH C. WILLIAMS.
EMMA WILLIAMS; born July 20, 1849; died July 13, 1912.
REV. JOHN C. WILLIAMS; born March 15, 1819; died Dec. 22, 1874.
REV. JOHN WILLIAMSON, died on the 14th of September 1842 in the 56th years of his age, and the 31st of his Ministry. He was by birth a South Carolinian, and was pastor of WAXHAW CHURCH in Sept. 1813. In 1818 he came to HOPEWELL as pastor. (Not the exact wording, but the substance).
SARAH E. WILLIAMSON; died Sept. 30, 1845, at the age of 41 years. We assume this was the wife of REV. JOHN WILLIAMSON above.

ELIZABETH WILLIS, daughter of S. S. and L. WILLIS; born Feb. 1, 1854; died July 154th 1857.
VIOLET L. WILSON, wife of DR. ISAAC WILSON; d. March 14, 1845, aged 33 years.
REBECCA I. WILSON, wife of DR. ISAAC WILSON; died Nov. 3, 1855, aged 49 years.
MARTHA E. L. WILSON, infant daughter of DR. I. & V. E. L. WILSON died 1838 age 8 mos.
THOMAS A. WILSON; born Dec. 11. 1827; died on Feb. 25, 1862.
REBECCA WILSON, infant of SAMUEL and HANNAH (WILSON) d. June 30, 1788, age 8 mos.
JOHN WILSON, died May 9, 1815 in the 24th yr. of his life.
OLIVE WILSON, daughter of J. A. and E. J. WILSON; b. Feb. 8, 1867; d. June16, 1924.
JAMES A. WILSON; born Sept. 18, 1839; died on July 21, 1924.
ELEANORA J. WILSON, wife of JAS. A. WILSON; b. April 27, 1841; d. May 16, 1907.
SUSAN M. WILSON, wife of DR. ISAAC WILSON; b. Feb. 13, 1816; died Jan. 28, 1894.
THOMAS C. WILSON; born Aug. 22, 1843; died on June 29, 1862.
HELEN ELEANORA WILSON, dau. of MAC and R. M. WILSON; born Aug. 12, 1901; d. 1910.
RHODA MAY WILSON, wife of MAC WILSON; born in 1879; died Jan. 11, 1907.
GILBREATH Mc. WILSON; July 17, 1841; June 1862.
DR. ISAAC WILSON; born Dec. 30, 1802; died Dec. 15, 1880.
R. M. WILSON, born 1847; died July 15, 1915.
MARGARET WILSON, wife of ROBERT WILSON 1793-1876.
WILLIAM WINDERS b. 1867- died 1920.
AUBRY W. WITHERS; b. March 21, 1898; died July 16, 1931.
MATTHEW WOODS died in December 1796 aged 32.
ELIZABETH WOODS died May 1802 aged 32 years.
LAURA HAMPTON WHITE; born 1846; died June 1874.

SUGAR CREEK CHURCH

REV. HENRY FOOTE, in 1846 wrote in his Sketches of North Carolina: "After passing CHARLOTTE, the first object of importance that meets the eye of one searching for localities, is the plain, brick meeting house of the SUGAR CREEK CONGREGATION, about three miles North of the village. This is the present place of worship of part of the oldest Presbyterian Congregation in the upper country, in some measure THE PARENT OF THE SEVEN CONGREGATIONS that formed the Convention in CHARLOTTE in 1775. The Indian name of the creek, which gave name to the congregation, was pronounced SUGAW or SOOGAW, and in the early records of the church was written SUGAW; but for many years it has been written according to the common pronunciation, ending the word with the letter R, instead of W. The brick church is the THIRD house of worship used by the congregation; the first stood about half a mile West from this, and the second a few steps South, the pulpit being over the place now occupied by the pastor's grave."

REV. ALEXANDER CRAIGHEAD. According to the same authority, the first Presbyterian minister that took his residence in Western North Carolina, and the third in the State, was Rev. Alexander Craighead. This statement is erroneous, in this, that REV. JOHN THOMSON, was residing in Mecklenburg County and preaching on the soil within the bounds of that county as now constitued, seven years prior to the arrival of MR. CRAIGHEAD on ROCKY RIVER to accept the call of the Congregation of the Church of that name, in the year 1758. But Mr. Craighead, frightened by the Indians, in 1755, left with many of his church members the Valley of Virginia, on the Cow Pasture, and came to what is now Mecklenburg or Cabarrus County. His first charge was at ROCKY RIVER, and following that at SUGAR CREEK. At the time of his arrival REV. JOHN THOMSON was no more, and until the month of March, 1765, REV. CRAIGHEAD was the solitary minister between the Yadkin and the Catawba rivers.

Just how many different edifices have housed the Sugar Creek Congregation since its establishment in the days of Rev. ALEXANDER CRAIGHEAD, the writer is not advised, but it is certain that it has occupied THREE DIFFERENT SITES, as was stated by Dr. FOOTE when he wrote in 1846. Today there are three different burial places containing the last remains of its members. The writer of these lines, within the past decade has visited all three of them and has copied the inscriptions from the gravestones of many of them, where they were marked, although, of course there are innumerable graves having no markers or identification tablets. Not all of the inscriptions were copied, and more particular attention was given to the more ancient ones. From the notebooks used on the occasion of these visits, the following copies are made.

In the oldest or original church yard site of SUGAR CREEK, we copied the following:

MEMORIAL TO REV. ALEXANDER CRAIGHEAD at the entrance to this burial plot, which is surrounded by a substantial fence, and kept in a fair state of preservation.
In memory of CAIRNS HENDERSON, who died May 25th, 1793, aged 69 years. (He was born in 1724.)
Sacred to the memory of ELIZABETH HENDERSON, who died October 4, 1805, aged 77 years.
In memory of DAVID ROBINSON, who died October 12 1808 aged 82 years. (B. 1726).
In memory of ISABELLA ROBINSON, who died Jan. 9, 1791, aged 71 years. (b. 1720).
In memory of ROBERT ROBINSON; died May 6, 1789; aged 32 years.
In memory of AGNES ROBINSON; died April 8, 1798, aged 22 years.
MARGARET ROBINSON died August 8, 1798, aged 18 years.
Sacred to the memory of ROBERT CARR; died April 5, 1789, aged 71 years. (born 1718).
Here lies the body of JOHN CARR; died March 12, 1780; aged 23 years.
In memory of JOHN GOFORTH; died June 2, 1791, age 12 years.
Sacred to the memory of JEMIMAH ALEXANDER; born January 9, 1727; died Sept. 1, 1797, aged 70 years; for 38 years a widow. (Her husband evidently died in 1759.)
SARAH SHARPE, daughter of JAMES and JEMIMAH SHARPE; born Sept. 16, 1755; died Sept. 16, 1794, aged 39 years.
JAMES WILSON, SR. died Nov. 20, 1836; aged 70 years.
CATHERINE WALLACE, died in 1823, aged 61 years.
In memory of JEAN WALLACE; died July 1, 1792, in her 80th year. (Born in 1712).
In memory of MARGARET WILSON, who died October 5 1800, at the age of 31 years.
JOHN McCORD, died Jan. 23, 1800, aged 68 years.
MARTHA McCORD died March 29, 1804, aged 62 years.

JANE McCORD, died Dec. 31, 1823, aged 16 years.
JOHN STARR, died Sept. 6, 1773, aged 48 years.
ELIZABETH ORR died Feb. 30, 1788, age 32 years.
ROBERT McGEE died Oct. 9, 1775 aged 75 years.

He was born in 1700, and he appears to have been the oldest person whose dates were copied.

LILLIE WILSON died June 17, 1799, aged 75 years.
HARRY BARNETT died 1775, aged 41 years.
HUGH BARNETT died Nov. 24, 1786, aged 53 years.
MARGARET BARNETT died Oct. 5, 1790, aged 30.
ANDREW ROBINSON, died June 31, 1792 at the age of 53 years. (b. 1739).
THOMAS ROBINSON died Sept. 17, 1806, aged 21.
CAPT. JOHN ROBINSON, died May 4, 1808 at the age of 59 years.
ROBERT ROBINSON died May 6, 1786 age 32 years.
EZEKIEL ALEXANDER, an infant, died 1793.
JOHN CAMPBELL died July 10, 1790 aged 26 years.
DUGAL CAMPBELL died Jan. 1, 1781, aged 15 yrs.
MARY CAMPBELL died Jan. 3, 1781, at the age of 11 years.

The inscriptions that follow are copied from the SECOND oldest SUGAR CREEK burial ground, which is only a short distance from the present day church:

In memory of HEZEKIAH ALEXANDER, who departed this life July 16, 1801 aged 78 years. Signed the Mecklenburg Declaration of Independence May 20, 1775.
ABRAHAM ALEXANDER died April 28, 1786, aged 68 years. Signed the Mecklenburg Declaration May 20, 1775.
DORCAS ALEXANDER (his wife)d. May 20, 1800 at age of 66 years.

JOAB ALEXANDER, died May 20, 1800, at the age of 66 years. (Born in 1734).
JOANAH ALEXANDER, died in the year 1823, at age of 58 years.
MARCUS ALEXANDER, died Nov. 15, 1815 aged 20 yrs.
MARGARET ALEXANDER, died in November, 1815, at the age of 18 years.
In memory of LIZA B. ALEXANDER, who died in 1813 at the age of 15 years.
In memory of MARTHA PARKS, who died October 10th 1803 at the age of 57 years. (Born 1746).
In memory of CYRUS ALEXANDER, who died March 24, 1790, aged 28 years.
In memory of JOHN M. ALEXANDER; died April 26th, 1818; aged 26 years.
RUTH ALEXANDER; died September 10, 1796; aged 36 years.
ELIZABETH WALLACE died in 1828 at age of 58 yrs.
In memory of WILLIAM WALLACE, who died May 20th, 1829, aged 58 years.
H. B. WALLACE, wife of WILLIAM WALLACE (relict) died in 1856, at the age of 70 years.
Sacred to the memory of ELIAS ALEXANDER; died September 21, 1812, aged 53 years.
JAMES B. ALEXANDER, died in 1842, aged 20 years.
HANNAH P. ALEXANDER, wife of OSWALD ALEXANDER, d. Feb. 9, 1823, aged 33 years.
JOEL ALEXANDER, died May 17, 1825, at the age of 52 years.
JOHN CAMPBELL, died January 27, 1851, at the age of 60 years.
ELIZABETH CAMPBELL, wife of JOHN CAMPBELL, died 1855, aged 81 years.
GEORGE W. HOUSTON; born November, 1778; died Jan 25, 1835.
JANE HOUSTON, wife of GEORGE W. HOUSTON; born August 10, 1780; died May 26, 1854, at the age of 73 years.
ROBERT A. HOUSTON, died August 9, 1841, at the age of 22 years.
JAMES A. HOUSTON; died August 4, 1847, aged 44 years.
MILTON BARNETT, died August 6, 1825, aged 24 yrs.
ROBERT BARNETT; died September 9, 1830, at the age of 80 years. (B. 1750).
JAMES F. TODD, an infant, died July 27, 1828, at the age of 7 years.
ROBERT M. TODD, an infant, died in 1831, aged 1 year.
ELIZABETH HENDERSON, died April 4, 1843, at the age of 84 years (b. 1759).
Sacred to the memory of ANDREW HENDERSON; died October 6, 1837, at the age of 84 years. (He was born in 1753).
MARGARET D. HENDERSON, consort of DAVID R. HENDERSON; born Nov. 24, 1797; died July 14th 1854.
MARY E. HENDERSON, daughter of DAVID R. HENDERSON; born in 1821; died 1837.
MARGARET D. HENDERSON; born May 6, 1791; died on December 12, 1871; aged 80 years.
NANCY B. HENDERSON; died April 14, 1856; born on November 14, 1788.
CAIRNS H. HENDERSON; died April 3, 1845; aged 58 years.
EDWARD YOUNG HENDERSON; died Sept. 12, 1833; age 8 years.
MARY K. HENDERSON; died Feb. 26, 1845; aged 15 years.
PHILO HENDERSON; died July 21, 1852 aged 30 yrs.
MATTHEW HENDERSON; died Jan. 9, 1847, aged 27 years.
HARRIET P. HENDERSON, wife of JAMES P. HENDERSON; died Nov. 25, 1857, aged 59 years.
JAMES RUFUS HENDERSON; died August 3rd, in 1831, at the age of 3 months.
MARY E. HENDERSON, daughter of DAVID and H. C. HENDERSON, died March 4, 1851; age 2 years.

MARTHA H. HENDERSON, daughter of DAVID and H. C. HENDERSON; died June 18, 1854 aged 7 years.
MINTY S. WALLACE HENDERSON, wife of DAVID HENDERSON; died March 20, 1835, at the age of 32 years.
MICHAEL O. FARRELL, native of Co. Langford, in IRELAND, died in January 1829, aged 48 yrs.
MARGARET ALEXANDER died in 1836 at the age of 83 years.
GEORGE DAVIES, died January 3, 1807, aged 71 years. (Born in 17360.
HANNAH DAVIES, died October 26, 1806, aged 57 years.
WILLIAM LUCKY died January 11, 1845, aged 67 years and 11 months.
MARY M. GRIER, wife of THOMAS J. GRIER, and late the widow of WILLIAM LUCKY, died March 19, 1843, aged 50 years.
INFANT SON, died July 8, 1822, aged 6 days.
INFANT son, died April 16, 1823, aged 6 days.
WILLIAM J. A. LUCKY, died Nov. 8, 1825 aged 8 months.
MARGARET LUCKY died Nov. 15, 1847 age 15.
PRUDENCE LUCKY died Apr. 2, 1826 age 16 years.
ALFRED B. LUCKY died August 18, 1826 age 11 yrs.
NANCY WALLACE died Oct. 24, 1811, aged 59 yrs.
FRANCIS Mc ALEXANDER died Dec. 23, 1846; at age of 54 years.
THOMAS KERNEY, born in June 1811; died April 16, 1855.
REBECKA KANADY, died March 4, 1845 aged 72 yrs.
THOMAS KANADY died July 4, 1857, aged 68 years
ISABELLA ROBINSON died Feb. 23, 1814 at the age of 29 years; also her infant child.
ROBERT ROBINSON died Jan. 17, 1814 aged 22 yrs.
EZEKIEL ROBINSON died Aug. 13, 1826 aged 44 years.
ROBERT ROBINSON, died Nov. 1, 1820 aged 7 yrs.
JANE ROBINSON died July 1, 1828 aged 8 years.
JAMES ROBINSON died in August 18___ aged 27.
JOSEPH WEDDINGTON died October 15, 1843 aged 22 years.
THOMAS L. HUTCHINSON died Nov. 4, 1846 at the age of 47 years.
ELVIRA E. HUTCHINSON, wife of THOMAS L. HUTCHINSON, died Jan. 20, 1842 aged 33 years.
GEORGE CALDWELL HUTCHINSON b. 1830; died 1830.
GEORGE NANCY HUTCHINSON; died August 29, 1838, aged 43 years; member of the bar 21 years.
JOSEPH Y. PARKS, died Dec. 10, 1843, in his 42nd year.
ROBERT PARKS died June 20, 1846 in his 75th year.
NANCY PARKS, died Feb. 5, 1841 in her 63rd yr.
ISABELLA SHIELDS, wife of DAVID SHIELDS, died October 9, 180__; aged 31 years.
MARY FLINN died Jan. 13, 1810, aged 75 years.
JOSEPH SAMPLE died August 4, 1842 aged 64 years.
C. G. ALEXANDER, died April 7, 1841 at the age of 45 years.
NANCY K. ALEXANDER, consort of C. G. ALEXANDER, died May 7, 1844, aged 33 years.
PHILANDER ALEXANDER, son of above, died May 20 1844.
NANCY MARGARET ALEXANDER, daughter of G. G. ALEXANDER, died June 7, 1845 aged 2 years.
JOSIAH ALEXANDER died July 13, 1828 aged 64 years.
MARY BAKER died April 9, 1846, aged 73 years.
ELAM MOORE died Jan. 30, 1840, aged 40 years.
Effieza C. MOORE died June 8, 1831, at the age of 33 years.
JAMES WILSON died August 8, 1844 at the age of 73 years.
MARTHA WILSON died May 5, 1822, at the age of 48 years.

ALBERT WILSON died June 28, 1873 aged 76 years.
ELIZABETH WILSON, wife of ALBERT WILSON, died Sept 2, 1870, at the age of 70 years.
ABBEY E. JONES, died August 26, 1833 aged 24 yrs.
REBECCA JONES died October 15, 1828 at the age of 30 years.
FRANKLIN and ISAAC JONES, two children of REBECCA JONES died about the same time she did.
LOUISA PARKS died January 18, 1839 aged 32 years.
ROBERT W. PARKS died September 3, 1844 aged 33 yrs
JAMES PARKS died August 22, 1824 at the age of 22 years.
SARAH PARKS died Feb. 17, 1834 at the age of 59 years.
ROBERT PARKS died June 19, 1844 at the age of 82 years. Probably father of them all.
JAMES A. HOUSTON died August 4, 1847 at the age of 44 years.
ROBERT A. HOUSTON died August 19, 1844 at the age of 22 years.
G. W. HOUSTON; born November 12, 1778; died January 25, 1835.
JANE HOUSTON, wife of G. W. HOUSTON; born August 10, 1770; died March 26, 1854.

INSCRIPTIONS ON TOMBSTONES OF THE PRESENT SUGAR CREEK CHURCH :

JAMES FLOW; born October 5, 1810; died March 3rd 1895.
MARY E. FLOW; born May 5, 1811; died Nov. 26 in 1866.
J. OMI FLOW; born Sept 16, 1837; died September 6 1856.
JOHN W. MOORE; born Feb. 9, 1813; died Nov. 8th 1867.
SAMUEL M. MOORE; died on August 13, 1858, at the age of 53 years.
MATTHEW WALLACE MOORE; died July 27, 1851, at the age of 15 years.
GRACE ELIZABETH KNOX, wife of G. W. ROBINSON, b. Ma ch 15, 1868; died January 30, 1914.
BATTE ERWIN; died July 28, 1854, at the age of 44 years 11 months and 22 days.
MARR ROBINSON ERWIN, wife of BATTE ERWIN and daughter of REV. JOHN ROBINSON; born Feb. 2, 1813; died June 26, 1888.

In memory of AUNT SUSAN MOORE, wife of WILLIAM C. MOORE; died July 30, 1860 in her 59th year.
JANE ELIZA IXLES, wife of E. W. LYLES, and a daughter of CAPT. DAVID MOORE; born August 25, 1832; died March 11, 1885 at the age of 52 years.
MARGARET ALEXANDER, wife of MATTHEW ALEXANDER; born December 20, 1796; died December 14, 1881.
T. MARTIN ALEXANDER; born 1811; died 1904.
JAMES HARVEY HENDERSON; born October 31, 1834; died Sept. 11, 1901.
MRS. CORDELIA HENDERSON born 1839; died 1875.
DAVID HENDERSON, born July 20, 1805; died Nov. 24, 1879.
HARRIETT C. HENDERSON, wife of DAVID HENDERSON born Sept. 28, 1815; died March 26, 1883.
THOMAS C. HENDERSON; born April 26, 1837; d. August 10, 1888.
JOSEPH RUMPLE; born Oct. 9, 1809; died Oct. 26, 1893.
BARBARA LAWRENCE RUMPLE, his wife, born April 1, 1807; died June 20, 1897.
DR. JOSEPH McKNITT HENDERSON; born November 23 1828; died Jan. 5, 1877.
LEONRA E. SIMREL HENDERSON, his wife; born March 16, 1832; died July 29, 1907.
MARGARET EVELYN ALEXANDER; born July 30, 1830; died April 28, 1905.
MARY A. ALEXANDER; born Sept. 24, 1832; died Jan. 20, 1918.
NORA NEAL MOORE, wife of REV. CHALMERS MOORE, born May 2, 1855; died May 8, 1930.
REV. ROBERT H. LAFFERTY, Pastor of the SUGAR CREEK CHURCH; born March 10, 1812; died July 18, 1864.
MARY SAMPLE, wife of R. F. BARNETT; born Aug. 1, 1805; died July 7, 1884.
MARY BALDWIN ERWIN, oldest child of BATTE ERWIN and MARY ROBINSON, died Sept. 21, 1855 aged 7 years, 11 months and 18 days.
CATHERINE ELIZABETH ERWIN, daughter of BATTE ERWIN; died Oct. 2, 1855 aged 5 years.
EVELINE CATHERINE WALLACE, wife of SAMUEL MOORE, died July 2, 1857; aged 57 years.
LIZZIE ANN MOORE (Dau.) died 1855 aged 16 yrs.

MARY WILLIAMSON MOORE, wife of JOHN MOORE, dau. of Z. L. and H. P. WILLIAMSON; b. 1846; died Jan. 1907

ROCK SPRINGS BURYING GROUNDS

BURIAL PLACE of COLONEL ADAM ALEXANDER

In his HISTORY OF MECKLENBURG COUNTY, Dr. J. B. Alexander presents an account of what he calls the OLD ROCK SPRINGS BURIAL GROUNDS, which he says is located somewhere in the general neighborhood of PHILADELPHIA CHURCH, out in the country some miles South and East of the town of CHARLOTTE, and for which, in its isolated location, he seems unable to account for, although many of the old graves are well marked, and it is apparent were at one time well kept up and cared for. In his account he gives the inscriptions from some of the gravestones, which we include in this account. We found there were several such old graveyards in MECKLENBURG COUNTY, with no Church or other identification near them, such as BAKERS GRAVEYARD and OLD BETHESDA, not far from the one called ROCK SPRINGS. Here are the inscriptions as given by Dr. Alexander:

MAJ. JAMES HARRIS; born Dec. 25, 1772; died Sept. 7, 1811.
SAMUEL L. HARRIS; born 1767; died 1798.
MARY HARRIS; born July 14 in 1749, aged 73 years.
CATHERINE MAXWELL; born 1774; died 1825.
ELIZABETH WILSON; born in the year 1800; died 1832
ADAM ALEXANDER (Signer) d. Nov. 13, 1798; 70 yaers.
MARY ALEXANDER (his wife)d. Nov. 26, 1813 aged 78.
ROBERT QUEARY; died Aug. 25, 1827, aged 64 years.

SAMUEL HARRIS, died 1825, aged 83 years.
MARGARET HARRIS, died 1782, aged 58 years.
JANE HARRIS, died 1797, aged 42.
WILLIAM MORRIS, died 1804 at age of 59 years.
ELIZABETH MORRIS; born 1750; died 1821.
HANNAH MOORE died in 1821 aged 58 years.
ELIZABETH MOORE died in 1792 at age of 18 yrs.
ELIZABETH BABB, died in 1792 at the age of 40.
ANDREW ROGERS; died in 1792 at age of 25 years.
ELIZABETH WILSON died in the year 1802. No age.

POPLAR TENT CHURCH

POPLAR TENT MEETING HOUSE was in that part of MECKLENBURG COUNTY, N. C., which is now a part of CABARRUS COUNTY, cut off from Mecklenburg in 1791, after the first U. S. Census was taken. It is one of the SEVEN OLDEST CHURCHES traditionally credited to the early missionary activities of JOHN THOMSON, ALEXANDER CRAIGHEAD and their colleagues.

The location of this old Church, according to WILLIAM HENRY FOOTE, was about seven miles from the town of CONCORD, on the road (at that time) leading to BEATTIE'S FORD, and about fourteen miles East of Davidson College. By the word "TENT" as used in this name was meant a stand or place for holding public worship, in the absence of a building specially erected and built for that purpose, such as was commonly used by religious congregations in the earliest days of the settlement of this and other regions like it. The emigrants to the Carolinas used these "tents" in all seasons of the year, till they could build a house of worship. This particular "tent" - so-called, even after a church building had been erected, was organized about the year 1764 or 1765, at which time the boundaries of the congregation was ascertained and agreed upon.

The first regular pastor of POPLAR TENT CHURCH appears to have been the REV. HEZEKIAH JAMES BALCH, a member of what was called the "Presbytery of Hanover" but previous thereto of the "Presbytery of Donegal". At the time he came to POPLAR TENT he with other noted Presbyterian leaders had been set off to form still another Presbytery, called the "Presbytery of Orange", the latter being composed of a half dozen ministers only: Rev. HUGH McADEN, who had visited North Carolina in 1755, leaving an interesting Journal, detailing his adventures on the journey, including a reference to his visit with COL. ADAM ALEXANDER on Rocky River; Rev. HENRY PATILLO, a noted Minister and teacher, of Granville County, N. C., and sometimes of GUILFORD, and father in law of COL. RICHARD HARRISON, of the Revolution; Rev. JAMES CRISWELL; REV. JOSEPH ALEXANDER, son of THEOPHILUS ALEXANDER, an older brother of JOHN McKNITT ALEXANDER; REV. HEZEKIAH BALCH, who settled in that part of North Carolina, which afterwards was made a part of the State of Tennessee, and REV. HEZEKIAH JAMES BALCH, who was pastor of POPLAR TENT from sometime in 1770 to the time of his death sometime in 1776. His grave is probably at Poplar Tent, but was never marked and its location is unknown, notwithstanding the fact that in 1775 he served as a member of the famous MECKLENBURG CONVENTION which adopted the ringing resolutions of absolute independence of the King of England.

What became known as the POPLAR TENT CONGREGATION was taken from ROCKY RIVER, a still older organization. Among the elders of ROCKY RIVER were AARON ALEXANDER, NATHANIEL ALEXANDER and DAVID REESE, who thereafter became elders of the Poplar Tent Church.

Other elders of the POPLAR TENT CONGREGATION, added in 1771, by the choice of the congregation, were JAMES BARR, ROBERT HARRIS, JAMES ALEXANDER, GEORGE ALEXANDER and JAMES REESE.

After the death of REV. HEZEKIAH JAMES BALCH, Rev. ROBERT ARCHIBALD became pastor of POPLAR TENT CHURCH, where he remained until about 1792, having been installed as such October 7, 1778. Dr. Foote, in his "Sketches" declares that there is nowhere a monument or tradition to direct to the grave of HEZEKIAH JAMES BALCH, or anywhere a LIVING MORTAL to claim him as their ANCESTOR, which implies that, if he ever married, he left no descendants, or else the line became extinct. It is probable that he was born in Scotland or Ireland.

After the passing of DR. ARCHIBALD, the Poplar Tent Congregation obtained the services of DR. JOHN ROBINSON, who was born in the bounds of SUGAR CREEK CHURCH, on Jan. 8, 1768, and who was raised in the Charlotte neighborhood, who remained as pastor until his death Dec. 15, 1843. This DR. JOHN ROBINSON was a member of an interesting family. See later.

ROCKY RIVER CHURCH

On page 480 of Foote's Sketches of North Carolina it is said: ROCKY RIVER was one of the SEVEN CONGREGATIONS that covered the region of country represented in the Convention at CHARLOTTE, of Declaration memory, and was no disinterested spectator of the doings & catastrophe of the Regulation. Among the first settlers in the bounds of the congregation, who, seemingly, came in a company, were: COL. ROBERT HARRIS on Reedy Creek; his brother SAMUEL HARRIS, on CLEAR CREEK; ANDREW DAVIS, on REEDY CREEK; MOSES SHELBY on CLEAR CREEK; WILLIAM, JAMES and ARCHIBALD WHITE on or near ROCKY RIVER; DAVID CALDWELL, on Caldwell's Creek, and ADAM ALEXANDER on Clear Creek. The MORRISON FAMILY also came early to ROCKY RIVER, and it is said they came from SCOTLAND.

Of these known early comers to this settlement, JAMES WHITE was the father of JAMES, WILLIAM and JOHN WHITE; ANDREW DAVIS had a son ROBERT DAVIS, and of the same generation were ROBERT CARUTHERS and BENJAMIN COCHRAN of this same locality, all of whom were participants with WILLIAM (Black Billy) ALEXANDER in what has been called the North Carolina "Gun powder Plot", described in some detail in Foote's account.

The outstanding minister of ROCKY RIVER CHURCH, after the death of ALEXANDER CRAIGHEAD, first sent by the Presbytery to serve the congregation, was JOHN McKAMIE WILSON, boyhood friend & near kinsman of ANDREW JACKSON, who was born in 1769. Foote says that his father was from England and in early life was engaged in the mercantile business in PHILADELPHIA. No account I have ever found gives the name of the father, and later I shall indulge in some speculation on this subject. John McKamie Wilson were to school at Hampden-Sidney College in Prince Edward County, Virginia, & completed his course there. The parents of JOHN McKAMIE WILSON had three sons, and one of the brothers served as Sheriff of Mecklenburg County. Dr. Isaac Wilson (1825-1875) of Mecklenburg County was a son of Sheriff Wilson, and the five sons of JOHN McKAMIE WILSON were his first cousins. One of them was JOHN WILSON and another ALEXANDER E. WILSON, who was a Missionary in Africa, and who died in that country. JOHN QUEARY, a "Signer" and ADAM ALEXANDER, another, lived in the bounds of ROCKY RIVER.

STEELE CREEK CHURCH

FOOTE, on whom one can rely, says that it is probable that what is known as STEELE CREEK CHURCH, in Mecklenburg County, was organised by REVS. ELIHU SPENCER and ALEXANDER McWHORTER, who were sent by the Synod in 1764 to the back parts of North Carolina, to aid the people in organizing their churches, settle their boundaries and take proper steps to obtain regular pastoral services. He adds that the settlement of all these congregations commenced about the same time, SUGAR CREEK and ROCKY RIVER taking the precedence somewhat in point of time.

In 1767, the REV. ROBERT HENRY, who for some time had served as pastor of the Church on CUB CREEK, in CHARLOTTE COUNTY, VIRGINIA, resigned that charge and accepted a call from STEELE CREEK and PROVIDENCE CHURCHES in Mecklenburg County. This man appears to have been the first regular settled minister of both these interesting congregations. There is not the slightest doubt in the mind of this writer but what many members of these two congregations who called him to this work came from the same general locality in Virginia, and had heard him preach there. The records contained in these notes will bear out this statement. He lived only a short time after coming to North Carolina, dying the same year of his arrival. Other preachers had preceded him to both places as the deliverers of occasional sermons as "supplies", but he appears to have been the first regular minister. From 1778 to 1797 Steele Creek had for its pastor Rev. DR. McCREE, who had been pastor of Centre Church, serving many Mecklenburgers in the Northern part of the County for years previous thereto.

DR. FOOTE in his interesting account of this Church declared that it had no history, but that it had RECORDS - not written with pen and ink, but graven in the enduring rock - records brief, concise, numerous and characteristic. By which he had reference to the gravestones that stand like immortal sentinels guarding the last resting place of members of the congregation who found in its burial plot their final haven of rest with their neighbors and forefathers, who had preceded them. This is literally true. This writer has visited and examined many old cemeteries in his travels, but there are few, if any of them, can excell STEELE CREEK CHURCH in interest. I have walked among these ancient gravestones and markers; have read the inscriptions graven thereon with the awkward tools of the era in which they were made, but which are sunk deep into the hard stone on which they are written, so that the passage of time and the flight of the war-torn centuries have left them still plain and legible. And they do tell the story of a glorious past, of lives of service, of heroic service in the armies of the country, and of an enduring patriotism that did not falter or shudder when signing a defiance to the thrones of Europe on May 20, 1775, and transmitting that act to the assemblage that eventually affirmed their simple but firm denunciation of an out-moded tyranny.

As you stroll among these ancient stones and monuments you may read the names of the old families that formed the band of emigrants to this now populous neighborhood; the NEELYS, the HARTS, PORTERS, BIGHAMS, SLOANS, McDOWELLS, GRIERS, MARSHALLS, POTTS and others. Many of these same names may be found on the old records up in the Valley of Virginia, from whence, accompanied by the intrepid Pastor of their flock, they fled to North Carolina, when the defeat of Braddock opened the way for intrusions of the enemy into their midst. Rev. Hugh McAden tells of meeting a cavalcade of them on their way down, accompanied by ALEXANDER CRAIGHEAD, who when finally settled in the Carolinas gave free reign to his teaching of the doctrines of freedom and liberty that gave birth to the Mecklenburg Declaration a decade later, after his own demise. Among the "Signers" of that declaration was at least one or more of the Steele Creek members.

The writer regrets that time and facilities prevented his making a complete abstract of the markers in this old Churchyard, but those set down and which follow are fairly representative of the whole and will be of some aid to those who are searching for ancestors among the patriots who are buried there:

TABLET - STEELE CREEK PRESBYTERIAN CHURCH - Second Church in MECKLENBURG COUNTY; Organized in 1760; first pastor, REV. ROBERT HENRY.
Sacred to the memory of REV. HUMPHREY HUNTER, who departed this life August 21, 1827, in the 73 year of his age. He was a native of IRELAND and emigrated to America at an early period of his life, etc. **
WILLIAM McREE died October 30, 1780, aged 75.
DINAH McREE died March 23, 1798, aged 81.
W. SILAS MARKS; born January 27, 1826; died Dec. 20, 1899.
MARY E. MARKS, wife of W. SILAS MARKS; born 1828; died 1892.
REV. JOHN COVINGTON; born 1800; died in 1854.
S. WATSON REID; born Dec. 12, 1831; died December 24, 1902.
REV. JAMES PRESLEY, D. D., of DUE WEST, South Carolina; born 1835; died in 1872.
JANE P. PRESLEY, wife of REV. JAMES PRESLEY (no further date).
JONATHAN REID; born in 1801; died in 1860.
CAROLINE REID, wife of JONATHAN REID. (no date).
JOHN M. WILSON; died March 21, 1842, at the age of 35 years.

MARGARET RICHARDSON; died November 18, 1849 at the age of 35 years.
WILLIAM MARSHALL; born March 3, 1815; died March 20, 1884.
JAMES MARSHALL; born June 10, 1776; died Aug. 15, 1864.
JANE MARSHALL; born 1780; died 1864.
JOHN PRICE died May 28, 1882 at the age of 64 years.
SAMUEL B. KNOX died May 11, 1875 at the age of 76 years. (Born 1799).
SAMUEL J. SLOAN; born December 17, 1841, and died March 30, 1891.
MARY NEELY; died October 2, 1864, at the age of 90 years (b. 1774).
MAJ. JOHN M. POTTS; born May 15, 1810; died March 5, 1875.
MARTHA ISOBEL POTTS, wife of MAJ. JOHN M. POTTS; born 1817; died in 1872.
ALEXANDER GRIER NEEL; born April 5, 1815; and died Feb. 25, 1898. A ruling elder in Steele Creek Church for 55 years.
G. L. WILSON; born October 20, 1822; died on March 20, 1907.
JOHN S. NEELY; died on November 5, 1855 at the age of 31 years.

REV. JOHN DOUGLASS, son of JOHN and ELIZABETH DOUGLASS; born October 10, 1809, in CHESTER, S. C.; died October 8, 1879.

FRANCES G. DOUGLAS, wife of REV. JOHN DOUGLAS; died in WASHINGTON, D. C. in 1884, at the age of 84 years.

MARY M. WEBB; died March 8, 1880, aged 65 years.

JOHN P. BYRUM; born December 24, 1813, and died in 1877.

JAMES MORROW COFFEY; born in LANCASTER, S. C., Oct 9, 1805; died December 17, 1893.

ELIZA AGNES COFFEY, wife of JOHN MORROW COFFEY; b. January 9, 1809; died March 31, 1890.

JAMES S. COFFEY, died in 1858 at the age of 23 years.

AMANDA COFFEY, wife of RUFUS A. COFFEY; born 1843; died 1892.

JOHN BEATTY; born April 19, 1790; died in 1874.

ISABELLA BEATTY, wife of JOHN BEATTY, died in 1879 at the age of 79 years.

ALEXANDER BEATTY and JOHN A. BEATTY buried on the same plot.

JAMES LOGAN MARTIN; died July 7, 1815, at the age of 28 years.

Sacred to the memory of ANDREW CATHEY, who died JANUARY 20, 1785, at the age of 64 years. He was born in 1721.

JOHN PRICE, died October 22, in 1802 at the age of 87 years. He was born in 1715.

MARY PRICE died November 29, 1804, at the age of 79 years. She was born in 1725.

WILLIAM McKINLEY; died May 29, 1813, at the age of 72 years. (b. 1741).

MARGARET McKINLEY, wife of WILLIAM McKINLEY, died in 1800 at the age of 66. (b. in 1734).

RICHARD ROBINSON, died January 20, 1789, at the age of 76. Born 1713.

ALEXANDER ROBINSON, died July 12, 1786 at the age of 30 years.

NICHOLAS GIBBONEY, died April 7, 1821, at the age of 80 years. Born in 1741. (He was a revolutionary soldier).

ROBERT LINDSAY (Son of JOHN LINDSAY)and his wife MARY B. McDOWELL, daughter of HUGH McDOWELL, of DAVIDSON COUNTY. They died September 28, 1850, at the ages of 32 and 27 years.

HUGH McDOWELL, died May 16, 1835, at the age of 57 years.

CAPT. HUGH PARKS, died in 1830, at the age of 46 years.

In memory of THOMAS GRIER, son of JAMES and MARGARET GRIER, died January 20, 1828, aged 84 years; a revolutionary soldier. His wife SUSANNAH GRIER, daughter of JAMES C. SPRATT, the second wife of THOMAS GRIER. The children of THOMAS GRIER were nine: (Names appear thus on the gravestone)

    HANNAH
    JOHN S.
    SAMUEL
    ANDREW
    CATHERINE M.
    MARY B.
    WILLIAM M.
    ZANUS A.
    SUSAN GRIER

The wife SUSANNAH GRIER died July 4, 1853 at the age of 84 years.

REV. JAMES PRINGLE, Pastor of the ASSOCIATED CONGREGATION OF STEELE CREEK; died October 28th 1818, at the age of 50 years.

WILLIAM BARNETT, died August 23, 1785, aged 27 years.

MARY BARNETT, died April 11, 1785, at the age of 21 years.

JOHN KING, died May 20, 1820, aged 60 years.

NANCY KING, wife of JOHN KING, died 1797, aged 90 years. She may have been his grandmother; she born 1707; he in 1760.

MARY L. MARKS; died April 25, 1827 at the age of 16 years.

MARY CREEK died in 1833 in her 60th year. She was born in 1773.

JOHN S. MARKS died September 10, 1833 at the age of 18 years.

WILLIAM P. McNIGHT (McKNIGHT?), died October 27, 1826, at the age of 26 years.

JOSEPH HARTT died in October, 1778, at the age of 34 years.

ELIZABETH HARTT died in 1775 at the age of 42 years.

ANDREW HARTT died in 1788 aged 17 years.

ROBERT R. RAY; born October 18, 1823; died on September 9, 1888.

J. A. MARKS; born October 14, 1847; died April 29, 1935.

VIRGINIA E. MARKS, wife of J. A. MARKS, died in 1919; born 1853.

GEN. WILLIAM H. NEAL; born Nov. 21, 1799; died December 29, 1888.

HANNAH G. NEAL, wife of William H. NEAL; died November 21, 1880; she the daughter of ZENAS and M. ALEXANDER.

JAMES BROWN died in the month of October,1830, at the age of 86 years.

JOHN BIGHAM, died April 20, 1792, at the age of 52 years.

PHILLIP SADLER died August 11, 1836, aged 72 years.

JANE SADLER died May 16, 1832, aged 61 years.

ALEXANDER SADLER died April 3, 1813 at the age of 23 years.

GEORGE SADLER died June 7, 1820, aged 19 years

HENRY SADLER died October 30, 1821, at the age of 27 years.

MARGARET SADLER died October 21, 1829, at the age of 19 years.

BARTHOLOMEW HAYNES died in 1813 at the age of 50 years.

SARAH HAYNES died April 18, 1839 aged 69 yrs. Wife of BARTHOLOMEW HAYNES.

JOHN BLAIR, a native of SCOTLAND; member of the Anti Burgher Seceder Church; died in September 1823 in the 70th year of his age.

JANE BLAIR (his wife) native of SCOTLAND, and member of the Anti Burgher Seceder Church, died September, 1832, in the 70th year of her age.

JAMES WILSON died October 5, 1820.

CAPT. JOHN HARRIS died October 26, 1821 aged 61 years.

MARY MOORE, wife of ROBERT SLOAN, born May 5, 1817; died September 6, 1901.

LAVINIA ELIZABETH STEELE, wife of DR. WILLIAM A. PRESSLEY; born June 24, 1829; died Jan. 21, 1902.

DR. WILLIAM A. PRESSLEY; born August 6th 1813; died December 25, 1874.

DEBORAH C. ROSS died October 12, 1846 aged 23 years, 11 months and 21 days.

SAMUEL COX; born August 11, 1789; died June 24, 1848.

DEBORAH C. COX, wife of SAMUEL COX, died June 12, 1848, aged 41 years.

JONATHAN REID; born September 9, 1800; died May 9, 1860.

JOHN B. GRIER; born 1822; died 1896.

S. ELMIRA GRIER, wife of JOHN B. GRIER; died April 5, 1878 aged 37 years.

W. K. REID; born June 4, 1808; died August 29 1867.

MARGARET MARSHALL , wife of WILLIAM MARSHALL, born April 7, 1826; died Oct. 7, 1896.

HANNAH PRICE, wife of DR. I. J. SLOAN; born 1835; died 1873.

ESTHER M. REID; born December 15, 1809; died August 21, 1869.

MARY MOORE, wife of A. G. NEEL, daughter of WILLIAM and E. HANNA, of YORK DISTRICT, S. C., died August 29, 1860, aged 37 years.
N. B. RODDEN, Co. B. N. C. Inf. C. S. A. no date.
MARGARET RODDEN; born Oct. 9, 1816; died Nov. 20, 1860.
HANNAH RODDEN, wife of LEWIS RODDEN; died Oct.13, 1849 at the age of 60 years. Born 1789.
MAJ. JOHN B. LEWIS, died July 8, 1858, at the age of 35 years.
JAMES BIGHAM died Nov. 1, 1845, at the age of 31 years. He was a ruling elder in the Associate Reformed Church at Steele Creek. (This was known as LITTLE STEELE CREEK.)
REV. J. B. WATT, Pastor of Steele Creek Church; born April 4, 1820; died September 16, 1860.
NANCY M. WATT, wife of J. B. WATT, died April 10 1854, at the age of 34 years.
LOUISE ANGELINE WATTS, second wife of REV. JAMES BELL WATTS (above); born 1835; died 1917.

ELIZABETH REED WATTS; was born 1870, d. 1937
JAMES LOGAN MARTIN; died July 7th, 1815; aged 28 years.
ESTHER Y. HUTCHINSON, wife of THOMAS L HUTCHISON, and daughter of JOHN and REBECCA McDOWELL. She married first REESE PRICE and had three children, REBECCA E., JOHN M. and PAMELA R. PRICE; she then married THOMAS L. HUTCHISON. She died December 24, 1850, at the age of 52 years.
JOHN McDOWELL, revolutionary soldier, died July 30, 1793, at the age of 52 years. He was born in 1741. (Marker).
JAMES McDOWELL died Sept. 4, 1795 aged 18 yrs.
JOHN McKINLEY, died in 1797, at the age of 21 years.
WILLIAM McKINLEY died Nov. 29, 1797, age 14.
WILLIAM ANDREW McREE died March 8, 1792, at the age of 10 years; also graves of JEAN McREE and ROBERT McREE, children.

DAVIDSON PRIVATE BURIAL GROUND

MAJ. JOHN DAVIDSON - one of the "Signers" - lived about fifteen miles Northwest of the town of Charlotte, near the Catawba River, and not far from what was known as TOOLE'S FORD, between COWAN'S FORD and the bend of the river, where he died January 10, 1832 at the age of 97 years, one of the wealthiest as well as the most distinguished men of Mecklenburg County. His wife, who was VIOLET WILSON, had died fourteen years earlier, and she was buried in a plot of ground, said to have been selected by Maj. Davidson, near his home, and where he and members of the immediate family were afterwards interred.

In the History of the Hopewell Church this private cemetery of the Davidson family is referred to as the "RURAL HILL GRAVEYARD", and a descendant of the family HON. EDWARD LEE BAXTER DAVIDSON some years ago erected a wall around part of it and installed wrought iron entrance gates, all properly inscribed. The location is off the highway, but easily accessible.

The following inscriptions, which are copied from pages 317-318 of Sommerville's Hopewell History, are said to have been copied by MAY and JO GRAHAM DAVIDSON:

MAJ. JOHN DAVIDSON. This wall erected in memory of MAJOR JOHN DAVIDSON, a signer of the MECKLENBURG DECLARATION OF INDEPENDENCE, May 20, 1775, and his wife VIOLET WILSON DAVIDSON and their descendants. Erected by EDWARD LEE BAXTER DAVIDSON. Homestead built in 1788; burned in 1886.
Sacred to the memory of MAJOR JOHN DAVIDSON, who was born December 15th, 1735, and died January 10th, 1832, in the 97th year of his age. A signer of the Mecklenburg Declaration of Independence, May 20, 1775.
Sacred to the memory of VIOLET DAVIDSON, wife of JOHN DAVIDSON, who departed this life December 3, 1818, in the 77th year of her age.
MARGARET M. DAVIDSON, relict of ROBERT DAVIDSON & the daughter of COL. ADLAI and MARGARET OSBORN; born April 7, 1776; died January 9th, 1864.
ROBERT DAVIDSON; born April 7, 1769; died on June 14, 1853.
Among the unmarked graves is that of
MARY WINSLOW DAVIDSON, who was born September 19, 1803; was married to GEORGE W. DOBY, February 9th, 1831, by Rev. J. WILLIAMSON. She died December 31st, 1832.
SARAH R. DAVIDSON; born November 12, 1779; died April 20, 1870 (Aged 81 years).
SALLIE HARPER BREVARD, wife of JOHN DAVIDSON; born October 26, 1780; died in January 1864.
ALEXANDER BREVARD DAVIDSON; born March 13, 1808; died July 4, 1896.
MARY LAURA SPRINGS DAVIDSON, wife of A. BREVARD DAVIDSON; born November 3, 1813; died October 24, 1872. Names of their children on back of tombstone: WILLIAM LEE, ROBERT A., RICHARD AUSTIN, ADAM BREVARD, FANNY BAXTER.

LEROY DAVIDSON; born August 19, 1855; died on Sept. 15, 1915.
RICHARD AUSTIN DAVIDSON; born Dec. 10, 1843; died April 1, 1892.
ADAM BREVARD DAVIDSON; born March 20. 1852; died October 11, 1869.
ROBERT AUGUSTUS DAVIDSON, born March 13, 1842; died March 31, 1865.
FANNIE BAXTER DAVIDSON; born June 3, 1861; July 24, 1863.
WILLIAM LEE DAVIDSON; born July 20, 1840; d. July 27, 1857.
SALLIE H. DAVIDSON, daughter of A. B. and MARY SPRINGS DAVIDSON; born August 16th 1845; died March 26, 1935.
BLANDINA R. DAVIDSON, daughter of A. B. and MARY SPRINGS DAVIDSON; born October 15th 1853; died April 26, 1937.
E. CONSTANTINE DAVIDSON; born February 17th 1820; died May 15, 1892.
JANE HENDERSON; born September 26, 1831; died June 15, 1914.
A. DAISY; born October 28, 1864; died June 12 1865.
E. SYLVESTER, born April 6, 1866; died Sept. 18, 1869.
SADIE BREVARD DAVIDSON; born Sept. 28th 1872; died September 8, 1916.
DR. WILLIAM SINCLAIR DAVIDSON; born Oct. 21, 1860; died March 23, 1936.
JOHN SPRINGS DAVIDSON; born in 1838, and died in 1899.
MINNIE CALDWELL DAVIDSON; born 1840; died in 1898.
JOHN SPRINGS DAVIDSON, JR.; born 1878 d.1878.
THOMAS BREVARD DAVIDSON; born Jan. 6, 1866; died July 8, 1936.
INFANTS. Children of D.A. and M.A. CALDWELL.

PROVIDENCE CHURCH

The settlements within the bounds of PROVIDENCE CHURCH - first called NEW PROVIDENCE - situated twelve miles South of the town of Charlotte, near the present line of UNION COUNTY, but which did not then exist, but most of which belonged to Mecklenburg, were made about the same time as those in SUGAR CREEK, STEELE CREEK and ROCKY RIVER. Previous to the actual organization of the church in 1765, Rev. ALEXANDER CRAIGHEAD, had probably preached in the beautiful grove where the meeting house afterwards stood, as many of these who settled in the neighborhood had come with him from the Cow Pasture congregation in the Valley of Virginia, and were his old friends and neighbors. Foote says that the first elders in the Church were ANDREW REA, ARCHIBALD CROCKETT, JOSHUA (JOHN) CROCKETT and AARON HOWIE. At least the first three of these formerly resided on the Cow Pasture in Virginia and had head ALEXANDER CRAIGHEAD preach there many's the time.

Besides possibly a few sermons by CRAIGHEAD, when he had been available, the first ministerial labors the settlement enjoyed, were from the REV. WILLIAM RICHARDSON, who, with REV. HENRY PATILLO had been ordained to the work on July 18, 1758 at the home of MR. ANDERSON, in Cumberland County, Virginia. REV. WILLIAM RICHARDSON was the uncle of HON. WILLIAM RICHARDSON DAVIE, beloved Statesman of North Carolina, and Major in the revolutionary army in 1880; also Rev. Richardson, between the time of his ordination and his preaching to this congregation in Mecklenburg, had labored as a missionary among the Cherokee Indians. Just how long and how often he preached to the congregation at Providence is not known. His place of residence was near the old WAXHAW CHURCH in what is now a part of Lancaster County, S. C., but what was then - partly, at least - understood to be not only in North Carolina, but in MECKLENBURG COUNTY. See deeds on record from the "Waxhaws" - pages 317 to 334, this volume.

The first regularly employed pastor of PROVIDENCE CHURCH was REV. ROBERT HENRY, who had ministered for some time to the CUB CREEK CHURCH of the Caldwell settlement in Charlotte County, in Virginia. He was also - presumably at the same time - in charge of the STEELE CREEK CHURCH, only a few miles away in Mecklenburg County. In 1770 the CLEAR CREEK CONGREGATION and PROVIDENCE entered into a partnership arrangement. Clear Creek afterwards became PHILADELPHIA, as it is known today. At that date the elders for Clear Creek were ADAM ALEXANDER, MATTHEW STEWART, JOHN QUEARY, MICHAEL LEGGETT and JOHN FORD. (It will be noticed that no less than three of these were among the signers of the Mecklenburg Declaration). The then elders of PROVIDENCE CHURCH were JOHN RAMSEY, JAMES LINN, JOHN HAGENS, JAMES HOUSTON, ANDREW REA, JAMES IRAFFEN, JAMES JOHNSTON, JAMES TATE, THOMAS BLACK and ROBERT STEWART.

REV. JAMES WALLIS, after the death of ROBERT HENRY, which occurred in 1767, was the first minister of whom there is a record, who gave protracted service to PROVIDENCE. He was born in 1762 and spent his entire ministerial life in the congregation, being buried in the old churchyard with his wife. He was a son of EZEKIEL WALLACE of Sugar Creek. Beacuse there were so many persons of the name of JAMES WALLACE, this minister, we are reliably informed, by an act of the Assembly, had his name changed to WALLIS. He left a most interesting family, and was a son in law of JOHN McKNITT ALEXANDER, of Hopewell, and during his lifetime served on the Board of Trustees of the University of North Carolina. Later REV. SAMUEL WILLIAMSON served as pastor of PROVIDENCE.

The PROVIDENCE CHURCH BURIAL GROUND provides a similar interest to that of STEELE CREEK and others we have attempted to describe. Its gravestones contain the history of the church and its members. We regret that we could not copy all of them, but enough are here presented to give all those interested a pretty fair idea of what families lived within the bounds of this Church.

THE REV'D JAMES WALLIS died December 27, in 1819; aged 57 years; minister here since 1792.

MARY A. WALLIS; died May 18, 1815, at the age of 27 years. Wife of Rev'd James Wallis.

SARAH AMANDA CURETON; died January 27, 1844, aged 13 years.

WILLIAM POTTS, of UNION COUNTY; born September 10 1788; died January 22, 1856. Erected by the POTTS FAMILIES, of Pleasant Valley, South Carolina, Steele Creek and Charlotte, N. C., and the McILWAINE FAMILY of Union County, N. Carolina, his descendants.

WILLIAM POTTS, JR., died March 7, 1836, at the age of 27 years.

LEVICY POTTS, died February 8, 1827, at the age of 40 years.

ANN F. WALKUP, wife of JAMES A. WALKUP, died June 15, 1855, at the age of 65 years.

JAMES POTTS, died December 25, 1821 at the age of 38 years.

MARY POTTS, died March 26, 1846, at the age of 60 years.

JAMES POTTS, SR., died November 4, 1825, at the age of 52 years.

WILLIAM POTTS, died November 29, 1800, at the age of 49 years. (Born in 1751).

JAMES POTTS died May 8, 1781, at the age of 62 years. (Born 1719).

SOPHIA SPRINGS, wife of JOHN SPRINGS and JOHN SPRINGS. No date.

ALEXANDER MORRISON, died in December, 1806, at the age of 42 years.

JOHN POTTS, died May 28, 1809, at the age of 33 years.

NANCY POTTS died April 3, 1830, at the age of 70 years. Born in 1760.

GEORGE PARKS died January 6, 1827, at the age of 43 years.

ELIZABETH PARKS, wife of GEORGE PARKS, died in February 1844, aged 54.

DAVID HOUSTON died April 14, 1842, aged 75 yrs. He was born in 1767.

ANN M. HOUSTON died October 9, 1822, at the age of 57 years. Born 1765.

DR. WILLIAM MORRISON, died November 1, 1806; aged 45 years. Born in 1761.

MARY DAVIS, the consort of WALTER DAVIS, died February 2, 1849, aged 71 years.

ANN DAVIS, died July 23, 1842, at the age of 41 years.

MARY A. C. DAVIS, died October 17, 1842, at the age of 21 years.

LUCINDA DAVIS, died December 23, 1845, at the age of 30 years.

LEVICA L. REA, wife of GREEN L. REX, died May 26, 1865; aged 57 years.

JAMES M. REA, son of GREEN L. REA, killed in the C. S. A. at Chancellorsville.
JOHN McCULLOCH; died August 11, 1845, at the age of 76 years. (Born 1769).
MARY McCULLOCH, wife of JOHN McCULLOCH (She was a SHANKS) died in 1842, at the age of 73 years.
JOHN McCULLOCH, died October 20, 1848, at the age of 37 years.
JOHN M. PARKS, died May 8, 1849, at the age of 34 years.
SUSANNAH KERR, died October 10, 1841, at the age of 56 years.
SAMUEL KERR, died July 15, 1847, at the age of 68 years.
ELLEN KARR (so spelled), wife of SAMUEL KERR, died May 9, 1821, at the age of 42 years.
JEMIMAH REA, died September 5, 1829, at the age of 42 years.
THOMAS REA died December 23, 1824, at the age of 40 years.
SILAS REA, died June 5, 1852 at the age of 50 yrs.
ELIZABETH REA, wife of SILAS REA, died in 1885, at the age of 80 years.
DAVID J. REA, died February 24, 1891, at the age of 58 years.
A. H. HOWEY, died May 21, 1858, at the age of 68 years. (Buried on the same lot with the Rea family).
MARTHA F. HOWEY, died May 29, 1860 aged 48 years.
Sacred to the memory of JANE SHARP, wife of JOHN SHARP, died January 5, 1854, at the age of 40 years.
THOMAS SHARP, died October 10, 1835, at the age of 62 years. Born in 1773.
MARTHA SHARP, wife of THOMAS SHARP, died in the year 1837.
J. G. QUERY, died April 4, 1860 aged 45 years.
ELIZABETH A. QUERY, died in the year 1863, at the age of 39 years.
ELEANOR POTTS was born in 1782, and died in 1843.
DAVID S. COFFEY, born September 20, 1816; died on May 1, 1891.
JANE KERR COFFEY, born October 1, 1843; died July 23, 1893.
JANE HOUSTON, born March 17, 1809; died August 6, 1881.
JOHN REA, died August 1826, at the age of 47 yrs.
THOMAS DUNN, died December 10, 1838, at the age of 42 years.
JANE M. DUNN died in 1845, at the age of 47 years.
CAPT. ANDREW DUNN; died 1820 at the age of 45 yrs.
A. B. WILSON, died in 1832 at the age of 33 years.
MARGARET WILSON, wife of A. B. WILSON, died 1836, at the age of 27 years.
JOHN McKEE died May 17, 1764 aged 43 years. Born in 1721. This is one of the oldest graves in this cemetery.
PEGGY McKEE, wife of JOHN McKEE, died in 1795.
NANCY McKEE died July 10, 1806, at age of 22 yrs.
JONATHAN ORR, died in the month of March, 1828 at the age of 47 years.
SAMUEL W. ORR, died in 1843 at the age of 33 yrs.
WILLIAM P. REA, died June 20, 1862, at the age of 22 years.
ROBERT GRIER, born February 17, 1807; died on Feb. 5, 1899.
SOLOMON REID, born September 3, 1787; died May 27, 1863.
ELIAS ALEXANDER McKEE, born August 27, 1816; died January 8, 1890.
SAMUEL WATSON McKEE, born February 1, 1871; died in month of July, 1897.
WILLIAM McGILL MATTHEWS; born May 24, 1814; died September 16, 1874.
ANN REA MATTHEWS, wife of WILLIAM McGILL MATTHEWS born August 6, 1817; died July 7, 1883.
HUGH H. MATTHEWS; died August 15, 1822, at the age of 35 years.

WILLIAM S. CUNNINGHAM, died in the year 1841 at the age of 28 years.
LETITIA CUNNINGHAM, died October 5, 1857, at the age of 80 years. (Born 1777).
WILLIAM CUNNINGHAM, died October 21, 1843, at the age of 73 years. (Born 1770).
JAMES CUNNINGHAM, died in the year 1833, at the age of 57 years. (Born 1776).
JAMES HOUSTON died in February 1803, at the age of 29 years. Born 1774.
MARGARET MATTHEWS HOUSTON, died December 27, 1788, aged 41 years. (Born 1747).
AARON HOUSTON died January 10, 1777, aged 40 years. (Born in 1737).
ANDREW REA, died June 3, 1801, at the age of 69 years. (Born 1732).
J. K. REA died September 20, 1861, aged 30 years.
DAVID REA, soldier of the revolution, died Oct. 1, 1839, aged 82 years, 7 months. Born in March, 1757.
JOHN COLUMBUS REA died July 20, 1834, at the age of 16 months.
INFANT brother of JOHN COLUMBUS REA, born in 1826 and buried by his side.
JOHN REA, ESQ., died November 15, 1843, at the age of 79 years. (Born 1764).
JACOB M. REA died October 2, 1846, at the age of 33 years.
ROGER CUNNINGHAM, died November 24, 1807, at the age of 77 years. (Born 1730).
MARY CUNNINGHAM, wife of ROGER CUNNINGHAM, d. June 17, 1845. (Stone broken off).
AGNES HOWIE, died September 19, 1786, at the age of 22 years.
JAMES ORMAND, SR., died February 20, 1779, at the age of 91 years. This man was born in 1678; evidently the oldest person who is buried in Mecklenburg County. By his side is buried:
JAMES ORMOND, JR., died December 3, 1777 (before his father) at the age of 52 years.
MARY FLENNIKIN, wife of JOHN O. FLENNIKIN; a SIGNER of the Mecklenburg Declaration of Independence, died February 14, 1823; aged 47 years.

Mrs. Ray made the above note and says that it is correct, and the only explanation of the age of the wife is that JOHN FLENNIKIN married a very young person, perhaps is his second wife. The initial "O" in his name is certainly NEWS.

JAMES MORRISON, the "Signer".
ANNABEL MORRISON, wife of JAMES MORRISON, d. September 9, 1818, at the age of 89 yrs and 21 days.

And here all the time we have been told that NEILL MORRISON was the "signer". Are these old PROVIDENCE tombstones telling us the truth? If so, we will have to revise our History of Mecklenburg.

ISAAC POTTS; born May 30, 1817; died February 23, 1844.
DOROTHY L. POTTS, daughter of JOHN W. and ROCINDA POTTS; born 1845; died 1848.
JAMES POTTS, son of JOHN W. and ROCINDA POTTS born 1835; died 1848.
Two other infant sons of above, JOHN W. and BENJAMIN POTTS, died July 11, 1811.
JAMES POTTS died September 23, 1821, at the age of 38 years.

MARY POTTS died March 26, 1840 in her 60th year.
JAMES POTTS, SR. died November 4, 1827, aged 52 years (husband of MARY POTTS above).
LYDIA GRAHAM, consort of GEN. GEORGE GRAHAM, died October 23, 1843, aged about 80 years.
ANDREW BAXTER, JR. died December 31, 1798, at the age of 22 years.
ROBERT McDOWELL died December 12, 1781, aged 28 years. Born 1753.
JOHN POLK died July 9th, 1809, aged 34 years.
WALTER DAVIS died January 20, 1839, at the age of 71 years. Born 1768.
ANN DAVIS died February 4, 1808, aged 41 years.
MILAS J. ROBINSON, died July 3, 1825 aged 36 years
PHILLIP WEEKS died July 14, 1809, at the age of 71 years. (Born 1738).
ELIZABETH WEEKS, wife of PHILLIP WEEKS, died July 8, 1816, at the age of 73 years.
JOHN WYLIE died October 12, 1852, at the age of 24 years.
JOHN HOUSTON died June 20, 1812, aged 37 years.
WILLIAM GRIBBLE, born December 18, 1796; died July 5, 1859.
MARY A. GRIBBLE, wife of WILLIAM GRIBBLE, born Dec. 25, 1802; died June 19, 1880.
MOSES A. BARNETT; died December 8, 1848, aged 10 years.
R. C. BARNETT died October 20, 1854, aged 54 years.
ELIZABETH McLAUGHLIN, born in County Derry, Ireland in 1800, died in 1829.
KATHERINE McCULLOCH, daughter of JOHN and MARY McCULLOCH, died August 19, 1825, aged 17 years.
JANE McCULLOCH, daughter of JOHN and MARY McCULLOCH died September 20, 1825, aged 19 years.

JAMES DUNN died December 12, 1799, at the age of 77 years. (Born in 1722).
ANDREW DUNN, died June 30, 1805, at the age of 54 years.
MARY DUNN, died October 26, 1834, at the age of 84 years.
JAMES McCULLOCH died February 8, 1842 in his 68th year.
JANE McCULLOCH died March 10, 1843, in her 65th year.
KATHERINE McCULLOCH, daughter of JAMES and JANE McCULLOCH, died September 9, 1822, at the age of 17 years.
MARY McCULLOCH, daughter of JAMES and JANE McCULLOCH and wife of JAMES PARKS, died May 30, 1838, at the age of 25 years.
JOHN McCULLOCH died July 31, 1824, in his 78th year. (Born 1747).
KATHERINE McCULLOCH, died March 9, 1824 in her 78th year.
ELIZABETH McCULLOCH, wife of ISAAC McCULLOCH, died September 9, 1819, aged 52 years.
WILLIAM McCULLOCH, son of JOHN and KATHERINE McCULLOCH, died March 28, 1817, at the age of 47 years. Born 1770.
JAMES McCULLOCH, son of ELIJAH and JANEY McCULLOCH, died July 25, 1808, aged 4 months.
JAMES E. McCULLOCH, died October 3, 1831, at the age of 22 years.
AMOS McCULLOCH; born in 1798; died July 29th, 1823.
JAMES HOUSTON, died January 4th, 1802 aged 73.
GRIZEY HOUSTON died August 15, 1802 aged 63.
JAMES HOUSTON died April 1, 1812 aged 36 yrs.

TOMBSTONE INSCRIPTIONS IN UNION COUNTY, NORTH CAROLINA

Over the line in UNION COUNTY, NORTH CAROLINA - that part which was formerly in Mecklenberg County - there are several old churchyards, which this author visited. One is called HOPEWELL, another BETHLEHEM, and another EMANUEL PRESBYTERIAN.

HOPEWELL CHURCHYARD

WILLIAM GREEN LONG; born May 3, 1842; died Nov. 29 1928.
SARAH ELLEN LONG, wife of W. G. LONG; born Oct.27. 1849; died ____ (Still living in 1939).
ELIZA JANE FAULK, wife of HOSEA FAULK, 1845-1887.
JOSEPH WATKINS; born February 24, 1864; died March 12, 1929.
WALTER BANKS WATKINS; born 1893; died 1922.
FANNIE D. AUSTIN, wife of JAMES AUSTIN; born Oct. 29, 1849; died Feb. 17, 1911.
W. J. CONNELL; born December 5, 1849; died in the year 1926.
JULIA CONNELL, wife of W. J. CONNELL; born 1848; died in 1921.
JOHN M. CAMPBELL; died November 24, 1900, at the age of 70 years.
MARY C. CAMPBELL, wife of JOHN M. CAMPBELL; born in 1826; died in 1893.
REV. E. A. LEMMONS; born 1825; died in 1870.
MARTHA J. WILLIAMS, daughter of J. K. and J. J. WILLIAMS; born in 1885; died in 1907.
A. W. H. PRICE; born in 1841; died in 1915.

THE EMANUEL PRESBYTERIAN CHURCH CEMETERY

This old cemetery is on the highway North of UNIONVILLE between CONCORD and MONROE, North Carolina, about a mile South of where the highway crosses GOOSE CREEK. Many of the graves are unmarked, but, from some that have markers it appears that persons were buried here not long after the War Between the States. We were told there was an older graveyard that belonged to this church at another site not far away, but we were unable to locate the older site of this church.

We were told that it was perhaps on the North side of Goose Creek, about a mile distant from the one where the following inscriptions were copied:

MICHAEL CROWELL, born November 3, 1795; died March 24, 1865; his wife is buried on the same plot.
ANDREW S. CROWELL; born February 28, 1824; d. January 13, 1895.
THOMAS A. CROWELL; born 1816; died in 1846. (This is one of the older graves and shows a much earlier interment).
JOSHUA SIKES; born August 17, 1803; died May 8, 1878.
FRANCES SIKES, wife of JOSHUA SIKES; born in 1809; died 1878.
SAMUEL PYRON; born Sept. 6, 1810; died May 9, 1869.
M. H. McDAVIS; born June 7, 1838; died Jan. 23 1926.
HARRIETT J. BRIX, wife of MACK DAVIS died in 1909 aged 71 years.
GEORGE W. ROWELL; born 1866; died May, 1933.

BETHLEHEM CHURCH GRAVEYARD IN
UNION COUNTY, N. CAROLINA

We found this old burial place in Union County, South Carolina, in that part of the County, which at one time, was in MECKLENBURG COUNTY. We were told by old residents that the old Church had stood at one time close by the graves, now grown up in weeds and but few of them showing any signs of the slightest care. We were told that the Church building and site had been removed to some other location, just where we did not ascertain. The graveyard is not far from a bend in Goose Creek, and the names we copied will give some idea of the identity of the families who lived in this community. We copied the following inscriptions:

N. C. GLANTS, wife of JEREMIAH GLANTS; died July 1, 1858, at the age of 27 years.
BEVERLY (or BEACHLY) M. LONG, the wife of J. A. LONG; died August 7, 1855, at the age of 25 years.
LUCINDA C. CUTHBERTSON, died September 1, 1866.
ELIZABETH M. HUNTER, consort of JOHN G. HUNTER ; died June 30, 1855, at the age of 25 yrs.
THOMAS LONG; died October 8, 1874, at the age of 62 years.
SARAH LONG, wife of THOMAS LONG; born in the yr. 1801; died in 1896.
JACOB LONG was born April 1, 1769; and died Nov. 22, 1851.
MOSES W. CUTHBERTSON died October 11, 1844, at the age of 38 years.

BARBARA LONG, wife of JACOB LONG; was born on September 4, 1772 and died on October 18, 1856.
WILLIAM FRANKLIN LONG; born in the year 1836; died in 1886.
J. L. UUCE; born in 1859 and died in the year 1926.
CHARLES E. SEHORN, was born September 29, in 1808, and died June 18, 1850.
MARY SEHORN, wife of CHARLES E. SEHORN; born in 1814; died in 1874.
MARGARET SEHORN, daughter of CHARLES E. and MARY SEHORN, was born in 1844, and died in 1855.
RACHEL L. CUTHBERTSON, wife of MOSES W. CUTHBERTSON; born 1810; died in 1872.

NOTE: The LONGS appear to have been the oldest family in the community, and JACOB LONG and his wife BARBARA were plainly the ancestors of the family. The name of JAMES and HENRY LONG appear in the first census of this community in 1790, but the only Jacob lived at that time in what is or was then, ROWAN COUNTY. He may have moved across the line into Union or Mecklenburg later.

BAKERS GRAVEYARD IN IREDELL COUNTY, N. C.

There are two old graveyards that contain interesting histories in connection with the people of MECKLENBURG COUNTY, one being in Mecklenburg and one of them in IREDELL COUNTY. Both are not far from the old BEATTIE'S FORD crossing on the Catawba. The writer will have more to say about them later in this volume. From Sommerville's History of Hopewell Church, pages 316 and 317 are taken the following inscriptions from the IREDELL GRAVEYARD of the name:

MRS. LILLY CONNER, wife of JAMES CONNER; born April 1, 1773; died September 23, 1844.
JAMES CONNER, a patriot and soldier of the revolution. Born in IRELAND in 1754; died April 11 1835, at his seat in MECKLENBURG COUNTY, where he had resided for the past 60 years - in the 81st year of his age.
MARGARET J. BREVARD (MARGARET WILSON CONNER) wife of J. F. BREVARD, and daughter of JAMES and LILLY WILSON CONNER; born November 29, 1779 and died October 25; aged 67 years.
JOHN FRANKLIN BREVARD; born December 5, 1788; died February 13, 1827.
MOSES WILSON, son of WILLIAM J. WILSON and ROCINDA WILSON; born October 26, 1804; died October 30, 1805.
NEARIA LILLY BREVARD, daughter of JOHN F. and PEGGY J. BREVARD; born and died in 1821.
ALEXANDER F. BREVARD, son of JOHN F. and PEGGY J. BREVARD; born 1826; died June 4, 1831.
LILLY JULIA McDOWELL, daughter of R. L. and R. R. McDOWELL; born Sept. 3, 1854; died at the age of 6 years.
DAVID LAWSON, born December 15, 1799; died in the 26th year of his age.
MARY LAWSON; born April 28, 1776; died December 10, 1853.
BENJAMIN WILSON; born August 4th, 1800; died at the age of 56 years.
JOHN WILSON, born June 12, 1795 and died in the 43rd year of his life.

JOHN McCONNELL, died September 30, 1801 at the age of 80 years. (Born 1721).
SAMUEL WILSON, died March 13, 1778 (may be it was 1788) in his 68th year. (Born about 1720).
DORCAS WHITE; died June 24, 1832, aged 27 yrs
F. T. CARTER, born September 16, 1841; died November 25, 1862.
THOMAS GIVENS died May 10, 1780, aged 30 yrs.
EDWARD GIVENS, JR. died Feb. 16, 1792 in his 31st year.
ROBERT HANNAH died July 29, 1844, at the age of 71 years. (Born 1773).
ESTHER HANNAH, wife of ROBERT HANNAH, died January 23, 1856, aged 83 years.
MARY JANE FORTNER; born Sept. 9, 1855; died Feb. 11, 1897. Daughter of ABNER and NANCY MONTEITH.
MARY MASON, wife of ISAAC MASON, born Feb. 10 1803; died February 21, 1854.
T. P. WHITE, born April 14, 1802, and died Jan 19, 1867, at age of 59 years.
MARGARET WILSON, born February 12, 1804; died at the age of 58 years.
SARAH McCONNELL; born October 8, 1802, died at the age of 34 years. Wife of BENJAMIN McCONNELL.
SALLEY McCONNELL COOKE, died at the age of 7 years.
SARAH D. WHITE; died September 30, 1844, at the age of 64 years. (Born 1780).

```
: PRESBYTERIAN  CHURCH-YARD  - CHARLOTTE :
:                 NORTH CAROLINA           :
```

On the second block from the "Square" in the present City of Charlotte, N. C. stands the old Presbyterian Church fronting on TRADE STREET, but setting back in the block surrounded by magnificent trees and occupying the entire block of land. Immediately back of the Church comes a cross street, and then another block containing the Church Cemetery, well kept and preserved. In this cemetery are many ancient graves and tombs. To leave out the families here buried in a History of Mecklenburg County would be to rob such an account of its best flavor. In this thriving metropolis one realizes that a large double-block of its most valuable property has been here dedicated to the memory of its pioneer families.

We could not copy all of the inscriptions, and doubtless failed to make copies of many that should be here listed, but the following are representative of the whole:

MARY GRAHAM; she died July 7, 1791, at the age of 71 years. (Her body is buried in the oldest SUGAR CREEK CHURCHYARD, but the stone, which had fallen down was removed to this place & set up). The inscription continues: Her children were ESTHER, JOHN, GEORGE, JOSEPH, SARAH and ANN GRAHAM.
Immediately inside the entrance gate of the cemetery are the MORROW FAMILY GRAVES:
CATHERINE M. MORROW, wife of MAJ. BENJAMIN MORROW; died October 20, 1845, in the 48th year of her life.
ALLEN M. MORROW, son of MAJOR BENJAMIN MORROW and CATHERINE MORROW; died in 1840, at the age of 15 years.
In memory of MARY ANN MORROW, consort of J. W. MORROW; born September 22, 1823; died August 22, 1853.
JAMES BENJAMIN MORROW, son of J. W. and M. A. MORROW; born February 1840; died in 1856.
S. EMILY MORROW, consort of DR. H. M. PRITCHARD, & daughter of MAJ. B. and C. M. MORROW; died in 1848, at the age of 20 years.
ELIZABETH C. HARRIS, wife of DR. THOMAS HARRIS; d. in 1844, at the age of 36 years.
THOMAS HARRIS, M. D., died in 1848, at the age of 45 years.
SAMUEL TAYLOR, SR., died in the month of SEPTEMBER 1841 at the age of 79 years. (b. 1762).
SUSANNAH BOYD, the wife of COL. THOMAS BOYD, daughter of JOSEPH and WINNIFRED DARNELL; born in JUNE, 1777; died in November 1845.
SAMUEL B. McCOMB, son of SAMUEL and ALICE McCOMB; died in 1842 at the age of 32 years.
AUGUSTUS J. ORR; born in 1838; died in 1866.
MAJ. GENERAL GEORGE GRAHAM; died March 29, 1826 at the age of 68 years.
DAVID M. HENDERSON, died in 1862 at the age of 65 years.
DR. THOMAS HENDERSON, died August 5, 1816, in the 62nd year of his age. (Born 1754)
ISAAC S. HENDERSON, died in 1861 at the age of 82 years. (Born 1779).
LUCINDA HENDERSON, the wife of ISAAC S. HENDERSON, died in 1860; aged 78 years. (Born 1782).
MARY HENDERSON died in 1818. She was the wife of DR. THOMAS HENDERSON and she was 66 years old at the time of her death. (Born 1752).
PAMELA HENDERSON, died in 1801, at the age of 16 years.
JOEL BALDWIN, died October 21, 1776, at the age of 26 years.
Sacred to the memory of NATHANIEL ALEXANDER, Governor of NORTH CAROLINA, who died March 7th 1808, in the 52nd year of his age.
FRANCIS IRWIN, the son of JOHN IRWIN, died September 24th, 1837. Nineteen years of age when he died.

WASHINGTON MORRISON, an attorney; died September 28, 1836, at the age of 35 years.
JOHN BLAIR IRWIN, the fourth son of JOHN and MARY IRWIN; died an infant in 1825.
JOHN IRWIN, the third son of JOHN and MARY IRWIN, infant, died in 1823.
JUNIUS AUGUSTUS IRWIN, son of JOHN and MARY IRWIN, died aged 7 months in 1827.
THOMAS GILLESPIE, born March 12, 1796; died January 25, 1829.
MARGARET GILLESPIE, born July 13, 1784; died October 30, 1850.
MARGARET POLK ALEXANDER, wife of DR. ALEXANDER died in September, 1800, at the age of 42 years. (Born in 1758).
MARY LONG DAVIDSON died at the age of 6 years.
HON. WILLIAM DAVIDSON; born September 2, 1778; died September 16, 1857, at the age of 80 years.
MARSHALL T. POLK, died April 5, 1831, at the age of 27 years.
JOHN IRWIN; born September 30, 1787; died July 18, 1860, at the age of 73 years.
MRS. MARY IRWIN, wife of JOHN IRWIN, and the daughter of MR. JAMES PATTON; died April 6, 1833, at the age of 37 years.

The firm of PATTON & ERWIN owned the site on which the City of ASHVILLE, N. C. now stands and sold the town lots at the time it was established.

DR. JOSEPH W. CALDWELL; born March 22, 1833; died June 9, 1862.
ANNE P. THOMAS, daughter of MAJ. BENJAMIN and CATHERINE M. MORROW; born April 11,1816; died July 30, 1846.
INFANT CHILD of J. W. and M. A. MORROW, died in 1852.
MARY ANN MORROW, consort of J. W. (JOHN WHITE) MORROW; born September 22, 1823; died on August 22, 1853.
CALEB ERWIN; born April 12, 1794; died April 16, 1856.
MARGARET CAROLINE TAYLOR, daughter of SAMUEL and ELLENER TAYLOR; died February 19, 1841, aged 11 years.
ELLENER TAYLOR, consort of SAMUEL TAYLOR, JR. died June 30, 1751, at the age of 40 yrs.
NANCY CATHERINE ALLISON, wife of THOMAS C. ALLISON and daughter of SAMUEL and ELLENER TAYLOR; died August 1, 1858 aged 28.
JANE ELIZABETH OWENS, wife of HENRY C. OWENS & daughter of the late WILLIAM ALLISON; b. March 30, 1813; died May 28, 1867.
HENRY C. OWENS; born November 15, 1797; died June 24, 1848.

JOSEPH WASHINGTON OWENS, son of HENRY C. OWENS; Born 1839; died 1842.
SOPHIA GRAHAM, wife of DR. JOHN R. WITHERSPOON, of Alabama, and daughter of GEN. JOSEPH GRAHAM, of NORTH CAROLINA; born February 20, 1791; died December 30, 1865.
GEORGE CARRUTH died October 7, 1829, at the age of 39 years.
WILLIAM F. McLELLAND; born October 5th, 1808; d. Feb. 28, 1856.
THOMAS TROTTER; born December 7, 1800; died Ma..n 31, 1865.
MARGARET GRAHAM TROTTER, consort of THOMAS TROTTER; born June 7, 1810; died November 30th, 1847.
THOMAS B. TROTTER, C. S. A., born November 23rd, 1839; died July 22, 1864.
CATHERINE GRAHAM; born in SCOTLAND, emigrated to this country in the year 1820; died June 10, 1865, at the age of 81 years.
RICHARD CARSON; died Feb. 16, 1855, aged 46 yrs.
ANDREW SPRINGS; died October 15, 1860, at the age of 75 years.
MARY SPRINGS, wife of ANDREW SPRINGS, died October 20th, 1869, aged 75 years.
DELIA SPRINGS; died in 1861, at the age of 25 yrs
DR. JOSEPH W. CALDWELL; born March 22, 1823; died June 9, 1862.

HARRIETT ANN CARSON, wife of RICHARD CARSON; daughter of REV. J. M. WILSON, D. D.; born August 3rd, 1818; died April 7th, 1850, with her infant.
WILLIAM CARSON; born December 4, 1782, in Co. ANTRIM, IRELAND; landed in CHARLESTON, S. C. in April, 1801; died November 22, 1846.
JULIA ADELAIDE WILSON, wife of JOSEPH H. WILSON, youngest daughter of JAMES PATTON, SR.; born December 8th, 1815; died in August, 1846.
JONATHAN WILMARTH, of New York, died September 26, 1834, aged 41 years.
DR. D. F. CALDWELL; born April 4, 1799; died December 24, 1861.
ELIZA CALDWELL, wife of DR. D. F. CALDWELL & daughter of WILLIAM DAVIDSON, died July 11, 1845, at the age of 39 years.
GENERAL THOMAS POLK and wife SUSANNA POLK ; Signer. Memorial erected by his son WILLIAM POLK. No dates.
P. C. CALDWELL; born August 21, 1802; died on January 26, 1865.
S. R. CALDWELL, wife of P. C. CALDWELL; born August 22, 1810; died March 12, 1863.
MARSHALL T. POLK; died April 5, 1831; at the age of 27 years.

ELMWOOD CEMETERY

ELMWOOD CEMETERY is just the typical City Burial Place, used by the people of the modern municipality of CHARLOTTE. People were buried in this cemetery as far back as the Civil War, and perhaps earlier. It is an immense plot of ground and a complete list of its inscriptions would fill a small volume. We copied a comparatively few of the epitaphs, but in them will be found the names of many of the old families who date back to the beginning of the history of this "HORNET'S NEST OF THE REVOLUTION", in which the research workers will be interested, on account of the dates, names, etc.

JAMES PATTON IRWIN; born March 20, 1820; died on November 24, 1903.
HARRIETT MORRISON IRWIN, wife of JAMES PATTON IRWIN; born September 18, 1828; died May 27, 1897.
DR. JOHN IRWIN, son of JAMES PATTON IRWIN; born 1855; died in 1894.
JAMES BLACKBURN RANKIN; born May 17, 1830; died October 29, 1903.
MARTHA JOHNSTON RANKIN, wife of J. B. RANKIN; b. December 26, 1829; died October 23, 1887.
MARY B. RANKIN; born 1862; died in 1882.
JAMES B. RANKIN; born 1868; died in 1879.
THOMAS S. RANKIN; born 1880; died in 1897.
CALVIN M. RAY; born February 8, 1819; died APRIL 5, 1885.
MARTHA M. RAY; born August 8, 1821; Died June 7, 1900.
ROBERT CALVIN RAY; born April 22, 1883; died in 1884.
WILLIAM A. RAY; born April 25, 1858; died March 1, 1906.
MINOR JONES RAY; born January 8, 1879; died on October 19, 1918.
EDGAR C. RAY; born December 14, 1877; died Aug. 13, 1932.
ROBERT CALVIN RAY; born April 22, 1833; died on 1884.
MARY DOWNS RAY, wife of ROBERT R. RAY; born Sept 27, 1854; died June 17, 1936.
DR. JOHN H. GIBBONS; born February 14th, 1795; died December 16, 1868.
CATHERINE GIBBONS, wife of DR. JOHN H. GIBBONS; born March 31, 1799; died December 28th, 1874.
MARSHALL JONES; born October 3, 1847; died Feb. 3, 1871.

JOHN G. WILSON, born April 4, 1804; died November 11, 1881.
ELIZABETH WILSON, wife of JOHN G. WILSON; b. July 9, 1803; died May 10, 1888.
LYDIA WILSON, born May 9, 1835; died Nov. 21st 1923.
JOSEPHINE JAMISON; born March 26, 1848; died March 9, 1928. Wife of S. NEAL JAMISON.
MRS. MARY CRAY; born Feb. 22, 1812; died June 15, 1881.
JANE C. CRAY; born July 29, 1834; died April 23, 1881.
KATHERINE T. ANDREWS, the wife of C. M. DAVIDSON; born 1867; died in 1926.
MARY LAURA SPRINGS, wife of JOHN J. BLACKWOOD; born July 12, 1823; died December 2nd, 1908.
JOHN J. BLACKWOOD; born April 10, 1810; died December 4, 1881.
ELI SPRINGS BLACKWOOD, son of JOHN J. BLACKWOOD; born Sept. 30, 1842; died August 7th, 1921.
W. C. BLACKWOOD; born Nov. 7, 1848; died Nov. 10, 1894.
JAMES J. BLACKWOOD; born January 7, 1816; died June 8, 1869.
J. J. BERRYHILL; born February 16, 1807; died November 2, 1862. (Killed).
HARRIETT BERRYHILL, died June 29, 1879; aged 74 years.
NINA CATHERINE HANNA; born 1835; died 1891.
MOSES ALLISON; born in ROWAN COUNTY, NORTH C., July 30, 1826; died in Mecklenburg County in 1874.
MARY ANN DAVIDSON, the wife of REV. ALEXANDER SINCLAIR; born Rural Hill, N. C., in 1837; died in 1902.

CHARLOTTE M. DAVIDSON, wife of W. F. DAVIDSON;
born August 20, 1828; died June 18, 1885.
SAMUEL E. LINTON; born 1835; died in 1912.
WILLIAM MAXWELL; born September 9, 1809; died on
October 26, 1890.
NANCY ADELINE MAXWELL; born 1817; died 1895.
CHARLES C. LEE; died 1862 in the C. S. army.
JAMES WALKER OSBORNE; born December 25, 1811; d.
August 11, 1869.
MARY ANN IRWIN, wife of JAMES WALKER OSBORNE, also buried here.
JULIA BAXTER, the wife of A. BAXTER SPRINGS; born
October 24, 1827; died Feb. 27, 1902.
COL. A. BAXTER SPRINGS; born October 21, 1819; d.
January 27, 1886.
A. B. SPRINGS, JR., born December 18, 1857; died
at BOERNE, TEXAS, May 30, 1881.
JOHN SPRINGS; born August 20, 1853; died January
6, 1890.
JOHN GRAHAM, an emigrant from Scotland; died in
February, 1880, aged 82 years.
ALEXANDER GRAHAM died in 1873 at the age of 73
years. He was a Ruling Elder in the Presbyterian Church of Charlotte.
WORTH A. DAVIDSON; born in 1895; died in 1898.
W. V. KIDD; born in 1879 and died in the year 1918

BREVARD DAVIDSON SPRINGS was born in the year
1860, and died in 1936.
CAROLINE CLARKSON SPRINGS was born in the year
1861, and died in 1938.
JOHN S. MEANS, was born April 13, 1846; died
July 28, 1900.
ROBERT GIBBONS, M. D., was born December 31st
1822; died May 14, 1898.
MARY GIBBONS was born January 25, 1825; died
April 17, 1907.
DAVID PARKS was born February 5, 1797; died on
June 13, 1873.
ANN ADELINE ORR, wife of DAVID PARKS (m. in
1827) born 1803; died 1835.
ANNE CHAMBERS LOCKE, wife of DAVID PARKS (m.
in 1837) born 1800; died in 1890.
DUNCAN CALDER; died May 19, 1883 at the age of
72 years.
FERDINAND KUESTER died on April 10, 1882; aged
53 years.
WILLIS I. HENDERSON; born October 4, 1861; d.
August 18, 1917.
THOS. HENDERSON PRITCHARD, D. D., born in 1832;
died in 1898.
JOSEPH GRAHAM, M. D., born April 15, 1837; d.
August 13, 1907. Beloved Physician.

GILEAD CHURCH INSCRIPTIONS

GILEAD PRESBYTERIAN CHURCH (A. P. R.) is located some four or five miles North of the
HOPEWELL CHURCH on the Beattie's Ford road in the Northern part of Mecklenburg County and not very
far South of BEATTY'S FORD. Baker's Graveyard, the burial place of REV. JOHN THOMSON is only about
a mile or so North of it. In fact the Church may have been located at the Baker's graveyard site
in the beginning, though all records that far back are unavailable. In the Sommerville History of
Hopewell we are told that the first pastor was perhaps a REV. JOHN BOYCE, and that REV. JAMES McKNIGHT (installed in 1797) preached to this congregation for thirty-five years, at the same time
serving COODLE CREEK and HOPEWELL in S.C. Among the early Ruling Elders of GILEAD are found the
names of WILLIAM HENDERSON, DAVID SMITH, HUGH LUCAS, PATRICK JOHNSON, GILBREATH McKNIGHT, JASPER
BLAKELY, WHITE MORROW, ALEXANDER GIBSON, JESSE WHITLOW, JOHN and EWART BELL and JOHN PRICE, JR.,
names that like that of EZEKIEL ALEXANDER, another one, recall the elder and earliest families of
MECKLENBURG COUNTY. There are many unmarked graves in the old GILEAD CHURCHYARD and one can only
surmise the names of the families whose members were here buried and left unmarked and unidentified
for future generations. The following are among the inscriptions there at this time:

JOHN M. ALEXANDER, born June 3, 1811; died in the
month of August, 1848.
GEO. SIDNEY HOUSTON
RACHEL HOUSTON, wife of GEORGE SIDNEY HOUSTON; b.
1796; died 1848.
JAMES HOUSTON, died July 23, 1843.
HOUSTON JOHNSTON
REBECCA CATHERINE JOHNSTON, wife of HOUSTON JOHNSTON; born Nov. 10, 1809; died Feb.7, 1837.
R. H. JOHNSTON born in 1806; died 1867.
MARY LOWRIE (JOHNSTON?) married first M. S. LOWRIE; married second D. O. McBAVEN; she d.
July 25, 1849.
JAMES S. JOHNSTON; born March 9, 1840; died Mar.
30, 1867.
J. ALEX JOHNSTON, died May 8, 1871.
PATRICK HUNTER JOHNSTON; died January 25, 1858.
ELIZA SMITH died November 14, 1854, at the age of
80 years. Born 1774.
JAMES SMITH, born ANTRIM COUNTY, IRELAND; Came
to America November 1827; died May 27th in
1860.
ESTHER SMITH, born ANTRIM COUNTY, IRELAND; Came
to America November 1826; died in 1868 at
the age of 75 years.
SARAH V. BELL; born January 2, 1796; died March
21, 1867.
WILL D. HANNA died on January 1, 1822, at the
age of 69 years. (Born 1753).
MOSES WILHEIM d. June 21, 1876 at age of 60 yrs.
S. W. DUCKWORTH d. Jan. 7, 1861, 78 years of age.

JANE BELL, daughter of JOHN and RACHEL BELL;
born April 20, 1799; and died September
5, 1886.
PAMILLA BERNICE OSBORNE, daughter of MILTON
and ANN OSBORNE; born September 17th
1839; died September 19, 1843.
ELIZABETH M. OSBORNE, daughter of MILTON and
ANN OSBORNE; born January 25, 1826; d.
August 31, 1841.
NANCY HENDERSON, wife of WILLIAM HENDERSON;
died June 25, 1813, aged 78 years. She
was born 1735.
DAVID SMITH, died January 12, 1833, at the age
of 81 years.
NANCY SMITH, died January 28, 1822 age 79 yrs.
MARY McKNIGHT, born Dec. 26, 1779; died July
26, 1811.
ELI ALEXANDER; born November 5th, 1784; died
July 26, 1834.
PRUDENCE McAULEY, died Sept. 19, 1816, at the
age of 50 years.
MRS. MARY M. SIFFORD, born March 17, 1803; d.
July 7, 1839.
WILL BEARD, born in 1766; died June 8, 1844.
SARAH B. RILEY, daughter of S. A. RILEY, d.
August 27, 1858, aged 48 years.
DANIEL McAULEY, revolutionary soldier; born
July 1, 1756; died Dec. 24, 1840.
GEORGE ROGERS, born June, 1739; died in 1814.
THOMAS D. PRICE, son of JAMES and ELLEN PRICE
d. Oct. 3, 1845 at the age of 12 years.

THE SIX MILE CHURCH BURIAL GROUNDS

There are TWO DIFFERENT SIX MILE CHURCH BURIAL GROUNDS. Neither of these cemeteries are in the present MECKLENBURG COUNTY, but the first, or eldest one of them, I am quite sure is within what was one time considered a part of Mecklenburg. It is now in what is called by some the BELLE AIRE section of SOUTH CAROLINA. The original SIX MILE CHURCH (Presbyterian) named for the Creek not far distant, is some four miles North of the present CHURCH of that name. The original Church has completely disappeared, with only the leaning and weather beaten tombstones of the old graveyard left to mark the spot. One of the leading spirits of the first Church was undoubtedly JAMES McKNIGHT MORROW, whose tombstone, with that of his wife SUSAN is still standing, along with those of many of his kin and his old neighbors, while his son ALLEN MORROW was the builder of the new Church, some miles South, and is there buried. Practically all readable inscriptions of the elder graveyard are copied, and not all, but many of these at the new site.

FROM THE OLD SIX MILE CEMETERY:

In memory of JAMES MORROW, SR.; died October 5th 1829, aged 64 years, 7 months, 14 days.
Sacred to the memory of SUSAN MORROW, Sen., wife of JAMES MORROW; died October 7, 1837, aged 72 years, 3 months and 22 days.
WILLIAM MORROW died October 18, 1831, at the age of 19 years.
SUSAN MORROW, daughter of JAMES MORROW and SUSANAH MORROW; died September 3, 1835, aged 32 years and 7 months.
MARGARET E. MORROW, died October 2, 1840 aged 9 years.
NANCY H. MORROW; died March 30, 1833, aged 20 yr and 11 months.
JOHN M. COFFEY, died October 1, 1842, aged of 31 years.
ELSY S. COFFEY, died May 16, 1839, at the age of 31 years.
JANE COFFEY died September 24, 1842, at the age of 31 years and 7 months.
ALEXANDER S. BIGGER; born March 28, 1785; died November 3, 1815.
ELIZABETH P. HAGINS, died March 27, 1820, at the age of 17 years.
JOSEPH HAGINS, died November 25, 1807, at the age of 43 years.
MARTHA HUTCHISON, who departed this life Dec. 16 1813 in the 21st year of her age.
In memory of MARY PATTON, who died March 8, 1820 at the age of 22 years.

FROM THE NEW SIX MILE CHURCHYARD:

MARY E. DOBY, only daughter of JOHN M. and ELIZABETH E. DOBY; died in 1828, aged 4 years.
ELIZABETH P. DOBY, wife of JOHN M. DOBY, died June 22, 1837 at the age of 32 years and 8 months.
JAMES W. WHITE, died May 18, 1849, at the age of 47 years.
ELIZABETH T. WHITE, died July 23, 1865, at the age of 54 years.
JAMES MILLER, died December 27, 1835, at the age of 55 years.
JOEL CHERRY died June 10, 1848, at the age of 79 years (Born 1769).
MRS. NANCY CHERRY, died June 24, 1859, at the age of 75 years.
MARY REBECCA MASSEY, wife of JOHN MASSEY; born September 21, 1808; died December 24, 1829.
GEORGE WASHINGTON BECKHAM, son of GEORGE D. and ELIZABETH BECKHAM; born June 3, 1829, and died September 9, 1844.
MARGARET SAINS, wife of THOMAS SAINS, died June 30, 1853, aged 61 years.
MARY GIBBONS, first wife of THOMAS GIBBONS; d. Aug. 8, 1831, at the age of 49 years.

DAVID HAGINS, died June 27, 1847, at the age of 50 years.
ANN C. HAGINS, only daughter of DAVID and LOUISA HAGINS, died in 1827 at the age of 5 years.
JOHN CULP, died October 7, 1842 at the age of 59 years.
MARY ANN CULP, died in 1851, aged 72 years.
NIMIRA COFFEY, wife of A. A. COFFEY, died March 1, 1858 at the age of 37 years.
Here lie the remains of ISAAC ROSSER, son of MAJ. JOSEPH ROSSER; born in CHATHAM COUNTY, N. C. October 7, 1783; d. March 15, 1851.
ELIZABETH ROSSER, wife of ISAAC ROSSER, d. November 9, 1847 at the age of 58 yrs.
KATE LUCKY, wife of COL. R. M. SIMS; born December 3, 1835; died Oct. 21, 1867.
JOHN P. STEWART, died March 9, 1857 at the age of 33 years.
JAMES H. STEWART, C. S. A., died in 1868 at the age of 37 years.
In memory of ALLEN MORROW; died October 6, 1883, aged 84 years 5 mos. 10 days.
CLARA A. MORROW, wife of ALLEN MORROW; d. February 13, 1879 aged 58 years.
W. C. GIBBONS, born March 22, 1821; died September 16, 1867, aged 46 years.
THOS. M. BLAKENEY; born September 20, 1854; died December 30, 1886.
SALLY J. MORROW, daughter of ALLEN and CLARA MORROW; born November 9, 1843; died May 27, 1918. She married a BURLEYSON.
M. C. HEATH; born February 21, 1806; died May 30, 1867.
MARY MORROW HEATH, wife of M. C. HEATH; b. February 19, 1809; died February 28, 1903.
EUGENIA A. HEATH; born November 24, 1846; died June 14, 1854.
HENRY B. HEATH; born May 22, 1851; died August 7, 1858.
WILLIAM D. HEATH; born in 1842, and died in 1865.
SARAH W. HEATH, born in 1853, and died in 1856.
CHARLOTTE L. HEATH, an infant, died February 10, 1830.
WILLIAM J. CURETON; born February 4, 1816; died April 18, 1863.
BENJAMIN JAMES CURETON; born August 28, 1839; died November 12, 1876.
NANNIE AZILEE CURETON, daughter of BENJ. J. and J. A. CURETON; born 1870; d. 1871.
LILLIAN STEWART CURETON, daughter of BENJ. J. and J. A. CURETON; b. 1864; d. 1865.
MARGARET SCALES, wife of THOMAS SCALES; died June 30, 1853, aged 61 years & 6 months.
ILA STEWART, infant daughter of JOHN P. and E. L. HEATH, Camilla, Ga. 1869-1890.

MRS. SARAH MASSIE, died February 18, 1861, aged 79 years. Born 1782.
ELIZABETH MASSIE, the wife of JOHN MASSIE; born April 15, 1805; died March 16, 1835.
WILLIAM ALFRED MASSIE, born in 1841; died 1846.
JOSEPH HAGINS died December 5, 1848, at the age of 47 years.
B. C. HAGINS, son of JOSEPH HAGINS and his wife JANE HAGINS, died September 29, 1841, at the age of 37 years.
JOSEPH GILLESPIE died March 21, 1839, at the age of 72 years. (Born 1787).
MINERVA MELVINA GILLESPIE, the daughter of JOSEPH and TEMPERANCE GILLESPIE, died July 20th, 1843, at the age of 16 years.
JAMES DELANEY; born November 11, 1819; died Oct. 9, 1897.
CATHERINE CALPHENIA DELANEY; born December 26th 1823; died September 17th, 1901; wife of JAMES DELANEY.
LT. ROBERT H. PORTER, C. S. A., died August 23rd 1864, at the age of 32 years.
MARGARET P. S. PORTER, wife of ROBERT H. PORTER; died September 18, 1856, aged 23 years.

JOHN MOORE died September 2, 1833, at the age of 60 years and 8 months. Born 1773.
OLIVIA MOORE died December 17, 1857, at the age of 84 years and 9 months.
JOHN P. MOORE, son of JOHN and OLIVIA MOORE, & husband of MARGARET Ma. MOORE; died Oct. 22, 1834, at the age of 39 years and 9 months.
HUGH MOORE, BARN December 28, 1799; died Sept. 11, 1843 at the age of 43 years and 8 months.
OLIVIA J. MILLER, wife of R. J. MILLER, daughter of JOHN and OLIVIA MOORE, died October 29, 1840 at the age of 23 years and 6 months.
RICHARD J. MILLER, died February 28, 1844, at the age of 28 years.
MAY SIMMLER, wife of JOHN SIMMLER; born June 28, 1819; died November 30th, 1848.
SMITH J. MILLER, died in 1849 aged 31 years & 10 months.
JAMES W. MILLER, son of SMITH and MARGARET MILler died in 1834 aged 14 years.
WALTER S. MILLER, died March 1836 aged 46 years.

THE OLD WAXHAW CHURCH CEMETERY

This ancient burial ground is in Lancaster County, South Carolina, but there was the time, doubtless, when it was considered a part of MECKLENBURG COUNTY, in North Carolina, when the location of the dividing line between the two Carolinas was undetermined and in doubt. In that section of this volume dealing with deeds to lands and wills registered at Charlotte Courthouse will be found many relating to lands on Waxhaw Creek and in what was called "Waxhaws" in Mecklenburg County. For that reason, and for the further reason that the names found on the list are of great historical interest, the inscriptions below are taken from the tombstones and included in this work. It is a rare list, but like others we have presented herein, not all of the inscriptions are included, but only those, in most instances, having relation to families who it is believed, or their kin, resided in Mecklenburg County. In other words, the inscriptions copied & given below relate to "neighbors" of the Mecklenburg Signers:

....

WILLIAM R. DAVIE, the Soldier, Jurist, Statesman, born in EDINBURG, SCOTLAND in 1756; died in South Carolina in 1820.
HYDER A. DAVIE; born October 29, 1786; died June 17, 1848.
ARCHIBALD DAVIE; born in Great Britain in the year 1764; died March 1, 1800; leaving three children: WILLIAM DAVIE, MARY DAVIE and a JOSEPH DAVIE
(The above inscriptions are in the private inclosure, with massive iron gates, just off to one side of the cemetery, and nearer the present Church building; all evergrown with vines and surrounded by evergreens.)
....

JAMES WALKUP died February 1, 1798.
MARGARET WALKUP, died December 22, 1793, at the age of 53 years.
JAMES WALKUP died September 23, 1807, at the age of 23 years.
ELIZABETH WALKUP died September 1, 1826, at the age of 39 years, and left behind a husband and seven children.
ROBERT WALKUP born January 25, 1780; died Sept. 22, 1846; aged 66 years.
JAMES ALEXANDER WALKUP aged 15 years;
JOHN HOBY WALKUP aged 12 years;
JOSEPH W. WALKUP, aged 10 years;
ROBERT WALKUP, aged 8 years; and
JOSEPH HOBY WALKUP aged 19 years, all expired amidst flames February 7, 1823. (They were burned to death.)

ANDREW GAMBLE; born August 4, 1771; died Sept. 3, 1853.
BETHIA GAMBLE, born October 11, 1788; died on March 3, 1856.
JAMES A. WHITE; born April 19, 1831; died in 1834.
MARGARET P. WHITE, died in the year 1831.
JAMES H. COFFEY, died in 1842.
WILLIAM A. COFFEY died in 1843.
DR. SAMUEL DUNLAP; born September 29, 1765; & died January 20, 1810.
ROBERT C. DUNLAP, born in 1829, and died year 1830.
ELIZABETH A. DUNLAP; born in the year 1795, & died in 1828.
JOHN CRAWFORD; born December 24, 1778; and died April 21, 1834. (Kin of ANDREW JACKSON).
JANE CRAWFORD; born April 3, 1762; died in the month of JULY, 1841.

....
"ere lies buried
ANDREW JACKSON, SR.
father of the 7th President of the United States; born in IRELAND; died in February in the year 1767.
Erected by CATAWBA CHAPTER D. A. R., of ROCK HILL, South Carolina.
....

JOHN FOSTER; born August 14, 1785; died June 28, 1868.
WILLIAM R. FOSTER, died in 1843, at the age of 16 years.
JAMES COWAN died in 1801, at the age of 28 yrs.

408

MARY DUNLAP died July 4, 1822, at the age of 68 years (Born 1754).
JAMES DUNLAP died February 26, 1846, at the age of 64 years, leaving a wife, three daughters and one son.
ELIZABETH DUNLAP, wife of JAMES DUNLAP, died May 26, 1858, at the age of 73 years.
ROBERT DUNLAP, died October 15, 1832, at the age of 54 years.
SARAH DUNLAP, died September 16, 1842, at the age of 60 years.
JAMES SOMERVILLE, died in August, 1790, at the age of 48 years.

GEORGE McKEMEY, died October 10, 1793, at the age of 79 years. (He was born in 1714)
MARGARET McKEMEY, wife of GEORGE McKEMEY, died on April 30, 1790, at the age of 60 years. (She was born in 1730.)

> MARGARET McKEMEY had been MARGA-
> RET HUTCHINSON, sister of the
> mother of PRESIDENT ANDREW JACK-
> SON.

ANN C. McKEMEY, wife of WILLIAM McKEMEY, died in 1818, at the age of 57 years. She was a Cowser, or COUSAR.

ROBERT HARPER, died May 15, 1800, at the age of 34 years. (Born in 1766).
DANIEL HARPER, died July 15, 1791, at the age of 46 years. (Born in 1745).
MARTHA E. HARPER died in 1805, at the age of one year.
MARTHA HARPER died January 11, 1815, at the age of 74 years. (Born in 1741).
BENJAMIN HARPER died June 12, 1801, at the age of 66 years. (Born in 1735).
WILLIAM HARPER died July 21, 1799, at the age of 36 years. (Born in 1763).
ROBERT HARPER died in 1806, at the age of 34 yrs.
HERCULES HUEY, died in the month of September in 1775, at the age of 50 years. (Born 1725).
CATHERINE HUEY, died November 6, 1808, at the age of 80 years. (Born in 1728).
JOSEPH BAKER died August 24, 1800, at the age of 30 years.
W. M. HADDEN, member of the First S. C. Regiment in the Revolutionary War.
REBECCA M. FOSTER, consort of HENRY FOSTER, and the daughter of WILLIAM and NANCY DUNLAP; died October 7, 1833, aged 23 years.
WILLIAM G. MASSIE, the youngest son of JAMES and MARY MASSIE, died March 20, 1841, at the age of 34 years. Left a wife and one daughter.

JAMES CROW, died July 17, 1775, at the age of 59 years.

> His wife was GRACE HUTCHINSON,
> sister of MRS. ANDREW JACKSON,
> SR. and aunt of the PRESIDENT.

MARTHA GREER, wife of JAMES GREER, of North Caro-lina. She went to pay her daughter MARGARET DAVIS a visit and was there arrested by death October 18, 1805, in the 53rd year of her age, leaving a husband and four children: ALEXANDER, MARGARET, AGNES and JAMES GREER.
JOHN RODGERS died on October 31, 1813, at the age of 70 years. (Born 1743).
JAMES JOHNSTON died on April 20, 1805, at the age of 40 years.

JENNIET BLAIR, the wife of JOHN BLAIR, died on August 29, 1817, at the age of 55 years.
JOHN LATTA, Lay Elder of WAXHAW CHURCH, died January 9, 1795, at the age of 68 years. (Born in 1727).
WILLIAM DAVIES, B. S., died on November 17th 1799, at the age of 24 years.

MR. WILLIAM BLAIR, born in County Antrim, Ire-land; died July 2, 1824, aged 66 years; born March 21, 1759, and when about 13 years old came with his father's family to America. He was a Revolutionary Patri-ot. His wife, MRS. SARAH BLAIR was the daughter of GEORGE DOUGLASS, and was born July 18, 1765, in this vicinity, and she died September 17, 1816. She was the mother of
MARY BLAIR
JAMES BLAIR
JANE BLAIR
DORCAS BLAIR
GEORGE BLAIR
ELIZABETH BLAIR
WILLIAM BLAIR

AGNES BARNETT died March 24, 1778, at the age of 55 years. (Born in 1723).
MARTHA BARNETT died September 26, 1775 at the age of 53 years.
SAMUEL BARNETT died November 23, 1774, in the 22nd year of his age.
JOSEPH BARNETT, died February 12, 1779, in the 24th year of his age.
MARGARET BARNETT died October 29, 1784, at the age of 25 years.
SAMUEL DUNLAP, ESQ. died September 17, 1801, at the age of 61 years. (Born in 1740).
WILLIAM TAYLOR died January 8, 1798 at the age of 39 years.
HENRY F. COUTZON; born in 1798, and died in the year 1865.
JAMES M. MOORE, born December 5, 1849; died on September 3, 1886. His wife was R. M. MOORE, buried on the same plot.
ROBERT HOWARD died in 1776.
JOSEPH HOWARD, died April 15, 1799, at the age of 25 years.
LETITIA DUNLAP died in the year 1805, at the age of 48 years.
JAMES WALKUP died September 23, 1807, at the age of 33 years.
MARGARET WALKUP died December 22, 1793, at the age of 53 years.
ELIZABETH JOHNSTON died November 19, 1805, at the age of 53 years.
SARAH HOWE (HUEY - HOWIE, Etc.) died September 20, 1791, at the age of 55 years.
JOHN STEWART, died April 2, 1851, at the age of 78 years.
SUSANNAH HART, died on September 6th, 1817, at the age of 82 years.
JAMES COUSART, born in Ireland; died September 29, 1801, in the 28th year of his age.
ELIZABETH COUSART, his wife (stone broken).
DAVID COUSART or COUSAR, a native of County Armagh, Ireland, died July 17, 1807, at the age of 30 years.
DAVID COUSART; died October 20, 1805, at the age of 33 years.
ARCHIBALD COUSART, died in the month of June in 1791, at the age of 45 years.
SUSANNAH H. COUSART; born February 20th, 1816; died October 12, 1856.
MARTHA COUSART, consort of WILLIAM; born Nov. 4, 1776; died Jan. 18, 1830 aged 53 yrs.

TOMBSTONE INSCRIPTIONS OF DAVID MORROW
AND CROCKETT FAMILY IN THE OLD
WAXHAW CHURCH-YARD

```
..........................
:                        :
:          IN            :
:        MEMORY          :
:       OF DAVID         :
:      MORROW WHO        :
:      DEPARTED THIS     :
:      LIFE FEBRUARY     :
:      THE 18 1785       :
:      AGED 54 YEARS     :
:                        :
:..........................
```

(The above is the exact wording and lineage of the DAVID MORROW inscription, with CROCKETT GRAVES located around it.)

JOHN CROCKETT died December 16, in the year of 1800, aged 70 years, and 5 months.(He was born about 1730).
JOHN CROCKETT died December 1776, aged 12 years.
ELIJAH CROCKETT died March 3, 1798, at the age of 41 years.
MARY D. CROCKETT died November 9, 1815, at the age of 56 years.
ANDREW CROCKETT died November 2, 1853 at the age of 84 years. (He was born about 1769).
AGNES CROCKETT, wife of ANDREW CROCKETT, died on ____ 1846, at the age of 57 years.

DAVID M. CROCKETT (DAVID MORROW CROCKETT) born October 29, 1821; died December 28, 1896.
ELI D. CROCKETT, died July 8, 1875, at the age of 63 years.
GEORGE HYDER CROCKETT, son of ANDREW CROCKETT, died 1843, at the age of 30 years.
ROBERT CROCKETT, born August 12, 1755; died March 17, 1820.
JANET CROCKETT, wife of ROBERT CROCKETT; b. September 9, 1749; died December 15th 1813.
ISABELLA N. CROCKETT, daughter of JAMES P. CROCKETT and his wife ISABELLA; b. 1836, died 1846.
JAMES P. CROCKETT, born March 16, 1791; d. July 20, 1856.
ISABELLA M. CROCKETT (ISABELLA MORROW?) b. April 22, 1802; died April 3, 1844.
ROBERT E. CROCKETT, eldest son of JOHN M. CROCKETT (JOHN MORROW?) and LEVICEY C. CROCKETT; died December 24, 1839, at the age of 10 years and 4 days.
ANDREW B. CROCKETT, third son of JOHN M. and LEVICEY C. CROCKETT; died December 30, 1839, aged 5 years and four months.
NANCY L. CROCKETT, second daughter of JOHN M. and LEVICEY C. CROCKETT, died January 9, 1843; aged 16 months.
R. H. CROCKETT 1811-1877. SARAH A., wife.

The family records of some of these CROCKETTS will be found in other parts of this volume. These are the members of the family of the famous DAVID CROCKETT who served in the U. S. Congress from Tennessee and died in the ALAMO in Texas in 1836. The name of DAVID came down from DAVID MORROW, the ancient Patriarch buried in the WAXHAW CHURCHYARD.

```
:                                    :
:           BETHEL CHURCH            :
:                                    :
```

BETHEL CHURCH, according to the information furnished by Mr. Walter S. Henderson, of Davidson, taken from the History of that congregation, was organized in the year 1828, and is therefore about 120 years old.

It is located South of Davidson Creek and some two miles from the Iredell County line in Mecklenburg, and near both Davidson and the present Cornelius. The following bits of information comes from the same source:

ROBERT HENDERSON, who married ZELINDA POTTS, was a member of this church in 1830.
ROBERT POTTS HENDERSON was a member in 1849.
WILLIAM WHITE, ROBERT WHITE and MOSES WHITE were all members of this Church in the year 1830. The claim has been made that the original MOSES WHITE (whose son JAMES WHITE married MARY, the daughter of HUGH LAWSON) lived in IREDELL COUNTY. This item indicates that some of the descendants, at least, probably lived in MECKLENBURG COUNTY.
MRS. DORCAS E. WHITE joined the BETHEL CONGREGATION in 1830, and EMMA WHITE joined the BETHEL CHURCH in 1864.
EDWIN POTTS HENDERSON married MARY WASHAM and was killed by a falling tree in the year 1899. They had sons: WILLIAM S., SAMUEL, THOMAS, JAMES, JOHN and RUFUS KLAM HENDERSON, who had a son WALTER S. HENDERSON, but not the one who furnished this information. RUFUS KLAM HENDERSON was a member of BETHEL in 1901 and died in 1943. WALTER S. HENDERSON, his son, was a member of BETHEL CHURCH in 1915.

The BLAKENEY and MORROW FAMILIES were members of BETHEL CHURCH, according to its records, from about 1870 up to 1900 and perhaps later.

PHIHAM MORROW was an ELDER of BETHEL CHURCH in 1892. His wife was MARGARET and they had a son named ROBERT MORROW, baptised December 4, 1892.

RACHEL E. MORROW joined the Church in 1874.
LAURAE MORROW (who married a CALDWELL) joined the Church in 1877.
CORNELIA MORROW (who also married a CALDWELL) joined BETHEL CHURCH in 1877.
LUELLA MORROW (who married one of the CATHEYS) joined the Church in 1877.

PELHAM MORROW (married MARGARET) joined the BETHEL CHURCH in 1877.
MARGARET MORROW (married an OCHLER) joined the Bethel Church in 1877.
LeROY MORROW joined BETHEL CHURCH in 188?
ROBERT B. MORROW joined BETHEL CHURCH in 1896.
CLIFF MORROW joined BETHEL CHURCH in 1898.
FANNIE MORROW joined the BETHEL CHURCH in 1900. She also married an OCHLER.
JAMES BARKKLEY joined the BETHEL CHURCH in 1890.
The sons of ROBERT HENDERSON and his wife ZELINDA POTTS were NEWT HENDERSON, EDWIN POTTS HENDERSON and WILLIAM HENDERSON who was killed in the War Between the States. EDWIN POTTS HENDERSON was born in 1825 and died in 1899. WILLIAM HENDERSON was born in 1827 and died 1862. NEWTON HENDERSON moved to MISSOURI.

NAMES AND DATES FROM THE BETHEL CHURCH RECORDS

EDWIN POTTS was born August 2, 1793 and died October 7, 1851.
ELIZABETH POTTS was born August 17, 1798 and died May 10, 1860.
CLEMENT NANTZ died August 26, 1853.
JAMES NANTZ died March 19, 1853.
JOHN NANTZ died November 30, 1837.   (The name afterwards spelled NANCE).
ELIZABETH JETTON died September 5, 1835.
ELIZABETH JETTON died June 15, 1876.

ELIZABETH PATTERSON born in September 1839; died November 22, 1855.
ALICE J. C. PATTERSON, born November 24, 1849; died December 30, 1862.
MARGARET JULIA PATTERSON, born August 3, 1836; died November 26, 1847.
JAMES PATTERSON, born February 26, 1812; died March 14, 1858.
AMANDA PATTERSON died November 14, 1849. She was the wife of JOHN POTTS PATTERSON.

W. G. POTTS died August 3, 1865.
REBECCA POTTS wife of W. G. POTTS, died March 23, 1880.
ROBERT POTTS born May 21, 1786; died November 20, 1859.
NANCY R. POTTS born February 11, 1794; died February 6, 1845.
ZEB. N. POTTS born January 4, 1816; died September 5, 1843.
ROBERT POTTS died July 1, 1863 aged 54 years.

MARY B. KNOX born October 28, 1794; died April 28, 1874.
JOHN KNOX born May 22, 1777; died July 16, 1860.
ANDREW S. KOX born January 15, 1834; died November 17, 1861.
JOHN R. KNOX, born March 18, 1830; died January 4, 1863.
R. J. W. KNOX, born September 26, 1829; died January 31, 1899.
MARTHA N. KNOX, wife of R. J. W. KNOX, born Dec. 25, 1824; died Nov. 27, 1904.

THOMAS WASHAM, born September 26, 1799; died June 7, 1882.
W. F. POTTS died May 30, 1877.
SARAH C. WASHAM, born July 26, 1792; died September 13, 1871.
WILLIAM PINCKNEY BUMGARNER (BUMGARDNER) born August 15, 1849; died Jan. 16, 1926.
CANDICE HOLLAR BUMGARDNER, wife of WILLIAM PINCKNEY, born December 23, 1848, and died April 7, 1915.
ZELINDA HENDERSON, wife of ROBERT HENDERSON, died May 25, 1850.
EDWIN P. HENDERSON, born September 19, 1825; died November 12, 1899.
LOVEY A. HALL (Mrs. F. W. Hall) born Oct. 8, 1848; died May 3, 1916.
F. W. HALL died June 18, 1888.
W. H. POTTS born August 10, 1849; died November 19, 1898.
W. F. HENDERSON died July 12, 1879.
NANCY EUNICE WASHAM (MRS. T. L. WASHAM) died July 14, 1884.
SIDNEY POTTS, son of W. G. and W. G. and REBECCA POTTS; born April 24, 1844; died January 17, 1925.
JAMES M. POTTS died September 21, 1869.
N. C. POTTS died October 14, 1869.
WILL L. STEWART born January 12, 1837; died August 8, 1860.
SAM S. STEWART died October 14, 1872.
NANCY E. GILLESPIE born November 6, 1852; died September 10, 1875.
JANE E. GILLESPIE (Mrs. WILLIAM A. GILLESPIE) born March 28, 1828; died Jan. 1857.
MARY A. GILLESPIE born October 20, 1835; died April 5, 1910.
WILLIAM A. GILLESPIE born October 27, 1823; died June 22, 1902.
MARY C. GILLESPIE, daughter of HENRY A. and REBECCA CATHEY; born February 6, 1835; died in the year 1874.
ISABELLA A. GILLESPIE died November 28, 1862.
R. B. MORROW died May 19, 1912.
RACHEL E. MORROW (wife of R. B.) died May 8, 1897.
J. LAWRENCE WILSON, born December 8, 1859; died February 20, 1902.
J. M. WILSON died July 26, 1910.
L. P. WILSON born November 13, 1833; died August 29, 1914.
JOHN A. KNOX, born May 29, 1846; died November 1, 1920.
T. E. POTTS born September 10, 1829; died April 13, 1897.
C. REBECCA POTTS, wife of T. E. POTTS, born November 13, 1830; died September 1917.
HIRAM V. HALL, born October 11, 1813; died June 24, 1890.
RACHEL HALL, born February 1, 1821; died March 4, 1879.

NOTES FROM AN UNPUBLISHED HISTORY OF BETHEL CHURCH: (Furnished by Mr. W. S. HENDERSON, of Davidson, N. C.) REV. THOMAS ESPY accepted an invitation to preach a THIRD part of his time, in July, 1829. In September Messrs. PATRICK JOHNSTON, ROBERT POTTS, A. B. JETTON and CHAS. MITCHELL were electd Ruling Elders, and in November (1829) were ordained by REV. DR. ROBINSON. In October (the 12th) 1830, HUGH L. WILSON, EDGAR RODGERS and KIRBY POPE were appointed stated Clerks; JAMES JOHNSTON, treasurer, and JOHN NANTZ, JOSEPH GILLESPIE, ALEXANDER WASHAM and EDWIN POTTS, trustees.

REV. THOMAS ESPEY was born in 1800. He came to North Carolina from Romney, Hampshire County, Virginia, where he had taught school for a time, and served as tutor in the family of MRS. DANDRIDGE in Jefferson County, Virginia, in the fall of 1825. In 1828 he received a commission from the "Young Men's Missionary Society of Concord Presbytery" and served in BURKE County, N. C. for about a year, and thereafter was invited to preach in different congregations, and commenced his labors in CENTRE, in IREDELL, & BETHEL, formerly a part of CENTRE, in Mecklenburg County. * In the Spring of 1831 he removed to SALISBURY, and about the same time was married to Miss Sarah Louisa Tate, of Burke County. His health not long afterwards failed, and he died April 16, 1833, and his remains were carried to SALISBURY for interment. The last few weeks of his life were passed at the house of R. H. BURTON, Esq. near Beattie's Ford, in the bounds of Unity Congregation. - Extracted from FOOTE'S SKETCHES pp. 363, 366.

On March 3, 1831, REV. PATRICK J. SPARROW was secured as Minister for BETHEL for one half of his time.

July 8, 1833, REV. JAMES A. ADAMS was secured as minister for a period of fifteen months, and on October 15, 1834, WILLIAM L. DAVIDSON was appointed Secretary of BETHEL CONGREGATION. This WILLIAM L. DAVIDSON gave the land on which DAVIDSON COLLEGE now stands, in honor of his father GEN. WILLIAM LEE DAVIDSON, who was killed at COWAN'S FORD during the revolutionary war. MAJ. ROBERT DAVIDSON was also a member of BETHEL according to the first list of members. On March 9, 1835, BETHEL and UNITY (a Church across the Catawba in Lincoln County) united in a call to REV. JAMES A. ADAMS.

There is no record of a pastor of BETHEL CHURCH for the next twenty years.

A subscription list, dated June 1841 is for one half of the time of REV. JOHN McPHERSON, as pastor at BETHEL. REV. S. O. B. WILSON and DR. SAMUEL WILLIAMSON are recorded as stated supplies about this time.

REV. E. D. JUNKINS began as supply pastor in January, 1855, and was installed as pastor in October that year. He served until October, 1860. The name deacon first appeared in the Church record in 1856, when S. M. WETHERS and JOHN KNOX were elected to that office. CONCORD PRESBYTERY met with BETHEL CHURCH in April, 1858, with REV. JUNKIN as Moderator. Rev. JAMES H. COLTON supplied from June to December 31, 1861.

REV. R. B. ANDERSON was ordained and installed as pastor of BETHEL, May 24, 1862. He later, in 1863, was granted a leave of absence to become a Chaplain in the army; and REV. T. E. DAVIS supplied the Church during his absence. The pastoral relation was later dissolved between Rev. Anderson and Bethel.

There is no record of a pastor in 1866.

DR. E. F. ROCKWELL, from Davidson College, supplied in 1867. DR. J. M. ANDERSON followed Dr. Rockwell from 1868 to 1876. During the latter part of his pastorate he was not able to serve and Dr. Charles Phillips of Davidson College supplied during 1875.

REV. L. K. GLASGOW began his ministry March 12, 1876, as supply for one half of his time. He became pastor August 18, 1878 and was installed April 24, 1879, during the meeting of Presbytery at BETHEL CHURCH. He served until October 14, 1885. In addition to his work as pastor he conducted a private school known as BETHEL ACADEMY, near the church. (A son of his, BENJ. WADDELL GLASGOW, was connected with the schools of DALLAS, TEXAS, until his death in 1941 -1942. Glasgow Street, in the City of Dallas, a cross-town Boulivard which runs in front of WOODROW WILSON HIGH SCHOOOL, is named for him.)

REV. R. W. CULBERTSON supplied from January to October 1886.

REV. HORACE LACY, a student from Union Thelogical Seminary, from May to October 1887.

Rev. R. A. WEBB was pastor from October 9, 1887 to October, 1888.

Rev. ROBERT S. ARROWOOD until December 1889.

BETHEL was transferred from CONCORD to MECKLENBERG Presbytery in 1890.

REV. R. W. BOYD was supply pastor part of 1890 and 1891.

REV. R. L. McNAIR supplied during the summer of 1892.

REV. J. M. GRIER began his ministry in the fall of 1892, with Bethel Ramah and Huntersville. Huntersville was dropped out and REV. GRIER remained with the other two until January 7, 1906, the longest pastorate in the history of BETHEL CHURCH - thirteen years.

REV. WILLIAM MILLS supplied in the summer of 1906. Bethel and Ramah dissolved their connection at this time and Bethel united with SHEARER CHAPEL and CORNELIUS May 5, 1907 in securing Rev. C. W. ERWIN as supply during the summer. DR. M. E. SEWLETTE, Dean of Davidson College supplied from November 1907 to November 1908.

REV. J. E. WOOL was pastor of BETHEL from 1908 to 1914.

REV. BOLLING HOBSON served from October 1914 to January, 1916.

REV. W. C. WAUCHOPE from October 1916 to February 1918. Became Chaplain in the army.

REV. R. C. CLANTZ began as supply in 1918, later pastor until 1924.

Presbytery met at BETHEL in April, 1923, for the third time in its history.

REV. WILSON MOORE supplied from May, 1925 to July, 1926.

REV. W. T. SMITH was pastor from September 1, 1926 until September 1930.

REV. W. H. JOHNSTON began his ministry in September 1931 and served until March 1st, 1940. During 1930 various ministers and ministerial students supplied the church. REV. J. L. RUSSELL began his pastorate in 1940.

SKETCHES OF THE MECKLENBURG SIGNERS

These names are here taken up and continued in the order in which they are numbered on the preceding map, showing the location of their homes. The genealogical data of these men will be mostly considered in notes which will follow later on. The data here presented has been obtained from numerous sources, all of which does not fully agree, but the writer believes that as here presented the information given is approximately correct and true.

(1) ROBERT IRWIN

He was a delegate in the Mecklenburg Convention of May 20, 1775, from the STEELE CREEK CHURCH settlement. He belonged to the IRWIN FAMILY of Prince George County, Virginia, and was born there in the year 1738, instead of 1740, as stated by Dr. J. B. ALEXANDER (p. 404) who says he came from Pennsylvania. He obtained his date from the list of the children of a WILLIAM IRWIN who died in Pennsylvania, who was not even related to this signer. He died December 23, 1800, at the age of 62 years. (Hunter, p. 51). He married MARY ALEXANDER, a daughter of ZEBULON ALEXANDER, from MARYLAND, and was one of the first bench elders of STEELE CREEK CHURCH. In 1776, after the Mecklenburg Convention, he and WILLIAM ALEXANDER, his wife's relative, commanded (each of them) a regiment under General Griffith Rutherford, in the expedition to subdue the Cherokee Indians in Western North Carolina and what is now a part of Tennessee, their troops being made up of men from Mecklenburg, Rowan, Lincoln (then Tryon) and other adjoining counties. In 1781 Colonel Irwin again commanded a regiment under General Rutherford in the Wilmington campaign. He was a delegate to the Provincial Congress which met at Halifax, April 4, 1776 with JOHN McKNITT ALEXANDER and JOHN PHIFER, both of whom had signed the Mecklenburg Declaration with him the year previous. In the month of November, following, he was again a member of the Halifax body, which formed the first Constitution. Shortly before his death (1797-1799) he was the Senator of Mecklenburg County.

(2) EPHRAIM BREVARD

DR. EPHRAIM BREVARD has been called the reputed author of the Mecklenburg Declaration of Independence, which was signed on May 20, 1775, in the town of Charlotte. He was born in CECIL COUNTY, MARYLAND, in 1744, according to the weight of authority, the son of JOHN BREVARD and his wife JANE McWHORTER. Ephraim Brevard, therefore, was a nephew of the celebrated early North Carolina missionary, ALEXANDER McWHORTER, a brother of John Brevard's wife Jane.. EPHRAIM BREVARD was also a nephew of ALEXANDER OSBORNE, whose wife was AGNES McWHORTER, another sister of ALEXANDER McWHORTER, one time President of the QUEEN'S MUSEUM in Charlotte. He and ADLAI OSBORNE were first cousins and together were students of a grammar school in Prince Edward County, Virginia, probably the forerunner of Hampden-Sidney College; thereafter he and Osborne and THOMAS REESE (a brother of DAVID REESE, also one of the Signers) graduated at Princeton. Under Dr. Alexander Ramsey, of South Carolina, he studied medicine, and in 1776, accompanied General RUTHERFORD'S expedition against the Indians in his professional capacity, being doubtless attached to COL. ROBERT IRWIN'S Mecklenburg regiment of militia.

DR. BREVARD, after this service settled in the town of Charlotte and Mecklenburg County for the practice of his profession, although JOHN BREVARD, his father, was considered a citizen of ROWAN COUNTY, residing somewhere North of the present DAVIDSON'S COLLEGE, perhaps within the old bounds of CENTRE CHURCH. He married a daughter of one of the richest and most influential citizens of Mecklenburg, COL. THOMAS POLK, and was therefore not only a signer himself, but the son in law of a signer of the Declaration. Dr. Brevard and his wife had only one child, MARTHA BREVARD, who married MR. DICKERSON. A son of this couple and the grandson of DR. BREVARD, was JAMES P. DICKERSON, a Lieutenant-Colonel in the South Carolina Regiment in the war with Mexico, who died from wounds received during that campaign near the City of Mexico. Before the end of the revolution and after the death of his young wife in 1780 he entered the service as a surgeon, and was made a prisoner at the surrender of Charleston. Due to his confinement his health gave way and he made his painful way homeward, only to reach the home of his friend and fellow patriot and signer, some miles North of Charlotte, JOHN McKNITT ALEXANDER, where he died, without ever reaching his own home a few miles further North. He died sometime in the year 1781, only about 37 years old. Dr. Brevard was a one-eyed man. Many children were named for him. He is buried in Charlotte.

(3) ZACCHEUS WILSON

ZACCHEUS WILSON and his brothers (known) ROBERT and DAVID, were probably the sons of ROBERT WILSON, who died in AUGUSTA COUNTY, VIRGINIA, in 1745, of whose estate, COL. JOHN WILSON, who was the first member of the House of Burgesses from that section, was administrator. They are believed to have been nephews of this COL. JOHN WILSON, of that county, and descendants of THOMAS WILSON, of York and PRINCESS ANNE COUNTY, Virginia, Master of the good ship DESIRE before 1650. PETER WILSON, of PITTSYLVANIA COUNTY, who lived on the DAN RIVER in an early day, may have been their uncle also. This PETER WILSON also had a son known during the Revolution as COL. JOHN WILSON. When ZACCHEUS, ROBERT and DAVID WILSON came to Mecklenburg County about 1755, with part of the Augusta Congregation of REV. ALEXANDER CRAIGHEAD, it is believed that their mother, the WIDOW WILSON, accompanied them. Their coming at this time, with the pastor of their old flock followed the defeat of BRADDOCK'S army in the North, which had unloosed a hysteria of fear among the settlers on the Little Calf Pasture and Hays Creek, in Augusta. At least one sister also came along who afterwards became the wife of CAPT. STEPHEN ALEXANDER, but whose first name is not known to the

413

writer. As stated by HUNTER, the brother ROBERT lived within the bounds of STEELE CREEK CHURCH in the Southeastern part of Mecklenburg, where he died, leaving a will in 1793, and had eleven sons, seven of whom are said to have served in the revolution; DAVID WILSON moved to SUMNER COUNTY, TENNESSEE, of JAMES WILSON, the oldest son there appears to be no record, while ZACCHEUS WILSON (the signer) married a MRS. ROSS, a widow with two daughters, one of whom married a man named MORGAN. This ZACCHEUS WILSON, Dr. Alexander says, was a surveyor, and a Captain at King's Mountain, where among the plunder taken, was an English surveyor's compass and platting instruments, which were assigned to him in the division and are yet preserved by one of his descendants. He was a member of the Mecklenburg Convention and of the Provincial Congress of November, 1776, for making laws and forming a Constitution. In 1788 he was also a member of the North Carolina Convention for the consideration of the Federal Constitution, and was among the large number that refused to give the draft their approval, as wanting in a proper protection of the rights of the people.

In 1796 CAPT. ZACCHEUS WILSON, having lost his wife, followed his brother MAJ. DAVID WILSON, to SUMNER COUNTY, Tennessee, who had settled there same nine years previously. His home in Sumner County was one mile Northeast of the town of GALLATIN, and twenty-six miles North of NASHVILLE, where he died in 1824. Little is known of his immediate descendants.

(4) THOMAS POLK

This distinguished signer, THOMAS POLK, according to one of the early writers and historians, when he arrived in what is now MECKLENBURG COUNTY at the frontier cabin of the intrepid THOMAS SPRATT, in the edge of the Indian settlement, "had only a knapsack on his back and a goodly share of indomitable enterprise". Soon thereafter he married SUSANNA SPRATT, the daughter of this earlier settler, who had been the first man to cross the rapids of the Yadkin on wheels a few months or years previously. This same writer says that he was born in SUMMERSET COUNTY, Maryland about 1730. In a separate article the POLK FAMILY as a whole will be discussed. His father "in about 1750" moved from MARYLAND to near Carlisle, Pennsylvania. It is not known that his son THOMAS even went to Pennsylvania, but it is a settled proposition that he was not native to that Colony, as were many other Virginia dk Maryland born residents who were drawn temporarily to WILLIAM PENN'S domain, only to remain there for a brief stay. It is not improbable, in fact that this young "knapsack traveler" was actually born in ACCOMAC COUNTY, VIRGINIA, since the KNOX FAMILY, ----sometimes NOCKS, on the old records of Accomac - to which his grandmother JOANNA belonged, was a Virginian by birth. THOMAS SPRATT and his family were also from ACCOMAC COUNTY, and doubtless had known THOMAS POLK when a child or young boy, before his parents made the Pennsylvania move. THOMAS POLK was a member of the Colonial Assembly of North Carolina in 1771 and 1775, associated with ABRAHAM ALEXANDER from Mecklenburg, and in 1775 - the year of the Declaration - he was appointed Colonel of the "Minute Men" with ADAM ALEXANDER as Lieut-Colonel and CHARLES McLEAN as the Major. As Colonel of the militia, he issued orders to the Captains of the several beats or districts to elect and send two delegates each to the Convention in Charlotte, which convened on May 19th in 1775, and which Convention adopted the Resolutions or Declaration the following day. Historians tell us that it was no small gathering, but a regular "outpouring" of the residents of the country. Following this at the Provincial Congress which met at Halifax April 4, 1776, Col. POLK was appointed Colonel of the fourth regiment of the Continental troops, with James THAXTON Lieutenant Colonel and WILLIAM (LEE) DAVIDSON as Major. Major Davidson was afterwards appointed a Brigadier General and held that rank when he was killed at Cowan's ford on the CATAWBA on February 1st, 1781. WILLIAM POLK, son of Col. Thomas Polk was also a revolutionary soldier and was born in the year 1759, which would place the date of Thomas Polk's marriage to Susan Spratt back of that date. Col. Thomas Polk and his son WILLIAM POLK were both surveyors, and in 1786, COL. POLK, who was a man of large means purchased many land warrants from his disbanded troops and in company with his four sons penetrated the Tennessee Duck River country to locate and survey these lands, his son doing most of the surveying. His younger brother, EZEKIEL POLK, shortly thereafter moved to Tennessee and settled near the present town of BOLIVAR with his sons, including SAMUEL, the father of JAMES KNOX POLK who became President of the United States.

COL. THOMAS POLK died in 1793, full of years and of honors and his mortal remains repose in the Presbyterian Churchyard in the City of Charlotte. His home was a short distance from PINEVILLE, on the banks of BIG SUGAR CREEK, as shown approximately on the accompanying map.

(5) ABRAHAM ALEXANDER

Dr. J. G. M. Ramsay, the Tennessee Historian, says that ABRAHAM ALEXANDER, the signer, was a cousin of JOHN McKNITT and HEZEKIAH ALEXANDER, and Dr. Ramsey should know, because he was a grandson of JOHN McKNITT ALEXANDER.

ABRAHAM ALEXANDER was born in CECIL COUNTY, MARYLAND, and JAMES ALEXANDER (father of JOHN McKNITT ALEXANDER) left a will which is on record in the courthouse in ELKTON, MARYLAND. He owned large tracts of land in Cecil County, on Elk River, from which the town derives its name. Thus circumstances, as well as family tradition, indicate that Dr. Ramsay is probably correct in his statement of the relationship.

This distingished signer was Chairman of the Convention which met in Charlotte, N. C. on May 19th and adjourned May 20, 1775, after adopting the "Mecklenburg Declaration of Independence". He was not only one of the leading spirits of the convention and its Chairman, but thereafter, during the whole period the revolution, both as a member of the Justice Court and as its Chairman and Chairman of the Committee of Safety. Dr. HUNTER in his "Sketches" observes that under the administration of ABRAHAM ALEXANDER, as Chairman of the Committee of Safety, the laws passed by that body were strictly enforced and generally observed, and each citizen, when he left the cCounty, was required to carry with him a certificate of his political standing, officially signed by the Chairman. He died April 28, 1786 aged 68 years, and is buried in the second oldest Sugar Creek burial ground. The name of his wife was DORCAS (last name unknown) who survived him apparently just one month to the day, when she also passed away at the age of 67 years. In Dr. Alexander's history it is said they had five sons and one daughter, ABRAHAM, ISAAC, NATHANIEL, ELIAS, JOAB and ELIZABETH, who married WILLIAM ALEXANDER, a son of HEZEKIAH ALEXANDER.

(6) HEZEKIAH ALEXANDER

HEZEKIAH ALEXANDER, according to his tombstone inscription in the second oldest of the three Sugar Creek Church graveyards died on July 16, 1801, at the age of 73 years. He was the son of JAMES ALEXANDER, whose will was written in CECIL COUNTY, MARYLAND in 1772, and pro bated at the same place in 1779, therefore it is safe to assume that he was a native of MARYLAND, and not of PENNSYLVANIA, as has been so often stated. He was a brother of JOHN McKNITT ALEXANDER. He signed the Mecklenburg Declaration of Independence May 20, 1775. Of HEZEKIAH ALEXANDER, Dr. Hunter in his interesting "Sketches" declares that he was more of a statesman than a soldier. He was appointed a member of the Committee of Safety, for the Salisbury District by the Provincial Congress which met at HILLSBORO in August, 1775, along with such men as General Griffith Rutherford, JOHN BREVARD, BENJAMIN PATTON and other outstanding patriots of the time and place. He served on the Council of Safety with his kinsman, WILLIAM SHARPE, and served in the Provincial Congress himself, from Mecklenburg County in 1776, with WAIGHTSTILL AVERY, ROBERT IRWIN, JOHN PHIFER and ZACCHEUS WILSON, all of whom, like himself, had signed the famous resolutions of May 20, 1775. In 1776 he was appointed paymaster of Col' Polk's regiment of Continentals, and also served afterwards as treasurer of the famous "LIBERTY HALL ACADEMY" in Charlotte. He was born in 1728 and died in July 1801, and is buried in the SUGAR CREEK GRAVEYARD near Charlotte.

(7) JOHN McKNITT ALEXANDER

JOHN McKNITT ALEXANDER was born in 1733, in the Northeastern portion of CECIL COUNTY, MARYLAND, where his father, JAMES ALEXANDER, settled on a tract of land called NEW MUNSTER, in the year 1714, and shortly thereafter married a sister of JOHN McKNITT, an early emigrant to the Southern part of the same County (at a point across the bay almost East of BALTIMORE). The writers say his son JOHN McKNITT ALEXANDER migrated to MECKLENBURG COUNTY, North Carolina in 1754, when he was about 21 years old, after he had served his apprenticeship to a tailor; that JOHN McKNITT was accompanied on this move by his brother HEZEKIAH ALEXANDER and his sister, JEMIMAH and her husband MAJ. THOMAS SHARPE, also of CECIL COUNTY, Maryland. After his arrival in Mecklenburg he also became a surveyor of lands and acquired several large tracts in his own name. The old records reflect that the above members of the ALEXANDER FAMILY of Cecil County, Maryland, were not the only ones of the same breed and name who settled in Mecklenburg, although they were probably the first comers. It must be confessed, however, that segregating the various families and persons of this migration and identifying their connection with the family is a heavy task for the modern writer, aided though he may be, by the accumulated records of the centuries, and the observation of the numerous scribes who have undertaken heretofore to set down the story.

This SIGNER is said to have married his wife JANE, or JEAN BANE in 1759. Again we are told that JANE BANE was from PENNSYLVANIA. Maybe so; but if one will take the trouble to examine the old deed and court records of the Valley of Virginia, he will discover that the BANE FAMILY lived in that section before this marriage took place. So, instead of traveling all the way to Pennsylvania or back to his old home in CECIL COUNTY, MARYLAND to claim his bride, JOHN McKNITT ALEXANDER may only have ridden the 100 to 150 miles or so across the old Indian path to the mountain regions of Virginia, for his wedding.

In addition to being one of the signers of the immortal Declaration of 1775, the subject of this sketch is referred to as the Secretary of the Convention. That he also served in the Provincial Congress of North Carolina is well established. History further records that despite his age this patriot rendered material and personal aid to General Nathaniel Greeny during the American Revolution and was actively employed in the work of sinking ferry boats on the Yadkin and Dan Rivers in behalf of the patriot army.

Of all of the ALEXANDERS, including the six who were signers, the family of this native of MARYLAND, is perhaps the most interesting. He only had two sons who survived him at his death to keep the name alive, so far as his immediate family line was concerned, but at least three of his five daughters became ancestresses of as many important families. One of his grandsons, HON. J. G. M. RAMSAY, of Tennessee, by his learning and talent, preserved the history of that commonwealth for all time; another set of grandchildren sprang from the daughter who married REV. SAMUEL C. CALDWELL, and a third set from REV. JAMES WALLIS, famous minister of PROVIDENCE CHURCH, who sent pioneer empire builders to ALABAMA and TEXAS where they played important roles in History.

He was an elder and one of the back-bone leaders in the HOPEWELL PRESBYTERIAN CHURCH, and at his death was buried in the old churchyard, alongside GEN. WILLIAM LEE DAVIDSON, RICHARD BARRY and others. His wife JANE BANE ALEXANDER is buried in the same plot. He died July 10, 1817 at the age of 84 years, living to be old, blind and infirm, but with the respect and reverence of his neighbors and friends around him. He was not an orator; he made no claims to being a statesman, but of his patriotism it may be said,none excelled him. Well blessed with this world's goods, he left them to his children, but to his descendants a still richer heritage in the humble record of a fearless and unwavering fight for human liberty and the rights of the "common man".

(8) MAJ. JOHN DAVIDSON

In a little family burial plot, not far from the site of HOPEWELL CHURCH and some twelve or fourteen miles North of the City of Charlotte, close to the Catawba River in Mecklenburg County, North Carolina, sleeps the remains of another one of the patriots who signed the Declaration of Independence of May 20, 1775 - MAJ. JOHN DAVIDSON. This man is another product of CECIL COUNTY, in "MARYLAND, m. MARYLAND!" His father was ROBERT DAVIDSON, whom SONDLEY declares was born in ELKTON, Maryland, also the home town of at least two of the ALEXANDERS whose names are appended to the DECLARATION. Without attempting to go into the genealogy of the DAVIDSON family in this brief note, it has been reasonably established that the THREE PRINCIPAL Davidson ancestors who settled between the CATAWBA and YADKIN rivers were brothers, all springing from a common source, and all, more than likely, originating in the State of Maryland.

The mother of MAJ. JOHN DAVIDSON and the wife of ROBERT DAVIDSON was an ISABELLA RAMSAY, and the claim has long been advanced that she was born in Pennsylvania, without any proof being adduced in support of the claim. There are instances where she is spoken of on the records as MARY RAMSAY, so that it is possible that she had the double name of MARY ISABELLA. From all accounts she came to NORTH CAROLINA as a widow, with her two children, JOHN (The MAJOR) and MARY DAVIDSON; her husband ROBERT DAVIDSON having died before her migration. MAJ. JOHN DAVIDSON, with that rank was a field officer in the Regiment of COLONEL ADAM ALEXANDER (another one of the signers), and he was with General Sumter in August, 1780, at the battle of HANGING ROCK, and was a General in the Militia service. As a business man, Maj Davidson was a success and had many interests. In 1790 he was one of the wealthiest slave holders in Mecklenburg County and owned considerable land which he was able to cultivate successfully on that account. Hunter gives him credit with having established the VESUVIUS FURNACE in Lincoln County, with his two sons in law, ALEXANDER BREVARD and JOSEPH GRAHAM. He married VIOLET, the daughter of SAMUEL WILSON, SR. and raised a large and interesting family of children, which will be reviewed in later genealogical notes herein; though he had only two sons, JACK and ROBERT DAVIDSON. He was located in his home only about one mile from what was called TOOLE'S FORD, on the Catawba River in Mecklenburg County.

(9) RICHARD BARRY

That RICHARD BARRY, the signer of the Mecklenburg Declaration of Independence was of Scotch-Irish descent, as has been often stated, there is little doubt, but that he was born in the Colony of PENNSYLVANIA in 1726 there is doubt. It is conceded that his wife was ANNE PRICE, and that she was "of Maryland", therefore, in the absence of some concrete evidence to the contrary, it is much safer to assume that her husband was also of MARYLAND, which appears to have furnished a large share of the leading patriots of Mecklenburg to the CATAWBA-YADKIN area. Ascribing verity to his tombstone record as it appears in the old HOPEWELL CHURCHYARD, Richard Barry was born in the year 1726 as stated. The coming of RICHARD BARRY to the banks of the Catawba River dates back to the time when REV. JOHN THOMSON, the pioneer minister and missionary, delivered his soul-stirring sermons to the inhabitants of the surrounding country - "in the bounds of what was afterwards Centre Church" - under the spreading oaks near the Barry Home. In fact, through his brother, HUGH BARRY, this signer was related to REV. JOHN THOMSON - Hugh having married a LAWSON, sister of the LAWSON who married HANNAH, the youngest daughter of JOHN THOMSON. But that is for the genealogical account of the BARRY FAMILY, which will come later.

This RICHARD BARRY was 55 years of age when, with other members of the MECKLENBURG TROOPS he disputed the passage of CORNWALLIS' army at COWAN'S FORD, a close distance from his home; in February, 1781, and it was RICHARD BARRY, who on that lamentable occasion when the gallant WILLIAM LEE DAVIDSON was slain, with other comrades, carried the patriot soldier's remains at the dead hours of night to the old HOPEWELL CHURCHYARD and reverently laid them by the side of his deceased neighbors and other patriots who were then sleeping there.

(11) ROBERT HARRIS, JR.

ROBERT HARRIS JR., as a signer, is not credited therewith on the Monument erected in Charlotte County, which is supposed to contain an authenticated list of the men who thus fearlessly defied a great dynasty of Europe, regardless of the consequences; neither does his name appear on the two lists published by MARTIN and RAMSAY. Instead the name of RICHARD HARRIS, as one of the signers appears on both the latter, and on the monument. Dr. Alexander says that the name of RICHARD HARRIS was placed on the monument and on the authenticated list through the evidence of REV. HUMPHREY HUNTER, but in the remarkable "Sketches" written by his son, which includes names of the signers, the name of neither RICHARD or ROBERT HARRIS is mentioned. In ALEXANDER'S history the statement is made that ROBERT HARRIS SR. was a signer, and that he was born in 1742, and a brother of JAMES HARRIS, still another signer, and repeats the oft-quoted phrase, unaccompanied by a scintilla of proof, that he was probably born in Pennsylvania.

The truth of the matter is that all of the evidence available, which is scant, tends to show that ROBERT HARRIS was one of the signers; that he was the son of CHARLES HARRIS, ancestor of WILLIAM SHAKESPEARE HARRIS, of the now CABARRUS COUNTY, and that he was born in PRINCE EDWARD or AMELIA COUNTY, VIRGINIA, where his father CHARLES HARRIS was living in the year 1755 between Buffalo Creek and the line of Charlotte County - or, what afterwards became the line, and where he is listed among the tithables. His mother was JANE McILHENNEY, and after her death his father married ELIZABETH (THOMSON) BAKER, a daughter of REV. JOHN THOMSON, and the widow of SAMUEL BAKER, whom he had known in PRINCE EDWARD COUNTY, Virginia, where she married SAMUEL BAKER. This ROBERT HARRIS was twice married, first to MARY WILSON, and second to MRS. MARY BREVARD DAVIDSON. ROBERT HARRIS, the signer, was NOT a brother of JAMES HARRIS, the other signer, but his cousin. This compiler has been unable to find any account of the death of this signer, nor is there anywhere, evidence of the year of his birth, which is a matter of speculation. We only know that he belonged to the HARRIS FAMILY that lived and thrived and multiplied in that part of MECKLENBURG COUNTY that in 1791 Became CABARRUS COUNTY; and nowhere on the records of either County, on the tax lists, census, deed or other books, have we run across the name of a RICHARD HARRIS, who might have lived in that section of the country and who might or could have been the signer, in whose place ROBERT is here in good faith substituted. His SECOND WIFE was the widow and relict of GEN. WILLIAM LEE DAVIDSON.

(12) JOHN PHIFER

The account of this signer of the Mecklenburg Declaration cannot be better presented than in the exact language of CYRUS L. HUNTER, that son of the famous HUMPHREY HUNTER, early minister of STEELE CREEK and other ancient Churches, as same appears on pages 53 and 54 of his "SKETCHES of WESTERN NORTH CAROLINA." He says:

JOHN PHIFER was born in CABARRUS COUNTY (when a part of Bladen) in 1745. He was the son of MARTIN PHIFER, a native of SWITZERLAND, and of MARGARET BLACKWELDER. He raised a numerous family, who inherited the patriotic spirit of their ancestors. The original spelling of the name was PFEIFER. He resided on "Dutch Buffalo Creek" at the Red Hill, known to this day as "PHIFER'S HILL". He was the father of GEN. PAUL PHIFER, grandfather of GEN. JOHN L. PHIFER, of MISSISSIPPI, and great grandfather of GENERAL CHARLES H. PHIFER, a distinguished officer in the battle of "SHI-

LOE", in the late war between the States. At the provincial Council held at JOHNSTON Courthouse in December, 1775, he was appointed Lieutenant Colonel of the first battalion of "Minute Men", in the Salisbury District; General Griffith Rutherford, Colonel, and JOHN PAISLEY, Major. He was a member of the Provincial Congress which met at Hillsboro on the 21st of August, 1775, associated with THOMAS POLK, WAIGHTSTILL AVERY, JAMES HOUSTON, SAMUEL MARTIN and JOHN McKNITT ALEXANDER; and also of the Congress which met at HALIFAX on the 4th of April, 1776, with ROBERT IRWIN and JOHN McKNITT ALEXANDER. By this latter body he was appointed Lieutenant Colonel of the regiment commanded by COL. ADAM ALEXANDER. He was also a member of the Provincial Congress which met at Halifax in November, 1776, which formed our first Constitution, associated with HEZEKIAH ALEXANDER, WAIGHTSTILL AVERY, ROBERT IRWIN & ZACCHEUS WILSON, as colleagues; (All of whom had signed the Mecklenburg Declaration at Charlotte in the year 1775). His wife was CATHERINE BARRINGER, which latter name was originally spelled as BEHRINGER. JOHN PHIFER filled an early grave, and lies buried at "RED HILL" on the Salisbury Road, where a decaying headstone, scarcely legible (in 1877) marks the last resting place of this true patriot.

(13) NEILL MORRISON

In one rather reliable book we are told that the MORRISON FAMILY came from SCOTLAND to PENNSYLVANIA in 1750, and removed to North Carolina (CABARRUS COUNTY now, but MECKLENBURG then) in 1757; in another, an erudite Historian informs us that NEILL MORRISON was born in PHILADELPHIA in 1728, and engaged in business there before coming to MECKLENBURG COUNTY, North Carolina, with his father, JAMES MORRISON. The latter writer says his father JAMES lived to be an old man, 81 years, and is buried in PROVIDENCE BURIAL GROUND. At Providence we find the grave of a JAMES MORRISON and on the tombstone he is called the "Signer". The NEILL MORRISON tombstone may be there but we did not find it, or, if we did, we misread it "JAMES" - possibly because of its decadent condition. The name of NEILL MORRISON as a signer appears on the Monument in the courthouse yard at CHARLOTTE and it appears that way also on all the other lists, except that CYRUS HUNTER in his "Sketches" of the signers, does not mention him at all. Why?

Every inference points to the fact that NEILL MORRISON belonged to the same family as that of REV. ROBERT HALL MORRISON, D. D., founder and first President of DAVIDSON COLLEGE, and which originally settled in what is now CABARRUS COUNTY on the North side of ROCKY RIVER. The grandfather of REV. ROBERT HALL MORRISON (father in law of STONEWALL JACKSON) was ROBERT MORRISON, who had a brother JAMES MORRISON, also a brother JOHN, and it so happens that DR. ALEXANDER says that the father of NEILL MORRISON - JAMES - had three sons; though from this attempt to straighten out the family, he must have had four. But there is such a divergence of statements about the origin of the MORRISONS, one does not know just WHERE they came from. The SCOTTISH origin is probably correct, but the dates must be wrong, and as usual, no proof is shown that the family ever lived in PENNSYLVANIA. Therefore we doubt seriously, if there was a residence in that Colony at any time. We accept the statement of DR. ALEXANDER that NEILL MORRISON and his father JAMES lived within the bounds of PROVIDENCE, and perhaps on FOUR MILE CREEK, as suggested, but undoubtedly members of the family also resided within the bounds of ROCKY RIVER and in what is now CABARRUS COUNTY.

NEILL MORRISON himself died on September 13, 1784, at the age of 56 years, and his wife, ANNABELL MORRISON lived until September 9, 1818, when she died in her 89th year, according to the inscription in PROVIDENCE CHURCHYARD. Evidently she was born in 1829. NEILL MORRISON and his wife ANNABELL were the parents of one daughter, who became the wife of MAJ. THOMAS ALEXANDER, and of three sons, DR. WILLIAM MORRISON, who served in the Revolution, and afterwards became a prominent physician, and of ALEXANDER and JAMES MORRISON. All three brothers died in 1806, twelve years before the death of their mother, who survived them. It is not improbable that NEILL MORRISON'S wife was an ALEXANDER.

(14) COL. JAMES HARRIS

In 1780 he was in fact a MAJOR of Col. Irwin's regiment and participated in the battle at RAMSOUR'S MILL in Lincoln County, though we find him called Captain at some places on the record and also COLONEL. His brother THOMAS HARRIS was the first Sheriff of Mecklenburg, long before the revolution, the exact dates having been lost or destroyed. JAMES HARRIS was the son of SAMUEL HARRIS and his wife MARTHA LAIRD and was the second of eleven children. His father moved to GREENE COUNTY, GEORGIA, and several of his children settled in that State also, some in HANCOCK, an adjoining County. As has been stated before JAMES HARRIS the signer was NOT a brother of ROBERT HARRIS, also a signer, but they were cousins, Robert Harris being the son of SAMUEL HARRIS' brother CHARLES HARRIS. In the year 1785 JAMES HARRIS was chosen to represent Mecklenburg County in the State Senate. According to the family chart he was born in 1739, and his death occurred September 27th in the year 1797 at which time he was 59 years old. He had a younger brother, SAMUEL HARRIS, who was a soldier of the revolution. The wife of JAMES HARRIS, the signer, was MARTHA HARRIS, a daughter of his uncle ROBERT HARRIS and his wife FANNY CUNNINGHAM. He and his brother Samuel Harris married sisters. More will be said about the HARRIS FAMILY in later genealogical notes. I am quite sure that the parents of this man lived at one time in VIRGINIA, though whether his sons were born there is problematical.

(15) COL. ADAM ALEXANDER

COL. ADAM ALEXANDER, of Clear Creek and Rocky River, is said by ALEXANDER, the Historian, to have been a cousin of JOHN McKNITT and HEZEKIAH ALEXANDER, and he was perhaps a native of CECIL COUNTY, Maryland, where he was born in 1728, which fact is deduced from his tombstone record in the old ROCK SPRINGS BURIAL GROUNDS in the Clear Creek section of Mecklenburg County, which states that he died Nov. 13, 1798, at the age of 70 years and 7 months, and that MARY, his wife died Nov. 26, 1813 at the age of 78 years. She was MARY SHELBY, a cousin of the famous General Shelby of King's Mountain fame.

As early as JUNE, 1770, he was living in the Eastern part of Mecklenburg County, and was a member of Clear Creek congregation. He was for many years a prominent magistrate and member of the County Court, and in May, 1775 was one of the signers of the Mecklenburg Declaration of Independence.

In September, 1775, ADAM ALEXANDER was appointed Lieutenant Colonel under Colonel Polk and served in what was called the Snow campaign against the Tories in South Carolina. In the following April he was chosen to command one of the Mecklenburg Continental regiments, succeeding Col. Thomas Polk. He led his forces against the Cherokee Indians at the head of the Catawba in 1776, under General Griffith Rutherford. Colonel ADAM ALEXANDER was living on Rocky River near the mouth of Clear Creek, or in that general locality away back in 1755-6, when Rev. Hugh McAden passed through the country on his way South, and is mentioned as Colonel Alexander in the minister's very interesting Journal. These notes show that Rev. McAden was a guest in the Alexander home on at least two different occasions in that early day.

This signer had an interesting family, including four sons and at least one daughter, who became the wife of the wealthiest slave holder in MECKLENBURG COUNTY after its establishment in the year 1762. One of his sons graduated at Princeton in 1787, and afterwards served in Congress from North Carolina. He was a distinguished lawyer, but left no descendants. Another son held various offices of trust in the County, and still another resided in the old homestead until well into the nineteenth century, with an interesting family of his own. Col. John Springs, his son in law, left a large family, whose descendants are widely scattered over the Southern States, and some of whom distinguished themselves in the service of their country.

(16) JOHN FORD

JOHN FORD was a member of CLEAR CREEK CONGREGATION as early as January 27, 1770, and he may have been in Mecklenburg County several years prior thereto. He came of a Presbyterian family from SOMERSET COUNTY, Maryland, where he had known the POLK family prior to the time they had left the same parts. The statement has been made heretofore that not only the POLK family, but the SPRATTS, KNOX and many other Mecklenburg early comers were from that part of Virginia and Maryland. JOHN FORD was not only one of the signers of the famous Mecklenburg Declaration in 1775, but he also served as a magistrate and member of the County Court afterwards, if not before. Like other patriots of that section he served his country in the wars and was a private in Charles Polk's Dragoons in 1781 on waht is called the Raft Swamp Expedition, whatever that may have been.

The old Mecklenburg records frequently give up the name of Fords, who were contemporaneous with the signer, but the relationship between all of them is undisclosed, so far as this writer has been able to determine. His will was written on April 25, 1798, and William Shakespeare Harris declared that he was perhaps deceased by the year 1800. There are still persons bearing the name of Ford in this section, and one JOHN FORD is found on the records of that part of South Carolina once believed to have been a part of Mecklenburg, which leads this writer to believe that he may have had a son or sons, not mentioned, who went to that section before his death. The statement is made that none of his lineal descendants remain in Mecklenburg County at this time, though there are collateral relatives still living there.

JOHN FORD, notwithstanding the statements above, which are gleaned from other brief accounts we have found of him, is listed on the census of 1790, and we are quite sure from the phraseology used the reference is to this signer. He is called JOHN FORD, ESQ., an indication that he was a man of some importance in his community, who had perhaps rendered some signal service to the country, which is thus recognised. The entry shows that he had only one daughter, and no sons, but by that time his sons may have been married and settled down for themselves, as immediately next to him there is a ZEBULON FORD listed, who could easily have been a son with an already large and growing family around him, consisting of FIVE SONS, all under the age of 16 years, and doubtless grandsons of the old signer, their grandfather.

(17) JOHN QUEARY

Here we have another PRESBYTERIAN ELDER who was a signer of the famous MECKLENBURG DECLARATION, who lived within the bounds of ROCKY RIVER and CLEAR CREEK (Now known as PHILADELPHIA) and whose name appears on the old Church records as early as 1770. Very little information is now available about his family. We only know, from the Census records of 1790, that he was a neighbor of ISAAC RAY, of ANDREW, DAVID and HUGH MOORE, who lived on Four Mile and Geese Creek, and that there was a WILLIAM QUEARY SR. and a William Jr. and a JOHN and an ALEXANDER QUEARY also listed, so that it is not improbable that the family to which he belonged was more or less numerous, in spite of the fact that it is not often mentioned on the records. This is often true about many families of that day and time. Dr. Alexander says that he had been told that JOHN QUEARY was a man of vigorous intellect, was well to do and a good scholar; that he accumulated considerable property and died at an early period, without giving the date of his death.

Having signed the famous Declaration he was unquestionably a patriot and doubtless done his part in the American Revolution, which he certainly survived. He lived in that part of Mecklenburg which is now in Union County, where he is buried. His immediate descendants, if any, have not been certainly identified at this writing.

JOHN QUEARY was a Scotchman, as were the others bearing the name, and so far as known, probably came direct from a port of entry to Mecklenburg County.

(18) WAIGHTSTILL AVERY

This distinguished signer of the DECLARATION was a native of GROTON, CONNECTICUT, where he was born in 1747 according to his chroniclers. He graduated at Princeton in 1766. He first went to the Eastern Shore of Maryland or Virginia (from whence came the Polks and others) where he entered upon the study of the law and after a residence there of some three years came to North Carolina and obtained his license to practice the following year. He married a Mrs. Frank, the daughter of a WILLIAM PROBART, a wealthy merchant of SNOW HILL, Somerset County, Maryland, in 1778. Meantime he had been a resident of the Charlotte community for several years, making his home before his marriage with the family of HEZEKIAH ALEXANDER, also one of the signers. After participating in the signing of the Declaration, in the year 1777 he was appointed one of the trustees of Liberty Hall Academy and was also chosen as one of the two members to represent Mecklenburg in the House of Commons, & served on the Committee to revise the public laws of the State. In 1778 he was appointed and commissioned Attorney General for North Carolina. It was shortly after this that he married and for a time took up his residence in JONES COUNTY, from whence in the next year or two he removed to Burke County on the upper reaches of the Catawba, where he called his home Swan Pond, which was afterwards the home of his son ISAAC T. AVERY. He represented Burke County in the Legislature several terms. In his lifetime in North Carolina he practiced law throughout the entire state and was well and favorably known throughout its domains. His wife, though living at the time of their marriage in Jones County, not far from New Bern, was from SNOW HILL, Maryland. His son, Col. ISAAC T. AVERY had several distinguished sons, including Col. Waightstill W. Avery, Col. Moulten Avery and Judge Alphonso C. Avery who served well and long on the bench of his native State. He was related to the Leneir family, of revolutionary fame. Col. Waightstill Avery lived until the year, 1821 when he died in the enjoyment of an ample estate, the patriarch of the North Carolina Bar, and especially of Western North Carolina. His descendants still reside in Hillsboro and its environs, respected and renowned.

(19) HENRY DOWNS

Mr. Hunter in his excellent work "Sketches of Western North Carolina", who gives a brief biography of each of the signers, fails to mention the name of HENRY DOWNS, though his name appears as such on the momument erected in their memory, and all of the other various lists that have been published, so there can be no question but what he was one of the patrots who attached their names to that famous document on May 20, 1775. Dr. Alexander, however, who mentions him, declares that he was "PROBABLY born in Pennsylvania", which is PROBABLY a mistake. He was born in 1728, in VIRGINIA, where on the Augusta records in 1758, when he was thirty years of age, he sold a tract of land to JOSEPH HANNAH, consisting of 300 acres, in Augusta County. He is mentioned in the Journal of THOMAS LEWIS, the early surveyor of Augusta County, who in 1746 undertook to establish a part of the line of the Lord Fairfax grant (p. 467 Waddell), or else the reference is to his father, an older HENRY DOWNS! In the note dated September 10, 1746 he is called Captain Downs, and it is appended thereto that Captain Downs was probably the HENRY DOWNS who was presented by the grand jury of Orange County in 1740 "for Sabbath-breaking by traveling with loaded horses to the Shenandoah" (page 385).
At any rate HENRY DOWNS the signer, was perhaps one of the "flock" who followed Rev. ALEXANDER CRAIGHEAD, from Jackson's River and the Cow Pasture settlement to the Rocky River in Mecklenberg County, an in all likelihood a native of ORANGE COUNTY, VIRGINIA, where the name of HENRY DOWNS either father or son often appears on the records. He may have been of Scotch-Irish descent, but he was not from Pennsylvania. His name and that of his two sons THOMAS and SAMUEL DOWNS appears on the United States Census of Mecklenburg in the year 1790, from the 19th and last District, as shewn on the map herein. He settled in that part of Mecklenburg which was later cut off and made a part of Union County, but not in his life-time. He lived to be 70 years of age and died on October 8th, 1798, and is buried in the old PROVIDENCE CHURCYARD.

(20) HEZEKIAH JAMES BALCH

The name of JAMES has always followed the first name of this signer, obviously to distinguish him from another HEZEKIAH BALCH, who played an important roll in the early History of that part of North Carolina which became a part of Tennessee. Both were ministers and contemporaneous, but the relationship between them - there must have been a relationship - has never been disclosed by any of the writers or documents we have seen. His name appears on the "Signer" monument as plain HEZEKIAH BALCH, but Dr. Foote in his account of him, always refers to him as HEZEKIAH JAMES BALCH. This signer was born in HARFORD COUNTY, MARYLAND, on what was called DEER CREEK, in the year 1746 & is said to have been a great grandson of COL. JAMES BALCH, a native of ENGLAND. Here is at least one signer who was not of the Scotch-Irish clan, as has been claimed for so many of them - often absent proof or evidence, save conjecture. The father of HEZEKIAH JAMES BALCH is said to have moved from Maryland to Mecklenburg when the signer was yet a youth in years.
HEZEKIAH JAMES BALCH went from Mecklenburg County to PRINCETON COLLEGE, where he graduated in 1766 in the same class with another signer, HON. WAIGHTSTILL AVERY. In 1767 he was licensed to preach by the Presbytery of Donegal and in 1769 was sent as a missionary to ROCKY RIVER and POPLAR TENT Churches in Mecklenburg. He is believed to have married a MISS McCONNELL, of the family of that name that lived almost directly on the line between Mecklenburg and Iredell County (after the latter was established) and they settled six miles West of the present town of Concord, not far from the home of his wife's parents, on the Beattie's Ford road. He did a splendid piece of pioneer work for these two churches, and demonstrated his patriotism by being one of the signers of the Mecklenburg Declaration just about a year prior to his death, he having died at the early age of 30 years, in the summer of 1776. After his death his widow married one of the younger members of that well known McWHORTER family, who died shortly thereafter, whereupon the widow moved with her children beyond the mountains to the West and settled in Tennessee, where all trace of them disappears. By her marriage to HEZEKIAH JAMES BALCH, Mrs. McWHORTER had two or more children. This signer is known to have had thre, brothers: Rev. Steven B. Balch, of Georgetown, Rev. JAMES BALCH, of Kentucky, and WILLIAM BLACH who settled in the State of Georgia.
He is buried in the graveyard of POPLAR TENT CHURCH and it was not until the year 1847 that funds were raised to erect a marker or monument over his grave to perpetuate his memory. He was the first pastor of POPLAR TENT CONGREGATION.

(21) EZRA ALEXANDER

EZRA ALEXANDER is said by DR. CYRUS L. HUNTER, in his "Sketches" to have been a son of ABRAHAM ALEXANDER, the President of the Mecklenburg Convention of 1775, although DR. J. B. ALEXANDER in his History of Mecklenburg does not list him among the Chairman's children. If he WAS a son of

ABRAHAM then here is one instance where both father and son were signers of the Declaration, and it is perhaps the only instance. He and William Alexander each commanded a company in Colonel William Davidson's command during the revolution, during the Tory uprising and the fight at RAMSOUR'S MILL in Lincoln County. He also served in Captain John Brownfield's company according to Dr. Alexander's account. In the census of 1790 he is listed as EZRA ALEXANDER SR. in the first, or Steele Creek District which extended North as far as Long Creek to the West of Charlotte, with a family consisting of four sons and two daughters, and his wife.

EZRA ALEXANDER died in the summer of 1800 at an advanced age, in Mecklenburg County. He was listed as a road overseer in 1778. (Page 352).

(22) CHARLES ALEXANDER

The identity of CHARLES ALEXANDER, the signer, is not clear. He lived, Dr. Alexander says, on the line from Charlotte to the Waxhaws, and in that part of Mecklenburg County which is now part of Union County. He belonged to the same ALEXANDER FAMILY as the others, and originated, through his ancestors, in CECIL COUNTY, MARYLAND. We find him listed on the United States census of 1790 in District No. 19, somewhere on the upper waters of Twelve Mile Creek, with a family consisting of three sons and as many daughters, if he is the "Capt. Charles Alexander", of that list, of which we are not sure. That he was one of the patriots who signed the Declaration on May 20, 1775, has not been questioned, even by HUNTER, who omits some known signers from his list.

There is a story connected with him, gleaned from Dr. Alexander's accounts, that he became an infidel and renounced all connection with the Churches. A society of infidels was established at one time in Mecklenburg County, and it is said that he became one of its members. Another statement is made that he may have followed Zaccheus Wilson and others to Tennessee. But Alexander says he died in 1801 - apparently in Mecklenburg County - and that he had a grandson who was an officer and soldier in the War with Mexico. Dr. C. L. HUNTER makes the statement that both he and JOHN FORD were members of CAPT. CHARLES POLK'S company of "Light Horse" in 1776 in the Wilmington campaign and that he rendered other military services during the revolution. It is possible that we can throw more light on CHARLES ALEXANDER the signer, when we get to the Alexander Family in the genealogical section of these notes.

(23) BENJAMIN PATTON

This BENJAMIN PATTON, who signed the Mecklenburg Declaration in 1775, was the previous year a delegate to the Provincial Congress which met at New Bern on August 25, 1774, and against which JOSIAH MARTIN, the then Governor, proclaimed against in behalf of the high and mighty KING of England. He is said to have walked the entire distance from his home in what is now Cabarrus County, rather than fail to be there and cast his vote. He was a man of iron firmness and indomitable courage and hasitated not one minute to attach his name to that Mecklenburg document which threw the defy into the teeth of a foreign potentate in behalf of a people hungry for freedom and anxious to shake off their political shackles. He has been classed as "an early and devoted friend of liberty".

BENJAMIN PATTON came from Virginia, and was followed to the Carolinas by many other members of the same family. Due to the fact that he settled on the North side of Rocky River not far from the first charges of REV. ALEXANDER CRAIGHEAD, it is not improbable that he too, came from the COW PASTURE section of Virginia, where his kinsman COL. JAMES PATTON had located as military commander of the Virginia troops in the early Indian days.

At the Provincial Congress which met at Hillsboro, August 21, 1775, shortly after the Mecklenburg demonstration, BENJAMIN PATTON, though somewhat advanced in years was appointed MAJOR of the Second Continental Regiment under Col. Robert Howe and Lieutenant Colonel Alexander Martin. He was a member of the Committee of Safety for Mecklenburg County, associated with two of his close ROCKY RIVER friends and neighbors, JOHN PAUL BARRINGER and MARTIN PHIFER, and these three and their other associates are said to have been a "Terror unto evil doers" of that day and time.

BENJAMIN PATTON died, it is said, at his home near CONCORD, in CABARRUS COUNTY at a ripe age, and his remains were interred on the banks of BUFFALO CREEK. The date of his death does not seem to be of record, nor is there a statement showing when he was born, as no monument markes his last resting place. MATTHEW PATTON, who married a MISS MOORE, daughter of PROF. CHARLES MOORE, who lived in the Waxhaw settlement in the old part of Mecklenburg County at one time, is believed to have been a son of BENJAMIN PATTON. His son's wife was a second cousin of GEN. JOSEPH GRAHAM.

(24) MATTHEW McCLURE

MATTHEW McCLURE came to Mecklenburg County, or what is now Mecklenburg, about 1751, and he was therefore among the early arrivals. The chroniclers say he was born in IRELAND about 1725; that he and his wife married there, and came direct to Mecklenburg section when they arrived in America. They settled about five miles South of Davidson College, somewhere North of HOPEWELL CHURCH where members of the family are buried. On the old tombstones at Hopewell the name is spelled in two ways: McCLURE and McLURE. He was one of the signers of the Declaration. His daughter JANE McCLURE was the wife of GEORGE HOUSTON, who belonged to the squad of brave Mecklenburg soldiers, who chased a whole Tory army out of the community at McIntyre's branch, with the aid of a few bees or hornets, and thus earned the title of "The Hornet's Nest" for Mecklenburg County, coined by the followers of the man who gave up his sword to George Washington at Yorktown not long afterwards. A son of GEORGE HOUSTON and his wife JANE McCLURE served throughout the revolution.

After the death of GEORGE HOUSTON his widow married another Irishman by the name of "BILLY" KERNS. She died in 1820, but left three KERNS children, THOMAS, MARY and HARPER KERNS, all descendants of MATTHEW McCLURE, the signer.

JOHN and ARTHUR McCLURE, sons of MATTHEW McCLURE, and their wives are buried at HOPEWELL Churchyard. JOHN McCLURE died April 11, 1817 at the age of 78 years and ten months, and ARTHUR McCLURE died March 18, 1817 at the age of 68 years.

HUGH McCLURE, a grandson of the signer, died November 10, 1840, in the 59th year of his age and is also buried there. Which son was his father does not appear.

(25) JOHN FLENNIKIN

JOHN FLENNIKIN, the signer, is not mentioned among the sketches written by CYRUS L. HUNTER, which were published in 1877, although his name appears on the monument and in all of the other lists published, so far as we have seen. JOHN FLENNIKIN is said to have been the seventh of nine children, born to either JAMES or JOHN FLENNIKIN, two brothers who settled in Mecklenburg County in an early day. He is said to have been born on March 7, 1744. His parents were Scotch-Irish emigrants who landed in Pennsylvania and came South. This signer may have been born in PENNSYLVANIA, though no proof is offered to that effect. It appears that they settled in the lower part of Mecklenburg and that JOHN FLENNIKIN lived on McALPIN'S CREEK, though his brother DAVID FLENNIKIN lived down in the Waxhaw section in what is now Union County, where he is listed on the U. S. Census in 1790. A CHARLES FLENNIKIN lived in 1790 in the HOPEWELL section of the County. The brother DAVID FLENNIKIN died April 26th, 1826, and drew a pension for wounds received when serving under General IRWIN and SUMPTER during the revolution.

The wife of JOHN FLENNIKIN was named MARY, and she died and is buried at PROVIDENCE BURIAL GROUND. Her death occurred February 14, 1823, when she was only 47 years of age, so that she was born in 1775, the same year that the Mecklenburg Declaration was signed by her husband, the explaination of which seems to be that she must have been a second wife and much younger than her husband. On her tombstone (See PROVIDENCE CHURCH RECORDS) the name of her husband is wrotten JOHN O. FLENNIKIN, described thereon as one of the Mecklenburg signers.

Neighbors of the FLENNIKINS on McALPINE CREEK was the ROGER CUNNINGHAM family, into which the FLENNIKINS must have married, because JOHN FLENNIKIN and SAMUEL FLENNIKIN, who were sons of the signer, moved to KNOXVILLE, TENNESSEE and are buried in what was called the old CUNNINGHAM graveyard just outside of the town; one of the oldest in that section. The signer is buried at Providence Church beside his young wife, though there seems to be no marker on his grave; or at least we failed to find one.

(26) DAVID REESE

DAVID REESE, the signer, was a native of WALES, and the son of a DAVID REESE, Presbyterian Preacher, who is said to have taken part in the terrible seige of Londonderry; the son DAVID was perhaps born in Wales, to which his father had returned, in about the year 1711 or 1712, since he had a brother, WILLIAM REESE, who lived in what is now the Southwest corner of IREDELL COUNTY, and who died in 1808 at the age of ninety-nine years.

The wife of DAVID REESE was SUSAN POLK, a sister of GEN. THOMAS and EZEKIEL POLK, whom he probably married in SOMERSET COUNTY, on the Eastern shore of MARYLAND, and they probably came to what is now Mecklenburg County, about the same time that the POLK FAMILY arrived. The date of his marriage to SUSAN POLK can be placed at approximately 1750, maybe earlier, since their son REV. THOMAS REESE, who married JANE HARRIS, was born in 1752.

DAVID REESE was an educated man and settled in the POPLAR TENT region in what is now CABARRUS COUNTY, where in 1751 he was elected an elder in that congregation, according to ALEXANDER, who, however, appears to lose sight of the fact that at that period this church had not yet been organized, so far as the records show. Anyway, we will assume, that DAVID REESE was one of the earliest elders in POPLAR TENT. In 1767, DAVID REESE and his wife SUSAN POLK had a grown son, to whom they executed a deed to lands. This may have been their son REV. THOMAS REESE, who married JANE HARRIS, daughter of CHARLES HARRIS, by his first wife, JANE McILHENNY. The statement on page 58 of HUNTER'S SKETCHES that DAVID REESE was a brother of Rev. Thomas Reese, is an error, although the signer and and his wife may have had also a son DAVID who was a brother of THOMAS.

REV. THOMAS HARRIS, a distinguished minister in the Presbyterian Church, removed to PENDLETON DISTRICT, S. C. where in 1792 he became pastor of HOPEWELL and CARMEL CHURCHES, near the home of JOHN C. CALHOUN'S family. Four years later, in 1796, he died at the age of 54 years and was the first person to buried at what is known as the "OLD STONE CHURCH". Afterwards the remains of GEN. PICKENS, GEN. ANDERSON and numerous other revolutionary patriots were buried beside him. The site of Hopewell Church there, of which he was pastor, is now marked by a marble shaft. The old Stone Church was built out of native stone by an old stone mason from Virginia, named JOHN HUSK, who is also buried there, the father of GEN. THOMAS J. HUSK, commander of forces at the battle of SAN JACINTO in the Texas revolution in 1836, and right hand aide to GEN. SAM HOUSTON.

(27) WILLIAM KENNON

He is supposed to have lived in ROWAN COUNTY, where he was a prominent lawyer and wealthy citizen who was chosen as a member of the Comitee of Safety of that County in 1774. In 1775 he was a member of the Provincial Congress, and he held other positions of trust and confidence at the instance of his neighbors. He was born in VIRGINIA, where his forbears obtained liberal and extensive grants of lands in a very early day, the family being widely connected, with the LEWIS and other well known families. His signature on the Declaration is attributed by EMPIE to the fact that the committee on credentials were rather careless. This writer does not so think, but believes that Kennon resided somewhere near the line of ROWAN in MECKLENBURG, that his county of residence at that time was undetermined, and that he was accepted as a MECKLENBURG man as a member. To GEORGIA.

(10) WILLIAM GRAHAM
(Omitted from its proper place)

WILLIAM GRAHAM appears to have been an unpretentious, but substantial farmer, who resided somewhere near the Beattie's Ford road, not far from HOPEWELL CHURCH in the northern part of MECKLENBURG COUNTY. The Historians profess to know little about him. He was from VIRGINIA, though he may have been of Irish parents. He probably came to Mecklenburg with the migrating congregation of REV. ALEXANDER CRAIGHEAD in about 1755. His wife's first name was MARGARET, and both are buried at Hopewell Church. He was born in 1740 and died July 17, 1818 aged 78 years. His wife MARGARET died in 1821 aged 71 years. He belonged to the interesting GRAHAM family. More about them later.

THE BEATTIE'S FORD SETTLEMENT

In CHARLOTTE, North Carolina, even today, if one wants to get directions to visit the old Hopewell Presbyterian Church, the scene of the McIntyre fight during the revolution, Gilleed's, Long Creek and other places too numerous to mention, he is told to "Go out the Beattie's Ford Road". When we were searching for the old "Baker's Graveyard", Mr. Hubbard and Dr. Alexander told us to "go out the Beattie's Ford Road", etc. One who is unacquainted with the history of Mecklenburg County, will naturally wonder, in this day and time, just where was and what was this "Beattie's Ford"?

Well, of course, it is just a place on the CATAWBA RIVER, where during the earliest days when all Mecklenburg County was part of ANSON or CRAVEN COUNTY, and there was no MECKLENBURG, NO ROWAN, NO TRYON and no LINCOLN COUNTY. JOHN BEATTIE, who came from VIRGINIA, most likely, was the first man to cross it on horseback, and when he did so he thought, rightly, that he was taking his own life in his hands, as he must have crossed over knowing that there were wild Indians on every hand throughout the wilderness he was entering. The date was about 1745-47. Historians have tried to certainly date it, without success. He settled near the "ford that bears his name", they say, and the place and name continued, though John Beattie and his descendants multiplied and scattered, but not before TRYON was erected in 1768, and abolished ten years later to give way to LINCOLN, next to the river and Rutherford joining it on the West and reaching to the line of the "Cherokee Country". BEATTIE, however, seems to have settled on the SOUTH or WEST side of the CATAWBA, at his "ford", and although until 1768 - after 1762 - it was MECKLENBURG, when the shifting of county names was concluded the BEATTIES found themselves living in and residents of LINCOLN COUNTY. Their names, however, have frequently been found on the records of MECKLENBURG for the reasons just stated, and for the further reason that some of them have lived in MECKLENBURG as it is today. But the name of "BEATTIE'S FORD" survived it all.

At this point it is well to explain that there were a string of fords up and down the CATAWBA river in those days and a little later several ferries, all bearing names of persons who established them or owned the land along the river banks where they were located. Beginning almost opposite the old HOPEWELL PRESBYTERIAN CHURCH "on the Beattie's Ford Road" and not far from the location of the home of MAJ. JOHN DAVIDSON, and his mother MRS. HENRY, there was what is still known as TOOLE'S FORD, at least in the writings one finds today. An old Indian Trader, with the usual Indian wife, who lived at this point, and it is said on the present Mecklenburg side of the river, was the "daddy" of this Ford. Then traveling North, a mile or so, one comes to the old ford called "COWAN's ford", and it was at this point Gen. William Lee Davidson was mortally wounded and died during the revolution. Then there is a skip of some four or five miles until you reach John "Beattie's Ford", which seems to be the last ford crossing from Lincoln into the present Mecklenburg. LINCOLN COUNTY, however, when first established in 1779 extended on Northward and embraced all of that territory now included in CATAWBA COUNTY, and SHERRILL'S FORD, located several miles North from Beattie's Ford was established nearly as early. One ADAM SHERRILL, by making the first crossing and settling nearby gave it the name.

There seems to be a total lack of information in regard to the COWAN for whom COWAN'S FORD was named, but the writer finds from his investigation that there was a connection between a family of this name and the ARMSTRONGS, of "Armstrong's Ford" on the South Fork of the Catawba, not so far distant. There is an occasional mention of the COWAN FAMILY on the records of Rowan County, and these were probably of the same stock.

But if we read the old records intelligently, there was not only a "Beattie's Ford" - meaning a place to cross the river with teams or on horseback - but a small town of the name, but it was across the river in what is now LINCOLN COUNTY, but built around the location of the "ford" mentioned. More properly speaking it may have been just a good sized "settlement", at most a kind of village or "town" as that term would have been used in the era of its existence. But it was the home of some personages of importance in the History of North Carolina.

Among these important personages were two brothers, ROBERT HUTCHINS BURTON, and ALFRED M. BURTON, sons of COL. ROBERT BURTON, of GRANVILLE COUNTY, North Carolina (who married Agatha Williams, daughter of JUDGE JOHN WILLIAMS, noted Jurist of North Carolina) and who married sisters.

ROBERT H. BURTON was married May 11, 1813 to Mary Fullinwider, daughter of JOHN FULLINWIDER, in Lincoln County.

ALFRED M. BURTON was married to ELIZABETH FULLINWIDER, daughter of JOHN FULLINWIDER, June 1, 1811.

ALFRED M. BURTON (From Sherrill's History of Lincoln County) was a lawyer and had a good practice, which, together with his large landed interests, took all of his time. He married Elizabeth, daughter of JOHN FULLINWIDER, and lived at Beattie's Ford. He ranked high among the men of mark in his profession, including JAMES GRAHAM, ROBERT WILLIAMSON, MICHAEL HOKE and others. He reared a large family among whom were Mrs. Sarah V. Young, Mrs. Eli Hoyle, Mrs. Connor and Miss Fannie Burton. The late ALFRED BURTON YOUNG, of Concord (Cabarrus County) was his grandson, and Burton H. Smith, of Charlotte a great grandson. He died in 1859 and was buried in the family plot in the UNITY CHURCH CEMETERY.

JUDGE ROBERT HENDERSON BURTON (from Sherrill) son of COL. ROBERT BURTON of GRANVILLE County, North Carolina, was born in 1781 in Granville County, and died at BEATTIE'S FORD, April 26, 1842. He was educated at the University of North Carolina and came to LINCOLN COUNTY, where he was admitted to the bar and began the practice of law. In 1818 he was elected JUDGE OF THE SUPERIOR COURT and after one year on the neck resigned and resumed his lucrative practice. While on the neck his courts were held at Salisbury, Buncombe and Rutherford and elsewhere in the wide district, including HILLSBORO. In 1830 he declined the office of State Treasurer, which was offered him by the Legislature. He was married to MARY (POLLY) FULLINWIDER in 1813 and settled on a plantation at BEATTIE'S FORD. He and his wife raised a family of 11 children, only four of whom married:

1. FRANCES BURTON married COL. MICHAEL HOKE.
2. ELIZABETH BURTON married J. M. H. ADAMS, a Presbyterian Minister.
3. AUGUSTUS W. BURTON married JULIA L. OLMSTEAD
4. HENRY W. BURTON married MRS. SARAH (HOYLE) KEENAN.

Of the other children of JUDGE ROBERT H. BURTON we have found no record.

AUGUSTUS W. BURTON, son of JUDGE ROBERT H. BURTON, married April 25, 1849, to JULIA L. OLMSTEAD, sister of REV. A. F. OLMSTEAD, an Episcopal Rector of Lincolnton. He and his wife settled in the town of SHELBY, North Carolina, (CLEVELAND COUNTY), where he practiced law until 1861 when he volunteered in the Civil War and went to the front as Captain of the Cleveland Guards. He was afterwards promoted to Major. After two years active service he was transferred to the Commissary Department and stationed in CHARLOTTE until the close of the conflict in 1865. Before the war he had represented Cleveland County in the House of Commons and was elected State Solicitor for the Western District of North Carolina, which office he held until 1858. Thereafter before volunteering in the C. S. A. he was State Senator from Cleveland County. He had two sons:

1. FRANK O. BURTON (b. 1851) went to Dakota. Died at Custer, 1898.
2. ROBERT H. BURTON an Episcopal Minister, went to Connecticut, where he died.

COL. ROBERT BURTON was a delegate from North Carolina; born in Mecklenburg County, VIRGINIA October 20, 1747; moved to GRANVILLE COUNTY, N. C. in 1775, where he married AGATHA WILLIAMS, the daughter of the famous JUDGE JOHN WILLIAMS, by whom he became the father of JUDGE ROBERT H. BURTON and ALFRED H. BURTON, who lived at BEATTIE'S FORD. COL. BURTON served in the revolutionary Army and attained the rank of COLONEL; sat in the CONTINENTAL CONGRESS 1787-1788; member of the Commission which established the boundary line between North Carolina and South Carolina, and Georgia, in 1801; died in GRANVILLE COUNTY, N. C., May 31, 1825. For a complete list of all his children and the Burton Family Bible records see pages 241-242 of this Volume.
JOHN BURTON, a brother of COLONEL ROBERT BURTON and an uncle of ROBERT H. and ALFRED H. BURTON was the father of HUTCHINS GORDON BURTON, who became Governor of North Carolina, and lived in HALIFAX COUNTY. Governor Burton was on his way to BEATTIE'S FORD to pay a visit to his cousins, Robert H. and Alfred H. Burton, at the time of his death, which overtook him in IREDELL COUNTY, just before he had reached his destination. It is the writer's understanding that JOHN BURTON and his wife MARY GORDON also settled near BEATTIE'S FORD, and that GOVERNOR BURTON was born, possibly in Mecklenburg County. However, we cannot verify this.

MAJOR HENRY W. CONNOR

Another distinguished resident of BEATTIE'S FORD, on the Lincoln County side, was MAJOR HENRY W. CONNOR, who was born near AMELIA COURTHOUSE, in VIRGINIA, August 5, 1793 - possibly in Prince Edward County. He served ten terms in the United States Congress from Lincoln County, N. C. and at that time the County included what is now CATAWBA COUNTY, but of course he represented a large part of the entire Old North State. It is said his parents came to MECKLENBURG COUNTY in 1800, and perhaps settled on the East or North side of the CATAWBA. The map made by GEN. JOSEPH GRAHAM shows "CONNOR'S STORE" located in the Northern Part of MECKLENBURG on DAVIDSON'S CREEK at the time the map was drawn in 1787. This shows that CAPT. CHARLES CONNOR and his wife ANN EPPES, parents of HENRY W. CONNOR came to MECKLENBURG in 1800 to join their relatives, and it also shows that the CONNORS of Northern Mecklenburg had come there from VIRGINIA and not PENNSYLVANIA or other foreign parts, as has been stated.

MAJOR HENRY W. CONNOR was a son in law of GOV. WILLIAM HAWKINS of WARREN and GRANVILLE COUNTIES, North Carolina, having married April 9, 1839, MRS. LUCY (HAWKINS) COLEMAN, in Washington, D. C. He was a brother in law (by this marriage) of JOHN WHITE MORROW (son of BENJAMIN ton, D. C. He was a brother in law (by this marriage) of HON. BENJAMIN MORROW, (also a Major in the war of 1812) who belonged to another old BEATTIE'S FORD family that resided on the Mecklenberg side of the river, who married MARY JANE HAWKINS, another daughter of GOV. WILLIAM HAWKINS.

This close relationship between the CONNORS and MORROWS, of Mecklenburg (around BEATTIE'S FORD) accounts for the following item, taken from an old newspaper:

MARRIED, at the residence of MAJ. HENRY W. CONNOR, by Rev. Jacob Hill, March 30, 1848, Mr. John W. Morrow of Mecklenburg County, to MISS MARY ANN NUTTALL, of GRANVILLE COUNTY.

This has reference to JOHN WHITE MORROW, a son of BENJAMIN MORROW, who was the father of PICKNEY MORROW, who was living at the old Morrow homestead near PINEVILLE in 1939.

CAPT. CHARLES CONNOR, who married ANN EPPES, the daughter of PETER EPPES, of PRINCE GEORGE COUNTY, Virginia, and who was the father of HON. HENRY W. CONNOR, is said to have been a merchant and sea Captain on ships plying between LIVERPOOL and NORFOLK, Virginia. He was, according to tradition, a wealthy man, and received his title as an active soldier of the revolution. The same authority quoted, says that he came to MECKLENBURG COUNTY, N. C. and settled near BEATTIE'S FORD, where he died in 1803. He is credited with only two children:

1. HON. HENRY W. CONNOR, M. C.
2. BETSY CONNOR married JOHN D. GRAHAM, son of GEN. JOSEPH GRAHAM.

JAMES CONNOR (1754-1835) was a brother of CAPT. CHARLES CONNOR, and married LILLIS WILSON, the daughter of SAMUEL WILSON and his wife (the third) MARGARET JACK, sister of CAPT. JAMES JACK. They were married in MECKLENBURG COUNTY and lived and died there "across the river from Beattie's Ford" (by which is meant the TOWN of Beattie's Ford, across the river in LINCOLN COUNTY, of course). They were married BEFORE 1800, because their son, CHARLES D. CONNOR was a representative in the State Senate from 1817 to 1820. LILLIS WILSON was born April 1, 1773 and died September 23, 1844 (Tombstone). They were the parents of CHARLES D. CONNOR (State Senator) and HENRY WORKMAN CONNOR, who settled in Charleston, S. C.

There is an interesting chapter in the life of this JAMES CONNOR (born in 1754) which has been entirely overlooked by the historians. His tombstone states that he was born in 1754 and that he died April 11, 1835, at his seat in Mecklenburg County "where he had resided for the last sixty years" in the 81st year of his life. The statement on the tombstone is not strictly true, for the reason that the sixty years he is supposed to have resided in Mecklenburg County, has a gap of many years in it, when he was absent in Tennessee, as will be explained below.

THE MOSES WHITE FAMILY

Among the other families who settled along DAVIDSON CREEK in the upper part of MECKLENBURG COUNTY and the lower edge of what is now IREDELL, but the line between which was uncertain for many years after Mecklenburg had been established, according to Dr. J. B. Alexander, was the MOSES WHITE FAMILY. We class the Whites among those who lived on the Mecklenburg side of BEATTIE'S FORD, because they lived between the present site of Davidson College and the Ford in Mecklenburg. There was a close association between the WHITES and the CONNORS, as well as the LAWSONS, MORROWS, BEATTIES, DAVIDSONS and others. ISAAC WHITE, a cousin of MOSES WHITE lived in LINCOLN, and at least two of his children married into the BEATTIE FAMILY; JAMES WHITE, son of MOSES, married MARY LAWSON, daughter of HUGH LAWSON whose home stood on the banks of DAVIDSON CREEK. Isaac White moved over into the Watauga Valley, when it was a part of NORTH CAROLINA, and became a member of the first court, and also served in the N. C. Legislature. JAMES WHITE, son of MOSES, migrated across the country and the mountains into the Holston Valley, and settled a few miles South of the junction of the Holston and the French Broad rivers, where he and one JAMES CONNOR erected a Fort and a cabin, and laid the foundation of the present City of Knoxville. We copy an extract from the history of this settlement:

> The Act granting Western lands to soldiers for services in the revolution was passed in 1783. This is what prompted JAMES WHITE, along with JAMES CONNOR, Robert Love and FRANCIS RAMSEY to explore the valleys of the French Broad as far down as the Little Tennessee for new homesites. They went back to their farms in Iredell (sic) County, North Carolina, packed up their families and goods and moved west.

Francis Ramsey was the son in law of JOHN McKNITT ALEXANDER, of Mecklenburg; JAMES CONNOR was the revolutionary soldier of DAVIDSON'S CREEK or BEATTIE'S FORD, in Mecklenburg County & the uncle of (afterwards) Hon. HENRY W. CONNOR, M. C.; JAMES WHITE was the son of MOSES WHITE and the son in law of HUGH LAWSON, who is buried about two miles from Beattie's Ford on the MECKLENBURG SIDE of the CATAWBA in the old Baker's Graveyard, with REV. JOHN THOMSON, MARY (DAVIDSON) PRICE, and others. Just how long JAMES CONNOR remained in White's Fort and Knoxville and vicinity, has not been recorded, but, he must have spent some length of time there; possible several years, since he and WHITE came back after their families. Perhaps an absence of some years from the neighborhood, and the presence of other members of the Connor family along DAVIDSON'S CREEK, had been so near forgotten, that the lapse of time had erased it from the memories of those who marked his grave. At any rate, it is thus recorded that JAMES CONNOR pioneered along the French Broad in Tennessee, with his friend JAMES WHITE and his wife MARY LAWSON, for some time, at least.

JOHN HILL WHEELER

Another notable resident of BEATTIE'S FORD, on the Lincoln side (the town) was the notable JOHN HILL WHEELER. It was here, in the old home plantation or home of JUDGE ROBERT H. BURTON, that Mr. Wheeler wrote for publication the widely quoted and voluminous "Wheeler's History of North Carolina" and his notable "Reminiscenses" which may be found in every Library of any consequence in the United States today. Here in the very midst of the scenes he pictured so adequately, surrounded by neighbors who bore the names of the ancestors he wrote about, such as the FORNEYS and others, and within sound of the rippling shoals of the Catawba fords, which Davidson's gallant band guarded so zealously to hold back the British army, this distinguished and gifted historian wrote the indelible record of their achievements. From 1837 to 1841 he had been Superintendent of the United States Mint at Charlotte, but on retirement he sought the tranquility and peace of a quiet home near Unity Church and at BEATTIE'S FORD to complete his monumental work. Later in life he gave up his home in Lincoln, however, and removed to Washington, D. C., where his biographers tell us he died on December 7, 1882.

REV. JOHN THOMSON AND HIS FAMILY

ANDERSON	CALDWELL	DANIEL	GRAHAM	LEEPER	ROE-ROWE
BAKER	COMBE	ELLIOTT	HARRIS	LOWE	SANKEY
BOOTH	CRAIG	EWING	HENRY	PASTEUR	WILLIAMSON
BROOKE	CROCKETT	FINLEY	HICKMAN	PATILLO	WILSON
BUTLER	CUNNINGHAM	GILLIAM	JARRETT	PATTON	UNDERWOOD

SAMUEL BAKER was the son in law of REV. JOHN THOMSON, and not "JOHN BAKER" as written by PROF. E. F. ROCKWELL, of DAVIDSON COLLEGE. Of the BAKER'S GRAVEYARD, Prof. Rockwell says:

"It dates from 1753, and its first grave was that of REV. JOHN THOMSON, probably the first missionary in these parts, who died in September, 1753, and was buried near his cabin in which he lived. JOHN (sic) BAKER, who lived near by was buried near the side of his father in law and gives name to the ground. HUGH LAWSON, grandfather of HUGH LAWSON WHITE, lies there, as do soldiers and godly church members, among them MRS. ISABELLA HENRY, mother of MAJ. JOHN DAVIDSON, JAMES PRICE and his wife MARY DAVIDSON PRICE. Quite a number of crude rock shafts, all grown over with moss, stand as sentinels in this lonely place, overshadowed by giant oaks".

Dr. J. B. ALEXANDER in his History of Mecklenburg County, N. C., says:

"BAKER'S GRAVEYARD is seven miles northwest of HOPEWELL on the west side of Beattie's Ford Road, and two miles east of the Catawba River."

To which Mr. James Price, of Charlotte, adds:

"Half mile or so west of Gilead's Church on the way to Johnson(s mill * * and there is buried MARY (DAVIDSON) PRICE; but her husband, JAMES PRICE, killed at the Iron Furnace in Lincoln County, is not buried with her."

To which they all might have added, as does this writer, who has himself visited the spot, that it is in MECKLENBURG and not in IREDELL COUNTY, as has been so many times erroneously stated. There are still many crude stones marking the head and foot of graves, but no inscriptions, no dressed stones and no identification of any kind. In 1877, nearly 70 years ago, according to MR. HUNTER, there was one rough slate rock, about one foot high and nine inches broad, on which had been rudely chiseled "HL", the initials of the early settler, HUGH LAWSON, grandfather of HUGH LAWSON WHITE, and whose son ROGER LAWSON had married the youngest daughter of REV. JOHN THOMSON.

In 1943, Dr. John Goodwin Herndon, of Haverford College, in Pennsylvania, one of REV. JOHN THOMSON'S descendants, through the CUNNINGHAM FAMILY, wrote a sketch of this distinguished early North Carolina minister, which was privately printed and distributed among the members of the family. It was a scholarly production and worthy of the erudite writer who produced it, but much lacking in the color that belonged to the subject.

In this admirable sketch Dr. Herndon quotes from records showing that REV. JOHN THOMSON entered the University of Glasgow in 1706, that he was probably born about 1790; thereafter, about 1715 he came to America and with his wife and probably one child, landed at "YORK" (interpreting that to mean NEW YORK). Two years afterwards he was called to the Church at Lewes, Delaware, where he remained until the latter part of 1729, or nearly 1730, after which he went to various places in Pennsylvania, meantime making various trips to VIRGINIA, where, at some unknown exact date he settled at Buffalo Church in Prince Edward County, Virginia. Thereafter in 1751 he went to North Carolina on "visits", preached there for a year or so, and died in 1753 and is buried at Baker's Graveyard in IREDELL COUNTY, though the author credits this writer, with contending otherwise. The author reviews the literary work of Rev· Thomson in a most interesting way, and devotes the last chapter to a very accurate and complete account of his family and thirteen children, and some of their connections. The sources of most of the information used by Dr. Herndon are the Presbyterian Church records, which are not to be impeached.

My brief comment on this work is that it pictures REV. JOHN THOMSON as coming to this country, a strange young man, with his wife, and casting his lot among utter strangers, absent all relatives and friends; forming no connections except among members of his flock, and being allied only with those families into which his children married, whereas the notes which I shall set out below give a widely different picture of the man and his family and his own connections. This picture may or may not be correct, but it is the writer's conception, based on his knowledge of all of the persons and families mentioned, and the records I have found in my research in Virginia and North Carolina. The writer is not a descendant of this man, but his wife is, though he is connected directly with the DANIEL FAMILY, about whom several erroneous statements were made by the same writer, in his article about the "CUNNINGHAMS OF CUB CREEK" (Virginia). Va. Mag. of Hist. & Biog. Vol. 52 pages 135 et seq., 1944.

REV. JOHN THOMSON, the young Glasgow student, was licensed by the ULSTER SYNOD meeting at ANTRIM on June 23, 1713 (Dr. Herndon's record). He probably came to Virginia that year, or it might have been in 1714. Rev. FRANCIS McKAMIE and his associated had formed the Presbytery of Philadelphia in 1706, while Thomson was attending the University. McKamie died in the year 1708 leaving a will in ACCOMAC COUNTY, VIRGINIA. Young Thomson's arrival was a half dozen years later, but it is conceded generally that he was the ultimate and almost immediate successor of FRANCIS McKAMIE in VIRGINIA and MARYLAND. The Presbytery itself did not receive notice of THOMSON'S arrival with "his wife and family" at "York" until 1715, at which time he had probably been in the country at least one year. It was not until two years later that he became pastor of the Church at Lewes, Delaware. REV. JOHN THOMSON "and his family" as the record describes him, did not come through the port of NEW YORK, but by way of "YORK" - in other words, YORKTOWN, VIRGINIA.

He did not help his wife and children (perhaps at least two of them) ashore at Yorktown, in 1713-14, among strangers, but was greeted by his own relatives and a host of their friends. He did not spend the two or three years interval between his arrival and his removal to Lewes, Delaware, in isolated idleness. He had a wife and a growing family to support and immediately "went about his master's business". In doing that he formed friends and ties among his relatives and their neighbors, which lasted throughout his long life. Nearby Williamsburg was the capital, and doubtless for a suitable remuneration he spent some of his time teaching, in order to take care of himself and family. If we could open the doors of the dim years of nearly 250 years ago, the writing of this man's career would be made much simpler. But a review of some of the records help a little:

REV. JOHN THOMSON AND SOME OF HIS YORKTOWN CONNECTIONS

The basis of the claim that REV. JOHN THOMSON with his wife and family landed in NEW YORK is a letter presented by REV. GEORGE McNISH to the Presbytery of Philadelphia in 1715 relating to Rev. Thomson, which read:

"There is one Mr. Thomson now arrived at York with his wife and family"

and which our perverse chroniclers insist meant they had arrived at New York. The last paragraph of the Journal of Rev. SAMUEL DAVIES, preserved on page 218 of Foote's Sketches of Virginia, reads:

"Arrived in YORK, February 13, 1755. The next day called in WILLIAMSBURG, waited on the Governor, and rode to Mr. HOLT'S that night".

Certainly no one would contend that YORK, as used by Mr. Davies, had reference to the port of NEW YORK. The term YORK in those days had reference to YORKTOWN, VIRGINIA.

THE THOMSON KIN: There were THOMPSONS living in York County, Virginia, long before the young Glasgow student, REV. JOHN THOMSON and his family, arrived there in 1713-14. On the records their names were usually spelled THOMPSON. Because in many instances the Rev. John Thomson spelled his name without the "p", members of the family often insist that was the correct spelling. This is possibly true, but his own name appears on some records spelled WITH the "p", thus, THOMPSON. However, while, to the mind of this writer, this alleged form of spelling, cannot be relied upon as a determinative factor in distinguishing our subject's family, from others who spell it THOMSON, it is tantalizingly indicative sometimes of a relationship between his branch of the THOMSONS and the others. But not always so, because we find many THOMPSONS who apparently must have been his kinsmen, notwithstanding.

In York County, Virginia, as early as 1646, a JOHN THOMPSON confessed judgment in favor of Elias Wigmore. (Vol.25, Fleet's Colonial Abstracts, p. 31) Thereafter the names of ROBERT, RICHARD, GEORGE, STEPHEN, WILLIAM (Minister), JOHN, BARTHOLOMEW, DANIEL and HENRY THOMPSON appear at periods even prior to the time that Rev. John and his "family" arrived there.

In one instance HENRY THOMPSON SR. and JR. both witnessed a deed. HENRY THOMPSON, JR. married MARY HURD, daughter of MAURICE HURD (probably HEARD). But here is the interesting note:

HENRY THOMPSON, JR. and his wife MARY became a planter in James City County, and in the year 1690 they deeded a tract of 140 acres of land in BRUTON PARISH, YORK COUNTY, lying next to JOHN DANIEL, which land was a part of MARY'S inheritance from her father MAURICE HURD.

Standing alone, this item from the records of York County seems meaningless, but in the light of what follows it is plainer:

We have traced this JOHN DANIEL of BRUTON PARISH, who had been or was a neighbor of HENRY THOMPSON JR. with unerring accuracy, and he has been identified as the Grandfather of JAMES, JOHN and WILLIAM DANIEL, of Prince Edward County, Virginia, who married respectively ELIZABETH, SARAH and HANNAH CUNNINGHAM, grand-daughters of REV. JOHN THOMSON.

They were the daughters of JAMES CUNNINGHAM who married ANNE THOMSON, one of the daughters of REV. JOHN THOMSON.

JAMES CUNNINGHAM who married ANNE THOMSON was born in either YORK or ELIZABETH CITY COUNTY, Virginia. Is it not plausible, if not even patent, that among the friends of YORKTOWN or York County, Virginia, whom Rev. John Thomson knew while living there for two or three years, were the parents of JAMES CUNNINGHAM? Does not the statement of Dr. Herndon that among THOMSON'S fellow students at the University of Glasgow were ROBERT, WILLIAM, HUGH and JAMES CUNNINGHAM, sound significant?

A previous note records that in 1646 one JOHN THOMPSON of York County confessed judgment to one ELIAS WIGMORE; we now find another note from the same record of the same year to the effect that this same ELIAS WIGMORE confessed judgment to THOMAS SWANN. This SWANN FAMILY was prominent in the Jamestown settlement for perhaps two centuries. ELIZABETH THOMPSON, supposed to have been a daughter of WILLIAM THOMPSON, of NANSEMOND COUNTY (South of the James) married CAPT. THOMAS SWANN, who was a Burgess in 1692. They had a son THOMAS SWANN, who was father of THOMPSON SWANN, Clerk of Cumberland County, Virginia in 1754. And JOSIAH THOMPSON, a son of HENRY THOMPSON, of York Co. (Jr.) married THOMPSON SWANN'S sister MARY ANN SWANN. The children of JOSIAH THOMPSON and his wife MARY ANN SWANN, from what we gather, included:

        WILLIAM MAURICE THOMPSON
        JOHN DANIEL THOMPSON
        WADDY THOMPSON

The first son was named for his grandfather MAURICE HURD or HEARD; the second was named for JOHN DANIEL, of YORK COUNTY, their old neighbor and probable kinsman in some way, while the third derived his name from the THOMPSON family connection with the descendants of old ANTHONY WADDY of YORK and New Kent Counties. Probably WILLIAM THOMPSON (father of ELIZABETH who married THOMAS SWANN) or else HENRY THOMPSON, SR. married a WADDY. WADDY THOMPSON, of this record died in GREENVILLE, S. C. Following is his tombstone inscription:

    Sacred to the memory of WADDY THOMPSON, who was born in
    Cumberland County, Virginia, the 18th day of November,
    1769, and died in this place on Feb. 8, 1845. He filled
    the office of CHANCELLOR of this State (S.C.) for twenty-
    three years with signal ability and was an able and vir-
    tuous magistrate and an upright and honorable man.

This WADDY THOMPSON was the famous Chancellor Thompson of S. C., as recorded on the in-scription. His wife was ELIZABETH WILLIAMS THOMPSON, the daughter of a certain COL. JAMES WILLIAMS (but not the one of King's Mountain fame). For a hundred years the genealogists have been claiming that this WADDY THOMPSON married ELIZABETH ANDERSON; that they were married in LOUISA COUNTY, Virginia, August 7, 1787; that he was the son of another WADDY THOMPSON who married as his second wife MARY LEWIS, daughter of ROBERT LEWIS, etc.

The explaination is that there were not several, but innumerable persons bearing the name of WADDY THOMPSON, all resulting from a first marriage between an early THOMPSON of YORK COUNTY and some one of the family of ANTHONY WADDY. HANOVER COUNTY, LOUISA COUNTY, GOOCHLAND COUNTY and ALBEMARLE COUNTY, Virginia, all have their WADDY THOMPSONS, showing on their records. Some of them even spelled the name THOMPSON as "THOMSON" without the "p". They were all descendants of the YORK COUNTY THOMPSONS, and possibly related to REV. JOHN THOMSON, the principal subject of these notes. This statement is bourne out by the obvious fact that ANTHONY WADDY was the ancestor of all the WADDY FAMILY, and lived in YORK COUNTY. At a meeting of the YORK COUNTY COURT on December 20,1645 this entry on the minutes appears:

    "ANTHONY WADDY arrested at the suit of ROBERT LEWIS,
    and not appearing, etc."
    — Vol. 24, p. 31 Fleet's Abstracts.

This little entry is significant in the light of added facts: That ANTHONY WADDY lived in YORK COUNTY, Virginia, in 1645; that ROBERT LEWIS was his neighbor, and they had frequent business transactions; that ROBERT LEWIS was the emmigrant ancestor of the famous "WARNER HALL" Lewis family, so-called, and was the supposed Great Great grandfather of ROBERT LEWIS of "Belvoir" whose daughter MARY LEWIS became the second wife of a WADDY THOMPSON, she having been the first wife of a SAMUEL COBBS, also of a YORK COUNTY FAMILY. Incidentally there were innumerable SAMUEL COBBS, all springing from the same stem, apparently the original AMBROSE COBBS. Last the reader jump at the conclusion that we are wandering far astray of our subject, be it known, that it was from a SAMUEL COBBS (but not the one mentioned immediately above) that REV. JOHN THOMSON and his son in law JAMES CUNNINGHAM boht lands in PRINCE EDWARD (then AMELIA) County, Virginia, before the year 1750. Here it is necessary to consider some more items from the YORK COUNTY records:

    August 31, 1717: JEAN PASTEUR, D. BLOUIT and THOMAS
    JONES are witnesses to the will of JEAN MAROT.

    March, 1720. JEAN PASTEUR, JOSEPH DAVENPORT and LEWIS
    DELONEY appraise the estate of SUSANNAH ALLEN.

    Feb. 20, 1720. JEAN PASTEUR, JOSEPH DAVENPORT and LEWIS
    DELONEY appraise the estate of DAVID CUNNINGHAM.

JEAN PASTEUR was the old "Barber and Paruke Maker", associate of DR. GEORGE GILMER, the brother in law of DR. THOMAS WALKER, and who died in WILLIAMSBURG in 1741, leaving a will, in which it is shown that his daughter ANNE, married SAMUEL COBBS, his daughter LUCHETIA married MATTHEW SHIELDS, and that D. BLOUIT was also his son in law.

LEWIS DELONEY is the same one who moved to LUNENBURG COUNTY and was the tythe taker for the territory immediately adjoining PRINCE EDWARD COUNTY in 1748.

DAVID CUNNINGHAM, also a "Barber and Paruke Maker" — otherwise a Physician and Surgeon — was an uncle of JAMES CUNNINGHAM, who married ANNE, the daughter of REV. JOHN THOMSON, and who died in 1719 in YORK COUNTY. His will was dated Jan. 13, 1719 and was proved February 19th of the same year. It was witnessed by LEWIS DELONEY, JOSEPH DAVENPORT and JAMES MORRIS, the executors being WILLIAM ROBERTSON and SAMUEL COBBS. His two children, DAVID and MARY CUNNINGHAM were placed under the care of SUSANKAH ALLEN, their grandmother, who died in 1720.

JEAN MAROT left a will in YORK COUNTY, Virginia, written in August 1717, and proved in December of the same year. He was murdered. In his will he mentions only his three daughters, EDITH, ANNE and RACHEL MAROT. (2 Tyler p. 205). His wife's name was ANNE.

EDITH MAROT married SAMUEL COBBS (Executor of DAVID CUNNINGHAM).
ANNE MAROT married (1) JAMES INGLES (2) JAMES SHIELDS.
RACHEL MAROT married RICHARD BOOKER.

There were two brothers SAMUEL and ROBERT COBBS. ROBERT COBBS married a daughter of WILLIAM PINKETHMAN (witness to the will of JOHN DANIEL in 1687) as his first wife, having a daughter ELIZABETH COBBS who married JAMES SHIELDS. This couple had a son JOHN SHIELDS who married MARGARET THOMSON, daughter of REV. JOHN THOMSON, of this record. ROBERT COBBS married second ELIZABETH ALLEN, daughter of DANIEL ALLEN and his wife SUSANNAH, and a sister of the wife of DAVID CUNNINGHAM. MRS. SUSANNAH ALLEN ran an Ordinary, or Inn in WILLIAMSBURG. After the death of his first wife JAMES SHIELDS married ANN MAROT, then the widow of JAMES INGLES, a descendant of MUNGO INGLIS. After the death of JEAN MAROT his widow married TIM SULLIVAN and moved to AMELIA COUNTY. SAMUEL COBBS and his wife EDITH also moved to the same locality, as did RICHARD BOOKER who married RACHEL MAROT. The BOOKERS and SHIELDS were also related to the FERGUSONS, and ROGER THOMSON, the son of REV. JOHN THOMSON, married ANN FERGUSON in AMELIA COUNTY, May 12, 1750. SARAH COBBS, daughter of ROBERT COBBS by Elizabeth Allen, married ROBERT JONES JR., of GRANVILLE COUNTY, North Carolina, prominent lawyer, and whose last wife was a daughter of COL. WILLIAM EATON; MARTHA COBBS, her sister, married first DUDLEY RICHARDSON and second SAMUEL WELDON. ROBERT COBBS and DAVID CUNNINGHAM married sisters, both daughters of DANIEL ALLEN and his wife SUSANNAH.

The above paragraph, based on the records, is enough to show the intimate relationship existing between the family of REV. JOHN THOMSON, JAMES CUNNINGHAM and the SAMUEL COBBS, Clerk of AMELIA COUNTY, from whom both were induced to purchase lands in AMELIA (later PRINCE EDWARD) County, on the dates shown below.

In 1745 REV. JOHN THOMSON bought 386 acres from SAMUEL COBBS on Spring Creek in AMELIA (now PRINCE EDWARD COUNTY) Virginia.

Nov. 1, 1742, JAMES CUNNINGHAM bought 900 acres on Spring Creek in the same locality, from SAMUEL COBBS.

These facts disclose that the CUNNINGHAMS and COBBS were intimately connected; that JAMES SHIELDS and RICHARD BOOKER had married sisters; that a son of JAMES SHIELDS by his first wife married JOHN THOMSON'S daughter; that the mother of JOHN SHIELDS was a daughter of an old friend of the DANIEL FAMILY; that a nephew of DAVID CUNNINGHAM married a daughter of JOHN THOMSON, and that all these relationships, of necessity date away back to the time when REV. JOHN THOMSON first came to VIRGINIA, in about 1714.

REV. JOHN THOMSONS FIRST CONNECTION WITH THE CROCKETT FAMILY IN VIRGINIA

ESTHER THOMSON, daughter of REV. JOHN THOMSON married one SAMUEL CROCKETT. It is believed that she was perhaps his oldest child. There is a very beautiful and romantic story that has been told and retold in connection with this marriage, to the effect that when REV. JOHN THOMSON " and his family " came over from Europe, SAMUEL CROCKETT, a young man was a passenger on the same vessel, and fell in love with ESTHER THOMSON as a child, resolving to marry her at some future time, and did so. Unless Rev. Thomson and his wife at that time had several children, she was little more than a "babe in arms" and the story would not be convincing. Whether true or not, it is certain that they married and the chroniclers declare "their first child was born in Prince Edward County, Virginia in 1735" , regardless of the historical fact that PRINCE EDWARD COUNTY had never been heard of at that date, and Col. William Byrd and his party on their "Jorney to the Land of Eden" only a little more than a year previously had cut their way through the forest and given names to the various streams that water the country.

The CROCKETTS, however, were woodsmen and advanced deep into the Indian country, ahead of most settlers, and it is possible, that though it was then in AMELIA COUNTY, they had built a cabin somewhere along these streams and settled at that date.

Who were these CROCKETTS?

FREDERICK E. HASKINS a noted research worker, who delves into the mysteries of lost families and facts, will be permitted to answer the question:

"TANGIER ISLAND, in Chesapeake Bay, was settled in the year 1686 by JOHN CROCKETT, who with his eight sons and their families, chiefly of CORNISH descent, came over from the mainland of VIRGINIA. Today practically one-third of the Island's inhabitants, descendants of the original settlers, bear the surname of CROCKETT".

DAVID CROCKETT himself, a descendant of this family, and a great grandson of ROBERT CROCKETT, a brother of SAMUEL, apparently knew nothing of the origin of his family, members of which were living on the MAINLAND OF VIRGINIA, in YORK, JAMES CITY, ELIZABETH CITY or GLOUCESTER COUNTY, before 1686. How long before is problematical.

The writer dislikes to destroy beautiful family traditions, such as the one about the beginning of the romance between SAMUEL CROCKETT and ESTHER THOMSON, which has been repeated so very often and so long, and which members of the family have cherished. Traditions grow. They usually grow out of something which becomes more and more distorted with the passage of time. There are many traditions of this particular kind where the couple "met on the ship coming over". It is a favorite story in hundreds of families, and in a few instances has some basis in fact. We believe there is a fact basis for this particular story, which summed up, is that SAMUEL CROCKETT did know ESTHER THOMSON when she was a child. Where? In YORKTOWN, VIRGINIA, or on TANGIER ISLAND.

The father of ESTHER THOMSON was a young University graduate, of a good family, well known in Yorktown, Williamsburg, Hampton and environs. During the probable THREE YEARS when the THOMSONS lived there, he frequently visited on the "Eastern Shore" in ACCOMAC, where at POKOMOKE, Rev. Francis McKamie had lived and died little more than a half dozen years previously. Doubtless he delivered occasional sermons, or taught pupils, sometimes across the Chesapeake. TANGIER ISLAND, the home of JOHN CROCKETT and his EIGHT SONS and their families, lies between the mainland - mouth of the York River - and the mainland on the "Eastern Shore". It is a part now and was then a part of ACCOMAC COUNTY. SAMUEL CROCKETT had met Rev. Thomson perhaps at Williamsburg or the landing at Yorktown, and on his visits across the bay the young minister may have visited on the Island populated so thickly by the Crocketts. His removal with his family up the bay and across to LEWES, DELAWARE in 1717 did not destroy his relationship with his friends lower down the peninsula, whom he doubtless visited occasionally, or with the CUNNINGHAMS, and others around Yorktown. So romance between SAMUEL CROCKETT and ESTHER THOMSON did not die, but reached its final fruition about 1733-4, when they married and pushed Westward up the JAMES RIVER via the NOTTOWAY to the vicinity of the mouth of BUFFALO, where they settled. Others of the Tangier Island Crocketts came with them, and the brother ROBERT CROCKETT bought lands from his friend BEVERLY along the Cowpasture. BEVERLY was from the town of HAMPTON, close by Tangier, and knew the CROCKETT FAMILY.

With a son in law and daughter, and after 1735, grandchildren pioneering in the BUFFALO settlement; with an old YORKTOWN friend, SAMUEL COBBS, Clerk of AMELIA COUNTY, dealing in lands & constantly boosting the locality around him, it is hard to believe that REV. JOHN THOMSON, who was ever an active and energetic traveler, failed to show up in that part of the country until as late as 1744. It is the writer's opinion that his visits to that section of the Virginia he evidently loved, began at least as early as 1735, when his first grandchild was born. Meantime WILLIAM BEVERLY of Hampton, was promoting the sale of lots (of land) in his "Manor" tract around AUGUSTA. One of his first customers was an old neighbor, JOHN CUNNINGHAM, who bought lot No. 1, in Staunton. ROBERT, his brother, also invested in "Manor" lands and shortly thereafter was elected to serve as a "Burgess" over at Williamsburg. SAMUEL CUNNINGHAM, still another brother, married MARY McKAMIE, grand-daughter of one of the TWO FRANCIS McKAMIES who were nephews of REV. FRANCIS McKAMIE, mentioned in his will. And the THOMPSONS - they just went over there in droves, and multiplied and replenished the earth. Thus we have the obvious magnets that drew REV. JOHN THOMSON to Virginia in those early days. Again we doubt that his first appearance in BEVERLY MANOR (Augusta County) was as late as 1739, as has been represented.

———

Among other persons whom REV. JOHN THOMSON possibly knew in the days when he resided among his kinsmen in York County, Virginia, was one SAMUEL WALLACE. In 1748 this SAMUEL WALLACE patented 2017 acres of land in the BUFFALO SECTION of Prince Edward County, Virginia. On January 3, 1733, SAMUEL WALLACE was one of the guests at a QUAKER WEDDING, at the home of JAMES BATES on Skimino Cr. in YORK COUNTY, Virginia, at which HANNAH BATES, daughter of JAMES married SAMUEL JORDAN. The parents of JAMES BATES, the father, were JOHN BATES and ELIZABETH DANIEL. They were also the uncle and aunt of JOHN DANIEL whose farm adjoined that of HENRY THOMPSON in Bruton Parish (On Skimino Creek). SAMUEL WALLACE married ESTHER BAKER, a daughter of CALEB BAKER, of PRINCE EDWARD COUNTY, VIRGINIA. No less than THREE of the daughters of REV. JOHN THOMSON, married three of the brothers of CALEB BAKER. SAMUEL WALLACE was the father of REV. CALEB BAKER, distinguished Kentuckyan, who witnessed the will of JAMES CUNNINGHAM, son in law of REV. JOHN THOMSON, in 1775, but having left the State before his death, could not serve. In a separate note we will discuss the BAKER FAMILY. SAMUEL BAKER, buried at Bakers Graveyard in MECKLENBURG COUNTY, N. C. was one of the three brothers.

———

In his lifetime of activity, especially that spent in Virginia, many young ministers had been the recipients of encouragement and aid at the hands of REV. JOHN THOMSON, the result of which lead to their ultimate success. Two notable instances have been cited, as in the case of REV. JOHN CRAIG, of Tinkling Spring, in AUGUSTA COUNTY, and REV. HENRY PATILLO, of North Carolina.

> REV. JOHN CRAIG. He was the minister of the TINKLING SPRING Congregation near Staunton, Virginia, In APRIL 1757 he witnessed the will of HUGH THOMPSON, Augusta County, Virginia, with his brother JAMES CRAIG, then in Halifax County. REV. JAMES CRAIG was the minister of CUMBERLAND PARISH in Lunenburg County for many years, and his wife, whom he married Feb. 19, 1776, was MARY BOOKER TERRY, daughter of MARY BOOKER and SAMUEL TERRY, and MARY BOOKER was the daughter of RICHARD BOOKER and RACHEL MAROT, sister of EDITH MAROT, who was the wife of SAMUEL COBBS, and ANNE MAROT who married JAMES SHIELDS. MARY BOOKER was first cousin of JAMES SHIELDS, a son in law of REV. JOHN THOMSON. - Bell's Cumberland Parish pp. 113-114.

REV. HENRY PATILLO. From REV. HENRY FOOTE'S "Sketches of North Carolina" we quote the following paragraph:

In the year 1751, the REV. SAMUEL DAVIES, then residing in HANOVER, VIRGINIA, made an excursion for preaching to the Roanoke. In the course of his journeyings, he became acquainted with HENRY PATILLO, then a young man, desirous of commencing his studies in preparation of the Gospel Ministry, and invited him to come and commence his course with him in Hanover. This invitation Mr. Patillo first declined, as he had engaged to go to PENNSYLVANIA (error) with another young man, and commence his studies under the care and tuition of the REV. MR. JOHN THOMSON, who was at this time in CAROLINA on a mission to the new settlements.

Rev. Foote's account further on says that in August 1754, Henry Patillo commenced a Journal, only a part of which remains, and that from the fragments that remain Mr. Foote gathered the following facts:

"Born in SCOTLAND, of pious parents, who were well situated in point of religious privileges, he was early placed with a merchant to learn the duties of a counting-house. He was later induced to seek for better things in the Province of Virginia, a region to which many young Scotchmen turned their eyes with empty pockets and hearts full of hope," etc.

Was REV. HENRY PATILLO born in Scotland? Foote says he was, and is relying upon a Journal, supposedly written by Patillo himself. It is no disgrace to be born in Scotland, and even REV. JOHN THOMSON, the subject of this study is supposed to have been born there, though proof is lacking. If REV. HENRY PATILLO was in fact born in SCOTLAND, how do we account for the following records:

First: Executive Journals of the Council of Colonial Virginia, Vol. 4, by H. R. McIlwaine:

At the Council Held at the Capital, December 12, 1733:
Present:
The Governor.

Mr. Commissioner BLAIR.		John Custis
Cole Digges	Later:	Will. Randolph
John Robinson	Present, John Carter, Esq.	John Tayloe
John Grymes		Phil. Lightfoot
Will. Dandridge	(Some items omitted.)	Thomas Lee, Esq.

1. JOSEPH NORFLEET appointed inspector at Lawrence's warehouse in room of Nicholas Parker.

2. WILLIAM BEVERLY, GENT., complains of patent or caveat for lands on Shenandoah to Jacob Stover. Patent issued.

3. JAMES PATILLO, OF PRINCE GEORGE, granted a patent.

4. ARTHUR HOPKINS granted patent to 2000a in Goochland County, etc.

5. STEPHEN HUGHES and TARLETON FLEMING granted six thousand acres in Goochland County on both sides of WILLIS CREEK and between the lines of Col. Benjamin Harrison, Mr. William Maye, JAMES CUNNINGHAM (*), Jacob Winfrey, George Briggs and Mr. Henry Cary, including 400 acres already surveyed for the petitioners.

6. JOSEPH DABBS and THOMAS WALKER 2500 acres on upper side of WILLIS CREEK.

7. SAMUEL COBBS asks patent to certain lands on South side of Swift Creek. 4000 acres granted.

* This JAMES CUNNINGHAM was the father of JAMES CUNNINGHAM, who married ANNE THOMSON, the daughter of REV. JOHN THOMSON.

JAMES PATILLO. In 1728 James Patillo was one of those appointed to inspect tobacco, and he was also one of those processioning the lands.
In an odd, undated page of land grants he was given "all the vacant land joining round his own plantation in Prince George County" not to exceed 1200 acres.
The surname of his wife has not been found, but

1. JAMES PATILLO (b. 1725)
2. ANN PATILLO (b. 1728)
3. HENRY PATILLO (b. 1730)

are given as the children of JAMES PATILLO and his wife MARY.

(BRISTOL PARISH - Slaughter - pp. 41-49 - 350-353, and 16. Virginia Magazine p. 155).

If the JAMES PATILLO of the above notes was the father of REV. HENRY PATILLO, born in 1730, and the father was living in VIRGINIA and a tobacco inspector in 1728, it is hard to conceive how his son HENRY could have been born in SCOTLAND. Nowhere have I been able to find any other HENRY PATILLO on the records, and the date 1730 just about fits the young man, whom REV. JOHN THOMSON had probably encouraged in his ministerial ambitions prior to his trip to Mecklenburg County, N. C., when Patillo would have been about 19 or 20 years of age.

THE CUNNINGHAMS AND CALDWELLS. JAMES CUNNINGHAM, to whom reference is made in note 5, of the previous page, obtained lands with HENRY CARY, BENJAMIN HARRISON, WILLIAM MAYO and others on WILLIS RIVER sometime prior to 1733. No other inference can be drawn from this statement relating to the patent granted STEPHEN HUGHES and TARLTON FLEMING. JAMES DANIEL, three of whose sons married grand-daughters of REV. JOHN THOMSON and also grand-daughters of this same JAMES CUNNINGHAM, also took up land on WILLIS RIVER about the same time. JAMES DANIEL moved there and settled on his property, but it is not known whether the first JAMES DANIEL ever left YORK COUNTY and came to that section to live. He may have sold his lands to others and remained in the neighborhood of Hampton or Yorktown, though his sons, probably after his death, settled all the way from New Kent to the Cowpasture settlement (Beverly's Manor) in the Valley of Virginia. JAMES CUNNINGHAM, the son, was induced by his uncle's executor, SAMUEL COBBS, to purchase lands near those of his father in law, REV. JOHN THOMSON, on CUB CREEK - not far from BUFFALO - then in Lunenburg, but later in CHARLOTTE COUNTY, in what became known as the "CALDWELL SETTLEMENT". JOHN CALDWELL, with children, WILLIAM, THOMAS, DAVID, MARGARET, JOHN, ROBERT and JAMES CALDWELL came there about 1750 from over in the Shenandoah Valley; they were joined there by other CALDWELLS, who came from the neighborhood of YORK COUNTY, in Eastern Virginia. The Shenandoah Valley Caldwells, headed by JOHN, came to this country after landing at NewCastle, Delaware, and stopping for a short time somewhere in Pennsylvania, thence going Southward to the Shenandoah in VIRGINIA. In the most reliable account the writer has found of this family, it is stated that they were relatives of CROMWELL, and that JOSEPH, a brother of JOHN, died in IRELAND, but that several of his children came to VIRGINIA about the same time JOHN came to DELAWARE, and settled on the JAMES RIVER. As a matter of fact, they settled in YORK COUNTY, VIRGINIA, for on the records there in 1687, their names appear on the old records I have in my possession at this writing. This note is made to show that NOT ALL OF THE CALDWELLS who settled along CUB CREEK and BUFFALO in Virginia, were of the Shenandoah Valley, or Pennsylvania set. As they had and bore similar names, the records became confused, and it is difficult to identify one set from the other, but BOTH SETS LIVED THERE TOGETHER.

SOME OF REV. JOHN THOMSON'S TRAVELS AND CONTACTS IN VIRGINIA

Heretofore it has been shown that REV. JOHN THOMSON with his wife and family came to YORKTOWN, VIRGINIA, and remained there perhaps for nearly three years before he took up his work at LEWES, DELAWARE, where he remained until the first part of 1730, or for about thirteen years. Then, that he evidently took his family and did missionary work in different parts of Pennsylvania, and perhaps Maryland, but perhaps often visited and worked during this time in various sections of Virginia, his son-in-law SAMUEL CROCKETT having settled in what is now PRINCE EDWARD COUNTY before 1735, when and where his first child was born.

It was TEN YEARS after this grandchild of JOHN THOMSON'S was born on BUFFALO CREEK, in AMELIA COUNTY (later Prince Edward)that SAMUEL COBBS sold his old friend REV. JOHN THOMSON a farm of 386 acres in the same locality, though his son in law, JAMES CUNNINGHAM, had purchased lands from SAMUEL COBBS in the same general locality three years previously. And it was about this time that another son in law, REV. RICHARD SANKEY, settled there, from Pennsylvania, he having no doubt met SARAH THOMSON in that Province and married her before coming to Virginia.

During this long period, the Church records show, there was a constant urge that impelled the subject of these notes to make visit after visit to VIRGINIA, where the lovers of religious freedom sought his counsel and advice. Dr. Herndon tells us that from about 1744 to 1750 he lived on his land on Spring Creek that he bought from SAMUEL COBBS in 1745, in AMELIA COUNTY.

And it was at about this time that he lost his first wife. Not long afterwards he married his second wife, who came to live with him on the Spring Creek property.

Dr. Herndon further observes:

> "It is not known how many times he visited the "back parts" of Virginia between 1733 and 1744, but it is of RECORD that he supplied (preached occasionally) in the neighborhood of WINCHESTER and STAUNTON in 1739, and preached in the Opekon neighborhood at Rockfish Gap, now in NELSON COUNTY; at CUB CREEK in Lunenburg (now CHARLOTTE County), at BUFFALO and WALKER'S in Amelia County (now Prince Edward) and at Hat Creek and Concord in what became CAMPBELL COUNTY."

And the good Doctor might have added, had he not been bound by the actual RECORDS of the Church, nor is it known at how many other parts of the Old Dominion REV. JOHN THOMSON, prior to 1739 and afterwards either lived or preached, before the end of 1750. We know that he ministered in HANOVER COUNTY - the home of the good Dr. SAMUEL DAVIES, his friend and co-worker. This is testified to by no less a personage than REV. PATRICK HENRY, uncle of PATRICK, the statesman and orator, who wrote a letter to REV. WILLIAM DAWSON, of Williamsburg, under date of February 13, 1744, in which he said:

> "I sent and invited THOMSON to my house. He entertained me with a distinct account of these New Light men, their peculiar tenets and practices; their rise and progress to this time. He is, in my opinion, a man of learning and good sense,

a strenuous opposer of these new preachers, and I believe he is a man of piety and veracity, so that his information may be looked upon as true.

PATRICK HENRY".

NOTE: At about this point in the writer's wandering narrative pertaining to the innumerable relationships of this great pioneer minister, supposed to have arrived in a strange land among a strange people, with his "wife and family" less than twenty years previous to the date of REV. PATRICK HENRY'S letter, quoted above, I imagine I can see some of my tradition-bound friends, whose credulity is being taxed to the limit, shake their heads, as much as to say:

"Well! I suspect the author will now have REV. JOHN THOMSON 'related' in some way to REV. PATRICK HENRY, in his next paragraph! "

Correct! Here it is:

SARAH THOMSON, his daughter became the wife of REV. RICHARD SANKEY, minister of the BUFFALOE Church, near CUB CREEK. They were probably married by 1730, and had one son and several daughters. One of their daughters became the wife of ROBERT GILLIAM. This ROBERT GILLIAM was the son of JOHN GILLIAM who married LUCY HENRY, a daughter of REV. PATRICK HENRY, who invited REV. JOHN THOMSON into his home and wrote his favorable appraisal of him to REV. WILLIAM DAWSON. In other words, a grand-son of REV. PATRICK HENRY married a grand-daughter of REV. JOHN THOMSON.

A more extended account of these GILLIAMS will appear further along in this book.

WERE THE THOMPSONS OF "TINKLING SPRING" IN AUGUSTA COUNTY MEMBERS OF THE FAMILY OF REV. JOHN THOMSON? - A STUDY OF THE QUESTION.

JOSEPH A. WADDELL in his "ANNALS OF AUGUSTA COUNTY, VIRGINIA", says that in the year 1747, WILLIAM and JOHN THOMPSON, deeded 110 acres of land for the use of the Presbyterian Congregation of Tinkling Spring. The deed was made to JAMES PATTON, JOHN CHRISTIAN, JOHN FINLEY, JAMES ALEXANDER and WILLIAM WRIGHT, as Trustees for the Congregation.

A JOHN FINLEY, JR. married a daughter of REV. JOHN THOMSON, and settled in MECKLENBURG County, North Carolina, where they were living in 1771, on lands which joined those of JOHN SHIELDS and his wife MARGARET THOMSON, as shown by a deed to be found among those abstracted in these notes.

MOSES THOMSON and ADAM THOMSON, apparently brothers, bought land from WILLIAM BEVERLY out of "Beverly's Manor" in Augusta County, sometime prior to 1744. This land was on CHRISTIAN'S CREEK, and adjoined the lands of JOHN RAMSEY and JAMES ARMSTRONG. Sometime the next year, MOSES THOMSON (they so spelled their names) moved to SOUTH CAROLINA (Just what part the records do not state) and December 12, 1745, MOSES THOMSON (in S. C.) executed the following deed:

MOSES THOMSON, of the Province of North Carolina, to JOHN MADISON, of Augusta for 110 pounds currency, sells 731 acres, part of 1041 acres sold to THOMSON by WILLIAM BEVERLY, out of 118,491 acres, known as Beverly's Manor, corner to ADAM THOMSON'S land; corner to JOHN RAMSEY. The witnesses were JAMES PATTON, THOMAS CHEW and HENRY DOWNS, JR.

The witness HENRY DOWNS, JR. moved to Mecklenburg County in 1773, and was one of the signers of the MECKLENBURG DECLARATION. On the same date as the above deed THOMSON executed, with JAMES PATTON, the following instrument:

MOSES THOMSON, late of AUGUSTA COUNTY, now an inhabitant of South Carolina, and JAMES PATTON, to JOHN MADISON, bond conditioned to defend against the right of dower in said land of JANE THOMSON, wife of MOSES THOMSON. Land adjoins JAMES ARMSTRONG and JOHN RAMSEY.

JOHN RAMSEY, whose lands adjoined those sold by MOSES THOMSON in the above conveyance, married the widow of ROBERT CROCKETT, brother of SAMUEL CROCKETT, who married ESTHER THOMSON, the daughter of REV. JOHN THOMSON. After his marriage to MARGARET CROCKETT (widow of ROBERT) JOHN RAMSEY moved to Mecklenburg County, North Carolina, and he and his step son, ARCHIBALD CROCKETT were among the first elders of what was then called NEW PROVIDENCE CHURCH. (Foote pp 245-6).

JAMES PATTON was killed by the Indians at Draper's in Augusta County, in 1755, as near as can be ascertained, and among the persons mentioned in the settlement of his estate, were WILLIAM SAYERS and his wife ESTHER. Esther Sayers (at that time) had been ESTHER THOMSON, the daughter of REV. JOHN THOMSON, who died in Mecklenburg County, who first married SAMUEL CROCKETT, and after his death became the wife of WILLIAM SAYERS, a young man, who owned the adjoining farm to SAMUEL CROCKETT before his death. SAMUEL and ESTHER (THOMSON) CROCKETT, having left Prince Edward County sometime around 1747-8, and settled in AUGUSTA COUNTY in the same neighborhood where MOSES and ADAM THOMSON and their descendants lived.

From Waddell's "Annals of Augusta": The Presbytery of Augusta continued their "supplications"the the Presbytery of Donegal for a pastor to reside among them. In 1739 they first applied for the services of REV. JOHN THOMSON, who CAME AND PREACHED FOR THEM FOR A TIME.

From FOOTE'S SKETCHES: Mr. JOHN THOMSON of the Presbytery of Donegal visited VIRGINIA in the year 1739, and spent some time in the OPEKON neighborhood, in the neighborhood of STAUNTON, in ROCKFISH in NELSON COUNTY, on CUB CREEK, at BUFFALO and in CAMPBELL COUNTY. He was a man of great vigor and took an active part in the affairs of the Church. Through his instrumentality Messrs. BLACK and CRAIG were sent by the Presbytery, the one to TRIPPLE FORKS, the other to ROCKFISH. He lived for a SHORT TIME at BUFFALO, to which place Mr. RICHARD SANKEY his son in law removed with his congregation, and continued their pastor for many years.

The above notes disclose TWO IMPORTANT points: First, that REV. JOHN THOMSON came to the neighborhood of STAUNTON, VIRGINIA, in Augusta County, where HE PREACHED FOR A TIME; not just one sermon, but that he was stationed there; it was his home FOR A TIME. This was apparently very early, at least by 1739. But he had evidently been there PRIOR to that time, because the people knew him and knowing him and having heard him preach BEFORE THAT, sent out a call for him to come BACK and live among them. Second, that he only lived for a SHORT TIME at BUFFALO. He was there long before his son in law RICHARD SANKEY came, and had owned a farm on Spring Creek, which he had bought from SAMUEL COBBS at least two years before SANKEY and his wife moved there. His son in law SAMUEL CROCKETT lived there TEN YEARS BEFORE his father in law bought lands from SAMUEL COBBS. But SAMUEL CROCKETT and his brother ROBERT moved to AUGUSTA COUNTY, Robert before Samuel, and possibly the death in 1746 of his brother ROBERT, caused him to remove to the neighborhood of STAUNTON. How many times and how often was REV. JOHN THOMSON in Augusta County? Even after SAMUEL CROCKETT died his widow ESTHER married into the SAYERS FAMILY, and thus WILLIAM SAYERS (the ancestor of Gov. JOSEPH DRAPER SAYERS, of Texas) became a son in law of REV. JOHN THOMSON.

MOSES THOMSON and his descendants perhaps all moved to the vicinity of SPARTANBURG, in South Carolina. In later years they were joined by the sons of ROGER THOMSON, son of REV. JOHN THOMSON. These all spelled their name without the "p".

ADAM THOMSON died in Augusta County leaving a will in 1769. His wife was NAOMIE, and his children were ANDREW, MARGARET, REBECCA. Son Andrew was made executor, and when he qualified his bond was signed by JOHN THOMPSON and JOHN HANDLEY. ANDREW THOMSON and the other children appear on the records spelled THOMPSON, so there seems to be no consistency in the manner of spelling the name.

ABOUT HUGH THOMPSON WHO LIVED IN AUGUSTA COUNTY

The next name of interest in this THOMSON study is that of HUGH THOMPSON, an early settler in AUGUSTA COUNTY, VIRGINIA, and a neighbor and associate of all of the other THOMPSONS according to the records. He died about 1762, and his will was probated on Feb. 18, of that year. He mentions his wife, but not by name. The will of HUGH THOMPSON is exceedingly interesting for several reasons, one being that it is witnessed by both JOHN CRAIG and JAMES CRAIG. The will was written in 1757, five years before, so that HUGH THOMPSON must have been contemporaneous with MOSES and ADAM THOMSON. It was OFFERED for probate in February 1762, but was not admitted for the reason that JOHN CRAIG was the only witness, JAMES CRAIG being at that time over in Lunenburg County, Minister of CUMBERLAND PARISH, or elsewhere. On August 18th, however, six months later JAMES CRAIG came over and finished proving up the will, and it was admitted. This abstract of the will is taken from Chalkley Vol. 2, p. 71.

Will of HUGH THOMPSON (April 26, 1757)
1. To wife a note due him by "my son" BRYCE RUSSELL, the Great Bible and Books.
2. To son JAMES THOMPSON, the Great Bible and Confession of Faith and the "Whole Duty of Man".
3. To daughter ELINER, her Bible, Allen's "Call to the Unconverted" and "THOMPSON'S CATECHISM"
4. To grandson HUGH RUSSELL, a small Bible.
5. To grand-daughter ISABELLA HELENA RUSSELL.
6. To daughter MARY, now in IRELAND.
7. To Grand-children: HUGH LEEPER and ELIZABETH LEEPER.
8. To grand-daughter, RACHEL RUSSELL.
9. To grand-son GEORGE RUSSELL.
10. To Grandson, JAMES LEEPER
11. To Grand-daughter JANE LEEPER
12. To MARY SCOTT.
Witnesses: JAMES RISK or SINK, JOHN CRAIG, JAMES CRAIG.
Proved Feb. 19, 1762 by JOHN CRAIG.
Proved August 18, 1762 by JAMES CRAIG.
Executors: WILLIAM THOMPSON and SAMUEL HENDERSON.
Executors qualified with WILLIAM BASKINS and JAMES BELL as sureties.

Was this HUGH THOMPSON a minister? The will certainly sounds like he might have been. The bequest to his daughter ELINER of a copy of "THOMPSON'S CATECHISM" authored and published by REV. JOHN THOMSON is significant. The book had been written by "John Thomson of Amelia" and printed in WILLIAMSBURG, VIRGINIA, by WILLIAM PARKS in 1749, just eight years before HUGH THOMPSON'S will was executed.

The wife of CALEB BAKER, three of her husband's brothers being sons in law of REV. JOHN THOMSON, when her "belongings" were inventoried in 1759, included a copy of "THOMPSON'S POOR ORPHANS' LEGACY", written by REV. JOHN THOMSON and published by BENJAMIN FRANKLIN in 1735.

It will be noticed that among the grand-children of HUGH THOMPSON, mentioned in the foregoing will are HUGH, JAMES, JANE and ELIZABETH LEEPER. This is intensely interesting to the writer, for the reason that a certain JAMES LEEPER was a CATAWBA RIVER pioneer, at about the time or near the time that REV. JOHN THOMSON died (1753) and was buried at Baker's Graveyard near the old BEATTIE'S FORD. From the best information available JAMES LEEPER owned lands, which he had both patented and bought that almost fronted on the West bank of the Catawba river, opposite BAKERS GRAVEYARD. The following extracts from MINNIE STOWE PUETT'S History of Gaston County (N. C.) bear on this point:

"JAMES LEEPER was one of the CATAWBA RIVER pioneers. The date of his settlement is not known, but a grant to him by King George III was enrolled in the general office in Wilmington on the 8th day of April, 1765. It was for a tract of land containing 300 acres lying on the West side of the river in what is now Gaston County, joining his own plantation on beginning. The survey and plot were made by JOHN McKNITT ALEXANDER, a signer of the Mecklenburg Declaration (afterwards). The above proves that JAMES LEEPER owned a plantation and was living on the CATAWBA before the grant was made.(1765). An older grant in the same locality was one of the many to FREDERICK HAMBRIGHT. It was dated April 23, 1762, and JOINED THE WEST SIDE OF THE CATAWBA RIVER. It was near the JAMES LEEPER land and was later sold by Hambright to HIM. (James Leeper).

On still another page of Mrs. Puett's History this appears:

"MATTHEW LEEPER was born May 27, 1755, the son of JAMES LEEPER, pioneer and owner of large tracts of land on the CATAWBA RIVER. JAMES LEEPER had at least two sons, MATTHEW and JAMES, JR. Matthew was a "South Fork boy" who served in the Revolutionary War, taking part in the battle of KING'S MOUNTAIN. He died October 12, 1849."

Cumulative evidence tending to link HUGH THOMPSON of the will in Augusta County in 1757, with REV. JOHN THOMSON, is the fact that the will named as EXECUTORS, William Thompson and SAMUEL HENDERSON. This SAMUEL HENDERSON was the brother of JAMES HENDERSON (See page 224 of this completed work) who married VIOLET LAWSON, one of the daughters of HUGH LAWSON, whose brother ROGER LAWSON married the youngest daughter of REV. JOHN THOMSON; furthermore, almost in view of the early grant and lands of JAMES LEEPER, on the bank of the SOUTH FORK of the CATAWBA RIVER, this brother of SAMUEL HENDERSON (Executor of HUGH THOMPSON in 1757) lies sleeping his last sleep, on the top of a high hill overlooking the CATAWBA VALLEY. He it is, who was the grandfather of JAMES PINCKNEY HENDERSON, the first Governor of Texas.

COL. JAMES PATTON'S CONNECTION WITH THE THOMPSON FAMILY

Among the earliest and most prominent citizens of AUGUSTA COUNTY, VIRGINIA, was COL. JAMES PATTON. Nothing very authentic is known of him. Waddell in his "Annals" gives what is plainly a TRADITIONAL ACCOUNT; that he was a native of IRELAND; that he was bred to the sea; that he served in the ROYAL NAVY of England; that he was the owner of a passenger ship; that he traded (maybe lived) at what is known or was then known as HOBB'S HOLE on the RAPPAHANNOCK RIVER, and that he "had crossed the Atlantic as many as twenty-five times,"all, of course, previous to his settlement in William Beverly's Manor, in Augusta County. The voluminous pages of CHALKLEY'S ABSTRACTS and records of AUGUSTA County, Virginia, reflect innumerable land transactions by him with the settlers there, and particularly with the THOMPSONS and THOMSONS (some of which have already been referred to heretofore), the WILSONS, ALEXANDERS, CHRISTIANS, FINLEYS, CRAIGS, LEWIS' and CUNNINGHAMS. The name of HENRY DOWNS, both Sr. and Jr. often appears in these items, also.

The descendants of Col. James Patton, who left only two daughters and no sons, have it handed down to them that his wife was named OSBORNE. This is but a family tradition, but the writer is impressed with the fact that all the surrounding circumstances and family history tend to establish it as a FACT, which may be relied upon. I firmly believe that his wife (who is declared by Mrs. Gov. Floyd to have been a haughty woman) was a sister of HON. ROBERT OSBORNE, of NORTHUMBERLAND, ESSEX and OLD RAPPAHANNOCK COUNTY, Virginia, and of ALEXANDER OSBORNE who settled in the bounds of "CENTRE CHURCH" in that part which is now in IREDELL COUNTY, North Carolina, the father of ADLAI OSBORNE, somewhat distinguished in the annals of the Old North State.

So far as can be found no member of the OSBORNE FAMILY of the name married into the THOMPSON FAMILY, but ROBERT OSBORNE'S wife was a MISS WADDY, and certainly the WADDY FAMILY did intermarry with the THOMPSONS, particularly those in HANOVER and NEW KENT COUNTY.

But, (and this makes it of much interest in this study) MARY PATTON, one of the two daughters of COL. JAMES PATTON, became the wife of WILLIAM THOMPSON, while his other daughter, MARGARET PATTON married COL. JOHN BUCHANAN. Col. Patton was killed by the INDIANS, while on a trip to the DRAPERS about 1755 and his will was proven at the November term of the Augusta County

Court in November of the same year. However, the abstract shows that the will had been executed in the month of September, 1750, and in it he refers to "Mary, the wife of William Thompson" and "Margaret, wife of Col. John Buchanan" between whom his estate is to be divided, "and their children", presupposing they had children at that time. From this it can safely be inferred that in 1750 both daughters were married and had children, so that WILLIAM THOMPSON must have married MARY PATTON somewhere between 1745-48, at which time he would have been a grown man, born perhaps before 1720. He could have been contemporaneous with MOSES and ADAM THOMSON, or, on the other hand, he may have been the son of one or the other. It certainly seems inescapable that he must have been related to them very closely.

The writer has been unable to find a will of this WILLIAM THOMPSON, who married MARY PATTON, but from the papers in two lawsuits filed in Augusta and Montgomery Counties, what is believed to be a complete list of his children have been secured. They were Shaffey v. Cloyd (Vol. II Chalkley pp 206-7) and Patten Thompson v. James Thompson, from the same source and volume. From these papers it is shown that WILLIAM THOMPSON and his wife MARY had the following children:

1. PATTON THOMPSON, m. JUDITH.
2. JAMES THOMPSON m. JANE.
3. HENRY THOMPSON
4. MARY THOMPSON m. a McCARTY
5. NANCY THOMPSON m. HENSON GARDNER.
6. MARGARET THOMPSON m. SAMUEL HICKMAN.
7. ISABELLA THOMPSON m. WILLIAM GLOVER
8. SARAH THOMPSON m. PATRICK McMANNIS
9. JOHN THOMPSON.
10. ELIZABETH THOMPSON m. WILLIAM FARLEY.

Thus, WILLIAM THOMPSON and wife MARY PATTON had ten children. In examining the notes pertaining to these children, it becomes obvious that what has been said about COL. JAMES PATTON, the name of his wife, and previous place of residence on the RAPPAHANNOCK, that these facts are ceroberated by the names. For instance:

MARY THOMPSON married a man named McCARTY. The Montgomery County suit (Thompson v. Thompson) shows that Mary and her husband __ McCARTY had two daughters; that their names were VIOLET and LETTICE. Attention is called to these notes:

ROBERT OSBORNE (m. Miss Waddy) lived in NORTHUMBERLAND County, Virginia, and was a prominent lawyer. Probably a brother of the wife of COL. JAMES PATTON.

DENNIS McCARTY (patented lands) lived in NORTHUMBERLAND COUNTY, Virginia, 1691 and afterwards. His wife was a MISS BILLINGTON (Dau. of LUKE) whose sister MARY, married HUGH DANIEL. His son was DANIEL McCARTY.

DANIEL McCARTY was an eminent lawyer, contemporaneous with ROBERT OSBORNE. He left will in about 1724, and among the legatees was a daughter LETTICE. This name remained in the McCarty family, and thus shows that the daughter of WILLIAM THOMPSON married into this particular RAPPAHANNICK COUNTY family.

SAMUEL HICKMAN who married MARGARET THOMPSON appears to have been a descendant of THOMAS HICKMAN, who settled in YORK COUNTY, VIRGINIA, and whose name frequently appears on the records there before 1750. His father of brother, NATHANIEL HICKMAN, patented lands also in NORTHUMBERLAND COUNTY as early as 1653, according to one record. SAMUEL HICKMAN and MARGARET THOMPSON had three children: LETTICE (who married HOWARD BANE and finally went to Alabama), a JOHN and a WILLIAM HICKMAN. The two sons were revolutionary soldiers and moved to ORANGEBURG COUNTY, S. C., where their names are found on the BARNWELL COUNTY records. REBECCA HICKMAN, said to have been a daughter of JOHN, married ISAIAH WROTEN, whose daughter SARAH married JESSE RICE. JESSE RICE came to S. C. from HANOVER COUNTY, VIRGINIA, where so many THOMPSONS lived, and was a descendant of the RICE FAMILY of OLD RAPPAHANNOCK COUNTY, who were related in some way to the McCARTYS. Doubtless the name LETTICE, given to their daughter by SAMUEL HICKMAN, comes down from the previous connection of the HICKMANS with the McCARTY or CORBIN FAMILY. One THOMAS HICKMAN (died in YORK County in 1731) was Clerk of the Council, and his brother EDWIN was Sheriff of SPOTTSYLVANIA COUNTY in 1729-30.

WILLIAM THOMPSON, son in law of COL. JAMES PATTON (Assuming he was born about 1720) was nearly eighty years old at the time of his death in 1796.

PATTON GARDNER and CYNTHIA GARDNER were two of the children of NANCY THOMPSON and her husband HENSON GARDNER. They moved to GEORGIA and settled in JACKSON COUNTY. CYNTHIA became the wife of DAVID S. McCREARY, the son of an old neighbor of the Pattons and Thompsons in Augusta County, and WILLIAM HICKMAN, their cousin, visited them in the year 1804, when they executed a deed to some of the other heirs of COL. JAMES PATTTON, who had then been dead for nearly fifty years. It is an established FACT that some of the descendants of the WROTENS of Barnwell, S. C. into which family the daughter of JOHN HICKMAN married were descended from REV. JOHN THOMSON.

SOME NOTES RELATING TO THE WILSON AND CUNNINGHAM FAMILIES

OF AUGUSTA COUNTY, VIRGINIA

The significance of some of the relationships between the THOMPSONS, PATTONS and others of early AUGUSTA COUNTY, VIRGINIA, can be better understood in connection with facts about the WILSONS and CUNNINGHAMS, who were mixed up with them in various ways.

When WILLIAM BEVERLY obtained his immense grant of land where the town of STAUNTON was almost immediately thereafter located, the country was opened up and the settlers flocked in, and with the first contingent came the CUNNINGHAMS, the WILSONS, COL. JAMES PATTON and his brother in law JOHN PRESTON, IRISH JOHN LEWIS, the THOMPSONS, DUNLAPS, FINLEYS, CROCKETTS and various other clans. This newly opened country, which had been detached from ORANGE COUNTY, was entitled to representation in the House of Burgesses, and the first person selected to represent it in that capacity was ROBERT CUNNINGHAM. His brother JOHN CUNNINGHAM had bought the first lot sold by WILLIAM BEVERLY, and SAMUEL CUNNINGHAM, another brother had followed BEVERLY to his new Eldorado, and doubtless invested in some of his lands. Of course it may have been due to BEVERLY'S influence and Robert Cunningham's other connections that he was selected.

Mr. William G. Stannard in his COLONIAL VIRGINIA REGISTER prints the following interesting note on page 114 of his Volume:

> "There was a Mr. Lee, a member in 1742, and perhaps other years, and a MR. CUNNINGHAM in 1745, 1746 and 1747, who cannot be identified, or their counties fixed. A WILLIAM RANDOLPH was a member in 1745, 1746 and 1747, after the death of WILLIAM RANDOLPH of 'TUCKAHOE', who represented Goochland. This seems to be certainly WILLIAM RANDOLPH of'WILTON', but he did not apparently represent HENRICO or GOOCHLAND. Possibly it was Goochland."

Thus Mr. Stannard finds a CUNNINGHAM in the House of Burgesses of Virginia, whom he can not identify. But the identification is cleared up by the CHALKLEY records of AUGUSTA COUNTY. It appears that at that period the Counties or Districts were called upon to pay the members of the House who served from their different districts, by the collection of a tax levied for that particular purpose, and the Chalkley records contain this notation from the records of AUGUSTA COUNTY for the year 1747:

> 1747. ROBERT CUNNINGHAM for expenses in attending the Council and going down; 1670 tythables at 23 pounds of tobacco at three farthings per pound.

This settles the identity of the CUNNINGHAM who served from AUGUSTA COUNTY in the years 1745, 1746 and 1747.

These further items from the same source are of interest in this connection:

> ROBERT CUNNINGHAM in 1745 was surety for JOHN WILSON, administrator for ROBERT WILSON.
> In 1746 ROBERT CUNNINGHAM was surety for JAMES PATTON, administrator for JAMES JANNETT or JARRETT.
> 1752. ROBERT CUNNINGHAM mentioned in deed to "lands in BEVERLY MANOR on CHRISTIAN'S CREEK, corner of ROBERT CUNNINGHAM."
> 1752. ROBERT CUNNINGHAM and WILLIAM PRESTON attorneys for GEORGE RUTLEDGE.
> 1753. ROBERT CUNNINGHAM and wife MARTHA 322 acres in BEVERLY MANOR on CEDAR SPRINGS.

From the above we see that ROBERT CUNNINGHAM in 1746 was surety for COL. JAMES PATTON, whose daughter married WILLIAM THOMPSON.

That he and WILLIAM PRESTON were attorneys together. WILLIAM PRESTON was the son of JOHN PRESTON and his wife, who was a sister of COL. JAMES PATTON.

That he owned lands and probably lived on CHRISTIAN'S CREEK in Beverly Manor, having bought lands from WILLIAM BEVERLY.

That he was surety in 1745 for COL. JOHN WILSON. Col. John Wilson was either the son or a brother of ROBERT WILSON who died at about this time. COL. JOHN WILSON succeeded ROBERT CUNNINGHAM as a member of the House of Burgesses from AUGUSTA COUNTY. When COL. JOHN WILSON died in 1773, his son MATTHEW WILSON was given charge of his estate as administrator; and as there was an older MATTHEW WILSON shown on the AUGUSTA RECORDS, the writer is convinced that Colonel WILSON had a brother named MATTHEW WILSON. Note the following item from the records:

> 1750-51: Inhabitants hear CAPT. JOHN WILSON petition for a road from CAPT. JOHN WILSON and JOHN McCLERY'S field to JAMES WILSON's, to JOHN CHRISTIAN'S, there to join road from COLONEL PATTON'S MILL, to TINKLING SPRINGS MEETING HOUSE. ROBERT CAMPBELL, MATTHEW WILSON, and others.

It will be noted that COLONEL WILSON thus early was called CAPTAIN. Later he appears on the records invariably as COLONEL JOHN WILSON. It is hardly probable that the MATTHEW WILSON whose name is signed here in 1750, would be the son of 23 years later, intrusted with the management of COL. WILSON'S estate and called his "son". He was perhaps his brother.

436

The Christian name MATTHEW, according to the records we have examined, appears to have been in common and constant use in both the WILSON and the THOMPSON families of this time and place, as witness the will of a MATTHEW THOMPSON proved in AUGUSTA COUNTY, May 16, 1753, in which he mentions his wife MARTHA and sons MATTHEW, WILLIAM and JOHN THOMPSON, in which JOHN DAVISON and the testator's daughter MARGARET THOMPSON and her FIVE children are also referred to. The son MATTHEW THOMPSON was made executor. Thus MATTHEW THOMPSON dates back contemporaneously with ADAM, MOSES and HUGH THOMPSON. These same records also disclose that there was a JOHN THOMPSON of the same vintage, who was deceased by 1761, when a son THOMAS THOMPSON left a will, naming his wife MARY and a brother JAMES THOMPSON.

Thus, considering the records we have ADAM, MOSES, HUGH, WILLIAM, MATTHEW and JOHN THOMPSON living in AUGUSTA COUNTY in "Beverly's Manor" among the very first settlers. The reader can therefore, very easily, surmise that the records suggest a marriage between the THOMPSONS and the family of COL. JOHN WILSON may have been consummated at an early day.

As for the MATTHEW WILSONS. There was one whose will was proven in December, 1795, whose wife was MARY. The will appears in Will Book No. 1. He had sons THOMAS, JOHN, SAMUEL, MATTHEW, JANNET, BETSY, POLLY, SALLY and NANCY.

Still another MATTHEW WILSON had a wife named HELENA. His will was proved in June of 1804. He left his son WILLIAM WILSON land on Little Back Creek adjoining JOHN and THOMAS SHARP; also son MATTHEW WILSON, JOHN WILSON and daughters SARAH, MARTHA, ELEANOR, ELIZABETH and MARY. His executors were wife HELENA, son JOHN WILSON and JAMES MITCHELL. He also left two Grandsons by the name of MATTHEW WILSON. That is to say, at least two of his sons had a son named MATTHEW WILSON. I am of the opinion that one of the MATTHEW WILSONS who left the two above wills may have been the son of COL. JOHN WILSON, who had died in 1773, while the MATTHEW who died in 1804 may have been a son of a brother - maybe MATTHEW - of COL. JOHN WILSON. When these two died, we know from their wills that they left at least THREE or FOUR other MATTHEWS of a later generation.

COL. JOHN WILSON appears to have been a man of considerable influence and property as well. As he served in the House of Burgesses for about 20 years, he was probably a statesman of some note. But scattered notes from the records disclose that several members of this same WILSON family were ministers, although I have not been able to find a preacher among them named MATTHEW. That there was a REV. MATTHEW WILSON, however, of that day and time is established by the following item from Dr. John G. Herndon's life of REV. JOHN THOMSON:

> REV. JOHN THOMSON "lived from 1717 to 1729 in Sussex County, Delaware, while he was pastor of the Church at LEWES. In the Records of the United Presbyterian Churches of Lewes, Indian River and Cool Springs, Delaware, it is stated that the burial of 'WIDOW, ESTHER WARRENTON, ye REV. JOHN THOMSON'S sister' took place on April 6, 1768, and elsewhere it is noted that at her funeral the PREACHER WAS REV. MATTHEW WILSON".

So, we have thus found that REV. JOHN THOMSON (who died in Mecklenburg County, N. C, in 1753) had a sister ESTHER, for whom, no doubt, his daughter ESTHER (who became the wife of SAMUEL CROCKETT) was named; that she died on or about 1768, and that, although she was in DELAWARE at the time of her death, the officiating minister who attended her last rites was a MATTHEW WILSON. Whether he was the brother MATTHEW of Col. John Wilson, of Augusta County, we can only surmise.

Who were these Wilsons?

We think the ancestor of the family is referred to in the following items from the records of YORK COUNTY, VIRGINIA, before 1650:

> That WILLIAM KNIGHT stands indebted to the estate of EDW. CHISWELL, deceased, 800 lbs tobacco, which debt THOMAS BROUGHTON undertook to answer "for at the request of THOMAS WILSON, Master of the good ship DESIRE".
>
> THOMAS BROUGHTON to have attachment against the estate of THOMAS WILSON, Master of the ship DESIRE
>
> March 24, 1647/8. MR. DENNIS STEPHENS makes oath that he received the goods listed in this entry, out of the ship DESIRE, whereof THOMAS WILSON was Master, and delivered in YORK RIVER in Virginia by bill of lading to him from MR. WILLIAM CARY, of London, merchant.
> (Fleet's Colonial Abstracts Vol. 25 pp. 73-74-82)

From Vol. 25, Virginia Magazine of History & Biography, pp. 199-200, there is an attempt by some enterprising genealogist to give an account of a family, which the writer identifies as that of which MR. THOMAS WILSON, Master of the ship DESIRE was undoubtedly the ancestor. The writer of the account denominates his ancestor as

"THOMAS WILSON, emigrant from ENGLAND, who married a MISS WILLIS, and settled in PRINCESS ANNE COUNTY, Virginia."

The genealogist then says that this THOMAS WILSON had four sons, no daughters being mentioned. Nothing is said about his being "Master of the good ship DESIRE". The sons by his wife MISS WILLIS were:

1. JOHN WILSON who moved up the POTOMAC.
2. SOLOMON WILSON
3. WILLIS WILSON
4. SAMUEL WILSON married a MISS MASON, and adds that he died in NORFOLK in 1710. This is the only date mentioned. SAMUEL WILSON and his wife, the writer, volunteers, had a son named

WILLIS WILSON

who became a sea captain, and married a daughter of BENJAMIN GOODRICH. Her name was ELIZABETH and her sister was the wife of SAMUEL BOUSH, a good old NORFOLK name, familiar to research workers in Norfolk annals, as are the GOODRICHES of Isle of Wight and elsewhere.

(This is one of those tantalizing genealogies one finds tucked away in these old Magazines, that starts out like it would give a history of the family, then selects a lone son, out of anywhere from three to a dozen or more children, chases down some of his descendants and lets all the rest multiply and replenish the earth and ignores them all) But to continue:

WILLIS WILSON, grandson of the old sea dog of the DESIRE, himself became a sea Captain and he and his wife ELIZABETH GOODRICH had children, the Lord only knows how many, but notice is taken of just ONE:

BENJAMIN WILSON who married ANNE SEAY

ANNE SEAY was the daughter of JAMES SEAY of "York River". This BENJAMIN WILSON and his wife ANNE SEAY joined the tide of emigrants Westward Ho! and settled on lands situated on WILLIS RIVER, in Cumberland County, where JAMES CUNNINGHAM had lands already located in 1733, as shown by McILWAIN'S "Journals of the Council" heretofore quoted. Having given us thus much of the family history, somewhat sketchy though it is, our genealogist sets out the names of the children:

1. MARY WILSON
2. ELIZABETH WILSON
3. WILLIS WILSON
4. BENJAMIN WILSON
5. ANNE WILSON
6. JAMES WILSON
7. MASON WILSON
8. SAMUEL WILSON
9. MATTHEW WILSON
10. ALEXANDER WILSON
11. GOODRICH WILSON
12. MARTHA WILSON
13. UNITY WILSON

Then we are given three more dates to help us. BENJAMIN WILSON died in 1814. He had settled in Cumberland County about 1750, and his daughter MARY (who is said to have married THOMAS MUMFORD) died in Cumberland County in 1822.

So you see, examining this list of the children of BENJAMIN WILSON, we find another MATTHEW WILSON, of Cumberland County; we also find a GOODRICH WILSON. Can there be any question but what BENJAMIN WILSON and ANNE SEAY are the ancestors of our good friend, REV. GOODRICH WILSON of WILMINGTON, N. C. and LYNCHBURG, VIRGINIA?

From all of which we conclude that COL. JOHN WILSON, of BEVERLY MANOR, very likely was a descendant of CAPT. THOMAS WILSON, Master of the good ship DESIRE, but the family being so numerous and its branches so varied in extent, an ordinary mortal after some three hundred years with no records to guide him, would ever be able to find his parent stem among the children of the old sea Captain. The odds however, would be in favor of the oldest son JOHN "who moved up the POTOMAC". The tradition is that COL. JAMES PATTON "retired from the sea", so it would not be unreasonable to say that his neighbor and close friend COL. JOHN WILSON sprang also from that tribe of men who "go down to the sea in ships", in the light of the above family chart.

ESTHER THOMSON "WARRINGTON" who died in Sussex County, Delaware, in 1768, and whose funeral rites were performed by REV. MATTHEW WILSON, was sister of REV. JOHN THOMSON, the subject of these notes. We are indebted to DR. HERNDON'S notes for this information. He has, of course, copied correctly from the records referred to, but sometimes records by repeated transcriptions are slightly varied, and we believe that the correct name of her husband (then deceased) was WARRINGTON, and that he was related in some way to REV. THOMAS WARRINGTON, of Hampton, Virginia, the close friend of REV. DR. CAMM and REV. PATRICK HENRY, heretofore mentioned. Another close friend of REV. CAMM, REV. HENRY and WARRINGTON was REV. WILLIAM ROBERTSON (possibly the William Robertson, who with SAMUEL COBBS and SUSANNAH ALLEN was an executor of the will of DAVID CUNNINGHAM, in 1719/20 in YORK COUNTY). These were the men who were plaintiffs in the "parson's case" in which PATRICK HENRY, the younger, distinguished himself, when he started out in the law business at HANOVER COURTHOUSE. The case of WARRINGTON v. JEGITTS was tried at HAMPTON, VIRGINIA, in 1763, and was a prototype and companion case to the one tried for DR. MAURY at Hanover. Like MAURY, MR. WARRINGTON lost his case.

THE SETTLEMENT ON "CHRISTIAN'S CREEK" IN BEVERLY MANOR, AUGUSTA COUNTY

Below is shown an improvised map of the settlement immediately surrounding the town of STAUNTON, in AUGUSTA COUNTY, an on which CHRISTIAN'S CREEK is shown. Reference to previous notes disclose that JAMES PATTON, GENT, as early as 1744 bought land from MOSES THOMPSON, located on CHRISTIAN'S CREEK. MOSES THOMSON and JAMES PATTON sold this land to JOHN MADISON and it joined

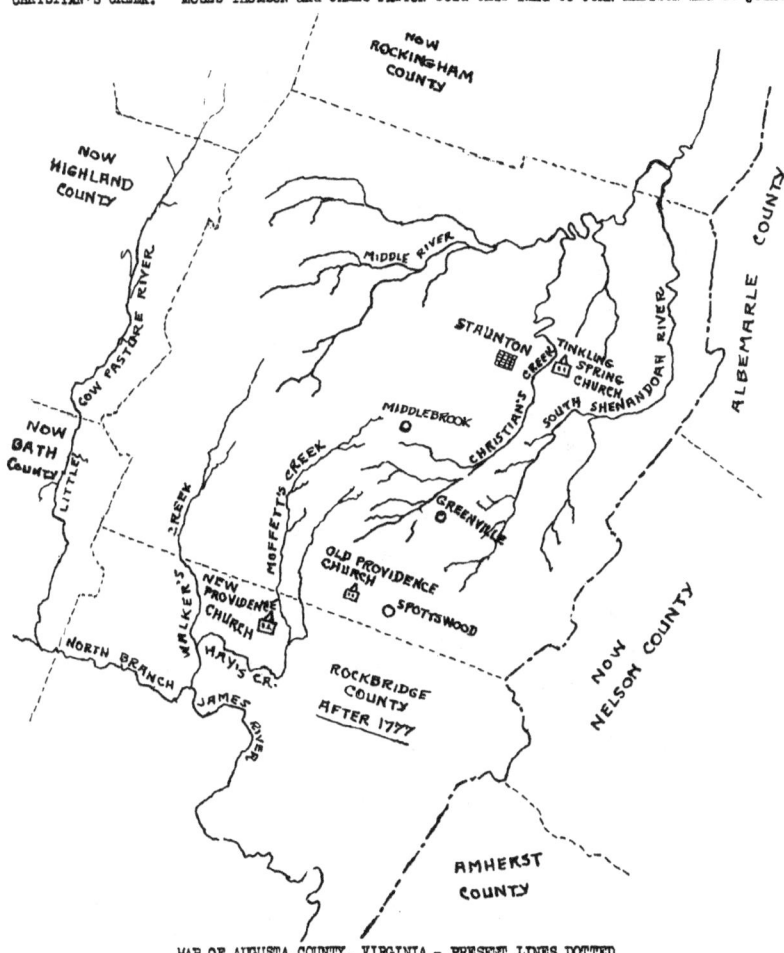

MAP OF AUGUSTA COUNTY, VIRGINIA - PRESENT LINES DOTTED

the land of JAMES ARMSTRONG, JOHN RAMSEY and ADAM THOMSON. The Tythe list of CAPTAIN (WILLIAM?) THOMPSON in 1755, contained, among others, the following names of land owners evidently residing in the same general community:

WIDOW THOMPSON	MATTHEW PATTON	JOHN FINLEY
WILLIAM THOMPSON	WILLIAM DYER	ROBERT FINLEY
ALEX THOMPSON	ISAAC WHITE	WILLIAM FINLEY
THOMAS THOMPSON	ADAM MORROW	JOHN FINLEY (JR.)

and JOHN RAMSEY. Of course, this is only a partial list, and many of the other families that have been mentioned in these notes had lands along CHRISTIAN'S CREEK, on which TINKLING SPRINGS CHURCH had been erected on lands sold by JOHN and WILLIAM THOMPSON in 1747 to JAMES PATTON, JOHN FINLEY & JOHN CHRISTIAN, Trustees for the Congregation. On LITTLE CALF PASTURE over across LITTLE NORTH MOUNTAIN lived ROBERT CROCKETT, ALEXANDER DUNLAP, THOMAS GILLIAM and others, on lands laid out and sold to them by COL. JAMES PATTON and IRISH JOHN LEWIS.

The preceding pages of this account have been devoted to a study of some of the people with whom the subject, REV. JOHN THOMSON, came in contact with, prior to the year 1751, when he came to what is now MECKLENBURG COUNTY, North Carolina, and the bounds of old CENTRE CHURCH, of which he was undoubtedly the first preacher, and which at that time embraced practically all of the northwestern part of what afterwards became MECKLENBURG COUNTY. This, in order that the student may more easily understand his various relationships, and determine for himself whether or not he was related by ties of blood and kinship to any of them, considering all the other circumstances.

(This compiler does not undertake to say that the young cleric, REV. JOHN THOMSON, supposedly fresh out of the University of Glasgow, landing at YORKTOWN, VIRGINIA in 1714, with his wife "and family" was a kinsman of all these other THOMSONS and THOMPSONS, at the time and place, and thereafter prominent in the affairs of the then young Colony of VIRGINIA. Speaking in the first person, I only know that the records, only part of which I have here reviewed, tell a most peculiar story, and a very convincing one, and that it would indeed be most singular, if not unreasonable, if in fact he actually landed among TOTAL STRANGERS, lived thus among them for at least TWO LONG YEARS, formed alliances between his own and their families of the most intimate nature, and afterwards had innumerable transactions with them, and yet was not related to them in any way. Further evidences of these intimacies will crop out in the study of his DESCENDANTS, in the pages that follow.)

DESCENDANTS OF REV. JOHN THOMSON, V.D.M.

REV. JOHN THOMSON was twice married. There are RECORDS to support the identity of his second wife, but the surname of his first wife is supported only by circumstantial evidence, and while her name, as so ascertained, may be doubtful, the compiler is taking the responsibility of using in this account of the THOMSON FAMILY.

His first wife was a MISS OSBORNE.
His second wife was a MRS. HEID, the widow of a THOMAS HEID. Her maiden name was MARY McKEAN, and she is described as a "Highland woman of dark complexion". By his second wife REV. JOHN THOMSON had only one child, HANNAH, who married ROGER LAWSON. His first wife was the mother of twelve children. He had thirteen children, altogether, born, it is believed, in the order as their names are given below:

1. ESTHER THOMSON (1709-10) m. (1) SAMUEL CROCKETT (2) WILLIAM SAYERS.
2. MARY THOMSON (1712) m. ROBERT BAKER, JR.
3. JOHN THOMSON (1714) m. MARGARET DAVIDSON
4. ABRAHAM THOMSON (1716) wife's identity unknown. Had son JOHN THOMSON.
5. SARAH THOMSON (1719) m. REV. RICHARD SANKEY.
6. _____ THOMSON (1721) m. JOHN GRAHAM.
7. ROGER THOMSON (1723) m. ANN FERGUSON
8. _____ THOMSON m. JOHN FINLEY, JR.
9. JANE THOMSON (1726) m. (1) DOUGLAS BAKER (2) WILLIAM WATSON.
10. ANN THOMSON (1728) m. JAMES CUNNINGHAM
11. MARGARET THOMSON (1730) m. JOHN SHIELDS
12. ELIZABETH THOMSON (1731-2) m. (1) SAMUEL BAKER (2) CHARLES HARRIS
13. HANNAH THOMSON (1735) m. ROGER LAWSON.

All of the dates of birth of these children are estimated, and the list as given is identicle with the list published in the "Life of Rev. John Thomson" by Dr. John Goodwin Herndon in 1942, who was good enough to give this compiler credit for having assisted him in securing the list of children named and in ascertaining the facts on which the dates are based. However, the writer has deviated just a little from Dr. Herndon's account of the dates of birth of some of the children, as well as the date of birth of REV. THOMSON himself, which he is convinced was earlier than 1790, as usually given.

We will now undertake to give some account of each one of these children, including such information as we have been able to find about their children and their descendants, and hope to do this without becoming too tiresome in the recital.

1. ESTHER THOMSON

ESTHER THOMSON was obviously born in Glasgow, Scotland, at the time when her father was a matriculated student in the University, which he had entered in 1706.

She was named for her father's sister, ESTHER, who married a man named WARRINGTON, whether in Scotland, Ireland or America, is not known. (She may have accompanied her brother REV. JOHN THOMSON when he came to Yorktown, Virginia, in 1714, and may have been a part of his "family" referred to in the letter read before the Presbytery the following year by REV. McNISH. That she came to Yorktown, where she met some relative of REV. THOMAS WARRINGTON, of Elizabeth City County or the town of HAMPTON, and there was married to him, is probable. The date of her husband's death is unknown, but she died in 1768, and REV. MATTHEW WILSON preached her funeral. This, of course, has reference to the sister, ESTHER.).

440

We have already repeated the tradition cherished by the descendants of ESTHER THOMSON, to the effect that when she was a child, she met SAMUEL CROCKETT on the ship coming to this country with her father and "his family", and that years afterwards they were married. This tradition the writer has discounted in the belief that the parents and perhaps grand-parents of SAMUEL CROCKETT were already here at that time and living on TANGIER ISLAND, in Accomac County, Virginia, but we shall not be hide-bound about it, and shall leave the reader to consider the facts we have offered and be his own judge. Anyway, SAMUEL and ESTHER THOMSON CROCKETT settled before 1735 in AMELIA COUNTY, VIRGINIA, where their first child was born, it is said in 1735. The place where they settled, while at that time (1735) was in AMELIA, it later became the part detached from AMELIA to form PRINCE EDWARD COUNTY. The children of SAMUEL and ESTHER CROCKETT were:

1. SAMUEL CROCKETT, JR. b. 1735 d. 1795 in Prince Edward County.
   m. (1) JANE STEELE   (2) MRS. ELIZABETH YOUNG.
2. ANN AGNES CROCKETT (b. 1736) m. JOHN MONTGOMERY in 1753.
3. JOHN CROCKETT (1737-1797) m. ELIZABETH MONTGOMERY.
4. JANE CROCKETT (b. 1739) m. HENRY DAVIS.
5. CATHERINE CROCKETT (b. 1741).
6. ROBERT CROCKETT (b. 1743). m. JANE STUART
7. ANDREW CROCKETT (b. 1745) m. SALLIE ELLIOTT
8. JAMES CROCKETT (b. 1749) d. 1826 m. MARY DRAKE.

The above is the list of children as same appears on page 12 of the "Crockett Family" by French and Armstrong, but we are advised that the list is based on Bible Records in possession of descendants.

Sometime prior to 1743, we imagine, SAMUEL CROCKETT and ESTHER his wife left what was to become PRINCE EDWARD COUNTY, and went to AUGUSTA COUNTY, where SAMUEL CROCKETT bought land from COL. JAMES PATTON, on which he and his family settled, and where he apparently died. This land adjoined other lands owned by a young man named WILLIAM SAYERS. After the death of SAMUEL CROCKETT, the widow, ESTHER, married this WILLIAM SAYERS, by whom she had, according to the family Bible, three sons: ROBERT SAYERS (b. 1754), ALEXANDER SAYERS (b. 1756), and JOHN THOMSON SAYERS (b. July 19, 1758).

JOHN THOMPSON SAYERS married SUSANNAH CROCKETT in 1784, and had a daughter ESTHER ARMSTRONG SAYERS, who married a cousin ABNER SAYERS. ABNER SAYERS was the father of DR. DAVID SAYERS, who settled at BASTROP, TEXAS, and whose son HON. JOSEPH DRAPER SAYERS, served for many years in the Congress of the United States, and afterwards two terms as GOVERNOR OF TEXAS. Thus GOVERNOR SAYERS, of Texas, was a great grandson of JOHN THOMSON SAYERS, and a great great great grandson of REV. JOHN THOMSON.

(What motive impelled ESTHER THOMSON and her husband SAMUEL CROCKETT to leave PRINCE EDWARD COUNTY, Virginia, (before that county was erected) and purchase land in AUGUSTA COUNTY from Col. James Patton? Did the possibility or probability that COL. PATTON'S wife was an OSBORNE, and ESTHER THOMSON'S mother was also an OSBORNE, have anything to do with it?)

SAMUEL CROCKETT, the first son of SAMUEL and ESTHER is said to have lived and died in Prince Edward County. If so, he must have had other relatives in PRINCE EDWARD besides his parents, or else he came back there from AUGUSTA COUNTY, because he could not have been over 10 years old when they left there and moved to Augusta. The children of SAMUEL JR. were JOSEPH (who is said to have gone to Georgia), MAJ. ROBERT CROCKETT (who married JANE LEWIS STUART, daughter of the LEWIS FAMILY - and of MRS. FROGG), JANE, ESTHER, MARGARET, JOHN, CATHERINE (who married ROBERT RUTLEDGE), and SAMUEL CROCKETT, III, who married FRANCES DUDLEY, a descendant of CHRISTOPHER DUDLEY and his wife MISS DANIEL, of Granville County, N. C.

CATHERINE CROCKETT (b. 1771 in AUGUSTA COUNTY, Va.) married ROBERT RUTLEDGE (1764-1853) and they had seven children; among them being NELLY RUTLEDGE, who married GEORGE KEYES, a soldier under ANDREW JACKSON in 1812, and who moved with his family to ALABAMA, where their son, HON. WADE RUTLEDGE, a prominent and brilliant lawyer in that State who became CHANCELLOR KEYES of ALABAMA, who lived at DEMOPOLIS, his wife being a daughter of GEN. GEORGE WHITFIELD. A daughter of Chancellor WADE KEYES became the wife of HON. NORMAN GOREE KITTRELL, of Houston, Texas, noted orator and jurist, and a direct descendant of the KITTRELL FAMILY of the town of KITTRELL in GRANVILLE COUNTY, North Carolina. I have often heard JUDGE KITTRELL (before whom I have tried cases in Texas courts) boast of the fact that through the veins of his children flowed the blood of the immortal DAVID CROCKETT. His eulogies on the "Immortal David Crockett" were gems and are to be found in several of the interesting volumes of which he was the author.

DR. SAMUEL CROCKETT III, son of SAMUEL CROCKETT JR. and his first wife JANE STEELE married FRANCES BLAND DUDLEY, of FRANKLIN, TENNESSEE, who was born June 30, 1786 and who was the daughter of HON. GUILFORD DUDLEY (Son of Christopher Dudley) and his wife ANNE EATON. The mother of GUILFORD DUDLEY was ELIZABETH DANIEL, daughter of JOHN DANIEL, who was born in YORK COUNTY in old BRUTON PARISH, and died in GRANVILLE COUNTY, N. C. leaving a will in 1763, in which he mentions his daughter ELIZABETH wife of CHRISTOPHER DUDLEY. The mother of the wife of DR. SAMUEL CROCKETT III was ANNE EATON, daughter of GEN. THOMAS EATON, and grand-daughter of COL. WILLIAM EATON, one of the original founders of GRANVILLE COUNTY and the commander of its militia troops in 1754. Both the EATONS and DUDLEYS, as well as the DANIELS were YORK COUNTY, VIRGINIA, stock, and the children of DR. SAMUEL CROCKETT III, Great Grandson of REV. JOHN THOMSON are thus remitted to York County, for their ancestry. It follows, logically, that the CROCKETTS may be safely placed in the same category.

The children of DR. SAMUEL CROCKETT III and FRANCES BLAND DUDLEY, were MYRA LEWIS, SARAH J. (who married WILLIAM PARK) MARY, FRANCES, ANNA (m. ROBERT GORDON and CHARLES (d. 1844).

ANDREW CROCKETT, son of SAMUEL CROCKETT and ESTHER THOMSON, married SARAH ELLIOTT, who was the daughter of ROBERT ELLIOTT, of PRINCE EDWARD COUNTY, Virginia, who had married MARY BAKER. MARY BAKER was a sister of ROBERT, DOUGLAS and SAMUEL BAKER, each of whom had married a sister of ESTHER CROCKETT, his mother; therefore he and his wife were first cousins. The date of ANDREW CROCKETT'S birth is given as 1745, in AUGUSTA COUNTY, which shows that SAMUEL and ESTHER had thus early left AMELIA COUNTY and purchased lands from COL. JAMES PATTON. ANDREW CROCKETT and his wife moved to and settled in DAVIDSON COUNTY, TENNESSEE, (now WILLIAMSON), where he received lands for his services as a revolutionary soldier. He and his wife are buried at BRENTWOOD, not far from FRANKLIN, TENNESSEE. It may not be tiresome to the reader to see a list of their children:

1. SARAH CROCKETT m. JOHN MALLORY.
2. POLLY CROCKETT m. JOSEPH CROCKETT, her cousin, son of JOHN.
3. JAMES CROCKETT m. MARTHA BELL
4. SAMUEL CROCKETT m. JOANNAH SAYERS, a cousin.
5. JOHN HAMILTON CROCKETT m. NANCY CROCKETT, her cousin, daughter of JOHN.
6. NANCY BAKER CROCKETT m. ROBERT SAYERS, brother of JOANNAH.
7. ANDREW CROCKETT, JR. m. ANNIE POWELL.
8. ROBERT SAYERS m. ELIZABETH GIBSON

Practically all of the descendants of these children are given in the "CROCKETT FAMILY" by ZELLA ARMSTRONG and MRS. FRENCH.

JAMES CROCKETT was the youngest son of SAMUEL CROCKETT and his wife ESTHER THOMSON, and he was born in AUGUSTA COUNTY, VIRGINIA, in 1750. When he was 21 years old he married MARY DRAKE a daughter of SAMUEL DRAKE. No, I do not believe he was a son of SIR FRANCIS DRAKE, as claimed, but of course he may have belonged to the same family or some of its branches. We are cautioned not to mistake this JAMES CROCKETT for the one who served in the House of Burgesses for VIRGINIA, laying that honor to another JAMES, son of a ROBERT WATKINS CROCKETT (meaning, of course, plain ROBERT CROCKETT) whose name we have never found on the records except as ROBERT, and whose son JAMES was living in MECKLENBURG COUNTY, N. C. at the time he is supposed to have been a Burgess. JAMES CROCKETT and his wife MARY DRAKE had twelve children, whose names would be of little value to the reader, with the exception of a daughter:

ESTHER CROCKETT, named for her grandmother, ESTHER THOMSON. Esther was born in January, 1780 and died July 9, 1870, over 90 years of age, and is buried at MADISONVILLE, TENNESSEE, the birthplace of this writer, in the old Baptist Churchyard. ESTHER CROCKETT married FRANCIS JACKSON CARTER, in Virginia. The "CROCKETT FAMILY" thus identifies FRANCIS J. CARTER:

"He was the son of GEORGE CARTER and wife "MARY" (probably "Craig') * * and brother of WILLIAM CARTER, who married UNITY BATES; also a brother of ROBERT CARTER who married JANE CROCKETT, daughter of COL. WALTER CROCKETT. These CARTERS were descendants of ROBERT CARTER (KING CARTER) who settled on the JAMES RIVER, near RICHMOND, in VIRGINIA."

(In Virginia genealogy ALL CARTERS are supposed to come down from old KING CARTER, otherwise the accounts would not be orthodox; but my information is that old "King" lived in Lancaster County, some distance from the JAMES RIVER). However, here we find the CROCKETTS, marrying into the old F. F. Vs from EASTERN VIRGINIA, which does not seem to conform to MR. MAURY'S description of the flying CROCKETTAIRES frightened by the annulment of the EDICT OF NANTES.

THERESA NEWELL CARTER, daughter of ESTHER CROCKETT and FRANCIS J. CARTER, married REV. JOHN SCRUGGS of TUSCULUM COLLEGE, of GREENEVILLE, TENNESSEE. He was also a BAPTIST MINISTER and was a son of RICHARD SCRUGGS and ELIZABETH McMAKIN, as well as a descendant of the family of the old GROSS SCRUGGS, of BEDFORD COUNTY, VIRGINIA, who in turn came from the marriage of one of his name to a young lady named GROCE, back in ISLE OF WIGHT or some of those early divisions immediately outside of JAMESTOWN. Again we find the CROCKETTS intermarrying with the early Eastern Virginia families. REV. JOHN SCRUGGS and his wife THERESA CARTER were the parents of ELEVEN children, and among them was

ELIZABETH ESTHER SCRUGGS, born in MADISONVILLE, TENNESSEE, who married HORACE BURTON YEARWOOD, and LAVINIA WALKER SCRUGGS who married THOMAS YEARWOOD. This last couple were the parents of EIGHT CHILDREN, including:

JOHN FRANCIS YEARWOOD, who was born in 1859, and who moved to Texas and became a noted ranchman employed on the famous I. X. L. Ranch in the PANHANDLE OF TEXAS, which was owned by the syndicate that built a five million dollar CAPITOL in Austin in exchange for several million acres of land. JOHN FRANCIS YEARWOOD married ELLA JOSEPHINE COFFEE, daughter of CAPT. JOHN COFFEE, of the Andrew Jackson Coffee family in Tennessee. The writer knew MR. YEARWOOD, whose father THOMAS YEARWOOD was a brother of ELISHA YEARWOOD, who married JUDITH WALKER MORROW, the great aunt of this scribe, and sister of ARMSTRONG MORROW, of Madisonville, Tennessee, his own grandfather. JOHN F. YEARWOOD died about four years ago leaving a fine family of children.

To set out or attempt to here record all of the descendants of SAMUEL CROCKETT and wife ESTHER THOMSON, daughter of REV. JOHN THOMSON, would be not only tiresome, but practically impossible. What has been given should furnish the reader with a pretty fair idea of their part of the family. We will now take up the others.

THE BAKER FAMILY OF PRINCE EDWARD COUNTY, VIRGINIA, AND ITS CONNECTION

WITH THE FAMILY OF REV. JOHN THOMSON, V.D.M.

Since no less than THREE members of the BAKER FAMILY, of Prince Edward County, Virginia, married into the family of REV. JOHN THOMSON, who died in MECKLENBURG COUNTY, N. C. in the year 1753, it is essential for an understanding of the THOMSON FAMILY and its numerous connection, to give some kind of an account of the BAKERS. The THREE BAKER BROTHERS who married as many daughters of REV. JOHN THOMSON, were as follows:

      2. MARY THOMSON (b. about 1712) married ROBERT BAKER, JR.
      9. JANE THOMSON (b. about 1726) married DOUGLAS BAKER.
     12. ELIZABETH THOMSON (b. about 1730-31) married SAMUEL BAKER.

These THREE UNITS of the THOMSON DESCENDANTS, bearing the name of BAKER, by reason of the above marriages will be discussed jointly, though we shall try to so segregate the members of each family that their particular branch may be identified.

In an ably written article in Vol. 49, of the Virginia Magazine of History and Biography, beginning on page 311, a few years ago, DR. JOSEPH DUPUY EGGLESTON, then President of the Virginia Historical Society, presented an outline of this BAKER FAMILY, and I think pretty clearly established the parentage of these Baker sons who married Thomson daughters. Beyond the name of the father, however, no further ancestral lines were established. Dr. Eggleston's account is the basis of most of the material here presented, and this writer, is unable to add with any certainty to the ancestral history of this family. The father of the family appears to have been a certain ROBERT BAKER, SR., who died in the year 1728, in LANCASTER COUNTY, Pennsylvania, intestate, but with a CALEB BAKER as administrator, witnessed by a DOUGLAS BAKER. A subjoined signature to the papers was that of a "ROBERT BAKER, JR."

It is easy for this writer to conjecture, and by considering certain isolated notes to be found on the earliest records of the Colony of Virginia, to deduce, that although this family of Bakers are thus discovered first on the records of Pennsylvania, it is nevertheless possible that they may have gone there from either MARYLAND or VIRGINIA. However, the point is not important for the purposes of this study.

As to when this family first came to VIRGINIA, from Pennsylvania, we can draw on the fact that as late as July 14, 1741, ROBERT BAKER (then called Sr.), CALEB BAKER and his wife MARTHA, sold land in Lancaster County to one Jacob Good, in which it is stated that part of the land had originally belonged to 'ROBERT BAKER, father of CALEB BAKER'. If I mistake not, Dr. Eggleston drew some of this early material from the "Life of Caleb Baker Wallace" by DR. W. H. WHITSETT. In the light of this deed the Virginia pilgrimage (and it appears to have been made by the entire Baker family) took place after 1741. Subsequent dealings and intermarriages between the persons named, and their allied connections pretty conclusively establish the fact that all of these on the list given below, were the sons and daughters of the ROBERT BAKER SR., who died in 1728:

     1. SAMUEL BAKER m. ELIZABETH THOMSON.
     2. CALEB BAKER m. MARTHA BROOKS
     3. ROBERT BAKER, JR. m. MARY THOMSON
     4. DOUGLAS BAKER m. JANE THOMSON
     5. MARY BAKER m. ROBERT ELLIOTT.

CALEB BAKER had married his wife MARTHA and she was living in Pennsylvania when the Jacob Good deed was executed in 1741; the record further shows that a child, CALEB BAKER, son of CALEB and MARTHA was born in Pennsylvania in 1734. Considering these facts and the other dates of births and deaths in Dr. Eggleston's chart, it is not unreasonable to suppose that the five marriages of the five children of ROBERT BAKER, SR. may all have occurred in Pennsylvania, before the family moved to PRINCE EDWARD COUNTY, Virginia. This may not be true, but it does seem that it could be true.

FAMILY OF SAMUEL BAKER AND HIS WIFE ELIZABETH THOMSON

As has been stated at the beginning of this study of the family of THOMSON, the REV. JOHN THOMSON died at the home of his son in law SAMUEL BAKER in Mecklenburg County, North Carolina in 1753.

SAMUEL BAKER and his wife ELIZABETH are supposed to have had FIVE CHILDREN at the time of his death, which probably occurred in 1757, because his will was probated december 24th of that year, in ROWAN COUNTY. The fact that his will was recorded in ROWAN COUNTY does not mean that he lived in ROWAN COUNTY, but it means that SALISBURY was the nearest place where an instrument pertaining to land titles could be recorded at that time. There was then NO MECKLENBURG COUNTY. The latter County was not established until FIVE YEARS LATER, 1762, and even then for some years there was no office where a will could be placed of record; no books or regular courthouse.

WILL OF SAMUEL BAKER: Rowan County, N. C. Dec. 24, 1757.   Names his wife ELIZA BAKER. Sons ROBERT BAKER and JOHN BAKER. Daughters MARGARET BAKER and MARY BAKER.
Provides: "My loving friend HUGH LAWSON, overseer of my last will and testament."
Witnesses: MOSES WHITE, ANDREW McCONNELL and GEORGE DAVIDSON.

MOSES WHITE was the father of HON. HUGH LAWSON WHITE; ANDREW McCONNELL was a brother in law of MOSES WHITE; GEORGE DAVIDSON was the father of GENERAL WILLIAM LEE DAVIDSON.

It will be noticed that SAMUEL BAKER in his will mentions only FOUR of his children. We have never been able to ascertain the name of the fifth child. It is said that he had another son. Who was he? Was it GEORGE BAKER who lived in the Steele Creek census district (No. 1) in 1790 with four young sons and three daughters, or Christopher Baker of Sugar Creek District with the same number of children, at the same time? In District No. 9 East of Rocky River there was a JOHN, JOSHUA and CHRISTOPHER living on Scotch Buffalo, but they were perhaps a Dutch or Scotch family of Bakers and not related.

Of HUGH LAWSON, who was made the overseer of SAMUEL BAKER'S will, there is much yet to be said. He was buried four or five years later in Baker's Graveyard, where the remains of JOHN THOMSON and his son in law SAMUEL BAKER were interred. His son ROGER LAWSON married the youngest sister of SAMUEL BAKER'S wife, ELIZABETH THOMSON, and in that way was what is commonly called a brother in law of SAMUEL BAKER.

MOSES WHITE, one of the witnesses, whose home was on DAVIDSON'S CREEK in upper MECKLENBURG COUNTY, not far from the present DAVIDSON'S COLLEGE, had a son, JAMES WHITE, who married MARY LAWSON, a daughter of HUGH LAWSON, who became the mother of HUGH LAWSON WHITE, of TENNESSEE. The first wife of MOSES WHITE was a McCONNELL, and ANDREW McCONNELL may have been her brother, or a nephew. I have never seen another will so well illustrating the custom of using relatives and their connections as signatories and witnesses as this. But how about GEORGE DAVIDSON? Does this man, the father of GENERAL WILLIAM LEE DAVIDSON (killed at COWAN'S FORD during the revolution), come within the same category? The answer is in the affirmative.

HUGH LAWSON, made overseer of the will of SAMUEL BAKER in this ancient instrument, had a daughter who married GEORGE EWING, who had several sons, among them a HUGH EWING, who settled in what is now LINCOLN or GASTON COUNTY; also there were several EWING daughters. I believe my notes show that at least THREE of the off-spring of GEORGE EWING and his wife MISS LAWSON married persons named DAVIDSON, whose relationship with the witness GEORGE DAVIDSON was very close, as was their relationship also with the family of REV. JOHN THOMSON.

This writer is compelled to confess that, in all his researches conducted on the family of SAMUEL BAKER of the foregoing will, he has been unable to find and identify any record pertaining to either a ROBERT or a JOHN BAKER, who might have been one of the two sons mentioned by name in Samuel's will. The nearest approach to an identification of the son JOHN is in the will of a certain JOHN BAKER, with wife "POLLY" who died leaving a will in WARREN COUNTY, GEORGIA, near where ROGER LAWSON, who married his wife's sister, resided after the revolution, in which he mentioned children WILLIAM, AUSTIN, EDWIN, PEYTON, JONATHAN, HENRY, a daughter POLLY, who married a man named BATTLE and ELIZABETH who married a WILLIAMS. This will was witnessed by three members of the TORRENCE FAMILY, JOHN, SEPTIMUS and a JOHN W. TORRENCE. Since the TORRENCE FAMILY, including the "Widow Terrence" resided in the neighborhood of where DAVIDSON COLLEGE is now located, during the days of the revolution, the names of members of this family signed to the will of a JOHN BAKER suggests that he may have been JOHN BAKER, son of SAMUEL.

Neither have we been able to find trace of the daughters MARGARET and MARY BAKER mentioned in this will.

But after the death of SAMUEL BAKER, his widow, ELIZABETH THOMSON, daughter of REV. JOHN THOMSON, married a second time, and after we review the connections thus made by the widow, the intimacy between SAMUEL BAKER'S FAMILY and the old patriarch GEORGE DAVIDSON, becomes a bit more interesting.

ELIZABETH THOMSON MARRIED (2nd) CHARLES HARRIS

CHARLES HARRIS, the second husband of ELIZABETH(THOMSON) BAKER belonged to the HARRIS FAMILY of ROCKY RIVER, in CABARRUS COUNTY (now). He dates away back, and it is claimed that he was one of the eight children of a ROBERT HARRIS, whose wife was a DOROTHY WILEY, and all of whom, except the parents settled in what is now CABARRUS COUNTY before 1750. The CHARLES HARRIS, who became the second husband of the daughter ELIZABETH THOMSON, was the father (by his first wife)of ROBERT HARRIS, JR. the "signer".

The first wife of CHARLES HARRIS had been a JANE McILLHENNY, and by her he had all of his children except two, who were by his second marriage to ELIZABETH THOMSON, the widow of SAMUEL BAKER. Children by his first wife were MARTHA, ROBERT (the signer), THOMAS, MARGARET, JANE and a JAMES; by ELIZABETH (THOMSON) BAKER he had SAMUEL HARRIS, a graduate of PRINCETON in 1787, who became a tutor there, where he died in 1789, and the famous DR. CHARLES HARRIS, of CONCORD, who conducted a famous Medical school; the latter the ancestor of WILLIAM SHAKESPEARE HARRIS, well remembered in the annals of MECKLENBURG COUNTY.

ELIZABETH THOMSON, daughter of REV. JOHN THOMSON, helped to raise the children of her second husband by his first marriage, since she was their step-mother. Her step-daughter MARTHA, married her cousin SAMUEL HARRIS, and her step son ROBERT HARRIS, married first MARY WILSON, and after her death and after the death of GEN. WILLIAM DAVIDSON, he married his widow, who had been MARY BREVARD, the daughter of JOHN BREVARD. GEN. WILLIAM DAVIDSON being the son of GEORGE DAVIDSON who witnessed the will of SAMUEL BAKER, thus it happened that BAKER'S widow, having afterwards married CHARLES HARRIS, her step son married the widow of the distinguished son of this same GEORGE DAVIDSON. Further, it appears from the records that GEN. WILLIAM DAVIDSON'S posthumous son (not mentioned in his will) who bore the name of WILLIAM LEE DAVIDSON II, married ELIZABETH DAVIDSON, daughter of MAJ. JOHN DAVIDSON.

Another step-child of ELIZABETH (THOMSON) BAKER, was little JANE HARRIS, who became the wife of a young preacher, THOMAS REESE, the son of DAVID REESE, the "signer". Jane must have been a very young child at the time her father married MRS. SAMUEL BAKER. That she received the parental care and training in her childhood of one of the daughters of REV. JOHN THOMSON, she doubtless remembered "all the days of her long life" - for she did live a long life, and finally died in Pendleton District South Carolina, having outlived her distinguished husband and married another in her old age.

She became the third wife of COL. ROBERT ANDERSON, a distinguished revolutionary soldier of Pendleton District. And thereby hangs an interesting "tale" germane to this study.

444

Among the patriots of the American Revolution COL. ROBERT ANDERSON ranks high in the History of his country, and many outstanding members of the Sons and Daughters of the American Revolution boast of him as an ancestor. At the battle of the COWPENS he served under the daring and intrepid ANDREW PICKENS, and when Pickens was made a Brigadier General, Anderson became COL. ROBERT ANDERSON. From Louise Ayer Vandiver's traditions and History of Anderson County, S. C. we "lift" the following account of Col. Anderson's family history:

ROBERT ANDERSON was born in VIRGINIA in 1741, the fifth child and second son of JOHN and JANE ANDERSON, who owned a comfortable farm in AUGUSTA COUNTY about five miles from STAUNTON. Young Robert was baptised on the 15th day of November, 1741, by REV. JOHN CRAIG. He grew up living the ordinary life of a VIRGINIA Planter's son, receiving the average education of a Virginia gentleman; and became a surveyor by profession.

Among the neighbors of the ANDERSONS was a family whose name was THOMSON, having a daughter called ANNE, whom Robert regarded as his "best girl", though he used no such undignified term in telling her about it, prattling instead of starry eyes, soul's ideal, and other such poetical things. But though young Anderson talked sentiment, he had an eye to business; and in pursuance of his profession he left home, carrying a chain over trackless woods, bogs and marshes. In those days journeys took a long time, and such trips as young Anderson made required years. For two years he had been away, his destination was the new Cherokee Country, which had been opened up in South Carolina; and after so long with no word from him his friends believed that he must be dead.

To pretty ANN THOMSON or THOMPSON came other suitors * * the girl finally consented to wed one of her admirers, and * * the preparations went on. * *

The appointed day for the wedding dawned. A bevy of merry girls filled the THOMPSON home. Anne, surrounded by her bridesmaids, was in an upper room dressing for the ceremony, when looking out of an upper window she saw a rider approaching * * she exclaimed: "By my soul! Yonder comes ROBERT ANDERSON and I love his little finger better than I do the other man's whole body!" Thereupon she seized a shawl and throwing it over her head sped away to meet the man she really loved. The Young Lochinvar had come out of the West, and mounting his horse behind him, they rode away to seek for Eldorado. From that moment ANNE THOMPSON is lost to history, though she lived for twenty-five years longer, and left five children, ROBERT ANDERSON, JR. and four daughters, ANNE, ELIZABETH, MARY and LYDIA.

ROBERT ANDERSON married twice more, the second being MRS. MAVERICK, a wealthy widow of PENDLETON; Lydia Anderson, one of the daughters married young SAMUEL MAVERICK.

COLONEL ANDERSON becoming again a widower, asked MRS. REESE, widow of his former pastor REV. THOMAS REESE, to marry him, which she did, and he outlived her. MRS. REESE was JANE HARRIS, as a girl, and had been raised and cared for as her step daughter by MRS. CHARLES HARRIS, second wife of COLONEL CHARLES HARRIS, who as a girl was ELIZABETH THOMSON, daughter of REV. JOHN THOMSON, the early minister of MECKLENBURG COUNTY, North Carolina.

Thus, it seems, COL. ROBERT ANDERSON, appeared to be very fond of marrying into the THOMPSON FAMILY.

At this point it will be noticed that REV. JOHN CRAIG, of Augusta County, Virginia, who had baptised COL. ROBERT ANDERSON as a child in 1741, and known to have been a kind of protege of REV. JOHN THOMSON, had been one of the witnesses to the will of HUGH THOMPSON, of Augusta County, Virginia in 1750. The identity of the several THOMSONS and THOMPSONS of Augusta have been heretofore discussed, but there were several of the names of whose children have not been found, and ANNE THOMPSON who became the first wife of COL. ROBERT ANDERSON, must have been the daughter of one of these. Which one we have never ascertained, and we do not believe that the records show, or that any person, even descendants of the family, knew.

At this point it would be interesting to give a lot of information now available on the family and descendants, mostly through his daughters, of the family of COL. ROBERT ANDERSON, who to all intents and purposes married TWICE into the THOMPSON FAMILY, through his final marriage to a daughter of CHARLES HARRIS, as shown above, one of the patriarchs of the HARRIS FAMILY of Eastern Mecklenburg. But Col. Robert Anderson properly belongs to South Carolina's long list of interesting patriots, and for that reason, further of his family history will be reluctantly omitted from these annals of MECKLENBURG FAMILIES.

CALEB BAKER WHOSE WIFE WAS MARTHA BROOKS - FAMILY.

This CALEB BAKER was a brother of SAMUEL, ROBERT and DOUGLAS BAKER, the three sons in laws of REV. JOHN THOMSON, but his own wife is supposed to have been MARTHA BROOKS, a sister of CATHERINE BROOKS who married MAJ. JOHN HODNETT (b. in 1730, and a Major in the Revolution) whose son married into the COLLIER FAMILY, of York County, Virginia, and whose daughter CATHERINE married CALEB BAKER JR. That this family was close to the THOMSON family is attested by the fact that in her last will and testament, among the legacies handed down to their eight children by Martha (Brooks) Baker was a copy of "THOMSON'S SHORTER CATECHISM" and "THOMSON'S POOR ORPHAN'S LEGACY" by Rev. John Thomson.

The EIGHT CHILDREN of this couple were: SAMUEL BAKER (m. widow of HUGH RITCHIE); HENRY BAKER, Executor of his father's will; ABRAHAM BAKER whose son CALEB settled in South Carolina; RUTH BAKER who married SAMUEL JOHNSTON; MARTHA BAKER who married CHARLES EWING, and had no less than NINE CHILDREN, who scattered throughout the Western Country, with hundreds of descendants; MARY BAKER who married ROBERT EWING (brother of CHARLES) and ESTHER BAKER who became the wife of SAMUEL WALLACE.

Contrary to some of the genealogical material that has been going the rounds for some several years, SAMUEL WALLACE who married ESTHER BAKER, was not of the Scotch-Irish family who settled in ALBEMARLE COUNTY, Virginia, to which MICHAEL WOODS and his family belonged, but, while he had his family origin in SCOTLAND, he belonged to an old EASTERN VIRGINIA FAMILY, who lived in YORK and ELIZABETH CITY COUNTY, with the CUNNINGHAMS, DANIELS and others heretofore mentioned, and was himself a QUAKER, being one of the witnesses (QUAKERS), who on March 5, 1738, attended the wedding of SAMUEL JORDAN to HANNAH BATES, which took place in YORK COUNTY, VIRGINIA. (See Minutes of White Oak Swamp Meeting Record Book 1699-1756). Others who were present were EDMUND JORDAN, ARMINGER TROTTER, ROBERT PLEASANTS, CHARLES WOODSON, DOROTHY JORDAN (CARY), ELIZABETH WYATT, MARGARET JORDAN, SARAH BATES, BENJAMIN JORDAN. FLEMING JORDAN. etc.

SAMUEL WALLACE, who married ESTHER BAKER, was obviously a descendant, about three generations removed, of "THOMAS WALLACE, of the County of WARWICK RIVER, Virginia, "Docter in Phisick" who gave a mortgage the 15th of December, 1647, to GEORGE LUDLOW, on certain slaves and an indentured servant. He was NOT of Pennsylvania origin. He and ESTHER BAKER, his wife, were the parents of HON. CALEB BAKER WALLACE, one-time Chief Justice of the Supreme Court of KENTUCKY, and who, before migrating to the Western Country was appointed one of the Executors of the will of JAMES CUNNINGHAM, the son in law of REV. JOHN THOMSON, but five years later could not serve because of his absence from the main Commonwealth of Virginia. The CALEB WALLACE history belongs to KENTUCKY and will be omitted here.

ROBERT EWING, the husband of MARY BAKER, with his wife, became the ancestor of a noble line of descendants. They had twelve children: SYDNEY ANN, JOHN, MARTHA, ROBERT, BAKER, YOUNG, URBAN, REUBEN, POLLY, CHATHAM, JANE and FINIS EWING; also EPHRAIM BREVARD EWING.

The last named, REV. FINIS EWING, settled in the "western country, became a minister of the Presbyterian Church, and founder of the branch of that denomination, which for over 100 years was known as the CUMBERLAND PRESBYTERIAN CHURCH. He belongs to the History of the South, and his children served their country both in the wars and in Civil Life in High Places. His wife, whom he married in DAVIDSON COUNTY, TENNESSEE, January 15, 1793, was MARGARET DAVIDSON, who was born and raised in MECKLENBURG COUNTY, NORTH CAROLINA. She was the daughter of GEN. WILLIAM LEE DAVIDSON, the gallant revolutionary soldier, who fell at Cowan's Ford, and who is buried at old HOPEWELL CHURCHYARD. After the death of her father GEN. DAVIDSON, her mother married ROBERT HARRIS, JR., a "signer" of the MECKLENBURG DECLARATION OF INDEPENDENCE, and a step-son of ELIZABETH (THOMSON) BAKER, daughter of REV. JOHN THOMSON of these sketches.

SAMUEL BAKER, who married ELIZABETH THOMSON was the great uncle, by marriage of REV. FINIS EWING, and his distinguished sons WILLIAM LEE DAVIDSON EWING, United States Senator from the State of Illinois, THOMPSON McGREADY EWING, member of the Constitutional Convention of the State of MISSOURI, and another son, EPHRAIM BREVARD EWING, who was a member of the SUPREME COURT of the State of MISSOURI, were all grandsons of GEN. WILLIAM LEE DAVIDSON, the Mecklenburg patriot.

ROBERT BAKER, JR. WHO MARRIED MARY THOMSON

ROBERT BAKER, JR., brother of SAMUEL BAKER, married MARY THOMSON, the daughter of REV. JOHN THOMSON. March 20, 1746 he bought 400 acres of land in the Buffalo settlement of PRINCE EDWARD COUNTY "beginning at Cunningham's corner", which perhaps had reference to the land of his wife's sister's husband, JAMES CUNNINGHAM. In his will it is stated (so Dr. Eggleston wrote us) that he "was of the Buffalo settlement of Prince Edward County, Gentleman", so he apparently had the standing of a Virginia Gentleman, as that term was generally used and understood. His own will was dated in 1759, and that of his wife in 1760. Dr. Eggleston believed that he was perhaps a "gun smith". Only one son is known and his name was SAMUEL BAKER, but either his daughter or grand-daughter married a JAMES ANDERSON.

DOUGLAS BAKER WHOSE WIFE WAS JANE THOMSON

The last will and testament of DOUGLAS BAKER, who married JANE THOMSON, the daughter of REV. JOHN THOMSON was executed February 14, 1765) and the maker must have died shortly thereafter, because on Spetember 25, the same year his estate was appraised by WILLIAM WATSON, JOHN FULTON and JOSEPH CUNNINGHAM. The witnesses to the will were GEORGE SKILLADAY, SAMUEL BAKER and ANDREW BAKER. DR. JOSEPH D. EGGLESTON says: "The assumption is the more reasonable, if the tradition in the various branches of the family is correct, that DOUGLAS BAKER married JANE, daughter of REV. JOHN THOMSON".

DOUGLAS BAKER and his wife JANE THOMSON were the parents of a most interesting lot of children, as follows:

1. ROBERT BAKER who died in 1773, and who married MARGARET GRAHAM. Thomas Graham, James Graham and JOSEPH PARKS were the witnesses to his will. THOMAS and JAMES GRAHAM were the sons of JOHN GRAHAM who married another daughter of REV. JOHN THOMSON, whose Christian name has never been found, but who, with her husband located in Prince Edward County, Virginia. This writer believes that another son of JOHN GRAHAM and his wife MISS THOMSON was the WILLIAM GRAHAM, who settled in the Hopewell section of Mecklenburg County, North Carolina, who with his wife MARGARET is buried at Hopewell Churchyard, and who was one of the signers of the MECKLENBURG DECLARATION OF INDEPENDENCE.

2. JOSHUA BAKER, who never married, but who left a will in 1777.

3. DOUGLAS BAKER, JR. who died in 1778, and whose wife was his cousin MARY ELLIOTT, the daughter of ROBERT ELLIOTT and his wife MARY BAKER, sister of all the Baker brothers who married into the THOMSON FAMILY. Another daughter of ROBERT ELLIOTT and MARY BAKER became the wife of ANDREW CROCKETT, revolutionary soldier, who, like his second cousin, FINIS EWING, settled in DAVIDSON COUNTY, TENNESSEE, where he left hundreds of descendants. DOUGLAS BAKER JR. and his wife MARY ELLIOTT had three children, one of whom we knew was NANCY BAKER who married JOSEPH MORTON, of an old Virginia family; also sons ANDREW BAKER and DOUGLAS BAKER III.

4. JOSEPH BAKER was born in 1753 and died the year following.

5. ANDREW BAKER. He was known as ANDREW BAKER, SR., and his wife was CATHERINE. He died leaving will in January, 1804, and his wife CATHERINE thereafter in 1811 married her husband's first cousin, CALEB BAKER JR., by whom she had no children. CALEB BAKER, JR. was already the father of 10 children by his first marriage to CATHERINE HODNETT, deceased.

6. JEAN BAKER married JOHN ARMSTRONG. Just when JOHN ARMSTRONG left Prince Edward County we have no way of accurately telling, but he and his wife JEAN became the ancestors of a numerous tribe of ARMSTRONGS who settled at ROGERSVILLE, TENNESSEE, in close proximity to their cousins, the CROCKETTS and MORROWS. There in 1813 JOHN ARMSTRONG died, leaving a will which we found on record, in which he mentions the following legatees: JEAN, THOMAS, WILLIAM, BAKER, JOHN, and JAMES ARMSTRONG, and also a SAMUEL BAKER, who was the husband of ANNIE ARMSTRONG, probably and apparently a daughter. This SAMUEL BAKER, who married ANNIE ARMSTRONG suggests the possibility - even the probability - that here was the FIFTH CHILD of SAMUEL BAKER and ELIZABETH THOMSON, of Mecklenburg, who married his cousin ANNIE ARMSTRONG. The son WILLIAM ARMSTRONG died in 1817 following, and named JANE, THOMAS, ANNIE and NANCY ARMSTRONG, the latter -NANCY - having married a man named FORGEY.

7. ESTHER BAKER married one GEORGE SHILLADAY. A daughter ESTHER SHILLADAY married a VANCE down in Washington County, Virginia.

8. MARTHA BAKER married WILLIAM DAVIDSON.

9. SAMUEL BAKER who died in 1802, married MARY, and had seven children, whose names have not been found.

Dr. EGGLESTON believed that there was still one other daughter and that she also married a SHILLADAY, first name unknown, but could not establish this by the records.

After the death of DOUGLAS BAKER in 1765, his wife JANE THOMSON married an old friend and neighbor, WILLIAM WATSON, by whom she had no children, though, it appears her second husband was probably a widower with several grown children of his own by a first marriage.

MARY BAKER AND HER HUSBAND ROBERT ELLIOTT

ROBERT ELLIOTT who married MARY BAKER was brother of SOLOMON ELLIOTT "of the Province of Pennsylvania and County of Chester, Trader", who died in 1773, and also had brothers JOHN, JOSEPH, ANDREW, and sisters MARGARET ELLIS, MARTHA BOGGS, SARAH McLELLAN and ALICE and RACHEL ELLIOTT. The father of ROBERT and all these children was ANDREW ELLIOTT.

As near as can be ascertained from all available records, ROBERT ELIOTT and his wife MARY BAKER had the following children:

1. SARAH ELLIOTT married ANDREW CROCKETT.
2. MARY ELLIOTT married DOUGLAS BAKER, JR.
3. JAMES ELLIOTT married MARY (last name unknown).

3. JAMES ELLIOTT died leaving a will (Book C-p.49) in MECKLENBURG COUNTY, North Carolina, which was dated March 13, 1772, in which he names:
        Wife: MARY.
        Son: ROBERT ELLIOTT.
        Dau: MARTHA ELLIOTT
        Dau: ISABELLA ELLIOTT.
Father: ROBERT ELLIOTT and wife MARY, Executers.
Witnesses: ANDREW McNEAL and WALTER DAVIS.

In Book C of MECKLENBURG COUNTY, N. C. the will of SOLOMON ELLIOTT, brother of ROBERT ELLIOTT, apparently executed in Pennsylvania somewhere, where as a "trader" he must have been temporarily sojourning, is on record. In this will SOLOMON mentions his brothers ANDREW, JAMES and JOSEPH, and his sisters MARGARET and RACHEL.

The witnesses to this very interesting document were HEZEKIAH JAMES BALCH, LEMUEL PATTON, and one WILLIAM McWHORTER.

All of which shows that among the other connections of REV. JOHN THOMSON, who came to MECKLENBURG COUNTY, were the ELLIOTTS who, like his three daughters, married into the BAKERS.

This ELLIOTT family came to MECKLENBURG COUNTY at a very early day, and married into the families of some of the other families who came early. ANDREW ELLIOTT, born March 29, 1765, with later members of the family, is buried at HOPEWELL PRESBYTERIAN CHURCH, which is an indication that they were Presbyterians. "My daughter MARGARET ELLIOTT" is mentioned in the will of DAVID MOORE, proved in February, 1778, of which JOHN BARNETT was an executer. The will of SUSAN SMART in 1850, which will be found in this volume and section among the early wills, mentions various relatives named SPRATT, BARNETT and ELLIOTT, and she makes her "friend and relative" SAMUEL H. ELLIOTT her executor. The JACKS are also mentioned in her will.

ABRAHAM THOMSON, SON OF THE REV. JOHN THOMSON

The material relating to ABRAHAM THOMSON, one of the sons of REV. JOHN THOMSON is very scarce. Various deeds and documents pertaining to lands in the Buffalo region of Prince Edward County, Virginia, can only be explained by the assumption that he was a son of the subject of these sketches. In Volume 3, page 448, dated April 14, 1770, appears a record of the following deed:

> George Ewing, Alexander Ewing, William Ewing and Jane Ewing, John Caldwell and Ellener Caldwell, James Ewing Jr. & Margaret Ewing and Ann Ewing of Prince Edward and Betetourt Counties in the Colony of Virginia, all of the ONE PART, and JOHN THOMPSON, Smith, and ABRAHAM THOMPSON, of Prince Edward County, of the OTHER PART, for 120 pounds, 395 acres on both sides of the North Fork of Fort Creek, deed. Witnessed by SAMUEL WALLACE, JOSEPH PARKS, JOHN CALDWELL and ANDREW WALLACE.

In Volume 5, page 36, dated March 28, 1772:

> ABRAHAM THOMPSON, of Prince Edward County, to JOHN THOMPSON, of said County, his interest in the 395 acres described in the above deed.

SAMUEL EWING married MARGARET. Samuel died and his will was proved in PRINCE EDWARD COUNTY, Virginia September 30, 1758. In it he mentions his wife Margaret and the following children: GEORGE, ALEXANDER, JANE, ELLEANER, MARGARET and ANN. If you will check this list of children with the underscored names of the first parties mentioned in the first deed above, you will see they are the same. It shows that WILLIAM EWING married JANE, JOHN CALDWELL had married ELLENER and JAMES EWING JR. had married MARGARET EWING. The 395 acres of land belonged to the estate of SAMUEL EWING, who had been dead for many years, and the heirs sold it to JOHN THOMPSON and ABRAHAM THOMPSON, brothers, who were both sons of REV. JOHN THOMPSON.

To again use that hackneyed expression of the genealogists "It is interesting to note", Samuel Ewing in his will, mentions his grandson SAMUEL EWING, the son of his eldest son GEORGE EWING. Here we will insert a marriage record from Prince Edward County:

> JAN. 2, 1773: SAMUEL EWING and MARY DANIEL. Letter of consent from GEORGE EWING for his son to get the license.

MARY DANIEL who married SAMUEL EWING (son of GEORGE and grandson of SAMUEL) was the younger sister of JAMES, WILLIAM and JOHN DANIEL each of whom married a grand-daughter of REV. JOHN THOMSON, all three daughters of JAMES CUNNINGHAM and his wife ANN THOMSON.

DR. JOHN G. HERNDON, of Haverford College, in his "Life of Rev. John Thomson" is perhaps correct in evaluating these records and in his conclusion that, while the name of the wife of ABRAHAM THOMPSON is lost in obscurity, that he did marry and that he had one son, at least, named JOHN THOMPSON, who left a will in Prince Edward County, Virginia, in 1795.

The will of this JOHN THOMPSON, grandson of REV. JOHN THOMSON was dated March 26, 1793, but was proven in Court June 15, 1795. In it he does not mention his wife, but names three sons and two daughters:

1. ROBERT THOMPSON
2. ROGER THOMPSON
3. JOHN THOMPSON
4. SARAH THOMPSON
5. JANE THOMPSON
6. Grand-daughter SARAH BAKER.

ROBERT and ROGER THOMPSON were his Executors, and the witnesses were FRANCIS WATKINS, SAMUEL W. VENABLE, JOSEPH PARKS and WILLIAM WOMACK, JR.

JANE THOMPSON, one of the daughters, married CALEB BAKER (evidently a cousin) and had these children: THOMSON BAKER, MARY BAKER (m. JAMES RICE), SARAH BAKER (never married), NANCY BAKER (married THOMAS VERNON) and BETSY BAKER (m. WILLIAM THORNTON).

BETSY BAKER (Dau. of JANE THOMPSON and CALEB BAKER) and her husband, WILLIAM J. THORNTON were the parents of NANCY, JANE, HARRIETT and BETSY THORNTON.

The names of these grandchildren and great grand-children of JOHN THOMPSON (son of ABRAHAM) are taken from the papers in a suit for a division of property after the death of CALEB BAKER.

THE EWINGS, DAVIDSONS, CALDWELLS, LAWSONS, HENDERSONS AND BARRYS

AND THEIR RELATION TO THE REV. JOHN THOMSON

EVERY NAME in the above headline is represented numerously among the early settlers of MECKLENBURG COUNTY, North Carolina. That each of these families were related directly or indirectly to the distinguished pioneer apostle of the Presbyterian Faith who died near Beattie's Ford in Mecklenburg County in 1753, this writer is able to establish. Many of these families may have been preceded by him to the Yadkin-Catawba valley, but some of them came there and settled perhaps a short time before his "visit" to the section. Not only the above families, but several others, including ALEXANDER OSBORNE, whom the writer thinks was a brother of REV. JOHN THOMSON'S first wife and the uncle of all his children, save one - HANNAH.

Who were these people?

THE EWING FAMILY. The family came from NORTH OF IRELAND to CECIL COUNTY, MARYLAND, as did the ALEXANDER and other MECKLENBURG COUNTY (N. C.) families. WILLIAM EWING was the father of two sets of children, NATHANIEL EWING by his first marriage, and WILLIAM, JOSHUA, JAMES, SAMUEL and perhaps THOMAS by his second marriage, as well as ANNE and perhaps other daughters. A brother of the ancestor, WILLIAM, was the father of CHARLES and ROBERT EWING, who married the two BAKER SISTERS heretofore mentioned. CHARLES and ROBERT were first cousins of NATHANIEL and his half-brothers, whose families have been briefly sketched on a preceding page. With the EWING FAMILY were representatives of two other families, the PORTERS and GILLESPIES; these two families were also cousins of the EWINGS.

NATHANIEL EWING had married RACHEL PORTER. Rachel was the sister of JAMES PORTER, who had married his cousin ELLEN GILLESPIE, and also of JOHN PORTER who married MARY ANTHONY, and was the father of OLIVER PORTER (m. MARGARET WATSON), WILLIAM PORTER and FRANCIS PORTER. NATHANIEL EWING remained in MARYLAND for a long time (though his children came to Virginia) and his half-brothers settled in what is now PRINCE EDWARD COUNTY, VIRGINIA.

THE DAVIDSON FAMILY. GEORGE DAVIDSON (father of GEN. WILLIAM LEE DAVIDSON); JOHN DAVIDSON (father of MAJ. WILLIAM DAVIDSON, of SWANANOA, N. C.); and ROBERT DAVIDSON (father of MAJ. JOHN DAVIDSON) all apparently brothers, were the ancestors of most of the DAVIDSONS in and around MECKLENBURG COUNTY, N. C. However, there was another brother of this family that settled in VIRGINIA, whose descendants lived in AMELIA COUNTY, but afterwards in PRINCE EDWARD COUNTY, whose name was WILLIAM. His sons and grandsons married into the EWINGS, BAKERS and THOMSONS, of VIRGINIA. Each of the four brothers named became the head of a numerous and distinguished family of children, and apparently all four of these brothers were born at NIXTON, MARYLAND, on the SUSQUEHANNA RIVER, in CECIL COUNTY, MARYLAND, where the will of JAMES ALEXANDER (father of JOHN McKNITT ALEXANDER) appears of record.

THE LAWSON FAMILY. It has become customary among genealogical writers on the LAWSON family to say that HUGH LAWSON first settled in PENNSYLVANIA, from whence he came to VIRGINIA with brothers JOHN and ROGER. One who has traced his connecting lines back, however, states that he and his brothers were cousins, some degrees removed, from the early VIRGINIA EMIGRANTS, Rowland & EPAPHRODITUS LAWSON and CHRISTOPHER LAWSON. The exact statement of MRS. CAROLINE BELLE PRICE on this matter is:

"The record of EPAPHRODITUS LAWSON and ROWLAND LAWSON, of VIRGINIA, shows that their ancestor, SIR HENRY LAWSON of 'Brough Hall' (in ENGLAND) was the father of their cousin CAPT. JOHN LAWSON, from whom COL. HUGH LAWSON descended".

Mrs. Price further says:
"HUGH LAWSON married MARY MOORE, daughter of CHARLES MOORE and MARGARET BARRY."

THE HENDERSON FAMILY. A very complete account of this family will be found on pages 221 to 230 inclusive of this completed work (at first bound in a separate volume styled "COLONIAL GRANVILLE COUNTY AND ITS PEOPLE"), to which reference for data not set out under this particular headline, is made.

THE BARRY FAMILY. It is the intention to give a separate account of the BARRY FAMILY, but the REV. JOHN THOMSON connection will be given somewhat in the course of this particular note. THE BARRY FAMILY is a necessary part of MECKLENBURG COUNTY, since RICHARD BARRY was one of the signers of the Mecklenburg Declaration of Independence.

With above predicate the writer will now undertake, as briefly as possible to show how all these families were related to REV. JOHN THOMSON, and to each other.

COL. HUGH LAWSON

At the May Court, 1746, the County Court of LUNENBURG COUNTY, VIRGINIA, made appointments of tythe takers. Those appointed were JOHN PHELPS, MATTHEW TALBOT. GENT., WILLIAM CALDWELL, CORNELIUS CARGILL, WILLIAM HILL, LEWIS DELONEY (formerly of York County, who had appraised the estate of DAVID CUNNINGHAM, uncle of JAMES CUNNINGHAM, of Cub Creek), LIDDALL BACON and HUGH LAWSON, Gent.

the latter being "appointed to take the list of tythables in this county from the line that divides this from BRUNSWICK COUNTY, upwards to the mouth of HOUNDS CREEK.

The list taken for that year (1746) has never been found, but subsequent lists for the years 1748, 1749, 1750, 1751 and 1752, by Col. Lawson appear in the Landon C. Bell's "Sunlight on the Southside".

After 1752 the name of HUGH LAWSON does not appear on the VIRGINIA RECORDS, and he perhaps settled immediately thereafter in NORTH CAROLINA, where he owned lands on both sides of DAVIDSON'S CREEK, and where he built a home. Davidson's Creek is in the upper part of MECKLENBERG COUNTY and is NOT in IREDELL or ROWAN COUNTIES. He died sometime after writing his last will and testament, in 1764, which will be found elsewhere in this work, and in it he mentioned his sons HUGH and ROGER LAWSON, his daughter MARY (who married JAMES WHITE) and FOUR sons in laws, as follows:

1. THOMAS IRWIN
2. GEORGE EWING
3. HUGH BARRY
4. JAMES HENDERSON.

JAMES HENDERSON married VIOLET LAWSON. HUGH BARRY married MARGARET LAWSON. GEORGE EWING married CATHERINE LAWSON. We have never been able to identify the Christian name of the daughter who married THOMAS IRWIN. It is believed, however, that THOMAS IRWIN had married HANNAH LAWSON, who after his death became the second wife of ROGER LAWSON, who had first married ANN FERGUSON in AMELIA COUNTY, Virginia.

GEORGE EWING, who married CATHERINE LAWSON, daughter of HUGH LAWSON and his wife MARY MOORE, was the son of SAMUEL EWING, one of the half-brothers of NATHANIEL EWING, who settled in AMELIA, afterwards PRINCE EDWARD COUNTY, VIRGINIA. The names of all of the children of SAMUEL EWING, the first, are to be found in the notes on next to the preceding page. GEORGE EWING (the son of SAMUEL) had the following children:

1. SAMUEL EWING m. MARY DANIEL in 1773.
2. HUGH EWING
3. ELEANOR EWING m. JOHN DAVIDSON in 1775.
4. GEORGE EWING JR.
5. ELIZABETH EWING m. WILLIAM DAVIDSON.

To further enhance the interest in these family connections, the records show that JOHN THOMSON, son of REV. JOHN THOMSON married MARGARET DAVIDSON, and SAMUEL CALDWELL married SARAH CUNNINGHAM (Dau. of JAMES CUNNINGHAM and ANN THOMSON) grand-daughter of REV. JOHN THOMSON. MARGARET DAVIDSON who married JOHN THOMSON was a daughter of WILLIAM DAVIDSON and a first cousin of GEN. WILLIAM LEE DAVIDSON, of Mecklenburg County, North Carolina. ALEXANDER EWING, brother of the GEORGE EWING who married CATHERINE LAWSON moved to and settled in BOTETOURT COUNTY, then a part of AUGUSTA where TWO MATTHEW WILSONS left families and wills, and JAMES EWING, the emigrant, uncle of GEORGE and ALEXANDER, had preceded him there many years where he died and is buried in the same graveyard with COL. JOHN WILSON, previously mentioned.

GEORGE EWING, HUGH BARRY and JAMES HENDERSON, all sons in laws of HUGH LAWSON moved to what is now LINCOLN COUNTY, North Carolina, and settled on the South Fork of the Catawba River; or more strictly speaking the particular neighborhood may have been in GASTON COUNTY. GEORGE EWING and his son HUGH EWING were both revolutionary soldiers, and fought at the battle of KING'S MOUNTAIN, as did ANDREW BARRY, the son of HUGH BARRY and grandson of COL. HUGH LAWSON. (Puett's History of Gaston County, N. C.)

NOTE: What the compiler is setting down in the above notes is real HISTORY, which to his certain knowledge has never before been committed to the public prints. It is positively thrilling to have been able to work out here problems of family relationships that for 150 years have been in total obscurity. The reader, it is hoped, will appreciate the temerity with which such material is thus presented.

More than 100 years ago, a distinguished planter, whose domain is said to have extended for some ten miles along the country road near the famous Broad River settlement, bearing the name of SAMUEL EWING DANIEL, lived and flourished, died and left his broad acres to a numerous progeny who claim Virginia descent. This writer has visited with his great grand-children, who were asked about the origin of his name SAMUEL EWING, and which they have always been unable to explain. They had never heard, of course, what became of his grandfather's sister, MARY DANIEL, of VIRGINIA, who was the own aunt of CUNNINGHAM DANIEL, son of JAMES DANIEL and ELIZABETH CUNNINGHAM of Prince Edward County, Virginia, and which ELIZABETH CUNNINGHAM (grandmother of SAMUEL EWING DANIEL) was a grand-daughter of our old V.D.M. REV. JOHN THOMSON, who died in North Carolina. In delving into the History of the EWING FAMILY, the records on which these notes are based came very readily to light.

The mother of SAMUEL EWING DANIEL was JANE COFFEE, who married CUNNINGHAM DANIEL. This JANE COFFEE was the daughter of a certain PETER COFFEE, from Prince Edward County, Virginia, who followed the DANIEL and CUNNINGHAM FAMILY to GREENE and OGLETHORPE COUNTY, Georgia, after the opening up of lands for revolutionary soldiers along Broad River. PETER COFFEE, the father of JANE, who married CUNNINGHAM DANIEL, was the son of another PETER COFFEE, who is mentioned in the will of JAMES DANIEL, grandfather of CUNNINGHAM DANIEL, which provides among other things that "I give and bequeath to my son JAMES DANIEL, 400 acres of land (on which) JAMMY BARROT liveth, joining PETER COFFEE". Thus a descendant of an old neighbor in VIRGINIA, became the wife of the descendant of another old neighbor, a custom so often followed that it became practically a RULE OF CONDUCT.

HUGH EWING, son of GEORGE EWING and his wife CATHERINE LAWSON, is mentioned in the Colonial Records of North Carolina as being a road overseer, as serving in the revolution during the last year of the War and participating in the battle of King's Mountain, and as receiving pay for his military services. He married and raised a family of three sons and three daughters:

1. SAMUEL EWING
2. ROBERT EWING
3. HUGH EWING
4. MARGARET EWING married a man named SINGLES.
5. SALLIE EWING m. JAMES ALLISON.
6. MARY EWING married a DAVIS.

The following is copied from the HISTORY OF GASTON COUNTY (N. C.) written by MRS. MINNIE STOWE PUETT, of Gastonia:

On the hills and bluffs overlooking the CATAWBA and SOUTH FORK RIVERS, many places of unparalleled scenic beauty were the homes of the Gaston County pioneers * * one such settlement was that of the EWINGS on a hillside near the present location of the STOWE Thread Mill of BELMONT. The Spring from which the family used water was in the creek bottom near by. HUGH EWING, a son of the pioneer GEORGE EWING, was a revolutionary soldier, who, though only seventeen or eighteen years of age, took part in the battle of KING'S MOUNTAIN. After the battle HUGH EWING and ANDREW BARRY, brought home ROBERT HENRY, a youthful companion, who was badly wounded.
(ROBERT HENRY was afterwards a distinguished surveyor, teacher and pioneer of BUNCOMBE COUNTY).

JAMES HENDERSON, who married VIOLET LAWSON, daughter of COL. HUGH LAWSON and sister of the wife of GEORGE EWING and also the wife of HUGH BARRY, along with possibly his own father and several brothers, came down from AUGUSTA COUNTY, VIRGINIA, and settled in that territory which was first a part of ANSON, later Mecklenburg and afterwards TRYON and finally LINCOLN and GASTON COUNTIES. He established a mill in the same neighborhood with the EWINGS, his relatives, and lived and died there. His grave is on top of the high bluff, opposite the old mill site, now the STOWE MILLS, and the little mill town of McADENVILLE. In the same burial plot, surrounded by a high stone wall, is buried some of the LITTLES, and ABEM SPRINGS (grandson of ADAM ALEXANDER) who bought the Henderson property from the heirs of JAMES HENDERSON after his death. This JAMES HENDERSON was the grandfather of JAMES PINCKNEY HENDERSON who became the first Governor of the great State of Texas after it ceased to be a Republic.

(At this point, in order that the reader may more fully understand the relationships between these several families, kinsmen of REV. JOHN THOMSON, the compiler believes that it is best to give a kind of outline of the history of the CALDWELL FAMILY)

ABOUT THE CALDWELL FAMILY - CUB CREEK, VA.

(THE FAMILY TRADITION: That the family is of BURCH ORIGIN (This I doubt); that after the restoration of CHARLES II, in England, DAVID CALDWELL and ANDREW CALDWELL, brothers, and their nephew, JOHN, a son of their brother JOHN came to AMERICA, landing in DELAWARE; that two other brothers, JOSEPH and DANIEL, remained in IRELAND, but their sons came to AMERICA and settled on JAMES RIVER, in Virginia. The nephew JOHN CALDWELL settled in what is now CHARLOTTE COUNTY, Virginia, after having married MARGARET PHILLIPS (in Ireland?), and was the ancestor of what is known as the CUB CREEK CALDWELLS, of the "Caldwell Settlement". There are many variants of this tradition, none of which agree, all seemingly coming from persons who should know, but THEY ALL can not possibly be true, because they contradict each other, as to dates, places, etc.).

These CALDWELLS of CUB CREEK (Virginia) according to pretty well established accounts, were for a short time domiciled in Pennsylvania, from whence they found their way South to the Valley of Virginia, and at one time it is believed were members of a Presbyterian Congregation of which REV. RICHARD SANKEY (who married SARAH THOMSON, daughter of REV. JOHN THOMSON) was the minister. Rev. JOHN THOMSON, on frequent visits to the Valley of Virginia, brought glowing accounts of the Roanoke River country back with him, since his daughter ESTHER and her husband had settled there by 1735, and JOHN CALDWELL and his wife and children and four brothers in law went to "spy out the land" and moved down there. Rev. Richard Sankey was also interested and moved down into the same general locality and took charge of the BUFFALO Congregation, in what became Prince Edward County. The Caldwells settled along CUB CREEK and its tributaries in what became CHARLOTTE COUNTY. The Caldwell contingent consisted of:

1. JOHN CALDWELL, his wife, MARGARET (Phillips),six sons and daughter MARGARET.
2. GEORGE (Or ALEXANDER) MOORE, and wife a sister of JOHN CALDWELL.
3. ALEXANDER RIGGIN and wife, a sister of JOHN CALDWELL.
4. RICHARD DUNSON and wife, a sister of JOHN CALDWELL.
5. THOMAS DOUGHERTY and his wife, (MISS PHILLIPS) sister of the wife of JOHN CALDWELL.

According to the various family accounts, JOHN CALDWELL and his wife MARGARET PHILLIPS had six sons and one daughter, as follows:

1. WILLIAM CALDWELL
2. THOMAS CALDWELL
3. DAVID CALDWELL
4. MARGARET CALDWELL
5. JOHN CALDWELL
6. ROBERT CALDWELL
7. JAMES CALDWELL   (b. 1734?)

The Christian names of the FOUR brothers in law of JOHN CALDWELL have been supplied by extraneous sources, as all four of them are left blank in the family accounts, but the writer is reasonably sure the names, as given are correct.

7. JAMES CALDWELL, in the family account, is said to have been born in 1734, and to have been the youngest of the seven children. In the light of discoveries made by this writer in working on this family, this statement is greatly in error, or else the framework of this family has been given wrong, because in 1749 both JAMES CALDWELL, SR. and JAMES CALDWELL, JR. appear on the Cub Creek tythe list of WILLIAM CALDWELL, and under the rules followed in those days even the "Jr" would have then been over 18 years of age and born by 1731 to be listed. And also for the same year and the year preceding, 1748, and afterwards, there were TWO WILLIAM CALDWELLS, and no THOMAS or ROBERT. These records make it very awkward to reconcile the family history, for one finds it hard to escape the conclusion that there were three brothers who first settled on CUB CREEK in the then LUNENBURG COUNTY, named JOHN, WILLIAM and JAMES, and that each of these brothers had a numerous family, the members of which have been badly "mixed up" with the descendants of the JOHN who appears to have "hogged" all the history of the family. But the compiler, to save time and space will, in this case, assume that the family accounts are approximately correct and will endeavor as far as possible to follow up the descendants as far as possible. JOHN, the principal head of the family died in OCTOBER, 1750.

1. WILLIAM CALDWELL, the oldest son, married MARGARET PARKS, and died in 1761 in Lunenburg County, on CUBB CREEK. After his death, his widow and children moved to South Carolina and settled in NEWBERRY DISTRICT.
2. THOMAS CALDWELL died on CUBB CREEK. He was alive March 25, 1763, when he and his wife ELIENER CALDWELL witnessed the last will and testament of JAMES DANIEL, of Prince Edward County, who lived in what was known as the BUFFALO SETTLEMENT. He afterwards died and is buried with his brothers WILLIAM and DAVID in the old CUB CREEK Churchyard.
3. DAVID CALDWELL died at some uncertain time contemporaneous with his brother THOMAS, and after his death his widow and children moved to KENTUCKY.
4. MARGARET CALDWELL was the only daughter and she married, probably by 1740, a man by the name of RODGERS (either WILLIAM or THOMAS RODGERS), by whom she had FIVE CHILDREN. Her first husband died in OCTOBER, 1750, within fourteen days of the death of her father JOHN CALDWELL; she then married JAMES MITCHELL, by whom she also had five children. She lost three daughters (probably by the first marriage) in Virginia, and then she and her family removed to KENTUCKY. Her son ROBERT RODGERS died in KENTUCKY.
5. JOHN CALDWELL married MARGARET EWING, the daughter of SAMUEL EWING, who died in 1758, leaving a will in which his daughter and grandson SAMUEL EWING CALDWELL is mentioned. He moved down into MECKLENBURG, first, and settled West of the CATAWBA RIVER in what is now either LINCOLN or GASTON County (near the line), where he raised a numerous family, his son SAMUEL having fought at KING'S MOUNTAIN.
6. ROBERT CALDWELL. He died in MERCER COUNTY, Kentucky, it is said in 1806. He moved first to MECKLENBURG COUNTY, North Carolina, with his brother JOHN, but about 1787, moved to Kentucky. He is known to have been the father of JOHN CALDWELL, SAMUEL CALDWELL, ROBERT CALDWELL and MARY CALDWELL who became the wife of DR. B. C. PALMER. The son John Caldwell died while holding the office of Lieutenant Governor; the son SAMUEL, who married the daughter of REV. HEZEKIAH JAMES BALCH - one of the signers - in MECKLENBURG COUNTY, N. C., was a Major General in the war of 1812, and was the first Clerk of LOGAN COUNTY, KENTUCKY, at Russellville. He and his wife ANN BALCH had nine children.
7. JAMES CALDWELL (b. 1734) married HANNAH OGDEN. He graduated at PRINCETON in 1759, and after his marriage settled in ELIZABETHTOWN, N. J. where he was pastor of the Church. Both he and his wife were victims of malicious sharp shooters during the revolution. They had eight children, among them being HON. ELIAS BOUDINOT CALDWELL, who for 25 years served as Clerk of the Supreme Court of the United States in Washington, D. C. Another son, JOHN EDWARDS CALDWELL became a protege of GEN. LaFAYETTE and was educated in France. At the time of the death of REV. JAMES CALDWELL his children, all minors, were placed around his bier in the Church at Elizabethtown, by their father's friend, COL. ELIAS BOUDINOT, who delivered an eloquent and impassioned funeral oration on that occasion. A daughter HETTIE CALDWELL married REV. ROBERT FINLEY, who was later President of FRANKLIN COLLEGE, in GEORGIA.

A LIST OF THE GRANDCHILDREN OF JOHN CALDWELL AND HIS WIFE MARGARET
PHILLIPS - SO FAR AS CAN BE ASCERTAINED

1. WILLIAM CALDWELL (d. 1761) m. MARGARET PARKS: had:

100. MAJ. JOHN CALDWELL
101. WILLIAM CALDWELL
102. JAMES CALDWELL
103. DAVID CALDWELL
104. MARGARET CALDWELL
105. MARTHA CALDWELL
106. ELEANOR CALDWELL
107. ELIZABETH CALDWELL
108. REBECCA CALDWELL
109. SARAH CALDWELL

(Widow and above children all settled in NEWBERRY DISTRICT in South Carolina.)

6. ROBERT CALDWELL (Name of his wife unknown) He first went to MECKLENBURG COUNTY where one of his sons married a daughter of REV. HEZEKIAH JAMES BALCH. Afterwards he moved to MERCER COUNTY, KENTUCKY where he is supposed to have died in 1806.
Four children known:

114. JOHN CALDWELL
115. SAMUEL CALDWELL
116. ROBERT CALDWELL
117. MARY CALDWELL

(There were probably others whose names have not been found by the compiler.)

2. THOMAS CALDWELL (d. after 1763) m. ELLENER.........

(Buried on CUBB Creek in Va.)
(Names of children unknown..)

3. DAVID CALDWELL (d. after 1776) at which time he signed DISSENTERS PETITION)

(Name of his wife unknown and names of children also. Widow and children went to KENTUCKY)

4. MARGARET CALDWELL married (1) RODGERS (2) a JAMES MITCHELL (5 children by each marriage.) First husband, RODGERS, died 1750. She must have married ca. 1740 and born ca. 1721-2.

(Moved with her second husband and children to KENTUCKY)

7. REV. JAMES CALDWELL married HANNAH OGDEN He was a graduate of PRINCETON.
had children:

118. MARGARET CALDWELL m. MR. CAUFIELD, of New Jersey.
119. JAMES CALDWELL, JR. settled in East Jersey.
120. JOHN EDWARDS CALDWELL. Taken to France and educated by General LaFayette. Died in New York.
121. HETTIE CALDWELL married REV. ROBERT FINLEY (to Georgia).
122. SARAH CALDWELL m. REV. NOEL, of New Jersey.
123. HANNAH CALDWELL m. JAMES R. SMITH, merchant of New York.
124. ELIAS BOUDINOT CALDWELL, Clerk of U. S. Supreme Court.
125. JOSIAH F. CALDWELL, of WASHINGTON, D. C.

5. JOHN CALDWELL married ELENER EWING, daughter of SAMUEL EWING, who died in Va. 1758.
Had children:

110. ROBERT CALDWELL.
111. WILLIAM CALDWELL
112. JOHN CALDWELL
113. SAMUEL CALDWELL

He probably married by 1745 at least, as his sister MARGARET married and had FIVE children by 1750.

(JOHN CALDWELL moved to what is now LINCOLN or GASTON COUNTY, North Carolina, and it is known that WILLIAM and SAMUEL were Revolutionary soldiers at KING'S MOUNTAIN) ORIGINALLY settled in MECKLENBURG COUNTY territory.

---

100. MAJ. JOHN CALDWELL (Son of William Caldwell and Margaret Parks) married but had no children. He was killed during the revolution in South Carolina by "Bloody Bill" Cunningham.

101. WILLIAM CALDWELL was a revolutionary soldier in South Carolina and belonged to the Company of his brother, then CAPT. JOHN CALDWELL. He married a MISS WILLIAMS, daughter of MAJOR JOHN WILLIAMS, and was the father of ten children, five of whom survived him. They were JOHN, WILLIAMS, JAMES, PATRICK C. and ELIZABETH.

102. JAMES CALDWELL was born July 8, 1755. He took a prominent part in the revolution in South Carolina. He married a MISS FORREST, by whom he had ten children. We can't give their names. In 1807 he was elected SHERIFF of NEWBERRY DISTRICT, S. C. He died in 1813. He served one term in the Legislature. "Uncle Jimmie" Caldwell as he was called had a badly disfigured face, due to sabre wounds received during the revolution. One son was GEORGE CALHOUN CALDWELL.

103. DAVID CALDWELL. He was a mere boy in the revolution and was so deaf as to be, in a great degree, incapacitated for the active duties of life. However, he lived to be an old man, moved to ABBEVILLE DISTRICT and later to GEORGIA, where he lived with two of his sons. He had four sons, JOHN ELLIOTT, JOSEPH, ANDREW (died a bachelor in Wilkes County, Ga.) and MEREDITH CALDWELL. JOHN ELLIOTT CALDWELL married ELIZABETH GARDNER and had THOMAS, MILTON PASCHAL, FRANKLIN, JOHN CALHOUN, HENRY LEE, ANDREW HAMILTON, MIRIAM, ELIZABETH, MARTHA and LOUIS FRANCES CALDWELL.

104. MARGARET CALDWELL married JOHN RITCHIE, a grandson of ALEXANDER RITCHIE, whose wife was her father's aunt.

105. MARTHA CALDWELL became the second wife of PATRICK CALHOUN, whose first wife had been the daughter of REV. ALEXANDER CRAIGHEAD, and sister of the wife of REV. DAVID CALDWELL, the famous North Carolina minister and teacher. She was the mother of JOHN C. CALHOUN, the statesman.

106. ELEANOR CALDWELL married JOHN MOORE.
108. REBECCA CALDWELL became the wife of JOSIAH EAST.
109. SARAH CALDWELL married a DR. MARTIN.
107. ELIZABETH CALDWELL became the wife of ROBERT GILLIAM (*)

(*) ROBERT GILLIAM who married ELIZABETH CALDWELL, daughter of WILLIAM CALDWELL and his wife MARGARET PARKS, of CHARLOTTE COUNTY, VIRGINIA, through his mother, was a great grandson of REV. JOHN THOMSON, who died in Mecklenburg County, North Carolina in the year 1753.

SARAH THOMSON MARRIED REV. RICHARD SANKEY

SARAH THOMSON, daughter of REV. JOHN THOMSON was born about 1718-19, probably in LEWES, DELAWARE, where her father was pastor of the Presbyterian Church at that time. When Rev. John Thomson severed his connection with the Church at LEWES about the beginning of 1730, he spent several years at various points in MARYLAND and PENNSYLVANIA doing work for his Church, and in the mean-time making freqent visits and "tours" throughout VIRGINIA, sometimes visiting relatives and friends and always looking after the interest of his religious duties as a minister. During this period he had moved his family along with him, and while they were sojourning in Pennsylvania his daughter SARAH met and married a young Minister named RICHARD SANKEY. This RICHARD SANKEY, like her father, though of a later period, was a student of the University of Glasgow, Scotland. The name was sometimes spelled "SINQUE". Richard Sankey and SARAH THOMSON were married probably about 1735-6. Just how many children were born to this marriage is problematical. So far only a half dozen children have been certainly identified, as follows:

1. JOHN THOMSON SANKEY m. ANNE THOMSON DANIEL.
2. SARAH SANKEY m. WILLIAM HAMMERSLEY
3. MARY SANKEY who m. ARCHIBALD SIMPSON.
4. ELIZABETH SANKEY m. JAMES PARKS, JR.
5. ESTHER SANKEY m. JOSEPH PARKS
6. .... SANKEY m. ROBERT GILLIAM.

We shall not tire the reader by extending a table or chart of all of the long line of children and grand-children of these off-spring of SARAH THOMSON and REV. RICHARD SANKEY, who were all grand-children of REV. JOHN THOMSON. Just a few brief notes will be sufficient to show connecting links of this with other families mentioned in these notes. DR. JOHN THOMSON SANKEY of WILKES and GREENE COUNTY, GEORGIA, named a son WILLIAM DANIEL SANKEY, and he in turn, married a daughter of WILLIAM DANIEL, who was herself a great-grand-daughter of REV. JOHN THOMSON.

ESTHER SANKEY who married JOSEPH PARKS SR. was the mother of BETSY ANN PARKS who became the wife of REV. ROBERT MOORE CUNNINGHAM, whose first wife had been ELIZABETH MOORE, the daughter of PROF. CHARLES MOORE, of Mecklenburg County, N. C. and SPARTANBURG DISTRICT, South Carolina, a sister of the wife of ANDREW BARRY, brother of RICHARD BARRY, one of the "Signers". Rev. Robert Moore Cunningham was the son of ROGER CUNNINGHAM who is buried at PROVIDENCE CHURCH, in Mecklenburg County.

ELIZABETH SANKEY who married JAMES PARKS JR. was the ancestress of HON. CLARK HOWELL, of the ATLANTA CONSTITUTION, now deceased, and of JUDGE JAMES BILLINGSLEA PARKS, of the OCONEE Judicial Circuit of Greensboro, Georgia.

ARCHIBALD SIMPSON married MARY SANKEY as his second wife, his first marriage being to KITTIE NELSON. This writer has been unable to establish with certainty the parentage of this son in law of REV. RICHARD SANKEY, but he is constrained to believe that here was a son of that venerable and distinguished minister of the Presbyterian Church who spent some forty years, more or less in the Province of South Carolina, married a MISS MUIR in Scotland and had a number of children whose names are not mentioned. He, like REV. JOHN THOMSON and REV. RICHARD SANKEY was educated at the University of Glasgow, and in his old age returned to Scotland, where he died. The following is taken from BOWEN'S HISTORY of WILKES COUNTY, Georgia:

> The HOPEWELL PRESBYTERY met in 1797 in the Old LIBERTY CHURCH in Wilkes County Georgia. Present were Revs. Messrs. SPRINGER, WADDELL, NEWTON, CUNNINGHAM, (Rev. Robert Moore Cunningham) and MONTGOMERY; elders JAMES DANIEL, of Liberty, EZEKIEL GILLIAM of BETHSALEM and LUDWICK TUGGLE, first elder of Bethany.
>
> Old LIBERTY CHURCH was nearly nine miles southwest of WASHINGTON (Wilkes County). There is a burying ground on the other side of the road. There are no inscribed tombstones, but frequent head stones and foot stones. Here lies buried JAMES DANIEL (revolutionary soldier) and his wife; ARCHIBALD SIMPSON and KITTY NELSON (who rode on horseback from Virginia) & also MARY SANKEY, whom ARCHIBALD SIMPSON married when KITTY NELSON died.

Both JAMES DANIEL'S wife (ELIZABETH CUNNINGHAM) and MARY SANKEY, wife of ARCHIBALD SIMPSON, were grand-daughters of REV. JOHN THOMSON. EZEKIEL GILLIAM of Bethsalem (later LEXINGTON) was a relative of ROBERT GILLIAM, who married a sister of MARY SANKEY.

THE GILIAM FAMILY

MAJOR ROBERT GILLIAM, of Newberry District, South Carolina, who married .....SANKEY, daughter of REV. RICHARD SANKEY, of the Buffalo Settlement in PRINCE EDWARD COUNTY, Virginia, was the father of ROBERT GILLIAM who married ELIZABETH CALDWELL, daughter of WILLIAM CALDWELL and his wife MARGARET PARKS.

The father of MAJ. ROBERT GILLIAM was JOHN GILLIAM, whose wife was LUCY HENRY, Daughter of REV. PATRICK HENRY, uncle of the orator of the revolution, and friend of REV. JOHN THOMSON, who wrote the friendly appraisal of REV. THOMSON to REV. WILLIAM DAWSON in 1744, which has been previously mentioned, when the subject of these notes had been invited to the HENRY HOME.

Who were these GILLIAMS?   That is a large order.

After much and prolonged research the writer has concluded there were two parent stems of the GILLIAM FAMILY in early colonial Virginia, headed by a WILLIAM DEVEREAUX GILLIAM and a JOHN GILLIAM, branded by tradition only, as brothers.

JOHN GILLIAM died leaving a will in NORFOLK COUNTY in 1651, in which he mentions his "oldest son" JOHN GILLIAM and a brother in law ROGER FONTAINE. This implies other children.

WILLIAM GILLIAM (possibly William Devereaux Gilliam) by tradition only was the father of a RICHARD GILLIAM, of NEW KENT COUNTY (close by YORK and CHARLES CITY COUNTY, in both of which the name GILLIAM infrequently is to be found on the records), whose wife was MARGARET and to whom was born numerous children.

Thus there were two sets of GILLIAMS, the JOHN GILLIAM set we call No. 1, and the WILLIAM GILLIAM set No. 2. There are times when the evidence indicates there was really only one set, but other items compel the assumption that there were two. In as few lines as possible (for us) we will endeavor to describe them and differentiate between them, a difficulty that is greatly enhanced by the fact that they migrated together to different sections and were so intermingled as to make the identification almost impossible.

JOHN GILLIAM (Set No. 1) had a son JOHN who evidently married a MARGARET HENSHAW and left sons JOHN, HENSHAW (HINSHAN) and ELIZABETH. This second JOHN was granted land in 1683 in BRISTOL PARISH. Ten years later he had deserted the land and it was patented to HENRY RANDOLPH (Book 6 Virginia Land Office). Nearly a hundred years later (June 17, 1769) a later HENRY RANDOLPH in his will made MAJ. PETER POYTHRESS and JOHN GILLIAM SR. and JOHN GILLIAM JR. his executors. In that long interim a marriage had taken place between the GILLIAMS and the POYTHRESS family. Among the ancient members of this POYTHRESS family were PETER and JOSHUA POYTHRESS. Thereafter the names PETER and JOSHUA appear in this particular branch of the GILLIAM FAMILY, and for that reason this writer has dubbed the No. 1 GILLIAMS as the "POYTHRESS GILLIAMS". Dr. Phil Slaughter in his "BRISTOL PARISH" register is authority for the statement that WILLIAM GILLIAM married a POYTHRESS. ROBERT GILLIAM, who married MISS ....SANKEY, daughter of REV. RICHARD SANKEY, was a POYTHRESS GILLIAM. These POYTHRESS GILLIAMS are to be found on the records of PRINCE GEORGE, SUSSEX, LUNENBURG, ALBEMARLE, and HANOVER COUNTY, VIRGINIA, and GRANVILLE COUNTY, North Carolina, during the eighteenth century.

HINSHAW GILLIAM, CHARLES GILLIAM and JOHN GILLIAM each patented lands along the NOTTOWAY RIVER in SUSSEX COUNTY, Virginia, in 1714, 1715 and 1723. THOMAS POYTHRESS and HENRY, THOMAS and NATHANIEL HARRISON patented lands in the same exact localities approximately at the same time, as did WILLIAM GLOVER. The patent to THOMAS POYTHRESS and CHARLES GILLIAM were both issued on the same day and year, with practically the same description, March 23, 1715.

JOHN GLOVER, in 1757, sold land on the waters of NUTBUSH CREEK in GRANVILLE COUNTY, North Carolina, on what was afterwards known as GILLIAM'S CREEK, to JOHN GILLIAM, "of Lunenburg County, Va." In the year 1769 ROBERT GILLIAM (the then son in law of REV. RICHARD SANKEY) sold to EDMUND TAYLOR a tract of 1230 acres of land in GRANVILLE COUNTY, North Carolina, located on GILLIAM'S BRANCH near the Virginia line.

On page 327 of the Cumberland Parish Register (Lunenburg County, Virginia, at a meeting of the Vestry on September 8, 1747 it was ordered: "That to the County line be one precinct and that JAMES MITCHELL and JOHN GILLIAM be the processioners of same"; also that JOHN CARGILL and SAMUEL HARRIS be appointed processioners.

The JOHN GILLIAM above mentioned was the father of ROBERT GILLIAM, and JAMES MITCHELL married MARGARET CALDWELL, the aunt of ELIZABETH CALDWELL, who married ROBERT GILLIAM JR. in Newberry District, S. C. Also JANE THOMSON, daughter of JOHN THOMSON JR. (Son of Rev. John) married a MITCHELL and had a son named JAMES MITCHELL. Note should be made of the fact also that ANNE GILLIAM, a sister of JOHN and an aunt of ROBERT married NATHANIEL HARRISON (See patent in Sussex), and ELIZABETH HARRISON a cousin of NATHANIEL was the wife of JOHN CARGILL. On the tythe list of Lunenburg County, Virginia, in 1752, taken by FIELD JEFFERSON, the names of JOHN GILLIAM with a son ROBERT appears.

On the tythe list of PRINCE EDWARD COUNTY, Virginia, for 1755, appears the names of CHARLES GILLIAM and JOSHUA GILLIAM.

WILLIAM GILLIAM, a brother of MAJ. ROBERT GILLIAM, who married MISS SANKEY, died sometime prior to May 10, 1791, and either lived in or owned property subject to the management of his executors in HANOVER COUNTY, VIRGINIA. His sons JOHN, PETER and WILLIAM GILLIAM were the executors of the estate. The administration or winding up of this estate was not completed or finally distributed until 1799, when most of the heirs had removed from Virginia to GEORGIA and TENNESSEE. It is shown on the records of WILKES COUNTY, GEORGIA. The wife of WILLIAM GILLIAM was MARY JARRETT, and their children were:

1. SARAH GILLIAM m. MICAJAH WILLIAMSON
2. DEVEREAUX GILLIAM m. EDITH ELLIS
3. PETER GILLIAM m. ANNE or NANEY HEARD
4. CHARLES GILLIAM
5. JOHN GILLIAM
6. JARRETT GILLIAM m. THEODOSIA DAVIS
7. JOYCE GILLIAM m. JOHN HOOD
8. THOMAS GILLIAM m. WINNIFRED
9. WILLIAM GILLIAM m. ELIZABETH ELLIS.

JOHN GILLIAM and his wife LUCY HENRY (Daughter of REV. PATRICK HENRY) had a number of children, all of whom have not been certainly identified by the compiler, but the following list is believed to include at least part of them:

1. WILLIAM GILLIAM m. MARY JARRETT
2. ROBERT GILLIAM m. MISS SANKEY
3. CHARLES GILLIAM m. FRANCES
4. JOSHUA GILLIAM
5. PETER GILLIAM
6. JOHN GILLIAM

A list of the children of WILLIAM GILLIAM and his wife MARY JARRETT is given on the page just preceding. MARY JARRETT was the daughter of DEVEREAUX JARRETT, and a FIRST COUSIN of REV. DEVEREAUX JARRETT. Their oldest daughter, SARAH GILLIAM became the wife of MICAJAH WILLIAMSON, the famous Georgia revolutionary soldier, who was the grandfather of ROBERT McAlPIN WILLIAMSON, who was an early Texas patriot, known as "Three Legged Willie", and who was called "The Patrick Henry of Texas", and whose Great Great grandmother was in fact the daughter of the elder PATRICK HENRY.

2. MAJ. ROBERT GILLIAM and his wife MISS SANKEY were the parents of at least three children, though accounts of MAJ. ROBERT GILLIAM'S family indicate that he had a number of others. The three thus referred to were:

1. WILLIAM GILLIAM (will proved 1804)
2. ROBERT GILLIAM, JR. (Revolutionary soldier).
3. SUSAN GILLIAM m. her cousin .... FINLEY.

WILLIAM GILLIAM who died leaving a will in GRANVILLE COUNTY, N. C. in 1804, married ELIZABETH and in his will mentioned the following children:

1. WILLIAM H. GILLIAM
2. LESLIE GILLIAM (m. ELIZABETH BALLARD in 1801)
3. AMY GILLIAM m. ISHAM HARRISON in 1783.
4. PRISCILLA GILLIAM m. JAMES HARRIS in 1783.
5. ELIZABETH GILLIAM m. RANSOM HARRIS in 1785.
6. DOLLY GILLIAM m. WILLIAM KING in 1790.
7. DELILAH GILLIAM m. a THORNE.
8. LUNDY GILLIAM m. WILLIAM SIMS in 1800.

ROBERT GILLIAM JR. moved with his father to NEWBERRY DISTRICT, S. C. where both son and father, took a prominent part in the revolution as a soldier. He was born in GRANVILLE COUNTY, North Carolina on January 11, 1760. In October, 1781 he and his father both narrowly escaped the wrath and bloody sword of the notorious "Bloody Bill" Cunningham.
This ROBERT GILLIAM JR., following the revolution married ELIZABETH CALDWELL, daughter of WILLIAM CALDWELL, who had removed with her brothers, sisters and her mother to South Carolina, after the death of her father in Charlotte County (Cubb Creek), Virginia. They had two sons and four daughters. They lived on what is known as PAGE'S CREEK, in Newberry District. The two sons were:

1. WILLIAM GILLIAM.
2. GEN. JAMES GILLIAM

CHARLES and JOSHUA GILLIAM were living in PRINCE EDWARD COUNTY, VIRGINIA, in the year 1755, and the name of JOSHUA GILLIAM thereafter appears on the records of South Carolina. CHARLES GILLIAM moved over into GRANVILLE COUNTY, North Carolina, where he joined some of his kinsmen. His last will and testament was recorded there in 1780, and in it he mentions his wife FRANCES and the following other legatees:

11. ELIZABETH GILLIAM m. ATWOOD.
2. MARTHA GILLIAM m. JOHN MITCHELL

Grand-daughters:
ANN MITCHELL,
PATSY GILLIAM GLOVER.
FRANCES MITCHELL
FRANCES ATWOOD

Grand-sons:
CHARLES, JOSHUA and JAMES MITCHELL
(Sons of JOHN MITCHELL and daughter MARTHA GILLIAM).

(In the year 1763 in GRANVILLE COUNTY, N. C., JOHN GILLIAM deeded certain lands in that county to DAVID MITCHELL. JANE THOMSON (Daughter of JOHN THOMSON, JR.) married a MITCHELL and had a son JAMES MITCHELL)

WILLIAM GILLIAM had a son: RICHARD GILLIAM, of NEW KENT COUNTY (Set No. 2), married into the LAWSON FAMILY, by which is meant the old Eastern Virginia LAWSONS, who were distant cousins of COL. HUGH LAWSON. The wife of RICHARD GILLIAM, in New Kent County, Virginia, BEFORE 1687, was MARGARET LAWSON. The births and baptisms of SIX of their children are recorded in the old ST. PETERS PARISH REGISTER, as follows:

1. JOHN GILLIAM bapt. Aug. 25, 1687.
2. ELIZABETH GILLIAM bapt. October 5, 1790.
3. WILLIAM GILLIAM March 26, 1699.
4. MARGARET GILLIAM Bapt. Nov. 2, 1701.
5. RICHARD GILLIAM bapt. April 1, 1705.
6. EPAPRODITUS GILLIAM ....1707(?)

1. JOHN GILLIAM (Baptised Aug. 26, 1687). I have concluded, from all the records in regard to him that he had the following children:

    100. JAMES GILLIAM
    101. AGNES GILLIAM
    102. JOHN GILLIAM
    103. MARGARET GILLIAM
    104. ELIZABETH GILLIAM
    105. SARAH GILLIAM

The first child of the above JOHN GILLIAM having been born in 1711 and the last named in 1728, it is probable that he was twice married. His last wife was MARTHA on the old Register.

3. WILLIAM GILLIAM (born March 26, 1699) is believed to have married AGNES HARRIS, who was probably a daughter of either EDWARD or JOHN HARRIS of New Kent County. The ELIZABETH GILLIAM wife of a WILLIAM GILLIAM who died in 1723, may have been a first wife. This WILLIAM GILLIAM lived in LUNENBURG COUNTY (Cumberland Parish Records) VIRGINIA, for many years, but moved to and died in GRANVILLE COUNTY, N. C., where he left a last will and testament in 1778, in which he mentions his wife AGNES and his children. He had the following children:

    106. RICHARD GILLIAM
    107. HARRIS GILLIAM m. a JORDAN.
    108. WILLIAM GILLIAM
    109. WINNIFRED GILLIAM m. CHRISTOPHER ROBERTSON.
    110. AGNES GILLIAM
    111. AMEY GILLIAM.

4. EPAPRODITUS GILLIAM (b. in 1707(?) -) married, but we have been unable to locate the name of his wife, or any of his children, except:

    112. EPAPRODITUS GILLIAM.

112. EPAPRODITUS GILLIAM (Son of EPAPRODITUS). According to some of his direct descendants, the name of his wife was ELIZABETH - last name unknown. Based on all available records he appears to have been the father of THREE SONS:

    113. JOHN GILLIAM m. JUDITH ROBERTSON
    114. RICHARD GILLIAM m. ELIZABETH GLOVER
    115. WILLIAM GILLIAM (d. Sept. 16, 1800).

(NOTE: It has already been shown in these notes how MAJ. ROBERT GILLIAM, of "Set No. 1" of the GILLIAM FAMILY married a grand-daughter of REV. JOHN THOMSON, our subject. Below we attempt now to show how the descendants of "Set No. 2" also married into the descendants and family of REV. JOHN THOMSON.)

113. JOHN GILLIAM married JUDITH ROBERTSON, and became the father of at least two children:

    200. JOHN ROBERTSON GILLIAM m. MARGARET CALHOUN.
    201. MARGARET GILLIAM m. WILLIAM DANIEL MATTHEWS.

MARGARET CALHOUN, who married JOHN R. GILLIAM, was the daughter of JANE DANIEL who married ADAM CALHOUN, JR. JANE DANIEL was the daughter of JOHN DANIEL and his wife SARAH CUNNINGHAM, and the mother of SARAH CUNNINGHAM was ANNE THOMSON, daughter of REV. JOHN THOMSON.

WILLIAM DANIEL MATTHEWS, who married MARGARET GILLIAM, was the son of FRANCES DANIEL who married WILLIAM MATTHEWS, and the mother of FRANCES DANIEL was also SARAH CUNNINGHAM, whose mother was ANNE, the daughter of REV. JOHN THOMSON.

ADAM CALHOUN, who married JANE DANIEL, grand-daughter of REV. JOHN THOMSON, and his brother JAMES CALHOUN, of LUNENBURG and PRINCE EDWARD COUNTY, VIRGINIA, were cousins of the famous PATRICK CALHOUN, of South Carolina, who married MARTHA CALDWELL, sister of ELIZABETH CALDWELL, who became the wife of ROBERT GILLIAM JR., revolutionary soldier.

114. RICHARD GILLIAM married in 1798 ELIZABETH GLOVER, and from his old family BIBLE, which contains the names of all his children, we find he had a son RICHARD HOLLAND GILLIAM, who married MARY VIRGINIA HOLMAN; they had a son WILLIAM EDWARD GILLIAM who married his cousin MARGARET DANIEL MATTHEWS daughter of MARGARET GILLIAM and WILLIAM DANIEL MATTHEWS, the latter being also a descendant of REV. JOHN THOMSON. WILLIAM EDWARD GILLIAM was the father of EDWARD HOLLAND GILLIAM and his wife LUCY ELCAN who was a prominent business man in CHARLOTTE, North Carolina, until he met an untimely accidental death shortly before the PEARL HARBOR CONFLICT, which has just ended. Their daughter, MRS. MARGARET (GILLIAM) SHROCK still resides in Charlotte, MECKLENBURG COUNTY, and is thus a descendant of REV. JOHN THOMSON, who is buried at BAKER'S GRAVEYARD on the Catawba River "out the Beattie's Ford Road".

To the reader it may appear as a singular fact that EPAPRODITUS GILLIAM, according to this record was a descendant of the emigrant EPAPRODITUS LAWSON (which he was) and that his GILLIAM descendants married into the family of REV. JOHN THOMSON, one of whose sons and one of whose daughters married children of COL. HUGH LAWSON. To the compiler this is not singular, but a mere natural result of the social rules that prevailed during the seventeenth and eighteenth centuries among the old families of the early colonies, particularly VIRGINIA, i. e. that kinfolks should intermarry with their own cousins and their own kin. The fact that it happened in this instance verifies the rule.

MICAJAH WILLIAMSON married SARAH GILLIAM. (See fourth page back of this at bottom of the page.) SARAH GILLIAM was the daughter of WILLIAM GILLIAM and his wife MARY JARRETT, and the grand-daughter of JOHN GILLIAM and his wife LUCY HENRY. MICAJAH WILLIAMSON and SARAH GILLIAM were cousins. This relationship requires explanation and somewhat of the

WILLIAMSON FAMILY

The WILLIAMSON FAMILY of VIRGINIA, according to LANDON C. BELL in his "OLD FREE STATE" ❧ p. 375 ❧ are descendants of SIR JOSEPH WILLIAMSON, KNIGHT, the son of an English clergyman. This Sir Joseph Williamson was born in 1630, and purchased the large estate of the Duke of Richmond, in KENT, ENGLAND, with its magnificent seat COBHAM HALL. He married CATHERINE O'BRIEN STEWART, and was once Secretary of State. In the will of NATHANIEL WEST, Citizen and Mercer of London, proved September 8, 1630, he mentions cousins GEORGE, ELIZABETH, RICHARD and WILLIAM WILLIAMSON, and an uncle and aunt THOMAS and ANN WILLIAMSON.

As the "cousin" RICHARD WILLIAMSON mentioned came to VIRGINIA and was old enough to be the father of SIR JOSEPH WILLIAMSON, Mr. Bell's deduction should be amended to show that the WIL-LIAMSONS of Virginia, instead of being descendants, were "of the same family" as Sir. Joseph Williamson, because they were here so early that they could not possibly have been his "descendants". This RICHARD WILLIAMSON was the ancestor of all of the Virginia family of the name, and he could have been an uncle of Sir Joseph, and in all probability was, because the WILLIAMSON HOME, in SURRY COUNTY, across the river from JAMESTOWN was named COBHAM HALL, after the Kentish seat of SIR JOSEPH.

RICHARD WILLIAMSON was in Virginia by 1640, in which year he witnessed a deed in ISLE OF WIGHT COUNTY to Capt. John Upton, and in 1646, six years later, as "RICHARD WILLIAMSON, SR." he also witnessed a deed by WILLIAM YARRETT, a well known Quaker, in the same county. By 1659 RICHARD WILLIAMSON was deceased and his widow had married JOHN JARRETT. He and his wife had the following children:

1. RICHARD WILLIAMSON
2. DR. JAMES WILLIAMSON
3. JOHN WILLIAMSON
4. DR. ROBERT WILLIAMSON
5. HENRY WILLIAMSON

As to 1. RICHARD WILLIAMSON, we have no definite information as to the date of his death or the name of his wife. After the death of his father as RICHARD WILLIAMSON "son and heir" of RICHARD WILLIAMSON, SR. he sold a large tract of land to one ARTHUR DAVIS.

2. DR. JAMES WILLIAMSON married ANN UNDERWOOD, the step daughter of CAPT. JOHN UPTON, and Capt. Upton in his will January 16, 1652 left to his daughter "ANN WILLIAMSON, wife of JAMES WILLIAMSON, an equal share of my lands at RAPPAHANNOCK". Thereafter Dr. James Williamson and his wife moved over on the Rappahannock, where he played important roles in the life of the early Virginia settlers, and whose wide influence extended across the Potomac into Maryland. He and his brother in law WILLIAM UNDERWOOD left innumerable descendants, as did his wife's sisters, the Underwood girls.

4. DR. ROBERT WILLIAMSON married JOAN ALLEN, the daughter of COL. ARTHUR ALLEN, of SURRY COUNTY, Virginia, who is credited with having erected the first brick mansion South of the James River, which is known in History as "Bacon's Castle" due to its connection with the famous Bacon's Rebellion, and which, we are told perhaps still stands. Dr. ROBERT WILLIAMSON died sometime during the year 1669, and by 1678 his widow had married ROBERT BURNETT. He made ROBERT WILLIAMSON, his oldest son his principal heir. The will of DR. ROBERT WILLIAMSON was witnessed by JOHN HARDY and the famous lawyer, WILLIAM SHERWOOD. (See notes on the Jarretts, which follow). JOHN HARDY's sister had married CHARLES JARRETT, a nephew of WILLIAM SHERWOOD. DR. ROBERT WILLIAMSON and his wife JOAN ALLEN were the parents of the following children:

100. ROBERT WILLIAMSON
101. GEORGE WILLIAMSON
102. ARTHUR WILLIAMSON
103. FRANCIS WILLIAMSON.

100. ROBERT WILLIAMSON died in 1688 without issue and his brothers and sisters divided his estate long afterwards, including lands that had been patented to him on BLACKWATER, two years previous to his death. At that time most of his brothers and sisters had moved to HENRICO COUNTY, with the DAVIS and other families with whom they were intermarried or related. So far as the compiler can ascertain Arthur and Francis Williamson may not have left descendants, but 101 GEORGE WILLIAMSON married ESTHER BRIDGER, daughter of COL. JOSEPH BRIDGER and his wife HESTER PITT, and left the following children, as shown by his will: (Dated in 1723).

200. GEORGE WILLIAMSON m. FRANCES DAVIS
201. ROBERT WILLIAMSON (Moved to HENRICO).
202. THOMAS WILLIAMSON m. OLIVE EXUM.
203. PATIENCE WILLIAMSON m. ROBERT EXUM.
204. ELIZABETH WILLIAMSON m. JOYNER.
205. JULIANA WILLIAMSON (never married).
206. ANNE WILLIAMSON m. JACOB DARDEN.
207. JOHN WILLIAMSON m. SUSANNAH LOWE.

207. JOHN WILLIAMSON, the grandson of DR. ROBERT WILLIAMSON and his wife SUSANNAH LOWE were married about 1735-6, and they were the parents of MICAJAH WILLIAMSON, who married SARAH GILLIAM about 1755, according to one descendant, who relies on a Bible record, and which appears to be about what it ought to be, with respect to dates. Having thus identified the parents of MICAJAH WILLIAMSON, it is now necessary to identify his wife, which will be accomplished in the account of:

THE JARRETT FAMILY

RICHARD WILLIAMSON (father of DR. ROBERT WILLIAMSON) died prior to 1662, and his wife MARGARET married JOHN JARRETT. MARGARET (WILLIAMSON) JARRETT had been MARGARET SHERWOOD, the sister of JUDGE WILLIAM SHERWOOD. By her first marriage to RICHARD WILLIAMSON she had four known sons, whose names have been heretofore given. By her marriage to JOHN JARRETT she had the following children:

1. ROBERT JARRETT m. MARY.
2. CHARLES JARRETT m. MARY HARDY.
3. JOHN JARRETT m. JOANNA LOWE.

JOANNA LOWE was a sister of MICAJAH LOWE and the daughter of MICHAEL LOWE. MICHAEL LOWE and his wife were the parents of four known children:

1. MICAJAH LOWE who married SARAH.
2. JOANNA LOWE m. JOHN JARRETT
3. MARY LOWE
4. SUSANNAH LOWE m. JOHN WILLIAMSON.

MICAJAH LOWE and his three sisters above were nephew and nieces of MICAJAH PERRY, the wealthy London merchant and ship owner, head of the firm of PERRY, LANE & COMPANY, who for over a half century advanced funds to planters of the Jamestown area as well as other parts of Virginia, to finance their tobacco crops, as well as for other purposes. Incidentally MICAJAH LOWE represented his uncles vast interests among the planters of the Colony for many years. Perry, Lane & Company was composed of MICAJAH PERRY, THOMAS LANE and RICHARD PERRY, and PETER PERRY an older brother at one time had been their resident agent in Virginia. These PERRYS and LANES contributed considerable sums towards the establishment of William & Mary College, as shown by the records of the period. MICAJAH LOWE died in England, while there on business in 1703. His uncle, MICAJAH PERRY lived until 1820. His grandson MICAJAH PERRY was Lord Mayor of London in 1728. The Lowe children are mentioned in the will of their uncle MICAJAH PERRY, and neither MARY or SUSANNAH were married at that time.

JUDGE WILLIAM SHERWOOD (who appears to have been an uncle of DR. ROBERT WILLIAMSON and his brothers) who was certainly the uncle of ROBERT, CHARLES and JOHN JARRETT, was a distinguished lawyer in JAMES CITY and also in YORK COUNTY, VIRGINIA. The encyclopediac accounts say he was "bred to the bar". (W. & M. 17, pp. 205 et seq.) When a young man he served in the office of SIR JOSEPH WILLIAMSON, known kinsman to RICHARD WILLIAMSON, father of DR. ROBERT WILLIAMSON, and the story is that tempted into evil ways by high life in LONDON he had appropriated fines belonging to Williamson, but was saved from punishment by the latter's generous interposition. Naturally, this created a bond between JUDGE SHERWOOD and the WILLIAMSONS perhaps equally as strong as blood relationship, if we be mistaken about the latter. At any rate the records disclose that he witnessed and perhaps wrote DR. WILLIAMSON'S will, in 1669. He died in 1697, leaving his "history books" to JOANNA JARRETT and all his law books to WILLIAM EDWARDS and DIONYCIOUS WRIGHT.

ROBERT JARRETT, nephew of JUDGE WILLIAM SHERWOOD married MARY, and they were the parents of two sons and one daughter. The daughter became the wife of WALTER CLOPTON, of NEW KENT and YORK COUNTY, Virginia. The sons were:

1. ROBERT JARRETT m. SARAH BRADLEY.
2. DEVEREAUX JARRETT m. ELIZABETH

1. ROBERT JARRETT and his wife SARAH BRADLEY had three sons and a daughter who lived beyond infancy, viz, Robert, Joseph and REV. DEVEREAUX JARRETT, long minister of St. Peter's Parish in New Kent County. The daughter's name was Susannah.

2. DEVEREAUX JARRETT, the grand-nephew of JUDGE WILLIAM SHERWOOD, married ELIZABETH (her last name unknown) and on the old ST. PETER'S PARISH REGISTER is listed the names of their four children and the dates of their respective births, as follows:

1. MARY JARRETT, daughter of DEVEREAUX JARRETT, born May 5, 1724.
2. ARCHELAUS JARRETT, son of Devereaux Jarrett, born Jan. 5, 1725/6.
3. ANNIE JARRETT, daughter of DEVEREAUX JARRETT and wife ELIZABETH born Nov. 13, 1727.
4. FANNIE JARRETT, daughter of DEVEREAUX and ELIZABETH JARRETT b. Jan. 15, 1729/30.

1. MARY JARRETT, grand-daughter of ROBERT JARRETT and his wife MARY, married about the year, 1749, WILLIAM GILLIAM, son of JOHN GILLIAM and LUCY HENRY, and they were the parents of SARAH GILLIAM who married MICAJAH WILLIAMSON, her somewhat distant cousin.

MICAJAH WILLIAMSON, had among others, a son PETER WILLIAMSON, who became the father of ROBERT McALPIN WILLIAMSON, a famous Texas patriot. This ROBERT M. WILLIAMSON on April 21, 1837 married MARY JANE EDWARDS, the only child of GUSTAVUS E. EDWARDS, of Austin County, Texas. GUSTAVUS E. EDWARDS was the son of GEORGE EDWARDS and ELIZABETH MONROE who were married in KENTUCKY in 1788; and GEORGE EDWARDS was the son of HAYDEN EDWARDS (b. 1716) and his wife PENELOPE SANFORD; HAYDEN EDWARDS was the son of WILLIAM EDWARDS who married MARY HAYDEN; WILLIAM EDWARDS was the son of JOHN EDWARDS of SURRY COUNTY, VIRGINIA; JOHN EDWARDS was the son of WILLIAM EDWARDS mentioned in the will of JUDGE WILLIAM SHERWOOD and to whom, jointly with DIONYCIOUS WRIGHT, Judge Sherwood left his law library in 1697. The wife of WILLIAM EDWARDS was SARAH LOWE, the widow of MICAJAH LOWE, and the sister in law of SUSANNAH LOWE who married JOHN WILLIAMSON. William Edwards and Sarah Lowe had MICAJAH EDWARDS, JOHN EDWARDS and a THOMAS EDWARDS besides some daughters. After the death of SARAH LOWE, WILLIAM EDWARDS married ELIZABETH HARRISON, daughter of the second BENJAMIN HARRISON, of SURRY COUNTY.

459

A little more information on the GILLIAM FAMILY will help:

The family genealogist of one set tells me that the HINSHEA GILLIAM, who patented lands in SURRY COUNTY died in 1737, and his children were JOHN, THOMAS, CHARLES, WALTER, PRISCILLA, LYDIA and WILLIAM, also a son HINCHEA. It may have been his son who several years later (1723) patented lands in the same neighborhood. Anyway these SURRY COUNTY GILLIAMS, CHARLES, JOHN and HINCHEA, were probably sons of the first HINSHAW GILLIAM (son of JOHN) who had a brother named JOHN, and it is believed that the brother JOHN was the father of another set of children, and among them a WILLIAM GILLIAM, who married perhaps a sister of MAJ. PETER POYTHRESS. This latter WILLIAM GILLIAM was the father of JOHN GILLIAM, who married LUCY HENRY and settled in LUNENBURG COUNTY, being on the procession list with JAMES MITCHELL and SAMUEL HARRIS in Lunenburg in 1747. Later, he bought lands from JOHN GLOVER on Nutbush and Gilliam's Branch in Granville County, N. C. His son, JOHN GILLIAM, JR., who was one of the witnesses to the will of HENRY RANDOLPH and an executor thereof with his father and PETER POYTHRESS. This JOHN GILLIAM JR. was a revolutionary soldier, and had sons HINCHEA, ISHAM, CARTER and ANSELM GILLIAM. His son HINCHEA GILLIAM, left a will in SUSSEX COUNTY, Virginia, which somebody has dug up, which describes him as being the "heir of John Gilliam, revolutionary soldier", in which he names one son JOHN GILLIAM and six daughters, MARY, SARAH, LUCY, PEGGY, EDNA and ELIZABETH. The daughter LUCY married DAVID BARROW (of the later GEORGIA BARROWS) and two of the daughters married persons named JONES.

JOHN WILLIAMSON, the son of GEORGE WILLIAMSON and his wife HESTER BRIDGER, and who was the father of MICAJAH WILLIAMSON (who married SARAH GILLIAM) had moved to BRUNSWICK COUNTY at that time (which joined SUSSEX) and was one of the witnesses to this will. JOHN GILLIAM, JR., the revolutionary soldier, was an uncle of SARAH GILLIAM, and she and HINCHEA GILLIAM were first cousins. Some of the HINCHEA GILLIAM children moved to GEORGIA (Wilkes County) and some of them moved to KENTUCKY.

ROBERT POYTHRESS, we are told, was the grandson of CAPT. FRANCIS POYTHRESS, the emigrant of 1633. This may or may not be correct. ROBERT POYTHRESS had only one son, but NINE daughters. The son was PETER POYTHRESS, mentioned above. The names of NONE of the nine daughters have been found and identified, but in 7 Va. Mag pp. 438-9, what purports to be the surname of their husbands are given as follows: Goode (of Whitby); GILLIAM (this was WILLIAM, of course); EPPES, Rubsiman, Morrison, Lee, Cocke, Baird and HARRISON.

ROBERT GILLIAM, the oldest brother, according to Phillip Slaughter, married LUCY SKELTON. His brother JOHN GILLIAM married LUCY HENRY. LUCY SKELTON was the daughter of MARTHA WAYLES and her first husband BATHURST SKELTON, after whose death she married PRESIDENT THOMAS JEFFERSON. LUCY WAYLES was the daughter of JOHN WAYLES and MARTHA EPPES, sister of FRANCIS EPPES No. 4. An ANNE EPPES, sister of MARTHA EPPES (who first married Llewellen Eppes) married BENJAMIN HARRIS, who was a brother of AGNES HARRIS, who married WILLIAM GILLIAM, of New Kent County, born in 1899, the son of JOHN HARRIS. The wife of ROBERT POYTHRESS was ELIZABETH GILLIAM, sister of JOHN and HINCHA GILLIAM, of Bristol Parish. The children of ROBERT GILLIAM and LUCY SKELTON were JOHN, ELIZABETH, REUBEN, JAMES S., SUSANNAH, JANE, ANNE and MERIWETHER B. SKELTON, GILLIAM.

It will be noticed that the WILLIAM GILLIAM who left will in GRANVILLE COUNTY in 1804 had two daughters who married men by the name of HARRIS, RANSOM and JAMES, and one daughter AMEY, in 1783, married ISHAM HARRISON. This William Gilliam was 108 William, son of WILLIAM GILLIAM and his wife AGNES HARRIS (will in Granville in 1778). JAMES HARRIS who married PRISCILLA GILLIAM was the father of W. W. HARRIS (b. about 1795 in Granville County) who moved to SPARTANBURG DISTRICT, South Carolina, where he left a long line of descendants.

The family of CHARLES ELLIS, who died in AMHERST COUNTY, VIRGINIA, dated in 1760 and probated the same year is of interest in connection with the GILLIAM FAMILY. He and his wife SUSANNAH HARDING, who had moved there from HENRICO COUNTY, had the following children: HANNAH, EDITH, SUSANNAH, JOSIAH, MARION, CHARLES, SARAH, BETHENIA, ELIZABETH and ROSANNAH ELLIS. Two of these daughters married into the GILLIAM FAMILY, EDITH having married DEVEREAUX GILLIAM, while ELIZABETH married WILLIAM GILLIAM. William and Devereaux Gilliam were brothers of SARAH GILLIAM, who married MICAJAH WILLIAMSON. Devereaux Gilliam moved to the vicinity of KNOXVILLE, TENNESSEE, where he erected a fort against the Indians at the junction of the Holston and French Broad rivers. One of his daughters became the wife of HUGH DUNLAP, and their son GEN. ROBERT GILLIAM DUNLAP commanded the Tennessee troops in Alabama during the Indian campaign of 1836, in which a number of the relatives of this compiler participated under his command. HUGH DUNLAP's grave and monument is in the Presbyterian Churchyard at Paris, Tennessee, which this writer has visited and copied. THOMAS GILLIAM, another brother of the wife of MICAJAH WILLIAMSON, was murdered by Indians about 15 miles from the town of KNOXVILLE, TENNESSEE in 1793.

These notes will be of additional interest:

ARCHELAUS JARRETT, brother of MARY JARRETT (wife of WILLIAM GILLIAM), like the WILLIAMSONS, moved to GEORGIA. Either he or a son of the same name died in ELBERT COUNTY in 1727, in which he named his children and makes provision for them.

DEVEREAUX JARRETT and wife ELIZABETH, of BURKE COUNTY, GA. on July 17, 1777, sold to ROBERT JONES, of Richmond County, Ga. 300 acres of land originally granted said JARRETT in 1770 and 1774, bounded by the lands of JOEL WALKER, JOHN STUART and JOHN PHILLIPS. Final payment June 25, in 1790. (Page 229 Ga. D. A. R. Historical Collections, Vol. 2).

These extracts from the records tend to strengthen the supposition that the wife of WILLIAM GILLIAM was the MARY JARRETT born in St. Peter's Parish on May 5, 1724.

A DAUGHTER OF REV. JOHN THOMSON MARRIED A MAN NAMED JOHN GRAHAM, in PA.

The name of this daughter of REV. JOHN THOMSON is unknown. Her name could have been MARTHA THOMSON. Dr. Herndon says that this JOHN GRAHAM was the son of another JOHN GRAHAM who died leaving a will dated April 12, 1743, in Lancaster County, Pennsylvania, and probated in February 1743/4, and witnessed by REV. RICHARD SANKEY and a BRICE SANKEY. This JOHN GRAHAM removed to and lived in PRINCE EDWARD COUNTY, Virginia. ROBERT BAKER, the son of DOUGLAS BAKER, who married another daughter JANE THOMSON, married MARGARET GRAHAM, and when Robert Baker died in 1773, his will was witnessed by JOSEPH PARKS and THOMAS and JAMES GRAHAM. If we follow the natural trend of marital relationships in the Baker and Thomson families, as amply evidenced by the record, we very naturally conclude that ROBERT BAKER married his first cousin, MARGARET GRAHAM, and that THOMAS and JAMES were her brothers. Then we find in the Hopewell section of Mecklenburg County a certain WILLIAM GRAHAM, who was one of the signers; a modest, unassuming farmer, with his wife MARGARET, settled there among his kindred and pursuing the even tenor of his way, only to rest at last in the peaceful churchyard near his home with his wife MARGARET. Obviously, since he is otherwise unaccounted for, all of the surrounding circumstances convincingly testify to the fact that he was another son of JOHN GRAHAM and his wife MARTHA(?), who seem to have at least these children:

1. WILLIAM GRAHAM m. MARGARET
2. THOMAS GRAHAM
3. JAMES GRAHAM
4. MARGARET GRAHAM m. ROBERT BAKER.

In all probability, likewise, this JOHN GRAHAM, may have been related to GEN. JOSEPH GRAHAM, whose father, JAMES GRAHAM, is said to have died in Pennsylvania, and whose mother, MARY GRAHAM came to Mecklenburg County after 1780. To the Grahams themselves this relationship may have been well known, but the lapse of time has dimmed these recollections of kinship, so that no record has been left to testify to the same with certainty.

ROGER THOMSON MARRIED ANN FERGUSON IN AMELIA COUNTY

After a careful study of the fragmental records apparently relating to ROGER THOMSON (usually spelled THOMPSON thereon) the writer has concluded that he was twice married; That his first wife was ANN FERGUSON, whom he married in what is now PRINCE EDWARD COUNTY, VIRGINIA (then AMELIA) in 1750, and afterwards to HANNAH, the daughter of HUGH LAWSON, and sister of ROGER LAWSON, who married HANNAH THOMSON, his sister. The first husband of HANNAH LAWSON had been THOMAS ERVIN or IRVIN.

In previous notes herein on REV. JOHN THOMSON'S early connections with the COBBS and SHIELDS and BOOKERS, the reader will find evidence to convince him of the fact that there was a close connection between them all, as their history reveals. For that reason the notes below containing marriage records of AMELIA COUNTY, all contemporaneous, are interesting as further stengthening those facts:

EDWARD BOOKER and ANN COBBS were married Feb. 1, 1739.
EDWARD BOOKER and EDITH MAROT COBBS were married MAY 17, 1746.
GEORGE BOOKER and SARAH COBBS were married OCT. 12, 1749.
THOMAS TABB and REBECCA BOOKER were married Sept. 27, 1735.
ROGER THOMSON and ANN FERGUSON were married MAY 12, 1750.

The space available will not permit the setting forth of data obtained by the writer showing the COBBS and BOOKER connection with the FERGUSON FAMILY, to which ANN FERGUSON belonged, but they all belonged to the YORK COUNTY TRIBES who have been heretofore reviewed; and these included also the CUNNINGHAMS. By his last marriage to HANNAH LAWSON (the widow of THOMAS IRVIN) ROGER THOMSON may not have had any children. Just how many he did have has not been ascertained, and we think cannot be. For a time ROGER THOMSON lived in ROWAN and in Mecklenburg Counties, in North Carolina, but he probably later removed to the TIGER RIVER section of Upper South Carolina (once a part of Mecklenburg territory) with the BARRY FAMILY, who were kinsmen of his second wife, HANNAH LAWSON and his sister's husband ROGER LAWSON. We find some data on the THOMSON - THOMPSON family there afterwards. Among the children of ROGER THOMSON, we think, were these:

1. ANDREW THOMSON (So spelled).
2. LAWSON THOMSON (So spelled).
3. MATTHEW THOMSON (So spelled).

In 1899, COL. THOMAS MOORE, writing from the town of MOORE, S. C. (in Spartanburg County) said: "I have in my library a Greek testament with this inscription in a beautiful hand 'ANDREW THOMSON, Ejus Liber, Anno Domini 1772' thus showing his acquaintance with two classic languages. In the back of the same book is inscribed 'LAWSON THOMSON, A. D. 1791' and 'ANDREW W. THOMSON, A. D. 1809' thus showing for many years they studied the Scriptures of the New Testament in the original language".

I am firmly convinced that both ANDREW and LAWSON THOMSON, of Spartanburg County, S. C. were sons of ROGER THOMSON, and that ANDREW W. THOMSON, A. D. was a great grandson of REV. JOHN THOMSON, who died in MECKLENBURG COUNTY, N. C. in 1753.

An ANDREW BARRY, called CAPTAIN, settled on the TIGER RIVER, in Spartanburg District, & married MARGARET MOORE, daughter of CHARLES MOORE. This ANDREW BARRY was born in 1746, and was perhaps a nephew of RICHARD BARRY, the MECKLENBURG SIGNER. See later.

ANOTHER DAUGHTER OF REV. JOHN THOMSON MARRIED JOHN FINLEY

Apparently none of the researchers on the THOMSON family have ever been able to discover the given name of this daughter. Your guess would be as good as any. That this marriage occurred is a fact ascertained from an old letter written by REV. RICHARD SANKEY, who married SARAH THOMSON, which was a discovery made by our good friend DR. JOSEPH D. EGGLESTON, of Hampden-Sydney College many years ago and about which he wrote the compiler at the time. Contrary to the popular conception among numerous genealogists, the FINLEYS first settled in AMELIA, or PRINCE EDWARD COUNTIES and were long time neighbors of the EWINGS, CALDWELLS, FORTERS, GILLESPIES and CUNNINGHAMS, as well as the THOMSONS and CROCKETTS. GEORGE and WILLIAM FINLEY (brothers of JOHN) lived on BUFFALO in Prince Edward, as did their sister ELIZABETH, who married a GILLESPIE, and did move to AUGUSTA COUNTY.

The father of JOHN FINLEY was also named JOHN and his wife is said to have been THANKFUL DOAK, and one genealogist, at least, has stated that the wife of JOHN FINLEY JR. was MARY CALDWELL, daughter of MAJ. JOHN CALDWELL, of the Revolution. Maj. John Caldwell, of the revolution, lived in South Carolina, was the son of WILLIAM CALDWELL and the brother in law of MAJ. ROBERT GILLIAM and PATRICK CALHOUN, and while he married, he was slain by Bloody Bill Cunningham before they had children. As a matter of fact, SUSAN GILLIAM, a sister of MAJ. ROBERT GILLIAM, married a son of JOHN FINLEY and his wife MISS THOMSON. (See previous notes on the Gilliam family, herein).

JOHN FINLEY (the first), who lived on BUFFALO in Prince Edward County, Virginia, had the following children, according to what is probably a correct account:

1. JOHN FINLEY m. MISS THOMSON.
2. GEORGE FINLEY
3. ELIZABETH FINLEY m. GILLESPIE
4. ROBERT FINLEY (b. in 1726)
5. JAMES FINLEY (b. about 1728).
6. DAVID FINLEY
7. MARGARET FINLEY
8. SAMUEL FINLEY
9. WILLIAM FINLEY. (possibly others).

In the year 1771 there was a deed executed in MECKLENBURG COUNTY, North Carolina, which establishes as a fact that JOHN FINLEY at least had lived there, though he may not have been residing there at that date. The deed was by his wife's brother in law JOHN SHIELDS, who had married MARGARET THOMSON, which makes it doubly valuable as evidence of the presence in Mecklenburg of these two sons in law of REV. JOHN THOMSON. Although this deed will be found among the miscellaneous records published elsewhere herein, we reproduce the abstract here again:

JOHN SHIELDS and MARGARET, his wife, PLANTER, to DAVID BRADFORD, consideration 52 pounds, a tract of 205 acres, part of original grant to AMBROSE HARDING, on McCUISTIAN'S line to ROBERT MOFFETT, thence MOSES ANDREW'S line to JOHN FINLEY'S.
Wit: JAMES SHIELDS   (Signed) JOHN SHIELDS
     AGNES SHIELDS   MARGARET SHIELDS

The name of JOHN FINLEY, as a son in law of REV. JOHN THOMSON, about whom these sketches are being written, adds a colorful tinge to the THOMSON FAMILY. Eminent historians, like RAMSEY, whose wife was a native of MECKLENBURG, HAYWOOD, also a native of North Carolina, Collins, of Kentucky, and others have searched in vain for the life story of this great "long hunter" who was one of the trusty scouts and woodsmen who guided DANIEL BOONE, JUDGE RICHARD HENDERSON, COL. RICHARD CALLOWAY and others across Cumberland Gap and into the bloody grounds of Kentucky, when American Explorations were thrilling the country. The following tablet, erected on the corner of a busy street in the town of SALISBURY, NORTH CAROLINA, tells its historic story, as written by the Elizabeth Steele Chapter of the D. A. R.:

Boone Trail 1769.
From this town RICHARD HENDERSON, in behalf
of RICHARD HENDERSON & COMPANY
Dispatched
DANIEL BOONE, JOHN FINDLEY,
John Stuart, Joseph Holden, James Mooney
and William Cooley
to
Explore the wilderness of Kentucky.

Hon. BENNETT HENDERSON YOUNG in his wonderful History of JESSAMINE COUNTY, KENTUCKY, opens his enthralling story of that infant settlement with this paragraph:

"In 1767, JOHN FINLEY, a woodsman and hunter from NORTH CAROLINA, moved by a spirit of adventure and love for hunting, entered the country known as the Bluegrass region. He was the first white man, history asserts, that ever penetrated the wilderness and forests of Kentucky sufficiently to see the central part of the state. Who came with him, whither they went and how long the party remained, neither traveler, legend nor written story tells. Two years later Finley returned with DANIEL BOONE to that wonderful land he had described to his neighbors and associates in NORTH CAROLINA." The story is finished by Col. Young with the assumption that Finley was eventually killed by the Indians and sleeps under the leaves of the forest he loved.

ANNE THOMSON MARRIED JAMES CUNNINGHAM

It is estimated that ANNE THOMSON, daughter of REV. JOHN THOMSON, who married JAMES CUNNINGHAM, was born about 1727-8, and that he was born about 1720 to 1722, possibly a little earlier. Their children were:

(1) SAMUEL CUNNINGHAM (died Greene County Ga. in 1805).
(2) ELIZABETH CUNNINGHAM married JAMES DANIEL. (To Georgia).
(3) SARAH CUNNINGHAM married (1) SAMUEL CALDWELL (2) JOHN DANIEL.
(4) MARGARET CUNNINGHAM married RICHARD GAINES, JR.
(5) JANE CUNNINGHAM married JAMES ADAMS, JR.
(6) ANN CUNNINGHAM married ANDREW HANNAH (Son of GEORGE HANNAH).
(7) MARY CUNNINGHAM married WILLIAM JOHNSTON.
(8) HANNAH CUNNINGHAM married WILLIAM DANIEL (Died GREENE COUNTY, GA.)
(9) ANDREW CUNNINGHAM married ISABELLA HANNAH (Dau. of GEORGE HANNAH).
(10) JAMES CUNNINGHAM married FRANCES REDD (Died in 1812 in GEORGIA).

As a rule tables or charts containing long lists of names are boresome, but by the use of the above charted list of the children of JAMES CUNNINGHAM and his wife ANNE THOMSON, one is able to get a "bird's-eye view" of this set of grandchildren of REV. JOHN THOMSON, and some inkling of what became of them. Each one of the ten had a family of his or her own, and all had descendants, whose connections spread out over the entire South

JAMES CUNNINGHAM, father of the above list of children, was twice married. He married ANNE THOMSON, daughter of REV. JOHN THOMSON, perhaps about 1743-4. She was the mother of all of his children. After her death and in his old age he married JEAN (KELSO) DANIEL, mother of the three Daniel brothers, who married three of his own daughters. They had no children, and both died not very long afterwards.

Dr. John G. Herndon, in an able article in the Virginia Historical Magazine, beginning on page 135 of Volume 52, styled "The Cunninghams of Cub Creek", declares that JAMES CUNNINGHAM was "born probably about 1720, presumably at Cunningham Manor, Northern Ireland". That this compiler differs with his erudite and accomplished friend of Haverford College, should not and does not disturb a long friendship and the common desire of both to ascertain the true facts, and when the writer here asserts that JAMES CUNNINGHAM never saw Northern Ireland, but was a native of the Colony of Virginia and an intimate and in many instances a kinsman of some of its oldest and most distinguished families, he does not desire to detract one iota from the high esteem in which he holds his fellow research worker on the Cunningham family. Furthermore, save and except for one thing, there is not a scintilla of evidence, or any slightest record tending to establish it as a fact that the CUNNINGHAMS OF CUB CREEK (headed by this particular JAMES CUNNINGHAM) were Scotch-Irish themselves, or of Scotch-Irish descent. The exception is that the Cub Creek Settlement did have a considerable quota of Scotch-Irish families, but on the contrary the older Virginia families from York, Henrico, Warwick, Hanover, Essex, Richmond, Lancaster, Spottsylvania and even old RAPPAHANNOCK COUNTY, likewise were seated in that neighborhood and in AMELIA and PRINCE EDWARD COUNTIES, and the children of JAMES CUNNINGHAM and his wife ANNE THOMSON preponderantly intermarried, they and their descendants, into these older VIRGINIA FAMILIES. Their business transactions, as shown on the old records, were with these older families, as witness:

JAMES CUNNINGHAM's first land transaction was the purchase of 900 acres of land on Spring Creek, from SAMUEL COBBS, Clerk of AMELIA COUNTY, who in 1720 was the executor of the will of DAVID CUNNINGHAM, in York County, Virginia.

In 1756 he sold 700 acres of this land to WILLIAM RANDOLPH, who had served as a member of the House of Burgesses of Virginia (about that time) with ROBERT CUNNINGHAM, the first Burgess from the Augusta area of Virginia.

His daughter, JANE CUNNINGHAM married JAMES ADAMS, JR., a member of a well known HENRICO COUNTY family, and kinsman of ROBERT ADAMS, Quaker, who married into other Quaker families from York and other Eastern Virginia parts.

His daughter MARY CUNNINGHAM married CAPT. WILLIAM JOHNSTON, of an old Colonial family of Eastern Virginia.

His daughter MARGARET CUNNINGHAM married a scion of the House of GAINES, one of the very oldest families of the YORK and RAPPAHANNOCK section of VIRGINIA.

His son JAMES CUNNINGHAM married FRANCES REDD, who, (according to Dr. Herndon) was a direct descendant of the HANOVER ANDERSONS, from ENGLAND, and the Great Great Grand-daughter of ROGER WILLIAMS, who died in Old Rappahannock County in 1677.

As the above chart of JAMES CUNNINGHAM'S children shows, no less than THREE of them married as many sons of JAMES DANIEL, of an old YORK COUNTY, VIRGINIA, family, of whom considerable mention has been heretofore made in these notes; while TWO of them married descendants of that GEORGE HANNAH, who was Provost Marshall of the BARBADOES, from England, whose brother ANDREW was living there at the same time. These HANNAHS came from the BARBADOES along with the first GEORGE CARRINGTON and other families in the early part of the eighteenth century, and were certainly not to be classed as Scotch-Irish, the category into which friend HERNDON attempts to place JAMES CUNNINGHAM, of Charlotte County.

That the name CUNNINGHAM is widely prevalent in SCOTLAND, or that there were nowadaysmany of Cunninghams (even in Charlotte and Prince Edward County) of the Scotch-Irish persuasion or lineage the writer admits, but the "CUB CREEK CUNNINGHAMS" were of a different set altogether.

THE CUNNINGHAMS OF CUB CREEK AND THEIR VIRGINIA ANCESTORS

JAMES CUNNINGHAM who married ANNE THOMSON, daughter of REV. JOHN THOMSON, who died in Mecklenburg County, North Carolina in 1753, belonged to what is known as the "CUB CREEK CUNNINGHAMS" of CHARLOTTE COUNTY, VIRGINIA. The ancestor of this JAMES CUNNINGHAM was the emigrant WILLIAM CUNNINGHAM, who came to Virginia on the "SPEEDWELL", which weighed anchor and sailed from Gravesend, England on May 28, 1635.

CAPT. WILLIAM CUNNINGHAM belonged to a family of merchants in ENGLAND, and his first visit to the Colony of Virginia, was probably in the capacity of a seaman, or the agent of his family in charge of business interests of the firm. Thereafter, apparently, he made other trips back and forth across the Atlantic, bringing over two sons, JONATHAN and NEHEMIAH CUNNINGHAM on later trips. Capt. Cunningham's name does not appear among the patentees of lands in York County, probably for the reason that he traded his own headright twice, and that of his two sons, for other lands in York County. His own first headright was bought by SAMUEL EDWARDS, of JAMESTOWN, of an old family afterwards established there and in Old Rappahannock County; his second went to his old neighbor and friend, nineteen years later, CAPT. THOMAS BALLARD, of York County, into whose family the Cunninghams later intermarried.

CAPT. THOMAS PAULETT purchased the headright of JONATHAN CUNNINGHAM, and WILLIAM BURDETT, who married ALICE TRAVELER in Accomac, a connection of the STONE and GRAVES FAMILY, secured the headright of NEHEMIAH CUNNINGHAM in 1641. The lands owned thereafter by the emigrant WILLIAM CUNNINGHAM were apparently located on QUEEN'S CREEK in York County, near to the DANIEL, WHITE, GRAVES, WEST, BOOTH, PINKETHMAN, BENNETT and WROE FAMILIES, data regarding which will be hereafter given.

The compiler must admit that the direct evidence BY THE RECORD, to support the presence in YORK COUNTY before 1650 of a CUNNINGHAM FAMILY headed by the emigrant WILLIAM is represented by only a few sketchy fragments, which are included in the following tabulated paragraph of just **FIVE LINES;**

WILLIAM CUNNINGHAM came in the "SPEEDWELL" to Virginia in 1635 (Hotten).
JOHN CUNNINGHAM died in Lower Norfolk 1670 (Lower Norfolk Wills).
ARCHIBALD CUNNINGHAM on LANCASTER COUNTY, (Va.) records 1663. (Book 2 p. 295).
WILLIAM CUNNINGHAM of OLD RAPPAHANNOCK COUNTY in 1683 (39 Va. Mag p. 75).
GEORGE CUNNINGHAM and wife JEAN, York County, Va. 1696. (Chas. Parish Register).

Even as the scientific wizzards of the Smithsonia variety take a fragment of jaw bone, a short length of vertebra and a petrified foot-print a million years old and from them construct a complete skeleton of a monster of pre-flood days, who stalked across the plains of Hindustan and scared the living daylights out of lesser animals, this compiler must, from the fragments in this paragraph reconstruct and rebuild the chart of this CUNNINGHAM FAMILY buried under the debres of centuries and make its members move about among their friends, relatives and neighbors and live again. As, declares the cartoonist of strange things, "believe it or not!"

(I expect the foregoing paragraph to shock my genealogical public. It is so intended that it should. But after all everything set down will be based upon RECORDS. Not records which say in so many words that so and so was the son of so and so, or the father of this or that person. Anybody can copy what a record says - if they can find one they can read. But, first, not everybody can read a record, and many who can read them do not understand them. So, the scientist reads the BONES OF EXTINCT ANIMALS because he knows BONES, while the average person would not be sure it was a bone in the first place. Some persons don't know a record any better than they would know a bone, so of course they would not understand what a record means even if they could read what it says. The scientists interpret the meaning of bones. The genealogist must know how to interpret records and analyze their meaning. What records? All records that tend to throw light on the meaning of such fragments as are available to be interpreted. Selah.)

Now to start with we are trying to establish, first, the indenty of the Cunninghams of Cub Creek; second, that they were related to the DANIEL FAMILY of Prince Edward County. Both the Daniel family of Prince Edward County and the Cunninghams of Cub Creek had forebears who knew each other a hundred years earlier in YORK COUNTY, Virginia. They may even have known each other back in ENGLAND before coming to this country. Is there any record to that effect? Well, not much - but some.

It is established by record evidence that there were CUNNINGHAMS in Northumberland and Lancaster Counties, Virginia. (Book 2 p. 295). This particular entry shows that a JOHN DANIEL was a notary in ENGLAND in 1663, and that an ARCHIBALD CUNNINGHAM's name is attached to an instrument pertaining to the collection of certain indebtedness from planters in LANCASTER COUNTY, VIRGINIA, at that time. JOHN DANIEL, Notary.

This is not much evidence, but it is some. Follow these notes and see it develop.

THE CUNNINGHAMS OF THE COLONY OF VIRGINIA PRIOR TO THE YEAR 1700, A. D.

WILLIAM CUNNINGHAM
had

- **JONATHAN CUNNINGHAM** — Descendants unknown.
  - **ARCHIBALD CUNNINGHAM** had
    - **THOMAS CUNNINGHAM** — Left will in NORTHUMBERLAND CO. 1727. Had daughter WINNIFRED CUNNINGHAM.
- **NEHEMIAH CUNNINGHAM** had
- **JOHN CUNNINGHAM** — No children. Left will Lower Norfolk 1670.
  - **WILLIAM CUNNINGHAM** — No record of his descendants.

1. **ALEXANDER CUNNINGHAM** had
   - 10. WILLIAM CUNNINGHAM
   - 11. CHRISTOPHER CUNNINGHAM
   - 12. ALEXANDER CUNNINGHAM
   - 13. JOHN CUNNINGHAM
   - 14. ROBERT CUNNINGHAM
   - 15. JAMES CUNNINGHAM

2. **WILLIAM CUNNINGHAM** had
   - 16. WILLIAM CUNNINGHAM
   - 17. JAMES CUNNINGHAM
   - 18. ALEXANDER CUNNINGHAM
   - 19. GEORGE CUNNINGHAM
   - 20. DAVID CUNNINGHAM
   - 21. JOHN CUNNINGHAM

3. **JAMES CUNNINGHAM** had
   - 22. THOMAS CUNNINGHAM
   - 23. JOSEPH CUNNINGHAM
   - 24. ANDREW CUNNINGHAM
   - 26. JAMES CUNNINGHAM

The above chart contains what we believe is a list of the ancestors of the CUNNINGHAMS, all of whom were born and lived in the Colony of Virginia, prior to A. D. 1700. (Except as otherwise explained).

16. WILLIAM CUNNINGHAM
18. ALEXANDER CUNNINGHAM) From Vol III, Chalkley's Augusta Records: THOMAS SLAUGHTER and ANN, his wife, to ROBERT SLAUGHTER, JR., of FREDERICK COUNTY (Va.) for 5 shillings, on Shenandoah River, 465 acres which JACOB COGAR sold to THOMAS McCREDIE, late of Fredericksburg, merchant, deceased MAY 24, 1763, recorded in General Court and purchased by THOMAS SLAUGHTER of ALEXANDER CUNNINGHAM, late merchant of FALMOUTH, VIRGINIA.
From the SPOTTSYLVANIA RECORDS: APRIL 6, 1762. JOHN SEMPLE, of KING & QUEEN COUNTY, a surviving partner of ROBERT BAYLOR, Gent., deceased, and the said JOHN SEMPLE, late merchants and partners, and ELIZABETH SEMPLE, his wife, make a conveyance to WILLIAM CUNNINGHAM, ALEXANDER CUNNINGHAM and JOHN STUART, of FREDERICKSBURG, VIRGINIA, said three persons being merchants and partners, to the tenement and store known as NEW MARKET, and 400 acres in ST. GEORGE'S PARISH, Spottsylvania County, adjoining.
21. JOHN CUNNINGHAM. APRIL 3, 1750. JAMES JACKSON, of Albemarle County, planter, and his wife SUSANNAH, to OWEN THOMAS, of Spottsylvania County, 300 acres in ST. GEORGE'S PARISH. Witnessed by NICHOLAS HAWKINS, JOHN CUNNINGHAM, MUMFORD STEVENS and ISAAC SCOTT.
20. DAVID CUNNINGHAM. From the records of YORK COUNTY, VIRGINIA: Will of David Cunningham dated January 13, 1719, and witnessed by LEWIS DELONEY, JOSEPH DAVENPORT and JAMES MORRIS, the executors being SUSANNAH ALLEN, WILLIAM ROBERTSON and SAMUEL COBBS. His two children, DAVID CUNNINGHAM and MARY CUNNINGHAM were placed under the care of SUSANNAH ALLEN, who died in 1720.
17. JAMES CUNNINGHAM. Proceedings of the VIRGINIA COUNCIL, December 12, 1733: STEPHEN HUGHES AND TARLTON FLEMING (the latter guardian of HANNAH DANIEL, daughter of JOHN) granted 6000 acres in GOOCHLAND COUNTY on both sides of WILLIS CREEK and between the lines of COL. BENJAMIN HARRISON, Mr. WILLIAM MAYO, JAMES CUNNINGHAM, Jacob Winfrey, George Briggs and MR. HENRY CARY, including 400 acres already surveyed for the petitioners.
19. GEORGE CUNNINGHAM and wife JEAN, 1696. (Charles Parish Register, YORK COUNTY, Va.)

2. WILLIAM CUNNINGHAM, OF SITTINGBOURNE PARISH, IN OLD RAPPAHANNOCK COUNTY.

2. WILLIAM CUNNINGHAM of SITTINGBOURNE PARISH, Old Rappahannock County, Virginia (Virginia Magazine od History & Biography Vol. 39, page 75) was a grandson of WILLIAM CUNNINGHAM, who arrived in VIRGINIA on the "SPEEDWELL" in 1636, and it is believed, the son of NEHEMIAH CUNNINGHAM, as shown on the above chart. The headright of NEHEMIAH CUNNINGHAM, his father, was used in taking up lands by WILLIAM BURDETT, of the "EASTERN SHORE" called ACCOMAC. BURDETT'S son THOMAS, married the widow of REV. WILLIAM COTTON, after the latter's death in 1640, and COTTON was succeeded as Minister of

HUNGAR'S PARISH by one REV. JOHN ROSIER, whose son JOHN ROSIER afterwards married a niece of CAPT. WILLIAM UNDERWOOD, as the genealogists say, "whom see!"

The following note from Virginia Magazine of History & Biography Vol. 39, page 35, based on the abstract of a record of Old Rappahannock Volume for 1683-1686, relates to 2. WILLIAM CUN-NINGHAM:

> WILLIAM COMBE is apprenticed to WILLIAM CUNNINGHAM, by the Vestry of SITTINGBOURNE PARISH. He was probably the half-brother of WILLIAM UNDERWOOD. In the records of 1666, ARCHDALE COMBE conveyed to his "son in law" (a term then used in lieu of step-son) one black cow and calf and 1500 pounds of tobacco. This deed was witnessed by WILLIAM MOSELEY and RICHARD MORLEY.

Who was this WILLIAM COMBE?

JOHN COMBE, merchant of London, married in 1587, MARGARET ARCHDALE, who was born in 1589, the daughter of THOMAS ARCHDALE. (The family later began to call and write the name plain COMBS). Their son ARCHDALE COMBE, who died in 1666, settled in OLD RAPPAHANNOCK COUNTY, in VIRGINIA, and married in 1663 ELIZABETH BUTLER, the second wife and widow of CAPT. WILLIAM UNDERWOOD. They had a son WILLIAM COMBE, referred to in the above note, who was apprenticed to WILLIAM CUNNINGHAM (above) after his father's death. WILLIAM COMBE afterwards married MARY ROE, the daughter of EDWARD ROE and his wife MARY. The WROE or ROE family was related by marriage to the CUNNINGHAM FAMILY, and it is believed that the wife of WILLIAM CUNNINGHAM was the sister of EDWARD ROE. WILLIAM COMBE settled in WESTMORELAND COUNTY, where his will was dated AUGUST 7, 1717, naming several children.

The will of JOHN CUNNINGHAM, uncle of 2. WILLIAM CUNNINGHAM (of the note - see chart) in LOWER NORFOLK in 1670 was proved by the affidavit of ANNE WROE.

THE INTERESTING UNDERWOOD FAMILY

Two brothers, JOHN UNDERWOOD and WILLIAM UNDERWOOD came to Virginia shortly after the INDIAN MASSACRE of 1623, and settled in YORK COUNTY.

JOHN UNDERWOOD

JOHN UNDERWOOD married DOROTHY CAYNEHOOE, the widow of REV. WILLIAM CAYNEHOOE, of YORK PARISH, after the latter's death. The REV. CAYNEHOOE left a daughter SYBELLA, who became the wife of MATTHEW HUBBARD and the ancestress of a lot of HARRISONS. Incidentally ROBERT HARRISON and JOHN UNDERWOOD in 1646 had a "run in" which reached the County Court, over the tobacco crop raised on the CAYNEHOOE plantation, after the Parson's death, while JOHN UNDERWOOD was the administrator of the estate, many of the details of which controversy can be gleaned from Beverly Fleet's enlightening Colonial Abstracts, Vols. 24 and 25.

That this JOHN UNDERWOOD was the brother of the first WILLIAM UNDERWOOD is clearly shown by certain records covering his business transactions from time to time.

For instance: At a Court held in YORK COUNTY, July 24, 1646, the following note appears on the proceedings:

> Record, p. 149. That by confession of JOHN UNDERWOOD he owes TOBY SMITH for certain clothes and SMITH owes JOHN UNDERWOOD for tobacco; this debt was assigned to RICHARD LEE (sic) and all was referred to the next Court. Fleet's Abstracts.

Now, who was TOBY SMITH? He was Lieut. Col. TOBY SMITH, who had left York County by about 1650 and settled in LANCASTER, and when in 1656 OLD RAPPAHANNOCK was organized he became a member of the first court of that county, with MR. WILLIAM UNDERWOOD, MR. THOMAS LUCAS SR., and MR. RICHARD LONS - possibly the "Richard Lee" of the above note, to whom JOHN UNDERWOOD assigned the debt in question. Again:

> TOBY SMITH was granted a patent to 650 acres in WARWICK COUNTY, upon the head of BACK RIVER, called "Smith's Ford", adjoining THOMAS FAULKNER and THOMAS BOULDING. Was formerly granted to said TOBY SMITH, February 14, 1640. The later patent was January 10, 1643.

WILLIAM UNDERWOOD

WILLIAM UNDERWOOD, the brother of JOHN UNDERWOOD, had a most remarkable and interesting family, whose history absorbs this writer. The identity of this man has been heretofore relegated to the background by those writers who have had occasion to mention his family and descendants. It is common knowledge among genealogists that his wife MARGARET, after she became a widow about 1642, married CAPT. JOHN UPTON, the ancient planter and neighbor of CHRISTOPHER REYNOLDS, CAPT. WILLIAM PIERCE, JUSTINIAN COOPER and others, but it seems so very obvious and plain that MARGARET was the daughter of CAPT. JOHN MASON that the writer cannot understand why they have not said so. WILLIAM UNDERWOOD, the first husband of MARGARET MASON left no will and we therefore have to look to the will of CAPT. JOHN UPTON, in 1652, for a list of the Underwood children. Nor is it generally noticed that MARGARET UPTON married a third husband after Capt. Upton's death, in the person of MR. THOMAS LUCAS, SR., who was also a member of the first court in OLD RAPPAHANNOCK COUNTY in 1656.

UNDERWOOD FAMILY CHART

WILLIAM UNDERWOOD married **MARGARET MASON** and had:

CAPT. WILLIAM UNDERWOOD
m. (1) MARY MOSELEY
m. (2) ELIZABETH BUTLER

His first wife was daughter of WILLIAM MOSELEY, of the LYNHAVEN MOSELEYS in Lower Norfolk.
His second wife was ELIZA BUTLER, sister of WILLIAM and AMORY BUTLER.
He had 2 sons by 1st mar:
JOHN UNDERWOOD (d. in KING GEORGE COUNTY, 1722, leaving son WILLIAM who married a STROTHER and had one son JOHN; also a daughter MARGARET m. BENJ. EDMONDSON.
WILLIAM UNDERWOOD died in RICHMOND COUNTY in 1718 leaving sons JOHN and WILLIAM and daughters MARY, ELIZABETH and SARAH.

After CAPT. UNDERWOOD'S death about 1661 his widow ELIZABETH married ARCHDALE COMBE and left a son WILLIAM COMBE, apprenticed to WILLIAM CUNNINGHAM. Also a son JOHN COMBE, RICHMOND COUNTY (will) children:
MASON COMBES
ARCHDALE COMBES
ELIZABETH KENDALL
JOHN (
MARY (MARY
SARAH (SARAH
AMYE COMBES

MARGARET UNDERWOOD
m. HUMPHREY BOOTH
had

HUMPHREY BOOTH, JR.
GRACE BOOTH
CATHERINE BOOTH
m. ROBERT BROOKE

ROBERT BOOTH, Clerk of YORK County (Va.) died in 1651,& had:
HUMPHREY BOOTH
m. MARGARET UNDERWOOD
ELIZABETH BOOTH
...ROBERT BOOTH m. ANN BRAY
WILLIAM BOOTH m. MRS. CHAPMAN.

They had daughter
ELIZABETH BOOTH who married CAPT. ROBT. ARMISTEAD and they had:
...ELYSON ARMISTEAD and
BOOTH ARMISTEAD

He had ROBERT BOOTH ARMISTEAD who married
ANNE SHIELDS, a relative of the CUNNINGHAMS -YORK CO.

ELIZABETH UNDERWOOD
m. (1) JR. JAMES TAYLOR
m. (2) CAPT. FRANCIS SLAUGHTER
m. (3) JOHN CATLETT
m. (4) REV. AMORY BUTLER

Her will 1673 (21 Va-Mag 307)
FRANCIS SLAUGHTER (Richmond Co)
died 1718 m. MARGARET HUDSON
(Ancestors of all the Slaughters)
JOHN CATLETT (son) m. ELIZABETH GAINES dau. of DANIEL GAINES
Mentions FOUR CHILDREN of her husband JOHN CATLETT
Her cousin CAPT. THOS. HAWKINS
Cousins HUMPHREY and CATHERINE BOOTH
Her daughter SARAH
Her daughter ELIZABETH
Her sister PIERCE.
Her "beloved husband" AMORY BUTLER.
"My brother" EDWARD ROWZEE and MR. DANIEL GAINES overseers of her will.

REV. AMORY BUTLER was a brother of REV. WILLIAM BUTLER, of WESTMORELAND COUNTY.

REV. WILLIAM BUTLER was the "gossip WILLIAM BUTLER" mentioned in the will of ANTHONY PARHAM, of MULBERRY ISLAND, Warwick County, Virginia, in 1641 (Colonial p. 237), who also mentions WIFE JOANE PIERCE wife of WILLIAM PIERCE, whose son WILLIAM married SARAH UNDERWOOD her sister.

BUTLER

THOMAS, JOHN and CHRISTOPHER BUTLER were also brothers of AMORY BUTLER who married ELIZABETH UNDERWOOD.
JANE BUTLER the first wife of AUGUSTINE WASHINGTON was of this family. MARY BALL second wife descends from MARGARET WILLIAMSON, daughter of her sister ANN UNDERWOOD.
AUGUSTINE WASHINGTON, JR. son of MARY BALL; BUTLER WASHINGTON son of JANE BUTLER; in will 1762:

"Children of my sister LEWIS (Betty), and my sister in law MRS. BOOTH, wife of WILLIAM BOOTH."

A CATHERINE BROOKE m. MAJ. JOHN HODNETT and her sister MARTHA BROOKE m. CALEB BAKER, three of whose brothers married daughters of REV. JOHN THOMSON. (See CALEB BAKER NOTES) elsewhere. Another daughter became wife of JAMES CUNNINGHAM, of CUB CREEK.
CALEB BUTLER (will 1708) Westmoreland names daughter m. JOHN BAKER who had BUTLER, JOHN and dau. comes CALEB.

ANN UNDERWOOD
m. DR. JAMES WILLIAMSON
(Oldest daughter)

They had THREE CHILDREN:

WILLIAM WILLIAMSON
no issue.
MARGARET WILLIAMSON
m. WILLIAM BALL
(Disputed by the BALL descendants)
MARY WILLIAMSON
m. JOHN ROSIER.

JOHN ROSIER was the son of REV. JOHN ROSIER, who succeeded in 1640, the REV. WILLIAM COTTON, of Hungar's Parish in ACCOMAC COUNTY.

Both father and son settled in OLD RAPPAHANNOCK and WESTMORELAND after they left the "EASTERN SHORE" of Virginia.

DEED in Westmoreland County, August, 1674:
From JOHN ROSIER of WESTMORELAND, Gent., son of JOHN ROSIER, Clerk, to his father in law ANTHONY BRIDGES, Gentleman, whose NEW wife ELIZABETH BRIDGES, was the widow of REV. JOHN ROSIER and mother of said JOHN ROSIER.

SARAH UNDERWOOD
m. WILLIAM PIERCE

(Son of CAPT. WILLIAM PIERCE of MULBERRY ISLAND)
He left will 1702
(W & M 9 p 270)
JOHN PIERCE
(Dau) m. BAYLEY.
ELIZABETH m. BRIDGES;(2)
MARGARET m. GRAHAM
MARY m. EDWARD ROWZEE.
(Dau) m. FRANCIS GOWER.

Gr. Dau. ELIZABETH POPE
had son in law
GOV. WILLIAM POPE DUVAL
She m. (2) WILLIAM WROE.
And through the WROE -ROE family was related to the CUNNINGHAM FAMILY.
(HENRY WILLIAMSON, brother of DR. JAMES WILLIAMSON married a daughter of COL. RICHARD LOWE, of OLD RAPPAHANNOCK and LANCASTER COUNTIES, erroneously spelled LOES on the record. He was employed in 1628 in VIRGINIA by PERRY & LANE's predecessors. p 11 George Sherwood's Vols.)

JULY 22, 1663. WILLIAM UNDERWOOD, son and heir of WILLIAM UNDERWOOD, late of RAPPAHANNOCK, in VIRGINIA, in the parts of AMERICA, appoints UNCLE, WILLIAM MOSELEY, guardian and Attorney for me to dispose of * * given and bequeathed to me by his last will and testament; to my uncle EDWARD BURTON, in County of Worcester, Gent. I, the said WILLIAM UNDERWOOD am under age, - that is fourteen and one-fourth years. Before Thomas Hartwell, Notary, in the City of Bristol. -- 7 Vir. Mag. of Hist & Biog. p. 62.

DEC. 8, 1656. MR. JAMES WILLIAMSON died intestate and MR. WILLIAM UNDERWOOD, UNCLE of his orphans on the mother's side, was appointed administrator and guardian to the said orphans. Vol. 38 Va. Mag. p. 391.

A. D. 1644. CAPT. JOHN UPTON and his wife MARGARET, of Isle of Wight County, Virginia, conveyed certain land to JOHN MASON, of said County. Vol. 38 Va. Mag p. 386.

March 8, 1655. Mrs. MARGARET UPTON refers in deed in Isle of Wight County, to her son in law FRANCIS SLAUGHTER.

ELIZABETH UNDERWOOD married DR. JAMES TAYLOR, but in 1655 she asked separation of the Governor and Council, to go and live with her mother. Dr. Taylor, however, died, and on MAY 1, 1655, his Estate came up for settlement and MR. SLAUGHTER in right of his wife asked for his one-third of the Estate. The returns were made by MAJ. NICHOLAS HILL and LAWRENCE BAKER, with JAMES MASON and WILLIAM BATTE as witnesses or bondsmen. - Va. Mag Vol. 38 p. 270.

DEC. 11, 1691. WILLIAM UNDERWOOD, JR. conveys land on RAPPAHANNOCK, whereof 600 acres was conveyed by MR. AMORY BUTLER to MR. WILLIAM UNDERWOOD, SR., as marrying the SISTER of Mr. Amory BUTLER, and afterwards conveyed with the consent of MRS. ELIZABETH COMBS to WILLIAM UNDERWOOD, JR., JOHN COMBS and WILLIAM COMBS. 17 W. & M. p. 78.

AUGUST 3, 1696. WILLIAM UNDERWOOD, of RICHMOND COUNTY to NATHANIEL POPE als BRIDGES, of same County, land he now liveth on. Ibid.

MAY 30, 1659. WILLIAM UNDERWOOD and his wife MARY, for 20 pounds Sterling, sells lands on the North side of the Rappahannock River to CAPT. RICHARD LOES (LOWE) and RICE JONES. 7 Tyler 62.

From RECORDS OF LANCASTER COUNTY (22 Fleet's Col. Abs. p. 66) AUG. 6, 1653. RICHARD LOES records a heifer given by him and MR. TOBY SMITH to HENRY WILLIAMSON, son in law to the said RICHARD LOES.

From GEORGE SHERWOOD'S EARLY EMIGRANT NOTES, Vol. II (p. 11) Chancery Bills and Answers, Charles 1 F. 68/60½ PERRY v. LOWE. July 2, 1628. RICHARD PERRY, of LONDON, Merchant, and BRYAN HARRISON, of WAPPING, Mariner, and wife SUSAN, late wife of JAMES CARTER, Master of the Ship "ANNIE of LONDON". Voyage to Virginia. RICHARD LOWE, in Virginia, employed to collect CARTERS debts.

CATHERINE BOOTH, daughter of MARGARET UNDERWOOD and HUMPHREY BOOTH, married ROBERT BROOKE (b. 1653) and had ROBERT, HUMPHREY and WILLIAM BROOKE. ROBERT BROOKE JR. was a Deputy Clerk of ESSEX COUNTY, Va. in 1700. He was a "Knight of the Golden Horseshoe". His father was still alive in 1700. WILLIAM BROOKE married SARAH TALIAFERRO, daughter of LAWRENCE TALIAFERRO and grand-daughter of JOHN CATLETT, son of JOHN CATLETT and ELIZABETH UNDERWOOD. A daughter of HUMPHREY BROOK is believed to have married a CUNNINGHAM, though proof is lacking, but there was a HUMPHREY CUNNINGHAM, of this period and we have seen that the CUNNINGHAMS lived in SITTINGBOURNE PARISH. The will of ROBERT BROOKE JR. (W. B. 7 p. 275) proved April 5, 1736, names his children: WILLIAM BROOKE (to be under care of COL. WILLIAM BEVERLY until 21); ROBERT BROOKE (land the testator bought from WILLIAM MOSELEY); RICHARD BROOKE; HUMPHREY BROOKE; daughters KATHERINE BROOKE, SUSANNAH BROOKE, MOLLIE (MARTHA) BROOKE (the one who married CALEB BAKER) and ELIZABETH BROOKE. His will was made at the time when he was leaving "to finish the survey" of BEVERLY MANOR, granted to his close friend and associate COL. WILLIAM BEVERLY, April 23, 1735, in the "forks of the Shenandoah". PHOEBE, the wife of ROBERT BROOKE JR. at the time of his death (1736) was the great grand-daughter of COL. TOBY SMITH, an old friend of the Underwood family, heretofore mentioned, from YORK COUNTY. Her surname was either HODGKINS or PEACHY. (9 Virginia Magazine 436).

CAPT. FRANCIS SLAUGHTER, the ancestor of the SLAUGHTER FAMILY of Virginia, came from ISLE of WIGHT COUNTY. THE BAKER FAMILY of ESSEX, and ST. ANNE'S PARISH, also came from the LAWRENCE and HENRY BAKER FAMILY of Isle of Wight County. DR. JAMES WILLIAMSON and his brother HENRY WILLIAMSON, who married the daughter of RICHARD LOWE came also from ISLE OF WIGHT. RICHARD LOWE was a relative, if not a brother, of MICHAEL LOWE, father of MICAJAH LOWE, whose sister married a JOHN WILLIAMSON. All of these WILLIAMSONS were of the "COBHAM" WILLIAMSONS, of SURRY COUNTY.

WILLIAM COMBE (apprenticed to WILLIAM CUNNINGHAM) married MARY ROE, the daughter of EDWARD ROE. WILLIAM CUNNINGHAM, nephew of the elder WILLIAM, also married a daughter of EDWARD ROE the brother in law of WILLIAM COMBE. William Combe had a son IGNATIUS ROE. These ROES lived in MARYLAND for a time, but finally came back over into VIRGINIA. In MARYLAND they intermarried with the RICHARDSONS (from ACCOMAC) and the family of MARQUIS CAIMES. Out of these intermarriages came MARQUIS COMBES of Frederick County. The name of RICHARD LOWE appears on the records of VIRGINIA always as RICHARD LOES, and it is only in SHERWOOD'S AMERICAN IMMIGRANTS that the name is properly spelled LOWE. He was appointed the agent of one CARTER in behalf of the estate, and BRIAN HARRISON had married the widow of CARTER, the first record of an intermarriage between these two notable families - a habit that continued until this day.

The foregoing notes tend to explain statements on the Underwood Chart. Lack of space precludes going into further details.

SOME NOTES RELATING TO THE DESCENDANTS OF 1 ALEXANDER CUNNINGHAM
THE SON OF NEHEMIAH CUNNINGHAM (SEE THE CHART)

10 WILLIAM CUNNINGHAM (Son of ALEXANDER and grandson of NEHEMIAH) married a sister of the EDWARD ROE, whose daughter MARY became the wife of WILLIAM COMBES and the mother of IGNATIUS COMBES. This EDWARD ROE had a son EDWARD ROE who married and had JOHN ROE and a daughter who became the wife of REV. DAVID MOSSOM, minister of ST. PETER'S PARISH preceding REV. DEVEREAUX JARRETT (See WILLIAMSON and GILLIAM NOTES), and who is said to have performed the wedding ceremony between GEN. GEORGE WASHINGTON and the widow MARTHA CUSTIS at the "White House", the Custis home on PAMUNKY, in NEW KENT COUNTY. REV. DAVID MOSSOM had a son DAVID and a daughter NELLY. David Mossom was a CAPTAIN in the American Revolution, and NELLIE MOSSOM married her cousin, WILLIAM ROE CUNNINGHAM, a Lieutenant in the Navy, who served on the Schooner "LIBERTY" as testified to by COMMODORE BARRON, a relative of the ROES and CUNNINGHAMS. (Tyler's Hampton p. 41. Burgess Va. Soldiers of '76).

WILLIAM ROE CUNNINGHAM, son of 10 WILLIAM CUNNINGHAM and his wife MARY ROE, had the following children:

    1. JAMES CUNNINGHAM m. MARY ROE
    2. DAVID CUNNINGHAM
    3. WILLIAM ROE CUNNINGHAM (II) m. SUSANNAH ROE.
    4. JOHN CUNNINGHAM m. (1) ANN BENNETT (2) ELIZA HOLSTON.
    5. MARY CUNNINGHAM.

JOHN ROE (son of EDWARD ROE 2nd) had MARY ROE, who married JAMES CUNNINGHAM; SUSANNAH ROE, who married WILLIAM ROE CUNNINGHAM; ELIZABETH ROE who married (1) RICHARD BARRON SERVANT (2) CHARLES PASTEUR; CATHERINE ROE married ADAM BOUTTELL, and it also appears, though this is not plain, that there was a MARGARET ROE who married DAVID MOSSOM. (Burgess).

JAMES CUNNINGHAM (Son of WILLIAM and grandson of 10 WILLIAM) and his wife MARY ROE had, as near as can be ascertained from the jumbled records, the following children:

    (1) WILLIAM ROE CUNNINGHAM
    (2) ELIZABETH ROE CUNNINGHAM
    (3) MARY CUNNINGHAM married JAMES LATTIMORE.
        Had son ROE LATTIMORE.

WILLIAM ROE CUNNINGHAM (II) and his wife SUSANNAH ROE had the following children:

    (6) SAMUEL BARRON CUNNINGHAM
    (7) ANNE CUNNINGHAM married THOMAS GATEWOOD.
    (8) ELIZABETH CUNNINGHAM married RICHARD GATEWOOD
    (9) ROBERT BARRON CUNNINGHAM
    (10) JOHN CUNNINGHAM
    (11) MARY CUNNINGHAM married ALEXANDER WILSON.

JOHN CUNNINGHAM (Son of WILLIAM R. CUNNINGHAM and MARY ROE) married ANN BENNETT as his first wife and had MARY, ANNE, JOHN, THOMAS, WILLIAM ROE, JAMES, SAMUEL, ELIZABETH and ELLENER CUNNINGHAM. By his second marriage he had CATHERINE CUNNINGHAM who married MARSHALL WHITEHURST of Portsmouth, Virginia. ROE LATTIMORE, son of MARY had children BARBARA, PORCHO and JOHN LATTIMORE.

ANNE CUNNINGHAM and her husband THOMAS GATEWOOD were the parents of PHILEMON GATEWOOD, WILLIAM CUNNINGHAM GATEWOOD and ELIZABETH A. GATEWOOD.

ELIZABETH GATEWOOD, the grand-daughter of WILLIAM ROE CUNNINGHAM (II) of the Navy service married GABRIEL GALT WILLIAMSON, son of THOMAS WILLIAMSON and the great grandson of another THOMAS WILLIAMSON and his wife JUDITH FLEMING (Dau. of TARLTON FLEMING).

TARLTON FLEMING was a first cousin of JOHN DANIEL (will YORK County in 1723) and the guardian of HANNAH DANIEL, sister of JAMES DANIEL, whose three sons married each a CUNNINGHAM and the grand-daughters of REV. JOHN THOMSON. THOMAS WILLIAMSON was the son of JOHN WILLIAMSON, member of the vestry of CURLE'S CHURCH, and who married REBECCA CHAMBERLAINE of New Kent County. He was a cousin, some degrees removed in a later generation of DR. JAMES WILLIAMSON and HENRY WILLIAMSON, of the Underwood Chart. The old Williamson home was called "COBHAMS" and was located in SURRY COUNTY, just across the JAMES RIVER from Jamestown Island.

----

11 CHRISTOPHER CUNNINGHAM (Son of ALEXANDER and grandson of NEHEMIAH) was the father of a bevy of sons who settled on the "North Fork" of Shenandoah County, Virginia, including a son CHRISTOPHER who probably married a daughter of JACOB PATTON, in whose will he appears as a legatee. This son CHRISTOPHER CUNNINGHAM died leaving a will in WASHINGTON COUNTY, TENNESSEE (then N. C.) in 1782, in which he mentioned MARY "my dearly beloved wife" - who was perhaps his second or third, and who was a daughter of JOHN MORGAN. The will names 15 children, and was witnessed by MATTHEW TALBOTT, JOSEPH TIPTON, and Executored by ROBERT ORR and ISAAC TAYLOR, whose wife, as I recall, was a PATTON.

The 15 children were ELIZABETH, SUSANNAH, LYDIA, JOHN, MARY, ANN, SARAH, JANE, JACOB, JOSEPH, MATTHEW, MOSES, AARON, ELEANOR and DAVID CUNNINGHAM. Robert Orr married ANN. Most of the West Tennessee Cunninghams and some in Texas come down from CHRISTOPHER and his fifteen.

----

12 ALEXANDER CUNNINGHAM moved to GOOCHLAND COUNTY, with the DANIEL FAMILY, and where his children intermarried with a French Huguenot family named MICHAUX. He was the father of MAJ. WILLIAM CUNNINGHAM, who after the revolution settled in TENNESSEE. One of his daughters married PHILLIP MAURY. MAJOR WILLIAM had nine children. Revolutionary warrants were issued to them based on a statement witnessed by JOHN PATERSON or PETERSON and one WILLIAM LATTIMORE, a relative of the ROE LATTIMORE family of ELIZABETH CITY and YORK COUNTY, VIRGINIA.

NOTES RELATING TO THE FAMILY OF 2 WILLIAM CUNNINGHAM, SON OF NEHEMIAH
THE SON OF WILLIAM CUNNINGHAM, THE EMIGRANT TO YORK

This 2. WILLIAM CUNNINGHAM, according to the conclusions of this compiler, was the grandfather of JAMES CUNNINGHAM, of CUB CREEK, Charlotte County, Virginia, who married ANNE THOMSON, the daughter of REV. JOHN THOMSON, of Mecklenburg County, North Carolina. His oldest son, perhaps, was 16 WILLIAM CUNNINGHAM (See Chart). The name of the wife of 16 WILLIAM CUNNINGHAM has not been ascertained, but it is not improbable that she was a BUTLER and a sister of REV. AMORY BUTLER, or a SLAUGHTER. They had children: (1) WILLIAM CUNNINGHAM (2) JAMES CUNNINGHAM (3) JOHN CUNNINGHAM (4) JOSIAS CUNNINGHAM (5) ROBERT CUNNINGHAM (6) THOMAS CUNNINGHAM.

(1) WILLIAM CUNNINGHAM married a LEWIS and died in Fairfax County, Virginia, in 1797, naming brothers JOHN and JOSIAS. (King's Fairfax Records p. 60).
(2) JAMES CUNNINGHAM died in SPOTTSYLVANIA COUNTY (Va.) in 1782. His wife was ANN ELEY, & she was a sister of EDWARD ELEY of the ISLE OF WIGHT COUNTY family of the name. The widow ANNE died leaving will dated April 23, 1789, named "my brother" EDWARD ELEY and children ELIZABETH, ANN, JAMES, NELLIE, WILLIAM, HENRY and GEORGE CUNNINGHAM. John Herndon was guardian of the two youngest children HENRY and GEORGE. This (2) JAMES CUNNINGHAM was a first cousin of JAMES CUNNINGHAM, of CHARLOTTE County (Cub Creek) who married ANNE THOMSON.
(5) ROBERT CUNNINGHAM moved to Frederick County (Va.) where his father had left him property and died there, where his will was probated in 1769. The will was proven by his son GEORGE CUNNINGHAM and JAMES CHEW of Spottsylvania County. He obtained lands from Lord Fairfax in 1760. His children named in his will were JAMES, GEORGE, WILLIAM, ROBERT, ELIZABETH, ELLENER and JANE CUNNINGHAM.
(6) THOMAS CUNNINGHAM married JANE McKEMIE, a sister of MARY McKEMIE, the wife of his first cousin SAMUEL CUNNINGHAM, and his will, probated in 1761, names his wife and JOHN McKEMIE as executors of the will. (These McKemies were the collateral relatives of REV. FRANCIS McKAMIE, Presbyterian Minister of POKOMOKE (Va.) whose successor in America was REV. JOHN THOMSON.
(The SLAUGHTERS, some of them, were associated with 16 WILLIAM CUNNINGHAM and his children. They owned lands in FREDERICK COUNTY, also. See notes on same page with the CUNNINGHAM CHART).

17 JAMES CUNNINGHAM (see later).

18 ALEXANDER CUNNINGHAM. He was associated with his brother WILLIAM CUNNINGHAM, and they engaged in the mercantile business together in SPOTTSYLVANIA and STAFFORD and PRINCE WILLIAM COUNTIES during the first half of the eighteenth century. One of their enterprises was located at what is now called FALMOUTH old trading post, but which was then a flourishing little town at the head of navigation on the RAPPAHANNOCK RIVER, first in KING GEORGE and later STAFFORD COUNTY. The SLAUGHTER family, descendants of CAPT. FRANCIS SLAUGHTER who married ELIZABETH UNDERWOOD and cousins of the WILLIAM COMBES (raised by WILLIAM CUNNINGHAM) were their neighbors and sometimes business associates. These CUNNINGHAMS had establishments in SPOTTSYLVANIA, KING GEORGE, STAFFORD, PRINCE WILLIAM and over beyond the mountains, whence some of them drifted and took up lands. It is believed that the wife of 18 ALEXANDER CUNNINGHAM was a BELL, from whence came so many ALEXANDER BELLS, WILLIAM BROWN BELL and JANE BELL, wife of ROBERT CUNNINGHAM and RACHEL BELL wife of JOHN CUNNINGHAM, will March 3, 1813 in AUGUSTA COUNTY (Vol III, Chalkley p. 241), witnessed by SAMUEL BELL, WILLIAM CUNNINGHAM and FRANCIS BELL. WILLIAM CUNNINGHAM, son of ALEXANDER (18) became a merchant at DUMFRIES in Prince WILLIAM during revolutionary days. 18 ALEXANDER CUNNINGHAM had children: (1) WILLIAM CUNNINGHAM (2) DAVID CUNNINGHAM (3) ALEXANDER CUNNINGHAM (4) JAMES CUNNINGHAM. (2) DAVID CUNNINGHAM'S will proved Nov. 19th, 1774 in AUGUSTA COUNTY. His wife was ANN (perhaps EWING), and as near as we can tell he had children DAVID, PATRICK, WILLIAM, JOHN, JAMES, ALEXANDER, ANNE, MARY, JANE and SARAH CUNNINGHAM.

19. GEORGE CUNNINGHAM remained in YORK COUNTY, where he was probably born about the year 1665, and where the old CHARLES PARISH REGISTER shows he was married to a wife named JANE and had a daughter JANE CUNNINGHAM born July 11, 1696. While the actual relationship cannot be proven, every inference indulged points to the fact that he was probably the father of (1) WILLIAM CUNNINGHAM who died about 1731 in YORK COUNTY, whose wife was MARY and who had (10) WILLIAM CUNNINGHAM who died in 1787 leaving children: ELIZABETH, FRANCES, JAMES, MARY and THOMAS CUNNINGHAM and perhaps others. (Charles Parish Register).

20. DAVID CUNNINGHAM was probably the father of NATHANIEL CUNNINGHAM, the latter being the ancestor of the CUNNINGHAMS who settled in PITTSYLVANIA COUNTY, as shown by the records of that county. Nathaniel Cunningham's will was proven in ELIZABETH CITY COUNTY, Virginia, in 1762, and was witnessed by JOHN SHEPPARD, JAMES SHEPPARD and FRANCIS BALLARD. The children of NATHANIEL CUNNINGHAM, who settled in PITTSYLVANIA COUNTY, were NATHANIEL, JOSEPH and THOMAS CUNNINGHAM. MARY CUNNINGHAM, daughter of THOMAS married THOMAS SHIELDS in 1787, and her brother WILLIAM CUNNINGHAM married MARGARET DEAN; another sister MARTHA married LABAN GRISHAM in 1790; also a sister ELIZABETH CUNNINGHAM married her cousin JOSEPH, son of THOMAS CUNNINGHAM. THOMAS CUNNINGHAM left will in 1797 (D & W BOOK No. 11), which was witnessed by JOHN SHIELDS (All these SHIELDS were neighbors of the Cunningams in York County, as heretofore shown), and his children were JEAN, ELEANOR, ISABELL, JOSEPH, WILLIAM, ELIZABETH, PEGGY, MARTHA, EPHRAIM and THOMAS CUNNINGHAM.

21. JOHN CUNNINGHAM. Hard to place him accurately, but it is believed that he had a son who settled across the JAMES RIVER in Isle of Wight or Nansemond County, who was the father of JOHN CUNNINGHAM who married POLLY FULGHAM, daughter of JOSEPH FULGHAM in 1782, and PETER CUNNINGHAM who married her sister LOUISA FULGHAM Dec. 6, 1786 in Isle of Wight County.

THE CUNNINGHAM STORES: On Hyco, in Person County, N. C., in Georgia, in Tennessee, in Richmond, Virginia, were "Cunningam Stores". They were owned by CUNNINGHAM & CO. The owners were of this family and of the WILLIAM ROE CUNNINGHAMS of YORK and ELIZABETH CITY County, headed by a SAMUEL BARROW CUNNINGHAM, after the Revolution. (Calendar of Virginia State Papers, Vol. 1 p. ___).

17 JAMES CUNNINGHAM, GREAT GRANDSON OF WILLIAM CUNNINGHAM, THE EMIGRANT, AND HIS DESCENDANTS.

17. JAMES CUNNINGHAM (Son of 2 WILLIAM, grandson of NEHEMIAH and Great grandson of WILLIAM CUNNINGHAM, the emigrant, of YORK COUNTY, VIRGINIA, was the father of JAMES CUNNINGHAM of CUB CREEK, Charlotte County, Virginia. The name of the wife of 17 JAMES CUNNINGHAM, we do not know. It is the compiler's opinion that she belonged to one of the early and prominent families of the Old Dominion who perhaps lived in OLD RAPPAHANNOCK, from whence they had migrated Northward from YORK County. On page 430 of these notes appear some of the proceedings of the Virginia Council on Dec. 12, 1733, in which it is shown that this 17 JAMES CUNNINGHAM had already been granted patents to lands situated on WILLIS CREEK (or RIVER) in Goochland County, and that his immediate neighbors at that time were TARLTON FLEMING, STEPHEN HUGHES, COL. BENJAMIN HARRISON, WILLIAM MAYO, HENRY CARY and others; and we are justified in assuming that all these prominent persons, including the RANDOLPHS, some of whom, the records show, were associated with the CUNNINGHAMS, were his close friends, whom he knew intimately, as in the case of SAMUEL COBBS, who had been Executor of the estate of his brother DAVID CUNNINGHAM in York County, a few years previously.

SONS OF 17 JAMES CUNNINGHAM AND HIS WIFE (NAME UNKNOWN)

101. SAMUEL CUNNINGHAM m. MARY McKEMIE (Relative of REV. FRANCIS McKEMIE).
102. ROBERT CUNNINGHAM m. MARTHA KIRKPATRICK (Sister of SARAH KIRKPATRICK, the wife of REV. SAMUEL DAVIES of HANOVER.
103. CAPT. JOHN CUNNINGHAM of Staunton, Va., m. SARAH DAVIS.
104. WILLIAM CUNNINGHAM m. JEAN KIRKPATRICK (Sister of MARTHA and SARAH).
105. DAVID CUNNINGHAM. Died YORK COUNTY VA. 1719/20. SAMUEL COBBS, Executor.
106. CHARLES CUNNINGHAM of NEW KENT COUNTY. On petition with JOHN THOMSON.
107. JAMES CUNNINGHAM m. ANNE THOMSON, daughter of REV. JOHN THOMSON - died in MECKLENBURG COUNTY, North Carolina in 1753.

Doubtless there were also some daughters, who married, and for that reason the records are more difficult of identification.

1. SAMUEL CUNNINGHAM married MARY McKEMIE, daughter or sister of JOHN McKEMIE. SAMUEL CUNNINGHAM died a very young man in 1747, leaving one daughter MARGARET CUNNINGHAM, who married ROBERT ARMSTRONG. The widow MARY CUNNINGHAM married ANDREW MITCHELL, ROBERT ARMSTRONG and his wife MARGARET settled in the Watauga Valley, and finally in KNOX COUNTY, TENNESSEE, where they left a large family of children and grand-children; the genealogists have it that they came to Tennessee by way of South Carolina, where they resided for several years. JOHN ARMSTRONG, a brother of ROBERT, married JEAN BAKER, a daughter of DOUGLASS BAKER and his wife JANE THOMSON, daughter of REV. JOHN THOMSON and brother in law of JAMES CUNNINGHAM, of CUB CREEK, in Charlotte County. Both ROBERT ARMSTRONG and his brother JOHN ARMSTRONG moved to Tennessee.

2. ROBERT CUNNINGHAM married MARTHA KIRKPATRICK, daughter of CHARLES KIRKPATRICK, a descendant of ROGER KIRKPATRICK, head of an ENGLISH FAMILY of the name. JEAN KIRKPATRICK, sister of MARTHA married 4 WILLIAM CUNNINGHAM, and SARAH KIRKPATRICK, another daughter, became the first wife of REV. SAMUEL DAVIES, the friend and co-laborer of REV. JOHN THOMSON. SARAH DAVIES died Sept. 15, 1757, long before CHARLES KIRKPATRICK made his will, in which he mentions his son in law ROBERT CUNNINGHAM. ROBERT CUNNINGHAM was a member of the House of Burgesses of VIRGINIA, and served in the years 1745, 1746 and 1747, with WILLIAM RANDOLPH, of Wilton, to whom JAMES CUNNINGHAM, of CUB CREEK, sold lands he had bought from SAMUEL COBBS on Buffaloe Prince SPRING CREEK in AMELIA (later Prince Edward County) giving a deed therefor to Randolph in 1756. (52 Va. Mag p. 139).

3. CAPT. JOHN CUNNINGHAM, of Staunton, bought lots Nos. 1 and 7 from COL. WILLIAM BEVERLY in 1749. These Cunninghams had been induced to come to AUGUSTA COUNTY through the influence of their old friend and neighbor, the Clerk of ESSEX COUNTY, and also by their relative, ROBERT BROOKE, who had helped originally to survey the land, prior to his death. In 1761 JOHN CUNNINGHAM was witness to a deed by WILLIAM JOHNSON or JOHNSTON, and the same year WILLIAM JOHNSTON died and both JOHN and ROBERT CUNNINGHAM witnessed his will. It is not strange, therefore that a son, WILLIAM JOHNSTON, married MARY CUNNINGHAM, daughter of JAMES of CUB CREEK, and a grand-daughter of REV. JOHN THOMSON. CAPT. JOHN CUNNINGHAM had only one son, WALTER CUNNINGHAM, who in 1773, with the consent of SARAH, the widow of CAPT. JOHN CUNNINGHAM, gave bond as administrator of the estate of his father, with ROBERT ARMSTRONG, who had married his cousin MARGARET CUNNINGHAM, as surety. (This shows that ROBERT ARMSTRONG was still living in Augusta County in 1773, and had not yet moved either to South Carolina or Tennessee.) CAPT. JOHN CUNNINGHAM had at least one daughter, MARGARET CUNNINGHAM, who married ROBERT REID or REED, by whom she had three children, ROBERT REED, CATON REED and FRANCES, who married HUGH BALLENTINE (Of an old NORFOLK family, South of the James River). MARGARET (CUNNINGHAM) REED, after the death of her husband, married GOVERNOR GEORGE MATTHEWS, of GEORGIA. In 1769 WALTER CUNNINGHAM had witnessed a deed by COL. ANDREW LEWIS and GEORGE MATTHEWS. WALTER CUNNINGHAM moved to JESSAMINE COUNTY, Kentucky, where he died about 1807 leaving a will. He had MARY CUNNINGHAM, who became the wife of ROBERT LOWREY (another NORFOLK family), AGNESS, m. WILLIAM DRAKE, and daughters JEAN and ISABELLA CUNNINGHAM. Walter's wife was JEAN STEELE, of Augusta County.

4. WILLIAM CUNNINGHAM married JEAN or JENNETT KIRKPATRICK, sister of the wife of ROBERT CUNNINGHAM and of the wife of REV. SAMUEL DAVIES, of Hanover County. In 1755 he and his wife deeded a tract of land at the head of MOFFITT'S BRANCH to CHARLES KIRKPATRICK, witnessed by JAMES HOGSHEAD, JOHN DAVIS and JOHN McKEMIE. JOHN DAVIS, probably a brother in law of CAPT. JOHN CUNNINGHAM, bought from him his Lot No. 1 in the town of STAUNTON. The names of the children of 4 WILLIAM CUNNINGHAM and his wife JEAN have not been identified.

5. DAVID CUNNINGHAM, died in YORK COUNTY, VIRGINIA, in 1719/20, leaving a will in which he mentions two children, DAVID and JANE CUNNINGHAM. JANE became the wife of JOHN WHITE of ELIZ-

ABETH CITY COUNTY, and her brother DAVID CUNNINGHAM moved to AUGUSTA COUNTY, where in 1749 he witnessed a deed by WILLIAM BEVERLY, the proprietor of BEVERLY MANOR, who was born and raised in the town of HAMPTON, in Elizabeth City County, where many of the CUNNINGHAMS had grown up with and known him, before he went to ESSEX COUNTY and became Clerk of the Court.

6. CHARLES CUNNINGHAM lived in NEW KENT COUNTY and sometime in 1749 signed a petition with some of his neighbors as a protestant dissenter. On this list appears the names of BLACKMORE HUGHES, SIMON CLEMENT, ABRAHAM LEWIS and also the name of JOHN THOMSON, who, it is believed was REV. JOHN THOMSON, who frequently spent time in this neighborhood with some of his old friends, when on his way to WILLIAMSBURG and other points. This was just shortly before REV. THOMSON left Virginia and went down into South Carolina, where he died some three years later.

This brings us down to 107 JAMES CUNNINGHAM, of CUB CREEK, who married ANNE THOMSON. The names of their 10 children have already been given on page 463, to which reference is here made.

GRANDCHILDREN OF JAMES CUNNINGHAM OF CUB CREEK

(1) SAMUEL CUNNINGHAM (wife unknown) had children: SAMUEL, ANDREW and HANNAH. (GEORGIA.)

(2) ELIZABETH CUNNINGHAM married JAMES DANIEL, and had children: JAMES CUNNINGHAM DANIEL, CUNNINGHAM DANIEL, JOHN THOMSON DANIEL, WILLIAM T. DANIEL, JANE DANIEL, SARAH DANIEL, (Dau) m. COLBERT, SAMUEL DANIEL, THOMAS DANIEL, RICHARD SANKEY DANIEL and DAVID DANIEL. (To Georgia).

(3) SARAH CUNNINGHAM married (1) SAMUEL CALDWELL (2) JOHN DANIEL (brother of JAMES) and had children: JAMES KELSO DANIEL (To Georgia), BETSY ANN DANIEL, JANE DANIEL, SARAH DANIEL, POLLY DANIEL, MARGARET DANIEL, FRANCES DANIEL, SAMUEL J. DANIEL. JOHN DANIEL died in Va. and most of his children remained there.

(4) MARGARET CUNNINGHAM married RICHARD GAINES JR., and had children: HEIROM GAINES, MARY PENDLETON GAINES and ANNE GAINES. Perhaps others. (To Georgia).

(5) JANE CUNNINGHAM married JAMES ADAMS JR., and had children: WILLIAM, SAMUEL, ANNE T., ELIZABETH, JOHN C., THOMAS F., JAMES B., ANN THOMSON, MOURNING, CALVIN, RICHARD and ABNER ADAMS. (To Elbert County, Ga.)

(6) ANN CUNNINGHAM married ANDREW HANNAH and had children: ANN THOMSON, JOHN, GEORGE, JANE, ANDREW, JAMES CUNNINGHAM, MARY, WILLIAM and SAMUEL HANNAH. (Some to GEORGIA).

(7) MARY CUNNINGHAM married WILLIAM JOHNSTON. Only one child - ANN JOHNSON - identified.

(8) HANNAH CUNNINGHAM married WILLIAM DANIEL (brother of JAMES and JOHN) and had children: JAMES, ANN, MARY, JANE, SAMUEL C., and WILLIAM DANIEL.

(9) ANDREW CUNNINGHAM married ISABELLA HANNAH (Dau. of GEORGE HANNAH) Source furnishes no children, or history of his family.

(10) JAMES CUNNINGHAM married FRANCES REDD and they had children: THOMAS, ELIZABETH, JOHN, SAMUEL, MARY M., JAMES T., HARRIET FRANCES, MARTHA INDIANA, ELIZA EARLY and WILLIAM REDD CUNNINGHAM.

ELIZABETH CUNNINGHAM daughter of (10) JAMES CUNNINGHAM, first above, married JEREMIAH EARLY a brother of GOV. PETER EARLY, of GEORGIA, whose youngest sister LUCY EARLY married CHARLES MATTHEWS, son of GOV. GEORGE MATTHEWS, one of who's wives was MARGARET CUNNINGHAM, a daughter of CAPT. JOHN CUNNINGHAM, of Staunton, Virginia, brother of JAMES CUNNINGHAM OF CUB CREEK.

MARY HANNAH, daughter of ANN CUNNINGHAM and ANDREW HANNAH, married JOSIAH DABBS, the son of RICHARD DABBS, who married her mother ANN (CUNNINGHAM) HANNAH after ANDREW HANNAH'S death. This RICHARD DABBS and his son were descendants of JOSEPH DABBS, who with COL. THOMAS WALKER was granted 2500 acres of land on the upper side of WILLIS CREEK by the Council on December 12, 1733, the same day that the patent to JAMES CUNNINGHAM (father of 107 JAMES), HENRY CARY and others was mentioned. Also numerous transactions are mentioned between this JOSEPH DABBS and JAMES DANIEL on the records of GOOCHLAND COUNTY thereafter. (McIlwain's).

This genealogical story of the REV. JOHN THOMSON and his associated families, the Sankeys, Gilliams, Underwoods, Bakers, Cunninghams and others is based upon unimpeachable records, as to the essential facts, and some of it on that indefinable element of magnetism, equally as dependable, in the view of the writer, that has always impelled the human race, consciously or unconsciously, to seek homogenious fields of endeavor among fellow-beings of the same blood, origin and traditions; whose common experiences, environment and understanding leads more surely to happiness and contentment. In the days of which we have written it was the exception and not the rule, that muptual bonds, wills and intimate business transactions were celebrated or executed between utter strangers, or those outside the same cultural circle, and new acquaintances were only in rare instances commandeered as witnesses to such indentures. Even as the trends and laws of nature, familiar to the scientist, enables him to ponder the jaw bone of an ancient mammoth, in connection therewith, and reconstruct his entire skeleton, so a working knowledge of history and these customs and rules of action among the people of the past, enables the writer to fill in missing gaps and rebuild the story of these ancient families, which would otherwise be lost to the World.

THE JACK FAMILY OF MECKLENBURG

No history of old Southern families could be complete without some mention of the JACK FAMILY, of Mecklenburg County, North Carolina. This family and many of the men and women in it pro-duced, weilded a wide influence in practically all of the Southern States. There have been a few sketches of certain branches of this family appearing in print from time to time in the last hundred years, all of which have been inadequate to give the student of old families a true perspective of this particular clan. There are a few points this writer would like to bring out that have never before been mentioned, aside from a mere tabulated list of the descendants, so that the reader may get a better view of this family.

PATRICK JACK was the North Carolina ancestor of the family. WILLIAM JACK, presumably of Pennsylvania, has been called the "ancestor" of PATRICK of Mecklenburg, but those historians who have mentioned him were careful not to say that he was the FATHER. As a matter of fact they did not know, nor does the writer of these sketches. Undoubtedly the best outline of the family was written by Cyrus L. Hunter in his "Western North Carolina" in 1877. The following, appearing on page 62 of his rare volume, bears on the ancestry of PATRICK JACK:

> In the reign of Charles II, in 1661 * * that despotic monarch * in Ireland ejected from their benefices or livings, under Jeremiah Taylor, thirteen ministers of the Presbytery of Lagan, in the Northern part of Ireland, for their non-conformity to the Church of England. Among the honored names of these thirteen were:
> ROBERT WILSON, ancestor of the REV. FRANCIS McKEMIE, who twenty years later, was the first Presbyterian Preacher that had ever visited the Western Continent, and near relative of GEORGE McKEMIE, of the Waxhaw settlement, and brother in law of Mrs. Elizabeth Jackson, the mother of General ANDREW JACKSON.
> ROBERT CRAIGHEAD, ancestor of the Rev. Alexander Craighead, the first settled pastor of SUGAR CREEK CONGREGATION, the early apostle of civil and religious liberty in MECKLENBURG COUNTY, and who ended his days there in 1766.
> THOMAS DRUMMOND, a near relative of WILLIAM DRUMMOND, the first Royal Governor of NORTH CAROLINA, who was hung by BERKELEY.
> ADAM WHITE, ancestor of HUGH LAWSON WHITE, a native of NORTH CAROLINA (who rose to political hights of leadership in TENNESSEE).
> WILLIAM JACK, ancestor of PATRICK JACK, of CHARLOTTE, N. C. (and of CAPT. JAMES JACK, who carried the Mecklenburg Declaration of Independence to the convention in session at Philadelphia.)

At this point in these annals, and before precipitating an account of the descendants of PATRICK, the father of CAPT. JAMES JACK, the messenger, it is proper to state that there were TWO DIFFERENT PATRICK JACKS who lived, for a time at least, simultaneously in MECKLENBURG COUNTY, NORTH CAROLINA. One was the father of CAPT. JAMES JACK, of Charlotte, and the other the father of a JOHN FINLEY JACK, a distinguished lawyer, who settled in KNOXVILLE, TENNESSEE, and married ELIZABETH COCKE, the daughter of GEN. WILLIAM COCKE, Captain in the revolution, and member of the United States Congress from Tennessee, who died in COLUMBUS, MISSISSIPPI, in 1828, in his 87th year. His son, JOHN FINLEY JACK was the namesake of the intrepid indian fighter and companion of Daniel Boone, of whom mention has been heretofore made — the son in law of REV. JOHN THOMSON. John Finley and this second Patrick Jack were not only near neighbors in Mecklenburg County, on the Catawba River, but were kindred spirits with an adventurous disposition in common that made them close friends. For convenience the second PATRICK will be referred to as PATRICK JACK II.

PATRICK JACK II was an "armorer" and is one of the few persons who have been identified in history as having been at the fall of the garrison at FORT LOUDON, erected by the British on the Little Tennessee River, on its South Bank, in what is now MONROE COUNTY, TENNESSEE. At the general massacre of the inmates treacherously engineered by the indians, his was one of the three lives that were spared, through the influence of an Indian leader called the "Little Carpenter".

On page 68 of RAMSEY'S ANNALS of Tennessee, there is a note reading:

> A grant signed ARTHUR DOBBS, Governor of North Carolina; WILLIAM BEAMER, Sr., Superintendent and Deputy Adjutant in and for the CHEROKEE NATION; WILLIAM BEAMER, JR., interpreter; and the "Little Carpenter," half king of the Cherokee Nation of the Overhill Towns, and MATTHEW TOOLE, Interpreter, made to CAPT. PATRICK JACK, of the Province of Pennsylvania, is recorded in the Register's Office of KNOX COUNTY, TENNESSEE. It purports to have been made at a Council held at Tennessee River, on the first of March, 1757. The consideration is four hundred dollars, and conveys to CAPT. JACK fifteen miles square South of the Tennessee River. The grant itself, confirmatory of the purchase by Jack, is dated at a general council, MET AT THE CATAWBA RIVER, on the 7th of May, 1762, and is witnessed by NATHANIEL ALEXANDER.

MATTHEW TOOLE, mentioned in this note, lived on the eastern bank of the CATAWBA RIVER in Meclenburg County and after him TOOLE'S FORD was named.
NATHANIEL ALEXANDER, the subscribing witness, was then an acting magistrate of MECKLENBERG COUNTY, and a man of wide and extensive influence.

PATRICK JACK II, who was in Fort Loudon, according to Hunter, returned to Pennsylvania, where he became a gallant officer in the American Revolution. The writer trusts this personal note will not be considered out of place, in making the statement that he was born on a part of the land embraced in the "fifteen miles square" allegedly purchased by this Patrick Jack from the Indians in 1757, later (in 1762) confirmed at a Council held in Mecklenburg County, North Carolina. Since this Patrick returned to Pennsylvania, no further reference to him will be necessary here, but we will return to the family of PATRICK JACK, of MECKLENBURG COUNTY. We think the chart below will make it easier to understand the ramifications of this family:

(1) PATRICK JACK married LILLIS McADOO (In IRELAND?)
and had:

Sons:
100. JAMES JACK
101. JOHN JACK
102. SAMUEL JACK
103. ROBERT JACK

Daughters:
104. CHARITY JACK
105. JANE JACK
106. MARY JACK
107. MARGARET JACK
108. LILLIS JACK

100. CAPT. JAMES JACK m. MARGARET HOUSTON
They were married Nov. 20, 1766, and had five children, as follows:

200. CYNTHIA JACK (b. 1767)
201. PATRICK JACK (b. 1769)
202. WILLIAM HOUSTON JACK (b. 1771).
203. ARCHIBALD JACK (b. 1773). d. y.
204. JAMES JACK (b. 1775).

101. JOHN JACK married MARY BARNETT and had

220. ANNE JACK m. MOSES WILEY.
221. MARY A. JACK m. JOHN J. BARNETT
222. DR. THOMAS A. JACK
223. JOHN JACK
224. SAMUEL JACK m. ANNIE LESLIE
225. SUSAN JACK m. ALEXANDER BOWIE
(Moved to ALABAMA).

ALEXANDER BOWIE became a Judge of the Court of Chancery in ALABAMA, where he settled with his family before the Indians had given up the territory. He appears to have been a son of JOHN BOWIE who fought in the revolution.

102. SAMUEL JACK m. (1) MISS KNIGHT and
Ch: (2) MARGARET STEWART.

205. ELIZA D. JACK m. Rev. HODGE
206. JAMES JACK died young.

207. SAMUEL STEWART JACK m. ELIZA MEREDITH.
208. JOHN McCORMICK JACK
209. WILLIAM D. JACK
210. MARY E. JACK
211. AMANDA M. JACK

103. ROBERT JACK (Hampshire Co. Va.) He came there from MARYLAND and never lived in Mecklenburg County, N. C. Had:
212. JAMES JACK
213. JOHN JACK (b. 1763) Only one who married. His
214. CYNTHIA JACK wife REBECCA
215. MARGARET JACK SINGLETON.

213. JOHN JACK became a successful merchant and banker in ROMNEY, VIRGINIA. He and his wife Rebecca Singleton had the following children:

300. ROBERT Y. JACK
301. CARLTON T. JACK
302. JAMES R. JACK
303. JOHN JACK
304. MARGARET JACK
305. JULIETTE M. JACK
306. JOHN G. JACK (Louisville, Ky.)
307. EDWARD W. JACK (Salem, Va.)

108. LILLIS JACK m. JOSEPH NICHOLSON
and they had six children. They moved to GEORGIA, where the name of JOSEPH NICHOLSON and his children and descendants are often found on the records.

104. CHARITY JACK m. DR. CORNELIUS DYSART
They had two sons:
216. JAMES DYSART (To GEORGIA)
217. ROBERT DYSART (To GEORGIA)

105. JANE JACK m. WILLIAM BARNETT (Son of JOHN BARNETT and ANNE SPRATT (the first child born in what is now MECKLENBURG COUNTY, of English Speaking parents. They had:

218. ANNIE BARNETT m. 204 JAMES JACK
219. SAMUEL BARNETT m. (1) ELIZA JOYNER
(2) ELIZA WORSHAM.

106. MARY JACK m. CAPT. ROBERT ALEXANDER
(Of Lincoln County, N. C.)
They had:

226. MARGARET ALEXANDER m. SAMUEL LOWRIE
227. LILLIS ALEXANDER m. CAPT. JAMES MARTIN
228. ROBERT W. ALEXANDER m. LOUISA MOORE
229. MARY ALEXANDER m. (1) JAMES J. SCOTT
(2) GEN. JOHN MOORE
230. ANNIE ALEXANDER m. JOHN SUMPTER

231. ELIZA ALEXANDER
232. EVALINE ALEXANDER
233. AMANDA ALEXANDER m. DR. J. C. RUDISILL.
(By 2nd wife MARGARET REILY)

107. MARGARET JACK m. SAMUEL WILSON (His third wife) and had:
234. SARAH WILSON m. BENJ. McCONNELL.
235. CHARITY WILSON d. y.
236. ROBERT WILSON m. MARG. ALEXANDER
237. LILLIS WILSON m. JAMES CONNOR
238. WILLIAM JACK WILSON m. ROCINDA WINSLOW, daughter of MOSES WINSLOW.

William J. Wilson and wife Rocinda left FOUR children.

DESCENDANTS OF CAPT. JAMES JACK OF MECKLENBURG

100   CAPT. JAMES JACK, of Charlotte, was the son of PATRICK JACK, the old hotel keeper on South Trade Street, about a block from where the Mecklenburg Declaration was signed on May 20th, 1775, who made the trecherous and perilous journey all the way from Charlotte to Philadelphia, Pennsylvania, where the Colonial Convention was then deliberating to present them with the immortal document. Of all of the sons of PATRICK JACK, perhaps CAPT. JAMES is best known in History, but not a great deal is known about his family. Thanks to Dr. Cyrus L. Hunter (son of the old Steele Creek Minister, HUMPHREY HUNTER) some of this information has been preserved, and, together with other items found here and there, is presented below:

-----

200. CYNTHIA JACK (Oldest child and only daughter of CAPT. JAMES JACK) married A. S. COSBY and moved with him to MISSISSIPPI, and after his death with her family of children went on over into LOUISIANA about 1814. Their children were

        308. MARGARET COSBY
        309. CYNTHIA COSBY
        310. JAMES COSBY
        311. DR. CHARLES COSBY

No further history of CYNTHIA JACK'S family has been found and identified.

201. PATRICK JACK (Oldest son of CAPT. JAMES JACK) married and raised a family of at least three sons, but the name of their mother is not contained in the account by Dr. Hunter. His mother, the wife of CAPT. JAMES JACK, as shown heretofore, was MARGARET HOUSTON, for whom 201 PATRICK named one of his sons. The children were:

        312. PATRICK JACK
        313. WILLIAM HOUSTON JACK
        314. JAMES W. JACK.

Information as to the families of the last two sons is lacking. There is a well authenticated statement, however, that PATRICK JACK, their father, was Colonel of the 8th Regiment of the U. S. Infantry in the war of 1812.

312. PATRICK JACK, (Son of PATRICK, the COLONEL) married HARRIETT SPENCER, a member of an old Southern family; and the SPENCER FAMILY as well as the JACK FAMILY, left GEORGIA, where CAPT. JAMES JACK the grandfather had moved, after the revolutionary war, and settled around GREENESBORO, in Greene County, Alabama. The children of 312 PATRICK JACK and HARRIETT SPENCER, some of whom, at least, were born in GEORGIA, according to Dr. Hunter's account, were as follows:

        400. JAMES JACK
        401. WILLIAM H. JACK
        402. PATRICK C. JACK
        403. SPENCER JACK
        404. ABNER JACK
        405. CHURCHILL JACK
        406. HARRIETT JACK
        407. MARGARET JACK.

400. JAMES JACK   Oldest son of PATRICK JACK and HARRIETT SPENCER) was born May 7, 1800, in ELBERT COUNTY, Georgia. He was the Great Grandson of CAPT. JAMES JACK and his wife MARGARET HOUSTON. He was twice married (1) to ANN SCOTT GRAY (Of GEORGIA) and (2) to MARY JANE WITHERSPOON. Dr. Hunter says he was the father of ten children by his first marriage and eleven by the second. We have found the names of fourteen only, as follows:

        500. EDWARD JACK   (Moved to Mississippi).
        501. JAMES M. JACK, C.SA. m. MARY SPENCER of Tuscaloosa Co. Ala.
        502. HEZEKIAH JACK
        503. PATRICK JACK never married.
        504. HARRIETT JACK m. J. T. B. COCKE, of MISSISSIPPI.
        505. SAMUEL JACK m. DELIA MILLER.
        506. JOHN H. JACK m. (1) LENA STICKNEY (2) SUSIE EDWARDS
        507. GRACE JACK m. W. C. CHRISTIAN
        508. JULIA M. JACK m. A. C. CHRISTIAN, CORSICANA, TEXAS.
        509. NVIE JACK m. JUDGE J. S. CALLICUT, CORSICANA, TEXAS.
        510. LILLIE JACK m. .... RANSOM, of CORSICANA, TEXAS.
        511. WILLIAM SPENCER JACK m. ANNIE STOLLINWERCK.
        512. CHARLES ELBERT JACK
        513. THOMAS HOWARD JACK, ATTORNEY, BLOOMING GROVE, TEXAS.

501. JAMES M. JACK (Confederate Soldier, of GREENESBORO, ALABAMA, who married MARY SPENCER, of the same place) had one son:
        600. THEODORE HENLEY JACK, a distinguished teacher and educator, who at this writing (1946) is connected with College Work in VIRGINIA.

401. WILLIAM H. JACK (Son of 312 PATRICK JACK and HARRIETT SPENCER and GREAT GRANDSON of CAPT. JAMES JACK) married LAURA HARRISON, and thus connected himself with another old North Carolina and Virginia family - the HARRISONS. LAURA HARRISON was the second daughter and child of ISHAM HARRISON and his wife HARRIETT KELLEY, and ISHAM HARRISON was the son of JAMES HARRISON and his wife ELIZABETH HAMPTON, sister of Col. Wade Hampton, of the Revolution, who was the son of ANTHONY HAMPTON who was massacred by the Indians on Tyger River in South Carolina, before the Revolution started, or about the time of its beginning. (See pages 255 and 253 of this work for an account of this family of HARRISONS). Hon. William H. Jack, with two of his brothers and many members of the HARRISON FAMILY emigrated to Texas from Alabama about 1831. The brothers were PATRICK C. and SPENCER JACK, and all three were prominent and successful lawyers. PATRICK C. JACK, one of the brothers was captured by the Mexicans and the settlers raised a small army for their rescue, from Gen. Bradburn, at Anahuac, led by ROBERT M. WILLIAMSON and others. WILLIAM H. JACK was in the battle of San Jacinto with Sam Houston's forces. He died in 1844 in Galveston, as did his brother PATRICK C., where both are buried. WILLIAM H. JACK left one son, THOMAS McKINNEY JACK, a noted Texas jurist, and two daughters. One of his daughters married GUY M. BRYAN, and the other became the wife of HON. WILLIAM PITT BALLINGER, of Galveston, the grandfather of JUDGE BALLINGER MILLS, who is at this writing (1946) still one of the leading lawyers of the Galveston bar and of the State of Texas. Spencer H. Jack, died young without leaving issue.

402. PATRICK C. JACK, died and is buried at Galveston, Texas. (See above paragraph).
403. SPENCER JACK, died leaving no issue. (See above pargarpah).
404. ABNER JACK. We have no record of his family.
405. CHURCHILL JACK was still alive and residing in ARKANSAS in the year 1876. He was the only one of the sons of PATRICK JACK and HARRIETT SPENCER who was alive at that time.

----

202. WILLIAM HOUSTON JACK (Second son of CAPT. JAMES JACK) was one of the first settlers and was a successful and prosperous merchant at AUGUSTA, GEORGIA. Eventually, however, he retired from the mercantile business and settled in WILKES COUNTY, GEORGIA, where he took care of his aged father and mother until their death. The wife of 202. WILLIAM HOUSTON JACK, was FRANCES CUMMINS, daughter of the REV. FRANCIS CUMMINS, one of the youthful witnesses, with SUSAN (BARNETT) SPRATT, of the actual signing of the MECKLENBURG DECLARATION OF INDEPENDENCE in 1775. REV. FRANCIS CUMMINS was the son of a CHARLES CUMMINS, whose will is to be found on p. 334 of these notes. FRANCIS CUMMINS was both a teacher and a preacher, and one of his pupils was ANDREW JACKSON, afterwards President of the United States. WILLIAM HOUSTON JACK left one son, WILLIAM CUMMINS JACK, who became a teacher by profession and a profound classical scholar, who in 1876 was living with his second son, also named WILLIAM HOUSTON JACK, a distinguished lawyer of NATCHITOCHES, LOUISIANA, who had one brother, DR. SAMUEL JACK of COLUMBIA COUNTY, ARKANSAS, as well as two other brothers, who were industrious and successful farmers.

203. ARCHIBALD JACK (Third son of CAPT. JAMES JACK) died young without issue.

204. JAMES W. JACK (Son of CAPT. JAMES) married ANNIE BARNETT, a daughter of JOHN BARNETT and his wife ANN SPRATT (the old pioneer -first to wheel across the Yadkin River), and had the following children:

315. SAMUEL T. JACK
316. JANE JACK
317. JAMES C. JACK
318. LILLIS JACK
319. PATRICK JACK
320. CYNTHIA JACK

315. SAMUEL T. JACK married MARTHA WEBSTER, of MISSISSIPPI.
316. JANE JACK married DR. JAMES JARRETT.
317. JAMES C. JACK was a volunteer soldier in the Texas Revolution and was a second corporal in the Company of Capt. Isaac Ticknor, under JAMES W. FANNIN, at Goliad, where he was slaughtered through the treachery of the Mexicans in the Spring campaign of 1836, with other members of his command.
318. LILLIS JACK married OSBORNE EDWARDS and
319. PATRICK JACK married EMILY HANSON, of Texas.

101. JOHN JACK, SON OF PATRICK

101. JOHN JACK, second son of the pioneer Inn Keeper, PATRICK JACK, lived on McALPIN'S Creek in Mecklenburg County, and served in the Revolution. This writer thinks he was the JOHN JACK who married MARY BARNETT, but DR. HUNTER makes the very positive statement that this JOHN JACK was a cousin and not a brother of CAPT. JAMES JACK. If so, the elder PATRICK JACK must have had a brother living in MECKLENBURG COUNTY at an early day, though PATRICK II (heretofore mentioned) is said to have been the first PATRICK'S nephew.

102. SAMUEL JACK was a Revolutionary soldier. Lived in SUGAR CREEK settlement.

THE BARRY AND MOORE FAMILY

RICHARD BARRY was one of the "SIGNERS" of the MECKLENBURG DECLARATION.
CHARLES MOORE was the SPARTANBURG SCHOOL TEACHER, who was a cousin of MRS. MARY GRAHAM, the mother of GEN. JOSEPH GRAHAM.
MRS. MARY GRAHAM, as a girl, was MARY McCONNELL, daughter of MARY BARRY and HUGH McCONNELL, JR., and grand-daughter of CATHERINE MOORE and ANDREW BARRY.
ROBERT MOORE CUNNINGHAM, son of ROGER CUNNINGHAM, who is buried at PROVIDENCE CHURCH married ELIZABETH MOORE, daughter of CHARLES MOORE.
ROBERT HANNA or HANNAH, was the old Deputy Surveyor of South Carolina, whose son ROBERT HANNAH married a daughter of CHARLES MOORE; who went to INDIANA, where two of his descendants served in the UNITED STATES SENATE from that State.
ANDREW BARRY married MARGARET CATHERINE MOORE, daughter of CHARLES MOORE, and his brother RICHARD BARRY married ROSANNA MOORE her sister.
HUGH BARRY, another brother of ANDREW and RICHARD BARRY, married KATE or CATHERINE LAWSON, daughter of HUGH LAWSON and his wife MARY MOORE, the latter a sister of CHARLES MOORE.
CHARLES MOORE, JR., son of the SPARTANBURG SCHOOL TEACHER, married JANE BARRY, daughter of RICHARD BARRY and sister of ANDREW, RICHARD and HUGH BARRY, and was the father of ANDREW BARRY MOORE, who became Governor of ALABAMA.
ALICE MOORE, another daughter of CHARLES MOORE, became the wife of JOHN LAWSON, a cousin of CATHERINE LAWSON who married HUGH BARRY.
GEN. THOMAS MOORE and his brother CHARLES MOORE, JR., both sons of CHARLES MOORE, School teacher, each had a son named CHARLES HAMILTON MOORE.
CHARLES HAMILTON, brother of ALEXANDER, ROBERT and ANDREW HAMILTON, who were on the tythe lists of PRINCE EDWARD COUNTY, VIRGINIA, in 1755, with GEORGE MOORE and CHARLES MOORE.

Thus it will be seen that it would be practically impossible to write a connected story of the family of either the MOORE or BARRY families without including both of them; also without numerous references to the McCONNELL, LAWSON, HANNA and other families with which they were connected.

THE EARLY EMIGRANTS

BARRY FAMILY: ANDREW BARRY who married CATHERINE MOORE, and MARGARET BARRY who married CHARLES MOORE.

CALDWELL FAMILY: ANDREW CALDWELL, the father of JOHN CALDWELL, of CUB CREEK, Virginia; MARY CALDWELL, his sister, who married HUGH McCONNELL. The wife of ANDREW CALDWELL was MARGARET MOORE.

McCONNELL FAMILY: HUGH McCONNELL, who married MARY CALDWELL, and MARY McCONNELL, who married JOHN LAWSON; JOHN McCONNELL who married VIOLET LAWSON; ALEXANDER McCONNELL.

MOORE FAMILY: (1) CHARLES MOORE, (2) EPHRAIM MOORE, (3) ALEXANDER MOORE, (4) ROBERT MOORE, (5) CATHERINE MOORE and (6) MARGARET MOORE.

LAWSON FAMILY: JOHN LAWSON who married MARY McCONNELL, VIOLET LAWSON who married JOHN McCONNELL.

That is about as brief an account of the ancestry of the BARRY and MOORE families as can be contrived. If space would permit it would be comparatively simple to spend a few pages of space copying some of the English notes on these families - also Ireland and Scotland - embraced in an interesting little tome by MRS. CAROLINE BEALL PRICE, a descendant of the LAWSON, McCONNELL, McKISSICK and HENDERSON FAMILIES, in which she goes back to "BROUGH HALL" in England and shows how these LAWSONS connect with and belong to the same family as EPAPRODITUS and ROWLAND LAWSON of early Virginia; how Lawson descendants, through HUGH, are eligible to the "Barons of Runnimede", the "Colonial Dames" and other patriotic societies.

In what follows an effort will be made to give as clear an account as possible of the descendants of the above ancestors. We will start off with

CHARLES MOORE who married MARGARET BARRY

CHARLES MOORE and his wife MARGARET BARRY were the parents of several children and we cannot be sure, either that the list is complete, or that, in every instance it is correct. No will has been found and no Bible Records are available to substantiate what contemporaneous and extraneous evidence seem to reveal. They seem to have been the parents of:

100. CHARLES MOORE m. MISS HAMILTON.
101. DAVID MOORE m. MARGARET CAMPBELL.
102. MARY MOORE m. HUGH LAWSON.
103. HUGH MOORE m. MARTHA CALDWELL.
104. GEORGE MOORE m. MISS CALDWELL.

105. WILLIAM MOORE m. MARY
106. JAMES MOORE
107. JOSEPH MOORE
108. JOHN MOORE.
109. VIOLET MOORE m. WiLLIAM WATSON.

100. CHARLES MOORE m. MISS HAMILTON, was the School Teacher of SPARTANBURG COUNTY, S. C., heretofore mentioned, and the cousin of MRS. MARY GRAHAM, mother of GEN. JOSEPH GRAHAM. A list of his children will be given later.

101. DAVID MOORE, who married MARGARET CAMPBELL, died in MECKLENBURG COUNTY, N. C. in 1778. An abstract of his will is shown on page 322. His will was witnessed by his brother, JAMES MOORE and by ARCHIBALD CAMPBELL.

102. MARY MOORE was the wife of COL. HUGH LAWSON, who died leaving a will in 1774, which had been executed in 1764. The will was placed on record in ROWAN COUNTY, as there was an unsettled line near his land on DAVIDSON'S CREEK. (See map pp. 369 and 380). HUGH LAWSON was buried in BAKERS GRAVEYARD in Mecklenburg County.

103. HUGH MOORE married MARTHA CALDWELL, and died leaving will in HALIFAX COUNTY, Virginia, in 1760, in which he mentions his wife MARTHA and his brother JOHN MOORE.

104. GEORGE MOORE married a sister of the wife of HUGH MOORE. Their wives were SISTERS of JOHN CALDWELL, of CUB CREEK, in Charlotte County, Virginia, and daughters of ANDREW CALDWELL and his wife MARGARET MOORE, the sister of CHARLES MOORE who married MARGARET BARRY. GEORGE MOORE, like his brother CHARLES, moved to SOUTH CAROLINA, where his name appears frequently on the records.

105. WILLIAM MOORE married MARY (her last name unknown) and moved to and settled in MECKLENBURG COUNTY, before TRYON was established, but in that part which later became TRYON and then LINCOLN. In 1768 he was one of the Commissioners to divide MECKLENBURG and TRYON COUNTIES.

106. JAMES MOORE is said to have married RACHEL BLACK, of a family of BLACKS who settled in what is now LINCOLN or GASTON, from VIRGINIA. James Moore and Rachel Black were married in Virginia. Before coming to North Carolina the Blacks lived in AUGUSTA COUNTY, VIRGINIA.

107. JOSEPH MOORE, while undoubtedly one of the brothers, is shown by a deed to have come to MECKLENBURG COUNTY in 1765, from the "Colony of PENNSYLVANIA". Twin deeds, executed the same day by JOHN McDOWELL and his wife ANN (June 8, 1765), one to JAMES MOORE and the other to JOSEPH MOORE furnish ample proof of their relationship. Both deeds had the same witnesses: RICHARD BARRY, WILLIAM BARRY and CHARLES MOORE. The lands were on McDOWELL'S CREEK in upper Mecklenburg.

108. JOHN MOORE. The will of HUGH MOORE in 1760 in VIRGINIA mentions JOHN MOORE as being his brother. At that time JOHN was perhaps the only brother remaining in VIRGINIA. He also came later to North Carolina, and perhaps settled below the present line in SOUTH CAROLINA.

109. VIOLET MOORE was a namesake of VIOLET LAWSON, a sister of COL. HUGH LAWSON, who married her sister MARY MOORE. VIOLET LAWSON married a WILLIAM WATSON, of PRINCE EDWARD COUNTY, who moved to the North side of FISHING CREEK (then in Mecklenburg County) where he obtained a land grant in 1753, part of which he deeded to WILLIAM MOORE May 21, 1764.

---

100. CHARLES MOORE and his wife MISS HAMILTON

100. CHARLES MOORE (the SPARTANBURG S. C. SCHOOL MASTER) and his wife MISS HAMILTON, had the following children:

200. MARGARET CATHERINE MOORE m. ANDREW BARRY
201. ALICE MOORE m. JOHN LAWSON.
202. ROSANNA MOORE m. RICHARD BARRY
203. .... MOORE m. ROBERT HANNA, JR.
204. JANE MOORE m. MATTHEW PATTON.
205. .... MOORE m. MATTHEW PATTON (His 2nd wife).
206. GEN. THOMAS MOORE m. (1) PATSY PRICE (2) MARY REAGAN.
207. ELIZABETH MOORE m. REV. ROBERT MOORE CUNNINGHAM.
208. ANDREW BARRY MOORE m. (1) ANNE MAXWELL (2) NANCY MILLER MONTGOMERY.
209. CHARLES MOORE, JR. m. JANE BARRY.

200. MARGARET CATHERINE MOORE and husband ANDREW BARRY
had children:

300. JOHN BARRY married his cousin VIOLET WATSON.
301. CHARLES BARRY
302. ANDREW BARRY
303. HUGH BARRY m. MALINDA KILGORE.
304. RICHARD BARRY m. MARGARET KILGORE.
305. POLLY BARRY m. THOMPSON LAWSON (Son of ROGER LAWSON & grandson of HUGH LAWSON).
306. VIOLET BARRY m. JAMES HANNA.
307. MARGARET BARRY m. DAVID THOMAS
308. KATHERINE BARRY m. JESSE CROOK.
309. ALICE BARRY m. DR. FORREST ALLGOOD.
(LANDRUM'S SPARTANBURG COUNTY FOLLOWED).

206. GEN. THOMAS MOORE m. (1) PATSY PRICE; m. (2) MARY REAGAN

The will of GEN. THOMAS MOORE, dated October 26, 1817, proved August 2, 1822, is on record in SPARTANBURG COUNTY, S. C. From this will and the account given by DR. LANDRUM in his History of SPARTANBURG COUNTY, he appears to have had the following children by both marriages:

310. JOHN MOORE, who died while in School.
311. POLLY MOORE m. DR. EBER SMITH.
312. ELIZABETH CUNNINGHAM MOORE m. COL. S. N. EVINS.
313. VIOLET MOORE m. J. H. BARRY.
314. MARGARET MOORE m. JOHN RODDY.
315. RACHEL MOORE m. MR. MEANS, of MEMPHIS, TENN.
316. MARTHA MOORE m. MR. BENSON, of ALABAMA.

317. BARRY MOORE moved to the WEST.
318. THOMAS J. MOORE m. MISS IRWIN, of CHARLOTTE, N. C.
319. ANNE MOORE m. (1) MR. CRUMP, (2) DR. RICHARD HARRISON (3) a man named MARTIN, of MISSISSIPPI.
320. AMANDA MOORE (*) m. (1) HENDERSON, (2) DR. EFFINGER, of OREGON.

The first son (310) was named JOHN PRICE MOORE, and his mother was PATSY PRICE, who was a daughter or grand-daughter of JOHN PRICE who married MARY DAVIDSON, sister of MAJ. JOHN DAVIDSON, of MECKLENBURG COUNTY. MARY (DAVIDSON) PRICE is buried in the old BAKERS GRAVEYARD near COWAN'S FORD in Upper Mecklenburg, with HUGH LAWSON and REV. JOHN THOMSON.

(*) AMANDA MOORE is not mentioned in the will of GEN. THOMAS MOORE, for some reason, but her name appears in the account by DR. LANDRUM, and the abstract may have omitted it by mistake. GEN. THOMAS MOORE was born in 1759. (?) #Landrum.

208. ANDREW BARRY MOORE m. (1) ANNA A. MAXWELL, m. (2) NANCY MILLER MONTGOMERY.

ANDREW BARRY MOORE (b. 1772) had no children by his first marriage to ANNA A. MAXWELL, and all of his children, named below were by his second marriage to NANCY MILLER MONTGOMERY, who married second SAM N. EVINS, whose first wife had been ELIZABETH CUNNINGHAM MOORE, daughter of GEN. THOMAS MOORE. By NANCY MILLER MONTGOMERY, ANDREW BARRY MOORE had the following children:

321. MARGARET ANNA MOORE (b. 1834) m. CAPT. SAMUEL C. MEANS.
322. MARY ELIZABETH MOORE (b. 1836) and died the same year.
323. ANDREW CHARLES MOORE (b. 1838) Killed at MANASAS in 1862.
(*) 324. THOMAS J. MOORE (b. 1843) m. MARY ELIZABETH ANDERSON

(*) The children of THOMAS J. MOORE and MARY ELIZABETH ANDERSON were (1) ANDREW CHARLES, (2) JAMES ANDERSON, (3) THOMAS BROCKMAN (4) ANNIE MARY (5) PAUL VERNON (6) HARRIETT MEANS (7) HENRIETTA SUE and (8) NANCY MONTGOMERY MOORE.

209. CHARLES MOORE JR. (b. 1774) m. JANE BARRY

CHARLES MOORE, JR. was the tenth child of CHARLES MOORE and his wife MISS HAMILTON (if that was his wife's name?), and he moved to PERRY COUNTY, ALABAMA, whence a number of the SPARTANBURG old timers had migrated. CHARLES MOORE JR. died at the age of 62 years and 8 months. All of his children were born in SPARTANBURG COUNTY, near the town of MOORE, which was named for the family. He and his wife JANE BARRY had the following children:

325. WILLIAM MOORE
326. ANDREW BARRY MOORE (Governor of ALABAMA).
327. CHARLES HAMILTON MOORE
328. ALFRED MOORE m. MISS HANNA
329. MARY MOORE m. JAMES EVINS
330. JULIET MOORE m. DR. ROBERT FOSTER
331. ADALINE MOORE (never married)
332. ELIZABETH MOORE (never married).

325. WILLIAM MOORE married (wife's name unknown) and had the following children: (1) CHARLES HAMILTON MOORE (2) ANDREW MOORE (3) RHODA JANE MOORE m. DR. JAMES A. MOORE (4) JAMES A. MOORE (5) SAMUEL MOORE (6) MITTIE MOORE m. MR. WYATT.

326. GOV. ANDREW BARRY MOORE m. MARY GOREE, of an old and prominent South Carolina family, and had (1) MARTHA J. MOORE m. POWHATTAN LOCKETT (2) ANNIE MOORE m. ALBERT LOCKETT, and ANDREW BARRY MOORE m. MARY SMITH.

327. CHARLES HAMILTON MOORE m. MARY BILLINGSLEA, of a prominent GEORGIA FAMILY that was connected with JOHN TROTWOOD MOORE, of Tennessee fame, and had: (1) DR. JAMES A. MOORE, who married his cousin RHODA JANE MOORE (see above), (2) ANDREW BARRY MOORE (3) CORNELIA JOSEPHINE MOORE and (4) THOMAS MOORE.

328. ALFRED MOORE married MISS HANNA and had (1) WILLIAM J. MOORE and (2) EMMA MOORE.

329. MARY MOORE married JAMES EVINS (probably a son of COL. SAM N. EVINS). His full name was JAMES GILLILAND EVINS. They had children: (1) CHARLES ALEXANDER, (2) THAD A., (3) T. J., (4) JAMES S. (5) JULIA (GRAHAM), (6) ROBERT HAMILTON (7) ANDREW (8) LUCIUS SEPTIMUS and (8) JANE ANNA EVINS.

330. JULIET MOORE m. DR. R. FOSTER, and had children: (1) MARY J. FOSTER m. A. C. MOORE and m (2) DR. WILLIAM R. BARRON; (2) ELIZA FOSTER m. LEONARD H. SEAWELL (3) MATTIE FOSTER m. C. F. FENNELL (4) ROBENA FOSTER m. LUCIUS S. EVINS (5) LUTIE FOSTER m. PITTS (6) ROBERT m. BARRON.

202. ROSANNA MOORE and husband RICHARD BARRY

This RICHARD BARRY was the brother of ANDREW BARRY who married MARGARET CATHERINE MOORE, sister of ROSANNA. On page 204 of Landrum's History of Spartanburg County, S. C. is the following which refers to this Richard:

> RICHARD BARRY, brother of ANDREW and JOHN, was born in 1751; died July 29th, 1816, aged 65 years. Coming here with CHARLES MOORE, he married his daughter ROSA, who survived him and went West with some of her children, where she died. He is buried in the MOORE CEMETERY. What part he took in the Revolution is not known. He stuttered in conversation, but it is related that in his public prayers, in which he was fluent, he never did so.
>
> His children by ROSA MOORE are: RICHARD BARRY, familiarly known as "Devil Dick"; KATY, who married a SLOAN and lived about ROME, GEORGIA; Polly married COL. ISAAC SMITH.
> There may have been other children.

Note the statement that ROSANNA (MOORE) BARRY "went west with some of her children, where she died", and that "there may have been other children". This writer thinks it not improbable that she and possibly several sons went to COLUMBUS, MISSISSIPPI, together with their cousins, the sons and daughters of MARGARET CATHERINE MOORE and her husband ANDREW BARRY.

With respect to the children of ANDREW BARRY and MARGARET CATHERINE MOORE, Dr. Landrum has this to say in the same volume:

> All these (the children of ANDREW BARRY) moved westward except KATY, who married JESSE CROOK, and ANDREW BARRY, who was known as MAJOR BARRY, who located near the home of his father, one mile North of MOORE, S. C., on TIGER RIVER, dying there December 18th, 1860, aged 73 years, 3 months and 23 days (b. about 1787). He married SARAH P. HARRISON, who was born January 21st, 1791, and died November 30th, 1843. They were married September 19th, 1815.
> (For list of these children see bottom of page 478.)

From a HISTORY OF COLUMBUS, MISSISSIPPI, by WILLIAM LOWNDES LIPSCOMB, published only in the past few years we copy the following notes relating to the BARRY FAMILY of that place:

> RICHARD BARRY came in 1819 to what is now COLUMBUS and ran the first hotel. He had several brothers and sisters, including DR. B. C. BARRY. He had another brother ...... BARRY, who had a daughter NANCY BARRY who married COL. MADISON BROOKS. He had a sister ...... BARRY who married DR. B. C. HUNT. RICHARD BARRY'S children included a son W. S. BARRY, born in COLUMBUS, who was a graduate of YALE and who became Speaker of the ALABAMA LEGISLATURE. His oldest daughter .... BARRY married B. W. BENSON, and his second daughter married DR. R. F. MATTHEWS.

Dr. Landrum in the second quotation above says that all of the children of ANDREW BARRY and MARGARET CATHERINE MOORE left South Carolina except KATY and MAJOR ANDREW BARRY, and he further says that "RICHARD married MARGARET KILGORE and went to MISSISSIPPI". With these authentic clues it seems easy to identify the COLUMBUS, MISSISSIPPI, BARRY FAMILY.

DR. B. C. BARRY was the second son on the the list (p. 478), and the other brother, who had a daughter NANCY was either JOHN or HUGH BARRY, more likely HUGH. The sister who married DR. B. C. HUNT must have been one of those on the list whose first husband's name is given, who had died, and her marriage to Dr. Hunt would have been her second marriage.

NANCY BARRY, daughter of HUGH BARRY (possibly of JOHN) married COL. MADISON BROOKS. Col. Brooks was a man of considerable means and wealth, and after the close of the War between the States, he sold out his plantation and with his wife and family moved to Texas, where he arrived, it is said, with $140,000.00 in cash. A large part of this money he immediately invested in Texas lands, and some in good securities, including, we are told $40,000.00 in Tarrant County courthouse bonds (Fort Worth, Texas). His lands were mostly in KAUFMAN COUNTY, TEXAS, where he and his wife lived and died and are buried, in the little town of FORNEY, named for an old CATAWBA RIVER family in North Carolina. Their son MADISON MICAJAH BROOKS rose to prominence in the State of Texas, becoming a member of the highest criminal court in the State. He made the race for Governor of Texas, receiving an enormous vote, but was defeated, under the "pro rata" rule adopted for the conventions at that time. He and his brothers remained wealthy and were rated as millionaire in that part of the State where they lived. They left many descendants who reside in Kaufman and Dallas County (Texas) to this day. NANCY BARRY was a grand-daughter of ANDREW BARRY and his wife MARGARET CATHERINE MOORE.

302. ANDREW BARRY JR. who remained in SPARTANBURG and married SARAH PATILLO HARRISON, the daughter of RICHARD HARRISON and his wife ANN PATILLO (Daughter of REV. HENRY PATILLO) had (1) MARGARET ANN m. MAJ. WILLIAM HOY; (2) RICHARD ALBERT; (3) HENRY PATILLO m. MARY JANE EVINS; (4) CHARLES A., m. ANN MARIA SUDDUTH, and (5) EMILY AUGUSTA BARRY who married JOSEPH WOFFORD TUCKER, who was a brother of SAMUEL TUCKER, father of LOUIZA D. TUCKER, who married JAMES MADISON LANHAM - and they were the parents of HON. S. W. T. LANHAM, a long time member of the U. S. Congress from and GOVERNOR OF THE STATE OF TEXAS.

101. DAVID MOORE m. MARGARET CAMPBELL

This DAVID MOORE was the son of CHARLES MOORE and his wife MARGARET BERRY, and the brother of the CHARLES MOORE who married MISS HAMILTON. DAVID MOORE and his wife MARGARET left a "joint" will in MECKLENBURG COUNTY, N. C., dated February 5, 1778, an abstract of which is shown on page 322 of these notes, in which the following children are mentioned:

- 210. JOSEPH MOORE (d. 1797) twice married.
- 211. HUGH MOORE (d. between 1790-1793).
- 212. WILLIAM MOORE
- 213. DAVID MOORE
- 214. MARY MOORE m. McRORY.
- 215. MARGARET MOORE m. ELLIOTT.

210. JOSEPH MOORE left a will in MECKLENBURG COUNTY, dated November 3, 1797, in which he named his wife MARY; but the mention of two sets of children indicate a previous marriage. In the table below the older set is given first and the younger set last:

- 333. JOHN MOORE
- 334. MARY MOORE m. TENDER.
- 335. MARGARET MOORE m. (1) STONE (2) NELSON.
- 336. GEORGE MOORE
- 337. JANE MOORE m. HILL
- 338. SARAH MOORE m. DICKSON.
- 339. ESTHER MOORE m. DICKSON

- 340. ARAMINTA MOORE
- 341. JOSEPH MOORE
- 342. JAMES MOORE
- 343. LUCINDA MOORE
- 344. NARCISSA MOORE
- 345. EPHRAIM MOORE

211. HUGH MOORE died between 1790 and 1793, without leaving a will. The U. S. Census for that year (1790) shows him to have been the head of a considerable family - two males sixteen years of age and over (including himself) and four males under 16; also four females (probably including his wife - who may have been a CUMMINS). The names of his sons but not of his daughters are shown in a deed on record in MECKLENBURG COUNTY (Book 19, p. 21), executed November 3, 1807, in settlement of the 211 HUGH MOORE estate. An abstract of this deed is shown on page 331 of these notes. From family records and other sources we have obtained the names of his three daughters. His children were:

- 346. DAVID MOORE
- 347. JOHN MOORE
- 348. WILLIAM MOORE m. (1) POLLY FITTEN (2) MARTHA JACKSON(?)
- 349. HUGH MOORE
- 350. JOSEPH MOORE
- 351. MARTHA (PATSY) MOORE m. COL. SMITH.
- 352. FRANCES MOORE m. ALLEN REED
- 353. MARGARET MOORE m. ROBERT McKNIGHT.

212. WILLIAM MOORE appears to have settled in GREENE COUNTY, GEORGIA, for a time at least. In the will of DAVID MOORE and MARGARET CAMPBELL, his parents, JOHN HARRIS and JOHN BARNETT were named as executors. In the course of time JOHN HARRIS died and JAMES HARRIS was substituted as the executor. Thereafter the following entry appears on the records of GREENE COUNTY, GEORGIA:

> GREENE COUNTY, GEORGIA, COURTHOUSE: I, WILLIAM MOORE, of the County of GREENE, State of Georgia, ordain my friend JAMES ORR, of the County of MECKLENBURG, State of North Carolina, to sue JAMES HARRIS, of the said County of MECKLENBURG, N. C. October, 1790.

(JOHN HARRIS, the executor, married JANE MOORE, who was perhaps a daughter of one of the brothers of 101 DAVID MOORE. JOHN BARNETT, the other executor, was the father of the famous SUSAN (BARNETT) SMART, whose will appears on page 313 of these notes).

213. DAVID MOORE. These records disclose that there were innumerable persons by the name of DAVID MOORE; at least two of them were cousins and died at approximately the same time, and both had lived in the general vicinity of the PROVIDENCE CHURCH on McALPIN and GOOSE CREEK. After a great deal of study and research the one whose wife was AGNES, has been identified as the son of 101 DAVID MOORE and MARGARET CAMPBELL. His will was dated August 4, 1793 and was proved in MECKLENBURG COUNTY, and it was his descendants who remained in MECKLENBURG and many of them are there to this good day.

HOPEWELL PRESBYTERIAN CHURCH FAMILY. On pages 167 to 170 inclusive of DR. CHARLES WILLIAM SUMMERVILLE'S History of Hopewell Presbyterian Church (1939) appears an extended account of the family and descendants of JOHN WILSON MOORE, ancestor of the MOORES of that part of MECKLENBURG COUNTY of the present time. John V. Moore was the son of SAMUEL MOORE and his wife EVELYN WALLACE, who was the son of JAMES MOORE, one of the sons of 213 DAVID MOORE and his wife AGNES, as shown on the next page of these notes.

The will of 213 DAVID MOORE, whose wife was AGNES, as shown by the will, mentions NINE children and two grandchildren, as follows:

354. ANDREW MOORE
355. DAVID MOORE
356. JAMES MOORE
357. HANNAH MOORE
358. ELIZABETH MOORE m. SOLOMON STANFIELD.
359. JOSEPH MOORE
360. JACOB MOORE
361. AGNES MOORE m. EVAN ALEXANDER.
362. MARGARET MOORE m. BROWN.

WILLIAM BROWN and DANIEL BROWN are mentioned as grandchildren

An abstract of the will of 356 JAMES MOORE appears on page 332 of these notes, and among the children he mentions are SAMUEL MOORE and ELAM MOORE.
An abstract of ELAM MOORE'S will appears on the same page.
SAMUEL MOORE, son of 356 JAMES MOORE married EVELYN C. WALLACE in 1831 (See page 344) and they were the parents of four children (1) ANDREW MOORE (2) RUFUS MOORE (3) JOHN WILSON MOORE, and (4) ELIZABETH MOORE, who died at an early age.

(3) JOHN WILSON MOORE was a Confederate Soldier, and married MARGARET GIBBON of an old and prominent HOPEWELL family, although the SAMUEL MOORE family had lived in the SUGAR CREEK neighborhood all their lives. John W. Moore was an Elder of Hopewell Church, a member of the Legislature and an active civic worker and citizen. He and his wife MARGARET GIBBON had the following children:

1. REV. JOHN WALLACE MOORE, who was twice married.
2. DR. NICHOLAS GIBBON MOORE, of Mooresville. N. C.
3. REV. LYNFORD LARDNER MOORE m. MARY TORRENCE.
4. ELIZABETH C. MOORE, of TAYLORSVILLE, N. C.
5. MARGARET ANN MOORE who married ADRIAN M. SAMPLE.
6. MARY AMELIA MOORE m. THOMAS J. SMITH.
7. FRANCES LARDNER MOORE m. DANIEL T. McCARTY.

346. DAVID MOORE (Son of 211 HUGH MOORE). Neither space or the information available will permit an extended account of either him or his family. These notes from the records may disclose some records pertaining to him, but we confess an inability to segregate them. In 1807 he was living in MECKLENBURG and bought out the interest of his three brothers in the lands left them by their father's estate. Presumably he may have continued to live in Mecklenburg County.

347. JOHN MOORE. From his gravestone in the SIX MILE CHURCH, which is located now in South Carolina, a short distance over the line from the PROVIDENCE TOWNSHIP, we know that he died in 1833, and from his age that he was born in 1773, which gives us a fairly good idea of the dates of birth of his brothers and sisters. The name of his wife was OLIVIA, and the markers on the family tombstones disclose the names of three of their children:

400. HUGH MOORE
401. JOHN P. MOORE
402. OLIVIA MOORE m. RICHARD J. MILLER.

These tombstone records for SIX MILE CHURCH will be found on page 408 of these notes. In Howe's History of the Presbyterian Church in South Carolina, is the statement that when SIX MILE CHURCH was organized, it greatly depleted the membership of the OLD WAXHAW CHURCH further down in Lancaster County, though it is unlikely that this included the MOORE FAMILY, which probably came mostly from PROVIDENCE, farther North and East.
One wonders, however, if RICHARD J. MILLER, who married OLIVIA MOORE, was not a descendant of the old preacher ROBERT MILLER, of the earliest period of the WAXHAW CHURCH, who sold his farm to a MR. BARNETT in 1758, reserving lands for the Church which were deeded to ROBERT DAVIS, ROBERT RAMSEY, JOHN LYNN, SAMUEL DUNLAP and HENRY WHITE, which deed was witnessed by ROBERT McCLANAHAN, JOHN CROCKETT and ANDREW PICKENS.

348. WILLIAM MOORE. This is the WILLIAM MOORE who married POLLY FITTEN, in MECKLENBURG COUNTY, North Carolina, February 19, 1806, with JAMES REED as surety on the marriage bond (See page 344). That this WILLIAM MOORE removed from MECKLENBURG COUNTY, N. C. to GREENE COUNTY, Ga., by 1814, is evidenced by the fact that the will of ISAIAH CUNNINGHAM FITTEN, probated in GREENE COUNTY, GEORGIA, July 21st of that year, leaves a bequest in money "to be paid to WILLIAM MOORE, for the purpose of schooling the children of my sister POLLY MOORE", and he also leaves "to my brother, JOHN FITTEN all of my clothes", and " to my beloved friend, ROBERT MOORE CUNNINGHAM" $75.00 for buying a suit of clothes". Which also suggests very strongly a relationship between REV. ROBERT MOORE CUNNINGHAM (son of ROGER) and these particular MOORES.
A number of these MECKLENBURG people who moved to GREENE COUNTY, Georgia, about 1833 moved to and settled in CHAMBERS COUNTY, ALABAMA, as did both WILLIAM and HUGH MOORE; also JOHN FITTEN. But 348 WILLIAM MOORE appears to have married again, probably to MARTHA JACKSON, as the administrators of his estate in June, 1836 (Book 1, pp 117-118) were MARTHA MOORE and DANIEL M. JACKSON, with WILEY J. DEAN, THOMAS D. GORDON, CHARLES McLEMORE and JOSEPH MUSICK, who appointed EVAN G. RICHARDS to sign their names to the bond as sureties.

THE FAMILY OF 349 HUGH MOORE

349. HUGH MOORE moved from MECKLENBURG COUNTY, N. C. to GREENE COUNTY, GEORGIA, where his uncle 212 WILLIAM MOORE had evidently preceded him by several years, and may have been living there when he arrived. HUGH MOORE married MARTHA FITZGERALD, whose parentage has not been identified, but who is believed to have been of the same family of FITZGERALDS who married into the DANIEL and HILLIARD FAMILIES in GEORGIA, and at least one of whom settled in PERRY COUNTY, ALABAMA, before the Civil War and was associated in business with the MOORES from SPARTANBURG COUNTY, S. C., doing business, first, under the name of EVINS and BARRY, and later as MOORE & FITZGERALD.

The home of HUGH MOORE, when he lived in GREENE COUNTY, was located somewhere between UNION POINT and WHITE PLAINS adjacent to the OLD BETHANY PRESBYTERIAN CHURCH, of which he was a RULING ELDER, while the distinguished minister FRANCIS CUMMINS was pastor of the Church. The relationship between HUGH MOORE and REV. FRANCIS CUMMINS seems to have been so close and continued, that, notwithstanding the absence of positive proof, it is believed they were in some way related. It may be that the wife of 211 HUGH MOORE, father of 349 HUGH was the sister ELIZABETH or REBECCA CUMMINS mentioned in the will of CHARLES CUMMINS of Mecklenburg County in 1777. (See page 324 of these notes).

The children of HUGH MOORE and his wife MARTHA FITZGERALD were:

403. MARY MOORE (b. 1805) m. (1) DAVID RANKIN m. (2) ... EVANS.
404. ELIZABETH MOORE m. JAMES CARTER KING. (His first wife).
405. ADELINE MOORE in 1827 m. (1) WILLIAM HANNAH DANIEL
    m. (2) KINDRED JACKS
    m. (3) JAMES CARTER KING (Her sister's relict).
406. MARTHA SELINA MOORE (b. 1813) m.(1) HENRY F. DANIEL; m. (2) THOMAS BOYD.
    (Her daughter FRANCES m. FRANCIS BILLINSLEA, of ALABAMA).
407. CAROLINE MOORE m. (1) WILLIAM THOMAS, of CHAMBERS COUNTY, ALABAMA.
    m. (2) REV. JOSEPH BROWN, Presbyterian Minister.
408. WILLIAM MOORE (b. 1807-8) known on the records as WILLIAM MOORE JR.,
    an indication that 348 WILLIAM MOORE, brother of HUGH,
    was then living in GEORGIA also.
409. ALFRED CUMMINS MOORE. He settled in LA GRANGE, GEORGIA, married and
    had a family. Was killed in the C. S. A.
410. MILES MOORE (b. 1820). Lived in CHAMBERS COUNTY, Alabama, when the U.
    S. Census of 1850 was taken. He is also believed to
    have been killed while serving in the C. S. A.

There are several interesting points relating to these children of 349 HUGH MOORE that should here be mentioned, at the cost of a little space:

MARY MOORE married DAVID RANKIN. The following note is found on page 159 of Sherrill's annals of LINCOLN COUNTY, N. C. (1937)

"WILLIAM RANKIN was born January 10, 1761. He came to TRYON, afterwards LINCOLN COUNTY, when a young man. He married MARY MOORE, sister of GEN. JOHN MOORE. * * His son, COL. RICHARD RANKIN * represented LINCOLN COUNTY in the Legislature of 1844 and 1850, and GASTON in 1856."

According to the same authority (page 112) GEN. JOHN MOORE, son of WILLIAM MOORE, was born in 1759, in what was later LINCOLN, now GASTON COUNTY. WILLIAM had four sons, JAMES, WILLIAM, JOHN and ALEXANDER, all loyal patriots during the revolution. GEN. JOHN MOORE'S first wife was the sister of GOV. ADAIR, of KENTUCKY, and his second wife was MARY SCOTT, widow of JAMES SCOTT and daughter of ROBERT ALEXANDER.

The will of ELIZABETH M. HAMILTON was probated in RICHMOND COUNTY (Augusta) GEORGIA, Nov. 27, 1839, and same was witnessed by JOHN MOORE and WILLIAM RANKIN.

Children of MARY MOORE and DAVID RANKIN were:

(1) MARGARET A. RANKIN m. B. W. JONES (She died 1887).
(2) MARTHA MOORE RANKIN m. COL. JOHN W. DANIEL, of TEXAS (2nd wife).
(3) DAVID F. RANKIN (b. 1835)
(4) JESSE RANKIN (b. 1838). (RANKIN DRUG COMPANY, ATLANTA, GA.)

COL. JOHN W. DANIEL was the son of ADELINE MOORE and WILLIAM HANNAH DANIEL (above), was Colonel of the 15th Texas Infantry C. S.A. and the grandfather of MRS. WORTH S. RAY, the writer.

----

406. MARTHA SELINA MOORE and her husband HENRY F. DANIEL were married in 1832, and they had two daughters:

500. FRANCES GOULDING DANIEL m. FRANCIS BILLINGSLEA
501. CORNELIA CAROLINE DANIEL m. REV. WILLIAM WALKER MORRISON

CHARLES HAMILTON MOORE, brother of ANDREW BARRY MOORE, Governor of ALABAMA, married MARY BILLINSLEA, and had a daughter CORNELIA JOSEPHINE MOORE (See p. 479). JUDGE JOHN MOORE, father of HON. JOHN TROTWOOD MOORE, of TENNESSEE, married EMILY BILLINGSLEA, PERRY COUNTY, ALABAMA.

407. CAROLINE MOORE

This CAROLINE MOORE, daughter of HUGH MOORE and MARTHA FITZGERALD was twice married; the first time to WILLIAM THOMAS, of Chambers County, Alabama, whither HUGH MOORE and his family, together with his brother 348 WILLIAM MOORE, and HON. ROBERT REA, son in law of COL. SMITH, who had married their sister PATSY MOORE, and the DOZIERS, and FITZGERALDS and BILLINGSLEAS, all closely allied and associated in GEORGIA, from whence they came, had moved about 1835-6.

However, it was the second marriage of CAROLINE MOORE, after her first husband CAPTAIN WILLIAM THOMAS had lost his life as a Confederate soldier, that is of great interest in the development of this MOORE STUDY. When CAROLINE MOORE married REV. JOSEPH BROWN, the Mecklenburg County (N. C.) Moores and the AUGUSTA COUNTY (Va.) MOORES were united, for REV. JOSEPH BROWN was the son of REV. SAMUEL BROWN, of Rockbridge County, and his wife MARY MOORE "The Little Captive", famous in the annals of Southwest Virginia. MARY MOORE was the daughter of CAPT. JAMES MOORE and his wife MARTHA POAGUE, the first having been killed by the Indians, and the second carried away with her youngest child and daughter MARY, she never to return alive, while MARY MOORE lived to make her escape and return to the arms of her anxious relatives, where she married SAMUEL BROWN. The story of these MOORES OF ABB'S VALLEY is too long and complicated to detail in these notes, but their relationship embraces many interesting families, including the WALKERS, DABNEYS, HOUSTONS, TODDS and a long list of interesting personages. Also:

RACHEL MOORE, aunt of MARY MOORE and sister of CAPT. JAMES MOORE (who was killed by the Indians in "Abb's Valley, Virginia, in Tazewell County, about 1785-6) married WILLIAM McPHEETERS, and they were the parents of REV. WILLIAM McPHEETERS, D. D., who in 1840 was elected President of DAVIDSON COLLEGE, in Mecklenburg County, which he declined on account of ill health. REV. WILLIAM McPHEETERS, the son of RACHEL MOORE and cousin of MARY MOORE the Captive, married into still another branch of the MOORE FAMILY, of Virginia, when on MARCH 18, 1809, he married LAVINIA MOORE in Blount County, Tennessee, who was a daughter of ALEXANDER SPOTTSWOOD MOORE and his wife ELIZABETH AYLETTE, and grand-daughter of BERNARD MOORE and his wife ANN CATHERINE SPOTTSWOOD.

Again, FRANCES BROWN, a daughter of MARY MOORE, "The Little Captive" and her husband REV. SAMUEL BROWN, became the wife of REV. JAMES MORRISON, third Pastor of NEW PROVIDENCE CHURCH in Rockbridge County, Virginia. The father of REV. JAMES MORRISON was JOHN MORRISON; (1768-1846) was an elder in ROCKY RIVER CHURCH in what is now CABARRUS COUNTY, who married MARY McCURDY and had 10 children, of which REV. JAMES MORRISON was the oldest. REV. JAMES MORRISON and his wife FRANCES BROWN were the parents of eleven children, including REV. WILLIAM WALKER MORRISON, who on June 30th 1856 married CORNELIA CAROLINE DANIEL, daughter of 406 MARTHA SELINA MOORE and her husband HENRY F. DANIEL. Thus the MOORE FAMILY of GOOSE CREEK and the ROCKY RIVER section of MECKLENBURG furnish a descendant to become the wife of a grandson of MARY MOORE, whose father was one of the MORRISONS of the ROCKY RIVER Congregation, whose education was obtained under JOHN McKAMIE WILSON in Mecklenburg County. Two daughters of REV. WILLIAM WALKER MORRISON live at this writing in STATESVILLE.

------

349 HUGH MOORE died in CHAMBERS COUNTY, ALABAMA. His death must have occurred during the summer of the year 1848. On pages 161-162, of Will Book 2, of Chambers County, Alabama, we found set out the bond of the administrators of his estate, dated the 15th of July of that year. Slightly abstracted, it reads:

> Know all men, etc. * * that we, MILES MOORE, ALFRED C. MOORE, CYRUS BILLINGSLEA and ROBERT REA of the County and State aforesaid (State of Alabama, Chambers County) are held and firmly bound unto CLEMENT C. FORBES, Judge of the County and Orphans Court for said County * * in the penal sum of $50,000, for the payment of which, etc.
> The condition of the above * * the above bound MILES MOORE and ALFRED C. MOORE, have been appointed administrators of the estate of HUGH MOORE, deceased, etc."
> Acknowledged before me, this 15th day of July, 1848.
> C. C. FORBES, J. I. C.
>
>   MILES MOORE (Seal)
>   ALFRED C. MOORE (Seal)
>   CYRUS BILLINGSLEA (Seal)
>   ROBERT REA (Seal).

Alfred C. Moore's full name was ALFRED CUMMINS MOORE. His parents were married by REV. FRANCIS CUMMINS and all were from MECKLENBURG COUNTY, N. C., and his father HUGH MOORE was an elder in OLD BETHANY in Greene County, Georgia, while Rev. Francis Cummins was the minister. The question, however, still remains, were they related?

Again, we find the BILLINGSLEA connection with the MOORES. Hugh Moore's grand-daughter married FRANCES BILLINGSLEA in GEORGIA. CHARLES HAMILTON MOORE, of MARIAN, ALABAMA, married MARY BILLINGSLEA, and the mother of JOHN TROTWOOD MOORE, of Tennessee fame, was EMILY BILLINGSLEA, the daughter of DR. CLEMENT BILLINGSLEA, of Washington, Wilkes County, Georgia, who was a lineal descendant of FRANCIS BILLINGSLEA, the emigrant in 1657, from ENGLAND, to MARYLAND. And the MOORES of MECKLENBURG also came from MARYLAND.

The BILLINGSLEAS went to Texas with the DANIEL FAMILY, and a younger CYRUS BILLINGSLEA as well as a FRANCIS, was personally known to the writer. FRANCIS BILLINGSLEA is buried AUSTIN,TEX.

102. MARY MOORE, SISTER OF CHARLES AND DAVID MOORE, MARRIED HUGH LAWSON

COL. HUGH LAWSON is said to have come to VIRGINIA at some uncertain date, from PENNSYL-VANIA, but this has never been verified by any record. We think it probable that he came, like the MOORES surely did, from MARYLAND. The name of HUGH LAWSON is on the early tythe lists of VIRGINIA, and the records show that he was one of the tythe takers for LUNENBURG COUNTY, in the years 1748, 1749 and as late as 1752, after which time he had probably removed to the upper part of MECKLENBURG COUNTY, near the supposed line between the present Mecklenburg and Rowan County. Dr. Hunter in his SKETCHES says that he built a fine home on DAVIDSON'S CREEK and owned lands on both sides of that stream. See map on page 380 of these notes for its location. When HUGH LAWSON died his will was proven in ROWAN COUNTY, though it is well known that he was buried in BAKER'S GRAVEYARD near COWAN'S FORD in Mecklenburg County. Hugh Lawson and his wife MARY MOORE were the parents of the following children:

```
200.  ROGER LAWSON  m. (1) MISS IRWIN (2) HANNAH THOMSON.
202.  HUGH LAWSON, JR. m. REBECCA McCONNELL, May 26, 1770.
203.  HANNAH LAWSON m. (1) THOMAS IRWIN (2) ROGER THOMSON.
204.  JANE LAWSON  m. GEORGE EWING
205.  MARGARET LAWSON m. HUGH BARRY
206.  VIOLET LAWSON m. JAMES HENDERSON
207.  MARY LAWSON m. JAMES WHITE.
```

The only one of the several daughters whose name we are in doubt about is the one who married GEORGE EWING. Her name may not have been JANE, but we think it probably was. In his will, Colonel Lawson only gave the names of his sons in laws, and, with the exception of MARY (who had not then married JAMES WHITE,) none of their given names were mentioned. Their names have been obtained from other isolated records. The names of the witnesses to the HUGH LAWSON will were DAVID and JOHN BYARS, and JOHN and HUGH BARRY. At that time HUGH BARRY was the testator's son in law.

In regard to ROGER LAWSON, the following is taken from MECKLENBURG COUNTY (N. C.) Deed Records, Harris Register, Book 5 pages 156-157:

CHARLES MOORE (See p. 478) of ANSON COUNTY, Schoolmaster, purchased of ROGER LAWSON, 600 acres of land in ANSON COUNTY, on the South side of BROAD RIVER, and South side of PACOLET RIVER, on a large creek, now called LAWSON'S CREEK, which 600 acres was granted to said LAWSON, February 23, 1754. This deed dated December 23, 1762, and witnessed by WILLIAM ALEXANDER, ROBERT LOWERY & RICHARD BARRY,

which shows that ROGER LAWSON probably moved to the TYGER RIVER SECTION of upper South Carolina, by 1754, where he was granted lands, supposed at that time to have been in ANSON COUNTY, NORTH CAROLINA. At that time ROGER LAWSON'S father in law, REV. JOHN THOMSON, had been dead about one year. That COL. HUGH LAWSON also owned lands in the TYGER RIVER section of upper South Carolina, is evidenced by a deed from CHARLES MOORE "Of Tryon County" to his son in law, ANDREW BARRY, an abstract of which is shown on page 321. Also at the time ROGER LAWSON made the deed to CHARLES MOORE in 1762, ROGER LAWSON was living in GEORGIA. See deed on page 319.

204. JANE LAWSON m. GEORGE EWING. In the section of these notes dealing with REV. JOHN THOMSON we have already given some information in regard to the family of GEORGE EWING, that he was the father of HUGH EWING and others.

GEORGE EWING and JAMES HENDERSON who were both sons in laws of COL. HUGH LAWSON, were both living in the year 1785, in LINCOLN COUNTY (that part of it now GASTON) and were made executors of the will of WILLIAM CHRONICLE, the father of MAJ. WILLIAM CHRONICLE, who was killed in the battle of KING'S MOUNTAIN, and who, at the time of his death, was engaged to MARGARET ALEXANDER, daughter of ROBERT ALEXANDER. (Puett's History of Gaston County, p. 115). JOHN SCOTT, whose widow MARY afterwards married GEN. JOHN MOORE, was a grandson of this WILLIAM CHRONICLE.

205. MARGARET LAWSON and her husband HUGH BARRY in the year 1771, lived on the North side of the CATAWBA RIVER and the South side of McDowell's Creek, as shown by the deed on page 317. This was in MECKLENBURG COUNTY. In 1790 HUGH BARRY lived in what was then LINCOLN COUNTY, a close neighbor to his brother in law JAMES HENDERSON. See under the BARRY FAMILY.

---

206. VIOLET LAWSON m. JAMES HENDERSON

Much has already been said about JAMES HENDERSON and his wife VIOLET LAWSON in another section of these notes. (See pages 225 and 226 of the GRANVILLE COUNTY Section of this Volume). The names of their children and two sets of grandchildren, including HON. JAMES PINCKNEY HENDERSON, the first Governor of the State of Texas, are given on page 226, and the name of JAMES HENDERSON'S father (believed to have married a LOGAN) on pages 223-224. Since that account was written, however, this compiler, through the assistance of some of the North Carolina descendants and other records theretofore unavailable, has obtained more material bearing on this family, which will now be included in this "addenda" to the account, which should be considered in connection with that already written.

THE HENDERSON FAMILY

Some CORRECTIONS and ADDITIONS to the HENDERSON FAMILY, as same appears 223 to 226 of these notes, and a more particular account of the N. C. HENDERSONS

Where so much is written and so many families are discussed, as in these notes, considerable charity in judgment should be extended to the compiler, who will be forced to admit innumerable mistakes have occurred. Here an effort will be made to correct some of them and to add other information obtained since the material on pages 223 to 226 was collected.

First, the wife of (1) JOHN HENDERSON, of ALBEMARLE COUNTY, Virginia, one of the brothers of SAMUEL HENDERSON, the Granville County (N. C.) ancestor, was not named BENNETT, as there stated (p. 223), but she was a MISS GOODE, a daughter of BENNETT GOODE. BENNETT GOODE belonged to the GOODES of HENRICO COUNTY, and probably lived in CUMBERLAND COUNTY at the time his daughter (perhaps SUSAN or FRANCES) married (1) JOHN HENDERSON. BENNETT GOODE was closely allied to the WOODSONS, PLEASANTS and JORDANS of HENRICO. This fact accounts for one of the sons of (1) JOHN HENDERSON being named BENNETT HENDERSON, and for his also having a son named BENNETT (See page 224).

For a list and an account of the children of the above, see the pages referred to.

On page 224 the statement is made that (5) WILLIAM HENDERSON, another brother of SAMUEL HENDERSON, as well as of (1) JOHN HENDERSON, married, or probably married a LOGAN. That her Christian name was SUSAN was based on a will of a WILLIAM HENDERSON, shown on the Augusta Records, whose wife was SUSAN. This may not have been (5) WILLIAM. That her name was LOGAN, as a girl, was based on the use of the name LOGAN as a Christian name by JAMES, the son of this WILLIAM, who married VIOLET LAWSON. It now develops that there was a relationship between the IRWINS and LOGANS, and that THOMAS IRWIN married a sister of VIOLET LAWSON, as shown on the preceding page.

The writer has concluded, basing his idea on an account to be found on page 405 of WADDELL'S annals of AUGUSTA COUNTY, VIRGINIA, that WILLIAM HENDERSON married a daughter of JAMES LOGAN, who lived on KERR'S CREEK, in Augusta County, Virginia, in 1743, and whose son GEN. BENJAMIN LOGAN of Kentucky fame, was born there that year. His son JAMES LOGAN married HANNAH IRWIN (probably a brother of THOMAS IRWIN, whose first wife was HANNAH LAWSON) and their son, JOHN LOGAN married RACHEL McPHEETERS, daughter of WILLIAM McPHEETERS and his wife RACHEL MOORE, the sister of REV. WILLIAM McPHEETERS, who married LAVINIA MOORE, daughter of ALEXANDER SPOTTSWOOD MOORE and his wife MISS AYLETTE. RACHEL MOORE was the sister of JAMES MOORE who married MARTHA POAGE, the latter the parents of MARY MOORE, "The Little Captive" (p. 484) and also the sister of ELIZABETH MOORE, who married MICHAEL COULTER and JOSEPH MOORE who married MARGARET COULTER. This means that:

JAMES HENDERSON who married VIOLET LAWSON was a first cousin of GEN. BENJAMIN LOGAN of KENTUCKY, JAMES HENDERSON had son LOGAN - Logan County, Kentucky, was named for BENJAMIN LOGAN. DAVID COULTER, son of ELIZABETH MOORE and MICHAEL COULTER, moved to LINCOLN COUNTY, North Carolina, or the upper part of S. C., and an account written by REV. WILLIAM McPHEETERS declares that one of his daughters became the wife of U. S. Senator WILLIAM C. PRESTON.

(5) WILLIAM HENDERSON'S FAMILY

The account of this man's family, as same appears on page 224 of these notes, only mentions two of his sons, JAMES and SAMUEL HENDERSON. Since writing that further evidence has come to light and we are convinced that he had the following children:

(50) JAMES HENDERSON m. VIOLET LAWSON
(51) SAMUEL HENDERSON m. JEAN.
(52) JOHN HENDERSON (b. 1724) See p. 388.
(53) WILLIAM HENDERSON m. NANCY. See p. 406.

The children and descendants of (51) SAMUEL HENDERSON have been detailed at some length on pages 224 and 225, and the account shows he was the ancestor of a large progeny who went to KENTUCKY and TENNESSEE and settled; while JAMES HENDERSON (who married VIOLET LAWSON) had numerous children and grandchildren listed on page 226.

It now develops that (52) JOHN HENDERSON and his brother (53) WILLIAM HENDERSON accompanied (50) JAMES HENDERSON to the Catawba River section in North Carolina; JAMES HENDERSON becoming a pioneer of LINCOLN COUNTY, while JOHN and WILLIAM HENDERSON settled in MECKLENBURG COUNTY, and are to be found listed on the 1790 census in "District No. 7" as shown on the map on page 369. For this list see page 360.

NANCY HENDERSON, the wife of (53) WILLIAM HENDERSON, SR., died June 25, 1813, at the advanced age of 78 years and is buried at the old GILLEAD CHURCH GRAVEYARD in Upper MECKLENBURG COUNTY. The inscription on her tombstone will be found on page 406. The writer is indebted to MR. WALTER S. HENDERSON, of DAVIDSON, N. C., a descendant of JAMES HENDERSON and his wife VIOLET LAWSON for this and other valuable information, which follows:

Space available prohibits publishing here a list of the descendants of (52) JOHN and (53) WILLIAM HENDERSON, even if the writer could do so. Among their descendants, however, was the pioneer physician, DR. THOMAS HENDERSON, and numerous others who resided for a time in MECKLENBURG COUNTY. As before stated, JOHN HENDERSON died in MECKLENBURG COUNTY in 1794, and the wife of WILLIAM HENDERSON in 1813. Mr. W. S. Henderson writes that there are many unmarked graves in the GILEAD CHURCH burial ground, and it is more than probable that WILLIAM HENDERSON is buried there.

The names of the children of JAMES HENDERSON and his wife VIOLET LAWSON, who lived in LINCOLN COUNTY (the part now GASTON) will be found on page 226 of this completed work, and we will not repeat them here. However, they are all mentioned in the will of JAMES HENDERSON, who died in LINCOLN COUNTY sometime after he wrote and executed it on September 9, 1793. The will was as follows:

THE WILL OF JAMES HENDERSON OF LINCOLN COUNTY
Grandfather of GOVERNOR JAMES
PICKNEY HENDERSON.

IN THE NAME OF GOD AMEN. I, JAMES HENDERSON, being very weak in body but sound in mind and memory, calling to mind that it is appointed for all men wanst to die; I make this my last will and testament. I leve to my son JOHN PETERSON and to my son LAWSON HENDERSON and to my daughter MARTHA HENDERSON, six shillings to each of the before named for to buy the Gospel meetre of Santify Cation. I leave to my grandson JAMES HENDERSON, PETER'S son, two hundred acres of land on DUCK RIVER (in Tennessee), the track of land I bought JAMES HOLLAND. I also leve to my daughter CATRIN the tract of land of twelve hundred acres I bought of the Reverend ARGEBEL (Archibald)in WILSON'S VALLE and one negro wench about the age of twelve years, a good helthe sound wench and a hors and sadle worth thirty pounds, all to be delivered to her at the age of eighteen years.

I leve all the rest of my estate Real and personall to my beloved wife VIOLET HENDERSON and to my son JAMES HENDERSON and to WILLIAM HENDERSON in the way and manner as folling. I leve the land I now live on and all my other land that is not before mentioned to JAMES HENDERSON and WILLIAM HENDERSON and LOGAN HENDERSON only my beloved wife VIOLET HENDERSON is for to have a good soficint mantanenc out of said land during her life but if it sute them to sell said Land the are for to pay my well beloved wife VIOLET HENDERSON two hundred pounds out of the price of said land, and after my decese I order my personall Estate to be valued by two man on oah to be chosen by all partys or by a megorety of them and the above JAMES HENDERSON and WILLIAM and LOGAN HENDERSON is for to pay my beloved wife VIOLET HENDERSON the forth part of the value of said personal estate at any time or times she sees cause to demand the same; and I do testify this to be my last will and testament and do declare all other wills and testamens void and recommend my soul to God that gave it and my Body to be buried in decent form by my Executors which I appoint my beloved wife VIOLET HENDERSON and JAMES HENDERSON my son to execute this my last will and testiment. In witness I have here unto set my hand and Seal this ninth day of September, Yr. 1793.

JAMES HENDERSON (Seal).

Witness:
Sam Chatswell
HUGH EWING.

HUGH EWING the witness to the will of JAMES HENDERSON was the son of GEORGE EWING, who married JANE LAWSON, sister of VIOLET LAWSON, wife of the testator in the above will.

The statement on page 226 that all of the children of JAMES HENDERSON, the testator, moved to TENNESSEE with their mother VIOLET HENDERSON about 1803, is error. Both LAWSON (who m. ELIZABETH CARRUTH) and WILLIAM (who m. ELIZABETH ABERNATHY) remained and lived and died in Lincoln County, North Carolina.

JAMES, LOGAN and JOHN HENDERSON appears to have migrated to the "Duck River" section of Tennessee. KATHERINE HENDERSON married a cousin, WILLIAM M. LOGAN and lived in TENNESSEE, and MARGARET (daughter of JAMES) married DANIEL McKISSICK, of Lincoln County, and also moved to TENNESSEE with her parents. She and her husband were the ancestors of CAROLINE BEALL PRICE, whose life-time of intense research has enabled the writer to assemble these facts on the HENDERSON and LAWSON family.

MAJOR LAWSON HENDERSON, father of GOV. JAMES PINCKNEY HENDERSON, of Texas, was born MARCH 22, 1774 and died Nov. 21, 1843. He was a native of LINCOLN COUNTY. He married ELIZABETH CARRUTH (who died in CANTON, MISSISSIPPI) and was Sheriff of the County (LINCOLN, N. C.) from 1796 to 1801. When the Legislature of North Carolina changed the law by providing that sessions of the SUPERIOR COURT be held in each county MAJ. LAWSON HENDERSON (in 1807)was appointed Clerk of the SUPERIOR COURT for the term of his life. In 1832 the Legislature made the office elective, and JOHN D. HOKE was elected Clerk, but MAJ. HENDERSON, who had not been a candidate refused to vacate the office on the ground that it was his property for life. Hoke entered suit for it and lost when the SUPREME COURT in a decision written by JUDGE RUFFIN, sustained MAJ. HENDERSON'S claim to the office. Later in 1837, he resigned.

He was married to ELIZABETH CARRUTH, July 20, 1798. He was 70 years old at his death.

GOVERNOR JAMES PINCKNEY HENDERSON, OF TEXAS

JAMES PINCKNEY HENDERSON was the first Governor of the State of Texas, after it was admitted to the Union. In 1837 he was Minister to England and France, from the Republic of Texas, but in 1840 he returned to Texas and practiced law in East Texas, in partnership with KENNETH L. ANDERSON and THOMAS J. RUSK. By authority of the Legislature he commanded the Texas troops in the War with Mexico with the rank of Major-General of Volunteers. In 1857 he was elected United States Senator from Texas, but, according to the histories, died before taking his seat. He was the son of LAWSON HENDERSON, the old Clerk and Sheriff of LINCOLN COUNTY, and the grandson of JAMES HENDERSON and VIOLET LAWSON, his wife.

CHARLES COTESWORTH HENDERSON, a brother, visited him in Texas, a short time before his death and while he was still Governor. In 1856(?)in Lincoln County, North Carolina, he gave the following account of his visit to GOVERNOR HENDERSON at the Capitol in Austin:

"I went to New Orleans on business a few weeks ago and got through with the business quicker than I expected, and as I had not seen my brother PICKNEY, for fifteen years decided to take a stage and go to Austin, Texas, to visit him. When I reached Austin about 11 o'clock in the morning, I went to the hotel and prepared to meet my brother. Coming down into the lobby I enquired where I might find Governor Henderson. Some gentleman spoke up and said Governor Henderson was in the Senate Chamber addressing the Senate on some matter. So I went to the door and the door-keeper gave me a direct look and said, 'You must be a brother of the Governor,' and I told him I was, but my brother had not seen me for fifteen years and would not know me. He took me down the aisle and gave me an end seat. As I sat down I noticed my brother halt in his talk and give a look in my direction, and in a few words told the Senate he would finish what he had to say later. He picked up his hat and when he got to me caught me by the ear and led me out, saying:
" 'Even a HENDERSON can't get lost in Texas!' "

In an account of a Fourth of July celebration held in LINCOINTON in 1836 as reported by the Raleigh (N. C.) Standard, there were twelve revolutionary soldiers seated at the table of honor, and the account is ended with the statement that "Toasts were drunk to HENRY W. CONNOR, the Congressman, and to JAMES PINCKNEY HENDERSON, who was at the time doing valiant service with SAM HOUSTON, for TEXAS INDEPENDENCE."

JOHN PETER HENDERSON (So called in the will of his father JAMES HENDERSON) was living in Williamson County, Tennessee, when his brother in law, WILLIAM N. LOGAN died leaving a will, and with his sister CATHERINE LOGAN was made executor of the will. JOHN PETER HENDERSON married in North Carolina, before moving to Tennessee, since his son JAMES is mentioned in the will of JAMES HENDERSON, his grandfather in 1794. From all sources we gather the names of the following children of JOHN HENDERSON, though we do not find the name of his wife:

    100. ROBERT HENDERSON m. (1) PEGGY SHEPHERD (2) MARY WOOTEN.
    101. JAMES HENDERSON m. AMANDA M. VOORHEES.
    102. VIOLET HENDERSON m. WILLIAM F. LYTLE.
    103. JANE HENDERSON m. WILLIAM B. MOORE.

The "TENNESSEE RECORDS" suggest that JOHN HENDERSON went to Tennessee, not only with his brother JAMES and brother in law WILLIAM LOGAN, but that along with them went a large contingent of the McKNIGHT FAMILY, from the GILEAD-COWAN FORD neighborhood, who settled along STONE RIVER.

In 1818 LOGAN HENDERSON went to TENNESSEE and purchased much valuable land near MURFREES-BORO, in RUTHERFORD COUNTY. He married MARGARET EWART JOHNSTON, the daughter of COL. JAMES JOHNSTON and his wife JANE EWART, the daughter of ROBERT EWART. LOGAN HENDERSON died in 1846 and his wife Margaret died August 13, 1863.

The will of WILLIAM LOGAN, proved at FRANKLIN, in WILLIAMSON COUNTY, Tennessee, in October, 1823 shows that he had over a thousand acres of land, slaves, etc., with six sons and two daughters. He left his library to his son NEWTON WILSON LOGAN. The two daughters were VIOLET BARRY LOGAN and MARY PATTERSON LOGAN. The latter married (as his second wife) W. F. LYTLE, whose first wife had been 102 VIOLET HENDERSON, her cousin. Other sons of WILLIAM H. LOGAN and CATHERINE HENDERSON were JAMES HENDERSON LOGAN, WILLIAM H. LOGAN and ROBERT LOGAN. DR. THOMAS COBLE, of Shelbyville, BEDFORD COUNTY, TENNESSEE, is a descendant of VIOLET LOGAN and her husband WILLIAM F. LYTLE.

In the old private burial plot on top of the bluff, opposite the McADENVILLE, MILLS in what is now GASTON COUNTY, N. C., where the remains of JAMES HENDERSON (m. VIOLET LAWSON) are buried, this writer copied two tombstone inscriptions, besides that of ADAM ALEXANDER SPRINGS, which suggest the LITTLES were closely related to the HENDERSONS. They were:

    ADAM T. LITTLE, b. Aug. 13, 1838; d. April 1850.
    WILLIAM H. LITTLE 1841-1843.

The difference is that the name was spelled "LITTLE" and not "LYTLE" as it is over in TENNESSEE. But the writer is of the opinion that this was the same identical family.

FAMILY OF WILLIAM HENDERSON

This WILLIAM HENDERSON was the son of JAMES HENDERSON and his wife VIOLET LAWSON, the grandson of HUGH LAWSON and his wife MARY MOORE, and the uncle of JAMES PINCKNEY HENDERSON, the first GOVERNOR OF TEXAS.

He is mentioned in his father's will in LINCOLN COUNTY (N. C.) in 1793; was born JULY 27, 1774, and died OCTOBER 31, 1857. On January 2, 1798, he was married to ELIZABETH ABERNATHY, of LINCOLN COUNTY, who was born November 11, 1779, and died on May 4, 1839.

They had the following children:

104. JAMES ABERNATHY HENDERSON, born September 28, 1798, and died April 8, 1888, who married SINA PHARR ABERNATHY, who was born July 31, 1811, and died November 20, 1888.
105. LAWSON HENDERSON, born March 17, 1800.
106. ISABELLA HENDERSON, born February 2, 1802.
107. ROBERT HENDERSON, born March 21, 1804, died 1863.
108. ELIZABETH HENDERSON, born March 10, 1806.
109. ADALINE HENDERSON, born December 4, 1808.
110. POLLY HENDERSON, born May 13, 1811.
111. JANE A. HENDERSON, born August 17, 1813.
112. WILLIAM H. HENDERSON, born June 1, 1816; died AUGUST, 1855, in ARKANSAS.
113. JOHN HENDERSON, born February 4, 1819; died February 14, 1887.
114. AUGUSTUS L. HENDERSON, born March 6, 1825.
115. MARY HENDERSON, born December 10, 1823; died May 13, 1831.

Children of 104. JAMES ABERNATHY HENDERSON:

Mary Asinthe Adeline (1831-1855) m. 1853, S. W. Craig.
Susan Elizabeth (1832-1893) m. 1865, John Fite.
Jane Wilson (1835-1898) m. Calvin Abernathy.
Emiline Amanda (b. 1837).
James Lawson (1839-1864) died in War Between the States.
William Adolphus (1842-1862) died in War BEtween the States.
MILES ABERNATHY (1844-1908) m. Margaret Slagle in 1886.
Francis Augustus (b. 1847) m. Elizabeth Lineberger.
Isabella Adelaide (b. 1849) m. 1880, James M. Collins.
Lucinda Eliza (b. 1852) m. 1871 Will I. Friday.

Children of ROBERT HENDERSON and his wife MARTHA CAROLINE SAMPLE:

Isabella Elizabeth (b. 1834) married Theodore Newton McNeely.
James Sample Henderson m. Margaret E. Harry.
Martha Jane Louise m. 1892 Isaac Henderson, of Mooresville, N. C. No issue.
Lawson Pinckney died in War Between the States (1839-1861). Killed at Yorktown, Virginia.
William Augustus Henderson, died in Civil war (1844-1863). Both of these brothers are buried at HOPEWELL CHURCH.
Mary Margaret Caroline m. in 1898 J. S. Collins, of Steele Creek settlement.

106. ISABELLA HENDERSON m. in 1820, WILLIAM DAVENPORT, and had children:
JOHN W., ELIZABETH, MARY E., JAMES A. and WILLIAM L. DAVENPORT, who went to Texas.

Children of MILES ABERNATHY HENDERSON and his wife MARGARET SLAGLE:

Walter S. Henderson (Of DAVIDSON, N.C.)
Bessie E. Henderson
Mary Henderson
Miles Palmer Henderson
Annie Henderson
Gladys Henderson
Willie Rachael Henderson
Ruth E. Henderson.
(Data furnished by Walter S. Henderson above).

109. ADALINE HENDERSON (b. 1808) m. ROBERT MILAS SAMPLE (b. 1807) and had children:

Elizabeth Sample m. John Houston.
Harriet Sample m. A. J. Hunter, of Huntersville.
Mary Sample m. Clement Nance Blythe.
Martha Sample m. C. W. McCoy.
Agnes Sample m. Marion Ransom of Huntersville.
J. Wilson Sample, killed in War Between the States.
Leroy Sample, killed 1862 in Civil War.
Elam Augustus Sample, minister, m. Margaret McKey.

---

107. ROBERT HENDERSON, who married MARTHA CAROLINE SAMPLE, on December 15, 1832, is designated in the Sommerville History of Hopewell Presbyterian Church, as the ancestor of the "Henderson Family of Long Creek". He is said to have settled near Long Creek bridge one mile and a half southeast of Hopewell Church, probably after his marriage into the Sample family of Mecklenburg. One is left to infer that all of the other Hendersons in Mecklenburg County, belonged to a different family of the same name. We think this is error, and that ROBERT HENDERSON'S grandfather had at least two brothers, with many descendants, who settled in a few miles North of Long Creek, nearly a hundred years previous - coming there from Virginia. 107 ROBERT HENDERSON, however, was possibly the first of the Lincoln County Hendersons, who bulged across the Catawba into Mecklenburg to make it their home, unless his older brother, James Abernathy Henderson, also came, since some of his descendants now live at Davidson. The lapse of time has obliterated any memory of these HENDERSONS, and the records are so crowded by various Hendersons today, that the old ones cannot be successfully segregated.

207. MARY LAWSON m. JAMES WHITE

MARY LAWSON was the youngest daughter of HUGH LAWSON and his wife MARY MOORE. Her marriage to JAMES WHITE had not taken place when her father's will was written in 1764. They were married May 13, 1770. JAMES WHITE was the son of MOSES WHITE and his first wife MARY McCONNELL. The children of JAMES WHITE and his wife MARY LAWSON were as follows:

300. MARGARET WHITE born April 8, 1771.
301. HUGH LAWSON WHITE, born October 30, 1773.
302. MOSES WHITE, born April 22, 1775.
303. ANDREW WHITE born May 19, 1779.
304. MARY McCONNELL WHITE born November 11, 1782.
305. CYNTHIA BARRY WHITE, born April 7, 1786.
306. MALINDA WHITE, born February 15, 1789.

GEN. JAMES WHITE, according to the family Bible, died August 14, 1831; and MARY (LAWSON) WHITE, his wife, died March 10, 1819, aged 77 years. Therefore, MARY LAWSON, the youngest child of COL. HUGH LAWSON, was born about 1742.

---

301. HUGH LAWSON WHITE, a distinguished Judge and United States Senator, from TENNESSEE, and the son of JAMES WHITE and MARY LAWSON, had the following children by his marriage to ELIZABETH CARRICK, daughter of REV. SAMUEL CARRICK:

400. CHARLES ANDREW CARRICK WHITE (1797-1826)
401. JAMES MOON MAY WHITE (1801-1828) died TUSCALOOSA, ALABAMA.
402. BETSY MOON WHITE (b. 1803) m. JOHN NEWTON SCOTT.
403. MARY LAWSON WHITE (b. 1805) m. WILLIAM SWAN.
404. LUCINDA BLOUNT WHITE (1807-1827) never married.
405. MARGARET ANN WHITE (b. 1809) m. EBENEZER ALEXANDER.
406. CYNTHIA WILLIAMS WHITE (1812-1829).
407. MALINDA McDOWELL WHITE (1815-1830).
408. HUGH LAWSON WHITE (1818-1819).
409. ISABELLA HARVEY WHITE born May 19, 1820.
410. SAMUEL DAVIS CARRICK WHITE, born May 26, 1825.

GEN. HUGH LAWSON WHITE died April 10, 1840, at the age of 67 years, and his wife ELIZABETH CARRICK WHITE died March 25, 1831. REV. SAMUEL CARRICK, father of ELIZABETH CARRICK WHITE, and a distinguished Minister, died August 18, 1809.

THE WHITE FAMILY

On page 424 of these notes appears a brief mention of the "Moses White Family" bearing mostly on the history of where the family lived in North Carolina, and the migration of GEN. JAMES WHITE (son of MOSES) to Tennessee.

A few notes relating to the history of MOSES WHITE and his family, inserted here will enable the student to better understand, not only the WHITE FAMILY, but other families we have and will mention in these notes.

One JAMES CAMPBELL died in AUGUSTA COUNTY, Virginia, leaving a will dated November 5, 1753, at about the age of 71 years.

He was the ancestor of MARGARET CAMPBELL, who married DAVID MOORE (See pages 477-481), and of ARCHIBALD CAMPBELL, who witnessed the will of this DAVID MOORE.

From his will and other records JAMES CAMPBELL had the following children:

(1) JOHN CAMPBELL
(2) DAVID CAMPBELL
(3) MOSES CAMPBELL
(4) JANE CAMPBELL m. ISAAC WHITE
(5) SARAH CAMPBELL m. SAMUEL STEELE
(6) MARY CAMPBELL m. MOSES WHITE.

This will of JAMES CAMPBELL was witnessed by ROBERT CUNNINGHAM and BENJAMIN STUART. ROBERT CUNNINGHAM was a member of the House of Burgesses from AUGUSTA COUNTY, Virginia. The wife of ROBERT CUNNINGHAM was MARTHA HAMILTON, a widow, who had been MARTHA KIRKPATRICK, daughter of CHARLES KIRKPATRICK, and one of her daughters MARY HAMILTON became the wife of DAVID CAMPBELL, and still another the wife of 100. CHARLES MOORE, whose brother DAVID married MARGARET CAMPBELL.

ISAAC WHITE and MOSES WHITE, brothers, married respectively, JANE and MARY CAMPBELL, two of the daughters of JAMES CAMPBELL (who was born about 1682) who left the will in 1753. They were sisters of JOHN CAMPBELL. This much has been heretofore admitted by the genealogists, but the same source asserts that the JOHN CAMPBELL they mean, was the JOHN who came from IRELAND to AMERICA in 1726 with five or six grown sons and several daughters and settled first in LANCASTER COUNTY, PENNSYLVANIA, later in Augusta County, accompanied by sons PATRICK, ROBERT and DAVID CAMPBELL. This JOHN CAMPBELL was a different one - the son of JAMES CAMPBELL, whom they never mention.

ISAAC WHITE, who married JANE CAMPBELL left a will in AUGUSTA COUNTY, VIRGINIA, dated August 10, 1775 (Vol III Chalkley p. 162) in which he mentioned his wife JANE, and the following children:

1. DAVID WHITE
2. ISAAC WHITE (d. Jonesboro, Tenn.)
3. JAMES WHITE
4. GORDON WHITE
5. JANE WHITE
6. ISABELLA WHITE
7. MARGARET WHITE
8. MARY WHITE m. JOHN YOUNG
9. ELIZABETH WHITE m. ANDREW RUSSELL
10. SARAH RODGERS.

MOSES WHITE (brother of ISAAC, above) so far as we can find, left no will on the records, but according to a history of "The White Family" he married MARY "sister of John Campbell, the emigrant, great grandfather of Gen. William Campbell, of King's Mountain fame," and had one son (perhaps others) named:

1. MOSES WHITE

1. MOSES WHITE (the son of MOSES and MARY CAMPBELL WHITE) married first, MARY McCONNELL, and second, ELEANOR ...? His will, probated in ROWAN COUNTY, N. C., June 14, 1783, mentions the following children:

100. DAVID WHITE
101. WILLIAM WHITE
102. JOHN WHITE
103. JAMES WHITE m. MARY LAWSON in 1770.
104. JEAN WHITE m. .... TEMPLETON.
105. ELIZABETH WHITE m. SAMUEL PEDEN
106. MARY WHITE m. McGAY
107. SARAH m. JOSEPH WILSON (To Tennessee).
108. CATHERINE WHITE m. ...PEDEN

109. ELEANOR WHITE
110. MARGARET WHITE.

The last two children are not mentioned in the will, but their names do appear in the account of the family from which this data is taken. They were doubtless children of the second marriage. The wife ELEANOR and the testator's sons DAVID and JAMES were named Executors. The will is witnessed by SAMUEL PEDEN and JOHN MORTON. Samuel Peden was the son in law of MOSES WHITE, and after PEDEN died his widow married MORTON, by whom she had several children, lost her second husband, and again married - this time to SAMUEL MORROW, a revolutionary soldier, whose sons moved to MORGAN COUNTY, ALABAMA, and some of their descendants to TEXAS. Descendants of SAMUEL PEDEN, among them a MOSES WHITE PEDEN, also moved to Texas.

The children of 103. JAMES WHITE and his wife MARY LAWSON have been set out on the preceding page.

JOSEPH WILSON and his wife SARAH WHITE moved to TENNESSEE and settled in the vicinity of Nashville, where JOSEPH was killed by Indians. His widow SARAH WILSON, for her extraordinary heroism and pioneer courage finds an enviable place in Mrs. Ellett's "Women of the Revolution".

———

2. ISAAC WHITE (a cousin of 1. MOSES) married his cousin SARAH LAWSON, and his will is on record in W. B. No. 1, p. 136 at JONESBORO, Washington County, Tennessee, where it was probated May 5, 1819. All of his children are not mentioned in his will. He names

111. TERRY WHITE
112. WILLIAM WHITE
113. FLETCHER WHITE (May be STEPHEN).
114. RICHARD WHITE
115. MARY WHITE wife of THOMAS GIBSON.
116. SUSANNA WHITE wife of DANIEL DENTON.
117. ANNIE WHITE wife of ELIJAH KERR.
"My other sons already taken care of".
Wife and son TERRY WHITE named Executors.
NATHAN SHIPLEY and WILLIAM GOMERY witnesses.

114. RICHARD WHITE was twice married. Married (1) MISS LAWSON, his cousin; (2) MRS. HENRY, said to have been the widow of a son of PATRICK HENRY. There were two sets of children:

(1) ANNA WHITE m. ....WRIGHT
(2) ELIZA WHITE m. ...WRIGHT
(3) MARY WHITE m. DAVID RUSSELL
(4) THEODOSIA WHITE m. THOMAS FINLEY
(5) LAWSON WHITE m. BEATTIE
(6) RICHARD WHITE m. MISS BEATTIE
(7) CLAIBORN WHITE m. LEONIDAS HOGUE.

(8) ELLEN WHITE m. JOSIAH BEATTIE
(9) PAULINA WHITE m. ROBERT BEATTIE
(10) RHODA WHITE m. .. WITTEN
(11) REBECCA WHITE m. (1) SID HOGUE (2) BEATTIE
(12) RACHEL WHITE m. .... TRIGG.
(13) JOHN WHITE m. MARGARET AIKENS
(14) THOMAS WHITE m. JANE YOUNG.
had :
EWING YOUNG WHITE.

EWING YOUNG WHITE m. MARGARET MONROW, sister of the compiler's mother, SARAH LAVINIA MONROW.

2. ISAAC WHITE commanded a Company of what is called the "South Fork Boys" from the then LINCOLN COUNTY, in the battle of King's Mountain, though at the time CAPT. WHITE was with his kinsman, GEN. WILLIAM CAMPBELL, in charge of the contingent from the Watauga Valley and Washington County, Va., whither Captain White had previously moved. SAMUEL CALDWELL, the young man heretofore mentioned, was a member of his company. (page 153 Puett's Gaston County.) In 1779 Captain ISAAC WHITE probably lived in GRANVILLE COUNTY (page 213 of these notes).

THE CAMPBELL CLAN

What Mr. JOS. A. WADDELL, in his annals of AUGUSTA COUNTY, VIRGINIA, has had to say about the pioneers of that section from the beginning of its settlement has generally been accepted as final, and the same is true of his account of the CAMPBELL FAMILY. The writer joins in this universal acclaim except in instances where he finds a positive record to the contrary. Mr. Waddell's account of the family of GEN. WILLIAM CAMPBELL, which is to be found on pages 396 to 398, of his work, mentions only the descendants of a JOHN CAMPBELL, whose sons are PATRICK, ROBERT and DAVID. Patrick had a son CHARLES, who he says was the father of GEN. WILLIAM CAMPBELL. Thus Waddell's version is that GEN. WILLIAM CAMPBELL was the great grandson of JOHN CAMPBELL. Nothing is said about the JAMES CAMPBELL, who left will in Augusta in 1753, and who mentioned his son in law ISAAC WHITE, as well as a son JOHN CAMPBELL and others. Mr. Waddell ends his account, however, with the statement that:

"Several other families of CAMPBELLS, not related as far as known to those just mentioned, were among the early settlers of Augusta."

Descendants of the CAMPBELLS themselves are not sure about their ancestry, as shown by correspondence with some of them, nor of the identity of certain JOHN CAMPBELLS shown on the records. JOHN CAMPBELL was probably the ancestor of GEN. WILLIAM CAMPBELL, even as Waddell claims, but WHAT John Campbell? Could it not have been JOHN CAMPBELL, son of JAMES of this will? And, anyway, since there were other Campbells there, how does he know they were not related? If there was an earlier JOHN, could he not have had a brother James? We have found no record to foreclose such a conclusion, only the Waddell assertion that the other Campbells were "not related, as far as known". Certainly there was a JAMES CAMPBELL as well as a JOHN CAMPBELL, and they may or may NOT have been brothers, and they may or may not have been close kin. Though, as we see it, it makes no difference, yet how do the descendants know that JAMES and not JOHN was not the ancestor of the General?

Anyway:

(1) JOHN CAMPBELL (Son of JAMES) was a brother in law of ISAAC and MOSES WHITE, and became the father of a family of children. Among those children, apparently, were three, whose names occur in these records:

(10) JOHN CAMPBELL m. MARY EDWARDS
(11) ARCHIBALD CAMPBELL m. ELIZABETH
(12) MARGARET CAMPBELL m. 101 DAVID MOORE.

(10) JOHN CAMPBELL and his wife MARY EDWARDS had a son ARCHIBALD CAMPBELL (d. 1821). His wife was said to have been a REBECCA KEITH, and they were the parents of DUNCAN G. CAMPBELL, revolutionary soldier, who married MARY WILLIAMSON, daughter of MICAJAH WILLIAMSON and his wife SARAH GILLIAM (See GILLIAM notes herein) and they were the parents of JOHN A. CAMPBELL, who became a member of the Supreme Court of Alabama. John A. Campbell m. Anne Esther Goldthwaite and had CLARA CAMPBELL who married Frederick Morgan Colston (b. 1835), the parents of BESSIE MASON COLSTON, who became wife of COL. HUGH HAMPTON YOUNG. (Virkis 2 p. 334)

COL. HUGH HAMPTON YOUNG was the son of Brig. Gen. Hugh Young (b. 1838), the son of HUGH FRANKLIN YOUNG (b. 1808) who was the son of HUGH YOUNG (b. 1772) who married his cousin SARAH STEELE grand-daughter of JAMES STEELE and SARAH CAMPBELL. Hugh Young was the son of JOHN YOUNG and S. MARY WHITE, daughter of ISAAC WHITE and his wife JANE CAMPBELL. (Ibid).

(11) ARCHIBALD CAMPBELL lived in MECKLENBURG COUNTY, N. C., and in 1778 was one of the witnesses to the will of DAVID MOORE and his wife MARGARET, sister of ARCHIBALD. When 103, JAMES WHITE, grandson of MOSES WHITE and MARY CAMPBELL, settled in what is now KNOX COUNTY, TENNESSEE, ARCHIBALD CAMPBELL, nephew of MARY CAMPBELL, and a cousin of JAMES WHITE'S father, followed him to that section, where he died in 1800, leaving a will, in which he named his wife ELIZABETH, proved September 8, 1801. His children were AGNES, JAMES, JOHN, ELIZABETH, JANET, WILLIAM, SAMUEL and MARY. The will was witnessed by JOHN PAUL and JOHN DOUGAN.

(2) EPHRAIM MOORE

EPHRAIM MOORE (See p. 477) is supposed to have been a brother of CHARLES MOORE, whose wife was MARGARET BARRY, the ancestors of all of the MOORES we have been writing about, back to page 477, of these notes. Only one thing is known about him and his family. One of his daughters (and even her Christian name is unkown) became the wife of JOHN McLEAN, and she and her husband JOHN McLEAN had two sons:

100. EPHRAIM McLEAN m. ELIZABETH DAVIDSON
101. COL. CHARLES McLEAN m. SUSANNA HOWARD

100. EPHRAIM McLEAN was born, it is said in 1730, while COL. CHARLES McLEAN was perhaps three or four years older. They were both revolutionary soldiers, and their mother was a MOORE, they were cousins of CHARLES, DAVID and HUGH MOORE, sons of CHARLES MOORE and MARGARET BARRY.

100: EPHRAIM McLEAN married ELIZABETH DAVIDSON in 1761. Elizabeth was the daughter of JOHN DAVIDSON, a brother of ROBERT DAVIDSON and GEORGE DAVIDSON, of North Carolina, and of WILLIAM DAVIDSON, of Prince Edward County, Virginia. The children of EPHRAIM McLEAN and his wife ELIZABETH were, according to the McLEAN family history, as follows:

    200. JOHN McLEAN (b. 1762)
    201. GEORGE McLEAN of(Logan County, Ky.)
    202. EPHRAIM McLEAN (Maury County, Tenn.)
    203. JANE McLEAN b. 1769, m. GEN. ROBERT EWING.
    204. _____ McLEAN m. ROBERT BRANK
    205. SAMUEL McLEAN (b. 1772) of Lawrenceburg, Tenn.
    206. JUDGE OLNEY McLEAN (of Ky.)
    207. CHARLES McLEAN (b. 1776) of Maury County, Tenn.
    208. WILLIAM McLEAN (b. 1778) Snow Creek, Tenn.
    209. JAMES McLEAN (b. 1780) Hinds County, Miss.
    210. ROBERT McLEAN (b. 1782) Harrodsburg, Ky.

The father of this family lived for many years in his old age in Maury County, Tennessee, on Knobb Creek. In about 1820, at the age of 90 years he returned to his former home at HARRODSBURG, KENTUCKY to reside with his sons ROBERT and OLNEY, where he died in 1823, aged 93 years. The descendants of him and his children are innumerable and are scattered throughout practically all of the Southern States

206. JUDGE OLNEY McLEAN married in 1845, MARTHA J. MOORE, a sister of WILLIAM R. MOORE, of Memphis, Tenn. who was elected to Congress in 1882. He was born in HUNTSVILLE, ALABAMA (Moore) on March 28, 1830, his family having moved to Tennessee.

101. COL. CHARLES McLEAN married SUSAN HOWARD, who was the widow ALLISON, who had two sons by her first marriage, named ALLISON. Her first husband is said to have been THOMAS ALLISON, & the two sons were named
    (1) ROBERT ALLISON
    (2) SAMUEL TURNER ALLISON.

The children of COL. CHARLES McLEAN and his wife SUSAN (HOWARD) ALLISON were

    211. JOHN McLEAN (Died after King's Mountain).
    212. EPHRAIM McLEAN
    213. SUSANNA McLEAN married a WHITE.

About 1796, COL. CHARLES McLEAN and his wife (who outlived her husband several years) migrated to LOGAN COUNTY, KENTUCKY. They were accompanied by 212 EPHRAIM McLEAN and his wife and three children, and also, it is believed by SAMUEL TURNER ALLISON, whom the land records show, obtained lands on some of the streams traversing LOGAN COUNTY, he having been a revolutionary soldier.

THE MOORE AND ALLISON FAMILIES

The MOORE, ALLISON and McLEAN families were all related. COL. CHARLES McLEAN and his brother EPHRAIM were grandsons of (2) EPHRAIM McLEAN, a brother of CHARLES MOORE who married MARGARET BARRY. COL. CHARLES McLEAN married the widow ALLISON and became the step-father of ROBERT and SAMUEL ALLISON. ROBERT ALLISON then married a widow LAMPKIN, who had been JANE MOORE, and this JANE MOORE was the daughter of:

103. WILLIAM MOORE m. MARY

one of the brothers of 100 CHARLES MOORE, the School Master, of Spartanburg. (pp. 479-478). This WILLIAM MOORE, with COL. CHARLES McLEAN, JOHN HILL and CHRISTOPHER CARPENTER, was named on the commission to select the site of the first courthouse of TRYON COUNTY, and made their report on July 26, 1774. (Page 100 Puett's History of Gaston County). The name of WILLIAM MOORE'S wife MARY has not been found. He and MARY, his wife, made the following deed in 1765:

    WILLIAM MOORE and wife MARY, of MECKLENBURG COUNTY, to
    EPHRAIM McLEAN, of the same place, lease of land at the head of
    the South Fork of FISHING CREEK, adjoining lands on branches
    of TURKEY CREEK. October 19, 1765. (Harris Register, Book 3,
    pages 1 and 2, of Mecklenburg County. See also page 320 of
    these notes, which shows the instrument was witnessed by WILLIAM
    DUNLAP and JOHN WILSON.

This is the same WILLIAM MOORE who was appointed by the General Assembly in 1768 to collect the taxes for the new county of TRYON, set up from the Western territory of what had been regarded for several years as embraced in MECKLENBURG COUNTY. The lands he leased to EPHRAIM McLEAN down on FISHING CREEK are now in YORK COUNTY, South Carolina, though at that time they were considered in MECKLENBURG, and the deed or indenture, for that reason was recorded at CHARLOTTE. This WILLIAM MOORE was the father of GEN. JOHN MOORE who served for seventeen terms in the General Assembly.

In the ANNALS OF LINCOLN COUNTY, by William L. Sherrill (1937), appear the following items relating to 103. WILLIAM MOORE:

The Assembly appointed and empowered WILLIAM MOORE to collect Tryon County taxes for 1768. Colonial Records Vol. 8 p 293.

The Assembly of 1770 appointed THOMAS NEEL, WILLIAM MOORE, ROBERT ADAMS, EPHRAIM McLEAN and JOHN BEARD, a commission to agree upon a site for the courthouse, etc. Colonial Records Vol. 8 p. 344.

1773 and 1774. WILLIAM MOORE and CHRISTIAN REINHARDT mentioned. Colonial Records Vol. 9 p. 491.

Report of the Commission to select site for courthouse made and those signing it, July 26, 1774, were CHARLES McLEAN, WILLIAM MOORE, JOHN HILL and CHRISTOPHER CARPENTER. p. 17 of the "Annals".

District Court in Salisbury, June 1, 1775. The jurors from TRYON COUNTY were WILLIAM MOORE, FREDERICK HAMBRIGHT, MOSES MOORE, William Gilbert, James McIntyre, JOHN McKINNEY, JAMES JOHNSTON and ABRAM KERKIN-DALL. Colonial Records Vol. 10 p. 1.

1775. WILLIAM MOORE and WILLIAM ALSTON were the Assemblymen from TRYON in 1775. Colonial Records Vol. 9, p. 1189.

On page 112 of the "Annals" appears an account of WILLIAM MOORE, which gives the names of his four sons, but mentions no daughters.

103. WILLIAM MOORE and his wife MARY, according to the ANNALS of LINCOLN COUNTY and information obtained from other and numerous sources, had the following children:

```
200.  WILLIAM MOORE m. a GULLICK.
201.  ALEXANDER MOORE
202.  JAMES MOORE
203.  JOHN MOORE (1759-1836)
204.  AGNES MOORE m. JAMES DICKSON.
205.  MARY MOORE m. (1) THOMAS CAMPBELL (2) WILLIAM RANKIN.
206.  ROSANNAH MOORE, said to have married a HENRY.
207.  JANE MOORE m. (1) WILLIAM LAMKIN (2) ROBERT ALLISON.
```

The dates on 203. JOHN MOORE are copied from the Lincoln "Annals". They appear to be all right. The names of the daughters come to us originally in a "family account", but we have checked them with other data and believe they are probably correct. The "Annals" account has this to say about 203. JOHN:

"The first wife of GEN. JOHN MOORE was a sister of GOVERNOR ADAIR, of Kentucky. His second wife was MARY SCOTT, widow of JAMES SCOTT and a daughter of ROBERT ALEXANDER".

This means that his second wife was a grand-daughter of PATRICK JACK and a niece of CAPT. JAMES JACK, whose first wife, Mrs. Moore's mother, was MARY JACK, mentioned in the will of PATRICK JACK (p. 328 of these notes).

The HENRY who is said to have married ROSANNAH MOORE was related to the GULLICK, who became the wife of WILLIAM MOORE. MOSES HENRY married MARGARET BALDREICH, and after the death of MOSES HENRY she married JONATHAN GULLICK. Elizabeth GULLICK, a sister of JONATHAN, became the wife of SAMUEL CALDWELL, the young Revolutionary soldier, who was himself related to the MOORES.

COL. ROBERT ALEXANDER, whose daughter MARY married first JAMES SCOTT and second GEN. JOHN MOORE, had a sister ELLEN ALEXANDER, who married SAMUEL RANKIN. WILLIAM RANKIN, a son of this last couple, married MARY MOORE, sister of the WILLIAM MOORE who married the GULLICK. COL. RICHARD RANKIN was the son of WILLIAM RANKIN and his wife MARY MOORE, and his daughter CATHERINE RANKIN also married a MOORE.

Thus, considering the above, one gets a pretty fair idea of the relationship existing between the Moores, Rankins, Gullicks and Henrys.

207. JANE MOORE

This JANE MOORE was born January 27, 1753. She was six years older than her brother, GEN. JOHN MOORE, one time Speaker of the North Carolina Assembly, who was born in 1759, according to the "Annals of Lincoln County".

She married first, WILLIAM LAMKIN or LAMPKIN. He was perhaps a brother of GEORGE LAMKIN, who was Sheriff of TRYON COUNTY in 1772, and of SAMUEL LAMKIN. This note (1778) from the "Annals of Lincoln," page 26:

SAMUEL LAMKIN, BENJAMIN HARDIN, JOHN WALKER and JONATHAN GULLICK were appointed as commissioners to run the dividing line between the new counties (LINCOLN and RUTHERFORD) agreeable to the act creating them.

WILLIAM LAMPKIN, the first husband of 207 JANE MOORE, is said to have been killed while serving in the revolution. They had at least one son, WILLIAM LAMPKIN, born September 16, 1773, who married ROSANNAH WOODS on December 4, 1798, in Washington County, Tennessee, the ceremony being performed by REV. SAMUEL DOAK, the noted pioneer minister and educator.

SOME DESCENDANTS OF 107 JANE MOORE AND HER HUSBAND ROBERT ALLISON

107. JANE MOORE and her second husband, ROBERT ALLISON (page 493) moved over into what is now, perhaps, GREENE COUNTY, TENNESSEE, where ROBERT ALLISON'S step-son WILLIAM LAMPKIN met and married ROSANNAH WOODS. The children of JANE and ROBERT ALLISON were as follows:

(20) MARY MOORE ALLISON m. GEN. JOHN BROWN.
(21) URIAH ALLISON (b. Feb. 1, 1782); m. NANCY CLARK COX.
(22) MARGARET ALLISON m. MOSES PRESTON
(23) SUSAN ALLISON m. ISAAC COUNCIL
(24) AMYE ALLISON m. JAMES CRAIG.
(25) ROBERT ALLISON (b. 1805) m. NANCY BYRD.
(26) JANE MOORE ALLISON, m. JAMES PRESTON.
(See Chart Below)

GEN. JOHN BROWN m. (20) MARY M. ALLISON and had:

1. ROBERT ALLISON BROWN (b. 1808) m. MARY JANE GILLENWATERS.
2. SARAH TARVER BROWN m. NATHANIEL R. JARRETT.
3. THOMAS ALBERT BROWN.
4. MARY JANE BROWN
5. JOHN W. BROWN
6. WILLIAM L. BROWN
7. SUSAN HOWARD BROWN

m. (2) NANCY COX, widow of URIAH ALLISON and had:

8. BENJAMIN BROWN
9. RACHEL JACKSON BROWN m. JOHN COLEMAN
10. ELIZA JANE BROWN
11. GEORGE BARTLETT BROWN.

---

1. ROBERT ALLISON BROWN and JANE GILLEN-WATERS had: (among others)

12. ELIZABETH GILLENWATERS BROWN (b 1847) m. 1868 H. CLAY DANIEL, and had:

20. PEARL HALL DANIEL
21. CHARLES H. DANIEL
22. ROBERT BROWN DANIEL
23. H. CLAY DANIEL, JR.
24. ELIZABETH DANIEL m. WILLIAM BARNES
25. WILLIAM GILLENWATERS DANIEL
26. LOUISE MERRILL DANIEL
27. MARY MOORE DANIEL m. JOHN TROTWOOD MOORE, of NASHVILLE, TENN.

(25) ROBERT M. ALLISON m. NANCY BYRD and had: Children:

1. JESSE BYRD ALLISON
2. ROBERT ALLISON
3. WILLIAM ALLISON
4. RUFF ALLISON
5. SARAH ALLISON
6. MARIA ALLISON
7. EDNA ALLISON
8. URIAH ALLISON
9. LAVINIA LAMPKIN ALLISON m. (1) WORK (2) JOHN HENRY TAYLOR.

JOHN HENRY TAYLOR and his wife LAVINIA LAMPKIN (LOU) ALLISON (MRS. WORK) had:

10. ANN ELIZA TAYLOR m. MR. DURKEE.
11. SARAH MATILDA TAYLOR
12. JOHN HENRY TAYLOR
13. WILLIAM PEYTON TAYLOR
14. CORNELIA DIXIE TAYLOR
15. THOMAS ULVAN TAYLOR m. MARY MOON of VA.

DR. THOMAS ULVAN TAYLOR who married MARY MOON was the beloved "DEAN TAYLOR" of the Engineering Department of the great UNIVERSITY of TEXAS, who died within the past three years at an advanced age, but still active, author of the "CHISHOLM AND OTHER TRAILS", the "LIFE OF JESSE CHISHOLM" an innumerable other books. He wrote:

"My grandfather was ROBERT M. ALLISON, who married NANCY BYRD. My mother was LAVINIA LAMPKIN ALLISON. My father JOHN HENRY TAYLOR was born in ROANE County, Tenn. Feb. 8, 1815; died PARKER COUNTY, TEXAS, in 186V."

---

103. HUGH MOORE AND HIS WIFE MARTHA CALDWELL

The last will and testament of 103 HUGH MOORE (p. 477) was proved in HALIFAX COUNTY, VIRGINIA, July 9, 1760. He was ordered to take the tythe lists of the County just exactly ten years prior to that date. HUGH LAWSON was ordered to do the same thing at the same time. In 1746 Dame MARIA BYRD and CHARLES CARTER, executors of COL. WILLIAM BYRD, began to sell the lands North and South of the DAN RIVER in the large grant to COL. BYRD called "The Havila", and among the first purchasers of these lands were ALEXANDER IRVIN, HUGH LAWSON, DANIEL EVANS, JOHN BOYD and HUGH MOORE. -- Clemens' PITTSYLVANIA COUNTY.

In his will HUGH MOORE mentions his wife MARTHA.
He named four children:

275. JOHN MOORE
276. ALEXANDER MOORE
277. MARY MOORE
278. ANNE MOORE.

There may have been other children, for a part of the will is torn off and unreadable.

The will of 103 HUGH MOORE, in 1760 in HALIFAX COUNTY, Virginia, also mentions his brother 108 JOHN MOORE.

The two sons of 103 HUGH MOORE, JOHN MOORE and ALEXANDER MOORE, joined their relatives in the Catawba Valley, in North Carolina, JOHN having married MARY JACKSON and ALEXANDER married RACHEL BLACK. Space will not permit extending these notes to include their descendants.

108. JOHN MOORE, who was probably born as early as 1710, moved to ORANGE COUNTY, N. C., as soon as settlers could enter that territory. He probably lived in what is now either PERSON or CASWELL COUNTY - possibly ROCKINGHAM. Some of his sons remained in VIRGINIA, or else afterwards returned there to live for a time. His oldest son, William, settled, it is said in ALBEMARLE COUNTY at one time, or in GOOCHLAND, where he married MILDRED HARRISON, a daughter of ANDREW HARRISON. The children of 108 JOHN MOORE were:

(1) WILLIAM MOORE m. MILDRED HARRISON, daughter of ANDREW HARRISON.
(2) GEORGE MOORE
(3) MARK MOORE (To OGLETHORPE CO. GA.)
(4) DEMPSEY MOORE
(5) JOHN MOORE m. PHEREBY.
(6) HUGH MOORE.

MILDRED HARRISON, who became the wife of (1) WILLIAM MOORE was the cousin of RICHARD HARRISON, of SPARTANBURG COUNTY (then believed a part of MECKLENBURG, N. C.) who married ANNE PATILLO, the daughter of REV. HENRY PATILLO, and of his daughter SARAH PATILLO HARRISON who married an ANDREW BARRY. (See pages 479-480).

WILLIAM MOORE and MILDRED HARRISON had children:

100. JOHN MOORE m. MARTHA HARVIE.
101. WILLIAM MOORE m. MARY MARKS.
102. FRANCES MOORE m. JOHN HENDERSON.
103. EDWARD MOORE m. (it is said) MILDRED LEWIS.
104. MATTHEW R. MOORE m. LETITIA DALTON.
105. .... MOORE m. MR. MARTIN.
106. .... MOORE m. DAVID BULLOCK.
107. .... MOORE m. ANDREW McALLEY.

104. MATTHEW R. MOORE lived in STOKES COUNTY, North Carolina, and he and his wife LETITIA DALTON were the parents of

208. MATTHEW R. MOORE, JR.
209. HON. GABRIEL MOORE (Governor of Alabama).

208. MATTHEW R. MOORE, JR. and his son GABRIEL T. MOORE, served in the STATE SENATE of North Carolina, from STOKES COUNTY, from 1829 onward for several terms. -WHEELER, p. 407.

209. HON. GABRIEL MOORE was Governor of ALABAMA, and served in the United States Senate from that State. Back in his mother's family there had been a GABRIEL HARRISON, which may have accounted for his Christian name.

(5) JOHN MOORE AND HIS WIFE PHEREBY

PHEREBY, the wife of JOHN MOORE may have been a COUNCIL. A rather prominent family of that name lived in STOKES COUNTY, and reference to p. 495 of these notes will show that SUSAN ALLISON, grand-daughter of SUSAN HOWARD, married ISAAC COUNCIL. It is known that ISAAC COUNCIL was of this same family in STOKES COUNTY, and among their neighbors was the family of BENJAMIN HOWARD. (Arthur's Westrn North Carolina). Again, it is possible that she was PHEREBY WOOTEN, since JOHN MOORE had a son WOOTEN MOORE.

The children of JOHN MOORE and his wife PHEREBY were as follows:

310. COUNCIL MOORE
311. MARY MOORE m. HERNDON.
312. HENRY MOORE
313. ALFRED MOORE, of ALABAMA.
314. ELIZABETH MOORE m. a HUCKLEY.
315. SARAH MOORE m. a WARREN.
316. WOOTEN MOORE, of ALABAMA.

JOHN MOORE and his wife PHEREBY lived in CHATHAM COUNTY, North Carolina, of which the picturesque little town of PITTSBORO is the county seat. It was there in the quaint little old courthouse that the writer ran across the will of JOHN MOORE, in which he not only gave the names of his children but several of his grand-children. The will was dated September 19, 1843 and its execution was witnessed by THOMAS BELL, ALLEN ELLIS and THOMAS WHITEHEAD. (See p. 199).

JOHN MOORE and wife PHEREBY were the ancestors of HON. JOHN TROTWOOD MOORE, of TEN-

NESSEE, for several years deceased, whose widow, MRS. MARY MOORE (DANIEL) MOORE, has been for several years the head of the Department of Archives and History for the State of Tennessee.

316 WOOTEN MOORE, son of 5 JOHN MOORE and his wife PHEEEBY (the son of 108 JOHN MOORE), married ELIZABETH TOOLEY. He lived for a time in WAKE COUNTY, North Carolina, and is said to have removed to PERRY COUNTY, ALABAMA, in 1832, where he joined his cousins, the descendants of CHARLES MOORE and his wife MISS HAMILTON, who came there from Spartanburg, S. C. WOOTEN MOORE was a successful and substantial cotton planter, whose plantation was situated about 9 miles West of the town of MARION. He was the father of

400. JUDGE JOHN MOORE m. EMILY ADELIA BILLINGSLEA.

400. JUDGE JOHN MOORE attended the University of Alabama and Howard College, and in 1850 began the study of law in the town of MARION. In 1865 he was a member of the Alabama Legislature from PERRY COUNTY and in in 1866 was elected Judge of the district composed of AUTAUGA, BIBB, DALLAS and PERRY COUNTY, to which he was elected over HON. B. F. SAFFORD, who afterwards settled in Dallas, Texas. In 1860 Judge Moore was elected to the Fourth Circuit and re-elected in 1886. He was married to EMILY ADELIA BILLINGSLEA, February 18, 1851. She was the daughter of DR. C. C. BILLINGSLEA, of Montgomery, who came there from WASHINGTON, WILKES COUNTY, GEORGIA, where the BILLINGSLEA family, old neighbors and connections of the MOORES OF MARYLAND, had settled in an early day. JUDGE MOORE and his wife were the parents of two sons and 4 daughters; one of the sons being HON. JOHN TROTWOOD MOORE, distinguished writer and Historian of the State of Tennessee.

Deaths - from BIBLE: Ann Elizabeth Moore (d. March 15, 1853?); Clement Billinslea Moore (d. March 31, 1857); Emily Moore (d. Jan. 20, 1870); Elizabeth Tooley Moore (d. August 16, 1865); Judge John Moore, (d. at Greensboro, Ala., April 27, 1904); Emily Adelia Moore, the mother, wife of Judge John Moore, (d. December 14, 1903); JOHN TROTWOOD MOORE (d. May 10, 1929, at his home "ANDREW PLACE", Nashville, Tennessee.). - Acklin p. 226. These were all "kin" of GOVERNOR ANDREW BARRY MOORE, and of GOVERNOR GABRIEL MOORE, of Alabama. (p. 495-6).

---

106 JAMES MOORE and wife RACHEL

106. JAMES MOORE, another son of CHARLES MOORE and his wife MARGARET BARRY settled in the extreme Southeastern part of MECKLENBURG COUNTY, the part that was afterwards in YORK COUNTY, South Carolina, on ALLISON'S CREEK, and was a neighbor of the ALLISON FAMILY, into which one of his brother's daughters married. On May 17, 1754 he patented lands there. By the year 1768 this JAMES MOORE was dead and his oldest son WILLIAM MOORE applied for and obtained the lands for himself and the other heirs. According to the family historian he had the following children:

   270. WILLIAM MOORE
   271. ALEXANDER MOORE
   272. MAJ. JAMES MOORE m. JANE JACKSON.
   273. JOHN MOORE
   274. MARY MOORE m. WILLIAM ADAIR (Tradition).
   275. JANE MOORE m. JAMES McELHENNEY.
   276. RACHEL MOORE
   277. JOSIAH MOORE.

According to HOWE'S History of the Presbyterian Church in S. C., p. 338, these MOORES all belonged to BETHESDA CHURCH, which included a territory some sixteen miles square, and which had been organized about 1765 by REV. WILLIAM RICHARDSON, uncle of HON. WILLIAM RICHARDSON DAVIES. The son, JOHN MOORE, had the following children, according to the same authority:

   380. JOHN MOORE
   381. SAMUEL MOORE
   382. NATHANIEL MOORE
   383. WILLIAM MOORE,

and perhaps some daughters, whose names are not mentioned in the "History". Among the other members of the congregation were JOHN ADAIR and WILLIAM ADAIR, and CAPT. JOHN McCONNELL and REUBEN McCONNELL, the KUYKENDALLS and others. Many of these members, it is stated, lived across the line in WHAT is now NORTH CAROLINA.

272. JAMES MOORE and his wife JANE JACKSON moved to GEORGIA, where they left a flock of children and other descendants, in which the name HUGH MOORE almost predominated. HANCOCK and GREENE COUNTIES were the homes of these MOORES in GEORGIA.

Old Gum-Log MOORE'S house was built on FISHING CREEK, some twenty feet from the water; often it was surrounded with water. WILLIAM ADAIR'S house, also old RICHARD SADDLER'S, stood in the same way. They were built thus to be as safe as possible from the lurking CHEROKEES, who often waylaid them while going for water, or when washing.

At old WILLIAM ADAIR'S in Chester (sic) the old man and lady took hold of JOHN ADAIR, their son and detained him by force; he watched his chance, and springing from them, mounted his horse, and soon overtook his command, leaving his mother screaming. JOHN ADAIR afterwards went to KENTUCKY. Pages 62 and 63 of "LOGAN'S MANUSCRIPT", Vol III, Jos. Habersham D.A.R. Collections.

KING'S MOUNTAIN

OLD SIX MILE GRAVEYARD

OLD "WAXHAW" CEMETERY

THE ALLISONS

COL. CHARLES McLEAN, the revolutionary patriot of the original MECKLENBURG COUNTY territory (afterwards LINCOLN from TRYON) married a widow SUSANNA ALLISON, whose first husband had been THOMAS ALLISON. There is a tradition that SUSAN was the daughter of a DR. WILLIAM HOWARD, of Philadelphia, who, having refused her the right to marry the man of her choice, swore that she would marry the first man who asked her after that, and that THOMAS ALLISON, having overheard the remark, immediately "popped the question" and they eloped and went South to North Carolina. This tradition is groundless and is based on the joke they used to tell on her husband, in explanation of how he happened to capture so fine a looking young woman. Neither was THOMAS ALLISON from Philadelphia; nor was Susan.

THOMAS and JAMES ALLISON were original emigrants to VIRGINIA, as shown by the records of LANCASTER COUNTY, and were well settled in that county by 1752-3. - Vol 22 Va. Colonial Abstracts, page 7. JAMES was the headright of ABRAHAM MOON, while THOMAS was claimed as a headright by the obstreperous CAPT. HENRY FLEET, the "Daniel Boone of Virginia and Maryland".

Eventually, the descendants of these two ALLISONS settled in SOMERSET COUNTY, on the Eastern Shore of MARYLAND and VIRGINIA, while some of them located higher up the POTOMAC on both sides of that stream, some being in PRINCE GEORGES and CHARLES COUNTY in Maryland, and some in WESTMORELAND and FAIRFAX COUNTY, in Virginia. It was perhaps in WESTMORELAND COUNTY, Virginia, where the ALLISONS first contacted the MOORE and LAMPKIN FAMILIES, a connection that lasted all the way down through Virginia, the Carolinas and into TENNESSEE and GEORGIA. The records of WESTMORELAND COUNTY yields up very little information about the ALLISONS save and except the will of THOMAS ALLISON, dated September 2, 1701, his inventory revealing that his wife was MARGARET; the fact that HANNAH, the daughter of HENRY GARNER, married an ALLISON, and that the will of WILLIAM MOORE, as late as April, 1796, left a son VINCENT MOORE and a daughter MARY ALLISON.

But the ALLISON FAMILY unquestionably lived in WESTMORELAND and had many representatives in the settlements. Among these was a ROBERT ALLISON, who moved to FAIRFAX COUNTY. It was this ROBERT ALLISON who became the first "connection" of the DANIEL FAMILY, to which H. CLAY DANIEL, the father of MRS. JOHN TROTWOOD MOORE, belonged.

HUGH DANIEL married MARY BILLINGTON. DENNIS McCARTY married her sister BARBARA BILLINGTON. DENNIS McCARTY and BARBARA were grand-parents of (1) DANIEL and (2) DENNIS McCARTY. The last named settled in FAIRFAX COUNTY, where he died leaving a will in 1742. His children were sons DANIEL, DENNIS and THADEUS McCARTY, daughter SARAH, who married HON. GEORGE JOHNSTON, and ANNE who married COL. WILLIAM RAMSEY. One of the daughters of COL. WILLIAM RAMSEY married ROBERT ALLISON, & DANIEL McCARTY moved to LINCOLN COUNTY, North Carolina, with the ALLISONS, where he left a will in 1782. Incidentally, the ALLISONS were living in LINCOLN (or GASTON) at about the same time. One of the daughters of DANIEL McCARTY, of Lincoln, married SAMUEL JOHNSTON, her cousin, and his daughter, JEMIMAH McCARTY married HUGH BLAIR.

It was also in WESTMORELAND COUNTY (the home, by the way, DANIEL McCARTY grand-father of the LINCOLN DANIEL McCARTY) that the ALLISONS first - so far as known - had a neighborly connection with the LAMPKIN FAMILY, the fruition of which resulted in the marriage of JANE MOORE, daughter of WILLIAM (pp. 493-494) MOORE, to WILLIAM LAMPKIN. She was not the first JANE LAMPKIN to become JANE MOORE, for JOHN LAMPKIN, of Westmoreland County left a will dated Nov. 15, 1737, in which he mentioned daughters JANE MOORE and WINNIFRED HOWELL. In this case, of course, JANE LAMPKIN, the daughter, had married a MOORE. This JANE (LAMPKIN) MOORE lived until about 1775, when in her will she mentions the names of all her children. They were:

1. JAMES MOORE
2. DORCAS MOORE
3. HANNAH MOORE
4. JANE LAMPKIN MOORE
5. SAMMIE LAMPKIN MOORE
6. GARLAND MOORE.

The JANE MOORE who left the above will, was only ONE of the grand-children of DAME HANNAH DAMOURVEL, whose will was proved in WESTMORELAND COUNTY (Va.) September 25, 1744. The entire list of her grand-children includes JANE MOORE, HANNAH BROWN, MAGDALENE JACKSON, HANNAH HARTLEY, PETER, son of GEORGE LAMPKIN, JAMES LAMPKIN, SAMUEL LAMPKIN and MAGDALENE CLAUGHTON. Magdalene DAMOURVEL, a daughter of the testator, had married CHRISTOPHER DOMINICK JACKSON, while another daughter HANNAH had married a WILLIAM HARRISON. - Data from FOTHERGILL.

CHARLES ALLISON left will in CHARLES COUNTY, MARYLAND, Feb. 20, 1696, leaving a son THOMAS ALLISON; JOHN ALLISON witnessed the will of WILLIAM CASTOR, up around MT. VERNON in Prince GEORGES COUNTY (MA.) in 1726, and PATRICK ALLISON was in SOMERSET COUNTY, at SNOW HILL, signing the will of ROBERT MARTIN May 12, 1725. THOMAS MOORE, JAMES MOORE and ROBERT MOORE all left wills in WESTMORELAND COUNTY at the turn of the century around 1700. These MOORES, ALLISONS and LAMPKINS all belonged to what this writer has termed the MARYLAND MOORE FAMILY, from which the MOORES of MECKLENBURG, stemmed.

Space is not available - nor time at the disposal of the writer - to enter into the intricate details of all of these connections. Each family would make a book of its own. I am assuming that those who are patient and inquisitive enough to attempt to digest what we have set down here, will be intelligent enough to figure out most of these connections for themselves.

LAMPKIN WILLS IN WESTMORELAND: JOHN LAMPKIN, will in 1737, daughter JANE MOORE; GEORGE LAMPKIN in 1718, children ELLENER, PETER and GEORGE and mentions brother JAMES LAMPKIN; GEORGE LAMPKIN will in 1772, wife AGNES, daughter LUCY and son YOUKLL LAMPKIN; SAMUEL LAMPKIN, will AUGUST 27, 1751, married a daughter of MATTHEW HUST and had son DANIEL LAMPKIN, and mentions his brothers ASHTON and CHARLES LAMPKIN.

Can there being any question as to the original family of SAMUEL LAMPKIN, WILLIAM LAMPKIN (who married JANE MOORE) and GEORGE LAMPKIN, the old Sheriff of TRYON COUNTY?

THE ALLISONS of MECKLENBURG lived in Census District No. 1 in 1790. (See pages 357 and 369 of these notes). Their homes were down on the CATAWBA RIVER near the BIGGERS FERRY, near the present South Carolina line. ALLISON'S CREEK took its name from this family. There were many of the ALLISONS who settled in that section, and some lived on FISHING CREEK in what is now South Carolina. Only the names of THREE appear on the census. A number of them had departed before 1790. Among these was ALFRED ALLISON, who moved after the revolution to GREENE COUNTY, GEORGIA. ALFRED ALLISON married a sister of ANDREW JACKSON, SR., and an aunt of PRESIDENT ANDREW JACKSON. Another sister, it is believed, was JANE JACKSON who married MAJ. JAMES MOORE, and also moved to GREENE COUNTY, GEORGIA. In the "Life of ANDREW JACKSON" by Marquis James, it is stated that ANDREW JACKSON, SR. came to the WAXHAWS accompanied by his family and the balance of a small colony of emigrants that his brother HUGH JACKSON (who had already been fighting Indians in the Waxhaws) had induced to leave Ireland with him. HUGH "backed out" on his enterprise, but ANDY came on with the remnants, and it is certain that among them was two or more SISTERS of the JACKSON FAMILY. ALFRED ALLISON & his wife had several children. We are sure of the names of only two of the sons, but we know there were other children. They were:

190. DAVID ALLISON
191. GWINN ALLISON

Both DAVID and GWINN ALLISON were first cousins of PRESIDENT ANDREW JACKSON. This is a known and well established fact in the history of GREENE COUNTY, GEORGIA. (Page 31 "Tenants of the Almighty" by Raper.)

GWINN ALLISON lived between the present town of GREENSBORO, and UNION POINT, in GREENE COUNTY, GEORGIA. When a new railroad was projected between these points about 1835, he refused to give up a part of his land for the right of way. He was subject to suit, by which the land was awarded to the purposes sought. He then loaded his shot gun and proposed to shoot the first man who came on his place. Finally he was jailed for his conduct, released and the money for his land tendered him, which he refused to accept. He finally became reconciled, and at his death left a bequest, in the form of a trust fund of $20,000 towards the schooling of poor children in Greene County. He died in 1865. ANDREW JACKSON visited GWINN ALLISON and his father several times, and it is a historical fact that on one of these visits to his uncle ALLISON, Mr. Jackson was entertained at a sumptuous banquit attended by the most prominent citizens of GREENE COUNTY. While there he was always a guest at the home of the ALLISON FAMILY - his uncle and cousins. A part of the GWINN ALLISON trust fund, left to the Commissioners Court of Greene County, Georgia, in 1865, we are informed, still remains intact. The inauguration of the free school system, made its use impractical, and it was specified that the interest only, and never the principal, was to be used for the purposes mentioned in the bequest.

190 DAVID ALLISON, COUSIN OF ANDREW JACKSON

From page 4 of JOHN ALLISON'S "Dropped Stitches in Tennessee History", the following paragraph is copied:

On the old record books of the minutes of the proceedings of the Court of Pleas and Quarter Sessions kept at JONESBORO (Tenn) will be found the following entry: "State of North Carolina, Washington County, Monday the 12th day of May, A. D. One Thousand Seven Hundred and Eighty Eight. ANDREW JACKSON, ESQ. came into Court and produced a license as an Attorney, with a Certificate sufficiently attested of his taking the oaths necessary to said office and was admitted to practice as an Attorney in this County Court."

The entry immediately preceding recites that:

"Archibald Roane, DAVID ALLISON, and Joseph Hamilton, Esqs, produced sufficient licenses to practice as Attorneys, and were admitted, etc."

In August, 1788, DAVID ALLISON was commissioned "Master of the Rolls and Clerk in Equity of the Superior Court of Law and Equity" for Washington District at JONESBORO, by Judges Samuel Spencer and David Campbell. - p. 6 "Dropped Stitces".

I don't know why it is that Historians totally lose sight of all these interesting family connections, when they are making records of famous lives and characters. It could not be a mere coincidence that ANDREW JACKSON and his first cousin DAVID ALLISON arrived in JONESBORO, Tennessee, from across the mountains, in May, 1888, and were admitted to practice law in the courts of this part of the country on the same day, and apparently at the same hour. The historians do not tell us that ANDREW JACKSONS advent into the Watauga Valley was in company with others, including some of his close kinsmen, with whom he was intimately associated in the new country in numerous business adventures, as the sequel shows.

JOHN ALLISON, in his "Dropped Stitches in Tennessee History" says on page 6, that DAVID ALLISON held the office of Clerk in Equity in JONESBORO for about two years, resigning in 1790, when he went to the settlement on the CUMBERLAND - now NASHVILLE - and engaged - he thinks - in the mercantile business.

One account of the marriage of ROBERT ALLISON to a daughter of WILLIAM MOORE, furnished the writer - but not vouched for - by Mrs. Katie Prince W. Baker, of Washington, D. C., says that at the time of their marriage ROBERT ALLISON lived near COLUMBIA, TENNESSEE, which, at that time, was substantially a part of the Cumberland Settlement.

Other data from the same source, likewise largely charged to tradition and not relied upon absolutely, is to the effect that WILLIAM LAMPKIN (who married JANE MOORE) was born in VIRGINIA and that his son WILLIAM LAMPKIN, JR. was reared in TENNESSEE (apparently near Greenville, or the little town of LIMESTONE close by) by his grandfather, a MR. MOORE; the assumption being that WILLIAM MOORE, father of JANE, had left LINCOLN COUNTY, N. C. and settled in his later years over the mountains in that settlement.

Sherrill's History of Lincoln County, which contains an account of WILLIAM MOORE and the names of his sons, including the distinguished GEN. JOHN MOORE, called "brother in law of GOV. JOHN ADAIR", and who in 1808 served as Speaker of the Assembly of North Carolina, says nothing about the later years of the father WILLIAM MOORE. The inference is that the author KNEW NOTHING, or he would have written something. Therefore, there may be some basis for this claim, especially in the light of the fact that ANDREW JACKSON (who came from the same general part of North Carolina) evidently did not come alone. He may have made his TRIP OVER THE MOUNTAINS alone, "astride a fine race horse, leading another, and with his stuffed saddle bags and a pack of hounds" as the older residents testified, but when he arrived in JONESBORO - named for States-Rights WILLIE JONES, of Halifax County, N. C. - he found (or else they immediately followed him) the following interesting personalities:

1. DAVID ALLISON
2. JAMES ALLISON
3. CHARLES ALLISON
4. JOHN ALLISON
5. SAMUEL SHERRILL
6. JOHN PUGH
7. JONATHAN HAMPTON
8. ALEXANDER OUTLAW
9. WILLIAM MOORE
10. JOSEPH HAMILTON
11. ISAAC WHITE
12. FELIX WALKER

1. David Allison we have already mentioned.
2. James Allison MAY have been his brother.
3. Charles Allison MAY have been another brother.
4. John Allison was the grandfather of JOHN ALLISON who wrote "Dropped Stitches". This John Allison went to West Tennessee and settled. He married a daughter of JOHN CHESTER, of Sullivan County, Tennessee, who built the old CHESTER HOTEL in Jonesboro, where ANDREW JACKSON held forth when he was President on his visits to or through JONESBORO.
5. SAMUEL SHERRILL was one of the sons of ADAM SHERRILL, and the father in law of JOHN SEVIER. He had a son named URIAH and a brother URIAH. This being an old LINCOLN COUNTY, N. C. family, and neighbors of the ALLISONS, the writer has not the slightest doubt but what COL. URIAH ALLISON (son of ROBERT ALLISON and JANE MOORE) was named for URIAH SHERRILL. I would like to present the proof, but an obvious fact needs no further proof.
6. JOHN or JONATHAN PUGH was from ORANGE COUNTY, where he had been held in durance vile following the "regulator" troubles. The people of frontier WASHINGTON COUNTY made him SHERIFF.
7. JONATHAN HAMPTON was the son of the old soldier COL. ANDREW HAMPTON, well known on the records of North Carolina.
8. ALEXANDER OUTLAW was from Duplin County, the son of JAMES OUTLAW. for an abstract of his father's will see page 205, of these notes.
9. In 1779 a certain WILLIAM MORE is mentioned. "Ordered that the Sheriff collect from WILLIAM MORE four-fold; his taxable property being appraised by JOHN WOODS, JACOB BROWN and JONATHAN TIPTON". p. 45 Dropped Stitches.
10. JOSEPH HAMILTON may have been a relative of the HAMILTONS who were related to the Moore family, down in the present YORK COUNTY, S. C.
11. ISAAC WHITE. See page 491 of these notes.
12. FELIX WALKER, who served as Clerk of the County Court, and afterwards settled over in BUNCOMBE COUNTY, serving in Congress from that District for many years. He was the son of JOHN WALKER, who was the first signer and Chairman of the convention that issued the TRYON DECLARATION OF INDEPENDENCE, shortly after the MECKLENBURG DECLARATION was signed in 1775.

---

190 DAVID ALLISON may have gone to the Cumberland Settlement after he resigned his lucrative office in JONESBORO in 1790, and he may have there engaged in the "mercantile business" but in some mysterious way his fortunes took an upward turn, for just FIVE YEARS later (1795) he had removed his field of business activity to PHILADELPHIA, where if Marquis James' "Life of ANDREW JACKSON" can be relied upon, he was a "secret partner" in the mercantile firm of JOHN B. EVANS & CO., of that metropolis, and on the occasion of Andrew Jackson's visit to this city, DAVID ALLISON bought from him 28,810 acres of Tennessee lands lying along DUCK RIVER, paying therefor $10,000 in notes for it, which the doubty Jackson proceeded to discount, partly, in order to obtain much needed ready money for his Tennessee enterprises in the Cumberland Settlements. Allison's credit at that time was good in Philadelphia, though it appears that afterwards it greatly declined. The same chronicler declares that at the time General Jackson had no title to these lands, but they were to be acquired from the Indians. Ultimately the title, after some litigation, was acquired and General Jackson needed, as he nearly always did, more "ready money" and he began negotiations with "the heirs of DAVID ALLISON" (David having died in the meantime) down in GREENE COUNTY, GEORGIA. GWINN ALLISON was one of those heirs, and since the plural is used in the story, there were evidently others, who lived in GREENE COUNTY, GEORGIA. The negotiation of this purchase "from the heirs of DAVID ALLISON" furnished the motive for the several trips of ANDREW JACKSON to his cousin in GEORGIA.

THE BARRY FAMILY

On pages 478, 479 and 480 of these notes, in discussing the MOORE FAMILY some data was necessarily included about the BARRY FAMILY. What is said here should be considered in connection with that material.

CECIL COUNTY, MARYLAND, and not Pennsylvania, furnished the immediate ancestor of the BARRY FAMILY who settled in MECKLENBURG and in South Carolina, to which belonged RICHARD BARRY, who died in 1801, and who was a signer of the MECKLENBURG DECLARATION.

RICHARD BARRY and his brothers and sisters were the sons and daughters of the ANDREW BARRY, who on March 15, 1738, by his will was made one of the Executors of ALEXANDER EWING, of CECIL COUNTY, MARYLAND. The tradition that the wife of ANDREW BARRY was CATHERINE MOORE, the sister of CHARLES MOORE, while not established positively by the records, is nevertheless made plausible and probable by the immediate and contemporaneous presence in the same County and neighborhood of THOMAS, WILLIAM, JOSEPH and an ANDREW MOORE. See Baldwin's Calendar of Maryland Wills, Volumes 6, 7 and 8. Subsequent records, gathered from various sources establishes, until refuted by more direct evidence, that

ANDREW BARRY AND HIS WIFE CATHERINE MOORE

of CECIL COUNTY, MARYLAND, (the same County from whence came the EWINGS, LAWSONS, ALEXANDERS and others) were the parents of the following children:

1. RICHARD BARRY (b. in 1726) m. ANN PRICE
2. ANDREW BARRY (died about 1769 in MECKLENBURG COUNTY, N. C.)
3. JOHN BARRY (living in LUNENBURG COUNTY, Va. in 1748)
4. HUGH BARRY
5. WILLIAM BARRY

In the year 1748 in LUNENBURG COUNTY, VIRGINIA, Hugh Moore and HUGH LAWSON were the tax officers (called Tythe takers) in that County; and on the list turned in by HUGH LAWSON appears the names of JOHN BARRY, ANDREW McCONNELL and THOMAS IRWIN. A careful tracing of these lists, as shown by BELL'S "Sunlight on the South Side" discloses that JOHN BARRY remained in LUNENBURG COUNTY, where he named one son WILLIAM TAYLOR BARRY, who had two sons WILLIAM TAYLOR and ANDREW BARRY. JOHN BARRY'S grandson WILLIAM TAYLOR BARRY became a United States Senator, a Supreme Court Judge in Kentucky, and Postmaster General of the United States under ANDREW JACKSON.

GEORGE EWING, (son of SAMUEL EWING) a grandson of ALEXANDER EWING, for whose estate ANDREW BARRY, the first, was Executor in CECIL COUNTY, MARYLAND, and HUGH BARRY, a grandson of the Executor, both married sisters and the daughters of COL. HUGH LAWSON, the Lunenburg Tythe taker of 1748.

1. RICHARD BARRY (the oldest son of ANDREW BARRY) moved to MECKLENBURG COUNTY, NORTH CAROLINA, with his brothers, ANDREW, HUGH and WILLIAM BARRY. See deed of HUGH BARRY, page 317, and inventory of ANDREW BARRY, on same page. 1. RICHARD BARRY was one of the signers of the MECKLENBURG DECLARATION of INDEPENDENCE in 1775. ANNE PRICE, the wife of RICHARD BARRY, was born in CECIL COUNTY, Maryland, in 1735, and was the daughter of ALEXANDER PRICE, who witnessed the will of DR. PETER BOUCHELLE, August 22nd of that year, who owned lands adjoining and was a brother of the wife of DAVID LAWSON. Pages 186-187, Baldwin's Calendar of Maryland Wills. This writer has been unable to find any list of the children of RICHARD and ANN PRICE BARRY, which appears to be correct, or complete. Summerville's History of Hopewell Church and Landrum's History of Spartanburg both deal with this question, honestly and conscientiously, but inadequately, since both fail to understand the generations of the BARRY FAMILY. From all sources, however, it is safe to say they had:

100. RICHARD BARRY m. ROSA MOORE
101. ANDREW BARRY m. MARGARET MOORE (See p. 478)
102. HUGH BARRY m. MARGARET LAWSON
103. JOHN BARRY
104. KATE BARRY
105. VIOLET BARRY

MR. LANDRUM in his "Spartanburg County" professes to know nothing of JOHN BARRY, whom he lists as a brother of RICHARD AND ANDREW, whom he identifies as the OLDER RICHARD and ANDREW by mistake, but does assert that JOHN BARRY lived in the fork of the Middle and North Tyger rivers in Spartanburg County, and was the father of WILLIAM TAYLOR BARRY, of Kentucky, Postmaster General under ANDREW JACKSON. A certain WILLIAM TAYLOR BARRY (in Lunenburg County, Va.) WAS the father of William Taylor Barry, Postmaster General, but he was the JOHN BARRY who was an UNCLE of his RICHARD and ANDREW of South Carolina. From the CONGRESSIONAL DIRECTORY, 1774-1791:

WILLIAM TAYLOR BARRY, appointed Postmaster General by President JACKSON, March 9, 1829, resigned in 1835; taught in TRANSYLVANIA UNIVERSITY; Chief Justice of the Supreme Court of Kentucky; member of the ELEVENTH U. S. CONGRESS; U. S. Senator from Kentucky; minister to Spain. Died England; buried Frankfort, Ky; born February 15, 1784 in LUNENBURG COUNTY, VIRGINIA.

SAMUEL WILSON, SR.

One of the earliest settlers of MECKLENBURG COUNTY, North Carolina, was SAMUEL WILSON, SR., who, according to Hunter's Sketches of Western North Carolina, died March 13, 1778, in the sixty-eighth year of his age. He was therefore born about 1710. He really dates back. His name is not listed among the signers of the MECKLENBURG DECLARATION, though RAMSEY lists a WILLIAM WILSON, as well as ZACHEUS WILSON, the latter known to be a signer.

His son MAJOR DAVID WILSON, with RICHARD BARRY, both of whom participated in the skirmish at COWAN'S FORD on February 1, 1781, secured the body of GEN. WILLIAM LEE DAVIDSON, after he was killed, and carried it to the home of SAMUEL WILSON, SR., prepared it for burial there, sent for MRS. MARY BREVARD DAVIDSON, who resided some miles distant, perhaps about where DAVIDSON COLLEGE is now located, who was brought down immediately by a neighbor, GEORGE TEMPLETON. Then MAJ. WILSON & RICHARD BARRY, with the help of other neighbors, after nightfall carried the remains to HOPEWELL Church where they were buried by candle-light, late in the evening of the same day.

Dr. Hunter in his "Sketches" says that SAMUEL WILSON was of Scotch-Irish descent, while numerous other accounts say that he was an ENGLISHMAN and a kinsman of an English General, SIR ROBERT WILSON. Hunter adds that he emigrated from PENNSYLVANIA to MECKLENBURG about 1745, where he settled "in the bounds of Hopewell Church". Hopewell Church did not exist at that time. The compiler thinks he was of ENGLISH lineage and a descendant of that REV. ROBERT WILSON, who, about 1661-2 was ejected from the Presbytery of Lagen in the northern part of Ireland, with thirteen other ministers, for his non-conformist tendencies towards the Church of England. This does not mean that he was either a Scotchman or an Irishman. The same ROBERT WILSON was the ancestor of REV. FRANCIS McKEMIE, the early Presbyterian pioneer, of ACCOMAC COUNTY, VIRGINIA, and of the McKEMIES of the lower part of MECKLENBURG, who were related to the famous JOHN McKEMIE WILSON, well known in the annals of MECKLENBURG. With the exception of the date of his death and his age at the time, dates on the family of SAMUEL WILSON SR. are simply non-existant. An excellent out-line of his family is contained in SOMMERVILLE'S History of Hopewell, pp 195-199, but it is almost wholly devoid of dates to guide the historian.

The writer is inclined to the belief that SAMUEL WILSON, SR. was born in SOMERSET COUNTY, MARYLAND, where there was a family of WILSONS, who came there and settled during the life-time of REV. FRANCIS McKEMIE, who were probably his cousins. Among these was a WILLIAM WILSON and his wife AGNES, of STEPNEY PARISH, as early as 1709/10, which was about the time - if Mr. Hunter's dates are right - that SAMUEL WILSON was born. The statement has been made in several accounts that SAMUEL WILSON was "not related" to numerous other persons named WILSON who settled and resided in MECKLENBURG COUNTY. We think this is erroneous, also. SAMUEL WILSON, SR. was married three times, to the persons, and in the order named below:

1. MARY WINSLOW (A sister of MOSES WINSLOW m. JEAN OSBORNE).
2. MRS. HOWARD (A sister of JOHN and WILLIAM POTTS)
3. MARGARET JACK (A daughter of PATRICK JACK and LILLIS McADOO)

The children of SAMUEL WILSON, SR. and his first wife MARY WINSLOW, were as follows:

10. MAJ. DAVID WILSON m. SARAH McCONNELL
11. BENJAMIN WILSON (It is agreed he was NOT married).
12. SAMUEL WILSON, JR. married HANNAH KNOX.
13. SARAH WILSON m. BENJAMIN McCONNELL
14. VIOLET WILSON m. MAJOR JOHN DAVIDSON
15. MARY WILSON m. EZEKIEL POLK.
16. REBECCA WILSON m. JOHN HENDERSON

There appears to have been only one child by the second marriage:

17. MARGARET WILSON m. JOHN DAVIDSON (of S. C.)

The children of SAMUEL WILSON, SR. by his third wife, MARGARET JACK were as follows:

18. ROBERT WILSON m. MARGARET ALEXANDER (Daughter of THOMAS ALEXANDER).
19. WILLIAM JACK WILSON m. ROCINDA WINSLOW
20. LILLIS WILSON m. JAMES CONNOR.
21. SALLY WILSON m. LATTA McCONNELL.
22. CHARITY WILSON died at the age of 16 years.

DR. HUNTER is in error in saying that SARAH McCONNELL, who married 10 MAJ. DAVID WILSON, was sister of the wife of GEN. JAMES WHITE, father of HUGH LAWSON WHITE. GEN. JAMES WHITE (who removed to TENNESSEE) was the son of MOSES WHITE and his wife MARY McCONNELL, but HUGH LAWSON, JR., brother of the wife of GEN. JAMES WHITE, married REBECCA McCONNELL, daughter of JOHN McCONNELL, in Iredell County, N. C. May 26, 1770, which would be about contemporaneous with the marriage of MAJ. DAVID WILSON, some years before the Revolution began.

HANNAH KNOX, the wife of SAMUEL WILSON, JR., was a daughter of CAPT. PATRICK KNOX, who was killed at Ramsour's Mill, in Lincoln County, during the Revolution. Samuel Wilson Jr. and his wife Hannah raised a large family, among whom was POLLY WILSON who married her cousin BENJAMIN WILSON, a son of MAJ. DAVID WILSON. JEFF WILSON, the only son, left no issue, and the daughter PATSY WILSON became the wife of HUGH McKNIGHT, according to the Sommerville account.

BENJAMIN McCONNELL and LATTA McCONNELL, both of whom married daughters of SAMUEL WILSON, SR. were sons of JOHN McCONNELL, an early settler of the lower part of IREDELL COUNTY, near the MECKLENBURG LINE. HUGH LAWSON JR. had married their sister REBECCA, and MAJ. DAVID WILSON married their sister SARAH McCONNELL. DAVID WILSON and his wife SARAH McCONNELL named one of their sons JOSEPH LAWSON WILSON, and he married SARAH WHITE and moved to TENNESSEE. MARY McCONNELL, the first wife of MOSES WHITE, and the mother of JAMES WHITE, was a sister of JOHN McCONNELL and an aunt of SARAH McCONNELL, the wife of MAJ. DAVID WILSON.

MAJ. DAVID WILSON, revolutionary soldier, and son of SAMUEL WILSON, SR. died in Mecklenburg County, leaving a will dated in SEPTEMBER 1820 (Book 3) in which he gives names of his children alive at that time. The son LAWSON WILSON is not mentioned, as he was killed by the Indians in TENNESSEE some years previous. The children of MAJ. DAVID WILSON and his wife SARAH McCONNELL were:

30. SAMUEL WILSON
31. MOSES WINSLOW WILSON
32. POLLY WILSON m. MR. WAUGH.
33. JOSEPH LAWSON WILSON m. SARAH WHITE.

14. VIOLET WILSON married MAJ. JOHN DAVIDSON, of whom much has been said heretofore in these notes, the son of MORT. DAVIDSON and his wife ISABELLA RAMSEY. We have carefully checked the list of their children with DR. SOMMERVILLE and HUNTER'S "Sketches" and find them practically identical, but shall follow the order in which they are placed by HUNTER. They were:

100. ISABELLA DAVIDSON m. GEN. JOSEPH GRAHAM, of LINCOLN COUNTY.
101. REBECCA DAVIDSON m. CAPT. ALEXANDER BREVARD.
102. VIOLET DAVIDSON m. WILLIAM BAIN ALEXANDER.
103. ELIZABETH DAVIDSON m. WILLIAM LEE DAVIDSON (Son of GEN. WILLIAM).
104. MARY DAVIDSON m. DR. WILLIAM McKEAN, REVOLUTIONARY SURGEON.
105. SARAH DAVIDSON m. ALEXANDER CALDWELL, SON OF DR. DAVID.
106. MARGARET DAVIDSON m. MAJ. JAMES HARRIS
107. JOHN (JACKEY) DAVIDSON m. SALLIE BREVARD, DAU. OF ADAM.
108. ROBERT DAVIDSON m. MARGARET OSBORNE, DAUGHTER OF ADLAI.
109. BENJAMIN WILSON DAVIDSON m. ELIZABETH LATTA.

15. MARY WILSON, daughter of SAMUEL WILSON and his wife MARY WINSLOW, married EZEKIEL POLK, and her grandson, JAMES KNOX POLK became PRESIDENT OF THE UNITED STATES. Their son SAMUEL POLK was the father of the President. The ancestry and descendants of the POLK FAMILY will appear later in these notes.

16. REBECCA WILSON was the name of another daughter of SAMUEL WILSON and his wife MARY WINSLOW, according to HUNTER'S "Sketches", but about whom nothing is said in the account in SOMMERVILLE'S "History of the Hopewell Presbyterian Church". The Hunter account says that she married JOHN HENDERSON, and after two children had been born, they set out from MECKLENBURG, with the intention of moving to TENNESSEE, accompanied by a brother and sister of HENDERSON. On the way, while they were stopping for dinner, they were attacked by Indians and both HENDERSON and his wife were killed. The brother and sister each seized a child and made their escape. Later those living all made their way to TENNESSEE. (NOTE: This could have been the JOHN PETER HENDERSON mentioned in will of JAMES HENDERSON who married VIOLET LAWSON, mentioned on page 487).

17. MARGARET WILSON m. JOHN DAVIDSON. He was an uncle of HON. WILLIAM DAVIDSON, who was SENATOR from MECKLENBURG. After her husband JOHN DAVIDSON died, she and her three children removed to ALABAMA. The children were SAMUEL, JOHN and MARY DAVIDSON. 17. MARGARET DAVIDSON was the daughter of SAMUEL WILSON, SR. by his second marriage to MRS. HOWARD, a widow.

---

18. ROBERT WILSON, son of SAMUEL WILSON, SR. and his third wife MARGARET JACK, sister of CAPT. JAMES JACK, married MARGARET ALEXANDER. MARGARET ALEXANDER was the daughter of a THOMAS ALEXANDER and his wife a MISS MORRISON, the daughter of NEIL MORRISON, one of the signers of the MECKLENBURG DECLARATION OF INDEPENDENCE. THOMAS ALEXANDER was known as "MAJOR" and lived in the SUGAR CREEK SETTLEMENT. The children of 18 ROBERT WILSON and MARGARET ALEXANDER were:

111. DOVEY WILSON m. JUDGE GEORGE W. LOGAN.
112. MARGARET WILSON m. BEN. BRACKETT.
113. ANNABELLA WILSON m. JOHN LOGAN, a brother of JUDGE GEORGE LOGAN.
114. ANGELINA WILSON never married.
115. THOMAS WILSON, C. S. A., m. SALLIE JONES. Killed in CIVIL WAR.
116. CYNTHIA WILSON (1824-1896) m. JOSEPH WADE HAMPTON (1813-1855).

JOSEPH WADE HAMPTON was twice married. His first wife was SARA STIREWALT, by whom he had at least one daughter MARY ANNETTE HAMPTON, who married RICHARD S. HARRIS. His second wife was CYNTHIA WILSON, daughter of 18. ROBERT WILSON, and grandson of SAMUEL WILSON SR. CYNTHIA WILSON'S aunt MARY, being the wife of EZEKIEL POLK, CYNTHIA was therefore a first cousin of SAMUEL POLK, the father of JAMES K. POLK, the President.

About the year 1749-50 JOSEPH WADE HAMPTON, moved to Texas and settled with his wife and family at AUSTIN, where he was engaged in the newspaper business, and belonged to and was one of the original members and organizers of the FIRST PRESBYTERIAN CHURCH in that city. He died in AUSTIN in 1855, where he is buried, leaving two sons and three daughters, besides his widow, all of whom after his death returned to MECKLENBURG COUNTY. They are buried at the HOPEWELL PRESBYTERIAN CHURCH.

THE POLK FAMILY

The advent of the POLK FAMILY into the Yadkin-Catawba valley must not have been so very long after that memorable day when the pioneer adventurer THOMAS SPRATT and his little family in his "wheeled vehicle" crossed the swirling waters of the YADKIN somewhere North, perhaps, of the present town of SALISBURY. At the door of his rude cabin, in an undetermined spot, South of CHARLOTTE, as the long shadows of lofty pines softened an approaching twilight, the lone traveler, THOMAS POLK, weary and foot-sore, reached for the latch-string, and was welcomed by the lusty pioneer and his family, as an old friend. THOMAS POLK, considering the events which followed, must have been the hardy scout of a numerous clan bearing the same family name, sent ahead to "spy out the land" and send back word to the others, the date of whose appearance on the records bears out this theory.

The tradition is that the POLKS came to MECKLENBURG from PENNSYLVANIA, but this seems to be only a tradition, since the actual records show that here was an old established family from the "Eastern Shore" of perhaps both MARYLAND and VIRGINIA. This same tradition is coupled with another, by which it is claimed that the name was originally POLLOCK, shortened to POLK. The last, as well as the first, must be discounted.

Numerous writers have attempted to commit to print and writing the annals of this POLK family, and all cling to these ill founded traditions, as if for dear life. They all insist that the Ancestors of the POLKS were MARGARET POLK and ROBERT POLK, she who was a TASKER, and he the son of an IRISH BARONET named POLLOCK, whose descendants in North Carolina shortened the spelling to plain POLK. They even call him (the ancestor) ROBERT BRUCE POLLOCK, by what authority, we have been unable to ascertain - perhaps, this too, is based on tradition. The will of a MAGDALENE POLKOCK, who is said to have been 92 years of age, proved in SOMERSET COUNTY, MARYLAND, in 1729, is given as authority for the names of the first AMERICAN GENERATION of the family, including JOHN, WILLIAM, EPHRAIM, JAMES, ROBERT, JOSEPH, MARGARET and ANN POLK or POLLOCK. Then the first named son, JOHN POLK is given as the ancestor of the North Carolina set, through his only son, WILLIAM POLK, said to have married (1) PRISCILLA ROBERTS and (2) MARGARET TAYLOR. The wife of JOHN POLK was JOANNA KNOX, according to this account, and they were the supposed ancestors. Their son WILLIAM POLK, from the best we can gather, was the father of THOMAS, EZEKIEL and the other MECKLENBURG POLKS.

This well rounded, but wholly unauthenticated story of the POLLOCK or POLK family, fails to take into account the presence in SOMERSET COUNTY, MARYLAND, of numerous other persons named POLK and NONE called POLLOCK, who resided in the same general neighborhood at and about the same time. The marriage of a JOHN POLK to a JOANNA KNOX seems plausibly true, considering the fact that there was a KNOX family residing there in SOMERSET at the time, with whom the POLKS were evidently very closely, and perhaps intimately associated. Sometimes the name of KNOX was spelled differently, but this is accounted for by the fact that slight differences frequently occurred in the spelling of all the ancient Colonial names, on documents of the records. About the time THOMAS POLK left MARYLAND and went to NORTH CAROLINA, one HENRY KNOCK left a will up above SOMERSET in KENT COUNTY; and FOOTE in his "Virginia Sketches" says that one of the sisters of the wife of REV. FRANCIS McKEMIE married a man named "NOCK", quite evidently of the regular KNOX FAMILY.

Not only did the POLK FAMILY of SOMERSET have many dealings and intimate relations with the KNOX family in SOMERSET COUNTY, MARYLAND, but they were also intimately connected with the SPRATT family, of the same place, as well as with the CALDWELLS and ALEXANDERS and WILSONS. In 1736, the will of ROBERT WILSON, of MONOKIN, in SOMERSET, believed to have been a son of the REV. ROBERT WILSON of the Presbytery of LABAN, in IRELAND, and a relative of REV. FRANCIS McKEMIE, was witnessed by a DAVID POLK and a MOSES ALEXANDER, both obviously relatives of the same families of the name who afterwards flourished in MECKLENBURG COUNTY, N. C. In 1696, the will of WILLIAM PORTER in the County of SOMERSET was witnessed by JOHN POLK and WILLIAM POLK; and in 1698, JOHN POLK and WILLIAM KNOX together, were the overseers of the will of one WILLIAM OWENS. These instances could be multiplied several times by a minute search of the records. - Baldwin's Maryland Calendar of Wills.

ROBERT POLLOCK (Sic) and his wife MAGDALENE were the parents, according to traditional chroniclers of the POLK FAMILY, of SIX SONS and TWO DAUGHTERS. The table of descendants below only includes the POLKS who are said to descend from JOHN POLK and his wife JOANNA KNOX. At most these names include, perhaps, only ONE-SIXTH of the POLK FAMILY. What became of the remainder of them would require a good sized volume, even if we could give a list of them. But this inadequate list seems to include about all the MECKLENBURG SET we have ever heard about, from which the country selected at least ONE OF ITS PRESIDENTS.

JOHN POLK married JOANNA KNOX

and they were the parents of a son WILLIAM POLK, m. (1) PRISCILLA ROBERTS and (2) MARGARET TAYLOR and became the father of the following children:

1. THOMAS POLK m. SUSANNA SPRATT (Daughter of THOMAS SPRATT).
2. CHARLES POLK m. POLLY CLARK
3. DEBORAH POLK m. SAMUEL McCLEARY
4. SUSAN POLK m. BENJAMIN ALEXANDER (2) DAVID HESSE (?)
5. JOHN POLK m. ELLENER SHELBY
6. MARGARET POLK m. ROBERT McKEE
7. WILLIAM POLK m. ..... SPRATT
8. EZEKIEL POLK m. (1) MARY WILSON (2) SOPHIA NEELY

-- American Historical Magazine, Vol. 1.

505

1. THOMAS POLK, SON IN LAW OF THOMAS SPRATT

This THOMAS POLK, whose wife was SUSAN SPRATT, is the young man who arrived in what is now MECKLENBURG COUNTY, N. C. with what little he had carried in a knap-sack thrown over his tired shoulders, on foot, and whose "journey's end" was the door of THOMAS SPRATT'S cabin, somewhere below CHARLOTTE; though there was no town of Charlotte in Mecklenburg County in those early days. The writers say that he was the oldest of the several sons of WILLIAM POLK, the son of JOHN POLK and his wife JOANNA KNOX.

THOMAS POLK became a surveyor and was largely self-educated from necessity, but as early as 1770 was a representative in the Assembly from Mecklenburg County; he aided in running the western extension of the boundary line between North and South Carolina, about 1771; at the breaking out of the American Revolution he became Colonel of the Mecklenburg County Militia, which then included all of the present CABARRUS COUNTY, afterwards set apart and named for STEPHEN CABARRUS. As Colonel of the militia, in 1775, it was this THOMAS POLK, the tired, lonely traveler of much earlier years, who issued the call for the election of delegates in the various communities then embraced in MECKLENBURG COUNTY, to the famous convention of May 19 and 20, 1775, which brought forth the first real, genuine and uncompromising DECLARATION OF INDEPENDENCE ever written on American soil.

Though far advanced in years THOMAS POLK served through the revolution, and at his retirement was made a BRIGADIER GENERAL. His valuable service to his country was recognized by GEN. NATHANIEL GREENE and other leaders with whom he was intimately associated, and in the end he was rewarded with numerous valuable grants of lands set apart in what is now TENNESSEE for himself and his heirs. Next to COL. JOHN SPRINGS, Thomas Polk at one time was considered the wealthiest man in MECKLENBURG COUNTY (p. 337).

GEN. THOMAS POLK and his wife SUSANNA SPRATT were the parents of FOUR sons and several daughters. We have searched in vain for a complete list of these children, and still have two of his sons missing from the list. We know, however that among their children these belonged:

    10. COL. WILLIAM POLK
    11. CHARLES POLK, m. MISS ALEXANDER.
    12. MARGARET POLK m. EPHRAIM BREVARD
    13. EUNICE POLK m. ALEXANDER CUMMINS
    14. _____ POLK (Dau) m. a MR. BROWN.

-- ALEXANDER'S History of MECKLENBURG COUNTY.

After the revolution GEN. WILLIAM POLK accompanied his sons to what is now TENNESSEE, for the purpose of surveying the lands granted them for military services, the son COL. WILLIAM POLK, having been appointed to make the surveys. These lands were located in the DUCK RIVER VALLEY, the exact location unknown to the compiler, but it is believed they were located somewhat East of the lands of the sons of the brother EZEKIEL POLK, which were farther West in what is now HARDEMAN COUNTY, TENNESSEE.

10. COL. WILLIAM POLK had a brilliant career as a soldier of the Revolution and was an officer of distinction. At the signing of the MECKLENBURG DECLARATION he was only nineteen years of age. He joined the Army thereafter and served throughout the war. He was with General Washington at Brandywine and Germantown in 1777, where he was wounded. He was then ordered South and was with Gen. Horatio Gates at Camden, and with Greene at Guilford Courthouse and was wounded again at Eutaw Springs. In 1787 he represented Mecklenburg in the House of Commons. After that he moved to Wake County, where he engaged in the banking business. His wife was a daughter of GOVERNOR WILLIAM HAWKINS, of Granville County, and a sister of the second wife of MAJ. BENJAMIN MORROW, a distinguished officer in the War of 1812, from MECKLENBURG COUNTY, and a kinsman of the writer. At his death in 1830 he left a widow and several children, three of whom were:

    100. GEN. THOMAS G. POLK, of MISSISSIPPI.
    101. BISHOP LEONIDAS POLK, of LOUISIANA.
    102. MRS. KENNETH RAYNOR.

---WHEELER, p. 416.

The MISS ALEXANDER, who married 11 CHARLES POLK, son of GEN. THOMAS POLK was one of the daughters of HEZEKIAH ALEXANDER, one of the signers of the MECKLENBURG DECLARATION.

ALEXANDER CUMMINS who married EUNICE POLK, daughter of GEN. THOMAS POLK, was son of REV. ROBERT CUMMINS and his wife MISS BLAIR, sister of the celebrated REV. SAMUEL BLAIR, minister and teacher. MARY, a sister of ALEXANDER CUMMINS, married DR. ALEXANDER McWHORTER, one time President of the "QUEEN'S MUSEUM" in Charlotte, and an early missionary to the valley between the YADKIN and CATAWBA RIVERS. The husband of EUNICE POLK was the nephew of AGNES, the wife of the pioneer, ALEXANDER OSBORNE.

12. MARGARET POLK and her husband EPHRAIM BREVARD (the signer). They were parents of only one child: MARGARET POLK BREVARD who became the wife of GOV. NATHANIEL ALEXANDER, who died in CHARLOTTE, N. C., November 8, 1808, and she is buried in the PRESBYTERIAN CHURCHYARD in Charlotte. See p. 405. *

NOTE: One account says that GOV. NATHANIEL ALEXANDER married a daughter of GEN. THOMAS POLK (Alexander's History of Mecklenburg County, p. 98) while another account states that he married MARGARET POLK BREVARD, daughter of EPHRAIM BREVARD and MARGARET POLK, daughter of GEN. THOMAS POLK (Same authority, p. 396). Dr. Alexander just got mixed up a little in his efforts to keep all these ALEXANDERS, who were so numerous in Mecklenburg, straight.

2. CAPT. CHARLES POLK married POLLY CLARK

CHARLES POLK, brother of THOMAS and EZEKIEL POLK was a gallant soldier of the revolution and also commanded a company in the regiment of COL. GRIFFITH RUTHERFORD, in what is known as the Cherokee Indian campaign, which was mustered into the service on March 12, 1776.

According to an account, Vol 1, American Historical Magazine, CAPTAIN CHARLES POLK married POLLY CLARK, and had the following sons, no daughters being mentioned:

15. CHARLES POLK, JR.
16. THOMAS POLK
17. SHELBY POLK
18. MICHAEL POLK
19. WILLIAM POLK.

In this memorable campaign against the Cherokee Indians, CAPT. CHARLES POLK'S command and those with him, penetrated the Cherokee country clear over the mountains into what is now MONROE and BLOUNT Counties, in TENNESSEE. Rumple's Rowan County History, is authority for the statement that only three or four men in the entire command actually lost their lives in this campaign, but it was a successful effort and resulted in a gain of much valuable territory, which was ceded by the Indians afterwards, to white settlements. - On pages 89 and 90 of Hunter's Sketches of Western North Carolina, is preserved a roster of the members of CAPT. CHARLES POLK'S company, which is of great interest historically. Following is the roster:

1. CHARLES POLK, Captain.
2. WILLIAM RAMSEY, 1st Lieut.
3. JOHN LEMMOND, 2nd Lieut.
4. JOHN MONTGOMERY, 1st Sergt.
5. WILLIAM GALBRAITH, 2nd SGT.
   (erased)
6. HUGH LINDSAY, Drummer.
7. JOHN SMITH
8. JOHN POLK, SR. (erased).
9. JOHN WYLIE
10. JOHN FINDLEY
11. JOHN GALBRAITH
12. JAMES HALL
13. JOHN STANSILL
14. WILLIAM .. (illegible).
15. JOHN MILLER
16. HUMPHREY HUNTER
17. HENRY CARTER
18. JAMES MAXWELL
19. JOHN MAXWELL
20. ROBERT GALBRAITH
21. JOHN McCANDLIS
22. NICHOLAS SILER
23. SAMUEL LINTON
24. THOMAS SHELBY
25. JAMES ALEXANDER
26. ROBERT HARRIS, JR.
27. JOHN FOARD
28. JONATHAN BUCKALOE
29. CHARLES ALEXANDER, SR.
30. HENRY POWELL
31. WILLIAM REA
32. SAMUEL HUGHES
33. CHARLES ALEXANDER, JR.
34. WILLIAM SHIELDS
35. CHARLES POLK, JR.
36. JOHN PURSER
37. WILLIAM LEMMOND
    Clerk to the Company
    and also the SURGEON.

JAMES HALL, whose name appears on this roster was the REV. JAMES HALL, was afterwards the Captain in a company in the revolution, and Chaplain of a Regiment to which it was attached; and he was also the famous minister and teacher, an account of whose labors is given at great length in Foote's Sketches of North Carolina.

HUMPREY HUNTER, another whose name is listed above also became a distinguished minister and for many years was pastor of STEELE CREEK and other MECKLENBURG CHURCHES. When the authenticity of the Mecklenburg Declaration was brought into question many decades later, it was DR. HUNTER, JAMES JACK and REV. FRANCIS CUMMINS (together with SUSAN SMART) who testified that they were present at the signing and the meeting, though too young, or not delegates participating in its adoption themselves. This soldier was the father of DR. CYRUS HUNTER who wrote the SKETCHES of WESTERN NORTH CAROLINA and gave them to the World.

SAMUEL LINTON lived and died in MECKLENBURG COUNTY and was the ancestor of the LINTON FAMILY who settled in GREENE COUNTY, GEORGIA. This man was the son of EDWARD LINTON, an abstract of whose will appears on 324, dated 1776.

WILLIAM SHIELDS was, it is likely, a son of JAMES SHIELDS, and a grandson of REV. JOHN THOMSON. JOHN FINDLEY, on the same list, married his mother's sister and in that way was the uncle of WILLIAM SHIELDS. On this campaign with COL. RUTHERFORD, this WILLIAM SHIELDS found a bag of gold in the camp of the enemy, which he promptly turned over to his commanding officer to purchase much needed supplies for his fellow soldiers.

JOHN FOARD, listed here, was one of the "Signers" of the MECKLENBURG DECLARATION less than one year before he enlisted in CAPT. CHARLES POLK'S Company.

CAPT. CHARLES POLK kept a diary during this campaign, and among other items mentioned by him was the death while over the mountains of a soldier named HANCOCK POLK, whose identity has not been established. As JOHN POLK, Captain Polk's brother, appears to have had a son listed as TAYLOR POLK, it suggests that his full name may have been HANCOCK TAYLOR POLK, and that he was the Hancock Polk who died or was killed in this Indian campaign, though he appears not to have been a member of his uncle's company.

The record shows that CHARLES POLK, JR., was a member of his father's company, but there seems to be no available information before the writer in regard to his younger brothers, (16) THOMAS, (17) SHELBY, (18) MICHAEL and (19) WILLIAM POLK.

It would not be improbable that some, if not all of these sons of CAPT. CHARLES POLK, in after years followed their cousins over the mountains into TENNESSEE.

3. DEBORAH POLK married SAMUEL McCLEARY

The account of this couple, which is set down in the family chart which is being followed in a general way in these notes, says that they had no children.

4. SUSAN POLK married BENJAMIN ALEXANDER

The chart referred to makes no mention of a second marriage, and says that BENJAMIN ALEXANDER and SUSAN POLK were the parents of six children: (1) CHARLES, (2) THOMAS, (3) SUSAN, (4) WILLIAM (Captain in Revolution), (5) BENJAMIN and (6) TAYLOR ALEXANDER. A certain THOMAS ALEXANDER, married JANE MORRISON, daughter of NEIL MORRISON, one of the signers of the MECKLENBURG DECLARATION. He was called MAJOR THOMAS ALEXANDER, and may have been one of the sons of SUSAN POLK and her husband BENJAMIN ALEXANDER. Also, the son (4) CAPT. WILLIAM ALEXANDER, may have been the famous "Black Billy" ALEXANDER, who lead a bunch of patriots in what is called the "Gunpowder Plot" during the "Regulator" troubles. Further mention will be made under the account of the ALEXANDER FAMILY.

A certain SUSAN POLK, according to ALEXANDER'S HISTORY of MECKLENBURG COUNTY, married DAVID REESE, one of the signers of the DECLARATION, and was the father of REV. THOMAS REESE, minister, who settled in ANDERSON DISTRICT, S. C., where he died. Dr. Alexander declares, without specifice identification, that she was a "close kinsman" of THOMAS and EZEKIEL POLK. One would assume that, since they had a sister SUSAN POLK, she was that sister, but for the POLK FAMILY CHART, which declares she married BENJAMIN ALEXANDER. Possibly she, or one of them, was cousin to the other, which must presuppose that more than one family of POLKS came to MECKLENBURG. See notes under "DAVID REESE" page 421, in which inadvertently REV. THOMAS HARRIS is mentioned, where it should be REV. THOMAS REESE.

5. JOHN POLK married ELEANOR SHELBY

ELEANOR SHELBY, the chart says, was a daughter of ISAAC SHELBY, and she and her husband, JOHN POLK were the parents of four children:

20. CHARLES POLK
21. TAYLOR POLK
22. JOHN POLK
23. ELEANOR POLK.

6. MARGARET POLK married ROBERT McREE

No information whatever is furnished pertaining to the family of ROBERT McREE and his wife MARGARET POLK.

7. WILLIAM POLK married a MISS SPRATT

MISS SPRATT was one of the daughters of the old pioneer, THOMAS SPRATT, and a sister of SUSAN SPRATT who became the wife of 1. THOMAS POLK, the oldest son of WILLIAM POLK.

---

8. EZEKIEL POLK m. (1) MARY WILSON, (2) SOPHIA NEELY

Of the youthful days of EZEKIEL POLK, says DR. ALEXANDER, nothing is remembered. He early married MARY WILSON, daughter of SAMUEL WILSON, SR., and sister to the wife of MAJ. JOHN DAVIDSON. In 1769 he was the first Clerk of the County Court of Tryon County - the territory from which Lincoln, Rutherford and Catawba County have since been formed.

The claim is made that he was born in PENNSYLVANIA on December 7, 1747, though the fact is pretty well authenticated that the POLK FAMILY came from SOMERSET COUNTY, MARYLAND. This writer does not claim to KNOW that EZEKIEL POLK was born on the Eastern Shore of MARYLAND, but reserves the right to BELIEVE that he was.

EZEKIEL POLK lived in MECKLENBURG COUNTY, before TRYON COUNTY was established in 1769; and on his appointment as Clerk of the new County, he removed to that County. After TRYON COUNTY was abolished, about 1778-9 he removed to MECKLENBURG COUNTY again, and settled eleven miles South of CHARLOTTE, near the present PINEVILLE, where his grandson JAMES K. POLK was born. This was a period of quiet in this region, and remained so until the invasion of the country by Cornwallis in September, 1780. Dr. Alexander says that the Polk home was in the pathway of Cornwallis' army, and that when it reached the Polk place, on Big Sugar Creek, in order to save the burning of his home, the destruction of his property and the suffering of his family, COLONEL POLK was forced to take British protection, which merely was understood to have been for the purposes stated, without implying any pledge for sympathy or service. The following startling statement appears on page 78 of Alexander's History of Mecklenburg County:

> Of EZRA and CHARLES ALEXANDER (signers) diligent enquiry has revealed nothing that is satisfactory about them, from the oldest citizens. One informant was under the impression that they lived within the bounds of PROVIDENCE CHURCH and were neighbors of EZEKIEL POLK, and like him - WERE ATHEISTS. If this is true, they probably emigrated with him to Tennessee, carrying with them their CIRCULATING LIBRARY or infidel literature -* * and were a good riddance to their fellow citizens. (p. 420).

EZEKIEL POLK and his first wife MARY WILSON had four children, and by his second wife he was the father of eight children; his second wife being a MRS. LEONARD, who as a girl was SOPHIA NEELY. Children by both marriages are named below:

24. THOMAS POLK (had seven children).
25. WILLIAM POLK m. ELIZABETH DODD.
26. MATILDA POLK m. MR. CAMPBELL.
27. SAMUEL POLK m. JANE KNOX.
---
28. JOHN POLK
29. LOUISA POLK m. CAPT. CHARLES NEELY
30. CLARISSA POLK m. THOMAS McNEIL
31. MARY POLK m. THOMAS JONES HARDEMAN.
32. CHARLES POLK
33. HENIGRA POLK
34. EUGENIA POLK
35. EDWIN POLK.

27. SAMUEL POLK and his wife JANE KNOX, the daughter of JAMES KNOX, of MECKLENBURG COUNTY, North Carolina, were the parents of the following children:

100. JAMES KNOX POLK m. SARAH CHILDRESS.
101. JANE MARIA POLK m. JAMES WALKER.
102. ELIZA POLK
103. MARSHALL POLK
104. JOHN L. POLK (never married).
105. FRANKLIN POLK (never married).
106. NAOMI POLK m. MR. HARRIS.
107. OPHELIA POLK m. MR. HAYS.
108. WILLIAM POLK m. MARY WILLIAMS.
109. SAMUEL POLK (never married).

29. LOUISA POLK and her first husband, CAPT. CHARLES NEELY, were the parents of four children (possibly others):

110. MARY NEELY m. MR. ATWOOD.
111. RUFUS POLK NEELY m. MISS LEA.
112. ADELIA NEELY m. MR. BELL
113. JACKSON J. NEELY

110. MARY NEELY and her husband MR. ATWOOD were the parents of three daughters and one son, the latter having died in a Northern prison during the Civil War. The three daughters were:

200. OCTAVIA ATWOOD m. a LUTHERAN MINISTER.
201. JOSEPHINE ATWOOD m. MAJOR JAMES DURST
202. ADELIA ATWOOD m. AUGUST PAIM

31. MARY POLK and her husband, THOMAS JONES HARDEMAN, went to TEXAS, and were accompanied by BAILEY HARDEMAN, a brother of THOMAS JONES HARDEMAN. Bailey Hardeman was Secretary of the Treasury, in the Cabinet of the REPUBLIC of TEXAS during what is known as the "interim" period. He died in 1836. T. J. HARDEMAN and wife MARY had:

203. MONROE HARDEMAN
204. LEONIDAS HARDEMAN
205. MARY FENTRESS HARDEMAN
206. GEN. WILLIAM N. HARDEMAN.

Both the ATWOODS and the HARDEMANS moved to Texas in an early day, coming to that State from BOLIVAR, TENNESSEE, in HARDEMAN COUNTY. HARDEMAN COUNTY, TEXAS, as well as HARDEMAN COUNTY, in TENNESSEE were named for the HARDEMAN FAMILY. The three ATWOOD DAUGHTERS, after finishing school in TENNESSEE, settled in early day, AUSTIN, TEXAS, the Capitol of the REPUBLIC and later of the State, and attended the inaugural balls of all the Governors, from the time of SAM HOUSTON on. MRS. ADELE PAIM died only a few years ago, leaving many descendants, including one daughter, MISS MARY PAIM (who never married) and a grandson, DR. HENRY L. KILGARTNER, lately returned from service in World War No. 2.

A grandson of THOMAS JONES HARDEMAN and his wife MARY POLK has been for FIFTY YEARS the Executive officer (now President) of the AUSTIN NATIONAL BANK, of Austin, Texas.

100. JAMES KNOX POLK

as is well known to History, was PRESIDENT OF THE UNITED STATES, retiring, as he had declared he would do, at the end of his first term. He graduated at the University of North Carolina in 1818. His grandfather and his parents settled in HARDEMAN COUNTY, TENNESSEE. Goodspeed (p. 161) says:

Among the first comers and for whom the County (of Hardeman) was named, was Col. THOMAS J. HARDEMAN; also Col. EZEKIEL POLK, his son WILLIAM POLK and son in law THOMAS McNEIL. * * Jacob Purtle raised a crop in the neighborhood of THOMAS McNEIL'S in 1821. WILLIAM POLK made a crop the same year, five miles NORTH of BOLIVAR. Maj. John H. Bills and PRUDENCE McNEIL were the first couple united in marriage in that vicinity by the laws of Civilisation.

THE KNOX FAMILY

JAMES KNOX POLK, President of the United States, was born near LITTLE SUGAR CREEK, Mecklenburg County, N. C. November 2, 1795. Moved with his parents to TENNESSEE in 1806; graduated at the University of North Carolina in 1818; elected GOVERNOR of TENNESSEE in 1839, and was PRESIDENT OF THE UNITED STATES, from March 4, 1845 to March 3, 1849.
His parents were SAMUEL POLK and JEAN KNOX.
SAMUEL POLK was the son of EZEKIEL POLK.
EZEKIEL POLK was the son of WILLIAM POLK.
WILLIAM POLK was the son of JOHN POLK and his wife JOANNA KNOX.

Thus, the mother of PRESIDENT POLK was JEAN KNOX, and his GREAT GRANDMOTHER was JOANNA KNOX, the wife of JOHN KNOX.

JEAN KNOX, the mother of JAMES KNOX POLK was the daughter of JOHN KNOX and his wife JEAN GRACY (Sometimes spelled GRACEY and sometimes GRACIE).

JOHN KNOX who married JEAN GRACEY or GRACY was born in SOMERSET COUNTY, MARYLAND, probably the son or nephew of WILLIAM KNOX, who, with JOHN POLK in 1698 was the overseer of the will of WILLIAM OWENS in SOMERSET COUNTY, MARYLAND. (Baldwin's Calendar of Maryland Wills, Vol. 2 p. 181). According to Rumple's History of Rowan County, JOHN KNOX was born in 1708, and his wife JEAN in the same year. This KNOX FAMILY lived, apparently, in the upper part of ACCOMAC COUNTY, Virginia, until the war against "dissenters" drove them across the line into SOMERSET COUNTY, MARYLAND. They were intense in their religious convictions, and an uncle, JOHN KNOX, brother of WILLIAM, and possibly the father, instead of WILLIAM, became a QUAKER and is known to have come to VIRGINIA, where he was present as a visiting minister at the WHITE OAK SWAMP MEETING of FRIENDS in HENRICO COUNTY, Virginia, in DECEMBER 1723. -(Henrice County Monthly Meeting of Friends, Record Book for 1699 to 1756.) It is believed by this writer that the father of JOHN KNOX, who married JEAN GRACY (grandparents of JAMES KNOX POLK), whether WILLIAM or JOHN, was the father of the following children:

1. JOHN KNOX m. JEAN GRACY.
2. ANDREW KNOX m. CHRISTIAN ....(?)
3. AMBROSE KNOX (mentioned in ANDREW'S will).
4. MATTHEW KNOX (lived in MECKLENBURG COUNTY, N. C.)
5. KATHERINE KNOX m. HENRY JOHNSTON (Lincoln County, N. C.)

A certain HENRY KNOCK, who died in KENT COUNTY, Maryland, came from the same settlement in SOMERSET COUNTY, MARYLAND. He married a sister of the wife of REV. FRANCIS Mackemie, whose Church the KNOX FAMILY belonged to. She is mentioned in her father's will, she being an ANDERSON. Their first child was named FRANCIS. (Vol 2, Md. Cal. of Wills, p. 204; Foote's Sketches of Virginia, Vol. 1 p. 44.)

HENRY JOHNSTON, who married KATHERINE KNOX and owned large tracts of lands in old MECKLENBERG (new LINCOLN) COUNTY, appears to have been BROTHER of GOVERNOR GABRIEL JOHNSTON, of early North Carolina fame, and was the father of only one son, COL. JAMES JOHNSTON, of Lincoln County, who served in the Revolution in the N. C. Continental Line. He had a brother SAMUEL JOHNSTON, who with REV. HENRY PATILLO, the famous teacher and Minister and protege of REV. JOHN THOMSON and student and friend of REV. SAMUEL DAVIES was made guardian of the miner children of 2. ANDREW KNOX, by his last will and testament in PERQUIMANS COUNTY, proven January 20, 1776. (Vol. 2, Joseph Habersham Chap. D. A. Collections in Ga., pp. 487-8; Sherrill's Annals of Lincoln County, North Carolina p. 32.) Foote's account of the life of these early Ministers of the Presbyterian Church, shows that REV. SAMUEL DAVIES, REV. JOHN THOMSON and their friend REV. HENRY PATILLO frequently ministered to the same settlement in SOMERSET COUNTY, MARYLAND, where the KNOX and POLK family lived and affiliated with the earliest Congregations they served; and this certainly accounts for the fact that when ANDREW KNOX died in PERQUIMANS COUNTY, he named his old ministerial friend, REV. HENRY PATILLO of Granville County, and his near kinsman SAMUEL JOHNSTON to look after his orphan children. (See Hathaway's N. C. Historical & Genealogical Register, Vol. 3, page 176.).

JOHN KNOX AND HIS WIFE JEAN GRACY

who, according to RUMPLE'S History of ROWAN COUNTY, are buried at old THYATIRA CHURCH, are said to have been the parents of the following children:

10. WILLIAM KNOX
11. SAMUEL KNOX (See will p. 327.)
12. JAMES KNOX (Father of JEAN KNOX)
13. ABSALOM KNOX
14. JOSEPH KNOX
15. JOHN KNOX
16. BENJAMIN KNOX

And one daughter:
17. MARY KNOX.

The names of these children are taken from the memorial slab erected by the descendants of JOHN KNOX and his wife JEAN GRACY at old THYATIRA CHURCH, on which appears the date MAY 20, 1911 -- in comparatively recent years.

According to an older marker, which occupied the same spot, JOHN KNOX died in 1758 at the age of 50 years and his wife JEAN in 1772 at the age of 64 years. It is presumed that these descendants knew their family history as late as 1911.

This writer has been unable to find and identify any of the descendants or children of either 10 WILLIAM, 13 ABSALOM, 14 JOSEPH or 16 BENJAMIN KNOX. Perhaps some of them had no children, but it is certain that some of them did. ALLISON KNOX, on the 1790 census in the 7th District, and DAVID KNOX, whose name appears down in the Providence Section, as well as the ROBERT KNOX, who married MARY EWART, in LINCOLN COUNTY, whose brother in law COL. JAMES JOHNSTON, was a cousin of all of the children of JOHN KNOX and JEAN GRACY, must have been sons of these KNOX BROTHERS.

An abstract of the will of SAMUEL KNOX probated in MECKLENBURG COUNTY on May 8, 1794, will be found on page 327 of these notes. This will only mentions his daughters and sons in laws and some grand-children, the presumption being that he had no sons, but THIS COULD BE WRONG, as the sons may have been taken care of prior to the making of the will. Again, the JOSEPH KNOX who was one of the witnesses may have been a son, instead of a brother (No. 14). But, taking the will as a guide:

                11. SAMUEL KNOX married MARY....

and had the following named children:

                100. JANE KNOX.
                101. SARAH KNOX
                102. MARY KNOX
                103. ____ KNOX m. GEORGE PETTUS
                104. ____ KNOX m. ALEXANDER CANDISH.

    Grandchildren mentioned:

            JOHN PETTUS
            STEPHEN PETTUS
            AGNES PETTUS
            MARY PETTUS.

On the same page (327) of these notes, and immediately following the will of SAMUEL KNOX is an abstract of the will of a VIOLET PETTUS, dated January 26, 1828, which was 34 years later. This is a genealogical cross-word puzzle, which we have analyzed to mean:

That one of the grandsons of SAMUEL KNOX, a son of the daughter who married GEORGE PETTUS - perhaps STEPHEN - married a VIOLET WILSON. This conclusion is based on the fact that VIOLET'S will is witnessed by ROBERT and SAMUEL WILSON, and that the name VIOLET in this community had by this time come to be in general use in the WILSON FAMILY.

Many members of the PETTUS FAMILY lived on the Eastern Shore of VIRGINIA and MARYLAND, and afterwards removed to the mainland of VIRGINIA, though it was sometimes called PETTITS. "This was because PETTITS came across from the EASTERN SHORE by 1636 to JAMES CITY COUNTY" - 26 Tyler, p. 184. From JAMES CITY COUNTY the PETTUS FAMILY migrated Eastward to HANOVER COUNTY, VIRGINIA, and other points in the Old Dominion. "All STEPHEN PETTUS' descend from STEPHEN of HANOVER" - Ibid page 188.

11. SAMUEL KNOX was a tax assessor in MECKLENBURG COUNTY, N. C. in 1778, and a CAPTAIN in 1781 to 1785. See page 354. And there was a SAMUEL KNOX, JR. on the Mecklenburg Census of 1790, who must have been a son of SAMUEL KNOX, SR., also shown on the same list.

                12. JAMES KNOX

The name of his wife has not been found in any of the authorities consulted, and the only information in regard to him seems to be that he married and was the father of JEAN KNOX who married SAMUEL POLK, son of EZEKIEL POLK, and the father of President JAMES KNOX POLK. A JAMES KNOX appears on the 1790 census, with apparently one son and his wife (page 358) and his name also appears on the list of the Public Officers of Mecklenburg from 1775 to 1785. (Page 354.

                15. JOHN KNOX married HANNAH REID

and they were the parents of the following children:

                105. ROBERT KNOX m. MARY EWART.
                106. WILLIAM KNOX
                107. GEORGE KNOX (d. 1869, aged 95 years).
                108. JANE KNOX married DAVID REID.
                109. FRANCES KNOX married JAMES PATTERSON.
                110. MARY KNOX m. BENJAMIN BRANDON
                111. ANNE KNOX m. an ANDERSON
                112. MARGARET KNOX m. a MR. CHAMBERS.

            17. MARY KNOX, DAUGHTER OF JOHN KNOX AND JEAN GRACY

is said to have become the wife of one WILLIAM ROSEBOROUGH, but the names of no children are mentioned. Vol. 3 HATHAWAYS N. C. Historical & Genealogical Register, page 315.

MARY EWART, the daughter of ROBERT EWART, who married 105 ROBERT KNOX, was the sister of JANE EWART, who became the wife of COL. JAMES JOHNSTON, who was the son of HENRY JOHNSTON and his wife KATHERINE KNOX, the sister of JOHN KNOX who married JEAN GRACY.

THE JOHNSTON FAMILY OF NORTH CAROLINA

The research worker in genealogy, who has followed these crude notes will by this time have discovered that the relationship between all of the old families of North Carolina, down under the surface, is almost endless. This relationship is not always apparent on the surface, and it is only when one digs down deep into the origin of these families sometimes that it is discovered. This by way of preface to the remark that the distinguished JOHNSTON FAMILY of North Carolina was related to the KNOX FAMILY.

The first intimation of this relationship comes about through the SINCLAIR FAMILY. Although previous chroniclers have, in the writer's judgment, gone far astray in discussing the beginnings of the KNOX FAMILY, on other points they have been correct, for the reason that there is always some semblance of fact in "handed down" traditions on which so many of them rely, but which the writer always discounts in the face of actual records that are to be found refuting them.

Of JOHN KNOX who married JEAN GRACY, the known immediate ancestors of the KNOX FAMILY of ROWAN and MECKLENBURG COUNTY, the account in Rumple's History of Rowan County, says:

"JOHN KNOX married an Irish-Presbyterian, JEAN GRACY, whose mother's name was JEAN SINCLAIR, a relative of the mother (also a SINCLAIR) of JOHN KNOX, THE REFORMER."

Because the name SINCLAIR is obviously a SCOTTISH family name, writers have handled all references to these alliances as if they occurred in SCOTLAND, when as a matter of fact the SINCLAIR family was numerous in lower Eastern Virginia and in North Carolina, though of course, representatives of the same family in SCOTLAND.

GOVERNOR GABRIEL JOHNSTON

GABRIEL JOHNSTON, said to have been a son of JOHN JOHNSTON (or JOHNSTONE) was GOVERNOR of the Province of North Carolina under the CROWN, from October 27, 1734, until July 17, 1752. He was twice married. His first wife was PENELOPE EDEN, daughter of GOV. CHARLES EDEN, who was at the time the widow of her THIRD HUSBAND, GEORGE PHENNY; and his second marriage was to FRANCES JOHNSTON who was also a widow, MRS. BUTTON. By his first marriage GOV. GABRIEL JOHNSTON had one daughter, PENELOPE JOHNSTON, who became the wife of COL. JOHN DAWSON. In 1770 MRS. PENELOPE DAWSON, administered on the estate of JOHN DAWSON, in BERTIE COUNTY, and executed a bond with THOMAS BALLARD and SAMUEL JOHNSTON as sureties. (Vol. 3 N. C. Hist. & Gen. Register, p. 448.).

Following is an abstract of the last will and testament of GOV. GABRIEL JOHNSTON, as same appears on page 53 Vol. 1, N. C. Hist. & Gen. Register:

WILL of GABRIEL JOHNSTON, of EDEN HOUSE, BERTIE COUNTY, NORTH CAROLINA, May 16, 1752; probated April 10, 1753; wife FRANCES JOHNSTON, daughter PENELOPE, the property which I had by her mother, in case of her death to go to my brother SAMUEL'S children, HENRY JOHNSTON, now at school at NEW HAVEN, neice PENELOPE'S brothers two sons SAMUEL and JOHN; my books to William Cathcart, sister ELIZABETH SINCLAIR, of FIFE, North Britain, CAROLINE JOHNSTON, one-fifth of balance of my estate to my wife, two-fifths to William Cathcart, in trust for my brother, one-fifth to SISTER ELIZABETH SINCLAIR; one-fifth to HENRY JOHNSTON. SAMUEL JOHNSTON and WILLIAM CATHCART, Executors. Done at EDEN HOUSE, 16th of May, 1652".

GOV. GABRIEL JOHNSTON, who mentions his SISTER ELIZABETH SINCLAIR twice in his will, had a brother GILBERT JOHNSTON, a brother SAMUEL JOHNSTON, and a brother HENRY JOHNSTON.

HENRY JOHNSTON married KATHERINE KNOX, the sister of JOHN KNOX whose wife was JEAN GRACY, whose mother was a SINCLAIR.

HENRY JOHNSTON and his wife KATHERINE KNOX came to the neighborhood of BEATTIE'S FORD on the CATAWBA RIVER and settled in what was then MECKLENBURG, but later made a part of TRYON and then LINCOLN, and died there, having been buried, it is believed at UNITY CHURCHYARD. (MERRILL'S History of Lincoln County, N. C. p. 32.)

KATHERINE KNOX, wife of the pioneer HENRY JOHNSTON, died a few years after they had married and settled in what is now LINCOLN COUNTY, North Carolina, leaving only two children. See below:

HENRY JOHNSTON AND HIS WIFE KATHERINE KNOX

KATHERINE KNOX, the wife of HENRY JOHNSTON, was the sister of JOHN KNOX who married JEAN GRACY. They had only two children:

100. COL. JAMES JOHNSTON m. JEAN EWART.
101. MARY JOHNSTON m. MOSES SCOTT

MOSES SCOTT and his wife MARY JOHNSTON, who lived near GOSHEN CHURCH, had three sons, JAMES J. SCOTT, WILLIAM SCOTT and ABRAM SCOTT. JAMES JOHNSTON SCOTT married MARY ALEXANDER, daughter of CAPT. ROBERT ALEXANDER. JAMES J. died in 1809, leaving two children, ABRAM SCOTT and MARY SCOTT. MARY (ALEXANDER) SCOTT, the widow, married GEN. JOHN MOORE, son of WILLIAM MOORE, and sister of MARY MOORE, the wife of WILLIAM RANKIN, in what is now GASTON COUNTY.

COL. JAMES JOHNSTON AND HIS WIFE JANE EWART

100. COL. JAMES JOHNSTON, son of HENRY JOHNSTON, an early settler in what is now LINCOLN COUNTY, N. C. married sometime before the beginning of the revolutionary war, JANE EWART, daughter of ROBERT EWART, one of the early patriots of MECKLENBURG COUNTY, and a "neighbor" of the signers of the Mecklenburg Declaration. ROBERT EWART, with GRIFFITH RUTHERFORD, JOHN BREVARD, HEZEKIAH ALEXANDER, BENJAMIN PATTON and others served on the "Committee of Safety" for the Salisbury District, which included both ROWAN and Mecklenburg and other counties.

At the battle of KING'S MOUNTAIN, ROBERT EWART, JAMES EWART, ROBERT KNOX, JOSEPH JACK, THOMAS BELL, JONATHAN PRICE, ABRAM FORNEY and PETER FORNEY were members of the Company commanded by COL. JAMES JOHNSTON, their kinsman. The following marriage alliances are on record:

    JANE EWART m. COL. JAMES JOHNSTON.
    MARY EWART m. ROBERT KNOX.
    MARGARET EWART m. JOSEPH JACK.
    RACHEL EWART m. THOMAS BELL.
    BETSY EWART m. JONATHAN PRICE
    SALLIE EWART m. THOMAS HILL
    ROBERT EWART m. MARGARET ADAMS.

These records are to be found in the form of a statement by the author on page 246 of DR. CYRUS HUNTER'S "Sketches of Western North Carolina". The exact relationship of the parties is not set down, but it occurs to the writer that the bride's were probably sisters of the ROBERT EWART who married MARGARET ADAMS and that all of those named EWART were son and daughters of the ROBERT EWART, father of JANE, who married COL. JAMES JOHNSTON. No dates are appended.

COL. JAMES JOHNSTON, before the revolution and perhaps shortly after his marriage bought some valuable lands on the CATAWBA RIVER, one mile Southwest of TOOLE'S FORD, about opposite the HOPEWELL CHURCH section of Mecklenburg, in LINCOLN COUNTY (or, possibly the present GASTON) where he erected a fine home, which was known in subsequent years as "OAK GROVE". Here he was blessed with numerous off-spring. For many years preceding his death he was a member of the Presbyterian Congregation of UNITY and a Ruling Elder in the Church. He and his wife JANE EWART were the parents of the following children:

1. ROBERT JOHNSTON m. MARY M. REID (Dau. of CAPT. JOHN REID).
2. MARGARET EWART JOHNSTON m. LOGAN HENDERSON.
3. JAMES JOHNSTON, JR. died 1816. Never Married.
4. HENRY JOHNSTON, died 1818. No issue.
5. MARTHA JOHNSTON m. DR. JAMES M. BURTON.
6. JANE JOHNSTON m. REV. JOHN WILLIAMSON, Pastor of HOPEWELL CHURCH.
7. CATHERINE JOHNSTON m. JOHN HAYES, of TOOLE'S FORD
8. DR. WILLIAM JOHNSTON m. NANCY FORNEY, of LINCOLN COUNTY.

LOGAN HENDERSON, who married MARGARET EWART JOHNSTON, great niece of GOV. GABRIEL JOHNSTON emigrated with other relatives and friends from the CATAWBA RIVER VALLEY to MAURY COUNTY, TENNESSEE. He was the son of the pioneer JAMES HENDERSON, whose last will and testament will be found set out in the pages of these notes, and whose wife was VIOLET LAWSON, the daughter of COL. HUGH LAWSON, who is buried at "Baker's Graveyard" in Mecklenburg County. A list of the children of LOGAN HENDERSON and his wife have already been given under the heading of GOVERNOR JAMES PICKNEY HENDERSON, of TEXAS, who was a son of LAWSON HENDERSON, a brother of LOGAN HENDERSON.

ROBERT JOHNSTON AND HIS WIFE MARY M. REID

ROBERT JOHNSTON who married MARY M. REID, who was the oldest son of COL. JAMES JOHNSTON, was a revolutionary soldier's son in law, though too young to take part himself. He and his wife had the following interesting family:

10. SARAH JOHNSTON m. DR. BENJAMIN JOHNSON, of VIRGINIA.
11. JAMES A. JOHNSTON m. JANE BYERS of IREDELL COUNTY.
12. DR. SIDNEY X. JOHNSTON m. HARRIET K. CONNOR, OF LINCOLN COUNTY.
13. JANE JOHNSTON m. (1) JOHN D. GRAHAM (2) DR. WILLIAM B. McLEAN
14. JOHN R. JOHNSTON m. (1) DELIA TORRENCE (2) LAURA NAPPOLIT.
15. ROBERT JOHNSTON m. CAROLINE SHUFORD, OF LINCOLN COUNTY.
16. DR. THOMAS JOHNSTON m. DORCAS LUCKEY, OF MECKLENBURG.
17. HARRIET JOHNSTON m. WILLIAM T. SHIPP, of GASTON COUNTY.
18. MARY JOHNSTON m. DR. WILLIAM DAVIDSON, of MECKLENBURG.
19. MARTHA JOHNSTON m. COL. J. B. RANKIN, of McDOWELL COUNTY.
20. COL. WILLIAM JOHNSTON m. ANN GRAHAM, of MECKLENBURG COUNTY.
21. RUFUS M. JOHNSTON m. CELIA LATTA, of YORK COUNTY, S. C.

1. ROBERT JOHNSTON (who married MARY M. REID) was a resident of the town of CHARLOTTE at the time of his death in 1854. His son 21 RUFUS M. JOHNSTON was the first of the family to die.

20. COL. WILLIAM JOHNSTON was a lawyer, having studied law under the celebrated JUDGE RICHARD MUMFORD PEARSON. He married in 1846 MISS ANNA ELIZA GRAHAM, daughter of DR. GEORGE F. GRAHAM, who was a brother of WILLIAM A. GRAHAM. COL. JOHNSTON served as MAYOR OF CHARLOTTE for four terms and was defeated for GOVERNOR by the celebrated ZEBULON B. VANCE. He was an industrialist and railroad builder.

DR. C. L. HUNTER in his "Sketches" is authority for the statement that GEN. JOSEPH E. JOHNSTON and ALBERT SIDNEY JOHNSTON were members of this JOHNSTON FAMILY.

SOME RECORDS FROM MARYLAND

Here are some interesting records from MARYLAND which are inserted here because they relate to some of the "neighbors" of the MECKLENBURG SIGNERS, and their early AMERICAN ORIGIN. A few explanatory notes are added.

WILL OF THE REVEREND FRANCIS MACKEMIE

ACCOMAC COUNTY, VIRGINIA. Dated April 27, 1708; proved August 4, 1708. (His wife was NAOMI ANDERSON, eldest daughter of WILLIAM ANDERSON.
1. Wife and two daughters, each 40 volumes of English books.
2. Law books to Rev· JEDEDIAH ANDREWS, of Philadelphia.
3. MR. ANDREW HAMILTON certain other Law books to be found among his Library books, and those he already has in his possession.
4. Another bequest to JEDEDIAH ANDREWS.
5. His Executrix (wife) to dispose of his house and lot on the Eastern branch of ELIZABETH RIVER in PRINCESS ANNE COUNTY; and house and lot at URBANA on WORMLEY'S CREEK; also lot joining New meeting house lot in POCOMOKE.
6. Youngest SISTER ANNE MAKEMIE of the Kingdom of IRELAND, and the two eldest sons of my brothers JOHN and ROBERT MAKEMIE:
    FRANCIS MAKEMIE and (Son of ROBERT)
    FRANCIS MAKEMIE. (Son of JOHN)
7. Wife NAOMI MAKEMIE, and daughters:
    ELIZABETH MAKEMIE
    ANNE MAKEMIE
8. Ordains the HON. COL. FRANCIS JENKINS and his wife MARY JENKINS, Executors and Guardians of children, and providing for their education.

The daughter ELIZABETH died by OCTOBER 6, 1708.
The daughter ANNE married a man named HOLDEN and lived until 1787.
COL. FRANCIS JENKINS died soon after REV. MAKEMIE, leaving no children, but left a great estate to his wife MARY. MRS. MARY JENKINS had been MARY KING, the sister of ROBERT KING and of ELLENER KING, who married CAPT. CHARLES BALLARD.
After the death of COL. FRANCIS JENKINS his widow MARY became the wife of REV. JOHN HENRY, & after HENRY DIED she married REV. JOHN HAMPTON. Both of these well known MINISTERS had been sponsored and induced to come to AMERICA by the REV. FRANCIS MAKEMIE.
-- FOOTE, Vol. 1, pp 57, 58 and 59.

WILL OF MR. WILLIAM ANDERSON, MERCHANT

ACCOMAC COUNTY, VIRGINIA. Proved October 16, 1698. He was a Merchant in ACCOMAC, VA.
1. To FRANCIS MAKEMIE and his wife NAOMI, a tract of 1000 acres, a little South of the village of ONANCOCK, the COUNTY SEAT, near which village they HAD THEIR RESIDENCE, five or six miles from DRUMMONDSTOWN, the later County Seat; also a plantation of 950 acres at POCOMOKE.
2. My daughter COMFORT TAYLOR and heirs.
3. Three lots at ONANCOCK to FRANCIS MAKEMIE and his heirs.
4. My daughter NAOMI MAKEMIE.
5. My three SISTERS MRS. BARROW, MRS. HOPE and MRS. NOCK. (Knox?)
6. MR. FRANCIS MAKEMIE all the money lent him and he is made sole executor of the will.
REV. FRANCIS MAKEMIE lived next to JONATHAN LIVELEY'S at ONANCOCK. - FOOTE Vol. 1, 43-44.

FIRST APPEARANCE OF REV. FRANCIS MAKEMIE IN AMERICA.

FOOTE (Vol. 1, p. 43.) says: The first mention of MAKEMIE'S name by any record in the UNITED STATES, is found in the COUNTY OF ACCOMAC, VIRGINIA, and bears date FEB. 17, 1690.
This is an error, for see:

WILL OF WILLIAM LOWERY IN NORFOLK

Will dated JAN. 23, 1687; proved in MARCH, 1686/7 by Yorley Lowery and JANE RAY.
1. Wife JANE ANDERSON.
2. And all my children now surviving.
3. My oldest son JAMES LOWERY, if he appears in the country.
4. Ordains MR. THOMAS SCOTT and MR. FRANCIS MAKEMIE Executors.
5. Yalxby Lowery.
Witnesses FRANCIS SAYER, JANE RAY, YOXEL LOWERY.
    WILLIAM LOWERY (and Seal).

In some way the JANE ANDERSON, wife of WILLIAM LOWERY or LOWERRY, of the above will must have been related to the WILLIAM ANDERSON whose daughter married FRANCIS MAKEMIE.
This is a three-year earlier mention than is given by FOOTE.

WHEN REVS. JOHN HAMPTON, GEORGE McNISH and JOHN HAMPTON CAME TO ACCOMAC & SOMERSET.

In the fall of 1705 after his (REV. MAKEMIE) had returned from ENGLAND, we find Mr. MAKEMIE, in the month of NOVEMBER, before the County Court of SOMERSET (MD.), with two ministerial brethren, JOHN HAMPTON and GEORGE McNISH, whom the records style "his associates" for whom he demanded certificates. Foote Vol. 1 p. 53.
MR. JOHN HENRY, the successor of MR. MACKAMIE at REHOBOTH, came in the year 1710, an ordained minister from the Presbytery of DUBLIN and was installed pastor the same year. Foote Vol. 1 p. 58.
REV. SAMUEL DAVIES, ALEXANDER CUMMINS (the son in law of GEN. THOMAS POLK, of MECKLENBURG) and MR. HENRY, Dr· Foote says, attended SAMUEL BLAIR'S famous FAGG'S MANOR classical school in Pennsylvania. (p. 159). Mr. Foote appears to be mistaken in the identity of HENRY. It must have been one of his two sons, either ROBERT or JOHN HENRY, who went to the Blair School with The Smiths and Alexander Cummins, and also REV. SAMUEL DAVIES. (WSR).

REV. GEORGE McNISH in September, 1715, read a letter to the Presbytery of Philadelphia, then in session " from Mr. JOHN THOMSON, probationer, lately come into the country, desiring the advice and assistance of the Presbytery".
REV. GEORGE McNISH and REV. JOHN HAMPTON who are mentioned in the above notes, were responsible for REV. JOHN THOMSON'S acceptance of a call in 1717 to the Church at LEWES, DELAWARE, not very far from the line of SOMERSET, COUNTY, Md. - Dr. JOHN G. HERNDON'S "Life of JOHN THOMSON".
This was the REV. JOHN THOMSON buried at Baker's Graveyard in MECKLENBURG COUNTY, N. C.

The congregations that first worshipped in America according to the forms of the Presbyterian Church on the Geneva or Scotch model, still have a name and a place among the people of God. He that would visit these mother churches of the Presbyterian body in America, must go down to the narrow neck of land between the ocean and the Chesapeake. There he will find SNOW HILL in Worcester, formerly SOMERSET, and may walk among the monuments and burial mounds. * * Thence let him take an excursion to the head of WICOMICO and to the head of MONOKIN (or Princess Anne) and he will be walking over ground consecrated by such men as MAKAMIE, McNISH, HAMPTON, HENRY, ROBINSON, DAVIES, FINLEY and RODGERS.\- Foote, Vol. 1 page 46.

After the arrival in VIRGINIA, of REV. JOHN THOMSON, much of his ministerial work was performed in the same Congregations that had been served by REV. FRANCIS MAKEMIE. By direction of the Synod, as early as 1719, REV. JOHN THOMSON participated in the ordination of John Clement as minister at POCOMOKE, and William Stewart as minister at MONOKIN and WICOMICO. The service of their ordination was held at REHOBOTH, SOMERSET COUNTY, Maryland, in June, 1719. The minutes of the Presbytery in 1724/5 show:

Upon the supplication from the congregation of SNOW HILL, ordered that MR. THOMSON supply them one Sabbath in April, one in June and one in July.

And again at Philadelphia September 16, 1725, it was ordered that MR. JOHN THOMSON supply the people of SNOW HILL four Sabbaths before March next.

In 1719, when the Synod of the Church met at Philadelphia, REV. JOHN THOMSON was elected Moderator. He was again elected in 1722.

These are instances disclosed by the RECORDS OF THE CHURCH, showing that REV. JOHN THOMSON, the Mecklenburg (N. C.) Minister of early days, served the same Churches described in the opening paragraph on this page from the annals of DR. FOOTE. It is believed that he had ministered and preached in both ACCOMAC and SOMERSET many times prior to the dates given, immediately after his arrival in VIRGINIA, and evidence indicates that he was well known to JOHN HAMPTON, JOHN HENRY and other contemporaries with whom he worked, as well as to the members of the Church who resided in those communities.

WILL OF ROBERT WILSON AT MONOKIN, IN SOMERSET COUNTY, MARYLAND in 1736.

Dated March 15, 1735; proved April 27, 1736.
1. Wife SARAH, dwelling house and orchard.
2. To the Presbyterian Congregation of MONOKIN for the use of the Ministers 10 pounds.
3. To brother GEORGE WILSON and his wife MARY and their son by law WILLIAM SCOTT and heirs, conditioned that they shall come and live on said plantation within seven years from date hereof, otherwise to GEORGE WILSON and heirs, grandson to the aforesaid brother (GEORGE) and son of ANDREW WILSON, supposed to be IN THE COLONY OF VIRGINIA.
4. TO GEORGE WILSON, son of ANDREW WILSON, and heirs, residue of estate, to be looked after by my brother GEORGE for his grandson until of age.
5. Wife SARAH and brother GEORGE, Exrs.
Witnesses: Benjamin Cottman
DAVID POLK
Thomas Pullett
MOSES ALEXANDER.

(Among the honored names of 13 ejected ministers by Charles II in 1661 under Jeremy Taylor, in the Presbytery of Laban in Ireland, was ROBERT WILSON, ancestor of the REV. FRANCIS McKEMIE, who twenty years later, was the first Presbyterian Preacher that had ever visited the Western Continent, and near relative of GEORGE McKEMIE, of the Waxhaw settlement, brother in law of MRS. ELIZABETH JACKSON mother of Gen. ANDREW JACKSON, and uncle of REV. JOHN McKEMIE WILSON, of Mecklenburg County, North Carolina. - Hunter's Sketches of Western North Carolina, page 62.)

The ROBERT WILSON, of MONOKIN, in SOMERSET COUNTY, Md. and his brother, GEORGE, were possible sons of the old Minister of the Presbytery of LABAN. ANDREW WILSON his nephew was the father of the younger GEORGE WILSON, then living in the Colony of VIRGINIA, who married a sister of GEORGE Mackemie, of the Waxhaws and became the father of REV. JOHN McKEMIE WILSON.

It will be noted that the ROBERT WILSON of the above will was NOT A MINISTER, but was an intense PRESBYTERIAN, who settled at MONOKINS, a Congregation FOUNDED IN THE BEGINNING by the REV. FRANCIS MAKEMIE, his kinsman.

WILL OF REV. JOHN HAMPTON, MINISTER, OF SOMERSET COUNTY IN MARYLAND.

Proved February 2, 1721/2.
1. Cousin JAMES ROUND.
2. Cousin EDMUND, son of WILLIAM ROUND.
3. Brother in law ROBERT KING.
4. Sister in law ELLENER BALLARD, the wife of CAPT. CHARLES BALLARD.
5. My two sons in law:
ROBERT JENKINS HENRY
JOHN HENRY.
6. Brother, ROBERT HAMPTON, merchant in LONDONDERRY, IRELAND.
7. My two sisters: MARGERY and FRANCES.
8. Wife MARY.
Witnesses: JOHN CLEMENT
ALEXANDER LAKEY
JOHN CHAWAN
ROBERT TRUMAN.

JOHN CLEMENT, the witness was ordained as the Minister at POCOMOKE in June 1719, by the REV. JOHN THOMSON. (who is buried at Baker's Graveyard in Mecklenburg County) See note above.

ROBERT JENKINS HENRY and JOHN HENRY the "sons in laws" mentioned were step-sons, and the sons of MARY KING and her second husband, REV. JOHN HENRY.

ROBERT JENKINS HENRY was later in life the pastor of the CUB CREEK CHURCH in CHARLOTTE COUNTY, VIRGINIA, and later pastor of PROVIDENCE CHURCH in Mecklenburg County, North Carolina.

WILL OF WILLIAM PORTER OF SOMERSET

Dated Dec. 6, 1695; proved June 10, 1696.
Wife ELIZA sole legatee and executrix.
"Friend's Choice" to be sold.
Witnesses:
JOHN POLK
John Porter
Thomas Smith
John Bennett
William Polk.

Md. Cal. of Wills Vol 7, p 180; Vol 5 p 88. Vol 2 p. 103. And the other sources mentioned in the text.

PATRICK CALDWELL and THOMAS CALDWELL WITNESS
WILL OF MATTHEW FERRENSONE 1738.
IN SOMERSET COUNTY. Md. Cal Wills
p. 33.
Will of MATTHEW FERRENSONE, planter of SOMER-
SET COUNTY, MARYLAND, dated May 27, 1738; proved
May 28, 1738.
Sons: EZEKIEL, MATTHEW, JOSEPH and JAMES.
Sons in law: PATRICK CALDWELL and THOMAS
CALDWELL.
Witnesses: JOHN WILLIAMS, JOHN HECORDS and
CHARLES PARSONS.
(The CALDWELLS may have been step-sons, or
they may have married two daughters.)

JOHN CALDWELL LEFT WILL IN SOMERSET JAN. 5, 1742.

Proved Dec. 17, 1743.   Vol 8 Md Wills
1. Son, ROBERT CALDWELL.   p. 245.
2. Son JOSHUA CALDWELL
3. Daughter, ANN CALDWELL.
4. Sister, GIVEN CALLAWAY.
Son ROBERT to have charge of younger children until they are of age.
Witnesses: JOHN WILLIAMS, WILLIAM KENNEY &
WILLIAM GIVEN.

THOMAS CALDWELL WITNESS TO WILL OF ISAAC NOBLE IN
SOMERSET IN 1732.
(Md. Cal. of Wills 6 p. 245)
ISAAC NOBLE'S WILL, Nov. 21, 1732. His wife
was SUSAN.
Sons and Daughters: ISAAC, JOHN, GRACE and
JANE NOBLE. Also MARY, who m. PETER SURMAN.
Witnesses: BRENT NUTHALL, JOSEPH McCLELLAN
and THOMAS CALDWELL.

JAMES CALDWELL WITNESS TO WILL OF WILLIAM LANGS-
TON or LANGSDEN IN 1708/9.
(Md. Cal. of Wills III, p. 152)
WILLIAM LANGSDEN, of Stepney Parish, in SOM-
ERSET COUNTY, Maryland; dated March 8, 1708/9, &
Proved Sept. 26, 1709.
Wife ISABEL
Sons JOHN, SPIRE, WILLIAM & daughters SARAH
& PRISCILLA.
JAMES GIVEN and wife ISOBEL, Executors.
Witnesses: JAMES CALDWELL, Agnes Wilson,
William Wilson, William Piner and SARAH NIGAMANS.

WILLIAM CALDWELL WITNESS TO WILL OF ROBERT CATH-
KENWOOD IN SOMERSET, MD. IN 1715.
(Md. Cal. of Wills Vol. 4, page 42)
Dated April 27, 1715; proved August 23,1715.
His wife was ANNE.
Brother in law: SAMUEL WORTHINGTON and his
wife ABIGE, to have charge of daughter should his
wife die.
Witnesses: WILLIAM CALDWELL
MARGARET FITZGERALD
JOHN ELZEY
SAMUEL WORTHINGTON.*
* SAMUEL WORTHINGTON the ancestor of the N.
C. and TENNESSEE WORTHINGTON FAMILY.

WILLIAM CALDWELL WITNESS TO WILL OF ALEXANDER
KNOX IN SOMERSET IN 1716.
(Md. Cal. of Wills Vol 4 p 153)
Will of ALEXANDER KNOX, dated Jan. 2, 1716;
proved March 22, 1717.
1. JOHN GIBSON.
2. MAJ. ARNOLD ELZEY.
Witnesses: WILLIAM CALDWELL
WILLIAM BARRON
WILLIAM TURPIN
RISDEN BOZEMAN.

JOHN CALDWELL WITNESS TO WILL OF JOHN HOLDEN
IN SOMERSET COUNTY MD. IN 1721.
(Md. Cal. of Wills Vol 5 p. 88)
JOHN HOLDEN left will in Somerset dated DEC.
2, 1716; proved March 22, 1721.
His wife was MARGARET.
Sons JOHN and JOSEPH HOLDEN.
Witnesses: JOHN CALDWELL
JEREMIAH RIGHT
JOHN SLIVENS
CHRISTOPHER VAGON.
(ANNE MAKEMIE, daughter of REV. FRANCIS MAK-
EMIE, married HOLDEN - See Will).

JOHN CALDWELL SR. WITNESS TO WILL OF JAMES GIVEN
IN SOMERSET COUNTY, MD. IN 1723.
(Md. Cal. of Wills Vol 5 p. 164)
Will of JAMES GIVEN, of ROWASTICO, in SOMER-
SET COUNTY, GENT. Dated Oct. 5, 1723; proved
May 11, 1724. His wife was MARTHA.
Children mentioned: JAMES, WILLIAM, GEORGE,
MARGARET, JOHN, SARAH, MARTHA and JANE GIVEN.
Overseers of will: JOSEPH VENABLES
PATRICK DONELSON
JANE McKEAN
JOHN CALDWELL SR.
(See other references on this page to the
GIVEN family)

JOHN CALDWELL WITNESS TO WILL OF EDWARD McGLAM-
ERY IN SOMERSET, MD. IN YEAR 1721.
(Md. Cal. of Wills Vol 5 p. 149.)
EDWARD McGLAMERY will, dated March 25, in
1721; proved Oct. 21, 1723.
His wife was SARAH.
Children: GEORGE, EDWARD, WILLIAM.
Witnesses: JOHN CALDWELL
THOMAS GODDARD
ROBERT DOWNS or DOVAN.
(McGLAMERY in those days was a way the name
MONTGOMERY was often spelled and pronounced).

JOHN CALDWELL AND JOSHUA CALDWELL WITNESSES TO
WILL OF WILLIAM ALEXANDER IN SOMERSET
COUNTY, MARYLAND IN YEAR 1732.
(Md. Cal. of Wills Vol. 7 p. 141)
WILLIAM ALEXANDER, planter of SOMERSET COUN-
TY, MD., will dated March 7, 1732; proved June
18, 1735.
His wife was CATHERINE
1. Son SAMUEL ALEXANDER.
2. Son JAMES ALEXANDER and heirs.
3. Son MOSES ALEXANDER and heirs, to whom he
leaves land "where my father WILLIAM ALEXANDER
did live".
4. Son LISTON ALEXANDER.
5. Daughter AGNES ALEXANDER.
Executors: Wife CATHERINE and son SAMUEL
ALEXANDER.
Witnesses: JOHN CALDWELL
John Crawford.
William Dulaney
JOSHUA CALDWELL

JOHN CALDWELL and ROBERT CALDWELL WITNESS WILL
OF JAMES ALEXANDER, SOMERSET IN 1735.
(Md. Cal Wills Vol 7 p. 141)
JAMES ALEXANDER will (Brother of WILLIAM
ALEXANDER, above) Dated March 30, 1735; proved
June 18, 1735.
Brother: LISTON ALEXANDER
Sister: AGNES ALEXANDER
Brother: MOSES ALEXANDER and his son SAMUEL
ALEXANDER.
Sister: MARY ALEXANDER m. MILLS.
Witnesses: JOHN CALDWELL, JOHN FAIRION,
ROBERT BAIDWELL and ROBERT CORNWELL.

WILLIAM KNOX WITNESS TO WILL OF THOMAS SMITH IN SOMERSET, MD., IN YEAR 1697.
(Md. Cal of Wills Vol. 2 p.131)
THOMAS SMITH will dated September 20, 1697.
Names wife JANET.
Sons WILLIAM, JOHN and ROBERT.
Overseers JOHN GRAY and JOHN BROWN.
Witnesses: WILLIAM LANE
WILLIAM OWENS *
WILLIAM KNOX.
* See next will below.

JOHN POLK, WILLIAM POLK AND WILLIAM KNOX WITNESS WILL OF WILLIAM OWENS IN SOMERSET 1698.
(Md. Cal. of Wills Vol. 2, page 181)
Will of WILLIAM OWENS (the witness above) - Dated March 27, 1698.
Sons: WILLIAM, JOHN, ROBERT and SAMUEL OWENS.
Wife Executrix.
Overseers of will: JOHN POLK, WILLIAM KNOX.
Witnesses: WILLIAM POLK
ARCHIBALD SMITH
JOHN GOLDSMITH
JOHN BROWN.

HENRY ALEXANDER OF SOMERSET COUNTY, MARYLAND, WITNESSED WILL OF WILLIAM BEDDER, SR.
(Md. Cal. of Wills Vol. 4, p. 192.
Will dated in September, 1718.

SAMUEL ALEXANDER WITNESSES WILL OF WILLIAM GYLLOT IN SOMERSET COUNTY, MD. IN 1716.
(Md. Cal. of Wills Vol. 4 p 43.)
Will dated Jan. 21, 1716; proved March 20th, 1716, in SOMERSET COUNTY.
Witnessed by SAMUEL ALEXANDER.

JOHN CALDWELL OVERSEER OF THE WILL OF JOHN MILLS IN SOMERSET COUNTY, MARYLAND IN 1729.
(Md. Cal. of Wills Vol. 7, page 115)
Will of JOHN MILLS of SOMERSET dated Feb. 20, 1729/30; proved Nov. 19, 1734.
(The wife of JOHN MILLS was MARY ALEXANDER - See will of JAMES ALEXANDER.)
Children named: REBECCA, HANNAH, MARY, ESTHER, WILLIAM, ROBERT MILLS and heirs (part of land lying in Va.) , ALEXANDER MILLS and NATHANIEL MILLS.
Overseers: ROBERT KING (Uncle of ROBERT J. HENRY and JOHN HENRY, whose mother married REV. JOHN HENRY, Col. JENKINS and REV. JOHN HAMPTON), JOHN CALDWELL and THOMAS LAYFIELD.
Witnesses: WILLIAM MILLS, JOHN TAMPLIN and THOMAS LAYFIELD.

ROBERT JENKINS HENRY AND JOHN HENRY WITNESS WILL OF SAMUEL TOMLINSON IN SOMERSET IN 1733.
(Md. Cal. of Wills Vol. 7 p. 83).
Will of SAMUEL TOMLINSON, of Somerset County, Maryland, dated Feb. 18, 1733; proved April 3, 1744.
Wife ABIGAIL.
Children: SOLOMON, SOWARD, HAMPTON, SARAH TOMLINSON, RACHEL BOSTON and MARGARET CROPPER.
Wife and son SOLOMON TOMLINSON, Executors.
Witnesses: ROBERT JENKINS HENRY
JOHN HENRY
HENRY SCHOOLFIELD.

DEVISEE OF ALEXANDER KNOX LEAVES WILL SOMERSET.
(Md. Cal. of Wills Vol 7 p. 20)
Will of COL. ARNOLD ELZEY, dated Feb. 16, 1729; proved Jan. 13, 1733.
Leaves land devised to testator by ALEXANDER KNOX, to Dr. PATRICK STEWART and heirs.

ROBERT JENKINS HENRY, JOHN HENRY AND ADAM BELL WITNESS JOHN SMITH WILL IN SOMER. T, MD.
(Md. Cal. of Wills Vol. 7 p. 81,).
Will of JOHN SMITH, of SOMERSET, dated Dec. 20, 1732; proved June 6, 1733.
Names wife MARY.
Brother WILLIAM SMITH and daughter EASTER.
Sister: ELIZABETH by EDWARD HAMMOND, her children: MARTHA HAMMOND, LEAH HAMMOND and BETTY HAMMOND.
Brothers GEORGE and ANDREW SMITH by father's last wife.
Witnesses: ROBERT JENKINS HENRY
* ADAM BELL
JOHN HENRY.
The HENRYS were sons of REV. JOHN HENRY and ADAM BELL was a relative of GEORGE BELL who settled in PRINCE EDWARD COUNTY, VA.

JOHN CALDWELL AND JOHN MORROW WITNESSES TO WILL OF COL. WILLIAM WHITTINGTON IN SOMERSET.
(Md. Cal. of Wills Vol. 5 page 15)
Will of WILLIAM WHITTINGTON, of Coventry Parish, SOMERSET COUNTY, MD., dated April 11th, 1720.
Mentions RICHARD BAYLEY, of ACCOMAC COUNTY, and his wife URSULA, and their sons EDWARD and WHITTINGTON BAYLEY.
ADAM SPENCE and his heirs, including WILLIAM, SOUTHEY, ESTHER and HANNAH SPENCE.
STEPHEN WHITE, Executor.
Bros. in law: SAMUEL HOPKINS, JOHN CALDWELL and FRANCIS ALLEN.
Witnesses: JOHN MOROGH, PETER ROBINSON & SAMUEL DERRICKSON and LITTLETON BOULAN.

WILL OF OWEN MOROGH (MORROW) IN SOMERSET COUNTY, MARYLAND, IN THE YEAR OF 1691/2.
(Md. Cal. of Wills Vol. 2, p. 64)
OWEN MCROUGH will dated March 18, 1691/2; proved March 14, 1692/3.
1. Son OWEN MORROW and heirs.
2. Son WILLIAM MORROW
3. Son JOHN MORROW
4. Son RICHARD MORROW
5. Son DAVID MORROW
6. Daughter MARY MORROW at 16 years.
7. Wife MARY and her child, residue.
Overseers: COL. DAVID BROWN.
ROGER WOOLFORD.
Witnesses: JOHN BROWN and RICHARD CARY or CARIN - maybe CURRIE.

JAMES CALDWELL WITNESS TO WILL OF MAURICE MOORE IN SOMERSET CO. MD., IN 1716.
(Md. Cal. of Wills Vol 4, page ...)
Will of MORRIS MORRES (MAURICE MOORE) dated November 7, 1716.
Mentions lands on BROAD CREEK in SOMERSET COUNTY.
Witnesses: JAMES CALDWELL
JOHN IRELAND.

JOHN CALDWELL, SR. WITNESS TO WILL OF WILLIAM FYSER IN SOMERSET COUNTY, MD. 1733/4.
(Md. Cal. Wills Vol. 6, p 97-8).
Will of WILLIAM FYSER, dated 1733/4.
Children: SARAH, ANN, JOHN and JOSEPH.
Cousin: JAMES DASHIELL.
Brother: CHRISTOPHER FYSER.
Cousins:
HURT NUTTER.
GEORGE DASHIELL
JOHN CALDWELL, SR.

JAMES DASHIELL wit. will of THOMAS LARRIMORE in SOMERSET COUNTY, MD. in February, 1731.

517

CECIL COUNTY, MARYLAND, AND NOT PENNSYLVANIA, THE BIRTH PLACE OF THE MECKLENBURG DECLARATION.

The MECKLENBURG DECLARATION OF INDEPENDENCE was framed and signed by a convention of duly elected delegates, at CHARLOTTE, N. C. in 1775, but the actual BIRTH PLACE of the indomitable spirit and love of LIBERTY that brought forth this defiant demand for religious freedom and independence may be traced back to the "forks of the Elk" and the banks of the Susquehanna river in what is now CECIL COUNTY MARYLAND. It was NOT a product of PENNSYLVANIA or of PENNSYLVANIA emigrants, but was predominantly instigated by former residents of MARYLAND.

The ALEXANDERS, McKNIGHTS, PORTERS, CALDWELLS, BARRYS, GILLESPIES and EWINGS all settled in CECIL COUNTY, MARYLAND, and it was their influence, operating through the CRAIGHEADS, THOMSONS, HAMPTONS, HENRYS, FINLEYS, BLAIRS, SMITHS, MAKEMIES and WILSONS, off-shoots of those teeth-gritting, defiant and determined sons and daughters of the Highlands of Scotland who were besieged at LONDONDERRY, who flung the seeds of LIBERTY to the four winds of a New World and brought about a revolution in thought and action that startled the thrones of Europe.

Following herewith are a few items from the records of CECIL COUNTY, MARYLAND, that tend to throw light on the family history of some of these "independence instigators":

WILL OF ALEXANDER EWING OF CECIL COUNTY, MARYLAND, IN THE YEAR 1738.
(Md. Cal. of Wills Vol 8, p. 26).
1. Wife (not named) 1/3rd of personal estate.
2. Son JOHN EWING.
3. Son WILLIAM EWING.
(WILLIAM HUSBANDS to make the division between them.)*
4. Dau. MARGARET EWING, when 16.
5. Son SAMUEL EWING.
6. Son in law: ANDREW PORTER.
(Step- son)
7. Son JAMES EWING.
(Children JAMES, JOHN, WILLIAM and MARGARET to be bound to a trade.)
Executors:
ANDREW BARRY, ESQUIRE (Father of RICHARD BARRY the SIGNER)
JAMES PORTER
SAMUEL EWING
NATHANIEL EWING.
Witnesses:
WILLIAM MITCHELL
ROBERT GILLESPIE
RACHEL EWING.

Should sons incline to sell their portion of lands it shall be to their brother.
Probate taken in presence of JAMES EWING, the eldest son of testator.

NOTE: The executors, SAMUEL and NATHANIEL EWING were BROTHERS of the testator.
The witness RACHEL EWING was the wife of the testator, who had been RACHEL PORTER, the widow of a PORTER. ANDREW PORTER was her son by her former marriage.

"WILLIAM HUSBANDS, a friend of this family was the ancestor of the NORTH CAROLINA REGULATOR, the famous HERMAN HUSBANDS.
The witness ROBERT GILLESPIE was a relative of REV. GEORGE GILLESPIE, once defeated for MODERATOR of the NEW CASTLE PRESBYTERY in 1719 by REV. JOHN THOMSON.
These are the EWINGS who settled in PRINCE EDWARD COUNTY, VIRGINIA. See notes about them.

WILL OF JOHN GARNER OF CECIL COUNTY, MARYLAND
(Md. Cal. of Wills Vol 5 p. 204)
Will of JOHN GARNER, dated March 7, 1723; & probated October 22, 1725.
To GEORGE GILLESPIE
To JOSEPH STEELE and MARGARET STEELE
To Children of JAMES STEELE
To Children of GEORGE GILLESPIE
To children of JAMES ALEXANDER by MARY STEELE* Extra JOSEPH STEELE and JAMES STEELE.
Wits. JAMES & MOSES ALEXANDER and JNO STEELE

INTERESTING FACTS REVEALED BY THE CONTENTS OF THE WILL OF ALEXANDER EWING AND OF JOHN GARNER:

In other notes will be found the names of the children and an account of the descendants of SAMUEL EWING, the executor of ALEXANDER EWING'S will. This SAMUEL EWING died leaving a will in PRINCE EDWARD COUNTY, VIRGINIA. It was his son GEORGE EWING who married a daughter of COL. HUGH LAWSON.

The JOHN GARNER will shows the connection between the ALEXANDERS, the STEELES and the GILLESPIES in CECIL COUNTY, MARYLAND.
ROBERT GILLESPIE, who witnessed the will of ALEXANDER EWING settled in ROWAN COUNTY, N. C. & was one of the sons of the GEORGE GILLESPIE mentioned in the GARNER WILL, and was also a cousin of course to the children of JAMES ALEXANDER and his wife MARY STEELE, and the children of JAMES STEELE, among them a WILLIAM, who married ELIZABETH MAXWELL GILLESPIE, the widow of ROBERT GILLESPIE about 1763, in N. C.
Children of ROBERT GILLESPIE and ELIZABETH MAXWELL, in N. C., were:

1. RICHARD GILLESPIE (never married)
2. ROBERT GILLESPIE
3. MARGARET GILLESPIE.

Richard Gillespie was a revolutionary soldier in N. C. ROWAN COUNTY.
MARGARET GILLESPIE married REV. SAMUEL E. McCORKLE, a noted minister of the Presbyterian Church in N. C.
After the death of ROBERT GILLESPIE, his widow married WILLIAM STEELE, of SALISBURY, N. C., who was a cousin of her first husband, and a descendant of one of the STEELE brothers mentioned in the will of JOHN GARNER in 1723, in CECIL COUNTY, MARYLAND.
They were the parents of only one son:

4. GEN. JOHN STEELE.

Gen. John Steele was born November 1, 1764, it is said, in the town of SALISBURY. He served in the Legislature; was a member of the First U. S. Congress, and First Comptroller of the Treasury under Gen. George Washington.
He died August 14, 1815.
His mother, ELIZABETH MAXWELL (GILLESPIE) STEELE was a heroine of the American Revolution who, on the occasion of GEN. GREENE'S visit to SALISBURY, as a guest at her home, presented him with an apron load of GOLD, at a time when he was dispirited and without funds to finish his campaign.

COL. JAMES MAXWELL, OF MARYLAND, MARRIED DAUGHTER OF JOHN EWING BY 1709.
(Md. Cal. of Wills Vol. 3 p. 145)
Will of JOHN EWING (Spelled EWING, EWEN) in BALTIMORE COUNTY, dated April 12, 1709.
Daughter DORCAS and heirs.
Brother in law, COL. JAMES MAXWELL.
Brother in law, MOSES GROOME.
Witnesses: JOHN EDWARDS, ROBERT CUTCHIN and THOMAS BARTON.
(Some of the EWINGS of NASHVILLE, TENNESSEE, changed the spelling of the name EWING to EWEN, & claimed THAT was the original spelling.)

JOSEPH MOORE OF CECIL COUNTY, WITNESS TO WILL OF WILLIAM RICE, 1729.
(Md. Cal. of Wills Vol 6 p. 180)
Will of WILLIAM RICE, of CECIL COUNTY, MARYLAND, dated August 2, 1729.
Wife MARY.
Son: THOMAS RICE.
Brother: DAVID RICE.
Witnesses: JOSEPH MOORE, Nicholas Hyland & Edward Johnson.

DAVID LAWSON, OF CECIL COUNTY, SON IN LAW OF DR. PETER SLUYTER IN THE YEAR 1721.
(Md. Cal. of Wills Vol. 7, p. 187)
Will of DR. PETER SLUYTER -SLEETDER, dated Jan. 20, 1721/2; proved Nov. 10, 1722.
To son in law DAVID LAWSON and heirs.
To son in law SAMUEL BOUCHELLE.
To daughter in law ELIZABETH, wife of DAVID LAWSON.
To MAGDALENE, wife of RICHARD THOMPSON.
Witnesses: ARNOLD BASSETT, JAMES VANDEGRIFT and JOHN DICKSON.
Note relationship of DAVID LAWSON and RICHARD THOMPSON in this will..

DAVID LAWSON OWNED PLANTATION IN CECIL COUNTY, MD, IN 1735. WILL OF DR. BOUCHELLE.
(Md. Cal. of Wills Vol. 7 p. 186)
Will of DR. PETER BOUCHELLE, of CECIL COUNTY, MARYLAND, dated August 22, 1735; proved July 26, 1736.
Wife MARY.
Daughters RACHEL and MARY.
Son Sluyter and heirs; land that was JACOB VANDEGRIFT'S, part of dwelling plantation adjoining DAVID LAWSON'S.
Son PETER SLUYTER.
Witnesses: James Craig.
             Robert Wood
             ALEXANDER PRICE.
(RICHARD BARRY married ANNE PRICE, of MARYLAND).

PETER LAWSON LIVED IN CECIL COUNTY, MARYLAND IN THE YEAR 1704 AND WITNESSED WILL.
(Md. Cal. of Wills Vol. 8, p. 199)
Will of ELIAS WILLIAMS, of CECIL COUNTY, MD. was proved NOV. 24, 1742.
The will was witnessed by PETER LAWSON, DAVID THOMAS and NATHAN WILLIAMS.

GEORGE LAWSON OF CECIL COUNTY, MARYLAND and JOSEPH MOORE MENTIONED IN 1732.
(Md. Cal. of Wills Vol. 7 p. 2)
Will of MARY READ, of PRINCE GEORGE COUNTY, MARYLAND, dated May 9, 1732.
Mentions GEORGE LAWSON, of CECIL COUNTY, MARYLAND and JOSEPH MOORE. (See RICE WILL above).

(Some of the LAWSONS and MOORES of CECIL COUNTY moved to PRINCE GEORGE'S COUNTY, MARYLAND).

LAWSONS OF CECIL COUNTY, MD. RELATED TO REEDS OR READS OF DORCHESTER COUNTY, MD.
(Md. Cal. of Wills Vol. 6 p. 58)
Will of ROBERT REED, Planter, of DORCHESTER County, MARYLAND, dated Spet. 18, 1727; proved October 2, 1727.
To Cousin WILLIAM REED.   (REV. JOHN
To son in law SAMUEL LAWSON.   THOMSON m.
To three daughters in law: MARY McKEAN
            ANNE TUCKER   REED)
            ELIZABETH ROE
            MARGARET BRACHER.
Witnesses: REDMAN FALLEN, ANN JONES and a MARY GREEN.
(REDMAN FALLEN was a well known RAPPAHANNOCK Character in VIRGINIA.)

THOMAS AND WILLIAM LAWSON OF CHARLES COUNTY, MD. WERE THERE IN 1730/31.
(Md. Cal. of Wills Vol. 6 p. 182)
Will of JAMES GALWITH, of CHARLES COUNTY, MD, dated March 8, 1730/31.
Son JONAS GALWITH left in care of WILLIAM LAWSON, but of he should die to THOMAS LAWSON.
Wits: JAMES DAVIS, THOMAS LAWSON and JOHN STRANGE.

JOHN LAWSON ALSO IN CHARLES COUNTY, MARYLAND IN THE YEAR 1725.
(Md. Cal. of Wills Vol. 6 p. 90).
Will of MARY LENOIR, widow, of CHARLES COUNTY, MARYLAND, DECEMBER 22, 1725.
Leaves legacies to DR. DANIEL JENIFER and JOHN LAWSON.
(REV. JOHN THOMSON'S second wife was to a Mary McKean READ, and
(CHARLES COUNTY, MARYLAND, was just South of PRINCE GEORGE'S COUNTY).

THE LAWSON FAMILY IN MARYLAND AS EARLY AS 1667 WILL OF JOHN, FATHER OF PETER LAWSON.
(Md. Cal. of Wills Vol. 1, page 45)
Will of JOHN LAWSON, dated October 6, 1667.
To son PETER LAWSON, lands on CHOPTANK CREEK in TALBOT COUNTY, MD.
To daughter DORCAS LAWSON 1/2 of estate.
To daughter JANE LAWSON
To one of RANDELL (Randolph) HANSEN'S children and to JOHN TENNEHILL.
Executors: RANDOLPH HANSON and HENRY HIDE.
Witnesses: RICHARD RIDER and BARBARA HANSON.

THE WAIKUP FAMILY OF MARYLAND AND THE LAWSONS MENTIONED IN HARWOOD WILL 1663.
(Md. Cal. of Wills Vol. 1 p. 24.)
Will of ALICE HARWOOD, widow of JOHN HARWOOD dated April 30, 1663.
To JOHN WALLCOP'S (WAIKUP- WAUCHOPE) son & daughter ELIZA.
To DORCAS LAWSON.
To FRANCES PHILLIPS, daughter of one THOMAS PHILLIPS.
STANOP (STANHOPE) ROBERTS, residuary.
Witnesses: JOHN LAWSON, JOHN WILKINSON and DUNCOMB PHRIZELL. (Frizzell).

JOHN LAWSON OF ST. MARY'S COUNTY AND HIS SON JOHN, LEGATEES OF JAMES OWEN 1659.
(Md. Cal. of Wills Vol. 1 p. 14.)
To JOHN LAWSON, son of JOHN LAWSON
To REBECCA FRIZZELL, dau. of ALEX FRIZELL.
To HARBERT HOMAN   (JAMES OWEN WILL)
To REV. WILKINSON.
To KINSMAN, COL. JOHN PRICE, Exr. & Residue.
Witnesses: ALEXANDER FRIZZELL, SARAH FRIZZELL and RICHARD LLOYD.

**THE MECKLENBURG ALEXANDERS

Not all of the MECKLENBURG ALEXANDERS came from CECIL COUNTY, MARYLAND, for some of them were from SOMERSET COUNTY on the "EASTERN SHORE" of MARYLAND, and some of them had doubtless originated in ACCOMAC COUNTY, VIRGINIA, around ONANCOCK and DRUMMONDSTOWN, and members of the Presbyterian flock ministered to by REV. FRANCIS MAKEMIE, JOHN HAMPTON, and perhaps occasionally by the young JOHN THOMSON.

But we KNOW that JOHN McKNITT ALEXANDER was of the CECIL COUNTY, MARYLAND FAMILY, and have followed the history of the ALEXANDERS to the point where it seems that after all, those of CECIL COUNTY and those of SOMERSET were of the same Scotch Irish strain. We have found it much easier to trace the JOHN McKNITT ALEXANDERS, who lived in MECKLENBURG, and when it appears that one of the name was NOT of his stock, we just credit him to the SOMERSET FAMILY.

The ancestor of JOHN McKNITT (or McKNIGHT) ALEXANDER in CECIL COUNTY, MARYLAND, was one JOSEPH ALEXANDER. Just when he settled at NEW MUNSTER in CECIL COUNTY is a matter of conjecture, since his name does not appear on the records until four years before his death, when he executed his last will and testament. This JOSEPH ALEXANDER was a TANNER by trade, and that set him apart at once as a man of character and substance. It made him a leather worker and a craftsman of no slight importance. In those days the TAN YARD was an institution to be reckoned with in the commercial and industrial life of a community. It was a magnet that drew to its portals practically every citizen and family in the countryside, absent the more modern system of trade and traffic in leather goods. As the proprietor of this establishment JOSEPH ALEXANDER was not only a skilled craftsman, but a respected depository of public information and learning. His neighbors came to him for advice and counsel; his views were disseminated up and down the valley with its verdant farms and homes, and his opinions on the welfare of the country was respected. JOSEPH ALEXANDER'S busy tan yard, we can imagine, in those days, probably furnished the seeds of longing for religious freedom and liberty in the minds of his neighbors and his children and grand-children, which nourished into full fruition, the desires and trends among the people of that early period, which culminated in the "Mecklenburg Declaration" which his descendants helped to write nearly a HUNDRED YEARS LATER.

All that the chroniclers of the ALEXANDER FAMILY have told us about that clan is evidently based wholly upon family traditions. Save that his name was JOSEPH and that he had a son JAMES, who was the father of JOHN McKNITT ALEXANDER, with a long list of children, we have not been further enlightened. Thus the scope of information has been narrowed at the end of TWO CENTURIES and almost a HALF, to the descendants of ONE SON, JAMES ALEXANDER. How fortunate that JOSEPH ALEXANDER, the old TANNER of NEW MUNSTER, left a last will and testament, which has been preserved, at least in part. From its musty pages we can read a bit more of this absorbing story. We can see that he had other sons, even though we can largely only surmise what became of their descendants. The treck Southward across VIRGINIA, where doubtless some tarried, and on into the CAROLINAS where the grandson JOHN McKNITT brought his tape and broadcloth to follow his "trade of a tailor", accompanied by at least one sister and several brothers, and no telling how many cousins and other relatives we can visualize more fully by reading between the lines of this old document, in which the grandsire named his several children, his relatives and some neighbors. The abstracted copy of the will, taken from Baldwin's Calendar of Maryland Wills, Volume 7, page 195, is as follows:

```
THE LAST WILL AND TESTAMENT OF JOSEPH ALEXANDER,
TANNER, OF NEW MUNSTER, CECIL COUNTY,
                MARYLAND.

Dated December 13, 1726.
Proved March 9, 1730.

To son in law:   ELIAS ALEXANDER.
To daughter:     SOPHIA ALEXANDER.
To son:          FRANCIS ALEXANDER.
To daughter:     JANE MULEY.
To daughter:     ABIGAIL CLAPAN.
To son:          JAMES ALEXANDER ( residue ).

Witnesses to the will:
                 OWEN O'DANIEL
                 ANNE TAYLOR
                 JOHN DAIL
                 JOHN McKNIGHT.
```

The witness JOHN McKNIGHT (sometimes McKNITT) was the brother of the wife of JOSEPH ALEXANDER, who was ABIGAIL McKNIGHT.

JAMES ALEXANDER, the son and residuary legatee, married his cousin, MARGARET McKNIGHT, a daughter of the witness JOHN McKNIGHT. She was the mother of JOHN McKNITT ALEXANDER, one of the signers of the "Mecklenburg Declaration".

As to the descendants of FRANCIS ALEXANDER, the son, and ELIAS ALEXANDER, called the "son in law" in the will of the old tanner, JOSEPH ALEXANDER, in 1726, the record is neither absolutely clear or positive. What we do have tending to identify the progeny of these two will be found in a later paragraph, on the next page.

Knowing somewhat of human nature and the customs that prevailed among the Scotch Irish families of the period when JOSEPH ALEXANDER must have first come to MARYLAND and settled at NEW MUNSTER and set up his tan yard, is not a wild probability that he was not alone among the members of his own family when he came. His brother WILLIAM ALEXANDER, who seems to have settled on the Eastern Shore in SOMERSET COUNTY, probably came over about the same time, and it is not improbable that one or more other brothers of JOSEPH came with him and settled in CECIL COUNTY. Two of these may have been the MARTIN ALEXANDER and SAMUEL ALEXANDER who were living in CECIL COUNTY on APRIL 23, 1728, both of whom witnessed the will of JOHN HOLTHAM of Cecil County on that date. We can only speculate as to their identity. They all perhaps left descendants and since many of the ALEXANDERS appeared in the CAROLINAS and in VIRGINIA in the generations following, doubtless some of them belonged to these other brothers or near relatives. Constant research in time may yield up interesting identities.

JOHN McKNIGHT. That there was a family of McKNIGHTS who came from the vicinity of LONDONDERRY and settled in CECIL COUNTY, MARYLAND, with JOSEPH ALEXANDER and his family there is no question. They may have pronounced the name McKNITT, and it is certain that JOHN McKNITT ALEXANDER so spelled and pronounced it. But that it was spelled McKNIGHT there can be little question, either, for it was so written wherever found on the records. These McKNIGHTS came to parts of VIRGINIA and remained for a time, and then to the CAROLINAS, and REV. JAMES McKNIGHT was a very early Presbyterian Minister in MECKLENBURG COUNTY, where he left descendants, who intermarried with several of the older families of the County. We are impressed with the idea that there was no distinction, save in the pronunciation, between these persons, and that the REV. JAMES McKNIGHT was of the same family as JOHN McKNIGHT of Cecil County, Maryland, whose sister ABIGAIL married JOSEPH ALEXANDER and was the grandmother of JOHN McKNITT ALEXANDER.

JAMES ALEXANDER, the son of JOSEPH, whose will appears on the preceding page, married MARGARET McKNIGHT, the daughter of JOHN McKNIGHT, the witness, as his FIRST WIFE. By this marriage he had NINE children. After the death of MARGARET McKNIGHT, he married as his second wife ABIGAIL (her last name unknown) and they had FIVE CHILDREN. By the will of JOSEPH ALEXANDER it will be ascertained that JAMES ALEXANDER had a sister ABIGAIL, who was named for her mother, ABIGAIL McKNIGHT, and the chances are that the second wife, as well as the first, was a cousin. This implies as well as suggests that she may have been an ALEXANDER, or another ABIGAIL McKNIGHT, and if the former, that she was the daughter of a brother of JOSEPH ALEXANDER, the tanner.

The will of JAMES ALEXANDER is on record in ELKTON, MARYLAND (Cecil County). It is dated June 17, 1772; proved July 15, 1779, the year of the maker's death. His second wife ABIGAIL and all his children by his two marriages are named in his will. That the testator had acquired lands in MECKLENBURG COUNTY, N. C. appears from the will. At the time the will was written several of his children were living in MECKLENBURG and had been there for twenty years or more. Following herewith is a list of the children:

1. THEOPHILUS ALEXANDER.
2. EDITH ALEXANDER
3. KEZIAH ALEXANDER
4. HEZEKIAH ALEXANDER
5. EZEKIEL ALEXANDER
6. JEMIMAH ALEXANDER
7. AMOS ALEXANDER
8. JOHN McKNITT ALEXANDER
9. MARGARET ALEXANDER
----
10. ELIZABETH ALEXANDER
11. ABIGAIL ALEXANDER
12. MARGARET ALEXANDER
13. JOSIAH ALEXANDER
14. EZEKIEL ALEXANDER.

Since the list shows two EZEKIELS and two named MARGARET, it is apparent that the first ones so named had died at the birth of the second ones.

1. THEOPHILUS ALEXANDER married CATHERINE. He died in CECIL COUNTY, MARYLAND in 1668 & his widow and children came to MECKLENBURG COUNTY, N. C. He was the father of REV. JOSEPH ALEXANDER one time Minister of SUGAR CREEK CHURCH, who established a famous school on BULLOCK'S CREEK in YORK COUNTY, S. C. afterwards. For children of THEOPHILUS see page 332 of these notes.

6. JEMIMAH ALEXANDER married THOMAS SHARPE. They are said to have married in CECIL COUNTY, MARYLAND. See a later note on this family.

4. HEZEKIAH ALEXANDER was a "signer" of the MECKLENBURG DECLARATION OF INDEPENDENCE.

8. JOHN McKNITT ALEXANDER was also a "signer" of the MECKLENBURG DECLARATION, and is said to have been the SECRETARY OF THE CONVENTION. He married JANE BAIN in 1762, on a trip he had made for that purpose to PHILADELPHIA. He settled in what is now MECKLENBURG before it was set apart as a County, lived in the HOPEWELL CHURCH section, and raised a large and interesting family. A list of his children and grand-children are set out on page 323 of these notes.

FRANCIS ALEXANDER, BROTHER, and ELIAS ALEXANDER, THE BROTHER IN LAW
OF JAMES ALEXANDER, FATHER OF JOHN McKNITT ALEXANDER.

DR. J. B. ALEXANDER in his HISTORY OF MECKLENBURG COUNTY, says that HEZEKIAH and JOHN Mc-KNITT ALEXANDER were brothers, while ABRAHAM, ADAM, CHARLES and EZRA ALEXANDER were their cousins. If they were FULL FIRST COUSINS, and the JOSEPH ALEXANDER WILL can be relied upon, these four "cousins" are bound to have been the sons of FRANCIS ALEXANDER mentioned in the will. The term "son in law" applied to ELIAS ALEXANDER by JOSEPH in his will, at that day and time (1726) usually, but not always, denominated a "step-son" suggesting that the person named was a son of the wife, but not of the testator, by a former marriage. In regard to this matter, the compiler has reached the conclusion, based entirely upon suggestive conditions and the customs which then obtained among these ancient families, that MARGARET McKNITT (or McKNIGHT) the second wife of JAMES ALEXANDER, was the WIDOW, MARGARET ALEXANDER, sister of ABIGAIL (the first wife) and daughter of of JOHN McKNIGHT, and that there was a son by this first marriage named ELIAS ALEXANDER (mentioned in JOSEPH ALEXANDER'S will in 1726) who was not only a son in law (step-son) of JOSEPH, but who was also a nephew of the testator, Margaret's first husband having been a brother of JOSEPH, whose name is lost in antiquity. Thus, ELIAS ALEXANDER, while not a brother of FRANCIS and JAMES ALEXANDER, was their "double first cousin" an a half brother of their father's children by his second marriage. ELIAS, therefore, had legitimate claims to a right in the ALEXANDER family circle. That his children came with the other ALEXANDERS to MECKLENBURG there is no sort of doubt.

Thus by deduction, following DR. J. B. ALEXANDER, it would appear that FRANCIS ALEXANDER, brother of JAMES ALEXANDER, was the father of:

1. ABRAHAM ALEXANDER
2. ADAM ALEXANDER
3. CHARLES ALEXANDER
4. EZRA ALEXANDER

These four were "cousins" of JOHN McKNITT ALEXANDER and HEZEKIAH ALEXANDER. Every one of these six ALEXANDERS were "signers" of the Mecklenburg Declaration of Independence, and if the four named were sons of FRANCIS ALEXANDER, then all SIX OF THEM were grandsons of JOSEPH ALEXANDER, the CECIL COUNTY, Maryland TANNER, who left the will in 1726. According to Dr. J. B. Alexander, also, 1. ABRAHAM ALEXANDER had a son named ELIAS (see page 323) though this statement does not agree with ABRAHAM'S will.

1. ABRAHAM ALEXANDER lived in SUGAR CREEK DISTRICT, near the town of CHARLOTTE. According to his tombstone inscription in the Sugar Creek graveyard (NO. 2), ABRAHAM ALEXANDER died in 1786, and therefore his name does not appear on the 1790 census, but the census of that year does show an ELIAS ALEXANDER, JR. married and with two children, living in that community in 1790; also DORCAS, the widow of ABRAHAM, with four sons and two daughters still living at home. Also an ELIJAH ALEXANDER, DAVID, DANIEL, EZEKIEL, JR., CAPT. THOMAS, DR. JAMES, JOHN and WILLIAM, as well as CAPTAIN ANDREW, EZEKIAH and others. See page 358.

On pages 413 to 421 of these notes will be found an account of all of the supposed FOUR sons of FRANCIS ALEXANDER, who signed the DECLARATION, as well as of JOHN McKNITT and HEZEKIAH ALEXANDER, sons of his brother JAMES ALEXANDER.

ELIJAH ALEXANDER OF SUGAR CREEK

The writer's attention has been called to the contents of a "leaf from an old family BIBLE" on pages 596-597 of the Joseph Habersham Chapt. D. A. R, Vol. 2, giving the names of the children of an ELIJAH ALEXANDER, (born May 13, 1772) in Mecklenburg County, N. C., whose wife was SARAH, (born in 1770). This man was not old enough to have been the ELIJAH ALEXANDER of the 1790 census of Sugar Creek, but he could have been a son of that one. According to this old record he had the following children:

1. FANNIE ALEXANDER (b. 1792) m. JOHN PRICE.
2. WILLIAM ALEXANDER (b. 1794) m. HANNAH WATSON.
3. DANIEL ALEXANDER m. NANCY ROE.
4. GARLAND ALEXANDER (b. 1799) m. SWAFFORD.
5. FOUNTAIN ALEXANDER (b. 1801) m. WATSON.
6. ELIZABETH ALEXANDER (b. 1804) m. HARDEN PRICE.
7. ELIJAH ALEXANDER (b. 1809) m. ELIZABETH STEELE
8. SARAH ALEXANDER (b. 1812) m. ISAAC CANNON.
9. PLEASANT ALEXANDER (b. 1807) m. LYCENE NORTON.

The children of PLEASANT ALEXANDER and his wife are also given on the sheet, and included among them is a daughter LAURA ALEXANDER who married JAMES STEELE. These intermarriages with the STEELE FAMILY harks back to the will of JOHN GARNER, of CECIL COUNTY, MARYLAND, an abstract of which is shown on page 518 of these notes and suggests that the ELIJAH of this record certainly belonged SOMEWHERE on the family chart of the CECIL COUNTY, MARYLAND ALEXANDERS.

Appended, however, to the record of ELIJAH ALEXANDER, given immediately above, is a footnote which says:

"Ancestors of this ELIJAH ALEXANDER came from VIRGINIA to MECKLENBURG COUNTY, NORTH CAROLINA, and from there moved down into SOUTH CAROLINA.

THE ALEXANDERS OF MECKLENBURG IN THE EIGHTEENTH CENTURY

As shown by the ancient records.

AARON ALEXANDER	ELIAS ALEXANDER	JOHN RAMSEY ALEXANDER
ABIGAIL ALEXANDER	ELIJAH ALEXANDER	JOSEPH ALEXANDER, REV.
ABRAHAM ALEXANDER	EZEKIAH ALEXANDER	JOSEPH McKNITT ALEXANDER
ADAM ALEXANDER	EZEKIEL ALEXANDER	JOSIAH ALEXANDER
AMOS ALEXANDER	EZRA ALEXANDER	MARGARET McKNITT ALEXANDER
ALLEN ALEXANDER SR.	FRANCIS ALEXANDER	MATTHEW ALEXANDER
ALLEN ALEXANDER JR.	GEORGE ALEXANDER	MOSES ALEXANDER
ANDREW ALEXANDER	HELENA ALEXANDER	NATHANIEL ALEXANDER
ARTHUR ALEXANDER	HEZEKIAH ALEXANDER	PHINEAS ALEXANDER
BENJAMIN ALEXANDER SR.	ISAAC ALEXANDER	SOPHIA ALEXANDER
BENJAMIN ALEXANDER JR.	JAMES ALEXANDER	STEPHEN ALEXANDER
CATHERINE ALEXANDER	JAMES McKNITT ALEXANDER	THOMAS ALEXANDER, DR.
CHARLES ALEXANDER	JAMES ALEXANDER, DR.	THEOPHILUS ALEXANDER
DANIEL ALEXANDER	JOAB ALEXANDER	THOMAS ALEXANDER, MAJ.
DAVID ALEXANDER	JOEL ALEXANDER	WILLIAM ALEXANDER
DORCAS ALEXANDER	JOHN McKNITT ALEXANDER	ZEBULON ALEXANDER

THE ALEXANDERS OF MECKLENBURG IN THE TWENTIETH CENTURY

200 Years later, as shown by the Charlotte TELEPHONE DIRECTORY

A. E. ALEXANDER, 1827 N. Harrill.
A. H. ALEXANDER, Derita Springs.
A. L. ALEXANDER, MRS. 807 N. Pine.
A. T. ALEXANDER, Providence Road.
ALBERT L. ALEXANDER, 1705 N. Allen.
ALVA E. ALEXANDER, 1812 Beverly Drive.
ANSLEY Q. ALEXANDER, Sharon ln
B. T. ALEXANDER, 2300 Vail Ave.
B. H. ALEXANDER, MRS. 420 Cherokee Rd.
C. J. ALEXANDER, 1833 Mecklenburg Ave.
C. W. ALEXANDER, 1612 Kenilworth Ave.
CARL L. ALEXANDER, Sharon Road.
CHARLES L. ALEXANDER, MRS. 1035 Queen's Rd.
CORA B. ALEXANDER, MRS. Camel Rd.
CYRUS ALEXANDER, MRS. 1422 McCall.
D. P. ALEXANDER, 1228 Enderly Road.
E. A. ALEXANDER, DR. 103½ South Tryon.
E. D. ALEXANDER, 210 W. 11th St.
E. U. ALEXANDER, Providence Road.
Ed. ALEXANDER, Providence Road.
ELIHUE ALEXANDER, 1203 Oaklawn Ave.
ELIZABETH ALEXANDER, MISS, York Road.
ETTA ALEXANDER, A. E. Boundary.
EULIE L. ALEXANDER, 709 East 11th St.
F. D. ALEXANDER, 927 Parkwood Ave.
F. D. ALEXANDER, 2146 Sherwood Ave.
F. T. ALEXANDER, 1104 South Mint.
FRANK W. ALEXANDER, Providence Road.
GEORGE C. ALEXANDER, 1401 Plaza.
H. C. ALEXANDER, 720 BERKLEY Ave.
H. Y. ALEXANDER, 1021 E. Worthington Av.
HENRY ALEXANDER, 2427 Crescent Ave.
EUGENE J. ALEXANDER, DR. 328 Flint.
J. F. ALEXANDER, MRS. 208 W. Bland.
J. H. ALEXANDER, MRS. 2107 Sherwood Av.
J. K. A. ALEXANDER, 213 Latta Arc.
J. LEWIS ALEXANDER, Rocky River Rd.
J. O. ALEXANDER, 229 South Cedar.
JACKSON C. ALEXANDER 521 E.Worthington.
JAMES C. ALEXANDER, Salisbury Road.
JAMES E. ALEXANDER, 2025 Wilmore Drv.E.
JAMES L. ALEXANDER, 1813 Tippah Ave.
JAMES M. ALEXANDER, DR. 314 Fenton Pl.
JAMES R. ALEXANDER, DR. 1030 Arosa Ave.
JNO. B. ALEXANDER, 509 Clement Ave.
JOHN D. ALEXANDER, 344 N. Caswell Road.
K. O. ALEXANDER, 621 Cherry.
L. LEON ALEXANDER, 1515 Kenilworth Ave.

ION ALEXANDER, MRS. 1048 East 7th St.
L. S. ALEXANDER, 716 Grandin Road.
LEE A. ALEXANDER, 151 Jewell
LUCILE M. ALEXANDER, MISS, 525 N. Church.
M. C. ALEXANDER, MRS. 117 West Park Ave.
M. EDWARD ALEXANDER, Steele Creek Road.
M. G. ALEXANDER, 1912 N. Harrill.
MARGIE ALEXANDER, 308 North Pine.
MYRTLE E. ALEXANDER, 2208 Belvedere Ave.
N. S. ALEXANDER, Hickory Grove Road.
NELLIE LAW ALEXANDER, MRS., Paw Creek.
P. K. ALEXANDER, 229 South Cedar.
PETER D. ALEXANDER, 1542 Jefferson Ave.
R. F. ALEXANDER, Salisbury Road.
R. L. ALEXANDER, Providence Road.
R. M. ALEXANDER, Statesville Road.
R. O. ALEXANDER, MRS., 309 E. Park Ave.
R. W. ALEXANDER, Mallard Creek Road.
RAYMOND C. ALEXANDER, Tuckaseege Road.
REID ALEXANDER, 924 Peachtree.
ROBERT B. ALEXANDER, 135 Circle Ave.
RUSSELL ALEXANDER, 212 Mill Road.
S. A. ALEXANDER, 2115 Central Ave.
S. B. ALEXANDER, 250 Cherokee Road.
S. I. ALEXANDER, 517 Belmont Ave.
S. M. ALEXANDER, 2838 Plaza Road.
SPRINGS R. ALEXANDER, 1437 E. 7TH ST.
THOMAS ALEXANDER, 2248 Colony Road.
THOMAS W. ALEXANDER, 309 Hempstead Ct.
UHIMAN S. ALEXANDER, 324 Ridgewood Ave.
V. S. ALEXANDER, 2621 Tuckaseege Road.
VIOLET G. ALEXANDER, MISS, 228 E. Blvd.
VIRGINIA ALEXANDER, MISS, 2014 Belvedere
W. A. ALEXANDER, 616 E. Worthington Ave.
W. C. ALEXANDER, 1906 Camp Green Blvd.
W. D. ALEXANDER, 2249 Croydon Road.
W. G. ALEXANDER, 2726 Marston Road.
W. H. ALEXANDER, 2005 Ashland Ave.
W. H. ALEXANDER, Beatty Ford Road.
W. L. ALEXANDER, 428 E. Boulivard.
W. S. ALEXANDER, MRS. 1519 Fairview Ave.
W. SUTTON ALEXANDER, 257 Hillside Ave.
WALTER L. ALEXANDER, 307 Hillside Ave.
WILSON ALEXANDER, 2626 Shenandoah Ave.
WYATT H. ALEXANDER, 2125 Kirkwood Ave.
Z. ALEXANDER, 517 South Caldwell.
Z. ALEXANDER, JR., 628 Baldwin Ave.
ALEXANDER'S STORE. Lawyer's Road.

NOTE: It is possible some on this list are "colored folks". We can't tell.

THE SHARPE FAMILY OF MECKLENBURG

THE SHARPE FAMILY of MECKLENBURG COUNTY, NORTH CAROLINA, was allied by blood and marriage with the ALEXANDERS, CALDWELLS and POLKS, and the first SHARPE to arrive in AMERICA came on the ill-fated "VIRGINIA MERCHANT", bound for JAMESTOWN and loaded with many emigrants. In January, 1650 it was driven by a storm, and foundered among the islands of the CHISOTEAGUE BAY on the Atlantic coast of Maryland and Virginia. Upon one of those islands, adjacent to what is now SOMERSET and WORCESTER COUNTIES, Col. Norwood, Francis Morryson, William Stevens and perhaps WILLIAM SHARPE landed and from there found their way by use of a guide to the home of ARGALL YARDLEY, and later to the plantation of Col. Littleton, in ACCOMAC COUNTY, VIRGINIA.

COL. WILLIAM STEVENS and WILLIAM SHARPE later settled on POCOMOKE RIVER and DIVIDING CREEK in SOMERSET where through several generations they and their descendants were neighbors of the CALDWELLS, POLKS and ALEXANDERS. It was this COL. WILLIAM STEVENS, who had lived in ACCOMAC COUNTY, VIRGINIA several years, who addressed the letter to the Presbytery of LAGAN in IRELAND asking for young ministers to be sent to VIRGINIA, which resulted in the coming to that settlement of REV. FRANCIS MACKEMIE, and later JOHN HENRY, JOHN HAMPTON and JOHN THOMSON, an account of whom has been heretofore given in these notes.

WILLIAM SHARPE, the neighbor of COL. STEVENS, was the father of DR. PETER SHARPE, whose will was proven in CALVERT COUNTY, May 28, 1672, who left to his son, another WILLIAM SHARP and his heirs certain lands and properties of his estate in TALBOT COUNTY on TUCKAHOE CREEK or River. The PETER SHARPE who on April 28, 1718, in TALBOT COUNTY, witnessed the will of ELIZABETH EVINS with MARY ALEXANDER and ALICE FOSTER, was perhaps a great grandson of WILLIAM SHARPE of SOMERSET COUNTY. From TALBOT COUNTY the SHARPES and the ALEXANDERS pushed on North across the SASSAFRAS RIVER to the "forks of the Elk" and the Bohemia River into CECIL COUNTY, MARYLAND, where, in 1749 THOMAS SHARP died and left a will, in which he named the following children:

1. WALTER SHARP
2. THOMAS SHARP
3. JAMES SHARP
4. HANNAH SHARP
5. SARAH SHARP
6. JOSEPH SHARP
7. SAMUEL SHARP

and sons in law JAMES SMITH and DAVID WHERRY.

The compiler is indebted to the REV. E. M. SHARP, pastor of the M. E. Church, at ABERDEEN, MISSISSIPPI, for an abstract of the will of the above THOMAS SHARP and the list of his children, Rev. Sharp being one of the descendants of this family. To the same source we are indebted also for a list of the children of the two sons 2. THOMAS and 3. JAMES.

2. THOMAS SHARP married 6. JEMIMAH ALEXANDER, daughter of JAMES ALEXANDER and his first wife MARGARET McKNIGHT. They were married in CECIL COUNTY, MARYLAND, where their children, WILLIAM, JOHN, JAMES, JOSEPH and SAMUEL SHARPE were born. HON. WILLIAM SHARPE, the oldest son, was born in CECIL COUNTY, MARYLAND, December 13, 1742. (Congressional Directory p. 989). 2. THOMAS SHARP died in CECIL COUNTY, MARYLAND, but his widow and their children, came to MECKLENBURG COUNTY, NORTH CAROLINA and settled.

3. JAMES SHARPE, brother of 2. THOMAS also came to MECKLENBURG COUNTY and settled sometime after 1750 perhaps, at about the same time his brother's family and his kinsmen the ALEXANDERS came there. REV. DR. SHARP has furnished the following as a list of his children, and it is very interesting:

10. EZEKIEL SHARP m. CATHERINE ALEXANDER
11. JOHN SHARP m. MARTHA YOUNG
12. JAMES SHARP m. RACHEL CANNON
13. ISABELLA SHARP m. REV. MR. PRICE.
14. PRISCILLA SHARP m. LEWIS JETTON
15. SARAH SHARP died young.

The mother of this last list of children and the wife of 3. JAMES SHARP was perhaps MARGARET ALEXANDER, a sister or half-sister of JEMIMAH who married 2. THOMAS SHARP. CATHERINE ALEXANDER, who married EZEKIEL SHARPE, was the daughter of THEOPHILUS ALEXANDER, brother of JEMIMAH and MARGARET and the oldest son of JAMES ALEXANDER and MARGARET McKNIGHT. MARGARET was also the sister of REV. JOSEPH ALEXANDER, the second pastor of SUGAR CREEK CHURCH.

HON. WILLIAM SHARPE, SON OF THOMAS SHARPE

In 1779 he was a member of the Continental Congress from North Carolina, and he and his sons took a leading part in the American Revolution. He married RUTH REESE, daughter of DAVID REESE, the signer. The mother of RUTH REESE and the wife of DAVID was RUTH POLK, who belonged to the POLK FAMILY of MECKLENBURG and of SOMERSET COUNTY, MARYLAND. HON. WILLIAM SHARP died in 1818 in the 77th year of his age, leaving a widow and twelve children. They were:

20. MATILDA SHARPE m. WILLIAM W. ERVIN.
21. RUTH SHARPE m. COL. ANDREW CALDWELL
22. THOMAS SHARPE (Rev. Soldier)
23. WILLIAM SHARPE (Rev. Soldier)

24. BETSY, 25. DAVID, 26. ELAM, 27. MARCUS, 28. CYNTHIA, 29. ELVIRA m. CALDWELL, 30. EDWIN & CARLOS.

THE TWO DISTINGUISHED DAVID CALDWELLS WHO LIVED IN NORTH CAROLINA

There were two noted persons by the name of DAVID CALDWELL who made their homes in early NORTH CAROLINA.

One of these, the REV. DAVID CALDWELL, of GUILFORD, married RACHEL CARIGHEAD and was the son in law of REV. ALEXANDER CRAIGHEAD the first pastor of ROCKY RIVER and SUGAR CREEK CHURCH. The other DAVID CALDWELL was the distinguished son of COL. ANDREW CALDWELL who married RUTH SHARPE, the daughter of WILLIAM SHARPE, mentioned on the preceding page of these notes.

HON. DAVID FRANKLIN CALDWELL, son of ANDREW CALDWELL and his wife RUTH SHARPE was born in 1792 (Rumple's Rowan County, p. 223), and attended the University at Chapel Hill, after which he studied law in the office of HON. ARCHIBALD HENDERSON at Salisbury. He was the brother of HON. JOSEPH P. CALDWELL, of IREDELL and DR. ELAM CALDWELL, of Lincolnton, N. C. DAVID FRANKLIN CALDWELL was Judge of the Superior Court of North Carolina, to which position he was elected in 1844. He was twice married. His first wife was FANNY ALEXANDER, daughter of WILLIAM LEE ALEXANDER, who had married a sister of HON. ARCHIBALD HENDERSON. His children by the first marriage were WILLIAM LEE, ARCHIBALD H., ELIZABETH RUTH, RICHARD ALEXANDER, JR. JULIUS ANDREW, and FANNY McCAY. His second wife was REBECCA NESBIT, the widow of MATTHEW TROY. The second wife is buried at the Presbyterian Church in Salisbury.

The family genealogists have been unable to trace any relationship whatever between the two families of these two DAVID CALDWELLS, and while this writer must admit his inability to present an absolute record of the connecting links he entertains no doubt whatsoever of their being of the same family.

We have already shown in these notes how and when the CALDWELL FAMILY lived in SOMERSET COUNTY, Maryland, and that they were associated with the ALEXANDERS and the POLKS and SHARPES on the "Eastern Shore" of MARYLAND. By following the RECORDS that have been preserved of these Eastern Shore families, we trace the CALDWELLS on up the Eastern Shore through TALBOT, QUEEN ANNE and other counties into CECIL COUNTY in the "forks of the Elk river." The McCONNELL family, which became numerous in IREDELL and MECKLENBURG COUNTY, N. C., lived in QUEEN ANNE County, Md., and JAMES McCONNELL remained there until after 1790, when he appears on the Census of that year; and in the same year the names of DAVID CALDWELL and JAMES CALDWELL appear there on the same list as neighbors of the McCONNELL family. AN ANDREW CALDWELL of this family married MARGARET MOORE, whose descendants we have already discussed, and HUGH McCONNELL married MARY CALDWELL, of this same family. Both the MOORES - some of them - and the SHARPES lived in SOMERSET, and also in CECIL COUNTY, including an ANDREW MOORE and his brother JOHN, who are mentioned in the will of EDWARD COLLIER in SOMERSET, August 20, 1688; (Md/ Cal. of Wills Vol. 2, p. 36), while RICHARD MOORE was witness to the will of JOHN DAVIS in QUEEN ANNE'S COUNTY in 1710; (Md. Cal. of Wills Vol 3.); and THOMAS MOORE and WILLIAM MOORE were witnesses to the will of WALTER NEWMAN in CECIL COUNTY, MARYLAND, Nov. 20, 1728 (Md. Cal. of Wills Vol. 6, p. 151).

WILLIAM SHARPE, descendant of the WILLIAM SHARPE of ACCOMAC COUNTY, VA. and SOMERSET COUNTY, MARYLAND, (WILLIAM SHARPE'S name appears on the TYTHE LIST of NORTHAMPTON COUNTY, Virginia in the year 1666 - which was then called ACCOMAC) married a REESE, grand-daughter of a POLK from SOMERSET, and his mother was JEMIMAH ALEXANDER, a grand-daughter of JOSEPH ALEXANDER, of CECIL COUNTY, MARYLAND; his daughter RUTH SHARPE, married COL. ANDREW CALDWELL, of the CALDWELL family of SOMERSET and CECIL COUNTY, and had a DAVID CALDWELL.

The other DAVID CALDWELL married RACHEL CRAIGHEAD, a grand-daughter of REV. THOMAS CRAIGHEAD, a contemporary of REV. JOHN THOMSON, JOHN HENRY and REV. JOHN HAMPTON, who was one of the leaders of the New Castle Presbytery, which met "at the branches of the Elk" in CECIL COUNTY, MARYLAND, March 15, 1725/6, and who had doubtless often preached to the EWINGS, ALEXANDERS, CALDWELLS and others at NEW MUNSTER and other places on the "Eastern Shore". These intermarriages and early associations write a plain story of the intimate connections between the earlier DAVID CALDWELL, and the later one, who descended from the SHARPES and ALEXANDERS. They were Cousins, several degrees removed, and also belonged to and were cousins of the CALDWELLS OF CUB CREEK, some of whom also came to MECKLENBURG, ROWAN and IREDELL, drawn there by the magnet of consanguinity.

REV. ALEXANDER CRAIGHEAD

Rev. ALEXANDER CRAIGHEAD, save for REV. JOHN THOMSON, who died in MECKLENBURG in 1753, was the first resident pastor of a Church in that settlement. He was first called to preach to the Presbyterian Congregation of ROCKY RIVER, and then to SUGAR CREEK, which he seems to have organized. He was the son of REV. THOMAS CRAIGHEAD, who in turn was apparently the son of REV. ROBERT CRAIGHEAD, one of the thirteen ejected ministers, from the Presbytery of LAGEN in Northern Ireland, from whence sprang also JOHN HENRY and JOHN HAMPTON, of SOMERSET COUNTY, MARYLAND, and ROBERT WILSON, ancestor of REV. FRANCIS MAKEMIE, all heretofore mentioned.

DR. WILLIAM HENRY FOOTE, in his "SKETCHES OF NORTH CAROLINA" on page 183 has this to say about ALEXANDER CRAIGHEAD'S ancestry:

> The tradition in the family of Mr. CRAIGHEAD, was that his father and grandfather, and perhaps his ancestors further back, were ministers of the gospel strongly attached to the Church, and reputed as truly pious. A Mr. Thomas Craighead was among the first ministers of Donegal Presbytery, a native of Scotland, and ordained in IRELAND.

In all of the material the writer has accumulated about this early minister and patriot of MECKLENBURG COUNTY he is unable to find a clue to the name of the wife of ALEXANDER CRAIGHEAD. As to his children, Dr. Foote says, that he was the father of TWO SONS & SEVERAL DAUGHTERS. All we have been able to find are those named below. For these we are indebted to the "History of the Presbyterian Church in South Carolina", p. 331, Vol. 1:

1. REV. THOMAS CRAIGHEAD, Nashville, Tenn.
2. ROBERT CRAIGHEAD, Mecklenburg County, N. C. in 1790.
3. NANCY CRAIGHEAD married (1) REV. WILLIAM RICHARDSON,
   (2) GEORGE DUNLAP.
4. RACHEL CRAIGHEAD married REV. DAVID CAIDWELL.
5. MARGARET CRAIGHEAD married JOHN CARRUTH
6. MARY CRAIGHEAD married SAMUEL DUNLAP.
7. ELIZABETH CRAIGHEAD married ALEXANDER CRAWFORD.
8. JANE CRAIGHEAD married PATRICK CAIHOUN.

PATRICK CALHOUN, who married JANE CRAIGHEAD was the father of the celebrated South Carolina Statesman, JOHN CALDWELL CALHOUN, who, however, was his son by his second wife, MARTHA CALDWELL, the sister of MAJ. JOHN CALDWELL and the daughter of WILLIAM CALDWELL and his wife MARGARET PARKS. William Caldwell had died on CUBB CREEK in VIRGINIA in 1761, after which his widow and her children moved to NEWBERRY DISTRICT, South Carolina. DR. HOWE declares (p. 331) that while on a trip to ABBEVILLE DISTRICT, after the death of JANE CRAIGHEAD, his first wife, PATRICK CALHOUN fell in with the father of MARTHA CALDWELL, accompanied him home and married his daughter MARTHA. This was perhaps one of her brothers instead of her father, who was deceased at that time. By his first marriage to JANE CRAIGHEAD, Patrick Calhoun was brother in law to DAVID CALDWELL, the great minister and preacher, of GUILFORD COUNTY, while by his second marriage, he became the son in law of a son of JOHN CALDWELL, of CUB CREEK, Charlotte County, Virginia, who was the son of another ANDREW CALDWELL. In this connection see notes and chart on pages 452-453.

JOHN CARRUTH, another son in law of ALEXANDER CRAIGHEAD, having married his daughter MARGARET CRAIGHEAD, was the father of ELIZABETH CARRUTH, who became the wife of LAWSON HENDERSON, of LINCOLN COUNTY, whose son JAMES PINCKNEY HENDERSON was the first GOVERNOR OF TEXAS; thus ALEXANDER CRAIGHEAD was the great grandfather of JAMES PINCKNEY HENDERSON.

NANCY CRAIGHEAD and her husband by her first marriage, REV. WILLIAM RICHARDSON, had no children. WILLIAM RICHARDSON DAVIE, the famous Carolina Statesman, was their "foster son" and the nephew of the minister. By her second marriage to GEORGE DUNLAP, Nancy became the mother of the following sons and daughters:

10. DR. DAVID DUNLAP, Charlotte, N. C.
11. GEORGE DUNLAP, of Anson County.
12. MRS. ANDREW CROCKETT
13. MRS. EDWARD CRAWFORD
14. MRS. RACHEL NEELY.

REV. THOMAS CRAIGHEAD married ELIZABETH BROWN. She was a daughter of REV. JOHN BROWN, of Virginia, a contemporary of ALEXANDER CRAIGHEAD. THOMAS CRAIGHEAD, according to the marker on his grave, was born in MECKLENBURG COUNTY, N. C. in 1750 (p. 78-9 Acklen's Tennessee Tombstone Records), which is a mistake, since at that time his parents were living in the vicinity of Staunton, Virginia, and had not moved to MECKLENBURG COUNTY. In fact MECKLENBURG had not then been established. They had one daughter, JANE CRAIGHEAD. If there were other children I have not been able to identify them. REV. THOMAS CRAIGHEAD is said to have performed the wedding ceremony for ANDREW JACKSON and his wife RACHEL (DONELSON) ROBARDS.

T H E   R E V.   W I L L I A M   R I C H A R D S O N

REV. WILLIAM RICHARDSON is buried at the old WAXHAW CHURCH cemetery. He was a contemporary of ALEXANDER CRAIGHEAD and held the installation services for him at ROCKY RIVER CHURCH, in MECKLENBURG COUNTY, N. C. on Sept. 27, 1758, which dates the arrival of DR. CRAIGHEAD into Mecklenburg territory, and shows that his son THOMAS (who was born in 1750) was NOT born in Mecklenburg, as stated on his marker in NASHVILLE, TENNESSEE. REV. RICHARDSON was from WHITEHAVEN, in ENGLAND, where he was born in 1729. For a time after coming to AMERICA, REV. RICHARDSON lived in the home of REV. SAMUEL DAVIES, and before 1758 he was in the WAXHAWS. His sister, MARY RICHARDSON, had married in ENGLAND, one ARCHIBALD DAVIE, and they were the parents of HON. WILLIAM RICHARDSON DAVIE, who after a brilliant career in the Revolution as a soldier, and in North Carolina as a statesman, settled in the Waxhaw Church section in his old age and died and is buried there, with the RICHARDSONS. HON. WILLIAM RICHARDSON DAVIE was present as a boy when the MECKLENBURG DECLARATION was signed at CHARLOTTE, N. C. on May 20, 1775, and preserved a copy of the resolutions as adopted for the use and benefit of posterity.

The wife of REV. WILLIAM RICHARDSON was NANCY CRAIGHEAD, daughter of REV. ALEXANDER CRAIGHEAD, and sister of the JANE CRAIGHEAD, the first wife of PATRICK CAIHOUN. REV. SAMUEL DAVIES, friend and mentor of REV. WILLIAM RICHARDSON, and of REV. JOHN THOMSON and HENRY PATILLO, so far as known, was not related to ARCHIBALD DAVIE or his son WILLIAM RICHARDSON DAVIE, but there was a certain ROBERT DAVIES, an elder in the WAXHAW CHURCH in 1758, who was probably a son or brother of the President of Princeton. With the RICHARDSON FAMILY at WAXHAW lived a certain ROBERT CARR, an uncle of WILLIAM RICHARDSON DAVIE, who had brought the latter over from ENGLAND to live with REV. RICHARDSON and his wife NANCY CRAIGHEAD, who were childless. ROBERT CARR was a Revolutionary soldier under his nephew (whose mother was Carr's sister). After young Davie came over from ENGLAND his parents came and also settled in the Waxhaw Church neighborhood. ARCHIBALD DAVIE and his wife MISS CARR had three children:

    1. HON. WILLIAM RICHARDSON DAVIE
    2. MARY DAVIE
    3. JOSEPH DAVIE

It is a matter of general history, of course, that after the revolution, HON. WILLIAM RICHARDSON DAVIE moved to North Carolina, where he married SARAH JONES, the daughter of GENERAL ALLEN JONES, of "Mount Gallant" in Northampton County.

(GEN. ALLEN JONES, father in law of WILLIAM RICHARDSON DAVIE, who was the foster son and nephew of REV. WILLIAM RICHARDSON, was the son of ROBIN (ROBERT JONES JR.) JONES and his wife SARAH COBBS, of VIRGINIA. MARTHA COBBS, sister of the mother of Gens. ALLEN and WILLIE JONES, married DUDLEY RICHARDSON. However, this compiler knows of no other relationship that may have existed between REV. WILLIAM RICHARDSON, born near WHITE HAVEN, ENGLAND in 1729, & DUDLEY RICHARDSON, of the old Maryland-Virginia family of RICHARDSONS, the great uncle of the wife of WILLIAM RICHARDSON DAVIE).

HON. WILLIAM RICHARDSON DAVIE and his wife SARAH JONES, of Northampton County, North Carolina were the parents of six children, as follows:

    10. HYDER ALI DAVIE m. ELIZABETH JONES
    11. MAJ. ALLEN JONES DAVIE
    12. SARAH DAVIE
    13. REBECCA DAVIE married DR. CHURCHILL JONES.
    14. MARY DAVIE married JOHN CROCKETT
    15. COL. FREDERICK WILLIAM DAVIE.

11. MAJ. ALLEN JONES DAVIE married MARY WALL, and they were the parents of two sons:

    16. ALLEN JONES DAVIE, JR. m. (2) ROSE NORWOOD
        of HALIFAX, NORTH CAROLINA.
    17. WILLIAM R. DAVIE married MISS McKINZIE, and
        they were parents of:

        CAPT. WILLIAM R. DAVIE, for many years a well known
        lawyer and State official in AUSTIN, TEXAS.

** THE ANCESTRY OF DAVID CROCKETT

Few people know that the ancestry of DAVID CROCKETT, known in the history of TEXAS as the "hero of the Alamo" lived in MECKLENBURG COUNTY, or that his forbears lived within the bounds of two old churches about which much has been said in these rambling notes, PROVIDENCE and the WAXHAW CHURCH.

DAVID CROCKETT was a descendant of the TANGIER ISLAND family of the name, some of whom lived in SOMERSET COUNTY, MARYLAND, from whence came the POLKS, CALDWELLS, SHARPES and ALEXANDERS, of MECKLENBURG. (See p. 428 of these notes). The will of RICHARD CROCKETT, of SOMERSET COUNTY, Maryland, was written February 28, 1726, and proved April 26, 1728. (Maryland Cal. of Wills Vol. 5, p. 115). The three sons named in that will were 1. JOHN CROCKETT, 2. ROBERT CROCKETT and RICHARD CROCKETT. Three other children were referred to but not mentioned by name.

It is believed that the second son, ROBERT CROCKETT, was the father of SAMUEL CROCKETT, who married ESTHER THOMSON, and ROBERT CROCKETT, who was the great grandfather of DAVID. ROBERT and SAMUEL CROCKETT were brothers, and lived for a time in that part of AUGUSTA COUNTY, VIRGINIA, from whence ALEXANDER CRAIGHEAD, came in 1755-58 to MECKLENBURG COUNTY, to take up his work at ROCKY RIVER and later at SUGAR CREEK. Some of the members of Rev. Craighead's flock settled in the Rocky River section and others within the bounds of PROVIDENCE, where REV. WILLIAM RICHARDSON took temporary supervision over them, until the coming of ROBERT HENRY, in 1765-7. Among the first elders in PROVIDENCE CHURCH were JOHN RAMSEY and ARCHIBALD CROCKETT.

See the following notes from FOOTE'S SKETCHES, p. 245.

    The first ministerial labors the settlement enjoyed (Providence), beside what they could receive from Mr. Carighead, were from the REV. WILLIAM RICHARDSON.
    The first elders in the church (Providence) were ANDREW RAY (Rea), ARCHIBALD CROCKETT, JOHN RAMSEY (p. 246) and AARON HOWIE.
    About this time (1766) MR. ROBERT HENRY, who gathered the Church on CUB CREEK, VIRGINIA, resolved, after ministering there for a number of years, to leave them, and an engagement was made for his services in these two congregations (Rocky River and Providence.)

JOHN RAMSEY, one of the first elders in PROVIDENCE CHURCH in MECKLENBURG, with ARCHIBALD CROCKETT, married MARGARET CROCKETT, the mother of ARCHIBALD and widow of ROBERT CROCKETT on the COW PASTURE in Augusta County, Virginia, and was the step father of ARCHIBALD and his brothers.

ROBERT CROCKETT, SAMUEL CROCKETT, ANDREW CROCKETT, WILLIAM CROCKETT and others were all brothers and sons of ROBERT CROCKETT, son of RICHARD CROCKETT, of SOMERSET COUNTY, Maryland. MARGARET CROCKETT, mother of ARCHIBALD and others, who married JOHN RAMSEY, was an ALEXANDER, from SOMERSET COUNTY, Maryland.

The children of ROBERT CROCKETT and his wife MARGARET ALEXANDER included the following:

1. JOHN CROCKETT, born in 1730. (Tombstone).
2. ARCHIBALD CROCKETT m. MARY ANN KING.
3. ALEXANDER CROCKETT
4. ANDREW CROCKETT
5. ROBERT CROCKETT
6. SAMUEL CROCKETT.

There were perhaps other children. After the death of ROBERT CROCKETT, the father, in about the year 1745-6, the mother MARGARET married JOHN RAMSEY, and in about 1758, she and her second husband and most of the sons, and daughters, if there were any, moved to MECKLENBURG COUNTY, N. C. They arrived there a little before, or at about the same time as REV. ALEXANDER CRAIGHEAD, and had perhaps been members of his church at NEW PROVIDENCE in what is now ROCKBRIDGE COUNTY. Also, some of the children of the other brothers of the elder ROBERT CROCKETT perhaps were included in the migration, some coming direct from PRINCE EDWARD COUNTY, where Robert's brother SAMUEL and his wife ESTHER THOMSON had lived for many years, together with WILLIAM CROCKETT another brother of SAMUEL. ANDREW CROCKETT, an uncle of this younger generation, with his wife MARGARET, were living in MECKLENBURG, N. C. as early as 1758, after the death of the elder ROBERT in AUGUSTA COUNTY, Va., as shown by the following deed:

ANDREW CROCKETT, and (wife) MARGARET, of MECKLENBURG COUNTY, N. C., with JOHN RAMSEY, sell lands on the Cow Pasture to JAMES CROCKETT. The land had been patented to ANDREW and MARGARET CROCKETT, Sept. 5, 1749. Still another ANDREW CROCKETT, probably the son of SAMUEL CROCKETT and ESTHER THOMSON witnessed a deed from the executors of JAMES PATTON in Augusta County, Va. in 1769.

ROBERT CROCKETT, son of ROBERT and MARGARET, and brother of ARCHIBALD, was living in MECKLENBURG COUNTY, N. C. in 1767, as shown by the following deed:

JAMES CROCKETT and MARTHA of AUGUSTA COUNTY, Va., and ROBERT CROCKETT and JANE (or JENNET) CROCKETT, sold 370 acres of land on the CALF PASTURE, to WILLIAM THOMSON. ROBERT and JENNETT were then living in MECKLENBURG COUNTY, N. C., August 18, 1767.

In 1742 both ROBERT CROCKETT and his brother ALEXANDER CROCKETT were members of the Company of CAPT. JOHN WILSON, of Augusta County, as shown by his muster roll. These citations are all on CHALKLEY'S AUGUSTA RECORDS, and could be multiplied, but are sufficient to establish the point of the origin of the MECKLENBURG CROCKETTS.

The CROCKETTS, when they moved to MECKLENBURG COUNTY, were already related to the ALEXANDER FAMILY, and perhaps with many other of the old families; certainly to the family of REV. JOHN THOMSON, perhaps in more ways than one, through SAMUEL who married ESTHER, and perhaps to some of the other THOMPSONS in AUGUSTA. It is remarkable to note how, when we go back to the place of their origin, in SOMERSET COUNTY, we discover the influences that impelled the formation of later alliances that arose in the course of their history.

THE KING AND THE HENRY FAMILY

REV. ROBERT HENRY, as the notes on the preceding page show, was engaged to serve as the first REGULAR PASTOR of PROVIDENCE, also serving the Congregation of STEELE CREEK (p. 390). REV. ROBERT HENRY was born and raised in SOMERSET COUNTY, from whence the CROCKETT ANCESTRY came, and was a son of REV. JOHN HENRY, contemporary, friend and associate of REV. JOHN THOMSON. The mother of REV. ROBERT HENRY was MARY KING, of SOMERSET COUNTY, a scion of whose family, WILLIAM KING early came to MECKLENBURG COUNTY, but to that part South or East of the CATAWBA, which afterwards became LINCOLN COUNTY. ARCHIBALD CROCKETT, son of ROBERT CROCKETT, married MARY ANN KING, daughter of WILLIAM KING, whose son HON. THOMAS KING, moved to HAWKINS COUNTY, TENNESSEE, and was one of the original organizing commissioners for that county. His sister's husband's son, and his own nephew JOHN CROCKETT, and several of his brothers, also moved to HAWKINS COUNTY, TENNESSEE.

See page 325 of these notes for an abstract of the will of ARCHIBALD CROCKETT, in which he left lands in HAWKINS COUNTY, TENNESSEE, to his son JOHN CROCKETT.

The following is from SHERRILLS "Annals of Lincoln Cour ' North Carolina:

"In his autobiography DAVID CROCKETT say   ` born in 1786, in Lincoln County. He was a son of JOHN CROCK..., a member of the Lincoln County (N. C.) Militia, during the period of the Revolution".

The last will and testament of WILLIAM KING, a near relative of the ROBERT HENRY, who ministered at PROVIDENCE and STEELE CREEK Church, will be found in Will Book D, page 138 of the records of MECKLENBURG COUNTY, N. C., dated Nov. 1, 1788. He was the great grandfather of the celebrated DAVID CROCKETT of Tennessee and Texas. He was a man of prominence and should have been, because he was perhaps a great grandson of ROBERT KING, who aided in the Rebellion against Lord Baltimore and aided materially in depriving that worthy of some of his power and influence in MARYLAND, one of his daughters, MARY, having married REV. JOHN HAMPTON, the collateral relative of COL. ANDREW HAMPTON, a great military figure in the annals of North Carolina, whose ancestry has so long puzzled the genealogists.

In this will, WILLIAM KING mentions his wife MARY ANN KING, and his four children:

1. ARCHIBALD CROCKETT
2. JOHN KING
3. ELIZABETH McCORKLE
4. WILLIAM McCULLOCH.

The EXECUTORS to this will were ARCHIBALD CROCKETT and JOHN KING. The witnesses were ELI (ELIJAH) CROCKETT, JOHN ELLIOTT and HENRY DOWNS. This HENRY DOWNS, of course, was formerly from AUGUSTA COUNTY, Virginia, and one of the signers of the MECKLENBURG DECLARATION of INDEPENDENCE.

It would be well to explain here that there were SEVERAL persons named DAVID CROCKETT in the history of the CROCKETT CLAN. It is not improbable that ARCHIBALD CROCKETT had an uncle named DAVID, among the sons of the first ROBERT CROCKETT from SOMERSET COUNTY, MARYLAND, and he in turn may have had a DAVID. One DAVID CROCKETT is buried in the old WAXHAW CEMETERY in what is now LANCASTER COUNTY, South Carolina. (See page 410), and on page 321, a DAVID CROCKETT and his wife ELIZABETH made deed to a JOSEPH GALBRAITH in Mecklenburg County in 1782. In this connection, in David Crockett's own autobiography, which if he did not actually write, he certainly sponsored in 1834, in detailing the various moves of his father, JOHN CROCKETT, over in that part of North Carolina, which is now TENNESSEE, he says, page 21:

"The next move my father made was to the mouth of COVE CREEK, where he and a man by the name of THOMAS GALBREATH undertook to build a mill in partnership", etc.

This item suggests an undoubted connection between DAVID the "hero" and the DAVID of the GALBREATH DEED in MECKLENBURG in 1782. The DAVID (who it has been claimed was the grandfather of the TEXAS DAVID) was dead at that time, and according to the tablet erected by the TENNESSEE HISTORICAL SOCIETY at ROGERSVILLE, "killed by the Indians". If a DAVID CROCKETT was killed by the Indians at the time claimed, although no Tennessee History mentions it, he was NOT the grandfather, but an UNCLE of our Texas DAVID, and a son of JOHN CROCKETT, the revolutionary soldier of LINCOLN COUNTY, North Carolina.

The DAVID CROCKETT and his wife ELIZABETH, of Mecklenburg (Deed on page 321 of these notes) was the DAVID who with JOSEPH, SAMUEL and ROBERT CROCKETT moved to GREENE COUNTY, GEORGIA, after the Revolution, where they took up lands, as witness these deeds:

APRIL 12, 1792: DAVID CROCKETT, for and in consideration of the sum of 20 lbs conveys to WALTER DEBT, lands granted to JOSEPH PANNELL, surveyed for WASHINGTON COUNTY, GA. Signed by DAVID CROCKETT and ELIZABETH (x) CROCKETT.

OCTOBER 1, 1792: JOEL BARNETT, of WILKES COUNTY, GA. and DAVID CROCKETT of the same County and State, parties: BARNETT sells to DAVID CROCKETT 287½ acres on the South Fork of SHOULDERBONE CREEK in GREENE County, adjoining the lands of WILLIAM BARNETT. Signed JOEL BARNETT and witnessed by WEST HARRIS, JAMES BROWN and H. MOUNGER.

The children of ARCHIBALD CROCKETT and his wife MARY, or MARY ANN KING (daughter of COL. WILLIAM KING) were DAVID, ROBERT, JOHN, JOSEPH, JAMES, ELI (ELIJAH), ELIAS and perhaps MARY. When ARCHIBALD CROCKETT made his will in 1804, several of his sons were then dead. DAVID and his wife may have been killed by the Indians; a supposition based on the fact that an administration of a DAVID is found on the records of WASHINGTON COUNTY, VIRGINIA, about 1880, which makes some reference to an interest in lands on the Holston.

JOHN CROCKETT, the son of ARCHIBALD, was the father of the famous DAVID CROCKETT, who, according to the Congressional Directory, which is usually correct, was

"Born at the mouth of LIMESTONE RIVER, in GREENE COUNTY, TENNESSEE, August 17, 1786,"

which, at the time of his birth, was then a part of the State of North Carolina. So after all, the statement that he was "born in North Carolina" is correct, technically speaking.

DAVID CROCKETT was a member of the U. S. Congress from Tennessee in the Twentieth and Twenty-First Congresses, and actually served from March 4, 1827 to March 3, 1821; he was re-elected again at the end of two years and served from March 4, 1833 to March 3, 1835, was defeated for re-election, told his constituents they could go to h....l, as he was "going to Texas."

JOHN CROCKETT was a brother of ARCHIBALD CROCKETT, and a nephew of SAMUEL CROCKETT, who married ESTHER THOMSON, daughter of REV. JOHN THOMSON, who died in MECKLENBURG in 1753. He lived in the WAXHAW SETTLEMENT near the old Church of that name, and is buried there. On his tombstone is this inscription: "JOHN CROCKETT died DEC. 16, 1800, aged 70 years and 5 Months." The name of his wife was MARGARET McCORKELL. She was probably a daughter of that JAMES McCORKELL, whom ARCHIBALD selected as his guardian, after his father's death in 1745-6 in Augusta County. These two deeds from the record are of interest here:

ARCHIBALD CROCKETT is witness to a deed from JOHN CROCKETT, son and heir of ROBERT CROCKETT to JAMES MOORE in Augusta County, Va. March 20, 1753.

ARCHIBALD CROCKETT and (wife) MARY (KING?) of ANSON COUNTY, N. C. and JOHN CROCKETT and (wife) MARGARET, deed to JAMES BEARD, 340 acres on COW PASTURE, corner JAMES MOORE. Witnessed by SAMUEL CROCKET. August 10, 1761.

And then these deeds in MECKLENBURG COUNTY - from the records there:

JAN. 6, 1770: Deed by JOHN CROCKETT and his wife MARGARET to WILLIAM MOORE (all of MECKLENBURG COUNTY), 160 acres on South side of WAXHAW CREEK, adjoining WILLIAM NUTT. Signed JOHN CROCKETT and MARGARET CROCKETT.

JAN. 4, 1771: WILLIAM McCORKLE and wife ESTHER to THOMAS PUSLEY 200 acres on North Fork of WAXHAW creek. WILLIAM McCORKLE and ESTHER McCORKLE. JOHN CROCKETT a witness.

There are many other deeds and entries could be shown except for lack of space in this work, which verify the observations made.

JOHN CROCKETT and his wife MARGARET McCORKELL were the parents at least of the children named below:

1. ELIJAH CROCKETT (b. Oct. 6, 1757).
2. JOHN CROCKETT (b. 1764)
3. ANDREW CROCKETT (b. 1769)

1. ELIJAH CROCKETT, son of JOHN CROCKETT and his wife MARGARET McCORKELL, married MARY DAVIE, the sister of HON. WILLIAM RICHARDSON DAVIE, the distinguished and famous CAROLINA STATESMAN and REVOLUTIONARY SOLDIER. According to an old REGISTER kept by their son, ROBERT CARR CROCKETT, ancestor of a numerous family of TEXAS CROCKETTS, a photostat of which is in possession of the compiler, they had the following children:

10. MARY CROCKETT b. Feb. 24, 1784.
11. JOHN CROCKETT b. Feb. 28, 1785.
12. ARCHIBALD DAVIE CROCKETT b. May 22, 1786.
13. MARGARET McCORKLE CROCKETT b. Oct. 2, 1787.
14. WILLIAM CROCKETT b. March 22, 1789.
15. ANN CROCKETT born Jan. 11, 1791.
16. ROBERT CARR CROCKETT B. June 27, 1792.
17. SARAH CROCKETT b. April 3, 1794.
18. BETSY CROCKETT b. August 11, 1795.
19. ELIJAH CROCKETT b. Jan. 23, 1797.

16. ROBERT CARR CROCKETT, named of course, for the gallant ROBERT CARR, who served in the command of his nephew WILLIAM RICHARDSON DAVIE, married, according to this old register, ANGEROSIA RICHARDSON. In all of the accounts that have been written of REV. WILLIAM RICHARDSON he appears to have had no children, or so far as recorded, any brothers or sons of the name. Yet, ROBERT CARR CROCKETT, a son of his niece MARY DAVIE, married a RICHARDSON. We can only surmise as to the identity of her parents. She died in TEXAS May 30, 1886 and is buried in an old cemetery at FLATONIA, TEXAS among her grandchildren and children. The compiler thinks she was either a grand-daughter or a grand niece of REV. WILLIAM RICHARDSON, who must surely have had either a son or a brother, about whom the Historians and what they have written are silent. ANGEROSIA did not "just happen along" to marry ROBERT CARR CROCKETT. She "growed" and whatever grows must have a start.

There is much more information in this old REGISTER of ROBERT CARR CROCKETT, which, from necessity must be omitted here. The fortunes of the CROCKETT family will be enhanced further in the following account of the family of:

REV. JAMES WALLIS OF PROVIDENCE CHURCH

Odd to relate, the following interesting account of the family of REV. JAMES WALLIS, who succeeded REV. WILLIAM RICHARDSON and REV. ROBERT HENRY as pastor of PROVIDENCE CHURCH, is supposed to have been written for the "ENCYCLOPOEDIA OF THE NEW WEST" (beginning on page 45) by JOHN HENRY BROWN, the celebrated TEXAS HISTORIAN, who is noted for his painstaking care and accuracy in setting down historical facts, wherever he found them. Checking whatever is written by JOHN HENRY BROWN is merely a perfunctory matter of form among latter day writers, who have learned to rely upon his statements. What he has said in these notes pertaining to the CROCKETTS and ALEXANDERS conforms perfectly with the material gathered by the writer over a period of years, bearing on the same subject.

JANE BANE ALEXANDER, daughter of the pioneer JOHN McKNITT ALEXANDER (who was called Polly in her father's will, and MARY, on her tombstone at PROVIDENCE CHURCH, where she is buried with her husband,) married REV. JAMES WALLIS' (See pages 323 and 400).

REV. JAMES WALLIS was the son of EZEKIEL WALLACE and the grandson of MATTHEW WALLACE. REV. JAMES WALLIS, on account of so many relatives of the same name, and also because of a little family broil, changed the spelling of the name from WALLACE to WALLIS, by an Act of the Legislature, and lived at old PROVIDENCE in MECKLENBURG COUNTY, where he is buried.

REV. JAMES WALLIS and his wife MARY ALEXANDER WALLIS, were the parents of the following children:

1. JOHN McKNITT WALLIS
2. JAMES WALLIS
3. JOSEPH WALLIS
4. WILLIAM WALLIS (died young).
5. EZEKIEL WALLIS (Died in infancy).
6. EDMUND WALLIS (died at age of 17).

1. JOHN McKNITT WALLIS died in PICKENS COUNTY, Alabama. He married and had two sons:

10. EZEKIEL WALLIS
11. JAMES WALLIS.

2. JAMES WALLIS . It was this JAMES WALLIS, who made the famous speech on "The Mecklenburg Declaration of Independence" at SUGAR CREEK in 1809, when his uncle, REV. SAMUEL C. CALDWELL, was conducting a classical school there, and the speech was a commencement performance by one of his students. This JAMES WALLIS first moved to ALABAMA and later to TEXAS, and died in WASHINGTON COUNTY, TEXAS, in December, 1865. His wife was ANN CROCKETT, the daughter of ELIJAH CROCKETT, and they were the parents of the following children:

12. MARIAN WALLIS
13. JAMES WALLIS
14. ELIJAH WALLIS
15. WILLIAM WALLIS
16. JOHN WALLIS
17. MARY WALLIS
18. JULIA WALLIS
19. SARAH WALLIS

3. JOSEPH WALLIS married ELIZABETH CROCKETT, daughter of ELIJAH CROCKETT, and they had the following children:

20. EMILY WALLIS m. JOSEPH TOLAND, of MORGAN COUNTY, ALA.
21. ELMIRA CAROLINE WALLIS
22. JOHN CALHOUN WALLIS
23. JOSEPH EDMUND WALLIS
24. MARY ELIZABETH WALLIS

In 1880 there was an EZEKIEL WALLACE (so spelled) in RED RIVER COUNTY, Texas, with 4 sons and two daughters, MOLLIE and MATTIE WALLACE.

MARY CROCKETT, the oldest child of ELIJAH CROCKETT married REV. McCORKELL and they settled in East Tennessee.
11. JOHN CROCKETT married his cousin MARY H. DAVIE, the daughter of WILLIAM RICHARDSON DAVIE, and they had a son ELIJAH CROCKETT, who had a son WILLIAM DAVIE, with whom this writer served in the TEXAS LEGISLATURE in 1909. WILLIAM DAVIE CROCKETT was from WASHINGTON COUNTY, TEXAS.
13. MARGARET McCORKELL CROCKETT married JOHN McKNITT WALLIS, the oldest son of REV. JAMES WALLIS and were the parents of EZEKIEL and JAMES WALLIS, above listed. JOHN McKNITT WALLIS died in Alabama in 1858.
19. ELIJAH CROCKETT, son of ELIJAH, married MARY TROUPE and died in MORGAN COUNTY, ALA., in the year 1823.
3. JOSEPH WALLIS who married ELIZABETH CROCKETT located at CHAPPELL HILL in Washington County, Texas in 1848. His son JOHN CALHOUN WALLIS brought the slaves overland from MORGAN COUNTY, ALABAMA, and his daughter ELMIRA CAROLINE WALLIS married DR. JOHN W. LOCKHART, of Washington County. When JOSEPH WALLIS came to Texas, his son 23 JOSEPH EDMUND WALLIS was 13 years of age. His son JOHN CALHOUN WALLIS m. ANNE E. GOODSON and in 1852 built the second store in CHAPPELL HILL, TEXAS. The son JOSEPH EDMUND WALLIS married KATE LANDES, daughter of COL. D. LANDES, of AUSTIN COUNTY, TEXAS, and formed the firm of WALLIS, LANDES & CO., wholesale merchants of GALVESTON, TEXAS. COL. LANDES and ISAAC APPLEWHITE of Washington County, Texas, started the H. & T. C. Railway. JUDGE JAMES E. SHEPPARD defeated JOSEPH WALLIS SR., for the Legislature in Washington County.

JOSEPH EDMUND WALLIS, grandson of REV. JAMES WALLIS, and the Great Grandson of JOHN McKNITT ALEXANDER, of MECKLENBURG COUNTY, N. C., and his wife KATE LANDES, had the following children:

100. CHARLES L. WALLIS
101. DANIEL EDMUND WALLIS
102. LOCKHART HADEN WALLIS
103. HEWIE PERLIE WALLIS
104. BIRDIE MAY WALLIS.

THE MORROW FAMILY

In the old WAXHAW CEMETERY, within fifteen feet of the marker on the grave of ANDREW JACKSON, SR. is buried DAVID MORROW, who died in 1785 at the age of 54 years. Around him are the gravestones of the WALKUPS, HARPERS and CROCKETTS, innumerable. (See p. 410). Nearby also will be found the grave of GEORGE McKEMIE. All these names indicate a MARYLAND ORIGIN, and particular the "Eastern Shore" variety.

I think my mother - who was one of them - was right, and that the MORROWS were IRISH, and not SCOTCH-IRISH. They were dissenting protestants, who came to the Eastern Shore of VIRGINIA, perhaps in the last half of the 17th century. They followed the redoubtable STEPHEN HORSEY and his fellows across the line into SOMERSET COUNTY. They spelled the name MORROW ordinarily, but scriveners and and Clerks often mis-spelled it, sometimes MORHY, sometimes MOROUGH & even MORRAY. On the MARYLAND RECORDS I find JOHN MOROUGH a witness to the will of WILLIAM WHITTINGTON, whose forbear lived in ACCOMAC and NORTHAMPTON COUNTY, and I find numerous MORROWS and DANIEL MORRY in Talbot County. A DANIEL MORROUGH died in ACCOMAC COUNTY in 1727, and a DANIEL MARRA lived in York County still earlier. DAVID MORROW'S will was proven in Lower Norfolk County, Virginia in 1789, I believe it was, and was related to the CHURCH and WHITE FAMILIES.

SAMUEL and DAVID MORROW came to MECKLENBURG and later settled in the TIGER RIVER section of South Carolina, and were revolutionary soldiers. Their declarations for pensions show they were born in MARYLAND "near Baltimore". I have identified them as probable grandsons of SAMUEL and JOHN MORROW, of BALTIMORE COUNTY, the sons of WALTER MORROW who died in 1709 (Md. Cal. of Wills Vol 3 p. 130.) Baltimore county adjoins CECIL COUNTY, and the MORROWS were in that county at the same time the RUMSEYS and ALEXANDERS and EWINGS lived there.

JEREMIAH and DANIEL MORROW of Lunenburg County, Virginia, came there and were living in that section from about 1746 to the 1767 period, after which they were in NORTH CAROLINA. There they intermarried with the WHITES and CROCKETTS, and my guess is that DAVID, who is buried at the old WAXHAW CEMETERY was the father of SAMUEL and DAVID, and came there from BALTIMORE COUNTY, MARYLAND, being a son of either SAMUEL or JOHN MORROW of the Walter Morrow will.

In the 1790 census in MECKLENBURG COUNTY the MORROWS, MAXWELLS and McKNIGHTS were living in Districts 1 and 7; that is, in STEELE CREEK, and the BEATTIE'S FORD section. The MORROWS intermarried into the EWING FAMILY in CECIL COUNTY, MARYLAND, and this marriage brought into the family chart several EWING MORROWS; then, a full 100 years later, the ANDREW EWINGS, of Nashville, TENNESSEE, again intermarried with the MORROW FAMILY. Descendants of JEREMIAH MORROW settled in SPOTTSYLVANIA COUNTY and ORANGE COUNTY, Virginia, and a later generation moved across into BERKELEY COUNTY. There they were neighbors of the McKNIGHT FAMILY, and these were the same MORROWS who lived with the McKNIGHTS in early Mecklenburg County.

Old Six Mile Church is the burial place of JAMES MORROW and his wife SUSANNAH WATSON, a daughter of DRURY WATSON the revolutionary soldier of PRINCE EDWARD COUNTY, Virginia. JAMES MORROW was born in PRINCE EDWARD COUNTY, where the EWING family settled. He named one of his sons DRURY MORROW and another JAMES McKNIGHT MORROW. There were many other children. ALLEN MORROW, another son is said to have built and established the Lower Six Mile church, where he is buried. These were the ancestors of MAJ. BENJAMIN MORROW, who married a daughter of GOV. WILLIAM HAWKINS, and whose old home is at PINEVILLE in Mecklenburg.

We are extremely sorry that further space is not available for this family.

REV. FRANCIS CUMMINS

An abstract of the will of the father of REV. FRANCIS CUMMINS will be found on page 334 of these notes. He was a student at "Queen's Museum" in CHARLOTTE about the time the MECKLENBURG DECLARATION was signed in 1775, and testified in after years as to what occurred. One of the JACKS married his daughter. His mother was REBECCA McNICKLE, who married CHARLES CUMMINS. I am convinced that he was related to ALEXANDER CUMMINS who married a daughter of COL. THOMAS POLK. He was licensed to preach in 1780, conducted a classical school for a time, and is one of those innumerable educators whom tradition credits with having tutored ANDREW JACKSON. Later in life he moved to ABBEVILLE DISTRICT, S. C. and then to GEORGIA - Greene County. He married SARAH DAVIS, a daughter of DAVID DAVIS in 1778. They had the following children:

1. REBECCA CAROLINE m. JESSE BOUCHELLE (DR.)
2. REV. EBENEZER H. CUMMINS m. MARY ANN BORDLEY of BALTIMORE, MD.
3. ELIZABETH CUMMINS m. DR. ARCHIBALD CARLISLE McKINLEY.
4. SARAH A. CUMMINS m. WILLIAM C. JACK (To Arkansas).
5. FRANCIS D. CUMMINS (Major in War of 1812) never married.
6. ESTHER CUMMINS m. DR. EZRA FISKE.
7. DEMARIS CUMMINS (b. 1788) m. JAMES G. BALDWIN.
8. HANNAH CUMMINS (b. 1789) m. (1) STEPHEN UPSON (2) ELIJAH BOARDMAN.

DR. JESSE BOUCHELLE, who married REBECCA CAROLINE CUMMINS, sounds like a near relative or descendant of DR. PETER BOUCHELLE, son of SAMUEL BOUCHELLE, who was a brother in law of DAVID LAWSON in CECIL COUNTY, Maryland, in 1721 (Md. Cal. of Wills Vol 7, p. 187 and 186).

DR. ARCHIBALD CARLISLE McKINLEY (b. 1779) Abbeville, S. C. was the son of WILLIAM McKINLEY (b. August 10, 1744) a collateral relative of the ancestor of PRESIDENT WILLIAM McKINLEY. ELIZABETH CUMMINS and Dr. McKINLEY had a daughter, SARAH SERENA McKINLEY (b. 1812) who was the grandmother of JUDGE HENRY UPSON SIMS, of Birmingham, Alabama, former President of the American Bar Association and a friend of the compiler, who furnished the data here presented on the family.

We are sorry the poverty of space forbids a full presentation of the data furnished.

BURIAL PLACE OF THOMAS SPRATT

The pioneer THOMAS SPRATT, the grandfather of SUSAN SMART, and the first man to cross the YADKIN on wheels (p 313) is buried in the oldest graveyard in MECKLENBURG COUNTY. Dr. Cyrus Hunter in his "Sketches of Western North Carolina", on page 77, says: Near the residence of THOMAS SPRATT is one of the oldest private burial grounds in the County, in which his mortal remains repose. Here are found the gravestones of several members of the SPRATT, BARNETT and JACK families, who intermarried; also those of the BINGHAMS (Bighams?), McKNIGHTS and a few others. On the headstone of MARY BARNETT, wife of WILLIAM BARNETT, it is recorded she died on October 4th, 1764, aged forty-five years. A hickory tree, ten or twelve inches in diameter, is now (1877) growing on the grave, casting around its benificent shade. The primitive forest growth, once partially cut down, is here fast assuming its original sway, and peacefully overshadowing the mortal remains of these early sleepers in this ancient graveyard.

In 1939 the writer conducted a vain search for the location of this old burial ground, described by Dr. Hunter, and it is only within the month of February of this year (1946) that a gang of workmen unearthed the site of it, near the present Mercy Hospital at the corner of East 5th and Caswell Road, about two miles from the business center of the City of Charlotte. Tombstones bearing the following inscriptions were found:

"Here lies the body of JAMES McNIGHT, who deceased OCTOBER ye 23rd, 1764, aged 60 years."
"In memory of Catherine Peel, who departed this life May ye 24th, 1778, aged 50 years".
"Here lies the body of ESTHER JOHNSTON, who deceased October the 22nd, 1775 aged 31 years!
(NOTE: Strictly speaking, BAKER'S GRAVEYARD, near BEATTIE'S FORD, is the oldest burial place in MECKLENBURG COUNTY.)

From the above we know that MARY BARNETT was born in 1719; JAMES McKNIGHT in 1704; CATHERINE PEEL in 1728, and ESTHER JOHNSTON in 1744.

ALEXANDER OSBORNE

ALEXANDER OSBORNE was born in 1709, it is said, in NEW JERSEY. He married AGNES McWHORTER, sister of DR. ALEXANDER McWHORTER, the early missionary and one time President of "QUEEN'S MUSEUM" in Charlotte. His wife was also the sister of the wife of the pioneer JOHN BREVARD, and the mother of EPHRAIM BREVARD. ALEXANDER OSBORN had two sisters, one of whom married COL. JAMES PATTON, and the other was the first wife of REV. JOHN THOMSON. As some evidence of these relationships, in Deed Book No. 1 p. 323, dated APRIL 13, 1753, there is the record of a deed from ALEXANDER OSBORNE and his wife AGNES to JAMES HARRIS, to 600 acres of land just below the forks of ROCKY RIVER, and across to the South Fork adjoining McCULLOCK, which was witnessed by JOHN BREVARD (his brother in law) and ROGER LAWSON, (who married a daughter of REV. JOHN THOMSON). In the year following there is another deed signed by the same parties and by the same witnesses. REV. HUGH McADEN in his journal of 1755 mentions staying at the home of COL. OSBORNE. Both OSBORNE and his wife died in July, 1776, leaving two children: ADLAI OSBORNE and JEAN OSBORNE. ADLAI OSBORNE was Clerk of the Court of ROWAN COUNTY, and was killed in the War of 1812 at the massacre at FORT MIMMS, leaving SPRUCE McCAY OSBORNE and EDWIN JAY OSBORNE. JEAN OSBORNE married MOSES WINSLOW.

THE WINSLOW FAMILY

BENJAMIN WINSLOW was the ancestor of the WINSLOW FAMILY, who lived just over the line in what is now IREDELL COUNTY, in the Center Church neighborhood in the old days. As early as MARCH 25, 1752 he patented five hundred acres of land on both sides of DAVIDSON'S CREEK - the South Fork. Rumple's History of Rowan calls it "DAVISES CREEK", but I am quite sure it was DAVIDSON, and if so it was in the present MECKLENBURG instead of ROWAN or IREDELL. BENJAMIN WINSLOW had three children, (1) BENJAMIN, JR., (2) MOSES, and (3) MARY WINSLOW.

The mother of BENJAMIN WINSLOW was a daughter of HARRY BEVERLY, who married BENJAMIN WINSLOW, his father, and HARRY BEVERLY was the IREDELL BENJAMIN WINSLOW'S grandfather. WILLIAM BEVERLY who settled "BEVERLY'S MANOR" with the aid of emigrants brought in by COL. JAMES PATTON and others, was BENJAMIN WINSLOW'S mother's first cousin. BENJAMIN WINSLOW (father of MOSES, etc) had a brother BEVERLY WINSLOW, of BERKELEY PARISH, Spottsylvania County, who lived until 1793, leaving will in which he mentions sons THOMAS, WILLIAM and HENRY, and daughters ELIZABETH, MARY, CATHERINE, AGATHA and SUSANNAH WINSLOW. Thus the WINSLOWS had plenty of kinfolks left in VIRGINIA, from whence they came. It is established that COL. JAMES PATTON came from ESSEX COUNTY to Beverly's Manor, and that his wife was an OSBORNE, and thus it is shown that there was a relationship BACK IN VIRGINIA between the WINSLOWS and OSBORNES, before they came to NORTH CAROLINA. WILLIAM BEVERLY was a second cousin of BENJAMIN WINSLOW, and ALEXANDER OSBORNE'S sister, through her enterprising husband COL. PATTON, played no unimportant part in building up the new Colony. REV. JOHN THOMSON, who died a few miles from ALEXANDER OSBORNE at his son-in-law's SAMUEL BAKER, had married another sister of OSBORNE, as his first wife, and so, had plenty of connections around and near him at the time of his death. MOSES WINSLOW, son of BENJAMIN, married JEAN OSBORNE, and their daughter DOVIE WINSLOW became the wife of DR. JOSEPH McKNITT ALEXANDER, son of JOHN McKNITT ALEXANDER, the signer; another daughter, CYNTHIA WINSLOW married SAMUEL KING; MARY WINSLOW married SAMUEL WILSON, SR., and their daughter, MARY WILSON, married EZEKIEL POLK and became the grandmother of a PRESIDENT OF THE UNITED STATES. So, after a time, the OSBORNE and WINSLOW family connections included most of the prominent families of MECKLENBURG COUNTY and its environs.

THE SAMPLE FAMILY

ELIZABETH ALEXANDER, half-sister of JOHN McKNITT ALEXANDER (b. Nov. 17, 1746) married WILLIAM SAMPLE, said to have been from IRELAND, and settled in the HOPEWELL SECTION along the BEATTIE'S FORD road, and they had a son JAMES SAMPLE, who married MARTHA ROBINSON of Sugar Creek, and this couple became the ancestors of all the SAMPLES in the upper part of MECKLENBURG COUNTY, and especially in and around HOPEWELL CHURCH.

THE ROCKY RIVER HARRIS'

The HARRIS FAMILY of the ROCKY RIVER section of MECKLENBURG COUNTY (now a part of CABARRAS COUNTY), according to MISS CLARA C. HARRIS, the family historian, of Concord, North Carolina, are descendants of a certain ROBERT HARRIS who married DOROTHY WILEY, who had the following children:

1. JOHN HARRIS m. (1) GRIZZEL STEELE (2) REBECCA McBAY.
2. WILLIAM HARRIS m. ELIZABETH GLENN
3. JAMES HARRIS m. MARY McILHENNY
4. MARGARET HARRIS m. ALEXANDER POER.
5. THOMAS HARRIS m. (1) MARY McKINNEY (2) AGNES.
6. SAMUEL HARRIS m. MARTHA LAIRD
7. ROBERT HARRIS m. FRANCES CUNNINGHAM (2) ANN HARRIS CALDWELL.
8. CHARLES HARRIS m. (1) JANE McILHENNY (2) ELIZABETH (THOMSON) BAKER.

MISS HARRIS says these brothers came from PENNSYLVANIA to MECKLENBURG COUNTY, N. C. about 1750, all except the brother WILLIAM HARRIS, who stopped in CECIL COUNTY, MARYLAND, where he and his descendants remained. She is a descendant of JAMES HARRIS and his wife MARY McILHENNY, through his oldest son ROBERT, who married MARGARET HARPER (b. 1737), who had a son HEZEKIAH PRICE HARRIS (1800-1869), whose son RICHARD SADLER HARRIS (1835-1911) had WADE HAMPTON HARRIS (1858-1935) who married CORA SPRINGS.

(NOTE: The writer regrets inability to give the chart of this family in full, for lack of space. This HARRIS FAMILY was NOT, in his opinion, a Pennsylvania family, but just another one of those families from the EASTERN SHORE of MARYLAND, who came from the vicinity of SOMERSET COUNTY and the POCOMOKE RIVER, gradually worked their way Northward to the upper reaches of the SASAFRAS RIVER, into the "forks of the Elk" where JOSEPH ALEXANDER and ALEXANDER EWING lived" and joined those families in the trek Southward down through VIRGINIA and into NORTH CAROLINA. The traditional account relied upon by the HARRIS FAMILY is purely tradition in fact, and no evidence has been found identifying the family in PENNSYLVANIA. On page 439 of "Howe's History of the Presbyterian Church in South Carolina" an account of the life of REV. JOHN HARRIS, says he was born in 1725 of WELCH parents, who settled on the EASTERN SHORE OF MARYLAND, graduated at Princeton in 1753, and soon thereafter preached to the Churches of WICOMICO and MONOKIN, in SOMERSET COUNTY, in MARYLAND.)

WILLIAMSON FAMILY OF BETHESDA CHURCH IN YORK DISTRICT, S. C.

REV. HEZEKIAH BALCH was born in HARFORD COUNTY, MARYLAND, just across the river from CECIL COUNTY, MARYLAND, in the year 1741, but his parents removed to MECKLENBURG COUNTY, N. C. about 1750 when he was but a child. They sent him to PRINCETON where he graduated in 1762. That the BALCH family came to MECKLENBURG with the ALEXANDERS, SHARPES, HARRIS and other families, from CECIL COUNTY and the "forks of the Elk" there is no sort of doubt. He married HANNAH LEWIS, and preached for the Congregation of BETHESDA, in York County - over the line from MECKLENBURG. Among the members of his church was the WILLIAMSON FAMILY, the head of which was JAMES WILLIAMSON, who with his sons were patriots of the Revolution.

JAMES WILLIAMSON of the BETHESDA Congregation, had the following sons:

1. JOHN WILLIAMSON
2. ADAM WILLIAMSON
3. SAMUEL WILLIAMSON
4. GEORGE WILLIAMSON
5. JAMES WILLIAMSON.

3. SAMUEL WILLIAMSON was the father of two noted sons who settled in MECKLENBURG COUNTY, and became a part of its interesting history. They were: (1) REV. JOHN WILLIAMSON, D. D., who was the pastor of HOPEWELL PRESBYTERIAN CHURCH, in Mecklenburg County for twenty-four years; and (2) DR. SAMUEL WILLIAMSON, a President of DAVIDSON COLLEGE.

The REV. HEZEKIAH BALCH, of this record, moved over into TENNESSEE, where he assisted the REV. SAMUEL DOAK and others in the establishment of several educational institutions, including the famous WASHINGTON COLLEGE, and the UNIVERSITY OF TENNESSEE. He was most certainly of the same family as the HEZEKIAH JAMES BALCH, who on May 20, 1775 affixed his signature to the MECKLENBURG DECLARATION OF INDEPENDENCE.

MRS. MARY GRAHAM AND HER SIX CHILDREN

MRS. MARY GRAHAM died in 1791 at the age of 71 years. She had been as a girl MARY McCONNELL, who first married a BARBER and second JAMES GRAHAM. Her children were ESTHER BARBER, JOHN GRAHAM, JOSEPH GRAHAM, SARAH and ANN GRAHAM. They have markers in the Presbyterian Churchyard at Charlotte. (p. 404).

GEN. JOSEPH GRAHAM m. ISABELLA DAVIDSON, daughter of MAJ. JOHN DAVIDSON and had twelve children, SIX of whom were:

1. HON. JOHN D. GRAHAM m. BETSY CONNOR.
2. JAMES GRAHAM never married.
3. DR. GEORGE F. GRAHAM m. MARTHA A. HARRIS.
4. VIOLET GRAHAM m. DR. MOSES WINSLOW ALEXANDER.
5. MARY GRAHAM m. REV. ROBERT HALL MORRISON (Dau. m. STONEWALL JACKSON).
6. GOV. WILLIAM A. GRAHAM, who married SUSANNAH WASHINGTON of Newbern.

THE EASTERN SHORE OF MARYLAND AND IT'S INFLUENCE ON MECKLENBURG COUNTY AND THE DECLARATION

From others who have written about MECKLENBURG COUNTY, NORTH CAROLINA, this compiler was once seriously impressed with the idea that it was purely and solely PENNSYLVANIA'S baby.

From the work performed in gathering the information crudely set down in the nearly 250 pages preceding, from the actual records, he finds that impression entirely dispelled.

Some of the reasons:

The Scotch and Irish, some called Scotch-Irish, many of them, appear on the records of North Carolina earlier than they do in PENNSYLVANIA.

Those who did go to Penn's colony started from and originated in the same general area on the EASTERN SHORE OF VIRGINIA and MARYLAND, whose families at that time had already begun the migration to the Yadkin-Catawba valley.

Pennsylvania's Susquehannah Valley and the lands along its tributaries drew people from both VIRGINIA and MARYLAND - restless creatures, disgusted with slave-packed plantations, neighborhood overlords and state supervised and tax supported religious institutions to which they did not belong or subscribe. The records disclose that often members of the same family would go one way while others went another; one neighbor to Pennsylvania and another to the Carolinas.

Thus the familiar-sounding names found in the "Pennsylvania Archives" and other sources. But the most of them were either VIRGINIANS or MARYLANDERS - many of them natives. Some of them remained in Pennsylvania long enough to get their names on a rent or muster roll, or some other semblance of a record, which present day genealogists and historians have "snapped up" as evidence that they were from Pennsylvania.

But these people sojourned only a brief period among their Dutch associates, for they no sooner heard from relatives or a neighbor who had reached the Carolinas, than they unceremoniously pulled up stakes and headed due South.

Thus, we can surmise that when THOMAS SPRATT crossed the Yadkin "on wheels" and settled in what is now MECKLENBURG COUNTY, he hastened to communicate with his old SOMERSET neighbors, the POLKS, who at last accounts were on their way to Pennsylvania. The next scene shows young THOMAS POLK, tired and dusty, but merrily swinging his knapsack and knocking at the humble door of the SPRATT CABIN, a few miles South of the present sprightly town of CHARLOTTE.

So much for THAT.

MECKLENBURG COUNTY, NORTH CAROLINA, in its early days appears to have been the breeding place of PATRIOTS, instead of great ORATORS and STATESMEN. It also produced outstanding teachers and ministers of the Church. So far as statesmen were concerned there was glory enough in having furnished ANDREW JACKSON and JAMES K. POLK to serve as Presidents of the United States, in the light of whose accomplishments the county's fame has never languished, nor ever will. A five mile RING drawn a little East and South of the present PINEVILLE will encompass the ancestral homes of both these outstanding notables.

But there is another ring, which can be drawn on the map of MARYLAND in the extreme Northeastern corner, between the forks of the ELK RIVERS which would encircle the homes of many families, who made the most marvelous contribution to the history of MECKLENBURG COUNTY. Within this imaginary ring, populated by a race of people who loved and prized liberty above life, resided the ancestors of the ALEXANDERS, EWINGS, LAWSONS, DAVIDSONS, REESES, HARRISES, SHARPES, McWHORTERS, MOORES, CUNNINGHAMS, BARRYS and CALDWELLS, whose descendants blazed their way across plain and mountain to the valley of the CATAWBA and YADKIN, while the eighteenth century was in its swadling clothes.

Then from various points, further down the MARYLAND PENINSULA, from whence the ELK RIVER pioneers had earlier migrated Northward to CECIL COUNTY, beyond the SASAFRAS, CHESTER, CHOPTANK, WICOMICO and on down to the ANNEMESEXES and POCOMOKE, came another delegation, kinsmen of the ELKTON families, who joined them in the trek to the CAROLINAS. In this tribal migration will be found the names of SPRATT, POLK, CALDWELL, SHARPE, WILSON and HENRY.

If the names mentioned were omitted from the rolls the story of the MECKLENBURG DECLARATION OF INDEPENDENCE might never have been told.

Where did the members of this caravan originate?

Approximately a hundred years before the ALEXANDERS, POLKS, CALDWELLS and others mentioned began to settle along the Yadkin and Catawba persons of the same names, with one STEPHEN HORSEY, as their leader, left the Eastern Shore of VIRGINIA (then called ACCOMAC, and now ACCOMAC and NORTHAMPTON COUNTIES) and settled between the LITTLE and BIG ANNEMESSEX rivers in what is now SOMERSET COUNTY, MARYLAND. Their leader, HORSEY, and perhaps others, were tired of being taxed to maintain the so-called Established Church, when they did not belong to it, believe in it, or, except when forced by threats, attend it. Some were Quakers (called by the Indians QUACKERS), some DISSENTERS, and all were NON-CONFORMISTS. Maryland had made overtures to welcome them, so they moved across the line.

It was in the midst of these families that at the instance of WILLIAM STEPHENS, the REV. FRANCIS MaKEMIE was sent from the BARBADOES; it was by these families that the PRESBYTERIAN CHURCH was established on American soil. MaKEMIE lived over the line in ACCOMAC COUNTY, Virginia, but his labors included these folks. Then came REV. JOHN HAMPTON, JOHN HENRY, McNISH and REV. JOHN THOMSON, who labored to carry on the work that MaKEMIE had started. These great ministers and teachers began to sow the fertile seeds of Liberty and religious freedom that took firm root in the minds of HORSEY'S followers along the Annemessex and Pocomoke. The preaching of FRANCIS MaKEMIE, GEORGE McNISH, JOHN HENRY, JOHN HAMPTON and REV. JOHN THOMSON fanned the tiny flames of human hopes implanted thus early along the shores of Eastern Maryland, which eventually burst forth between the Yadkin and the Catawba in 1775, by being crystalized in the MECKLENBURG DECLARATION OF INDEPENDENCE. But the interesting part of this story is that the faded names on the Church rolls of POCOMOKE, SNOW HILL and MONIKINS tally so perfectly with the names signed to that immortal document.

The settlement on the Annemessex and Pocomoke occurred between 1666 and 1670. Their leader, STEPHEN HORSEY, died there in 1772, leaving a family of eight children named in his will. Even the witnesses to that document - JOHN WALKUP and HENRY POWELL - represent early and well known leaders in MECKLENBURG COUNTY, NORTH CAROLINA; families whose names are to be found at every turn on the musty records kept by the Harrises and Alexanders. There is no list of these people in existence, so far as the writer knows. Some settled in the JAMESTOWN section of Virginia, nearly a half century before; some had removed to the South side of the JAMES RIVER, along Elizabeth River in Norfolk, and the bays and inlets of Nansemond County, and like those who remained in ACCOMAC for sometime, joined the migration to the ANNEMESSEX and POCOMOKE. Among the latter were the sons of the persecuted JOHN PORTER. Some of them were straight out IRISH, some properly to be called SCOTCH-IRISH, and some who had come direct from SCOTLAND and ENGLAND to either the Western or Eastern Shore of Virginia. WILLIAM DURANT (father of GEORGE of DURANT'S NECK, already in North Carolina) lead some three hundred to the inlets of the CHOPTANK and WILLIAM STONE, once a puritan leader, and Sheriff of NORTHAMPTON, had been appointed GOVERNOR at ST. MARY'S, and carried some of his neighbors with him to Maryland, also, particularly the HARRISONS, who, like himself, came from NORTHAMPTONSHIRE, ENGLAND. From the "Northampton Engagement" and the "Northampton Protest", both signed by HORSEY before this migration occurred, and from the tythe list of NORTHAMPTON (Virginia) in 1666, we cull many of the names that went along with Stephen Horsey, because they lived and died in SOMERSET, leaving sons and daughters, who are later to be found on the records of CECIL COUNTY, TALBOT, KENT and DORCHESTER, further North, and finally in Mecklenburg County, N. C.

This, breifly, is the saga of a race of people, scourged through long centuries by the nine-tails of tyrany, in quest of religious freedom and liberty of action, whose humble forbears exiled themselves on the EASTERN SHORE OF MARYLAND, among the islands and inlets of its rugged coast; were found by REV. FRANCIS MaKEMIE and encouraged to hope for divine aid in an eventual political emancipation, and whose children and children's children clung to that hope for dear life through a long period of intrigue and scheming by the Calverts and the Berkeleys, only in the end to outwit the overlords and at times know what it was to wield the balance of power in their beloved Maryland. They educated their sons at Princeton, under most adverse circumstances, and made them teachers and leaders among their kind; improved their own circumstances at every opportunity and kept an eye on the vast open spaces of the West and South for the benefit of their posterity. The eldest sons went forth at times to "spy out the country" and brought back stories of new regions in the Carolinas, and new worlds to conquer. Occasional trials were made in Pennsylvania, generally abandoned in favor of a less rigid climate and more homogeneous surroundings, to end finally in a general exodus Southward, to join many who had preceded them to the new land of promise. Maryland had been their haven through several generations, and still retained the taint of feudal baronage. She had been their abiding place through the hard years, when the light of a free people glimmered first in the distance, which had been fanned into reality through the preaching and teaching of the MaKemies, Henrys, Thomsons and Craigheads. It was not that they did not love Maryland, but they loved liberty more. If the new country was not what it should be, they could reshape it to their own wishful ends, or at least try. How well they succeeded is now spread on the pages of History. The Old North State was the better for their coming, and the generations they multiplied and left to follow in their wake, can repeat in throbbing song the immortal lines of Maryland's own:

> Hark to the wand'ring son's appeal,
> Maryland!
> My mother State! To thee I kneel,
> Maryland!
> For life and death, for woe and weel,
> Thy peerless chivalry reveal,
> And gird thy beauticus limbs with steel,
> Maryland! My Maryland!

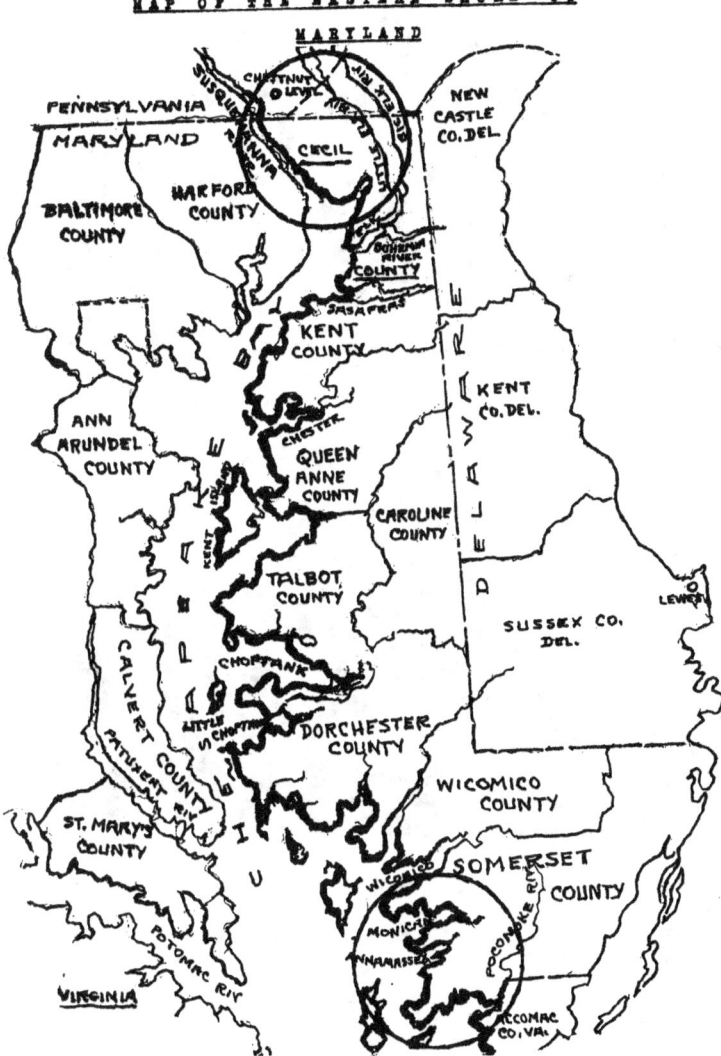

MAP OF THE EASTERN SHORE OF MARYLAND

UPPER RING: The territory embraced in the "upper ring" on the above map, was served by REV. JOHN THOMSON for many years (he who died in Mecklenburg County, North Carolina in 1753, and is buried at BAKERS GRAVEYARD), and also by his son in law REV. RICHARD SANKEY; they having often preached at CHESTNUT LEVEL, which falls within the RING. The CALDWELL FAMILY of CUB CREEK, Virginia, belonged to this CONGREGATION, and went with the EWINGS, BARRYS and MOORES to Virginia. The territory embraced in this upper ring furnished no less than SIX SIGNERS to the MECKLENBURG DECLARATION by the same name - ALEXANDER; it also furnished RICHARD BARRY, JOHN FORD and the two HARRISES and DAVID REESE, which we can recall. See text.

LOWER RING: This was the original home of the families of the upper ring, they having migrated up the Eastern Shore of Maryland to the BOHEMIA and ELK RIVERS. Among those families were the EWINGS, BARRYS, ALEXANDERS, CALDWELLS, SHARPES, DAVIDSONS, FORDS, HARRISES, CUNNINGHAMS, REESES and numerous others. They left behind them parts of the same families, including the POLK, KNOX, WILSON, HAMPTON, HENRY, KING, SPRATTS and others, and the lower ring sent its contingent to MECKLENBURG where it joined those from above. Thus there were families bearing the same names in MECKLENBURG, who were related to families of the same name from both the LOWER and UPPER ringed territory on the above map.

MORROW FAMILY GRAVES - PRESBYTERIAN CHURCHYARD

VIEW OF PROVIDENCE CHURCH BURYING GROUND

BETHEL CHURCH NEAR DAVIDSON COLLEGE (See PAGE 410)

SOURCES AND AUTHORITIES

ACKLEN, JEANNETTE TILLOTSON, Tennessee Tombstone Records 325, 526.
ACKLEN, JEANNETTE TILLOTSON, Tennessee Bible Records, 488, 497.
ALEXANDER, J. B., History of MECKLENBURG COUNTY - 316, 370, 371, 375, 382, 383, 395, 413, 414, 416, 417, 420, 425, 506, 508, 522.
ALLISON, JOHN, "DROPPED STITCHES OF TENNESSEE HISTORY", 500, 501.
AMERICAN HISTORICAL MAGAZINE, (Peabody Institute); 505, 507
ANNALS OF NEWBERRY DISTRICT, SOUTH CAROLINA, by J. BELTON O'NEAL, 456.
ARTHUR, JOHN PRESTON, HISTORY OF WESTERN NORTH CAROLINA, 451, 496.
BALDWIN'S MARYLAND CALENDAR OF WILLS, 502, 510, 514-520, 525, 527, 532.
BELL, LANDON C., "SUNLIGHT ON THE SOUTH SIDE", 450, 502
BELL, LANDON C., "OLD FREE STATE", 458.
BELL, LANDON C., "CUMBERLAND PARISH REGISTER, "429, 455, 457.
BETHEL CHURCH, MECKLENBURG COUNTY, N. C., NOTES FROM ITS UNPUBLISHED HISTORY, 412.
BODDIE, JOHN BENNETT, "SEVENTEENTH CENTURY ISLE OF WIGHT COUNTY", 458, 467.
BOWEN, ELIZA, "HISTORY OF WILKES COUNTY, GEORGIA", 454.
BRISTOL PARISH REGISTER, by SLAUGHTER, 430.
BRYANT, H. E. C., MATTHEWS, N. C., in the CHARLOTTE OBSERVER, 1946. Mr. BRYANT lives "seven miles from Matthews, and four miles from PINEVILLE", on R. F. D. No. 1, and is a retired member of the famous "GRIDIRON CLUB", of newspaper writers, of WASHINGTON, D. C., who loves fox hunting and who was born in Mecklenburg County, N. C. His frequent articles on Mecklenburg topics shows him to be one of the best informed persons we have ever contacted. He certainly knows his MECKLENBURG HISTORY.
BYRD, COLONEL WILLIAM, in his "JOURNEY TO THE LAND OF EDEN", 428.
CALENDAR OF VIRGINIA STATE PAPERS, 470.
CHALKLEY'S RECORDS OF AUGUSTA COUNTY, VIRGINIA, pp. 419, 421, 433-434, 465, 470, 528, 436.
CHARLES PARISH REGISTER, OF YORK COUNTY, VIRGINIA, by LANDON C. BELL, 464, 465, 470.
CLEMENT, MAUD CARTER, HISTORY OF PITTSYLVANIA CO. VIRGINIA, 495.
COLLINS' HISTORY OF KENTUCKY, 462.
COLONIAL RECORDS OF NORTH CAROLINA, 451, 494.
COMPENDIUM OF AMERICAN GENEALOGY, VIRKUS, 492.
CONGRESSIONAL DIRECTORY FOR 1774-1891, 502, 524.
CROCKETT FAMILY, by FRENCH & ARMSTRONG, 441.
CROCKETT, ROBERT CARR, REGISTER AND FAMILY RECORD KEPT BY HIM, photostatic copy in the files of the compiler, 530. The original of this unusual and rare record is in possession of MR. M. H. CROCKETT, a prominent social and business leader, of AUSTIN, TEXAS, a great great grandson of ELIJAH CROCKETT and his wife MARY DAVIE, sister of HON. WILLIAM RICHARDSON DAVIE, buried in the OLD WAXHAW CEMETERY in LANCASTER COUNTY, SOUTH CAROLINA. 530.
CUMBERLAND PARISH REGISTER, of LUNENBURG COUNTY, VA., by LANDON C. BELL, 429, 460.
"CUNNINGHAMS OF CUB CREEK" an article in the VIRGINIA MAGAZINE OF HISTORY & BIOGRAPHY, by DR. JOHN GOODWIN HERNDON, of Haverford College, 463.
DAVIES, REV. SAMUEL, JORNAL KEPT BY HIM, 426.
DEED AND WILL RECORDS OF MECKLENBURG COUNTY, NORTH CAROLINA, 317-334, 351-356.
DODD, HON. WILLIAM E., "THE OLD SOUTH", 314, 356.

EGGLESTON, DR. JOHN DUPUY, of HAMPDEN-SYDNEY COLLEGE, Farmville, Va., Article written on the BAKER FAMILY in the VIRGINIA MAGAZINE OF HISTORY & BIOGRAPHY in 1941,443.
EGGLESTON, DR. JOHN DUPUY, in letters and correspondence addressed to the compiler of this volume, 446, 447, 462.
ELLETT'S "WOMEN OF THE REVOLUTION", 491.
ENCYCLOPOEDIA OF THE NEW WEST, article written by JOHN HENRY BROWN, Texas Historian, in his life-time, 530.
ESKER, MRS. KATIE PRINCE W., of WASHINGTON, D. C., in letters to the compiler, 501.
EXECUTIVE JOURNALS OF THE COUNCIL OF COLONIAL VIRGINIA, by McILWAINE, 430.
FAIRFAX COUNTY, VIRGINIA; WILLS AND ADMINISTRATIONS OF, by ESTELLE KING, 470.
FOOTE, REV. WILLIAM HENRY, SKETCHES OF NORTH CAROLINA, 370, 382, 393, 397, 400, 412, 430, 525, 527.
FOOTE, REV. WILLIAM HENRY, SKETCHES OF VIRGINIA, 432, 433, 505, 510, 514.
FOTHERGILL'S, WILLS OF WESTMORELAND COUNTY, VIRGINIA, 499.
FLEET, BEVERLY, COLONIAL ABSTRACTS OF VIRGINIA RECORDS, 426, 427, 437, 466, 499.
FRENCH & ARMSTRONG'S genealogy of the "CROCKETT FAMILY", 442.
GEORGIA PUBLICATIONS of the JOSEPH HABERSHAM CHAPTER, D. A. R. (Vol. 2), 510;(Vol 1) 351, (Vol. 2) 522
GEORGIA PUBLICATIONS, of the GEORGIA CHAPTER, D. A. R. (Vol. 2) 460.
GOODSPEED'S HISTORY OF TENNESSEE, 509.
HARRIS, MISS CLARA C., of CONCORD, N. C., in correspondence with the writer, 534. MISS HARRIS has furnished valuable material relating to her family, which the writer regrets having been compelled to omit from these pages for lack of available space.
HASKINS, FREDERICK, commentator and historian, as well as researcher, 462.
HAYWOOD, JOHN, CIVIL AND POLITICAL HISTORY OF TENNESSEE, 462.
HENDERSON, MR. WALTER S., of DAVIDSON, NORTH CAROLINA, letters and information copied & furnished the compiler, 410, 412, 489 and 510. Mr. HENDERSON is descended from JAMES HENDERSON and VIOLET LAWSON, through the son WILLIAM HENDERSON (Chart p. 489).
HERNDON, DR. JOHN GOODWIN, "LIFE OF JOHN THOMSON", 425, 431, 437, 440, 438, 514, 448.
HOWE, REV. GEORGE, D. D., "HISTORY OF THE PRESBYTERIAN CHURCH IN SOUTH CAROLINA", 497, 526, 534.
HUNTER, CYRUS L., "SKETCHES OF WESTERN NORTH CAROLINA", 413-417, 419, 420, 473-475, 485, 503, 504, 507, 513, 515, 533.
JAMES, MARQUIS, "LIFE OF ANDREW JACKSON" 500, 501.
LANDRUM, REV. J. B. O., "HISTORY OF SPARTANBURG, SOUTH CAROLINA", 461, 478, 479, 480, 502.
LEWIS, THOMAS, of early Virginia, JOURNAL KEPT BY, 419.
LIPSCOMB, WILLIAM LOWNDES, "HISTORY OF COLUMBUS MISSISSIPPI", 480.
LOGAN'S MANUSCRIPT, published by JOSEPH HABERSHAM CHAPTER, D. A. R. COLLECTIONS, 497.
MARRIAGE RECORDS OF MECKLENBURG COUNTY, NORTH CAROLINA, 335-351.
MARTIN'S HISTORY OF NORTH CAROLINA, 315, 416.
MARYLAND CALENDAR OF WILLS, by BALDWIN, pp 510, 515.

539

McAIDEN, REV. HUGH, JOURNAL IN HIS TRIP THROUGH NORTH CAROLINA in 1755, 374, 382, 397, 396 533.
McILWAINE'S VIRGINIA COLONIAL REGISTER, 472.
NORTH CAROLINA COLONIAL RECORDS, 379.
NORTH CAROLINA HISTORICAL & GENEALOGICAL REGISTER, by HATHAWAY, 510-512.
NORTHUMBERLAND COUNTY, VIRGINIA, RECORDS, 464.
PATILLO, REV. HENRY, extracts of JOURNAL KEPT BY HIM, 430.
POLK, CAPT. CHARLES, of MECKLENBURG, data from a diary kept by him in INDIAN COUNTERY, 507.
PENNSYLVANIA ARCHIVES, reference to the, 535.
PRESBYTERIAN CHURCH HISTORY in AUSTIN, TEXAS, 504.
PRESBYTERY OF PHILADELPHIA, extracts from Minutes of the, 515.
PRICE, MRS. CAROLINE BEALL, "THE LAWSON, McCONNELL, McKISSICK and HENDERSON FAMILIES", 449, 477, 487.
PRINCE EDWARD COUNTY, VIRGINIA, data from RECORDS of the County, 428, 448.
PROCEEDINGS OF THE VIRGINIA COUNCIL, 465, 471.
PUETT, MINNIE STOWE, "HISTORY OF GASTON COUNTY, NORTH CAROLINA", 434, 450, 451, 485, 492.
RALEIGH (N. C.) STANDARD, 488.
RAMSEY'S ANNALS OF TENNESSEE, 315, 413, 414, 416, 462, 473, 503.
RAPER, ARTHUR F. (From material in the hands of DR. T. B. RICE, of GREENSBORO, GA.) "TENANTS of the ALMIGHTY", 500.
RECORDS FROM TOMBSTONES OF MECKLENBURG COUNTY, N. C., 383-411.
RECORDS OF MECKLENBURG COUNTY, NORTH CAROLINA, on file at the COUNTY COURTHOUSE, 481, 485, 530.
RECORDS OF CECIL COUNTY, MARYLAND, 449.
RECORDS OF CHAMBERS COUNTY, ALABAMA, 484.
RECORDS OF ESSEX COUNTY, VIRGINIA, 468.
RECORDS OF GREENE COUNTY, GEORGIA, 481.
RECORDS OF OLD RAPPAHANNOCK COUNTY, VIRGINIA, 466.
RECORDS OF YORK COUNTY, VIRGINIA, 437.
REVILL, MISS JANIE, of SUMPTER, S. C., numerous items of information bearing on the MOORE family of SPARTANBURG and TYGER RIVER, obtained from her "ABSTRACT OF MOORE RECORDS IN SOUTH CAROLINA".
RIVERS OF THE EASTERN SHORE by HULBERT FOOTNER, 524.
ROCKWELL, DR. E. F. from material written by him relating to REV. JOHN THOMSON, 425.
RUMPLE'S HISTORY OF ROWAN COUNTY, NORTH CAROLINA, 421, 376, 500, 510, 512, 525, 533.

SHARP, REV. E. M., ABERDEEN, MISSISSIPPI; from letters and information to the writer, 524.
SHERRILL, WILLIAM L, "ANNALS OF LINCOLN COUNTY, NORTH CAROLINA", 422, 467, 468, 483, 494, 501, 510, 512, 528.
SIMS, JUDGE HENRY UPSON, former President of the AMERICAN BAR ASSOCIATION, from letters and information sent the writer, 532. BIRMINGHAM ALABAMA.
SLAUGHTER'S "BRISTOL PARISH REGISTER", 455, 460.
SOMMERVILLE, CHARLES WILLIAM, Ph. D., D. D., "THE HISTORY OF HOPEWELL PRESBYTERIAN CHURCH", 351, 383, 399, 403, 406, 481, 489, 502.
STANNARD, WILLIAM G., COLONIAL VIRGINIA REGISTER, 436.
ST. PETER'S PARISH REGISTER, 456-457, 459.
SPOTTSYLVANIA COUNTY, VIRGINIA RECORDS, by CROZIER, 465.
STROCK, MRS. MARGARET GILLIAM, of CHARLOTTE NORTH CAROLINA, 457. (Material furnished the writer)
UNITED STATES CENSUS RECORDS OF MECKLENBURG COUNTY, NORTH CAROLINA, FOR 1790, 357-368.
UNITED STATES CENSUS REPORTS FOR 1790, 420, 419, 481, 483, 486, 511.
UNITED STATES CENSUS REPORTS FOR THE YEAR 1850, 483.
VANDIVER, LOUISE AYER, "TRADITIONS AND HISTORY OF ANDERSON COUNTY, SOUTH CAROLINA", 445.
VIRGINIA LAND OFFICE RECORDS AND BOOKS, 455.
VIRGINIA MAGAZINE OF HISTORY & BIOGRAPHY, 430, 437, 443, 460, 463, 465, 468, 471.
WADDELL'S ANNALS OF AUGUSTA COUNTY, VIRGINIA, 432-434, 419, 486, 492.
WELLS, EMMA MIDDLETON, "HISTORY OF ROANE COUNTY, TENNESSEE", 495.
WHEELER, JOHN H., "HISTORY OF NORTH CAROLINA" 424, 506.
WHEELER'S "REMINISCENSES" OF NORTH CAROLINA," 424.
WHITE OAK SWAMP QUAKER MEETING HOUSE, MINUTES 446, 510.
"WHITE'S FORT", by LUCILE DEADERICK, in KNOXVILLE (TENN) JOURNAL, 424.
WILLIAM AND MARY QUARTERLY HISTORICAL MAGAZINE, 459.
WISE, JENNINGS CROPPER, "EARLY HISTORY OF THE EASTERN SHORE OF VIRGINIA", 535, 536.
YORK COUNTY, VIRGINIA, COUNTY RECORDS, 427.
YOUNG, BENNETT H. "HISTORY OF JESSAMINE COUNTY, KENTUCKY", 462.

SUBJECT INDEX
PAGES 313 TO 536

ALABAMA COURT OF CHANCERY, occupied by the BOWIE kin of the JACK FAMILY, 474

ALEXANDERS OF MECKLENBURG, their kin and origin, 520-523.

ALEXANDERS OF MECKLENBURG of the eighteenth century, 523

ALEXANDERS OF MECKLENBURG of the twentieth century, 523.

ALEXANDER, ABRAHAM, and his parentage, 522.

ALEXANDER, ELIJAH, of SUGAR CREEK, and his GEORGIA FAMILY, 520.

ALEXANDER, FRANCIS, of CECIL COUNTY, MARYLAND, an uncle of JOHN McKNITT ALEXANDER, and his children, 522.

ALEXANDER, JOHN McKNITT, and his family, from the records, 323.

ALEXANDER, JOSEPH, grandfather of the MECKLENBURG ALEXANDER FAMILY, and his last will and testament in CECIL COUNTY, MARYLAND, 520.

ALLISON FAMILY, of MARYLAND, VIRGINIA, NORTH CAROLINA, GEORGIA and TENNESSEE, 499-501.

ALLISON FAMILY, of ROANE COUNTY, TENNESSEE; chart of, 495.

ALLISON FAMILY and its connection with the MOORE FAMILY 493-501.

ALLISON, DAVID, of the WATAUGA VALLEY, a cousin of ANDREW JACKSON, President, 500-501.

ALLISON, GWINN, of GREENE COUNTY, GEORGIA, and a trust fund left to the county, 500.

ALLISON, ROBERT, of ROANE COUNTY, TENNESSEE, and his family chart, 495.

ANDERSON, GEN. ROBERT, of ANDERSON COUNTY, S. C., and his connection with the HARRIS and THOMSON FAMILY, 444-445.

ARKANSAS JACK FAMILY, descendants of the MECKLENBURG JACK FAMILY, 476.

ALLISON, URIAH, obtained his name from the SHERRILL FAMILY of LINCOLN COUNTY, N. C., 501.

AUSTIN,NATIONAL BANK, of AUSTIN, TEXAS, official a descendant of the POLK FAMILY, 509.

BACON'S CASTLE in ISLE OF WIGHT COUNTY, built by the ALLENS, kin of WILLIAMSONS 458.

BAKER FAMILY, of PRINCE EDWARD COUNTY, VIRGINIA, and its connection with JOHN THOMSON family, 443.

BAKER FAMILY, of OLD RAPPAHANNOCK COUNTY, VIRGINIA, and its connection with the THOMSON and BROOKE FAMILY, 467.

BAKER'S GRAVEYARD in MECKLENBURG COUNTY, burial place of HUGH LAWSON and REV. JOHN THOMSON, 425.

BAKER'S GRAVEYARD in IREDELL COUNTY, with list of tombstone inscriptions, 403.

BALLINGER, HON. WILLIAM PITT, a descendant of the JACK FAMILY; home in GALVESTON, TEXAS, 475.

BARRY, ANDREW, of CECIL COUNTY, MARYLAND, the ancestor of the MECKLENBURG and LINCOLN COUNTY NORTH CAROLINA BARRY family, 518, 502.

BARRY and MOORE FAMILIES of VIRGINIA and NORTH CAROLINA, 477.

BATTLE OF SAN JACINTO and of GOLIAD, TEXAS, participated in by the JACK FAMILY, 476.

BEATTIE'S FORD SETTLEMENT in LINCOLN and MECKLENBURG COUNTY, and some of the families living there, 422-424.

BETHEL CHURCH, in UPPER MECKLENBURG, its History and some of its tombstone records, 410-412.

BETHLEHEM CHURCH in UNION COUNTY, NORTH CAROLINA and tombstone records found there, 403.

BEVERLY MANOR, in AUGUSTA COUNTY, VIRGINIA, 429, 439.

BOOKER FAMILY of Eastern Virginia, PRINCE EDWARD and other counties, and its connection with the CUNNINGHAMS and THOMSONS, 461.

BOOTH FAMILY of YORK, ESSEX, RICHMOND and OLD RAPPAHANNOCK COUNTIES, 468.

BROOKE and BROOKS FAMILIES, of Eastern Virginia and their connection with the THOMSON and CUNNINGHAM families, 446.

BROOKS, JUDGE M. M., of TEXAS, a direct descendent of the BARRY FAMILY of MECKLENBURG COUNTY, NORTH CAROLINA, 480.

BRYAN FAMILY, of GALVESTON, married into JACK FAMILY, from MECKLENBURG, 476.

BYRD, COLONEL WILLIAM, of early VIRGINIA, and lands sold to the MOORES, later of MECKLENBURG COUNTY, N. C., 495.

BROWN, JOHN HENRY, noted TEXAS HISTORIAN, writes on the subject of the CROCKETT and WALLIS FAMILIES in the ENCYCLOPEDIA OF THE NEW WEST, 530, 531.

CABARRUS COUNTY, notes on the HARRIS FAMILY of that section, 343, 534.

CAMPBELL FAMILY, OF VIRGINIA, and its connection with the MOORE FAMILY of MECKLENBURG COUNTY 481-484.

CAMPBELL FAMILY and its connection with the WHITE and STEELE FAMILIES, 492.

CHART OF CALDWELL FAMILY of CUB CREEK, in CHARLOTTE COUNTY, VIRGINIA, 453.

CALDWELL FAMILY of SOMERSET COUNTY, MARYLAND & mention in wills, 516.

CALDWELL, DAVID, including two prominent persons of the same name, 525.

CALHOUN, PATRICK, a son in law of REV. ALEXANDER CRAIGHEAD, 526.

CENSUS OF MECKLENBURG COUNTY, NORTH CAROLINA, by DISTRICTS, shown on map, in 1790, pages 357-368.

CENTRE CHURCH, its History and information relating to, 382.

CHESTER HOTEL in JONESBORO, TENNESSEE, and its connection with the ALLISON FAMILY, 501.

CHRISTIAN'S CREEK, in AUGUSTA COUNTY, VIRGINIA, as shown on MAP, 439.

CHURCH OF ENGLAND and ministers from the PRESbytery of LABAN, 473.

COMBE FAMILY, of OLD RAPPAHANNOCK and its connection with the CUNNINGHAMS, 468.

COMMITTEE OF SAFETY for the SALISBURY DISTRICT, names of members, 513.

CRAIGHEAD, REV. ALEXANDER, and the members of his family and children, 525.

CROCKETT FAMILY and its first connection with REV. JOHN THOMSON, 428.

CROCKETT FAMILY connections with the RICHARDSON, DAVIE and WALLIS FAMILIES, 527-531.

CROCKETT FAMILY of TANGIER ISLAND in ACCOMAC COUNTY, on the EASTERN SHORE of VIRGINIA, 428-429.

CROCKETT, DAVID, hero of the ALAMO, IN TEXAS, and his ANCESTRY and FAMILY, 527-531.

CROCKETT, WILLIAM DAVIE, a member of the TEXAS LEGISLATURE, 531.

CROCKETT FAMILY, tombstone records in the OLD WAXHAW CEMETERY, 410.

CROCKETT, SAMUEL and his wife ESTHER THOMSON and their descendants, 440-442.

CROMWELL, OLIVER, his kinfolks and influence on the MECKLENBURG DECLARATION, 314.

CUB CREEK, VIRGINIA, CALDWELL FAMILY, 451-453

CUMBERLAND PRESBYTERIAN CHURCH founded by a relative of the BAKER-THOMSON family,446.

CUMMINS, REV. FRANCIS, and his family and his children, 532.

CUNNINGHAM FAMILY, of EARLY VIRGINIA, with a chart, 465.

CUNNINGHAMS OF CUB CREEK, VIRGINIA, 463, 464, 465-472.

CUNNINGHAM MANOR, in NORTH IRELAND, 463.

CUNNINGHAM FAMILY of SITTINGBOURNE PARISH in ESSEX COUNTY, VIRGINIA, 465.

CUNNINGHAM FAMILY, of FREDERICKSBURG, VA. 470.

CUNNINGHAM, ALEXANDER, son of the emigrant NEHE-MIAH CUNNINGHAM, and his family, 469.
CUNNINGHAM, CHRISTOPER, and his family of early VIRGINIA and the WATAUGA VALLEY in TENNESSEE, 469.
CUNNINGHAM, JAMES, granted land on WILLIS RIVER CUMBERLAND COUNTY, VIRGINIA (afterwards), the father of the CUB CREEK FAMILY, 471.
CUNNINGHAM, JAMES, of CUB CREEK, VIRGINIA, and his children and grandchildren, many of whom removed to GEORGIA, 472.
CUNNINGHAM, NATHANIEL, his will and notes pertaining to his family, 334.
CUNNINGHAM, ROBERT, brother in law of REV. SAMUEL DAVIES, and member of the HOUSE OF BURGESSES, of VIRGINIA, with WILLIAM RANDOLPH, 436.
CUNNINGHAM, WILLIAM, original emigrant to VIRGINIA, and his FAMILY CHART, 465.

CUNNINGHAM FAMILY, connection with the ROE and BARRON FAMILIES in VIRGINIA, including COMMODORE BARRON, 469.
CUNNINGHAM STOKES, established in RICHMOND, PERSON COUNTY, N. C., GEORGIA and in TENNESSEE, by the Commodore Barron CUNNINGHAMS, 470.
D. A. R. MAGAZINE, list of early officers of MECKLENBURG COUNTY, taken from records and published by, 353-356.
DANIEL FAMILY and its connection with the MOORE FAMILY, 483, 484.
DANIEL, COL. JOHN W., of the 15th TEXAS INFANTRY C. S. A., of DALLAS, TEXAS, 483.
DANIEL, SAMUEL EWING, of GEORGIA, and his connection with the EWING FAMILY of PRINCE EDWARD COUNTY, VIRGINIA, 450.
WILLIAM RICHARDSON DAVIE, revolutionary patriot with his connections and descendants, 527.
DAVIE, HON. WILLIAM R., with tombstone inscriptions of his family in WAXHAW CEMETERY, 410.
DAVIE, CAPT. WILLIAM R., lawyer and TEXAS STATE OFFICIAL, AUSTIN, TEXAS, 527.
DAVIDSON FAMILY of VIRGINIA, MARYLAND and NORTH CAROLINA, 449.
DAVIDSON FAMILY, of MECKLENBURG COUNTY, with notes relating thereto, 504.
DAVIDSON FAMILY PRIVATE BURIAL GOUND, with tombstone inscriptions, 399.
GENERAL WILLIAM (LEE) DAVIDSON, picture of grave in HOPEWELL CHURCH CEMETERY, with inscription copied from monument, 386, 387.
DAVIS FAMILY of MECKLENBURG COUNTY, related to the PICKENS FAMILY, with notes on TENNESSEE connections, 325.
DEEDS FROM THE RECORDS OF MECKLENBURG COUNTY, 317-321.
DUNLAP, GEN. ROBERT GILLIAM, member of SAM HOUSTON'S cabinet of the REPUBLIC OF TEXAS, related to the GILLIAM FAMILY, 460.
EARLY MAP OF MECKLENBURG COUNTY, showing the area included in 1762, 379.
EASTERN SHORE OF MARYLAND and its influence on MECKLENBURG COUNTY and the DECLARATION, 535-536.
EDWARDS FAMILY and its connection with the WILLIAMSON FAMILY of Eastern VIRGINIA, 459.
ELLIOTT FAMILY and its connection with the THOMSON FAMILY and the BAKERS, 447.
ELLIS FAMILY, of ALBEMARLE COUNTY, and its connection with the HARRISONS and GILLIAMS, 460.
ELMWOOD CEMETERY, in CHARLOTTE, N. C., with some of its oldest tombstone inscriptions, 405-406.
EMANUEL PRESBYTERIAN CHURCH in UNION COUNTY, N. C. with tombstone inscriptions and records, 402.
EWING, ALEXANDER, of CECIL COUNTY, MARYLAND, the ancestor of the PRINCE EDWARD COUNTY, VIRGINIA FAMILY of that name; his will, 518.
EWING FAMILY and its connection with the THOMSON, BARRY and LAWSON FAMILIES, 518, 449-451.
FAGG'S MANOR, BLAIR school in PENNSYLVANIA, 514.

FITTEN FAMILY, of MECKLENBURG and GEORGIA, with wills and notes, 333.
FORKS OF THE ELK RIVER, in MARYLAND, 524.
FINLEY, JOHN, celebrated explorer and "long hunter" and son in law of REV. JOHN THOMSON, 462.
GILLEAD CHURCH, in UPPER MECKLENBURG, tombstone records, 406.
GILLESPIE, ROBERT, of CECIL COUNTY, MARYLAND, witness to will of ALEXANDER EWING in CECIL COUNTY, in 1738, 518.
GILLESPIE, ROBERT married ELIZABETH MAXWELL, later the mother of GEN. JOHN STEELE, of ROWAN COUNTY, N. C., 518.
GILLIAM FAMILY, and its connections in VIRGINIA and SOUTH CAROLINA, 454-457.
GILLIAM, MAJOR ROBERT, son in law of REV. RICHARD SANKEY, 454.
GILLIAM, JOHN, father of MAJ. ROBERT GILLIAM, married daughter of REV. PATRICK HENRY, 454.
GILLIAM, CAPT. DEVEREAUX, established fort at KNOXVILLE, TENNESSEE, 460.
GRAHAM, GEN. JOSEPH, and his map of MECKLENBURG COUNTY, followed, 380.
GRAHAM, MRS. MARY, and her children (mother of GEN. JOSEPH and others), 534.
GRAHAM, WILLIAM, the signer, picture of grave at HOPEWELL PRESBYTERIAN CHURCH, 387.
GUN POWDER PLOT and the REGULATORS, participated in by the "black boys" and WILLIAM ALEXANDER, 374, 396, 508.
HAMPTON, REV. JOHN, will in SOMERSET COUNTY, MARYLAND, 515.
HAMPTON, JOSEPH WADE, an early AUSTIN, TEXAS, newspaper man and Presbyterian, and his MECKLENBURG COUNTY, FAMILY, 504.
HARRIS FAMILY, of ROCKY RIVER, in early MECKLENBURG COUNTY, 534.
HARRIS, ROBERT and JAMES, signers of the DECLARATION, 416, 417.
HARRIS FAMILY and its connection with the THOMSON FAMILY, 444.
HARDEMAN, HON. BAILEY, an early member of the Cabinet of the TEXAS REPUBLIC, a descendant of the POLK FAMILY, 509.
HARDEMAN, THOMAS, JONES, a noted early TEXAN, and brother of BAILEY, 509.
HENDERSON FAMILY CHART, showing the descendants of WILLIAM HENDERSON, uncle of GOVERNOR JAMES PINCKNEY HENDERSON, of TEXAS, 489.
HENDERSON FAMILY of MECKLENBURG and LINCOLN COUNTIES, NORTH CAROLINA, 486.
HENDERSON, GOV. JAMES PINCKNEY, of TEXAS, 451, 481, 485.
HENDERSON, JAMES, son in law of HUGH LAWSON & grandfather of GOV. J. P. HENDERSON, his last will and testament in LINCOLN COUNTY NORTH CAROLINA, 487.
HENRY, REV. JOHN, minister in SOMERSET COUNTY, MARYLAND and contemporary and friend of REV. JOHN THOMSON, and father of REV. ROBERT HENRY, of PROVIDENCE CHURCH, 510.
HENRY, REV. PATRICK, uncle of the ORATOR and his friendship with REV. JOHN THOMSON, 432.
HENRY, REV. ROBERT, preacher at PROVIDENCE & STEELE CREEK and step-son of REV. JOHN HAMPTON, 515.
HOPEWELL PRESBYTERIAN CHURCH in MECKLENBURG COUNTY, its hstory and tombstone records, 383, 392.
HOPEWELL CHURCH in UNION COUNTY, N. C. and its tombstone records, 402.
HOPEWELL CHURCH and its ancient gravestones, a picture taken on the grounds, 387.
HORNET'S NEST, the name of a fight in MECKLENBURG COUNTY, during the revolution, 405, 372, 387.
HOUSTON FAMILY, of MECKLENBURG, relatives of the JACK FAMILY, 474, 475.

INDEPENDENCE HILL, home of the famous JOHN McKNITT ALEXANDER, the signer, 372.
JACK FAMILY of MECKLENBURG, GEORGIA, ALABAMA and TEXAS, 473-477.
JACK, JAMES, of MECKLENBURG, who carried the DECLARATION TO PHILADELPHIA, and his descendants chart, 475-476.
JACK, PATRICK, of MECKLENBURG (there were two of them); chart of his descendants and family, 474.
JACK, THOMAS McKINNEY, son of WILLIAM H. JACK, of TEXAS, 476.
JARRETT FAMILY and its connection with the WILLIAMSON and GILLIAM FAMILIES and the LOWES, 459.
JOHNSTON FAMILY, of MECKLENBURG and LINCOLN COUNTIES, NORTH CAROLINA and its connection with the SINCLAIRS and KNOX FAMILIES, 512.
KING FAMILY and its connection with the CROCKETT family of MECKLENBURG, 528, 529.
KING'S MOUNTAIN, a picture of the mountain itself, where the famous battle occurred, 498.
KING GEORGE III, the seventh year of his reign, as mentioned in DAVID MOORE DEED in 1767, 320.
KNOX FAMILY, its history and origin, 510, 511.
KNOX FAMILY, as mentioned in wills in SOMERSET COUNTY, MARYLAND, 516, 517.
KITTRELL, NORMAN G., of Texas, married into CROCKETT FAMILY through KEYES family of ALABAMA, 441.
LANHAM, GOV. S. W. T., a descendant and relative of the TUCKERS and BARRYS of SPARTANBURG, SOUTH CAROLINA, 480.
LAWSON FAMILY and the history of its origin and connections, 449.
LAWSON FAMILY and their relationship to the MOORE FAMILY of MECKLENBURG, 485.
LAWSON FAMILY of CECIL COUNTY, MARYLAND, as mentioned on MARYLAND RECORDS, 519.
LAWSON, DAVID, of CECIL COUNTY, MARYLAND, 519.
LEEPER FAMILY, originated in AUGUSTA COUNTY, VIRGINIA and settled in LINCOLN COUNTY, NORTH CAROLINA on the CATAWBA RIVER, 434.
LONDONDERRY, SIEGE OF, mentioned, 421.
LOVE FAMILY, of MECKLENBURG COUNTY, with wills of the LOVE FAMILY, 326.
MAP OF AUGUSTA COUNTY, VIRGINIA, showing streams and BEVERLY MANOR section, 439.
MAP SHOWING the ORIGINAL MECKLENBURG COUNTY, NORTH CAROLINA and attached territory, 379.
MAP OF U. S. CENSUS DISTRICTS into which MECKLENBURG COUNTY was divided, 369.
MAP SHOWING LOCATION OF HOMES OF THE SIGNERS and THEIR NEIGHBORS, 380.
MARRIAGE RECORDS and connections, from the records and the history of the families, 335-351.
MaKEMIE, REV. FRANCIS, his will and information about his family and connections, 514.
McKEMIE, GEORGE, descendant of REV. FRANCIS MaKEMIE, buried at WAXHAW CEMETERY, 409, 473.
McLEAN, EPHRAIM, and his family, showing connection with the MOORE FAMILY, 493.
MECKLENBURG CONVENTION mentioned, 315, 375, 396 & all through the book.
MECKLENBURG COUNTY (mentioned on nearly every page, and for that reason omitted from INDEX).
MECKLENBURG SIGNERS, three lists on page 315, and sketches on pages 419-421.
MILLS, JUDGE BALLENGER, of GALVESTON, TEXAS, a descendant and relative of the JACK FAMILY, 476.
MOORE, CHARLES, ancestor, and his children and descendants, 477.
MOORE and BARRY FAMILIES of SPARTANBURG COUNTY, S. C. the same as MECKLENBURG FAMILY, 478-480.
MOORE, EPHRAIM the ancestor of the McLEAN FAMILY of MECKLENBURG and ROWAN and ANSON, 492, 493.
MOORE, HUGH, wills and notes relating to his family, in MECKLENBURG and elsewhere, 331, 483.
MOORE, HON. JOHN TROTWOOD and family ancestry, 497.

MOORE, MRS. JOHN TROTWOOD (MARY MOORE DANIEL) and her ancestry. Chart of family, 495.
MOORE, GOV. GABRIEL, of ALABAMA, who died in HUNT COUNTY, TEXAS, and his ancestry, 496.
MOORE & FITZGERALD, firm in PERRY COUNTY, ALABAMA, 483.
MOORE FAMILY and the LAMKINS of WESTMORELAND COUNTY, VIRGINIA, 499.
MORROW FAMILY, of early VIRGINIA, MARYLAND, NORTH CAROLINA, SOUTH CAROLINA, GEORGIA and other STATES, 532.
MORROW FAMILY, wills and other information relating to, 322, 329.
MORROW FAMILY TOMBSTONE RECORDS at SIX MILE CHURCH, 407, 408.
MORROW, DAVID, his tombstone inscription in the OLD WAXHAW CHURCH CEMETERY, 410.
MORROW, JOHN, mentioned in wills in SOMERSET COUNTY, MARYLAND, 517.
MORROW, OWEN, abstract of will of in SOMERSET COUNTY, MARYLAND, 517.
MORROW, WALTER, will in BALTIMORE COUNTY, MARYLAND in 1709, 532.
MORROW, DAVID, will in LOWER NORFOIK COUNTY, Va. in 1689, 532.
MORROW, DANIEL, will or administration in ACCOMAC COUNTY, VA. in 1727, 532.
NEW CASTLE PRESBYTERY, JOHN THOMSON defeated GEORGE GILLESPIE for moderator, 518.
NOTES, GENEALOGICAL OBSERVATIONS on the MECKLENBURG CENSUS RECORDS for 1790, 370-376.
OCHILTREE, DUNCAN, possible signer of the DECLARATION, but never recognized because he became a BRITISH OFFICER, 316.
OFFICERS OF MECKLENBURG COUNTY from 1775 to 1785, from the records, 352-356.
OSBORNE, ALEXANDER, sketch, and connection with McWHORTER, THOMSON, BREVARDS and other MECKLENBURG FAMILIES, 533.
OVERHILL TOWNS of the Cherokee Indians, and the claim of another PATRICK JACK to lands along the TENNESSEE RIVER, 473.
PARSON'S CASE, famous lawsuit by PATRICK HENRY in VIRGINIA, 438.
PATILLO, REV. HENRY, his family and origin and connection with REV. JOHN THOMSON, 430, 431.
PATTON, COL. JAMES and his connection with the THOMSONS and OSBORNES, 434, 435.
PERRY, LANE & CO., famous LONDON MERCHANTS and the WILLIAMSON-LOWE connection, 459.
POPLAR TENT CHURCH, history and information relating to, 396.
PRESBYTERIAN CHURCH IN TOWN OF CHARLOTTE, including its history and tombstone records, 404, 405, 534.
POLK FAMILY from SOMERSET COUNTY, MARYLAND, with the KNOX FAMILY CONNECTIONS, 505-509.
POLK, CAPT. CHARLES and a roster of his company in the Cherokee INDIAN CAMPAIGN, 507.
POLK, EZEKIEL, grandfather of a PRESIDENT of the UNITED STATES, and his descendants, 509.
POLK, JAMES KNOX, President of the UNITED STATES and his family, 509.
PROVIDENCE CHURCH, its history and tombstone records copied from its gravestones, 400-402.
QUEARY, JOHN, a signer of the MECKLENBURG DECLARATION, sketch of, 418.
RAFT SWAMP EXPEDITION, in which CAPT. CHARLES POLK and his Company served, 418
REV. WILLIAM RICHARDSON, his history and family 526-7.
ROCK SPRINGS BURIAL GROUNDS, its location and inscriptions copied from tombstones, 374, 395.
ROCKY RIVER CHURCH and its first minister, REV. ALEXANDER CRAIGHEAD, from Cow Pasture section of VIRGINIA, 396.
RUSK, THOMAS J., of TEXAS, raised in the congregation of REV. THOMAS HARRIS in S. C., 421.
RUST FAMILY of WESTMORELAND COUNTY, VA. and its connection with MOORE and LAMKINS, 499.

SAFFORD, JUDGE B. F., of DALLAS, TEXAS, defeated for JUDGE in ALABAMA, by the father of JOHN TROTWOOD MOORE, of TENNESSEE, 497.

SAMPLE FAMILY of the upper part of MECKLENBURG, related to the ALEXANDER FAMILY, 533.

SANKEY, REV. RICHARD, son in law of REV. JOHN THOMSON and father in law of MAJOR ROBERT GILLIAM, of SOUTH CAROLINA, 451.

SAYERS, GOV. JOSEPH DRAPER, of TEXAS, a descendant of the CROCKETT FAMILY, 433, 441.

SHARPE FAMILY of MECKLENBURG COUNTY, NORTH CAROLINA, from CECIL COUNTY, MARYLAND, 524.

SEVEN OLDEST CHURCHES in MECKLENBURG (leaving out GILLEAD), 381.

SIGNERS OF THE MECKLENBURG DECLARATION and list of their neighbors, 381.

SKETCHES AND HISTORY OF THE MECKLENBURG DECLARATION SIGNERS, 413-421.

SLAUGHTER FAMILY and its connection with the CUNNINGHAM and GAINES FAMILIES, 468.

SMART, SUSAN, as a girl SUSAN BARNETT, witness to the signing of the DECLARATION, 313.

SPRATT, THOMAS, the first settler to come across the YADKIN "on wheels" and the place of his burial in the town of CHARLOTTE, 313, 533.

SIX MILE CHURCH, the old original one, with tombstone inscriptions, 407.

SIX MILE CHURCH, the later one, with tombstone inscriptions from the churchyard, 407, 408.

SIX MILE CHURCH - the old original one - picture of the gravestones, 498.

STEELE CREEK CHURCH, its history and some of its interesting tombstone inscriptions 397-399.

STEELE FAMILY, of CECIL COUNTY, MARYLAND, as disclosed by the will of JOHN GARNER, 518.

STEELE, GEN. JOHN, a son of ELIZABETH MAXWELL who was widow of ROBERT GILLESPIE, 518.

SUGAR CREEK CHURCHYARDS, the oldest, second oldest and the modern one, with records copied from the ancient tombstones, 393-395.

TANGIER ISLAND, ACCOMAC COUNTY, VIRGINIA, original home of the CROCKETT family, 428.

TARRANT COUNTY, TEXAS, original courthouse bonds, invested in by a descendant of the BARRY FAMILY, of MECKLENBURG COUNTY, 480.

TAYLOR, DEAN T. U., of the UNIVERSITY of TEXAS, a descendant of the ALLISON FAMILY, 495.

TEXAS CROCKETT FAMILY, an account of the WAXHAW and MECKLENBURG family, 530.

THOMPSON, REV. JOHN, his "POOR ORPHANS LEGACY" & "SHORTER CATECHISM", 433, 446.

THOMPSON, REV. JOHN, an account of his family, his coming to VIRGINIA, his VIRGINIA RELATIVES & connections and the families with which he was allied; this account includes all data from page 425 to 472, inclusive, including an account of those families associated with his own. Besides this there is much other scattered material, not included in these pages, but to be found in all sections of the book. RUN THE INDEX FOR OTHER MATERIAL.

THOMSON, REV. JOHN in AUGUSTA COUNTY, VIRGINIA, 432.

THOMSON, REV. JOHN, with list of his thirteen children, 440.

THOMSON, ABRAHAM, son of REV. JOHN THOMSON, 448.

THOMSON, ROGER, son of REV. JOHN THOMSON and son in law of HUGH LAWSON, 461.

THOMPSON FAMILY of AUGUSTA COUNTY, VIRGINIA, 433.

THOMPSONS of YORK COUNTY, VIRGINIA, 426-428.

TINKLING SPRINGS CHURCH, AUGUSTA COUNTY, VIRGINIA with MAP OF THE LOCALITY, 439.

TOOLE'S FORD in MECKLENBURG COUNTY, NORTH CAROLINA, 473.

TRYON COUNTY, NORTH CAROLINA, Declaration of Independence by Convention held, 501.

U. S. CENSUS DISTRICTS OF MECKLENBURG COUNTY in 1790, with MAP showing locations, 369.

UNITED STATES CENSUS RECORDS OF MECKLENBURG COUNTY, 1790, 357-368.

UNDERWOOD FAMILY of Early VIRGINIA, with chart showing family connections, 467, 466.

UNION COUNTY, NORTH CAROLINA CHURCHES and the records from old tombstones, 402.

WAIKUP FAMILY of MARYLAND and MECKLENBURG CO. NORTH CAROLINA, 519, 536, 408.

WALLIS, REV. JAMES, minister of PROVIDENCE & his family and connections with the ALEXANDERS and CROCKETTS, 530-531.

WASHINGTON COUNTY, TEXAS, where the WALLIS and CROCKETT family settled, 531.

WAXHAW CHURCH and the old tobstone inscriptions on its graves, 408-410.

WAXHAW CEMETERY, picture of the old graveyard near the CHURCH, 498.

WEALTHY LEADERS and slave owners of MECKLENBURG COUNTY in 1790, 377-378.

WHITE, JAMES, founder of KNOXVILLE, TENNESSEE, and his descendants, 490-492.

WHITE, MOSES and his family of the BEATTIE'S FORD settlement on the CATAWBA RIVER, 424.

WHITTINGTON, WILLIAM, of SOMERSET COUNTY MARYLAND, his will, 517. JOHN MORROW one of those named.

WILLS from the MARYLAND RECORDS, 514-519.

WILLS from the MECKLENBURG RECORDS, 322-334.

WILSON FAMILY, of AUGUSTA COUNTY, VIRGINIA, 436-438.

WILSON, ROBERT, of SOMERSET COUNTY, MARYLAND, his last will and testament, 514.

WILSON, SAMUEL, of MECKLENBURG, father in law of EZEKIEL POLK, and his family, 503-504.

WILLIAMSON FAMILY, of YORK COUNTY, SOUTH CAROLINA, father of the MECKLENBURG ministers, 534.

WILLIAMSON FAMILY of EASTERN VIRGINIA, and its earliest American origin, 458.

WILLIAMSON, ROBERT McALPIN, of TEXAS, known as "THREE LEGGED WILLIE", account of his family and relationship to the GILLIAMS, JARRETS and LOWES, 455-460.

WINSLOW FAMILY, and its relationship to the BEVERLY FAMILY of ESSEX COUNTY, VIRGINIA & other lines, 533.

WORTHINGTON, SAMUEL and his wife ALICE, of SOMERSET COUNTY, MARYLAND, the ancestors of the NORTH CAROLINA and TENNESSEE WORTHINGTON FAMILY, 516.

YEARWOOD, JOHN FRANCIS, of the famous I. X. L. TEXAS RANCH, and of WILLIAMSON COUNTY, TEXAS, a descendant of REV. JOHN THOMSON & the CROCKETT family, 442.

NAME INDEX
PAGES 313 TO 536

ABBOTT 366
ABERNATHY 335, 338, 340, 344, 346, 359, 381, 383, 489, 487.
ADAIR 483, 494, 497, 501.
ADAMS 366, 412, 423, 463,472 494, 513
ADAMSON 326
ADELMAN 362
AIKENS 491
AKER 352
ALEXANDER 314, 320, 323-326, 328-332, 340-352, 357-361, 364, 367, 368, 370-374, 376-378, 381, 383, 384, 393-396, 398, 400, 404, 406, 413-420, 422, 424, 432, 434, 449, 451, 473, 334-339, 474, 482-483, 485 490, 494, 502-508, 512,513 515-518, 520-525, 530-536.
ALLEN 322, 357, 358, 363, 364, 366, 373, 377, 384, 427, 428, 438, 458, 465, 517.
ALLISON 331, 335, 336, 339,349 350, 357, 361, 373, 377, 384.
ALSTON 494
ANDERSON 361, 400, 412, 425, 427, 444-446, 463, 479,488 510, 511, 514.
ANDREWS 318, 335-337, 348, 361 364, 373, 405, 449, 462, 514.
APPLETON 366
APPLEWHITE 531
ARCHIBALD 359, 377, 396, 487.
ARMISTEAD 467
ARMSTRONG 317-319, 432, 361, 364, 373, 377, 422, 439, 447, 471
ARROWOOD 412
ASHLEY 363
ATKINS 359
ATWOOD 456, 509
AUBREY 363
AUSTIN 402
AVENT 366, 378
AVERY 376, 381, 415, 417-419.
AYLETTE 484, 486.

BACON 449
BAILEY 358, 360, 364
BAIN 385
BAIRD 460
BAKER 322, 328, 336, 338, 340, 347, 350, 352, 357, 358, 361, 372, 373, 381, 385, 394, 409, 416, 429, 440, 442-444, 446-448, 461, 467, 468, 471, 533, 534.
BALCH 315, 316, 334, 336, 337, 358, 376, 381, 396, 419, 447, 452, 453, 534.
BALLINGER 476
BALLENTINE 471
BALDREICH 336, 340, 494
BALDWIN 336, 340, 404
BALL 467
BALLARD 456, 464, 470, 512, 514, 515
BAILEY 352
BANE 335, 385, 415, 435
BANKS 326
BARBARA 352
BARKER 314, 534
BARHAM 467
BARKLEY 385, 388, 411
BARLOW 358
BARNARD 327
BARNES 336, 347, 352, 361, 495
BARNHARDT 362, 363
BARNHILL 349, 352, 364
BARNETT 313, 314, 320-322, 324 326-328, 334, 336-339, 348, 349, 341, 352, 357, 358, 366-368, 370, 381, 382, 385 393-395, 398, 402, 409, 448 474, 476, 481, 482, 529,533
BARR 321, 334, 336, 352, 396.
BARRON 385, 469, 479, 516
BARROW 514
BARRINGER 352, 362, 363, 373, 378, 381, 417, 420
BARRY 314, 315, 317, 319, 320, 321, 323, 336, 343, 361, 373 376, 381-383, 385, 415,416, 449, 450, 454, 461,477-481, 483, 485, 492, 493, 496, 502, 503, 518, 519, 535.
BARTON 385, 519
BASDELL 366, 378
BASKINS 433
BATTLE 422
BATEY 358, 367
BATTE 468
BATES 429, 442, 446
BATTLE 444
BAWYERS 362
BAXTER 327, 328, 368, 378, 399 402, 406
BAYLEY 467, 517
BAYLOR 465
BAYS 368
BEACH 359
BEAMER 473
BEAN 364, 482
BEARD 494, 530.
BEASON 317, 320
BEATTY 317, 336, 346, 347, 350 352, 357, 370, 377, 378,382 398, 424
BEAVER 352
BECK 362
BECKHAM 407
BEDDER 517
BEGS 320
BEHRINGER 417
BELK 352, 366, 378, 381, 402
BELL 319, 346, 352, 360, 361 372, 385, 406, 433, 442, 458, 470, 496, 509,513,517
BENHAM 378
BENN 314
BENNEKLEW 352
BENNETT 464, 469, 486, 515
BENSON 361, 479, 480
BERGER 362
BERKELEY 314, 473, 536
BERRY 348, 360
BERRYHILL 319, 336, 347,352 357, 381, 405
BEST 362
BEVER 363
BEVERLY 429, 430, 432, 436, 468, 471, 472, 533
BICKETT 365
BIGGERS 317, 318, 349, 352, 361, 364, 370, 373, 381, 407
BIGHAM 329, 352, 357, 358,367 377, 397-399, 532
BIGHANS 350
BINGHAM 533
BILLS 509
BILLINGSLEA 479, 483, 484,497
BILLINGTON 435, 499
BIRD 337
BLACK 326 330, 345, 349, 352, 359, 360, 362, 364, 365, 367, 375, 377, 378, 385, 400, 478, 496
BLACKWELDER 352, 362, 363
BLACKWOOD 357, 359, 385, 405
BLAKELEY 336, 345, 406, 410
BLAKENEY 407
BLAIR 335, 336, 338, 345, 347 348, 352, 365, 398, 409, 430, 499, 506, 514, 518
BLASTER 363
BLESS 362
BLEWETT 326
BLOUITT 427
BLYTHE 328, 335, 336, 342, 345, 352, 360, 366, 372, 385, 499
BLUE 366
BOARDMAN 532
BOATWRIGHT 336, 350
BOGER 362
BOGGS 334, 336, 343, 447
BOND 336, 343, 345, 352, 366
BONHAM 368
BOOKER 361, 428, 429, 461
BOONE 462, 473
BOOTEN 334
BOOTH 425, 464, 467, 468
BORDLEY 532
BOUDINET 452
BOST 344, 349, 352, 363
BOSTION 363
BOSTON 517
BOSTWICK 339
BOUCHELLE 502, 519, 532
BOUGHFRIEND 359
BOULAN 517
BOUSH 438
BOUTWELL 469
BOWERS 336, 344
BOWIE 313, 474
BOWMAN 325, 377
BOYCE 406
BOYD 333, 336, 338, 404, 412 483, 495
BOZEMAN 516
BOZZELL 336, 346
BRABHAM 325
BRACKER 519
BRACKETT 504
BRADDOCK 413
BRADFORD 318, 361, 373, 462.

545

BRADLEY 352, 359, 385
BRADSHAW 325, 336, 345, 352, 359, 366
BRALEY 358
BRANDON 364, 511
BRANK 493
BRATTON 352
BRAY 467
BREVARD 315, 334, 335, 336, 338, 346, 352, 370, 376, 381, 382, 399, 403, 413, 415, 444, 504, 506, 513, 533
BREWSTER 352, 378
BRIDGER 458, 460
BRIDGES 363, 467, 468
BRIGGS 430, 465
BRIGHAM 319
BRINEGAR 363
BRINKLEY 345, 350
BROADNAX 360, 377
BROOKE 425, 443, 446, 467, 468, 471, 480
BROWN 317, 318, 322, 327-330, 336, 342, 344, 348, 349, 352, 357, 359, 361, 363, 364, 366, 368, 373, 381, 385, 398, 482, 483, 484, 495, 499, 501, 506, 517, 526, 529
BROWNFIELD 352, 357
BROUGHTON 437
BROUSTER 352
BRYAN 357, 364, 476
BRYANCE 362
BRYSON 334, 360
BUAM 357
BUCHANAN 335, 346, 352, 359, 365, 434, 435
BUCK 317
BUCKALOO 318, 339, 507
BUCKNER 339
BUGG 364
BULLOCK 496
BUMGARDNER 411
BURDETT 464, 465
BURLYSON 407
BURNS 364
BURNETT 351, 458
BURNEY 340
BURTON 336, 347, 412, 422, 423, 468, 513
BURWICK 317
BUSBY 336, 344, 346
BUSSARD 362, 378
BUTT 349
BUTLER 345, 385, 425, 466, 467, 468, 470
BUTNER 319
BUTTON 342
BYARS 485, 513
BYRD 428, 495
BYRUM 319, 328, 339, 347, 348, 398.

CABARRAS 344, 506
CAIGLE 363, 364
CAIN 336, 342
CAIRNS 352, 366, 378
CALDER 406
CALDWELL 314, 323, 332, 335-341, 344-346, 348-352, 359, 360, 371, 374, 381, 385, 396, 399, 404, 405, 410, 425, 431, 448, 449, 451-453, 455-457, 462, 463, 477, 478, 492, 494, 495, 504, 505, 516-518, 524-527, 534, 535.

CALHOUN 317, 337, 348, 358, 421, 453, 457, 462, 526.
CALLICUT 475
CALVERT 536
CAMM 438
CAMPBELL 322, 332, 337, 343, 352, 357, 358, 361, 362, 364, 374, 381, 386, 393, 394, 402, 436, 477, 478, 481, 490, 492, 494, 500, 509
CANDISH 327, 511
CANNON 326, 332, 352, 359, 361, 381, 385, 522, 524
CAPLE 362
CAPPS 385
CARGIE 365
CARGILL 449, 455
CARLOCK 337, 349
CARR 385, 393, 526, 527, 530
CARNEY 358
CARPENTER 321, 493, 494
CARRICK 316, 490
CARRIGAN 322, 352, 361, 365, 373, 381
CARRIGER 363
CARROLL 357, 377
CARRUTH 337, 339, 347, 352, 405, 487, 526
CARUTHERS 331, 337, 352, 357, 358, 361, 364, 365, 374, 378, 396
CARSON 313, 318, 352, 357, 360, 383, 385, 386, 405.
CARTER 430, 442, 468, 495, 507
CARY 430, 431, 437, 446, 465, 471, 472, 517
CARIE 517
CASEY 361
CASHON 337, 344, 346
CASTILLO 357
CASTOR 362, 499
CATHCART 512
CATHERWOOD 516
CATLETT 467, 468
CATHEY 337, 339, 352, 357, 360, 370, 397, 381, 382, 398, 410
CATTOR 357
CANFIELD 453
CAYNEHOOE 466
CERLAUGH 362
CHAMBERLAIN 362, 469
CHAMBERS 318, 367, 511
CHAINEY 366
CHAPPELL 337
CHAPMAN 467
CHARLES 365
CHATWELL 487
CHEEK 337, 342, 358, 377, 398
CHERRY 407
CHESTER 501
CHEW 432, 470
CHILES 350
CHILDRESS 432, 509
CHISWELL 437
CHRISTENBURY 332, 337, 343, 349, 351, 361
CHRISTIAN 432, 434, 436, 475
CHRISTMAN 352, 363
CHRONICLE 485
CHURCH 532
CLAIN 363
CLANTZ 412
CLAPAN 520
CLARK 332, 335-337, 342-344, 346, 349, 352, 357, 359, 361, 505, 507
CLAUGHTON 499
CLAY 365

CLAYBORNE 314
CLAYTON 557
CLEFFLAND 357
CLEMENTS 363, 472, 515
CLERICE 362
CLETMON 367
CLINE 363
CLONTS 362
CLOPTON 459
CLOSIAN 362
CLOTS 363
CLOUD 317, 320
CLUB 317
COAK 366
COAN 363
COBLE 362, 488
COBBS 427, 428, 430, 431, 433, 438, 461, 463, 465, 471, 527
COCKE 460, 473, 475
COCHRAN 318, 337, 346, 352, 360, 364, 366, 374, 378, 396
COFFEY 337, 341, 344, 370, 398, 401, 407, 408, 442, 450
COIE 363
COLLEGE 365
COLBERT 337, 342, 472
COLDWELL 364, 374
COLEMAN 362, 495
COLLAND 364
COLLIER 446, 525
COLLINGS 348
COLLINS 337, 386, 389
COLSTON 492
COLTON 412
COMBE 425, 466-469
COMBS 466, 468
CONNELL 336, 402
CONNINGHAM 367
CONNOR 377, 381, 403, 422-424, 474, 503, 513, 534
CONTS 365
COOK 325, 337, 344, 347, 353, 362, 364, 368, 377, 378
COOKE 360, 403
COOLEY 462
COOPER 337, 349, 357, 358, 361, 466
COPELAND 361, 373
CORBIN 435
CORCHAM 357
CORNWELL 516
CORZINE 362, 373
COSBY 341, 475
COTHRON 333
COTTISER 362
COTTON 465, 467
COUL 366, 378
COULTER 486
COUNCIL 495, 496
COUSAR 409
COUSART 409
COURTNEY 366
COUTSON 409
COVINGTON 397
COWAN 313, 337, 348, 349, 359, 408, 422
COX 362, 398, 495
CRAIG 337, 341, 366, 425, 429, 433, 434, 445, 495, 519
CRAIGHEAD 314, 336, 338, 353, 359, 371, 377, 383, 393, 396, 397, 400, 413, 419-421, 453, 473, 518, 625, 528, 536
CRAVEN 386
CRAWFORD 338, 365, 381, 408, 516, 526.

CHEATON 361
CREPS 363, 378
CRESCO 363
CRESWELL 322
CRICKETT 462
CRISWELL 396
CROCKETT 317, 321, 324, 325,
    327, 329, 336, 338, 339,
    345, 350, 353, 360, 367,
    372, 375, 378, 381, 400,
    410, 425, 428, 429, 430,
    431-433, 437, 439, 440-
    442, 447, 482, 526-528,
    530-532.
CROCKETTAIRE 442
CROMWELL 314, 431
CROOK 478
CROPPER 517
CROSS 349
CROUL 363
CROWLE 364, 365, 374
CROWELL 364, 374, 402
CROZIER 353
CRUM 365
CRUMELL 364
CRUMP 479
CRUSE 362, 373
CRUZINE 353
CRYE 366
CULBERTSON 366
CULP 362, 807
CUMMINS 313, 334, 341, 345,
    357, 381, 386, 476, 481,
    483, 484, 506, 507, 514,
    532
CUNNINGHAM 324, 327, 333-335,
    338-340, 347-349, 353, 368,
    367, 378, 381, 401, 417, 421
    425-431, 434, 436, 440, 446
    448-450, 453, 454, 456, 457
    461, 463-465, 467-472, 477
    478, 490, 534, 535, 375, 466
CURETON 346, 400, 407
CURRIE 517
CURRY 329, 360, 367, 372
CUSTIS 430
CUTHBERT 330
CUTHBERTSON 364, 365, 374, 403
    412
CUTHINS 519

DABBS 430, 472
DABNEY 391
DACRES 317
DAKER(BAKER?) 358
DAIL 520
DALTON 486
DAMOURVILLE 499
DANDRIDGE 412, 430
DANIEL 326, 327, 337, 341, 347
    348, 425, 426, 428, 429,
    431, 435, 441, 448, 450,
    452, 454, 457, 463, 465,
    464, 469, 472, 483, 484,
    495, 497, 499
DARBY 366
DARNELL 327, 333, 358, 377,
    404
DARROSOL 334
DASHIEL 517
DAVENPORT 335, 338, 427, 428,
    465, 489
DAVIE 338, 375, 400, 408, 497,
    526, 527, 530, 531
DAVIES 394, 409, 420, 426, 431,
    471, 510, 514, 515, 526
DAVISON 437

DAVIDSON 314, 315, 316, 319,
    320, 321, 323, 328, 334-
    338, 343, 346, 349-351, 353
    360, 370, 372, 376, 377,
    381-383, 386, 387, 405, 406
    412, 414-416, 420, 422, 440
    443, 447, 450, 479, 493,
    503, 504, 508, 513, 535
DAVIS 321, 324-326, 330, 334,
    338-340, 342, -345, 349, 353,
    357, 358, 360, 361, 364-366,
    372, 373, 377, 381, 396,
    400, 402, 412, 441, 447,
    451, 455, 458, 471, 482,
    519, 525, 532
DAWNS 367
DAWSON 431, 432, 455, 512
DEAN 470
DEATON 362
DELANEY 408
DELONEY 427, 428, 449, 465
DEMSEY 366
DENT 529
DENTON 327, 491
DERMOND 368
DERRICKSON 413
DICKSON 322, 332, 365, 413,
    481, 494, 519
DIGGES 430
DINKINS 358, 377
DIXON 337, 339, 344
DOAK 462, 495, 534
DOBY 399, 407
DOBBS 320, 473
DOBBINS 330, 351
DODD 509
DOHERTY 339, 346, 359, 360,
    361, 386
DOUGHERTY 350, 451
DOLIN 362
DONALDSON 321, 365, 367
DONELSON 516, 526
DORTON 364
DOUGLASS 338, 350, 353, 366,
    378, 386, 398, 409
DOVAN 516
DOVE 363
DOWNS 315, 317, 318, 325, 327
    328, 333, 338, 339, 348,
    353, 367, 375, 376, 378,
    381, 419, 432, 434, 516,
    529
DOSIER 366
DOZIER 484
DRAFFEN 353, 400
DRAKE 441, 442, 434
DRAPER 432
DRESHILL 353
DRUMMOND 473
DRY 363 353 362
DUCE 403
DUCK 360, 372
DUCKWORTH 329, 346, 353, 406
DUDGEON 451
DUDLEY 441
DUGAN 492
DUNKINS 322, 327
DULANEY 516
DUNBAR 366
DUNLAP 320, 324, 330, 336, 338
    342, 353, 408, 409, 436,
    439, 460, 482, 493, 526.
DUNN 339, 344, 353, 358, 360,
    364, 366, 381, 386, 401,
    402
DUNNE 386
DURANT 314, 536
DURKEE 495
DURST 509
DUVAL 467

DYER 439
DYSART 328, 339, 341, 353,
    474

EAFRIT 363
EAGER 364, 374, 378
EAGLEY 362
EAKINS 366
EARLY 472
EASENHART 362
EAST 453
EATON 428, 441
EDEN 512
EDENTON 353
EDMISTON 359
EDWARDS 353, 459, 464, 475,
    476, 492, 519
EFFINGER 479
EGGLESTON 443, 446
ELEY 470
ELGIN 357
ELLIOTT 313, 317, 318, 320,
    322, 326, 327, 334, 345,
    353, 358, 360, 386, 425,
    441-443, 447, 448, 481,
    529
ELLIS 334, 447, 455, 460, 496
ELZEY 516, 517
EMERSON 344, 358, 361, 377,
    386
EPPES 424, 460
ERWIN 326, 329, 347, 353, 358
    360, 368, 376, 381, 395,
    461, 524
ESPEY 412
ESSLEMAN 368
EVALT 362
EVANS 483, 495, 501
EVENSHINE 353
EVINS 479, 480, 483, 524
EVITTS 360
EWART 360, 488, 511-513
EWEN 519
EWING 381, 425, 444, 446-453,
    470, 485, 487, 493, 502,
    518, 519, 525, 532, 534,
    535
EXUM 458

FAGGENWINTER 362
FAGGETT 353, 363, 367, 378
FAIRLOE 516
FALLEN 519
FALLS 339, 343, 349
FANNER 353
FARLEY 435
FARR 343, 361, 362, 377, 378
FARRELL 394
FARRER 353
FAULK 402
FAULKNER 466
FENNELL 479
FERGUSON 319, 353, 358, 362,
    364, 378, 428, 440, 450,
    461
FERRILL 360
FESPERMAN 362
FINCHER 328, 366
FINK 363
FINLEY 318, 324, 353, 366,
    381, 425, 432, 434, 436
    439, 440, 452, 453, 456
    462, 473, 491, 507, 518
    518
FINNY 353
FIPPS 358
FISHER 353, 363, 365, 367
FISKE 532
FITE 489

FITTEN 330, 331, 333, 339, 341, 343, 344, 347, 382, 481
FITZGERALD 331, 339, 483, 484, 516
FLAUGH 365
FLEET 499
FLEMING 361, 430, 465, 471
FLENNIKEN 315, 339, 347, 348, 349, 353, 360, 368, 376, 381, 401, 421, 431
FLINN 394
FLITBREATH 333
FLOW 349, 351, 391
FLOYD 434, 435
FOGLEMAN 363
FOIL 363
FOIX 363
FONTAINE 455
FOOTE 525
FORBES 366, 484
FORD 315, 318, 339, 343, 353, 365, 374, 376, 378, 381, 400, 418, 507
FORNEY 381, 513
FORREST 453
FORRESTER 378
FOSTER 353, 408, 409, 479, 524
FORSYTHE 360, 366
FORTNER 403
FOWLER 366
FOX 351
FRANK 418
FRANKLIN 339, 433
FRAZIER 343, 353, 360, 361
FREEMAN 331, 353, 357, 365, 378
FRIDAY 489
FRIZZELL 519
FROGG 441
FROHACK 318, 320
FRUSELAND 363
FULGHAM 470
FULHAM 386
FULLENWIDER 422, 423
FULTON 446
FULWOOD 349, 391
FURR 334, 353, 362, 363, 378

————

GAINES 463, 467, 472
GALBRAITH 321, 353, 367, 375, 381, 507, 529
GALLIWAY 359
GALWITH 519
GAMBIE 408
GANTT 367
GARDNER 353, 359, 435, 453
GARMON (JARMON) 353, 365, 378
GARNATT 353
GARNER 499, 578, 522
GARRISON 349, 351, 353, 359, 360, 377, 386
GARTON 326
GASAWAY 261
GASTON 368
GATEWOOD 469
GIBBONS 344, 366, 405, 406, 407
GIBBONY 357, 370, 377, 398
GIBSON 360, 406, 442, 482, 491, 516
GIFFORD 353
GILBERT 494
GILES 353, 359
GILLEDEN 334
GILLELAND 350, 361
GILLENWATERS 495
INGLES 353, 364, 451

GILLESPIE 335, 360, 361, 366, 367, 372, 373, 404, 408, 411, 412, 449, 462, 518.
GILLIAM 425, 432, 439, 453-460, 462, 492.
GILMORE 353, 358-361, 372, 373
GIPSON 359
GIVENS 319, 353, 360, 366, 372, 377, 403, 516
GLANTS 403
GLASS 365
GLOVER 338, 345, 349, 361, 435, 455, 457
GODDARD 516
GOFORTH 359, 393
GOLDSMITH 517
GOLDTHWAITE 492
GONDER 362, 365
GOOD 443
GOODE 460, 486
GOODMAN 353, 362, 363
GOODNIGHT 353, 362
GOODRICH 438
GORDON 322, 327, 353, 366, 441, 482
GOREE 479
GORMLEY 491
GOWER 467
GRACY 510, 511, 512
GRAHAM 313-315, 319, 323, 324, 334, 335, 339, 343, 346, 357, 359, 360, 368, 370, 372, 353, 376, 377, 380-382, 384, 386, 387, 402, 404-406, 420-425, 440, 447, 461, 477, 478, 504, 513, 515, 534.
GRAVES 464
GRAY 351, 353, 366, 405, 475
GREEN 353, 402, 519
GREENE 357, 518
GREER 353, 358, 367, 377, 409
GREGORY 363, 373, 391.
GREY 386
GRIER 339, 349, 353, 394, 397, 398, 401, 412
GRIBBLE 319, 353, 402
GRIFFIN 339, 347, 367
GRIFFITH 333
GRIFFEY 357
GRISHAM 470
GROCE 442
GRONER 362
GROOME 519
GRUBBLE 365
GRUFF 363
GRYMES 430
GUIRE 367
GULLICK 494
GYLLOT 517

————

HADDEN 367, 409
HADDOCK 362
HADLEY 362
HAGENS 367, 378, 400, 407, 408
HAGLER 353, 363
HARGITT 366
HALL 331, 339, 346, 353, 361, 365, 411, 507
HAMBRIGHT 434, 494
HAMPTON 314, 339, 340, 350, 360, 377, 381, 386, 476, 501, 504, 514, 515, 517, 518, 520, 524, 525, 529, 535, 536.
HAMILTON 353, 360, 361, 477, 478, 479, 481, 483, 490, 497, 500, 501, 514
HAMMOND 317, 318, 360, 372
HANDLEY 433

HANNA 328, 399, 405, 406, 433, 477, 479
HANNAH 403, 419, 463, 472, 476, 477
HANNON 386
HANSEN 519
HANSIL 360
HAPPOLDT 513
HAPWORTH 357
HARKEY 342
HARBISON 365
HARDEMAN 509
HARDEN 320, 494
HARDING 318, 460, 462
HARDMAN 363
HARDY 458, 459
HARDWICK 363
HARGETT 353
HARNEY 363
HARGROVE 339, 346, 357
HARKEY 346, 353, 365
HARKNESS 367
HARMON 322
HARPER 334, 339, 340, 360, 409, 532
HARRIS 315, 316, 319, 320, 322, 328, 335-345, 347-351, 353, 358, 360, 361, 363-366, 372, 374, 376, 378, 381, 382, 395, 396, 398, 404, 416-418, 421, 425, 440, 444, 445, 455-457, 460, 481, 504, 507, 509, 529, 533-536
HARRISON 324, 351, 365, 367, 378, 381, 430, 455, 456, 459, 460, 465, 466, 468, 471, 476, 479, 480, 496, 499
HARRY 335, 340, 386, 489
HASKINS 428
HAWFIELD 333
HAWKINS 340, 344, 345, 346, 423, 428, 465, 467, 506, 532
HAYNES 353, 357, 398
HAY 318, 334
HAYDEN 459
HAYS 320, 364, 368, 509
HATES 353, 513
HANKS 357
HEARD 406, 426, 427, 455
HEATH 407
HEGANS (HAGENS) 322, 328, 329, 366
HEILY 474
HELMS 343, 366
HELLEMS 366
HENDRY 317, 319, 320
HENDERSON 314, 316, 320, 325, 326, 328 335-337, 339, 340, 344-348, 353, 358-360, 371, 377, 381, 384, 386, 388, 393-395, 399, 404, 406, 410, 411, 433, 434, 449, 450, 451, 462, 479, 485-489, 496, 503, 504, 513, 525, 526.
HENNEGAR 363
HENNEGAN 346
HENNINGER 366
HENRY 320, 334, 338, 340, 353, 360, 397, 400, 422, 425, 431, 432, 438, 451, 454-456, 459, 460, 491, 494, 514, 515, 517, 518, 524, 525, 527-530, 535, 536.
HENSHAW 455
HENSON 373
HERNDON 327, 463, 470, 496

548

HESE 363
HICKMAN 425, 435
HIDE 519
HIGAMANS 516
HILGARTNER 509
HIGGINS 329
HILL 324, 329, 332, 341, 345
  348, 351, 353, 360, 372,
  381, 449, 468, 481, 493,
  494, 513
HINMAN 363
HIPP 360
HISE 363, 366
HISS 353
HOAN 363
HOBLEY 362
HOBSON 412
HODGE 367, 474
HODGKINS 468
HODNETT 446, 447, 467
HOFFER 320
HOGANS 353
HOGDEN 357
HOGE 367
HOGUE 491
HOKE 422, 423, 487
HOLBROOK 353, 361
HOLLAND 353, 487
HOLDEN 462, 516
HOLMAN 457
HOLT 358
HOLSTON 469
HOLTHAM 521
HOMAN 519
HONEYCUTT 363
HOOD 322, 353, 365, 378, 455
HOOVER 354
HOPE 354, 359, 514
HOPKINS 327, 430, 517
HORLASHER 354
HORN 339
HORSEY 314, 361, 532, 535
HOUGHTON 326
HOUSE 329, 354, 363
HOUSTON 322, 325, 332, 337,
  340, 341, 345, 349, 354,
  359, 361, 366, 367, 373,
  375, 377, 378, 381, 388,
  394, 395, 400-402, 406,
  417, 420, 474-476, 484,
  488, 489, 509
HOWARD 328, 341, 345, 351, 366
  409, 493, 496, 499, 503,
  504
HOWE 358, 420
HOWELL 336, 364, 378, 454,
  499
HOEY 353
HOWEY 366, 401
HOWIE 336, 337, 341, 346, 366
  378, 400, 401, 409, 527
HOY 480
HOYLE 422, 423
HUBBARD 422, 466
HUBER 363
HUCKLEY 496
HUDSON 360, 467
HUEY 337, 341, 342, 409
HUGHES 430, 431, 465, 471,
  472, 507
HUGHEY 367
HUGHIE 354
HUNNICUTT 360
HUNT 360, 377, 480
HUNTER 316, 337, 339, 341, 349
  356, 357, 359, 374, 388,
  397, 403, 416, 419, 489,
  475, 507
HURD 426, 427
HURLAUGHER 363

HUSBANDS 518
HUTCHINS 334
HUTCHINSON (HUTCHISON) 351, 354
  357, 358, 361, 372, 394,
  399, 407, 409
HUTSON 328
HUTTER 517
HYLAND 519

———

INGLES 428
IRELAND 341, 403, 408, 420,
  517
IRWIN 315, 338, 341, 343, 344,
  354, 359-361, 365, 376, 388,
  404-406, 413, 415, 417, 421,
  450, 461, 479, 485, 486, 495,
  502
ISENHAKER 363
ISHAM 358
ISLER 357
IZEL 366

———

JACK 318, 328, 336, 339, 341,
  349, 350, 351, 354, 371,
  448, 473-475, 494, 503,
  507, 513, 532, 533
JACKS 483
JACKSON 313, 326, 327, 357,
  375, 378, 381, 396, 408,
  409, 441, 465, 473, 476,
  481, 482, 496, 497, 500,
  501, 502, 515, 526, 532,
  534, 535
JAMES 460
JAMISON 340, 341, 388, 405, 436
JARMON 365
JARRETT 354, 363, 425, 436, 455
  456, 458-460, 469, 476, 495
JEFFERSON 455, 460
JEGGITTS 438
JEMISON 360
JENIFER 519
JENKINS 514, 517
JETTON 335, 354, 360, 411, 412
  424
JIMISON 360
JINKINS 368
JOHN 341, 343, 344, 347, 348,
  367
JOHNSON 320, 332, 349, 388, 406
  513, 519
JOHNSTON 317, 318, 339, 341-
  343, 349, 350, 354, 359,
  360, 365, 400, 406, 409,
  412, 446, 463, 471, 472,
  488, 494, 499, 510-513,
  533
JONES 341, 344, 395, 405, 428,
  460, 468, 483, 501, 504,
  519, 527
JORDAN 446, 457, 486
JOYNER 458
JUKE 363
JULIAN 350
JUNKINS 412

———

KAIRNES 354
KANADY 394
KARR 401
KEECH 332
KEEN 491
KEENAN 423
KEITH 492
KELIAH 354

KELLEY 360, 476
KELSO 463
KELUGH 359
KENDALL 467
KENDRICK 327, 367
KENNEY 394, 516
KENNEDY 323, 341, 344, 354,
  358, 359, 365
KIMBERLY 388
KENTON 354, 381, 421
KERLOCK 362, 363
KERNS 335, 341, 350, 388, 420
KERR 317, 320, 333, 337, 341,
  342, 347, 348, 354, 357,
  360, 388, 401
KEW 320
KEVER 359
KEYES 441
KIDD 406
KIDWELL 365
KILGORE 314, 349, 478, 480
KILPATRICK 354
KIMMINS 364
KINCAID 388
KINDRICK 358
KING 325, 326, 327, 342, 347,
  354, 366, 368, 388, 398,
  456, 483, 514, 515, 517,
  528, 529, 530, 533
KIRK 341, 347
KIRKES 357
KIRKPATRICK 341, 347, 364, 368
  378, 471, 490
KITHCART 357
KITTRELL 441
KNEESE 363
KNIGHT 437, 474
KNOCK 505, 510
KNOX 317, 327, 341, 342, 345,
  349, 351, 354, 358, 360,
  368, 377, 381, 389, 395,
  397, 411, 412, 418, 503,
  505, 509-514, 506, 516,
  517
KREPPS 363
KUESTER 406
KUYKENDALL 317, 494, 497
KYGER 365
KYLES 361
KYSER 354, 365

———

LACKEY 367, 378
LACY 412
LAFAYETTE 452
LAIRD 340, 342, 417, 534
LAKEY 515
LAMPKIN (LAMKIN) 493, 494,
  495, 499, 500, 501
LANDES 531
LANGSTON 516
LANHAM 480
LANE 459, 517
LANLEY 367
LANNING 342, 344
LARRIMORE 517
LASHLEY 354, 367, 378
LATHLIN 367
LATTA 360, 389, 409, 469, 504
  513
LATTIMORE 469
LAWING 354, 360, 389
LAWRENCE 348
LAWSON 316, 319, 321, 322, 366
  372, 381, 403, 410, 416, 424
  425, 434, 440, 443, 449-451,
  444, 456, 457, 461, 477, 479
  485-491, 495, 502, 504, 513,
  518, 519, 533, 535.

LAYFIELD 517
LEA 509
LEACH 365
LEDIES 347
LEE 406, 430, 460, 466
LEES 329
LEEPER 317, 425, 433, 434
LEFEVER 358
LEGGITT 339, 342, 354, 365, 366, 400
LEIGH 365
LEMONS 344, 349, 359
LEMSONS 402
LEMMOND 354, 507
LENOIR 354, 419, 519
LEONARD 509
LESLEY 367, 381, 474
LEWING 360
LEWIS 317, 336, 342, 354, 361, 362, 366, 373, 377, 378, 399, 421, 427, 434, 436, 439, 441, 467, 470, 471, 472, 496
LIDAKER 363
LIEBEY 363
LIGHTFOOT 430
LINCOLN 422
LINDSAY 337, 343, 368, 398, 507
LINGLE 363
LINGO 361
LINEBERGER 489
LINKER 363
LINN 366, 400
LINTON 324, 327, 406, 507
LIPE 343, 348
LIPPE 365
LIPPARD 363, 378
LITAKER 354
LITTLE 363, 389, 451, 488
LITTLETON 524
LIVELEY 514
LIVINGSTON 337
LOCK 354, 361
LOCKE 377, 406
LOCKETT 479
LOCKHART 531
LOES 466, 468
LOFTON 343, 344, 363
LOGAN 486, 487, 488, 504
LLOYD 519
LONG 354, 360, 362, 363, 365, 373, 389, 402, 403
LOVE 326, 357, 381, 389
LOW 320
LOWE 425, 458, 459, 467, 468
LOWRANCE 360
LOWERY 354, 471, 485, 514
LOWRIE 335, 341, 342, 350, 406 466
LUCAS 354, 360, 406, 466
LUCKEY 327, 332, 349, 358, 359 394, 407, 513
LUDLOW 446
LUDAKER 378
LYLES 395
LYNN 482
LYPE 363
LYTLE 354, 488

———

MACK 354
MADISON 432, 439
MALLORY 442
MALEARY 321
MARINER 357
MARKS 337, 342, 397, 398, 496
MARLER 354

MAROT 428, 429
MARRA (MORROW) 532
MARSHALL 342, 345, 397
MARTIN 315, 316, 318, 325,336 342, 346, 354, 358, 361, 389, 398, 399, 417, 420, 453, 474, 479, 499
MARTINDALE 354
MASH 364
MASSER 354
MASSIE 408, 409
MASSEY 337, 342, 345, 407
MASON 349, 354, 358, 377,403 438, 466, 467, 468
MASTERS 362
MATTHEWS 325, 339, 345, 346, 354, 363, 367, 401, 457, 471, 472, 480
MAURY 438, 469
MAVERICK 445
MAXWELL 318, 342, 347-350,354 358, 360, 364, 381, 395, 406, 478, 479, 507, 518, 519, 532
MAYO 430, 431, 465, 471
McADEN 316, 332, 342, 343,533
McADOO 341, 474, 503
McALLEY 496
McANNULTY 354
McAULEY 342, 349, 388, 406
McBAY 534
McBEE 326, 343
McBOYD 367
McCABB 361
McCABBEN 366
McCABLUM 366
McCAFFERTY 354
McCAFREN 364
McCALL 325, 339, 342, 343,345 354, 359, 365, 366
McCALLISTER 359
McCALLUM 366
McCAMMON 364, 367
McCAIN 354, 366, 367, 378,381
McCANDLESS 359, 507
McCARIES 354
McCARTY 319, 336, 342, 345, 347, 435, 482, 499
McCAULE 340, 342
McCAULEY (McAULEY) 342, 367
McCAUSLIN 366
McCAY 491
McCLAIN 359, 364
McCLANACHAN 320
McCLANAHAN 360, 482
McCLARTY 361, 365
McCLARY 342, 357, 358, 377
McCLENACHAN 317
McCLELLAN 364, 517
McCLENDEN 341
McCLEARY 505, 508
McCLERRY 354, 436
McCLURE 325, 330, 342, 357, 359, 360, 372, 376, 420.
McCLURKEN 330
McCOLUM 365
McCOMBS 354, 358, 365, 378, 404
McCONNELL 314, 320, 350, 382, 403, 419, 443, 474, 485, 490, 491, 497, 502-504, 525, 534
McCONG 360
McCORKLE 319, 321, 322, 324, 327, 332, 337, 342, 343, 346, 354, 360, 366, 367, 377, 381, 382, 389, 518, 529, 530, 531.
McCORD 335, 354, 357, 393.

McCORMICK 357, 358
McCOREON 341, 342
McCOSTEN 328
McCOWN 361
McCOY 335, 336, 341, 343, 350, 354, 360, 365, 377, 378, 389, 489
McCRAY 361
McCRACKEN 360, 365, 389
McCRAVEN 365
McCREDIE 465
McCREARY 435
McCREE 355
McCRARY 366
McCRUM 358, 377
McCUISTION 318, 462
McCULLOCK 319, 321, 326, 334, 336, 344, 355, 358, 359, 361, 368, 378, 386, 401, 402, 529, 533
McCULLOUGH 320, 322, 327, 343
McCUMMINS 365
McCURDY 355, 364, 378, 484
McDANIEL 343, 347
McDAVIS 402
McDONALD 331, 350, 357
McDOWELL 319, 320, 329, 355, 357, 359, 370, 381, 397-399, 402, 403, 478
McDUGALD 328, 360
McEIRATH 345
McELROY 355, 367, 378, 381, 389
McENTIRE 389
McEWEN 343, 346, 347
McFADDEN 355, 364
McFALL 357
McFERSON 365
McGAUGH 328
McGEE 357, 371, 381, 393
McGEHEY 365
McGIBONY 337, 343
McGILL 358
McGIN 360, 389
McGINNIS 364, 365
McGINTEY 359, 365
McGLAMORY 516
McGOUGH 318
McGOUGHEN 367
McGRAW 362, 363
McGUIN 325
McGUIST 365
McILHENNY 339, 343, 416, 497, 534
McILWAIN 400
McINTIRE 360, 364, 365, 381, 422, 494
McKAY 359, 489
McKEAN 440, 516, 519
McKEE 328, 330, 346, 355, 357 358, 359, 367, 377, 401
McKEMIE (McKENZIE) 314, 381, 409, 426, 429, 470, 471, 473, 503, 505, 510, 514-516, 518, 520, 524, 532, 535, 536
McKIBBEN 326
McKINDLEY 318
McKINLEY 317, 332, 357, 361, 364, 398, 399, 532, 534
McKINNEY 340, 343, 494
McKINZIE 527
McKISSICK 314, 487
McKNIGHT 322, 324, 329, 339, 343, 355, 357, 381, 389, 398, 406, 481, 488, 503, 518, 520-522, 524, 532, 533
McKNITT 329, 415, 520, 522.

550

McLANTY 350
McLAUGHLIN 402
McLEAN 320, 334, 337, 339, 343, 350, 414, 492, 493, 494, 504, 513
McLEARY 349
McLELLAN(D) 334, 405, 447
McLEMORE 482
McLURE 389, 420
McMAHAN 363
McMAKIN 442
McMANNIS 435
McMEANS 327
McMURRAY 364, 365, 378
McNAIR 358, 412
McNEAL 334, 447
McNEELY 355, 357, 366, 389, 489
McNEIL 340, 343, 509
McNICKLE 532
McNIGHT 398
McNISH 426, 440, 514, 515, 535, 536
McPHEETERS 484, 486
McPHERSON 365
McQUAY 345, 348
McQUISTION 366
McQUOINS 320
McRACKIN 328
McREA 355, 361
McREE 323, 325, 339, 378, 397, 399, 505, 508
McRORY 322, 481
McSPANN 343, 346
McSPARREN 346, 367
McWHIRTER 340
McWHORTER 334, 336, 340, 343, 355, 366, 367, 381, 397, 413, 419, 447, 506, 533, 535
MEANS 354, 361, 367, 377, 406, 497
MEEK 329, 350, 354, 359
MEISENHEIMER 354
MELCHER 363
MELLER 367
MENSON 369
MERCHANT 368
MEREDITH 474
MESLAND 319
MICHEAUX 469
MILES 344, 350
MILLS 412, 476, 517
MILLER 321, 331, 339, 340, 341, 344, 347, 354, 359, 362, 363, 364, 365, 367, 368, 407, 408, 475, 482, 507
MINEY 365
MINSINGER 363
MINSTER 362
MISENHEIMER 362, 363
MITCHELL 321, 328, 354, 359, 362, 365, 412, 437, 452, 455, 456, 460, 518
MOCK 362
MOFFITT 350, 360, 361
MONEY 320
MONROE 459
MONTEITH 314, 336, 343, 360, 384, 389
MONTGOMERY 332, 337, 343, 349, 354, 357, 359, 365, 367, 381, 441, 478, 479, 507, 516
MOON 495, 462
MOONEY 462
MORRIS 327, 328, 343, 346, 349, 350, 354, 364, 365, 378, 395, 428, 465
MORGADINE 362
MORGAN 364, 369

MOORE 314, 317-322, 324, 325, 330-335, 337 - 347, 349, 350, 354, 357, 360, 365, 367, 375, 379, 381, 389, 394, 395, 398, 399, 408, 409, 412, 418, 420, 448, 450, 453, 454, 461, 474, 477-485, 488-490, 492-494, 497, 499-502, 512, 517, 519, 525, 530, 535.
MORRAY 532
MORROW 318, 322, 329, 330, 336, 338, 340, 341, 343-346, 348-351, 360, 370, 381, 404, 406, 407, 410, 411, 423, 439, 442, 506, 517, 532.
MOROGH (MORROW) 517
MORTON 325, 361, 447, 491
MOSELEY 467, 468
MOSSOM 469
MOUNGER 529
MOYER 354, 362, 363
MUIR 454
MULEY 520
MULLEN 360
MULLS 365
MULVEE 348, 354, 368
MURPH 362
MURPHY 320, 354, 361, 365
MUSICK 482.

NAIL 365, 382
NAILOR 355
NANCE (NANTZ) 335, 336, 345, 389, 390, 411, 412
NASH 334
NATION 357, 360
NEAL 318, 355, 398
NEEL 321, 331, 397, 399, 494
NEELY 318, 325, 327, 345-348, 355, 358, 359, 377, 397, 505, 509, 526
NELSON 332, 365, 391, 454, 481
NESBIT 333, 525
NETTERHAVER 363
NEUSMAN 363
NEWTON 328, 366
NEWELL 355, 364
NEWMAN 342, 345, 355, 359, 525
NICELER 355, 362
NICHOLSON 320, 328, 355, 357, 358, 360, 474
NOBLE 516
NOCK 505, 514
NOEL 453
NORFLEET 342, 430
NORMANT 350
NORTON 522
NORWOOD 524, 527
NULL 357, 358, 361, 367
NUTHALL 345, 423, 516
NUTT 321, 355, 530

OATES 337, 342, 350, 351, 367
OCHILTREE 316, 317, 355
OCHLER 411
O'DANIEL 520
ODOM 367
OGDEN 452, 453
OIMSTEAD 423
OLIPHANT 342, 348
OLIVER 351, 358
ORMOND 341, 345, 365-367, 401
OUDY 363
OUREY 363
OUTLAW 501

ORR 322, 334, 336, 345, 347, 349, 350, 355-359, 365-367, 377, 393, 401, 404, 406, 469, 481
OSBORNE 318, 323, 330, 345, 348, 351, 355, 360, 366-368, 375, 382, 399, 406, 413, 434, 435, 440, 441, 449, 503, 504, 506, 533
OVERBY 345, 348
OVERCASH 344, 345
OVENSHINE 363
OWENS 357, 404, 405, 505, 510, 517, 519

PAGE 368
PAISLEY 417
PALM 509
PALMER 452
PANNELL 529
PARKER 360
PARKS 324, 326, 332, 333, 337, 338, 340, 341, 343-347, 349, 350, 355, 357, 359, 367, 370, 377, 381, 390, 394, 395, 398, 400-402, 406, 433, 441, 448, 452-454, 526
PASINGER 362
PASTEUR 425, 427, 469
PATSON 367
PATTERSON 345, 346, 348, 355, 358, 362, 367, 375, 377, 381, 390, 411, 469, 571
PATILLO 326, 396, 425, 429, 430, 431, 480, 510
PATTISON 358
PATTON 315, 317, 329, 334, 355, 360, 361, 373, 376, 381, 404, 407, 415, 420, 425, 432, 434-436, 438, 439, 441, 442, 447, 469, 478, 513, 528, 533
PAUL 492
PAULETT 464
PAXTON 366
PEACHY 468
PEARSON 513
PEDEN 491
PEEL (PEELE) 332, 355, 361, 377, 390, 333
PEOPLES (PEEPLES) 330, 345, 360, 372, 390
PEOPARD 354
PENCE 363
PENNY 355, 361
PENN 314, 535
PERREYSONE 516
PERKINS 355
PERRY 459, 468
PERSONS 333
PETERSON 340, 469
PETTIT 511
PETTUS 327, 342, 345, 390, 511
PHARR 337, 340, 344, 390
PHELAN 350
PHELPS 449
PHIFER 315, 355, 361, 362, 373, 376, 377, 378, 386, 413, 415-417, 420
PHILLIPS 326, 355, 365, 368, 378, 451-453, 460, 519
PHRIZZELL 519
PICKENS 324, 326, 355, 359, 361, 365, 371, 373, 377, 381, 445, 482
PIERCE 466
PIERSON 357

PINCKNEY 411
PINER 516
PINKETHMAN 428
PITTMAN 437
PITTS 479
PLEASANTS 446, 486
PLOTT 362
PLUMMER 357
PLUNKETT 364, 378
PLYLER 355, 363
POAGE 484, 486
POER 534
POLK 313, 315, 316, 318, 320
    323, 328, 329, 335, 336,
    342, 345, 346, 349, 350,
    355, 358, 365, 370, 372,
    374, 376-378, 381, 389,
    402, 404, 405, 413-415,
    417, 418, 420, 421, 515,
    503-510, 524, 525, 527,
    532, 533, 535
POLL 318
POLLOCK 505
POPE 412, 467, 468
PORTER 324, 346, 355, 357,358
    366, 377, 397, 408, 449,
    505, 515, 518
POREY 363
POTTER 367
POTTS 317, 320, 321, 335, 338
    346, 348, 350, 355, 361,
    366, 367, 372, 375, 377,
    378, 381, 397, 400-402,
    411, 412, 503
POWELL 365, 442, 507, 536
POWERS 348
POYTHRESS 455, 460
PRESSLEY 397, 398
PRESTON 436, 486, 495
PRICE 314, 321, 338, 346, 355,
    358, 361, 363, 372, 377,
    381, 385, 397-399, 402,
    406, 416, 425, 449, 478,
    479, 502, 513, 519, 522
    524
PRIDE 322, 329
PRINGLE 398
PRITCHARD 404, 406
PROBART 418
PROCTOR 339
PROPS (PROBST) 363, 378
PUCKETT 342, 348, 349, 501
PUGH 501
PULLETT 515
PURSER 507
PUSLEY 321
PURVIANCE 340, 348
PURYEAR 365
PYRON 365, 374, 402
PYSER 517

QUEARY 315, 336, 338, 339,346
    374, 376, 381, 395, 396,
    400
QUERY 355, 359, 365, 371, 401
QUEBAN 366
QUIMAN 355, 363
QUINN 348

RABB 355, 365, 378, 395
RAMEY 358
RAMSEY 315-317, 321, 323, 335
    339, 340, 345, 346, 355,
    360, 365-367, 384, 400,
    414-416, 424, 432, 439,482
    499, 504, 507, 527, 528.

RANDOLPH 430, 436, 455, 463,
    471
RAINEY 321
RANKIN 339, 346, 390, 405,
    483, 494, 512, 513
RANSOM 349, 460, 475, 489
RAPE 363, 366
RAPHIL 360
RAY 337, 346, 365, 367, 375,
    381, 398, 405, 418, 483,
    514, 527
RAYNOR 506
REA 330, 331, 333, 336, 337,
    339-343, 345-349, 355,
    400, 401, 484, 507, 527
READ 519
REAGAN 478, 479
REAMS 324
REDD 463, 472
REDRICK 366
REDICK 367
REDFORD 366
REED 318, 321, 329, 330, 331,
    337, 339, 341-344, 346-
    351, 355, 357-359, 363,
    365, 367, 368, 481,482,
    519
REESE 315, 347, 355, 362,376
    381, 396, 421, 444, 454,
    508, 534, 525, 535
REID 350, 390, 397, 398, 401
    440, 447, 511, 513
REINHARDT 494
HENDRICKS 367
REYNOLDS 466
RHEA 347
RHODES 347
RICE 336, 347, 358, 435, 519
RICHARDS 482
RICHARDSON 366, 397, 400,428
    468, 497, 526, 527, 530
RICHEY 355, 359, 363
RICHIE 451
RIDER 519
RIDENAUR 363
RIGEY 363
RIGSBEY 363
RILEY 343, 349, 358, 406
RINHART 363
RISK 433
RITCHIE 446, 453
RITCHISON 355
RIVES 333, 334
RIVERS 334
ROANE 500
ROBARDS 526
ROBERSON 321
ROBERTS 505, 519
ROBERTSON 321, 428, 438, 457,
    465
ROBINSON 318, 319, 326, 333,
    334, 339, 340, 341, 347,
    349, 355, 371, 372, 378,
    390, 393, 394-396, 398,
    402, 430, 515, 517
ROBISON 358, 359, 360, 367,
    368, 384
ROCKWELL 412, 425
RODEN (RODDEN-RHOTEN-WROTEN)
    336, 337, 343, 339, 347,
    350, 399
RODDY 479
RODGERS 365, 390, 409, 412,
    452, 453, 479, 515
ROE 425, 466, 468, 469, 519,
    522
ROGERS 324, 341-345, 347-349
    355, 362, 363, 365-368,
    373, 377, 378-395, 406.
ROSEBOROUGH 363, 511

ROSIER 466, 467
ROSS 317, 326, 337, 340, 348,
    351, 355, 359, 361, 362,
    364, 374, 378, 390, 398.
ROSSER 407
ROUND 515
ROUTH 365
ROWAN 337, 347, 348, 367
ROWDEN (RODDEN, ETC.) 349
ROWE 425
ROWELL 402
ROWZEE 467
RUBSIMAN 460
RUDISILL 474
RUFFIN 487
RUMPLE 348, 395
RUMSEY 532
RUSK 421, 488
RUSSELL 345, 347, 348, 355,
    359, 360, 362, 364, 372,
    374, 378, 390, 412, 433,
    491
RUST 500
RUTHERFORD 417, 507, 513
RUTLEDGE 340, 388, 441

SADLER 355, 398, 497
SAFFORD 497
SAIES 324, 407
SAMPLE 314, 335, 340, 343,355
    359, 360, 390, 391, 394,
    395, 482, 489, 533
SANKEY 425, 431-433, 440, 451
    454-456, 459, 461, 462
SAVILLE 351
SAYERS 432, 433, 440, 441,442
    514
SCALES 362, 407
SCANNELL 362
SCHOOLFIELD 517
SCOTT 317, 319, 332, 348, 355
    358, 364, 374, 433, 465,
    474, 483, 485, 490, 494,
    512, 514, 515
SCRUGGS 442
SEAWELL 479
SEAY 438
SECREST 347, 348, 355, 366,
    378
SEIFERIT 363
SELF 365
SEHORN 403
SELL 363, 364
SELLERS 319
SELWIN 318
SEMBLER 408
SEMPLE 465
SEMIONS 363
SENLETTE 412
SERVANT 469
SEVIER 501
SHANKS 328, 355, 362, 367,378
SHANNON 367
SHARP 321, 324, 341, 344, 347
    348, 349, 355, 401, 437
SHARPE 318, 332, 333-336, 338
    348, 359, 360, 367, 368,
    371, 372, 375, 381, 393,
    415, 521, 524, 525, 527,
    534, 535
SHAVER 362, 365, 378
SHEFFLEY 435
SHELBY 331, 335, 356, 359,
    377, 396, 417, 505, 507,
    508
SHEPPARD 346, 348, 358, 366,
    470, 488, 531
SHERRILL 422, 458, 501.

552

SHIELDS 318, 332, 336, 337, 348, 351, 357, 359, 361, 391 394, 428, 429, 432, 440, 461, 462, 467, 470, 507
SHILLADAY 446, 447
SHINN 358, 362, 378
SHIP 513
SHIPLEY 491
SHIVE 362
SHORT 356
SHUFORD 513
SIBLEY 367
SIDES 363, 364
SIFFORD 406
SIKES 356, 402
SILER (See SYLER) 507
SIMINER 362, 378
SIMONS 364
SIMONTON 333
SIMS 317, 456, 532
SIMMONS 359
SIMPSON 317, 351, 356, 365, 367, 454
SINCLAIR 405, 512
SINGLETON 474
SINK 433
SINQUE (SANKEY) 454
SITTON 348
SKELTON 460
SKITLETON 362
SLAGLE 489
SLAUGH 363
SLAUGHTER 465, 467, 468, 470
SLEYDER 519
SLIVERS 516
SLOAN 330, 349, 356, 357, 359 361, 371, 372, 397, 398, 480
SLOWGH 362
SLUTTER 519
SMART 313, 326, 327, 336, 348 351, 356, 358, 370, 377, 448, 476, 481, 507
SMITH 313, 318, 320, 331, 333 336-338, 342, 348, 349, 356, 359, 361-363, 365, 367, 368, 377, 378, 406 412, 422, 453, 466, 468 479, 481, 482, 507, 514 515, 517, 518, 524
SNELL 336, 348, 365
SOMERVILLE 328, 351, 391, 409
SPARROW 412
SPEARS 344, 346, 348, 349, 358 364
SPEERS 351
SPECK 363
SPENCE 517
SPENCER 341, 349, 391, 397, 475
SPOTTSWOOD 484
SPRATT 313, 329, 336, 341, 346 349, 356, 357, 366, 370, 377, 381, 382, 398, 414, 418, 447, 476, 505, 506, 508, 533, 535
SPRINGS 322, 335, 338, 358, 367 377, 378, 400, 405, 406, 418, 451, 488
SPRIGS 358
STAFFORD 356, 364
STANDLEY 318
STAINS 365
STANFIELD 322, 344, 349, 482
STANLEY 320
STANSILL 365, 507
STARLING 359
STARNES 344, 349, 363, 364, 367
STARR 366 393
STARRETT 356

STEELE 345, 349, 351, 360, 361, 398, 441, 471, 490, 492, 518, 522, 534
STEEN 356
STEPHENS 335, 391, 437
STEVENS 337, 349, 365, 465, 524, 535
STEVENSON 341, 356, 360, 361, 366, 367, 378
STEWART 343, 344, 350, 356, 374, 391, 400, 407, 409, 411, 474, 515, 517
STIERWALT 363, 504
STILLWELL 365
STITT 367
STINSON 325, 326, 337, 349, 356, 357, 391
STOLLINWERCK 475
STONE 314, 464, 475, 481
STOREY 366, 378
STOUGH 363
STOVER 430
STOWE 322, 390, 391, 451
STRACHBACK 359
STRAIN 359
STRANGE 519
STRONG 349
STUCKER 363
STURGEON 321, 368, 381
STUART 314, 358, 359, 364, 460, 365, 366, 367, 391, 441, 462, 465, 490
SUDDUTH 480
SULLIVAN 360
SUMPTER 357, 377, 421, 474
SURMAN 516
SUTHER 364
SWAFFORD 522
SWANN 329, 338, 349, 356, 358 368, 378, 427, 490, 522
SYKES 350
SYLER (See SILER) 507
SYLVESTER 399

———

TAGERT 357
TALBOT 449, 469
TALIAFERRO 468
TALLEY 365
TAMPLIN 517
TANNER 332, 356, 361, 366
TARLTON 372
TASEY 359
TATE 317, 321, 400, 412
TAWNS 367
TAYLOR 325, 329, 333, 348, 349 356, 358, 361, 362, 368, 404, 409, 430, 455, 467, 468, 469, 470, 495, 505, 514, 515, 520
TEDFORD 362
TEEM 364
TEMPLE 356
TEMPLETON 356, 361, 373, 491 503
TENNEHILL (TANNYHILL) 519
TENNER 322, 481
TERRY 429
THOMAS 317, 330, 333, 356, 358 377, 404, 465, 478, 483, 484, 519
THOMSON 314, 318, 319, 338, 339 343, 372, 383, 391, 393, 406 416, 424-433, 435, 437-451 453-457, 461-464, 467, 470- 473, 479, 485, 507, 510, 514 515, 518-520, 524-528, 530, 533-536.

THOMPSON 320, 328, 334, 336, 338, 349, 360, 366, 382, 391, 426, 427, 432-437, 440, 472, 519
THORNE 456
THORNTON 448
TICKNOR 476
TIPTON 469, 501
TITUS 367
TODD 332, 339, 343, 344, 349 356, 360, 391, 394
TOLAND 531
TOMLINSON 517
TOOLE 473
TOOLEY 497
TORRENCE 332, 335, 337, 339, 346, 349, 361, 377, 382, 391, 444, 482, 513
TOTTER 365
TOWNS 367
TOWNSEND 362, 365, 373
TRAVELER 464
TRIGG 491
TROTTER 405, 446
TROY 525
TRUMAN 515
TUCKER 361, 364, 480, 519
TURFIN 516
TYGERT 356

———

UANS 366
UNDERWOOD 425, 458, 466-468, 391
UPSON 532
UPTON 458, 466, 468

———

VANCE 347, 349, 358, 365, 366 391, 513
VANDERGRIFT 519
VAN PELT 348, 349, 357
VENABLE 448, 516
VENABLES 516
VERNER 357
VERNON 448
VINAN 367
VOYLS 362, 364

———

WADDELL 337, 349
WADDIE (WADDELL) 356, 361
WADDY 427, 434
WAGGINER 364
WAGON 516
WALKER 320, 322, 328, 330, 331, 336, 345, 346, 348-350, 356-358, 363- 365, 367, 368, 375, 378 427, 430, 460, 472, 484 494, 501, 509
WALKUP (Same as WAUCHOB, WAUHOB, WAUCHOPE, etc) 322, 324, 329, 356, 373, 375, 378, 381, 400, 408, 409, 519, 532, 536
WALL 341, 527
WALLACE 321, 323, 326, 332, 344 349-351, 356, 359, 362, 364, 368, 373, 374, 376, 377, 381, 393-395, 400, 429, 446 448, 481, 482, 531
WALLIS (Same as WALLACE) 338, 350, 361, 391, 400, 415, 530, 531
WALTER 362

553

WARREN 365
WARREN 391, 496
WARRENTON 437, 438
WARRINGTON 438, 440
WASHAM 344, 350, 367, 410-412
WASHINGTON 368, 376, 420, 467, 534
WATTS 365, 399
WATKINS 360, 402, 448
WATSON 314, 320, 329, 344, 359 364, 440, 446, 447, 449, 478, 522, 532
WAUGH 329, 504
WAUCHOPE (See WALKUP) 324, 367, 412, 519
WAYNES 460
WEATHERS 329, 336, 350, 412
WEBB 324, 398, 412
WEAVER 364
WEBSTER 476
WEDDINGTON 394
WEEKS 356, 368, 402
WEIR 350, 384
WELCH 364
WELDON 428
WELLS 361
WEST 327, 358, 366, 458, 464
WHARTON 391
WHEELER 424
WHERRY 524
WHITE 314, 316, 320, 350, 356 362, 364, 366, 374, 378, 381, 392, 396, 403, 407, 408, 410, 424, 425, 439, 443, 450, 464, 471, 473, 482, 485, 490-493, 501, 503, 504, 517, 532
WHITFIELD 441
WHITEHEAD 496
WHITEHURST 469
WHITNEY 392
WHITLOW 406
WHITNEY 350

WHITSETT 358
WHITTEN 491
WHITTINGTON 517, 532
WIDINGTON 364
WIER 356
WIGMORE 426, 427
WILLIAMS 336, 345, 347, 350, 356, 360, 361, 367, 392, 402, 422, 423, 427, 444, 453, 463, 509, 516, 519
WILLIAMSON 313, 324, 344, 348 349, 366, 381, 399, 400, 412, 422, 425, 455, 456, 458, 460, 459, 467 -469, 476, 492, 513
WIHELM 364, 406
WILKINSON 357, 519
WILSON 314-317, 320, 321, 322, 325, 327-329, 334, 335-338, 343-346, 350, 351, 357, 358, 361, 366, 368, 370, 372, 376-378, 381, 392-395, 397-399, 401, 403, 405, 411-416, 420, 424, 425, 434 436-438, 444, 450, 469, 473 474, 484, 491, 493, 503-505 508, 509, 511, 516, 518, 525, 528, 533, 535
WILEY 321, 359, 361, 362, 364
WILLIFORD 351
WILLIS 392, 437, 438
WILMARTH 405
WINCHESTER 364
WINECOFF 356
WINESAUGH 362
WINFREY 430, 465
WININGS 359
WINSLOW 323, 328, 335, 346, 350, 351, 356, 382, 474, 503, 504
WINTERS 392
WISE 359, 361, 365
WISEHART 358, 328

WISER 364
WISENER 356
WISEL 363
WITH 364
WITHERS 358, 392
WITHERSPOON 356, 368, 475
WITENHOUSE 364
WITHERFORD 365
WODINGTON 362
WOLFE 330, 356, 363
WOMACK 448
WOOD 519
WOODS 356, 359, 360, 392, 495 501
WOODSON 446, 486
WOODWARD 347
WOOL 412
WOOLFORD 517
WOOTEN 488, 496
WORCESTER 515
WORK 495
WORLEY 345, 351
WORSHAM 342, 474
WORTHINGTON 516
WRIGHT 358, 432, 459, 491
WRON 464, 466
WROTEN 347, 435
WYATT 367, 446, 479
WYLIE 326, 331, 333, 340, 356 367, 372, 377, 378, 402, 474, 507
YANDELL (YANDIE) 356, .368

YANDELL (YANDIE) 356, 368
YARBEY 367
YARVOROUGH 321, 366
YARDLEY 524
YEARWOOD 442
YEWMAN 362
YOUNG 318, 356, 359, 362, 377 422, 441, 491, 492, 524
YURCE 358.

PLACES

ABBEVILLE DISTRICT, S. C.
532.................. 453
ABB'S VALLEY, VA....... 484
ACCOMAC COUNTY, VA. 314,.. 414
426, 429, 503, 510, 514, 515,
520, 524, 525......... 535
ALABAMA 341,415....... 373
ALAMO (TEXAS).......... 410
ALBEMARLE COUNTY, VA. 455,
465, 486.............. 496
ALLISON'S CREEK 497..... 500
AMELIA COUNTY, VA. 416, 423
428, 429, 449, 450, 461, 462
ANAHUAC, TEXAS......... 476
ANNE ESSEX RIVER......508.. 535
ANDERSON DIST. S. C..... 508
ANSON COUNTY, N. C. 317,
319, 323, 326, 379, 422,
485, 526.............. 530
ANTI BURGHER SECEDER CHURCH 398
ANTRIM COUNTY, IRELAND.. 406
ASSO. CONG. OF STEELE CREEK 398
AUGUSTA COUNTY, VA. 413,419
432-434,436, 437, 441,
442, 445,451, 462, 471,
476, 478, 490, 491,497,
527-529............... 530
AUSTIN, TEXAS, 386, 488... 509

BACK RIVER, YORK CO. VA.... 466
BAKER'S GRAVEYARD, 314, 346
372, 382, 381, 395, 403,
422, 425, 434, 457, 478,
479, 485, 513, 515..... 533
BALTIMORE, MARYLAND, 415,
519................... 532
BARRY'S CREEK........... 371
BASTROP, TEXAS.......... 441
BATTLE OF SAN JACINTO (TEX) 421
BEATTIE'S FORD.314,.382,...
403, 423, 424......... 434
BEATTIE'S FORD ROAD, 419,
421,425, 457.......... 533
BEATTIE'S FORD SETTLEMENT.. 422
BEATTIE'S FORD SECTION... 532
BEAVERDAM CREEK 319, 375.. 378
BEDFORD COUNTY. VA...... 442
BEDFORD COUNTY, TENN. 316.. 488
BERTIE COUNTY, N. C. 342.. 512
BELLE AIRE SECTION, S. C.. 407
BELMONT, N. C........... 451
BERKELEY PARISH, VA..... 533
BETHEL ACADEMY.......... 412
BETHEL CHURCH S. C..410.. 412
BETHESDA M. E. CHURCH... 332
BETHESDA CHURCH, S. C. 341,
343................... 497
BETHLEHEM CHURCH...402.. 403
BETHSALEM CHURCH (GA)... 454
BEVERLY MANOR, VA. 432, 436
437, 468, 472......... 533
BIBB COUNTY, ALA........ 497
BIGBYVILLE, TENN........ 325
BIGGERS' FERRY. 370,..... 500
BIG SUGAR CREEK..370..... 414
BIRMINGHAM, ALA......... 532
BLACKWATER RIVER, VA.... 458
BLADEN COUNTY........... 379
BLOOMING GROVE, TEXAS... 475
BLOUNT COUNTY, TENN, 484.. 507
BOHEMIA RIVER, MARYLAND. 524
BOLIVAR, TENN....414.... 509
BRADDOCK'S ARMY......... 413

BRENTWOOD, TENN......... 442
BRISTOL PARISH, VA...... 455
BROAD CREEK, MARYLAND... 517
BROAD RIVER............. 319
BROUGH HALL, ENGLAND.... 477
BRUNSWICK CO. VA. 450... 460
BRUTON PARISH, YORK CO VA
426.................. 441
BUFFALO CHURCH, CREEK AND
SETTLEMENT (VA). 420,
425, 429, 431, 433,446
451, 454..............462
BULLOCK'S CREEK S. C. 332 521
BURKE COUNTY? GA....... 460
BURKE CO. N. C. 412..... 419
BUNCOMBE COUNTY, N. C.327 423

CABARRUS COUNTY N. C. 322
329, 331, 339, 340,342
372, 396, 416, 417,420
422................... 506
CALDWELL SETTLEMENT in VA
337, 400, 431......... 451
CALF PASTURE, VA....... 528
CALVERT COUNTY, MARYLAND. 524
CAMPBELL COUNTY, VA. 431 433
CAMILLA, GEORGIA....... 407
CANE CREEK, in S. C...317 320
CANTON, MISS........... 487
CARLISLE, PENN......... 414
CARMEL CHURCH, S. C.... 421
CASWELL COUNTY, N. C... 496
CATAWBA RIVER 320 (and
many other places)... 321
CATHEY'S MEETING HOUSE... 370
CECIL COUNTY, MD. 415,417
420, 449, 502, 518-522
525, 532, 534......... 535
CEDAR SPRINGS, VA...... 436
CENTRE CHURCH 376, 382,
412, 413, 416, 434,
381, 440.............. 533
CHAMBERS COUNTY, ALA. 331
339, 482, 484......... 484
CHAPEL HILL, N. C...... 525
CHAPPELL HILL, TEXAS... 531
CHARLOTTE COUNTY, VA. 336
337, 351, 397, 431,451
453, 456, 470, 471... 526
CHARLES CITY CO. VA..... 455
CHARLES COUNTY, MD..... 499
CHARLOTTE, N. C. (mention
made often).......... 375
CHATHAM COUNTY, N. C. 407 496
CHEROKEE INDIANS...400.. 507
CHEROKEE COUNTRY..418,422 473
CHESTER COUNTY, PENN.....334
CHESTER COUNTY, S. C... 351
CHESTER RIVER (MD.).... 535
CHOPTANK RIVER (CREEK)MD.
519................... 535
CHRISTIAN'S CREEK VA. 432 436
COHAM HALL ..458........ 469
CODDLE CREEK CHURCH.... 406
CODDLE CREEK 346, 374... 382
COFFEY BRANCH.......... 370
COLLETON COUNTY S. C... 320
COLUMBIA, TENN......... 501
COLUMBUS, MISS, 473.... 480
CONCORD PRESBYTERY..... 412
CONCORD CHURCH......... 412
CONCORD, N. C., 372, 402,
419................... 420
CORNELIUS N.C. 342, 370.. 410

CORSICANNA, TEXAS....... 475
COUNTY DERRY, IRELAND.... 402
COW PASTURE CONGREGATION. 400
COW PASTURE RIVER (VA)
393, 528.............. 530
COWAN'S FORD, 372, 422,
446, 479, 485......... 503
CRAVEN COUNTY.......... 422
CROWDER'S CREEK,y ..318.. 370
CUB CREEK CHURCH (VA.)400
515...................525
CUB CREEK, CHARLOTTE CO.
VA.431, 433,449, 451,
453, 464, 467, 471... 526
CUMBERLAND COUNTY, VA 438 486
CUMBERLAND PARISH (VA.).. 433
CUMBERLAND SETTLEMENT... 501
CURLE'S CHURCH (VA.)... 469
CUSTER, S. D........... 423

DALLAS COUNTY, ALA..... 347
DALLAS, TEXAS.......... 412
DAN RIVER (VA.)........ 495
DAVIDSON COLLEGE 313, 342
382, 396, 412, 413,417
420, 425, 444......... 534
DAVIDSON COUNTY, N. C... 398
DAVIDSON CO. TENN, 442.. 446
DAVIDSON'S CREEK, 382,410
423, 424, 444, 450,478
485................... 533
DEMOPOLIS, ALA.......... 441
DILLEY, TEXAS........... 33
DIVIDING CREEK (MD.)... 524
DONEGAL PRESBYTERY..... 525
DORCHESTER CO. MD...... 519
DRUMMONDSTOWN VA....... 514
DUCK RIVER, IN TENN 487,
501................... 506
DUE WEST, S. C......... 397
DUMFRIES, VA........... 470
DUPLIN COUNTY, N. C.... 501
DUTCH BUFFALO CREEK, 373. 416

EASTERN SHORE OF MD., 418
505, 508, 520, 532,534 536
EASTERN SHORE OF VA., 313
467, 511, 532......... 535
EDEN HOUSE, EDENTON N.C.. 512
ELBERT COUNTY, GA., 472.. 475
ELKTON, MARYLAND, 415,.. 521
ELK RIVER in MD., 414... 535
ELIZABETH CITY CO. VA.428
440, 470.............. 469
ELIZABETH RIVER (VA.) 514 536
ELIZABETHTOWN, N. J.... 452
EMANUEL PRESBYTERIAN CH.. 402
ERWIN COUNTY, GA....... 324
ESSEX COUNTY, VA. 434,468
471, 472.............. 533

FAIRFAX COUNTY, VA., 470. 499
FALMOUTH, VA., 465...... 470
FISHING CREEK, 321, 478,
493................... 497
FORKS OF THE ELK, MD..... 534
FORNEY, TEXAS.......... 480
FORT LOUDON, TENN...... 473
FOUR MILE CREEK, 317... 321
FRANKLIN, TENN, 441..... 442
FRANKLIN COLLEGE, Ga.... 462

FREDERICK CO. VA., 465....470
FREDERICKSBURG, VA....... 465
FRENCH BROAD RIVER....... 460

GALLATIN, TENN........... 414
GALVESTON, TEXAS, 476.... 531
GASTON COUNTY, N. C., 318,
  320, 340, 434, 450,452,
  453, 478, 483, 485,487
  499, 512................ 513
GEORGIA, 341, 421........ 472
GILEAD CHURCH, 324, 340,
  349, 406, 425, 486.....487
GLASGOW, SCOTLAND........ 440
GLASGOW STREET, DALLAS... 412
GLOSTER, ENGLAND......... 318
GLOUCESTER CO. VA........ 428
GOOCHLAND CO. VA., 436,
  465, 469, 471........... 496
GOOSE CREEK, 320, 321,331
  374, 402, 481........... 484
GOSHEN CHURCH............ 512
GRANVILLE CO. N. C., 345,
  379, 396, 423, 428,456
  456, 460, 485, 486..... 506
GREENE CO. GA. 326, 327,
  333, 340, 345, 417,450
  454, 463, 475, 481,483
  497, 482, 500, 501,507
  529..................... 532
GREENE CO. TENN., 494.... 529
GREENSBORO, ALA.,475..... 497
GREENSBORO, GA.,326, 454. 500
GREENSBORO, N. C......... 337
GREENVILLE, TENN......... 501
GUILFORD, CO. N. C., 396. 526

HALIFAX, N. C., 413, 501,
  527..................... 527
HALIFAX CO. VA., 429, 478
  495..................... 496
HAMPSHIRE CO. VA., 412... 474
HAMPTON, VIRGINIA, 429... 431
HAMPDEN-SYDNEY COLLEGE,
  391, 396................ 413
HANCOCK CO. GA........... 497
HANGING ROCK FIGHT,...... 416
HANOVER CO. VA., 427, 431
  434, 435, 455........... 511
HARDEMAN CO. TENN....509.. 506
HARDEMAN CO. TEXAS....... 509
HARRODSBURG, KY.......... 493
HARFORD COUNTY, MD..419.. 534
HAWKINS CO. TENN. 325.... 528
HAYS CREEK, AUGUSTA CO VA 413
HENRICO CO. VA. 436, 458.
  460..................... 486
HILLSBORO, N. C., 415,417
  423..................... 493
HORR'S HOLE, VA.......... 434
HOLSTON RIVER (TENN) 424 529
HOPEWELL PRES. CHURCH 313
  325, 328, 334, 338, 343
  345, 349,350, 371, 382
  383, 392, 399, 400, 406
  415, 416, 420, 422, 421
  454, 481, 482, 489, 503
  504, 533................ 534
HOPEWELL CHURCH S. C..... 421
HOPEWELL CHURCH, UNION CO
  N. C.................... 402
HOPEWELL CHURCH SECTION
  446, 450, 461........... 513
HUNGAR'S PARISH (VA) 466. 467
HUNTERSVILLE, N. C. 370.. 489
HUNTSVILLE, ALABAMA..... 493

ILLINOIS (STATE)......... 446
INDEPENDENCE HILL........ 371
INDIAN CREEK, 317, 319... 320
IREDELL COUNTY, 349,375,
  382, 403, 410, 421, 423
  424, 425, 434, 503, 504
  525..................... 533
ISLE OF WIGHT CO. VA., 438
  442, 458, 468........... 470

JACKSON CO. GA........... 435
JAMES CITY CO. VA. 426,428 511
JACKSON'S RIVER, VA...... 419
JAMES RIVER, VA...451.... 471
JAMESTOWN, VA... 458.464. 524
JEFFERSON CO. VA......... 316
JESSAMINE CO. KY......... 471
JONESBORO, TENN. 491, 500 501

KAUFMAN CO. TEXAS........ 480
KENT COUNTY, MD.......... 505
KENTUCKY (STATE OF) 452.. 462
KERR'S CREEK (VA)........ 486
KENT, ENGLAND............ 458
KILLIAN'S CREEK.......... 317
KINGDOM OF IRELAND....... 514
KING GEORGE CO. VA....... 467
KING & QUEEN CO. VA...... 465
KING'S MOUNTAIN, 427, 434
  450-453, 491-493, 498...513
KITTRELL (TOWN OF)....... 441
KNOB CREEK, TENN......... 493
KNOX COUNTY, TENN. 471... 492
KNOXVILLE, TENN. 421, 424,
  460..................... 473

LA GRANGE, GA............ 483
LANCASTER COUNTY, S. C.,
  320, 400, 408, 443, 468
  499..................... 529
LAURENS CO. S. C......... 350
LAWRENCEBURG, TENN....... 493
LAWSON'S CREEK (S. C.)... 485
LEWES, DELAWARE, 431, 454. 514
LEXINGTON, VA............ 454
LIBERTY HALL ACADEMY, 415. 419
LIMESTONE RIVER, TENN.... 529
LIMESTONE DISTRICT....... 322
LIMESTONE, TENN.......... 501
LINCOLN COUNTY, N. C., 321
  339, 391, 413, 450, 452
  478, 483, 486-489, 492
  499, 501, 510-513, 528. 529
LINCOLNTON, N. C......... 423
LITTLE CALF PASTURE RIVER.
  413..................... 439
LITTLE CATAWBA RIVER..... 321
LITTLE NORTH MOUNTAIN, VA 439
LITTLE STEELE CREEK CHURCH 399
LITTLE TENNESSEE RIVER... 473
LIBERTY (OLD) CHURCH (GA.) 454
LOGAN COUNTY, KY. 452, 493 496
LONG CREEK, 371, 389, 420. 489
LONDONDERRY, IRELAND, 518. 521
LONDON, ENGLAND.......... 459
LORD GRANVILLE'S LINE.... 382
LOUISIANA (STATE OF)..... 506
LOUISVILLE, KY........... 474
LOVE SPRINGS (GA.)....... 326
LOWER NORFOLK CO VA.464-
  466..................... 582
LOWER SIX MILE CHURCH.... 532
LUNENBURG CO. VA. 427, 431
  433, 452, 455, 457, 460
  485..................... 532

LYNCHBURG, VIRGINIA...... 438
LYNCH'S CREEK............ 375
LYNHAVEN PARISH (VA.) 314.. 467

MADISONVILLE, TENN....... 442
MARION, ALABAMA.......... 497
MARYLAND (STATE OF) 336,348
  374, 474, 485........... 514
MATTHEWS CEMETERY (TENN). 325
MAURY COUNTY, TENN, 325,493 513
McADENVILLE, N. C., 451.. 488
McALPIN'S CREEK, 318, 324,
  333, 421...476.......... 481
McDOWELL'S CREEK 314, 317,
  319, 371, 478........... 485
McINTYRE'S BRANCH........ 420
MEMPHIS, TENN.......479.. 493
MERCER COUNTY, KY, 452... 453
METHODIST CHURCH.....342. 343
MEXICO, THE CITY OF...... 413
MICKEL CREEK............. 324
MISSISSIPPI (STATE) 344,416
  475..................... 506
MISSOURI (STATE)....411.. 446
MOFFITT'S BRANCH (VA).... 471
MONOKIN, MARYLAND, 515, 534 536
MONOKIN CHURCH (MD)...... 505
MONROE, N. C. 345........ 402
MONROE CO. TENN.. 473.... 507
MONTGOMERY, ALA... 378... 497
MONTGOMERY CO. N. C...... 378
MOORE, S. C.............. 461
MOORESVILLE, N. C.. 482.. 489
MORGAN COUNTY, ALA...495. 531
MOSES DICKEY'S CREEK..... 319
MOUNT GALLANT, N. C...... 527
MOUNT VERNON, VA......... 499
MULBERRY ISLAND, WARWICK CO
  VA...................... 467
MURPHREESBORO, TENNESSEE.. 488

NANSEMOND COUNTY, VA. 427,
  470..................... 536
NASHVILLE, TENN, 338, 371,
  414, 491, 501, 526...... 532
NATCHITOCHES, LA......... 476
NEWBERRY DIST. S. C.456,453 452
NEW BERN, N. C........... 420
NELSON COUNTY, VA. 431... 433
NEW JERSEY............... 533
NEW KENT CO. VA. 434, 456,
  459, 471................ 472
NEW MARKET, VA.....465, 520 521
NEW PROVIDENCE CHURCH IN VA
  400, 432................ 528
NEW YORK................. 425
NORFOLK, VIRGINIA. 434... 514
NORFOLK COUNTY, VA. 438.. 455
NORTH CAROLINA R. R. CO.. 330
NORTH FORK WAXHAW CREEK.. 321
NORTHAMPTON CO. N. C..... 527
NORTHAMPTON CO. VA., 314,
  525..................... 532
NORTHUMBERLAND CO. VA. 434,
  435..................... 465
NOTTOWAY RIVER (VA.)..... 455
NUTBUSH CREEK, N. C...... 455

OGLETHORPE CO. GA.... 450.. 496
OLD BETHANY CHURCH 395, 483 484
OLD RAPPAHANNOCK CO VA. 463
  464..................... 471
ONANCOCK, MD., SOMERSET CO. 514
OPEKON, VA....431........ 433
ORANGE CO. NC....496..... 501

PACOLET RIVER, S. C. 319.. 485
PAGE'S CREEK NEWBERRY DIST
    S. C.................. 456
PARIS, TENNESSEE........... 460
PARKER COUNTY, TEXAS....... 495
PAW CREEK, 335............. 370
PENDLETON DIST. S.C., 421. 444
PENNSYLVANIA, 320, 341,415
    421, 431, 446, 454, 505
    508, 518....535........ 534
PERRY CO. ALA. 479, 483... 497
PERSON COUNTY, N. C....... 496
PERQUIMANS CO. N. C....... 510
PHIFER'S HILL.............. 416
PHILADELPHIA CHURCH, 400,
    418................... 395
PHILADELPHIA, PENN.318,396
    417, 499, 501......... 521
PICKENS COUNTY, ALA....... 531
PINEVILLE, N. C., 313, 329
    342, 344, 370, 377,378
    423, 508.............. 535
PITTSYLVANIA CO. VA., 413. 470
PLEASANT VALLEY, S. C..... 400
POCOMOKE RIVER (MD) 314,
    524................... 535
POCOMOKE (MD) 429, 470,514
    515................... 535
POPLAR TENT CHURCH 316,374
    396................... 419
POPLAR TENT DISTRICT...... 378
PORTSMOUTH, VA............ 469
POTOMAC RIVER, 438, 458... 499
PRESBYTERIAN CHURCHYARD IN
    CHARLOTTE............. 404
PRESBYTERY OF DONEGAL.... 433
PRESBYTERY OF DUBLIN..... 514
PRESBYTERY OF LAGAN, 473.
    503, 505, 515, 524.... 525
PRESBYTERY OF PHILADELPHIA 514
PRINCE EDWARD CO. VA. 344
    396, 416, 423, 425, 426
    428, 431, 441-443, 446-
    450, 452, 455, 457, 461
    471, 477, 478, 493, 517
    518, 528.............. 532
PRINCE GEORGE CO. VA. 413 455
PRINCE GEORGES CO. MD, 470
    499................... 519
PRINCE WILLIAM CO. VA.....470
PRINCESS ANNE CO. VA. 413. 437
PRINCETON COLLEGE, 419,453 536
PROVIDENCE CHURCH, 317,321
    327, 330, 345, 348, 375
    397, 400, 401, 417, 419
    421, 454, 481, 482, 515
    527, 528, 530......... 531
PROVIDENCE BURIAL GROUND.. 400
PROVIDENCE CHURCH DIST.324 375

———

QUEEN ANNE CO. MD......... 525
QUEEN'S CREEK, YORK CO. VA 464
QUEEN'S MUSEUM, CHARLOTTE,
    413, 506, 532......... 533

———

RAMBUR'S MILL, 343, 349..
    391, 420.............. 503
RAPPAHANNOCK CO. (OLD) VA.
    435, 466.............. 468
RAPPAHANNOCK RIVER, VA.434
    458................... 468
RAPPAHANNOCK, VA..........519
RED HILL, SALISBURY ROAD . 417
REEDY CREEK, 318.......... 396
REHOBOTH, SOMERSET MD. 514 515
REPUBLIC OF TEXAS......... 509

RICHMOND CO. VA... 467... 468
ROCKFISH GAP, VA.......... 433
ROCK HILL, S. C...........408
ROCKINGHAM CO. N. C...... 496
ROCK SPRINGS BURIAL PLACE 417
ROCKY RIVER, 313, 316,338
    340, 341, 339, 371-375
    378, 382, 393, 417,418
    420, 444, 525, 527,533 534
ROCKY RIVER CHURCH, 396,
    397, 400, 484......... 525
ROGERSVILLE? TENN...447.. 529
ROCKBRIDGE COUNTY, VA.... 484
ROME, GEORGIA............. 480
ROMNEY, VA................ 474
ROWASTICO, SOMERSET, MD.. 516
ROWAN COUNTY, N. C., 317,
    319, 373, 382, 403,405
    413, 421, 443, 478,485
    491, 510.............. 518
RURAL HILL GRAVEYARD...... 399
RUSSELLVILLE, KY.......... 452
RUTHERFORD CO. N. C....... 494
RUTHERFORD COUNTY, TENN.. 488

———

SALEM, VIRGINIA... 348... 474
SALISBURY, N. C., 412,462
    505, 518.............. 525
SALISBURY DIST. N. C.,369
    417................... 513
SALISBURY ROAD............ 382
SAN ANTONIO, TEXAS........ 339
SASAFRAS RIVER (MD) 524,
    534................... 535
SCOTLAND, 417....430...... 431
SCOTCH BUFFALO CREEK...... 444
SELMA, ALABAMA............ 341
SHEARER'S CHAPEL.......... 412
SHELBYVILLE, TENN......... 316
SHERRILL'S FORD........... 422
SHOULDERBONE CREEK (GA).. 529
SHENANDOAH VALLEY, VA.... 431
SHENANDOAH CO. VA......... 469
SHENANDOAH RIVER (VA.)... 465
SITTINGBOURNE PARISH (VA)
    465, 466.............. 468
SIX MILE CH. BURIAL PLACE 407
SIX MILE (OLD) GRAVEYARD. 498
SIX MILE CHURCH, 330, 331
    344, 482.............. 532
SIX MILE CREEK...321..... 378
SNOW CREEK, TENNESSEE.... 493
SNOW HILL, MD. 418, 419..
    515................... 536
SOMERSET COUNTY, MD..314
    414, 418, 421, 499,503
    505, 508, 510, 514-517
    520, 524, 525, 527-529
    532, 534.............. 535
SOUTH CAROLINA, 321,..338
    376, 378.............. 522
S. FORK CATAWBA RIVER,321 451
SOUTH TRADE STREET, CHAR-
    LOTTE, N. C........... 475
SPARTANBURG, S. C., 433.. 477
SPARTANBURG CO. S. C. 314
    461, 478, 479......... 496
SPOTTSYLVANIA CO. VA.,435
    470, 532.............. 533
SPRING CREEK (VA.) 428,
    463................... 471
STAFFORD CO. VA........... 470
STATESVILLE, N. C......... 484
STAUNTON, VA., 431, 433,
    436, 439, 472......... 526
STEELE CREEK DISTRICT,351
    370................... 420
STEPNEY PARISH, MD....... 516

STEELE CREEK CHURCH, 317,
    340, 341, 349, 370, 397..
    400, 413, 414, 489, 507
    528, 529..............533
ST. GEORGE'S PARISH, VA... 465
ST. PETER'S PARISH, VA.... 460
STOKES CO. N. C........... 496
STONE RIVER (TENN)........ 488
STOWE THREAD MILLS (N.C.). 451
SUGAR CREEK BURIAL GROUNDS.
    318, 414..............415
SUGAR CREEK SETTLEMENT, 376
    444, 476, 504......... 522
SUGAR CREEK, 318, 321, 329
    340, 331.............. 350
SUGAR CREEK CHURCH 323, 393
    395, 397, 400, 473, 521
    525, 527.............. 531
SURRY COUNTY, VA. 458, 459,
    460, 468, 469......... 469
SUSSEX COUNTY, VA.....455.. 460
SUSSEX COUNTY, DELAWARE... 437
SUMNER COUNTY, TENN...370.. 414
SWANANOA, NORTH CAROLINA.. 449
SWIFT CREEK, VA........... 430

———

TALBOT COUNTY, MARYLAND... 524
TANGIER ISLAND (VA.), 441
    429................... 527
TAYLORSVILLE N. C......... 482
TAZEWELL COUNTY, VA....... 484
TENNESSEE (STATE OF)....336
    339, 340, 344, 346, 375
    424, 490, 497......... 506
TEXAS (STATE OF), 341, 344, 415
    WATIRA CHURCH......... 510
TINKLING SPRINGS MEETING
    HOUSE, AUGUSTA CO. VA..
    429, 436, 432......... 439
TOOLE'S FORD......399..... 513
TRADE STREET, CHARLOTTE,..
    315................... 404
TRANSYLVANIA UNIVERSITY,KY. 502
TRANSYLVANIA (KENTUCKY).. 316
TRYON COUNTY, N. C. 318,319
    321, 379, 413, 422, 478
    485, 493, 494, 499.... 512
TRYON STREET, CHARLOTTE... 315
TUCKAHOE CREEK, TALBOT CO.
    MARYLAND.............. 524
TURKEY CREEK (S.C.?)...... 493
TUSCALOOSA, ALABAMA....... 490
TWELVE MILE CREEK, 370, 375 420
TYGER RIVER (S. C.?),461,
    480, 485, 502......... 532

———

ULSTER, IRELAND,.......... 426
UNION COUNTY, N. C., 325,
    374, 375, 402, 403, 400, 421
UNION POINT, GA. 463...... 500
UNITY CHURCH (LINCOLN CO)..
    412, 422, 512......... 513
UNIVERSITY OF ALABAMA..... 497
UNIVERSITY OF GLASGOW, 425, 454
UNIVERSITY OF N. C.400, 510 525
UNIVERSITY OF TENN...316.. 534
VIRGINIA (STATE OF), 338,
    415, 417, 421, 446, 478. 522

———

WAKE COUNTY, N. C......... 497
WARREN CO. N. C... 340.... 344
WARREN COUNTY, GA......... 444
WARWICK COUNTY, VA........ 466
WARWICK RIVER (VA.)....... 446

WASHINGTON, GA............ 454	WESTERN DISTRICT (TENN) 325...................... 379	YADKIN-CATAWBA VALLEY N.C. 535
WASHINGTON COLLEGE (TENN). 534	WELCH NECK (N. C.)......... 344	YADKIN RIVER (N. C.) 313, 332, 476............... 505
WASHINGTON COUNTY, TENN... 469, 495............... 500	WESTMORELAND CO. VA. 466... 499	YORK COUNTY, S. C.321,333 493, 497, 501.......... 513
WASHINGTON, GA. 484, 497.. 529	WHITE HAVEN, ENGLAND....... 527	YORK DISTRICT, S.C. 324... 399
WASHINGTON CO. VA......... 529	WHITE'S FORT, KNOXVILLE.... 424	YORK COUNTY, VA. 413, 426 427, 428, 431, 446, 449 459, 461, 463, 465, 466 469...................... 471
WASHINGTON COUNTY, TEXAS.. 531	WICOMICO RIVER (MD) 515,534 535	
WATAUGA VALLEY, TENN., 316 471, 492................ 500	WILKES CO. GA 453, 455, 460, 476................ 529	
WAXHAW SETTLEMENT, 320,376 378, 473, 500, 515..... 530	WILLIS RIVER (CUMBERLAND CO. VA 430,465, 471.431. 472	YORK RIVER (VA.).......... 437
WAXHAW CEMETERY, 324, 498 529.................... 532	WILMINGTON, N. C........... 438	YORKTOWN, VA. 426, 429,437 440.................... 489
WAXHAW CHURCH, 375, 381, 392, 400, 482.......... 527	WINCHESTER, VA............. 431	
	WORCESTER CO. MD........... 524	
	WORMLEY'S CREEK (VA.)...... 514	WASHINGTON, D. C., 424.... 453

www.ingramcontent.com/pod-product-compliance
Lightning Source LLC
Chambersburg PA
CBHW072022240426
43667CB00044B/2255